Celebrating t... ...
of Literacy

The Twenty-Sixth Yearbook
A Peer Reviewed Publication of
The College Reading Association
2004

Co-Editors
Jo Ann R. Dugan
Ohio University

Patricia E. Linder
Mary Beth Sampson
Texas A&M University-Commerce

Barrie A. Brancato
Clarion University of Pennsylvania

Guest Editor
Laurie Elish-Piper
Northern Illinois University

Editorial Assistants
Michelle Miller   **Kimberly Klakamp**
Naga V. R. K. Burugapalli
Texas A&M University-Commerce
Cortney Cawley
Ohio University

ISBN 1-883604-32-X

Printed at Texas A&M University-Commerce
Cover Design: JoAnn R. Dugan
Cover Photograph: JoAnn R. Dugan

Committee and Commission Chairpersons
Conference/Research Focus
Conference Coordinator, Barbara Reinken, Grand Valley State University
Program, Wayne M. Linek, Texas A&M University-Commerce
Elections, Maria Valeri-Gold, Georgia State University
Awards, Jane Brady Matanzo, Florida Atlantic University
Research, Julie K. Kidd, George Mason University; Charlene E. Fleener, Old
    Dominion University
Publications, Timothy G. Morrison, Brigham Young University

Organization Focus
Membership, Angela M. Ferree, Western Illinois University; Linda Thistle-
    thwaite, Western Illinois University
Public Information, Marie F. Holbein, State University of West Georgia; Donna
    M. Harkins, State University of West Georgia
Media, Patricia Douville, University of North Carolina at Charlotte
Historian, Gary L. Shaffer, Middle Tennessee State University
Photographer, Frederick J. Fedorko, East Stroudsburg University (Emerita)
Resolutions & Rules, William Dee Nichols, Virginia Tech; John P. Helfeldt, Texas
    A&M University
Legislative & Social Issues, Barbara J. Fox, North Carolina State University

Ad Hoc Committee
Technology, Marino Alvarez, Tennessee State University

TABLE OF CONTENTS

ACKNOWLEDGEMENTS

A great deal of time and effort has gone into the creation of this book. It would not be possible without the contributions of the authors, editors, assistant editors, secretaries, and printers who have contributed their talents and time to the production of this volume.

We are extremely grateful for support from our universities who provided financial assistance, personnel, facilities and time over the past year. At Ohio University, we would like to thank Dr. Roderick McDavis, President; Dr. James Heap, Dean, College of Education; Dr. Scott Sparks, Chair, Department of Teacher Education.

At Texas A&M University-Commerce, we thank Dr. Keith McFarland, President; Dr. Edward Seifert, Interim Dean, College of Education and Human Services; Dr. Frank Ashley, Dean, College of Education and Human Services; and Dr. Martha Foote, Head, Department of Elementary Education. Also, we would like to thank Vivian Freeman, Printing Supervisor, who carefully prepared the final galleys of the book for printing.

At Clarion University, we thank Dr. Joseph Grunewald, President; and Dr. Nancy Sayre, Interim Dean, College of Education.

We also appreciate the help of our editorial assistants, Cortney Cawley, Ohio University; Michelle Miller, Kim Klakamp, and Naga Burugapalli, Texas A&M University-Commerce.

Last but not least, we extend a heartfelt thanks to our families for their devotion and understanding when we were busy reading and writing.

Best wishes for a beautiful holiday season and a Happy New Year too!

JoAnn R. Dugan, Co-Editor
Ohio University
December 15, 2004

INTRODUCTION:
CELEBRATING THE POWER OF LITERACY

With this 49th volume of the CRA Yearbook, we celebrate the power of literacy to make every child a life-long reader. The young child on the cover is immersed in a favorite picture story. The seeds of literacy were planted early in his life through shared book experiences with family and friends. At home and in school, these seeds must be nurtured so that the roots of literacy grow strong and deep.

I recall my days as a preschool teacher. I witnessed the powerful influence that literacy has on children's play and learning. Every child came to school with the belief that she or he could read and write. The children were enthusiastic and engaged as they participated in literate behaviors, listening to stories, writing their names, noticing environmental print, pretending to read menus and books, scribbling messages, and dictating stories. I remember the little boy who proudly showed me a drawing of his pet dog with "BR" (Bear) scribbled across the page and proceeded to describe all the tricks his dog could do. In the kitchen center, a little girl scribbled a breakfast order on a notepad, and served green eggs and ham to children seated at the table. Another boy asked every day to listen to the audiotape of "Jack and the Beanstalk" while he turned the pages and read the pictures intently. By midyear he knew the story by heart and read it from memory almost word for word. Stories we read aloud became the source and substance of the children's play, limited only by their imagination. On the playground, children could be seen blowing down the pigs' house, and running away from the troll who lived under the gym set.

The classroom was a literate community. Parents joined the community too. Language experience was a routine activity. Parents took dictation and read to children. We sang rhyming songs, recited nursery rhymes, marched around the alphabet, and read, told, and painted stories. Literacy was a creative, enjoyable and natural part of our daily lives. The impact of these early, informal and playful literacy experiences should not be underestimated. Although the children were just beginning their literate journeys, these were transformative experiences that would have a powerful influence on their acquisition of print concepts and self-efficacy as readers and writers.

As parents, teachers, or literacy educators, we celebrate the powerful impact that literacy can have on our children's and students' lives to become successful members of society. We recognize their ability to communicate more effectively. We encourage them to explore new and interesting topics through reading and writing. We share our appreciation for the aesthetic appeal of picture books. We have learned to use computers more effectively to access and share information and create web-based resources. We encourage inquiry, dialogue, and share multiple interpretations in an effort to elevate the level understanding. We value and cherish the right to express different points of view in a free and democratic society and empower our students by helping them exercise this right.

As literacy educators, we study a wide spectrum of literacy topics from processes and practices to educational policies. As members of an academic community, we live our work. Reading and writing are central to our profession and our lives. Like our students, we are transformed by the scholarship of inquiry, teaching and learning. As a result of our work, we know more about the literacy process than we ever did. We know there is no quick fix, no recipe for becoming literate. All children deserve richer, more meaningful reading and writing. Teachers must be more knowledgeable. Instruction must be flexible enough to address variations in individual and developmental needs of students. In this volume, we invite you to explore some current topics and issues in literacy as we celebrate the power of literacy to make a positive impact on the lives of our students, ourselves, and the world.

JoAnn R. Dugan, Co-Editor
Ohio University
December 15, 2004

MEET THE EDITORS

JoAnn R. Dugan is an Associate Professor of Language and Literacy at Ohio University where she teaches graduate and undergraduate literacy courses in the Teacher Education Department. Her scholarly interests focus on instruction for struggling readers, response to literature, and literature discussions. A former Preschool teacher and Reading Specialist, JoAnn earned her Ph.D. from the University of Pittsburgh. She has served as the Co-Editor of the CRA Yearbook for the past eight years.

Patricia E. Linder is an Associate Professor of Reading and Elementary Education at Texas A&M University-Commerce where she teaches undergraduate and graduate literacy courses. She has served as a co-editor of the College Reading Association Yearbook since 1997. She has also served two terms as Chair of the Resolutions and Rules Committee and was Chair of the Adult Learning division from 2002-2004. Pat is one of the center coordinators for the teacher education field-based professional development school at A&M-Commerce.

Mary Beth Sampson is a Professor of Reading and Elementary Education at Texas A&M University-Commerce where she teaches master's and doctoral students. She has more than 85 publications including articles, textbooks, book chapters, newspaper columns, curriculum materials, and children's books. Her latest textbook is *Total Literacy: Reading, Writing and Learning* (with Tim Rasinski and Michael Sampson). She has served as co-editor of the CRA Yearbook for three years and is currently Chair-Elect of the Teacher Education Division.

Barrie A. Brancato has a D.Ed. in Curriculum and Instruction from Indiana University of Pennsylvania. Her interests are multicultural education, instructional strategies and social studies. She is currently Education Department Chair at Clarion University.

Laurie Elish-Piper is an Associate Professor and Reading Clinic Director in the Department of Literacy Education at Northern Illinois University. Her scholarship focuses on elementary reading, family literacy, and school-university partnerships. She has authored over 50 publications including, *Teaching Beginning Readers* (with Johns & Lenski) and *Learning to Teach Language Arts in a Field-Based Setting* (with Wiseman & Wiseman).

PRESIDENTIAL ADDRESS

PREDICTING THE WHETHER: LESSONS LEARNED FROM THE PAST

Presidential Address

Robert J. Rickelman

University of North Carolina-Charlotte

Robert J. Rickelman has been an active member of CRA since attending his first conference in 1980 with John Readence, his major professor. He has served as President, President-Elect, an elected member of the Board of Directors, Co-Editor of Reading Research and Instruction *and* Reading News, *Chair of the Teacher Education Division, and Co-Chair of the Public Information Committee. He is currently a Professor and Department Chair in the Reading and Elementary Education Department at the University of North Carolina-Charlotte, and has taught in middle and secondary schools in Ohio and Pennsylvania. He received his B.A. and M.Ed. from Ohio University and the Ph.D. in Reading Education from the University of Georgia.*

Abstract

This Presidential Speech focused on looking at the history of the College Reading Association in order to predict some possible (the "whether") courses for the future of the organization. The author relied extensively on the History of the College Reading Association: 1958-1998 *(Alexander & Strode, 1999) as well as his own personal experiences from the past 25 years as a member and leader within the organization.*

I would like to state up front that the title of this paper is not mine. I am indebted to my good friend, Jim Cunningham, who came up with a form of this title about 10 years ago. Jim invited several literacy professors in North Carolina to take part in a panel for a meeting of the North Carolina Research Association. He asked us to predict 10 years into the future, to identify salient issues we thought we would be facing in the field of literacy education. Ironically, we were making predictions at that meeting for the present, and I do not recall our predictions being anywhere close to the recent truths.

In an effort to try another round of predicting the future, this time of the organization, I thought it would make good sense to look at past events that have shaped the current state of the College Reading Association (CRA). A benefit of predicting the "whether" is that no one can accurately dispute your predictions. After 10 years, it is likely that most have forgotten the predictions. So, in an age of accountability, I have found a way to escape the bean counters; my goal is to give this prognostication my best shot, and not worry much about the accuracy. At least the predictions will not be much worse than those of professional weather forecasters.

I would like to divide my paper into three sections. First, I would like to recount influential past events of the College Reading Association. In other words, I would like to examine events that likely shaped where the organization finds itself today. In addition, I would like to highlight comments made by past CRA Presidents who identified timely issues during their terms of office. This section will make up the bulk of my remarks. Second, I would like to reflect briefly on where I think the organization stands today. Finally, I would like to offer several "best guess" predictions about where the organization might be headed.

The Past

The College Reading Association was founded in 1958 by 10 or so college teachers from Pennsylvania, who met at Temple University in Philadelphia. They identified themselves as the Committee for a College Reading Association, which they envisioned as an organization for professional educators living in the Northeastern and Mid-Atlantic states who were interested in promoting college reading programs.

The first formal conference of the new organization was held at LaSalle College, also in Philadelphia, on October 11, 1958. About 50 participants representing 30 schools attended the meeting. The second conference was held the following May at Lehigh University, where the group adopted the first constitution and by-laws, written by Al Mazurkiewicz. Bruce Brigham was elected the first President of the new organization, but he resigned after four months. Mazurkiewicz became the new president, and served in that role for the following 3+ years. At this second conference, the registration fee was $1.00, and membership dues were set at $3.00/year.

The College Reading Association now has a number of standing committees and commissions, but the first was the Commission on the Use of Paperbacks, chaired by Jerry Weiss, who served 22 years in this position. The first newsletter was funded and edited by Al Mazurkiewicz, and was published in February of 1961. The first journal, *Journal of the Reading Specialist*, came out in September of 1962, with Al Mazurkiewicz as the first editor. He continued in that role until 1969. The journal title was later changed to *Reading World* in 1969, and then in 1985 to *Reading Research and Instruction*.

The organization was formally chartered in Northampton County, Pennsylvania on November 18, 1963. The charter was signed by John E. Daniel, Albert J. Mazurkiewicz, Charles J. Versacci, Clay A. Ketcham, and Paul N. Terwilliger. In 1968, the first recognition award was given to A.B. Herr, a past Secretary-Treasurer of the organization from Rochester Institute of Technology. Later, in 1972, the A.B. Herr Award for Outstanding Professional Service (service to the organization, research, teaching, professional activity and other professional contributions) was given for the first time to Uberto Price. The following year, the Award was split in two, as it remains today. The A.B. Herr Award is now given for outstanding contributions to the reading education profession, while the Special Services Award (later renamed the Albert J. Mazurkiewicz Special Services Award) is given for service to the organization. The first Master's Thesis Awards were given in 1978 to Patricia Fisher, Ernest Balajthy, and Sara Strous. In 1982, the first Dissertation Awards were given to Mary Ann Medley and Daniel Pearce. The Laureate Award was given for the first time in 1996 to the person who has documented an influence on other reading professionals through mentoring and teaching, longevity as a CRA member, research and publications with students, and participation at CRA conferences, on the Board of Directors, and on committees. Lillian R. Putnam was the first winner of this award.

Alexander and Strode (1999) divided up their CRA history into five year time increments, and it is interesting to see how they identified the "hot topics" in each of those time periods. This is especially important in terms of seeing where we now stand. At the end of each five-year period, here are the timely issues that concerned CRA members:

> 1968—i.t.a. (Initial Teaching Alphabet), Words in Color, the Joplin Plan, individualized reading, grouping practices
>
> 1973—phonics, linguistic readers, programmed instruction, mechanical and electronic apparati, team-teaching, non-grading, diversity in content and illustrations, compensatory teaching for disadvantaged children

1978—responding to NAEP evidence on "Why Johnny Can't Read," criticism of "anything goes" in the classroom, criticism for accepting non-standard English in the classroom

1983—Right to Read, Back to the Basics movement, instructional time vs. achievement, comprehension, reading-writing connection, theoretical frameworks, discourse analysis, schema theory, guided writing, metacognition, computers in reading

1988—declining availability of grant money in reading, staff cuts, teacher education reform, qualitative research methodologies

1993—continuing classroom cutbacks, low morale, pedagogy under attack

1998—assessment, continuing accountability, deprofessionalization of reading education

Since Alexander and Strode's (1999) reporting ended in 1998, I would like to take the opportunity to offer these "hot topics" from the past 5 year period:

2003—No Child Left Behind, performance-based assessment, paper-and-pencil tests, lateral entry teachers, alternative licensure, "evidence-based/science-based" funding formulas, scripted reading lessons

What is immediately noticeable from examining the past issues is that many of the topics on the current list have been building up over the past 20 years. These are not new issues. Concerns about the deprofessionalization of our field have been voiced since the mid-1970s. In 1992, CRA President Norm Stahl urged members, in his Presidential Address, to build well-coordinated, ongoing offensives, including building professional alliances, to create a united front to criticisms of higher education. With the recent debates in Washington over the reauthorization of the Higher Education Act, his advice continues to be timely a dozen years later.

Along with timely issues from the past, I would like to conclude this section with advice given by two CRA Past-Presidents during their terms of office. Bert Price, who was CRA President in 1970, listed the following critical areas that he felt needed to be addressed by members:

- Teacher training institutions need to prepare candidates more thoroughly
- We need to narrow the gap separating research and practice
- We should teach reading in a more serious manner
- We need more research on how people learn
- We need more information about the nature of reading and language
- We must match methods, materials, and techniques to the needs of learners

Price's recommendations continue to hold true to this day, especially in light of all the recent interest in "science-based instruction."

In a similar way, President George Mason, in 1984, issued the following challenges to the CRA divisions:

- Teacher Education—take a stand, draft resolutions, seek media coverage, express position on concerns about budget cuts in K-16 schools
- College—undertake a campaign to increase professional stature of its members in order to secure more support for needed college programs
- Clinical—college reading clinics are facing extinction, so prepare convincing justifications in the face of looming budget cuts
- Adult Learning—mount campaigns to educate the public on their programs

His advice to the organization still holds true today, as we struggle for credibility at the local, state, and national levels.

The Present

Currently there are many questions about what works in the literacy classroom. While bureaucrats debate science, teachers and children are left to sort it all out. I have a photograph from the Charlotte Observer, our local daily newspaper, showing a student who had a Roman numeral 4 shaved into his head. This brash act was in anticipation of taking the annual "end-of-grade" test, in which the goal of all students was to score a 4, the highest grade possible. While the newspaper reporter focused on the lengths that teachers and students went to in order to prepare and motivate themselves for the test, the fact that young children take the act of testing so seriously is concerning. Another reporter did a follow-up report on the negative stressors that result from high-stakes assessments.

One of my personal heroes is Ernest Boyer. Boyer used to be the Commissioner of Education under President Jimmy Carter, before this position became a Cabinet post. He was also the former President of the SUNY system. At the time of his death in 1995, he was the Director of the Carnegie Foundation for the Advancement of Teaching in Princeton. Boyer, based on his vision of what a school should be, developed the "Basic Schools" model, introduced in his book of the same name (1995). Boyer expressed concern that, for many children, school was becoming the "pursuit of trivial pursuit," with the focus on learning isolated facts. His vision for a Basic School was a place where kids made connections to the real world, where the goal was not a test score but a coherent view of knowledge. He was concerned that, for many students, clichés become substitutes for reason. I share this same concern about adults. Certainly no one would argue that some children should be left behind, just as you cannot argue that there should be no family values. But this polar distinction between the good guys and the bad guys is, unfortunately, skewed by politics; so that the cliché becomes the political focus rather than what is actually happening with real people in real classrooms. The challenges issued by George Mason 20 years ago are still timely!

The leaders of CRA have been engaged in discussions with leaders in other national literacy organizations, most notably the International Reading Association and the National Reading Conference, to try to present the united alliance Norm Stahl suggested over a decade ago. Some important questions, however, remain.

Boyer, in a speech to the Association of Supervision and Curriculum Development a dozen years ago, suggested several important questions, which should guide us in setting a national agenda for K-12 education. First, to give us an outline for where we need to focus our efforts in education, we should ask "What is an educated person?" Boyer suggested that an educated person is well-informed, acts wisely, continues to learn, and discovers the connectedness of things. Second, we should ask "What is a good teacher?" He suggests that a good teacher is knowledgeable, relates information to students, promotes active learning, and is an authentic and open human being. Interestingly, Boyer never stated that an educated person is one who scores well on multiple choice tests. If you asked the average person who they identified as the smartest person alive, I doubt that they would mention someone who was a noted test taker. I would guess they would likely mention divergent thinkers and problem solvers like Albert Einstein or Bill Gates. The scripted lessons I see in many of today's classrooms seem to take the human, creative element from students. I have heard about one local school principal who formally observes teachers by going into their classrooms with a script and a stopwatch, criticizing teachers for being a minute or more off of the script. All this is done, with good intentions, in the name of science. The basal used in that school touts itself as being based on scientific evidence, so the principal assumed that deviating from the script at all would contaminate the researched methodologies. Good teachers are leaving these schools, where they are most needed. Are children the benefactors of this "science" or are they quietly being left behind? Bert Price's suggestions are as real today as they were 35 years ago.

The Future?

So, we have a sense of time and place, based on our past as an organization. We have heard (but have we listened?) to advice from former leaders. Most would agree that our field is in a state of chaos today. So, is it possible to even predict the "whether," knowing the uncertainty of education today.

I think so, since there is no immediate penalty for me suggesting where it is we may be headed. Honestly, I have no scientific evidence to support any of my predictions!

Can we learn from past lessons? Plutarch suggested that history repeats itself. If true, it may be helpful to look at where we have been, where we are not, and think ahead to where we may be headed. Here are my ideas.

First, I think we need to heed the advice of George Mason, and respond to criticisms from within and outside the profession, advancing our own rich long-standing store of "scientific evidence" for how reading works and the best ways to teach it. Almost 100 years ago, Huey (1908) discussed the psychology and pedagogy of reading. Since then, a strong line of research has informed our field of reading. To ignore the best thinking of our forebears for practices forged in other arenas is to ignore the past. The fact is that kids did learn using whole language, that kids did learn using direct instruction, and kids did learn using eye movement pacing machines. On the flip side, there are, of course, children who did not learn to read using each of these methods. I would rather rely on an educated and informed teacher's methods than on a script written by someone who has never seen the community, the school, or the child. A script cannot react to a child who looks puzzled. It cannot make creative, informed decisions when things go awry. A book can never replace a good teacher. Ask any parent or child who has ever been in a classroom with an outstanding teacher, and they will tell you this.

Second, we need to be flexible rather than defensive. While we certainly can boast a rich history in literacy education, we must be flexible enough to recognize the efforts of others with a similarly rich research tradition, in areas such as special education and educational psychology. While using different paradigms, their research, blended with our own, can forge new pathways to learning that will benefit children. Rather than arguing about who is right, we need to put forth our best cooperative efforts at synthesizing the information that we know and how best to apply it to the classroom and to the community.

Third, we need to train and mentor the leaders of tomorrow, and foster in them the knowledge, skills, and dispositions to become outstanding and educated persons, who seek lifelong learning. We need people who do not over commit or shirk their responsibilities, and who will get things done. I am convinced that a major characteristic of most leaders in the field is not that they are incredibly smart (although many are!) or that they are incredibly organized (although some are!), but that they get things done when they agree to get them done. Those who talk the most about being incredibly busy often spend too much effort talking rather than doing. I don't know about you, but I'll take a doer every time!

Fourth, we need to connect with the media. I have certainly been guilty of avoiding the limelight. When called on to meet with a newspaper of television reporter, it is easy to discover schedule conflicts. However, who will best make our case? Who will be remembered when policies and legislation are being considered, the person who agreed to the radio interview or the person who hid? In a similar way, we need to connect with legislators, for the same reasons. I once went to a conference on how to be a department chair, and had breakfast with the Dean of Education at a major university. He said that the best move he made as a new dean was to go to his state capital with a bag full of stuffed university mascots. He scheduled meetings with any state legislator who agreed to meet with him. He asked for 30 minutes of their time, and awarded them with a stuffed dog at the end of the meeting. But what he found, and the reason he told the story to me as a new department chair, was that he became the "go to" person when education issues were brought before the state legislature. Rather than calling for the expert advice of someone else, the legislators with whom he met asked their secretaries to call "that guy who brought the dog" to seek his opinion, since he seemed to know a lot about education. In a similar way, we need to figure out how to be the "go to" person for our local and state legislators and media.

Fifth, we need to share, rather than hide, the good things (as well as the bad things) about the profession. There seems to be a conspiracy mentality in the general population today regarding teachers, including us. The feeling is that we are not doing a good job, but trying to hide this fact by being defensive. Everyone seems to be an expert in education. After all, I have had some people tell me that they went through the school system for 16 years, so why shouldn't they be experts? I wonder if these same folks would allow me to extract a tooth. After all, I have been going to the dentist religiously for over 40 years, so I surely should be an expert in dentistry by now, right?

The bottom line, I think, is that we need to be collaborators as much as we are allowed to collaborate. In spite of the fact that we are being told we don't know how to teach and that we should blow up the colleges of education, the fact is that many, many people were well taught, did learn, and are now successful in their jobs. Why not share some credit along with the blame?

References
Alexander, J.E., & Strode, S.L. (1999). *History of the College Reading Association, 1958-1998.* Commerce, TX: College Reading Association.

Boyer, E.L. (1995). *The Basic School: A community for learning.* Princeton, NJ: Carnegie Foundation for the Advancement of Teaching.

Huey, E.B. (1908). *The psychology and pedagogy of reading.* Cambridge, MA: M.I.T Press.

KEYNOTE
ADDRESSES

FAST START: SUCCESSFUL LITERACY INSTRUCTION THAT CONNECTS SCHOOLS AND HOMES

Keynote Address

Nancy Padak
Tim Rasinski

Kent State University

Nancy Padak and Tim Rasinski are professors of literacy education at Kent State University. Their research interests focus on fluency and family literacy. Each is a Past-President of CRA; they also edited the CRA Yearbook, as well as The Reading Teacher. They currently edit the Journal of Literacy Research. The program described in this paper is available from Scholastic (2005).

Abstract

In this article we describe Fast Start (FS), a parental involvement program for families with K-2 children. FS offers an alternative to typical approaches to parental involvement. The principles on which FS is based are described. We then explain the program itself and finally share research results based on several trials in public schools. These trials have shown that children involved in FS achieve significantly more in reading than their non-FS peers. Moreover, children and parents are nearly universally pleased with FS, and teachers believe FS to be worth the time invested.

R eading more often leads to reading better. Moreover, children who come to school having been read to typically have an advantage over their peers who did not have such preschool experiences. Both of these assertions, long accepted as givens in the literacy community, speak to the importance of engaging children in reading outside of school. Yet the unfortunate truth is that most students do very little reading out of school. The home can help here. Parental involvement in reading is an untapped source for increasing the sheer amount that students read, which in turn will increase children's proficiency in reading.

Parental involvement can significantly influence children's learning in general and reading achievement in particular. Ann Henderson (1988; Henderson & Berla, 1994), for example, concluded that parent involvement leads to improvements in student achievement, grades, test scores, and overall academic performance. Results from nearly every National Assessment of Educational Progress have indicated that students who are regularly involved with their families in literacy-related activities have higher levels of reading achievement than students whose parents are not actively involved in their reading. Similarly, an international study of reading instruction found that the "degree of parental cooperation" was the most potent of 56 significant characteristics of schools most successful in teaching reading (Postlethwaite & Ross, 1992).

Experimental research results likewise point to the value of parental involvement in children's reading. Children whose parents engage them in family literacy activities have accelerated oral language development (e.g., Senechal, LeFevre, & Thomas, 1998), greater phonemic awareness and decoding ability (e.g., Burgess, 1999; Purcell-Gates, 1996), and higher overall reading achievement (e.g., Cooter, Marrin, & Mills-House, 1999; Foertsch, 1992; Morrow & Young, 1997) compared to peers without such opportunities.

Unfortunately, ongoing and consistent efforts to involve parents in children's reading have proven difficult to sustain. Many teachers we know have described unsuccessful and unrewarding experiences when working with parents. Others believe they don't have time or energy for such a program when they seldom get release time, remuneration, or recognition. Most parent involvement programs in reading tend to be one-shot affairs such as talks by local experts in reading, "make it and take it" workshops, pre-packaged commercial programs, or short-term incentive programs. These approaches have little effect on students' reading achievement or attitudes, particularly for children who struggle with reading (Padak, Sapin, & Baycich, 2002).

We believe that Fast Start (FS), the parental involvement program we describe in this article, offers an alternative to typical approaches to parental involvement. The principles on which FS is based are described below. We then explain the program itself and finally share research results based on several trials in public schools.

Characteristics of Successful Parent Involvement Programs

Successful parent involvement in reading programs share several attributes (Rasinski & Padak, 2004). These characteristics provide the basis for FS. They can also be used as guidelines for teachers and schools to design their own programs to meet specific needs or to design evaluations of existing programs.

Use Proven and Effective Strategies

Parents often have limited time to devote to working with their children. Therefore, at-home activities must be based on proven and appropriate methods for achieving success in reading. Too often, at-home activities have questionable value for improving academic performance. Drawing and coloring pictures or cutting out photographs from magazines may not be the best use of parents and children's time together at home.

Provide Training, Communication, and Support

Most parents are not teachers. They need good and understandable training that includes demonstrations and opportunities for discussion and questions. Someone who is enthusiastic about and committed to parent involvement should provide the training.

Teachers need to understand the realities of busy family life and be sensitive to educational barriers that may impede parent–child reading activity. Some parents may feel uncomfortable reading aloud to their children because of their own real or perceived lack of reading ability. Parents of English Language Learners may not themselves be fluent readers of English. Parents whose own educational experiences were negative may hesitate to attend school functions. Yet all these parents want to help their children succeed. The teacher's challenge, then, is to find meaningful ways for all families to be involved in home reading activities. Making books on tape available is one way to promote all families' involvement. With some thought, resourceful teachers can find many more.

Continuing communication and support can provide parents with timely feedback about their questions and concerns and can encourage persistence with the at-home reading activities. Support can be in the form of a regular informative newsletter, monthly sessions in the school, or offers of personal contact by phone or email. Ongoing communication and support build bonds between home and school and demonstrate to parents that other people care about their children's reading growth.

Real Reading

One of the best things that parents can do for children of any age is to read to them. Reading aloud provides children with a model of fluent reading and offers parents natural opportunities to point out text features for young children. Similarly, when parents read with their children or listen to their children read, children grow as readers. Texts for these activities should be authentic (e.g., poems, song lyrics, jokes, jump rope rhymes); children should be able to read them successfully with enough support from parents. These simple activities—read to, read with, and listen to children—are powerful ways to promote student growth in reading.

Some parent involvement plans fail because parents lack appropriate texts or the time or resources to acquire them. Although periodic trips to the public library are advisable, requiring them as a condition of participation in at-home reading activities might discourage parental involvement. The easiest solution is to provide parents and children with reading materials. When the materials are provided, parents are more likely to remember to do the activities with their children. The materials themselves act as reminders to parents to get the job done.

Make Activities Easy, Consistent, and Enjoyable

Parents tell us that parent involvement activities don't work if they are too complex, take inordinate amounts of time, or change from day to day or week to week. They say it's hard to develop a routine of working with their children under these conditions. Therefore, at-home reading activities need to reflect this reality. At-home activities for young children should be relatively brief (10-15 minutes several times each week), simple routines with some variation to keep interest high. Such activities make it easier for parents and children to develop predictable, time-efficient routines. These, in turn, increase the likelihood that the at-home activities will be conducted regularly and successfully.

Consistency is important as well. Once an effective instructional routine is introduced, major changes or disruptions in the parent-child routine should be avoided. Rather, families should be able to develop a level of comfort with the routines. Variety can be introduced by changing the texts and the ways in which parents and children respond to what they read.

For parents and children to persist in academic tasks over the long term, the instructional activities must be enjoyable for everyone. A sense of informality and playfulness infused into the activities can help achieve this goal.

Parents should be reminded to be enthusiastic, provide positive encouragement, and support their children's attempts to read. Allowing children some control over activities also lends enjoyment to the sessions. If the reading is followed by some word games, for example, children can choose the games as well as the words to include.

Provide Ways to Document Home Activities
Documenting at-home activity permits teachers and schools to monitor parent–child involvement and evaluate the program's success in achieving its goal. More important, perhaps, documentation gives parents tacit encouragement and reminds them to continue reading with their children. Parents can use a log sheet to record their work with their children over a specified period of time. Parents tell us that posting the sheet in a prominent place reminds them to do the activity. At the end of the time period the log sheets are returned to the school.

We used these guidelines to develop FS. Teachers or school administrators can also use them to design other programs for parent involvement in reading. When home and school collaborate to provide enjoyable and authentic reading experiences, students benefit because they have multiple daily opportunities to grow as readers.

Fast Start in Reading
FS is a program we developed at Kent State University for involving parents of young readers (kindergarten through Grade 2) and struggling readers. In FS parents read short, highly predictable passages with their children. We have found that rhyming poetry, nursery rhymes, jokes and riddles for children, and short vignettes work very well. Each day parents and their children spend about 15 minutes on one of the passages. What we ask parents to do is specific and based on effective instructional principles:

1. The parent reads the passage to the child, and they talk about its content.
2. Parent and child read the passage together until the child is able to read it alone.
3. The parent listens to the child read and gives encouragement, support, and praise.
4. Parent and child select and then play several short word games from a menu of ideas.

These word games are generic and grouped to provide developmentally appropriate support for children. Group A activities (see Appendix) concentrate on concepts about print. Group B activities focus on phonemic awareness, and Group C activities are for children who are beginning to read independently. Teachers tell parents which group of activities to use for the word games.

School personnel invite parents to attend FS training sessions at the beginning of the school year. Several sessions are offered, morning and evening, so that parents can choose which session to attend. Sessions are typically led by children's teachers. Parents leave the sessions with informational packets (see Appendix), enough passages for one month, and log forms for recording their work with their children. Each month from October through May, teachers send home new sets of readings and new log sheets. The program is relatively inexpensive and time efficient. The major cost is duplication, and the major time commitment for teachers is in the initial training sessions.

Parent participation in FS has been exceptionally high, and student growth in reading is apparent and significant, especially among children who are most at risk for reading problems.

Kent State's Summer Reading Program

An adapted version of FS has been an integral part of Kent State's summer reading program, a five-week clinical tutoring program for children experiencing significant difficulty in learning to read. During the first week of the program parents are asked to attend an orientation session during which they are introduced to the adapted version of FS (adapted for children in intermediate and middle grades as well as primary grade students), provided with material (or it is provided by individual tutors on a daily basis), and asked to engage in FS tutoring daily. We have found a strong relationship ($r = .60$ to $.79$) between the parents' level of participation in FS tutoring with their children and their children's reading growth (word recognition and reading fluency) over the course of the brief summer reading program (Rasinski, 1995).

Fast Start in Worthington, Ohio

School psychologist Bruce Stevenson (2002) implemented FS over a three-month period with beginning first-grade students. Parents worked with their children on the program for a relatively short period of time— about ten minutes per day. Nevertheless, he found that FS had a statistically significant and substantial effect on the reading growth (letter and word recognition, reading fluency) of the lowest achieving first-graders, those who would normally be considered most at-risk for academic success. FS students made nearly twice the gain as a control group doing more traditional parent involvement activities in letter and word recognition and reading fluency. Moreover, he found that parents found the program easy to implement and valued the opportunity to employ it with their children.

Fast Start in Akron and Canton, Ohio

A couple of years ago we were talking about parental involvement and FS at an in-service session for teachers. After the session, Sharon Davis, a first-grade teacher at Seiberling School in Akron, indicated an interest in implementing FS at her school. Consequently, we worked with eight first-grade teachers and a kindergarten teacher to implement FS in 2001-02. We analyzed results of the Seiberling implementation in summer 2002 and shared them with Canton teachers early in the 2002-03 school year. As a result, Canton implemented FS in grades K and 1 in its 18 elementary schools during the 2002-03 school year.

Our evaluation of FS focuses on children's achievement as well as children's, parents', and teachers' perceptions. To evaluate achievement, we use the tests and measures currently in place in the schools. Perceptions are obtained through surveys (for parents and teachers) and interviews (with children) developed especially for this research. Interested readers may contact either of us for copies of these survey and interview instruments.

Analysis of children's reading achievement data for both K and 1 and in both school systems was based on a 2[time] X 3[level of involvement] design. The time variable was beginning and end of the school year. For level of involvement, we asked teachers to mark class rosters indicating whether students were actively involved in FS, somewhat involved in FS, or not at all involved in FS.

Kindergarten assessments in Canton are based on Clay's *Observation Survey* (2002). Analysis of these assessments showed that children who were involved in FS a) had significantly greater word vocabulary growth (p < .05), b) attained concepts about print more quickly (p < .05), and c) learned to identify upper and lower case letters more quickly (p < .05) than their non-FS counterparts.

Kindergartners in Akron and first graders in both school systems are assessed with the *Developmental Reading Assessment* (Beaver, 1997). Analysis of scores for these children showed that students who were at least somewhat involved in FS significantly outperformed their non-FS counterparts (p < .01). Taken together, these results show that the FS program was effective in increasing children's reading abilities, regardless of their measured ability at the beginning of the year. Being "somewhat" involved in FS was enough to lead to achievement gains.

Children who participated in FS were overwhelmingly positive about the experience (see Table 1). When commenting on the poems, in addition to general positive comments, children noted that they liked the content of the texts and that they enjoyed working with family members. Regarding content, for example, one child said, "I liked the rhyming words and they were funny." Another commented, "The poems were not hard or easy—they were just right." Children also enjoyed the word play activities. Sample comments show this: "They help you read a lot"; " 'cause I can learn stuff—how to do the sounds and how to make all the letters"; "because I got to play with my dad." The few children who had negative perceptions commented that the work was too hard or boring.

Table 1. Children's Perceptions of Fast Start*

	YES	A LITTLE	NO
Like poetry reading?	97 (89%)	9 (8%)	3 (3%)
Like word activities?	94 (86%)	3 (3%)	5 (5%)
Did (adult) enjoy?	93 (85%)	8 (8%)	3 (3%)
Did FS make you a better reader?	106 (97%)	1 (1%)	2 (2%)

individual interviews with children at Seiberling (spring, 2002; N=25) in Akron and 4 elementary schools (spring, 2003; N=84) in Canton.

As Table 1 shows, children firmly believed that FS helped them become better readers. Their reasons for this belief centered in three areas:

- Challenging content: "Because they had lots of words I didn't know"; "the words were hard but now I'm reading."

- Encouraged reading development: "The harder it gets, the better you get"; "because I couldn't read that much before and now I'm reading a lot of stuff"; "because they have hard words, and the more I read, the more I know."

- Encouraged interest in reading: "because all of a sudden I sat down and started reading"; "I read them every day after school. Sometimes I write poems myself."

Parents' perceptions about FS were also very positive (see Table 2). Many parents commented positively about their children's and their own reaction to FS: "The one-on-one time was nice"; "It gave him something to look forward to every night"; "I have always loved poetry. I see the same excitement in [my child] now"; "brought us closer together." The few negative reactions centered in difficulty maintaining the child's interest and the parent or child believing FS was a "chore."

In general, parents were also very positive about the impact that FS had on their children's reading ability and on whether the time they devoted to FS was well spent. With regard to the former, parents commented, "[Child] is eager to read now and without assistance"; "it seemed to help him with his fluency and expression"; "it has helped him recognize words and build confidence in reading." And about spending time in FS, sample parent comments were "To see your child read and want to read is priceless"; "this is a nice way for the family to spend time together"; "allows for quality time."

Table 2. Parents' Response*

	YES	SOMEWHAT	NO
Child enjoyed sessions	210 (68%)	86 (28%)	15 (5%)
Parent enjoyed sessions	222 (72%)	76 (25%)	20 (6%)
Child enjoyed poems	252 (81%)	54 (17%)	12 (4%)
Child enjoyed word play	224 (73%)	96 (31%)	17 (6%)
Made a difference in child's reading	158 (51%)	111 (36%)	38 (12%)
Time well spent	255 (84%)	34 (11%)	14 (5%)

*N= 31 Seiberling parents, 2001-02 and approximately 275 Canton parents, 2002-03

Teacher responses to the FS survey are summarized in Table 3. In general, teachers believed that FS time was well spent and that their students enjoyed the activity. Teachers were less sure about academic benefits or about parents' responses. We found it intriguing that of the three groups surveyed/interviewed, teachers' perceptions of FS were the least positive. Although we have no explanation for this finding, we are planning further research to learn more about teachers' ideas about FS.

Table 3. Teachers' Perceptions of Fast Start*

Among active participants:
- Reading improved (38%)
- No difference in reading ability (38%)

Among "somewhat active" participants:
- Reading improved (24%)
- No difference in reading ability (35%)

Parent response:
- Positive (39%)
- Negative (39%)
- Mixed (20%)

Student response:
- Liked (86%)
- Disliked (5%)

Time well spent?
- Yes (64%)
- No (13%)

*selected responses from teacher surveys in Akron and Canton

Conclusion

Fast Start has demonstrated to us that parents really do want to help their children in reading. In many cases they just don't know what to do or what materials and programs to choose. When schools get parents involved in a systematic way, using effective methods of instruction and providing support, materials, and communication, children make substantial and significant progress as readers.

Although parent involvement may not be a cure-all for every difficulty that children encounter in reading, we know that it does make a difference—in some cases, a huge difference. Our experiences lead us to recommend that all education professionals try and try again to involve parents actively in children's literacy development. The potential benefits are simply too great to pass up.

References

Beaver, J. (1997). *Developmental reading assessment.* Upper Saddle River, NJ: Pearson.

Burgess, S. (1999). The influence of speech perception, oral language ability, the home literacy environment, and prereading knowledge on the growth of phonological sensitivity: A 1-year longitudinal study. *Reading Research Quarterly, 34,* 400-402.

Clay, M. M. (2002). *An observation survey of early literacy achievement* (2nd ed.). Portsmouth, NH: Heinemann.

Cooter, R., Marrin, P., & Mills-House, E. (1999). Family and community involvement: The bedrock of reading success. *The Reading Teacher, 52,* 891-896.

Foertsch, M. (1992). *Reading in and out of school: Factors influencing the literacy achievement of American students in grades 4, 8, and 12 in 1988 and 1990.* (ERIC Document Reproduction Service No. ED 341 976)

Henderson, A. (1988). Parents are a school's best friends. *Phi Delta Kappan, 70,* 148-153.

Henderson, A., & Berla, N. (Eds.). (1994). *A new generation of evidence: The family is critical to student achievement.* Washington, DC: National Committee for Citizens in Education. (ERIC Document Reproduction Service No. ED 375 968)

Morrow, L., & Young, J. (1997). A family literacy project connecting school and home: Effects on attitude, motivation, and literacy achievement. *Journal of Educational Psychology, 89,* 736-742.

Padak, N., Sapin, C., & Baycich, D. (2002). *A decade of family literacy: Programs, outcomes, and the future.* Columbus, OH: ERIC Clearinghouse on Adult, Career, and Vocational Education.

Postlethwaite, T.N., & Ross, K.N. (1992). *Effective schools in reading: Implications for educational planners.* The Hague: International Association for the Evaluation of Educational Achievement.

Purcell-Gates, V. (1996). Stories, coupons, and the TV Guide: Relationships between home literacy experiences and emergent literacy. *Reading Research Quarterly, 31,* 406-428.

Rasinski, T. V. (1995). Fast Start: A parental involvement reading program for primary grade students. In W. Linek & E. Sturtevant (Eds.), *Generations of literacy. Seventeenth yearbook of the College Reading Association* (pp. 301-312). Harrisonburg, VA: College Reading Association.

Rasinski, T., & Padak, N. (2004). *Effective reading strategies: Teaching children who find reading difficult* (3rd ed.). Upper Saddle River, NJ: Pearson.

Senechal, M., LeFevre, J., & Thomas, E. (1998). Differential effects of home literacy experiences on the development of oral and written language. *Reading Research Quarterly, 33*, 96-116.

Stevenson, B. (2002). *The efficacy of the Fast Start parent tutoring program in the development of reading skills of first grade students*. Unpublished doctoral dissertation, The Ohio State University, Columbus.

Appendix. Daily Fast Start Lesson

Fast Start

FAST START has two parts—reading the poem or passage and playing with the words. Here are directions for each part. A FAST START session should take about 10-15 minutes. Please do FAST START at least 5 times each week.

Reading the Poem or Passage

1. Sit next to your child.
2. Hold the poem so both of you can see it.
3. Read the poem **to** your child. Do this two or three times. Read it slowly and expressively. Point to the words as you read.
4. Read the poem **with** your child. Do this two or three times. Again, read slowly and expressively. Point to the words as you read, or let your child point as you read.
5. **Listen** to your child read the poem by himself or herself. Do this two or three times. Have your child point to the words as he or she reads and be sure to tell your child what a good reader he or she is!

   Remember: Read to . . . read with . . . listen to your child read.

Playing With the Words

[Your child's teacher will tell you which group of word games you should use. Pick an activity or two from your child's group. Do different activities on different days so your child will enjoy the word work. Be sure to tell your child what a good job he or she is doing.]

Group A

1. Ask your child to count the lines in the poem. Ask him or her to point at each line as it is counted.
2. Have your child to count the words in the poem. Ask him or her to point to each word as it is counted.
3. Ask questions about the words—How many words are in line 1? Show me the third word in line 2. Which line has the most words? Which line has the fewest words?
4. Say a letter of the alphabet. Ask your child to find all the times that a particular letter is used in the poem. Repeat for several other letters.
5. Point to a word. Ask your child to tell you the letter that begins the word. Then ask him or her to tell you what letter ends the word. Repeat with several words.
6. Give your child a pencil or marker. Say a word from the poem and have your child find it and mark it some way—circle it, underline it, highlight it, etc.

Group B

1. Say two words from the poem. Ask your child to tell you if the words rhyme with one another. Repeat with several other pairs of words.
2. Find a word from the poem that is a simple rhyming word. Ask your child to say some words that rhyme with the word you chose. Write all these words in a list on the poetry sheet.
3. Say a word from the poem. Ask your child to say the word by breaking it into sounds. (For example, you might say "bat," and your child would say "buh—a—tuh.")
4. Do the opposite of #3—you say "buh—a—tuh" and ask your child to tell you what word it is: "bat." Then ask your child to find the word in the poem.
5. Say two words from the poem. Ask your child if they start with the same sound. Repeat several times. (Choose some words that do start with the same sounds and some that don't.)

Group C

1. Use the word cards. Ask your child to select a word or two from the poem to put on the cards. You also select a word or two.
2. After you have gathered 10-12 words over several days, play with them. If you make a duplicate set of cards, you can play "Concentration" or "Go Fish."
3. Find words from the poem that all have the same vowel. Put the words on word cards. Ask your child to sort the cards into categories according to the sounds that the vowel makes in the words.
4. Ask your child to sort the word cards into categories according to the consonant sound that is found in the word. For example, sort your words into all the words that begin with the "buh" sound. Or, sort your words into all the words that end with the "kuh" sound.
5. Select a word from the poem. Play guessing games with the word. For example, with the word "hat," you could ask, "What word would we have if we changed the /h/ to a /p/?" "What word would we have if we put an /e/ on the end?"
6. Ask your child to read the words as you flash them to him or her. Challenge him or her to read them as quickly as possible.

PREPARING ELEMENTARY TEACHERS IN READING: WILL UNIVERSITY-BASED PROGRAMS MOVE FORWARD OR BE "LEFT BEHIND"?

Keynote Address

James V. Hoffman

The University of Texas at Austin

James Hoffman is Professor of Language and Literacy Studies at the University of Texas at Austin. He teaches graduate courses and directs the undergraduate reading specialization program. Jim is a Past-President of the National Reading Conference and a former editor of the Reading Research Quarterly. He currently serves as editor for the Yearbook of the National Reading Conference. His research interests include texts, teaching, and teacher preparation.

Just one week after the closing of the College Reading Association's annual (2003) conference hosted in Corpus Christi, the Texas State Board of Educational Certification (SBEC) approved a procedure for certifying virtually anyone with a bachelor's degree in a relevant area to teach at the high school level. This procedure requires that the candidate pass a test but it does not require the completion of any accredited academic preparation program, nor does it require any practicum experiences as conditions for certification. The governor of Texas was not the only source of support for this initiative. The proposal was also supported by the State Association of School Boards in Texas. Teacher unions, professional associations for teachers, and teacher educators spoke in opposition to the proposal but fell short in their goal to block the action. The media tended to characterize the opponents of the proposal as "turf-protecting." The State Board of Education approved the new procedures in March of 2004 (Hoffman & Sailors, in press).

What motivated this action? Certainly some of the credit (or blame) falls on the federal *No Child Left Behind (NCLB) Act* of 2001 (United States Office of Education, 2003) that requires states to ensure that all teachers are highly qualified in every subject they teach by the end of the 2005-06 school year. It is left to the individual states to determine what counts as "highly qualified." Currently, the number of "highly qualified" teachers in most states, particularly in low-income areas, falls well short of the targets set by NCLB. The action taken by SBEC, and no doubt the source of support from the State Association of School Boards, was argued for explicitly in terms of NCLB and teacher supply. But clearly, this is not the only motivating factor. Public schools have been exposed in Texas over the past decade through the "high-stakes" testing movement. Schools portrayed as failing by politicians are vulnerable to radical reform. With the economy stalled and unemployment high even among the college educated, teaching now stands as a viable short-term option for employment. Finally, the tax-base for schools has shrunk with the economy. The choice between "opening doors" to all (a no-cost option on the front end) and investing in teacher education has become a point of deliberation. Policy makers are reluctant to invest in the same teacher education that has been characterized as the source of the problem with low performing schools.

Are the policy initiatives underway in the state of Texas an anomaly? Or, are these actions part of a national trend to "leave behind" traditional forms of preservice teacher preparation? Will the "open-door" policy be restricted to the certification of secondary teachers? Or, will it be extended to all levels? I believe there is sufficient evidence to suggest that the actions taken in Texas are indeed part of an effort that is national in scope to dismantle teacher preparation programs. Decisions made and actions taken over the next several years, as with the SBEC plan for certification, may well shape teaching and teacher education far into this millennium. Teacher education is "at risk" of being left behind in the face of such initiatives. As teacher educators concerned with the preparation of teachers in the area of reading, we cannot ignore this movement or its ramifications. How can educators, government officials, and the public ensure the high qualifications of all who teach reading in all elementary and secondary public schools? What is the best way to improve the quality of teacher preparation and increase the numbers of qualified teachers to the levels needed? How can we insure that teachers who are qualified and prepared in the area of reading will take and keep positions in high-poverty schools? How can teacher education regain the trust of the public?

This address explores these key questions with a particular focus on teacher preparation in reading. I have organized this report around the work of the International Reading Association's National Commission on Excellence in Teacher Preparation in Reading. I will offer a summary of the Commission's research and the findings. Most of these findings have been published previously in the research literature and will be referenced accordingly. The goal here is to bring together the total work of the Commission as a way of both addressing the concerns of the moment as well as setting an agenda for the future. I will use the findings from this research to frame a positive role for reading educators to take in addressing the challenges of public trust and public policy. I use the personal pronoun "we" throughout the manuscript. This usage acknowledges the contributions of the many educators, cited in the references who contributed to the work of the Commission. I also use the term "we" to situate myself with the community of reading teacher educators. This is my identity. While I cannot assume to speak for this community, I choose to speak from within it.

The Work of the Commission

In the spring of 1999 the International Reading Association (IRA) established a National Commission on Excellence in Teacher Preparation in Reading. The Board of Directors charged the Commission with developing and executing a program of research that would lead to the identification of the qualities of effective teacher preparation programs with a specific focus on reading. The work of the Commission was to focus on programs of initial teacher preparation offered in the context of four-year, university-based baccalaureate programs. The Commission organized a program of research around three distinct but interrelated studies.

Study 1: Preservice Teacher Preparation in Reading

A national survey of teacher education programs was conducted to determine the "status-quo" of teacher preparation programs across the United States (Hoffman & Roller, 2000). The national survey was designed to assess the status quo for reading teacher preparation programs and practices across the United States. Through this survey descriptive data on existing programs and program features as well as data on the judgments of quality were gathered. Over 900 reading teacher educators from across the United States, representing a wide variety of institutional contexts responded to this survey. The major findings from this IRA Commission survey study included:

- The average number of semester course hours in the area of reading was greater than six (two+ courses).
- Despite recent trends toward 5-year and fifth-year programs, 84% of the respondents described the 4-year baccalaureate as available to students.

- Undergraduate reading specializations were available in over 40% of the programs, with an average of 16+ semester hours required in these programs.
- Descriptions of course textbooks and course topics suggested that a comprehensive and "balanced approach" to reading was represented in most programs.
- Extensive field experiences in teaching reading prior to student teaching (supervised and connected to course content) were commonplace.
- The vast majority of the teaching faculty had both classroom experience in teaching, as well as advanced degrees in the area of reading.
- Teaching diverse learners was identified as a major focus in many programs.
- Over 85% of the respondents rated their programs as "very good" or "outstanding."

Clearly, teacher preparation in the area of reading is receiving greater attention today than in any previous period (Austin & Morrision, 1963; Hoffman & Pearson, 2000). However, variation within the IRA survey data suggests that the range in program characteristics and program quality is great. The results of this survey are useful in interpreting the findings from the other studies conducted by the Commission.

Study 2: Critical Features of Excellence in Teacher Preparation Programs

The second study focused on the identification of program features associated with "excellent" reading teacher preparation programs (Harmon, et.al, 2001; Hoffman, Roller & The National Commission on Reading Teacher Preparation, 2003). The selection panel worked to identify a set of excellent programs of teacher preparation in reading that could become the focus point for the identification of the critical features of programs. Through a competitive application process, a panel of prominent reading educators selected eight sites they judged to have outstanding preparation programs graduating excellent beginning teachers of reading. Twenty-eight colleges and universities applied to participate in the study, providing detailed descriptions of their programs, vignettes of classroom teaching, documentation of learning by recent program graduates, and critiques of these vignettes by program faculty and students and by public school principals and teachers. Some of the applicants nominated their entire teacher preparation programs for consideration, while others submitted just their reading specialization programs. In addition to the criterion of excellence in preparation, the panel also took into consideration the diversity of public and private institutions, large and small, in communities across the United States. The review panel identified eight programs. These were not the "eight best programs," but rather these were eight excellent programs representative of the many that exist in the country. Three of the programs offered undergraduates a choice of a "reading specialization." Only these reading specialization programs were studied. At the other five institutions the emphasis on reading was program wide. At the point in time when these programs were identified, the program directors and other interested faculty became part of the IRA Commission and full collaborators in the research effort

The Commission looked across these eight sites to identify critical program features using qualitative methods. In site visits, structured interviews, and small group meetings with program faculty, the Commission gathered data about each of the eight programs. The eight common features of excellence identified by the Commission through this qualitative analysis were:

- *Content.* Teacher educators engage preservice teachers with a comprehensive curriculum and guide them toward the development of a cohesive knowledge base for effective teacher decision-making.
- *Apprenticeship.* Teacher Educators engage their preservice teachers in a variety of course-related field experiences where they have opportunities to interact with excellent models and mentors.
- *Vision.* Teacher educators center their program around a vision of literacy, quality teaching, and quality teacher education.
- *Resources and Mission.* The teacher education program has sufficient resources (intellectual, financial, and professional) to support the mission for quality teacher preparation.
- *Personalized Teaching.* Teacher educators value diversity and are prepared to offer their preservice students responsive teaching and an adapted curriculum.
- *Autonomy.* Teacher educators are active in adapting and negotiating with their institutions to make sure their students receive the most effective preparation possible.
- *Community.* Teacher educators work to create an active learning community that includes the faculty, their students, and mentor teachers.
- *Assessment.* Teacher educators continually assess their students, their program, their graduates, and themselves to guided instructional decision-making and program development.

Study #3: Investigating the Experiences and
Practices of Commission Program Graduates: A Longitudinal Study

In the third and final line of research, the Commission followed a group of graduates from these "excellent" programs through their first years of teaching. This third study in the Commission research program was guided by two questions: (1) How do the graduates of IRA Commission programs transition into full-time teaching responsibilities? and, (2) How effective are graduates of IRA Commission programs in teaching reading? We adopted both quantitative and qualitative research methods to explore these basic research questions. The study was a longitudinal comparison study—spanning a three-year period of data collection.

The research perspective for the first year of the longitudinal study was qualitative. In large part the decision to adopt a qualitative perspective for Year 1 was based on the nature of the research question. We were interested in understanding the experiences of the first year teachers as interpreted by them and the ways in which these experiences connected to their preservice preparation. There were a total of 101 participants in Year 1 of the study. Forty of these participants were graduates of the three IRA Commission sites who had completed a reading specialization. Thirty-three of the graduates had completed one of the Commission's five reading embedded programs. Twenty-eight additional graduates were identified for participation in the study to serve as comparison teachers. These comparison teachers were graduates from the three Commission institutions that offered a reading specialization. However, these twenty-eight comparison teachers had completed a "general" program and not the specialization.

Structured telephone interviews were conducted at three points in the beginning teachers' first year of teaching (September, January, June). Inductive data-driven analyses yielded 4 overarching themes—instructional decision-making, negotiations, community, and valuing of teacher preparation—that distinguished the responses of graduates of the IRA exemplary programs from those of graduates of general education programs.

Instructional decision-making. Commission teachers reported creating learning experiences and alternative structures that reflected mindful and purposeful planning, such as flexibly grouping students, providing a range of reading material, and offering individual tutoring in response to varying student needs.

Negotiations. Commission teachers were more likely to mention specific actions or decisions taken by them to meet students' needs. These actions were often in the form of supplements to the curriculum but at times were even at odds with the prescribed program within the school they were working.

Community. Graduates of the Commission programs, in large part reported seeking out learning communities, drawing from their school community, as well as colleagues and peers from their teacher preparation programs.

Valuing Teacher Preparation. Finally, Commission teachers viewed their teacher preparation positively and related it to their current classroom practices. Commission graduates reported valuing a variety of features of their teacher preparation programs including college classroom practices, field experiences, and the knowledge base gained from course work.

These four themes revealed stark contrasts between graduates of Commission programs and the graduates of the general education programs. The beginning teachers' from the specialization programs definitive talk about valuing teacher preparation combined with their informed, knowledgeable talk of teaching and learning in their classrooms indicate a likely connection between quality reading teacher preparation and subsequent teaching (A complete report of findings from the first year of the study can be found in Maloch, et.al, 2003).

The methodology for Years 2 and 3 was expanded to include data collection on the classroom environment and classroom teaching that was descriptive and quantitative in nature. We also expanded the participant group to include teachers in the same schools as the Commission graduates. This addition was made to better ground the comparison of Commission teachers with other teachers in a context that was similar. The research questions for Year 2 were focused on a description of the teaching practices of Commission graduates and comparing these practices to other teachers: (1) What are the teaching practices associated with graduates of the Commission sites? and (2) How do these teaching practices compare to other teachers? All of the program teachers included in Year 1 of the study who were teaching in self-contained K-5 classroom settings were invited to continue participation, as were all of the original comparison graduates. Forty-six of the Commission graduates meeting these criteria agreed to continue into Year 2. All of the original program comparison teachers who participated in Year 1 were invited to continue in the study (These were the graduates of the three Commission sites who had completed a general program and not the reading specialization). Eleven of these original program comparison teachers agreed to continue participation. To augment the number of comparison teachers with the same years teaching experience, we actively recruited participation of teachers with the same years teaching experience in the same schools where the Commission gradates were teaching. Seventeen additional teachers meeting these criteria were identified through this process. Combining these two groups we created a group of 28 second-year comparison teachers. A second comparison group was added for Year 2. This group consisted of experienced teachers, matched as close as possible to the Commission teachers' grade level and recommended by the school principals at the Commission teachers' sites as being "excellent." Seventeen of these experienced (nominated as excellent) teachers were successfully identified and agreed to participate in the study following this procedure. The average years teaching experience for this group was thirteen years. We refer to this group as the "site-based experienced teacher" group. The total number of teacher participants for the second year of the study was 92. For Year 3 of this study we expanded the data collection in participating classrooms to include more frequent observations. We also expanded our data collection to include direct measures of student reading achievement with pre (early fall) and post (late spring) standardized testing. All of the program teachers included in Year 2 of the study were invited to continue participation into Year 3. Comparison teachers (same years experience and same grade levels as program teachers) and site-based experienced teachers at the same grade level (recommended by principals as excellent) were recruited. We were able to collect complete data, including student achievement, during Year Three on eighteen program teachers and fifteen "same years" comparison teachers.

Classroom teaching during years 2 and 3 was examined using the TEX-IN3 observation instrument (Hoffman, 2001). This instrument was selected because of its comprehensive focus on effective reading and literacy practices. The TEX-IN3 is focused on the literacy environment of the classroom. It is specifically designed and validated for use in self-contained elementary classrooms. The TEX-IN3 has three major components: a text *In*ventory; a text-*In*-use observation; and a series of text *In*terviews. The instrument has demonstrated excellent reliability and validity characteristics. The major components of the TEX-IN3 have been validated in terms of student achievement growth in reading (Hoffman, Sailors, Duffy & Beretvas, in press). Our focus on the literacy environment as a window to examine teacher effectiveness is consistent with a highly productive line of research into the teaching of reading and reflects findings from a number of studies that have shown the literacy environment created within the classroom is a critical feature of effective teaching. Data collection with the TEX-IN3 was conducted once during Year 2 and three times during Year 3 in all participating classrooms. Observers were trained to high levels of reliability on the TEX-IN3. They were "blind" to the status of the teachers they observed. We analyzed the data from the TEX-IN3 following the same procedures used in Year 2 to compare Program and Comparison Teachers (same years experience) classrooms.

I will share with you only selected findings from Year 2 and 3 observations. There was a statistically significant effect for Teacher Group (F=4.8, df=2, p<.01) on the ratings of teachers on the Holistic Text Environment. These ratings represent the average score on a 1 through 5 rubric with one the lowest score possible and five the highest. Post hoc analysis revealed the difference between the Commission program graduates and the Same Years teaching group was statistically significant (p<.01) and the difference between the Commission program graduates and the experienced teachers was not (p=.23).

The analysis of the data related to the observations of student engagement with texts in the classroom was restricted to the data gathered during the observations focused on reading instruction time (as designated by the classroom teacher). The snapshot QTE observation score is focused on the entire class. The snapshot differences were statistically significant (F=4.867, df=2, p<.01). Post hoc analysis revealed statistically significant differences favoring the Commission graduates over both the same year and site-base experience comparison groups (p<.05). The average student sweep QTE scores were also statistically significant (F=.5066, df=2, p<.01. Post hoc analysis revealed statistically significant differences favoring the Commission graduates over the same years comparison teachers.

The evidence gathered during Years 2 & 3 suggests that the graduates of high quality preparation programs continue to maintain their advantage over the "same years" comparison teachers that was documented in Year 1. The patterns of statistical significance are noteworthy given the power limitations associated with the relatively small numbers of teachers included in the study. Just as important, though, are the consistent patterns in the differences examined across the two years of data collection with the TEX-IN3. A complete report of the findings from the Years 2 & 3 follow-up study can be found in Hoffman, J.V., Roller, C.M., Maloch, B., Sailors, M., Duffy, G.G., Beretvas, S.N. (2004); The National Commission on Excellence in Elementary Teacher Preparation for Reading (2003).

Discussion

The evidence gathered through the work of the Commission suggests that participation in a high quality teacher preparation program that focuses specifically on the teaching of reading has a positive influence on the experience of the teachers entering the profession, and on the quality of and engagement with the literacy environment they create within their classrooms. These claims rest on both the qualitative data gathered in Year 1 and on the observational findings from Years 2 and 3 of the study. While these findings may come as no surprise to teacher educators, they offer scientifically based research evidence for the impact of the quality of teacher preparation on entry into teaching and classroom teaching practices. I am not aware of any study of reading teacher preparation that has followed this large of a sample of teachers over a period of three years with careful attention to the interpretive experiences of the participants, the direct observation of teaching practices. Of the eleven studies included in the NRP report on preservice teacher preparation in reading, the majority was limited to 4 to 6 weeks of data collection. None of the studies reviewed followed graduates into classrooms.

Reactions and Responses

Already, there have been attempts to discredit the work of the Commission.

Susan Neuman, in Education Weekly, was reported to have called the work of the Commission as "invalid" because the selection of Commission sites was not random. This criticism itself is invalid since there never was an attempt to generalize to all teacher education programs. The sample selection was purposeful.

Some reading teacher educators have criticized the report arguing that the programs were not the "best" programs. There was never an intention to identify the best programs, only to identify a set of quality programs that represent the diversity of programs in country. We could replicate this study tomorrow. We could cast the net again. If we did I suspect we would identify 8 different programs, but the findings related to features and the impact would be similar and that is the crucial test of scientific inquiry.

The research has been criticized for the lack of a theoretical framework. This research was never conceived as a test of a theory. It is an empirical study designed to provide the data that could become the basis for building a theory. It is research grounded in the reality of what exists. Our goal is to reveal and then explain. This is theory building. This is no different from what was so successful in the research in teaching literature for over two decades. This is not a study to answer questions but a study that should be useful in formulating theories and framing future research.

The work has been criticized from a "what's new" perspective. True, the findings are aligned with IRA/NCTE and even NCATE standards. However, we cannot assume anything that is obvious to reading educators as good teaching or teacher education will be accepted and supported without "scientific" support. There has been no research base for the IRA/NCTE standards for teacher preparation in reading–until now. We are not surprised that complexity and "good practices" shine in this study. We were not in search of a "silver bullet" solution. What is important to note in the findings is the significant discrepancy between most teacher education programs, as represented in the survey study, and the features of excellence. This is not said to discredit or devalue what we do but to inspire and direct our resolve to move forward.

Why the effort to discredit the research of the Commission? Could it be that the findings that suggest an investment in quality teacher preparation is a promising path are at odds with the current policy environment designed to dismantle teacher preparation programs? The work of the Commission suggests strongly that an investment in teachers and teacher education will have a positive impact on teaching and students. I began this address with a report on an effort in the state of Texas that would begin the dismantling of teacher preparation programs. I argued that this kind of effort is part of a larger national effort to discredit teacher preparation. If we remain passive we will be left behind. If we dig in our heels and become defensive, we will be dismissed as turf protecting by the public and the policy-makers. To move forward in reading teacher preparation, we must advocate for a positive agenda for reform that builds on the findings of the Commission on the one hand and supports future efforts for research into effective practices on the other. The work of the Commission provides a sound base to launch this effort. The choice is simple. It is move forward or be left behind. There is no in between position. The public will not tolerate nor should we tolerate "business as usual." The challenge is an individual one for each of us as teacher educators to make changes. It is also the responsibility of organizations like the College Reading Association (CRA), the International Reading Association (IRA), and the National Reading Conference (NRC) to assume a key role in supporting our efforts.

References

Austin, M.C., & Morrison, C. (1962). *The Torch lighters: Tomorrow's teachers of reading.* Cambridge, MA: Harvard University Press.

Harmon, J., Hedrick, W., Martinez, M., Perez, B., Keehn, S., Fine, J. C., Eldridge, D., Flint, A. S., Littleton, D. M., Bryant-Shanklin, M., Loven, R., Assaf, L., & Sailors, M. (2001). Features of Excellence of Reading Teacher Preparation Programs. In J. V. Hoffman, D. L. Schallert, C. M. Fairbanks, J. Worthy, & B. Maloch (Eds.), *Fiftieth Yearbook of the National Reading Conference.* Chicago: National Reading Conference.

Hoffman, J. V. (2001). The TEX-IN3: *Text Inventory, Text In-Use and Text Interview Observation System.* Unpublished manuscript. University of Texas at Austin.

Hoffman, J.V., & Pearson, P.D. (2000). Reading teacher education in the next millennium: What your grandmother's teacher didn't know that your granddaughter's teacher should. *Reading Research Quarterly, 35* (1), 28-44.

Hoffman, J. V., Roller, C. M. & The National Commission on Excellence in Elementary teacher Preparation for Reading Instruction. (2001). IRA excellence in reading teacher preparation: Current practices in reading teacher education at the undergraduate level in the United States. C. Roller (Ed.), *Learning to teach reading: Setting the research agenda* (pp. 32-79). Newark, DE: International Reading Association.

Hoffman, J. V. & Sailors, M. (2004). Those who can't teach can: Assessing the impact of *No Child Left Behind* on the teacher education. In K. Goodman, P. Shannon, and Y. Goodman (Eds.) *Saving Our Schools,* pp. 137-150. Berkeley, CA: RDR Books.

Hoffman, J.V., Sailors, M., Duffy, G.G., & Beretvas, N. (2004). The Effective Elementary Classroom Literacy Environment: Examining the Validity of the TEX-IN3 Observation System. *Journal of Literacy Research 36*(3), 303-334.

Hoffman, J.V., Roller, C.M., Maloch, B., Sailors, M., Duffy, G.G., Beretvas, S.N. (2004). Teachers' Preparation to Teach Reading and Their Experiences and Practices in The First Three Years of Teaching. *The Elementary School Journal 105*(3), 267-288.

Maloch, B. et al. (2003). Understandings, beliefs, and reported decision making of first-year teachers from different reading teacher preparation programs. *Elementary School Journal,* 103, 431-458.

The National Commission on Excellence in Elementary Teacher Preparation for Reading Instruction. (2003). *Prepared to make a difference.* Newark, DE: International Reading Association.

United States Office of Education (2003). *Inside No Child Left Behind.* Retrieved March 25, 2003 from http://www.ed.gov/legislation/ESEA02/pg2.html#sec1119

LATINO CHILDREN'S LITERATURE *IS* MAINSTREAM

Keynote Address

Becky Chavarría-Cháirez

Becky Chavarría-Cháirez is the author of Magda's Tortillas ~ Las tortillas de Magda, *and* Magda's Piñata Magic ~ Magda y la piñata mágica, *fully bilingual children's picture books published by Arte Público Press/Piñata Books. Becky Chavarría-Cháirez, also is owner of Chameleon Creek Press, a literary and arts communications group serving aspiring to accomplished writers. Based in New Mexico, the award-winning broadcast journalist, freelance writer, playwright, speaker and multiculturalist, can be reached at www.chameleoncreek press.com or chameleoncreek@aol.com.*

The children's book genre has come a long way in recent years, as children's literature has broadened its reach to speak to and about the infinite rainbow of readers. For those of us who care about and promote literacy, this is the time many of us have been waiting for. And, for me, this is what my life has prepared me for.

Consider, we live in a nation where all are afforded the promise of inalienable rights; individual freedoms, democratic principles, and ideals that sustain and bind us. Among the mix is the diversity of American life and culture, which ensures our ever-changing cultural landscape, will need and seek multicultural, multilingual stories to mirror the lives of our American children.

The American melting pot remains on simmer. This will likely be present throughout our lifetime and the lives of generations to come. Due to our geographic kinship to *las Américas* in this hemisphere, war, disease, political change and the desire for the American dream, these factors will ensure that our American culture and literature will continue evolving and that the need for Latino/Hispanic-themed and bilingual children's books will grow. And, for children's book authors and illustrators, this means our artistic assignment will be to capture this dynamic trend and accurately reflect our ever-shrinking planet for the children. This situation is precisely why I began writing for children about Latino children, their families, and many blendings of culture wrapped in universally understood terms *AND* in two languages, the two most spoken languages in the United States. This is not a prediction for the future, because the future *IS* now!

Each one of you here today has seen it, and at the very least, has certainly read about this American shift. And, the publishing industry and literary community have taken notice of this reality. Nearly everything Latino/Hispanic is influencing and flavoring our pop culture in many genres—from Hollywood, art, music, culinary trends, the media; the children's book market is no exception.

Diversity is here. Diversity matters. Diversity is no longer a foreign notion, neither misunderstood nor underrated. In my life, diversity has been a way of life. Diversity has been a cornerstone of what I consider life's university without walls.

Let's flash back to my upbringing. I grew up in one of America's most unique cities, San Antonio—home of sun, salsa and Cisneros, as I say. San Antonio offered an environment where my culture was dominant and in constant interaction with many cultures and peoples in the city which I lovingly refer to as the "military melting pot," a southern cousin to Ellis Island. But, unlike Ellis Island, San Antonio is just a few hours north of the U.S.-Mexico border.

In my old neighborhood, beyond each front doorstep, there were many worlds to discover. My old neighborhood, barrio or as I like to imagine, my own Ellis Island, was one residential block of 20 single-family dwellings was a place where Korean, German, Italian, Irish, Sicilian, Mexican-American, Polish, Czech, Scottish, French—and most likely a few others—interacted and blended in the simplest and yet most profound ways.

Across the United States, many cities much further from San Antonio, cities located in North Carolina, Georgia, Oregon, Arkansas and virtually every state in the union, are absorbing Latino culture. My San Antonio roots have traveled far and adopted many other Latino cultures along the way—through war, economic hardship, and the quest for American dream.

Let's further consider the numbers and the outlook: **The majority of Hispanic children in the United States were born here to U.S. citizens of Hispanic origin.** I am the offspring of U.S.-born, Mexican-American parents, whose parents came into the U.S. soon after the Mexican Revolution and the flu pandemic that killed untold millions.

The majority of Hispanic children in the U.S. are predominantly English speakers and yet, the continuous arrival of immigrants from Latin American countries coupled with the growing need for the practical use of Spanish in the workplace and, the desire of many Latinos to preserve culture through language, further ensure that there always will be a need for children's books, educational materials and *THEN SOME* in Spanish.

In recent years, Hispanic newspapers and magazines have begun featuring more advertising for Spanish-language audiences.

In the '80s and '90s, major U.S. cities like Dallas, Houston and San Antonio became one-newspaper towns—and those are just the ones in Texas. But, now, in the 21st century, Dallas and Fort Worth each have another daily paper. No, these are not new English-language dailies in direct competition—these are new dailies published in Spanish. The largest Spanish-language newspaper dailies in North Texas are in Dallas/Fort Worth—*Al Día*, which is owned by The Belo Corporation and *Diario La Estrella,* which is owned by the Fort Worth Star-Telegram. Both are corporate-owned, not a mom-and-pop periodical, like the majority of Latino publications that have been in existence.

Discount stores like Wal-Mart, Target and Toys 'R Us have expanded their book inventories to include Spanish and bilingual titles.

For those of you who own a DVD player - - - - (That reminds me . . . I have a knock-knock joke that I'm saving to tell you all later. Be sure to remind me.)

DVD's are making a tremendous impact on the exchange of cultures and languages. One can select from numerous options. You've probably noticed that now you can opt to view a DVD program/movie and supplemental features, activities and games in several languages.

Now if we turn on the tube to watch television, haven't you noticed some commercials in Spanish are being aired on English-language television? And, I'm not talking, *"Yo quiero Taco Bell."* The first time I saw these Spanish-language ads, I checked to see who flipped the channel and then, I realized it was *intentional* on the advertisers' part, if not inevitable. Spanish is creeping into the workplace and marketplace. Notice how often you now see signage and advertising in Spanish? Next time you step into your shower, take a close look at the product labels for your shampoo or look in your medicine cabinet and read the side panels on your over-the-counter medications.

Tune in your AM/FM shower radio and you will likely hear Latino rhythms and Hispanic recording artists spicing up the pop music charts. I haven't done a complete inventory, but I think all of the daytime soaps have their Latino characters and they aren't just maids and gardeners anymore.

In the classroom, bilingual education programs are also diversifying. Recently, dual-language programs in schools allow children to learn all subjects in English and Spanish, putting the languages to simultaneous use. Currently, the United States has more than 31 million Hispanics, making it or rather, us—*nosotros*, the fifth largest Spanish-speaking country in the world. *¿Qué?* you may be asking yourselves. Listen carefully and let this sink in. This is not only happening in the southwest region of the United States. For example, the 2000 census found that North Carolina's Hispanic population registered a 394 percent increase in population, making North Carolina one of the fastest-growing states with a growing Hispanic population. **By 2010, it is projected that only Mexico will have more Spanish-speakers.** (Yes, let's stop and allow me to repeat that sentence again. Write this down.) And by 2050, Hispanics will number 96 million, approximately 24% of the overall U.S. population. Before you attempt to fully fathom that estimate, consider the likelihood that this government projection may be somewhat conservative. So, why not round that up to 100 million!

Now for those of you who savor politics in America, the political parties are allocating additional funds and outreach efforts to court the growing Hispanic vote in several states, including Georgia, Arkansas, not to mention in those states generations ahead in that trend. On a recent ABC news show, George Stephanopoulos predicted that there is no turning back. Every future presidential candidate's political future will greatly benefit from the candidate's ability to speak Spanish and know how to court the many sectors in the Pan-Hispanic community.

Coming full circle—returning to the literary scene. More publishers will be publishing bilingual books and stories based in Hispanic culture or featuring Latino characters. Bilingual books are versatile and user-friendly, not only serving a greater number of readers, but also reaching across generations and their language proficiencies within extended Hispanic families. In some homes one parent or an entire generation may speak Spanish and the other parent may prefer English. And, in some, as my family—TEX-MEX or *Spanglish* was forbidden.

Publishers no longer ask if they should venture into the Hispanic book market. Some are sorry they hesitated entering the market, but can console themselves in knowing that the genre will remain in demand.

As more students enroll in dual-language programs, they will seek Spanish titles to reinforce their new language usage.

Perhaps one of the unexpected benefits of writing bilingual children's books is that my books and those of many other Latino children's book authors are not just for kids. Adults use them, too! English-as-a-Second Language students and Latinos who are learning to read in their native language, Spanish, and then bridging from their native language to English are taking these early steps into literacy and bilingualism with children's books. It makes sense— Absolutely, *¡Claro que sí!*

Teachers and librarians affirm that the bilingual children's book genre with Hispanic-themed stories is on target. Their enthusiastic acceptance and usage of these books in their libraries and classrooms is helping Hispanic children's books become instant classics. Diversity begets more diversity. Perhaps diversity is universal. Looking within the Latino demographic, there is much to consider beyond language—there are *other* nuances of culture to capture. But, this is not an easy task. There is immense diversity within this diverse ethnic group. For publishers and writers, this means they must carefully edit books that present this Pan-Hispanic rainbow in its many dimensions.

Hispanics are not from one country and they do not all share the same customs and language preferences, for that matter. They may be from one or more racial groups. And, not all Latin Americans speak Spanish. In South America, Brazilians speak Portuguese. One Central American country's official language is English. Which one? Belize.

Tortillas are considered Hispanic, but are not traditionally served in every Latin American country. The same goes for tamales, tacos, even chips and *salsa*—the spicy condiment that has been outselling catsup in the United States. Salsa is something you eat but is it also a style of music and dance style popularized in the Caribbean, a musical mélange of Afro-Cuban and Latino rhythms. *Mariachi* music is not universally played either. Did you know the *mariachi* is something the Mexicans borrowed from the French?

Book publishers—the mainstream, multi-cultural and Hispanic houses—have all taken notice. The surge in dual-language programming in the Southwest and other regions where the influx in Hispanic populations continues, further fuels this demand. Several Latino writers—myself included—decided to write children's books to meet their personal desire for stories which mirror the real-life cultures and traditions of Latino children in the U.S. In fact, this is the mission of my publisher, Arte Público Press and Piñata Books, its children's imprint.

Some of the best selling Spanish children's books are not written by Hispanics and they aren't about Hispanic children, i.e. *Clifford™*, *Barney™*, *Curious George™*, *Madeleine™* (well, okay, Pepito is Madeleine's *amigo*, a Spaniard) and others, yet they have universal appeal to youngsters. But, the real growth market and demand is for books for and about Latino characters and themes.

If you are interested in writing for the Latino market, keep in mind these criteria that most publishers want to see in their titles:
- Authentic characters, setting,—even in fiction, situations are and should be true to life, easy for Hispanic as well as all young readers to relate to.
- Positive portrayal of Hispanics as leaders, teachers, role models. Bio-

graphical books about Hispanic leaders are much needed as schools seek Latino heroes, writers, sports stars, artists, politicians, educators and others to focus on the contributions of Latino society in the U.S.

- Correct use of language, spelling, grammar and the text should be impeccably translated. Children's books are not just for entertainment. They can reinforce proper usage of Spanish. In bilingual books, the reader should receive a clear and easily understood message in either text. Translation is a fine art of utmost importance.
- The absence of stereotypical images. Not all Hispanics are short, dark-skinned, with black hair and use burros for transportation. These images were common in the earliest portrayals of Hispanics. Stereotypes are to be avoided in all depictions of Latino culture and lifestyles. Avoid stereotypical messages and images regarding economic, cultural, religious and lifestyle diversity to illustrate and model whom Latinos really are.
- Realistic portrayal of cultural issues, traditions to instill ethnic pride and cross-cultural awareness are desired in varying degrees.

Just as every child is individual and unique, the same is true of the Hispanic/Latino child. There is what I call The Latino Melting Pot to consider. While the majority of Latinos in the Southwestern United States are from Mexico, there are Latinos from dozens of Latin-American countries. It is important to remember, each Latino child is part of a unique family with his or her cultural fingerprint. More and more of these children are being born into multi-ethnic homes to Hispanic and non-Hispanic parents.

Keep a watch on the bookstore and library shelves; diversity in Latino-themed children's books will evolve into another literary trend. As children's stories explore the basic elements of Latino cultures with themes about holidays, celebrations, food and traditions, folklore, history and more this is only the beginning. Given the multitude of Hispanic groups and the number of blended Latino and non-Latino cultures, diversity in Latino books will be the next wave, or, rather a permanent fixture in American children's literature, an accurate reflection of the many peoples who make up Hispanic life in the U.S. and the greater Americas.

As publishers expand the scope of their stories and cultural situations, we will likely begin seeing more children's books featuring blended Latino families. Part of the American experience is the continual melting pot within our borders. Stories about how a Latino/Hispanic family must familiarize itself with another Latino's customs, foods and other ethnic/cultural traditions because mommy is Puerto Rican and daddy is Mexican. Grandma is German but Grandpa is Cuban. These are more common now. And, let's check out reality television—like it or not.

Recently, in the weeks before this conference, I have, like many of you, been watching The Bachelor. Quickly, tell me, there are three eligible ladies left in "Roseland" . . . Who are they? I am most intrigued by the dynamics and interaction millions witnessed a few nights ago with Bachelorette Mary and her Cuban-American family in Miami, Florida. All along, I thought that Mary was Latina but since the girls' surnames are never given I wasn't sure. Then Mary brings Bachelor Bob to her folks home to meet all her *hermanas* and her *padres*. A family member translates for Bob and the millions of viewers. And the body language: Did you notice how Bob was surrounded by Mary's relatives who talked to him well within his personal space? Well, I got a big kick out of this . . . This is happening all over the US. Couples like Mary and Bob are marrying, having children and adding to the need for bilingual children's books.

It used to be the old fables taught us how to act and behave and there were those nursery rhymes, fairy and moralistic tales. Today's children's books provide guidance on a whole new level. These stories will help families build understanding, mutual respect and find, if not foster, common ground—the stuff that binds families together. As different ethnic groups neighbor one another in the American landscapes, expect to see their stories side by side, sharing shelf space in bookstores and libraries. Beyond telling stories to entertain, they can enlighten and help draw families together, Hispanic-themed children's books. . . . are part of the literary melting pot. Hispanic-themed books help demonstrate empathy, appreciation and respect for our differences. It is not an act of political correctness, it is the right thing to do—I consider it just another dimension to what we call the all-American experience.

Now children's books like those in my Magda Madrigal series feature adventures that tell their stories, although fiction, they are reality-based.

Parents who just over a decade ago were wanting their children to learn Japanese, now realize there is a much greater likelihood that the next generation will be doing more business with the extended American family— the ones who share our hemisphere and speak Spanish. I would even venture to say that Arabic will be next language wave. It will be a necessity for national security and building cultural bridges.

Teachers can attest that their Hispanic youngsters derive a greater sense of belonging and gain a higher self-esteem. When Latino children are not just viewed as "an other" but as another in the American family, this has a vitally visceral and visible impact. I get the biggest kick out of reading my books to Hispanic children. I love watching the students' body language. They become fully entranced by Magda making tortillas or creating piñata magic for her little brother and hearing how the characters can speak both languages. The body language is strong: kids' pupils dilate and they hang on to every word. For Hispanic children, these stories validate who they are and will build their cultural self-awareness and boost their personal self-esteem. Who knows, this new genre in children's books could be the supplemental link that educators have needed to help Hispanic students stay in school and celebrate who they are. We won't know right away, but this book genre is something to experience. *Vamos a ver.* We shall see.

Lastly, for non-Hispanic children, I want them to discover the universal themes and emotions—Hispanic children have stories to tell about their first day at school, losing a pet, moving to a new house, having a new baby brother or sister. The situations are similar and the subtle differences in the details are only minor, not differences, just the details—the details of life.

My character, Magda Madrigal is like millions of Latino children in the U.S. and accurately captures a glimpse into their lives including their Spanish language, family traditions, and food customs—the universal elements of culture. Magda's stories underscore the universal connections we all share. Family, home, love, compassion, problem solving, and always, with a generous helping of adventure!

So, stay tuned and watch the bookshelves in your local libraries and bookstores. The first Latino U.S. president is probably in diapers right now. Oh, and don't touch that dial because Bachelor Bob will soon choose his bacherlorette. If it's Mary—the family will deal with questions of language, race, perhaps religion, customs, and traditions and blend every aspect of their lives as their hearts may intertwine. And, if Bob chooses Mary, we know the family WILL be able to do some things together—watch the same DVD's.

Which brings me back to my joke:
Knock-knock . . . or *'Tan-Tan'*
Who's there? *¿Quién es?*
DVD/DVD who. . . .? *¿Quién?*
DVDDVDVDVD—That's all folks!

Reflections, Remembrances and Resonances

Keynote Address

Albert J. Mazurkiewicz

Kean University

Dr. Albert J. Mazurkiewicz is a Professor Emeritus at Kean University. A founder of CRA, he has provided exemplary leadership and service to the Association from its beginning. Because of his immeasurable service to the CRA, the Service Award was renamed for him and now is the Albert J. Mazurkiewicz Special Services Award. His insights into the history of CRA are invaluable. The following is his keynote address for the J. Estill Alexander Forum for CRA Leaders in Literacy.

Before there was a CRA (College Reading Association) there was an IRA (International Reading Association) and an NCTE (National Council of Teachers of English). Before there was an IRA, there was an International Council for the Improvement of Reading Instruction (ICIRI) founded by Emmet A. Betts at Temple University in 1947 and a National Association for Remedial Teaching (NART) c. 1947. NART had sectional meetings for Pre-School & Primary, Middle & Upper Grades, High School, College and Adult & Clinical Reading. As can be seen, these covered three of the areas we in CRA have been interested in and where people in teacher education and in Reading & Study Skills programs might have found a home. Unfortunately, NART and ICIRI joined together as one organization in 1955 and these areas were lost. The focus in subsequent years, as with NCTE, was on the primary grades.

About the same time, Oscar Causey had established the Southwest Reading Conference in Texas, which on his death lapsed for a year or two to be reborn as the National Reading Conference, which, as we all know, eventually separated to form the NRC and ARF, the American Reading Forum. Only the North Central Reading Association, which existed at the same time as Causey's conference, focused on College Adult Problems. This organization was made up of Educators and Management Training Directors from such industries as Firestone Tire and Rubber Co., Standard Oil of Ohio, etc., and continued for a while meeting only in the mid-central areas and eventually disappeared.

In the early issues of bulletins produced by each of the two major organizations, *The Reading Teacher* of the ICIRI, which became the Reading Teacher we know today of IRA, carried short articles by such early luminaries as Francis Triggs (Triggs Diagnostic Reading Test) and Arthur Gates. Gates (1952) wrote tellingly that

> . . . . the significance of test norms is frequently misunderstood. The norm represents not an ideal achievement but merely an average or mediocre attainment. It reveals what the statistically average child in a large population does. Necessarily about half of the children in this large population fall at or below the norm score, and another half exceed the norm score. If a class is composed of pupils of superior mentality coming from superior homes and with superior teaching equipment, they should be expected to exceed the norm on average, whereas less privileged children should not be expected to equal the norm. (1-2)

He continued pointing out that "It should be realized that at this particular time the exact significant of norms, that is, of an average or grade score, is not as clear cut as it was a couple of decades ago." And that "all tests have a limited and not a perfect reliability. The score on any test will, on average, not be an absolute measure of the pupil's ability, but an approximation of it."

On the other hand, some of the early articles found in these early publications were superficial and/or descriptive of programs in place in schools. Needless to say, we college adult practitioners and teachers of teachers found such material mostly irrelevant. Moreover, a college instructor in the field had limited financial resources and could not readily travel large distances to keep up with or make contributions to the field. We felt alienated and met in small groups at local conferences to share ideas.

But what was Reading like in those days? When I began my graduate studies in 1950, reading was, at the University or Pennsylvania, found in Education and consisted of two courses. The completion of these two courses, taught by Drs. Preston and Bond, we were assured, made us qualified to direct a Reading & Study Skills Center. And, sure enough, that's what happened to me. It was only while working in the field that I discovered what I didn't know and sought help elsewhere.

At Temple University, on the other hand, where I continued my studies, a doctorate of some 20 courses in the Psychology of Reading was possible. True, a number of these courses were seminars with Dr. Betts, but others were by doctoral level teaching assistants my own age such as Marjorie Johnson, Roy Kress and Jules Abraams.

At that time college adult and even upper level grade school reading would be best characterized as "mechanical." We were taught to diagnose reading problems with the opthalmograph, later renamed the reading eye camera, and identified duration of fixations, return sweep, saccades, etc., using a continuous photograph of reflections from the eye in motion while reading a passage or short article. The difficulty in photographing the reflected light from the eyes was then compounded by the time spent having to have the film, which could be several feet in length, developed by a commercial photographer. This early device was eventually improved to contain the film and developer in one unit and became somewhat messy with leaks of the solution and was then known as the Reading Eye Camera.

Follow-up instruction, with or without such diagnosis, used devices such as the tachistoscope where words and phrases were flashed for recognition at 1/100 of a second, the Reading Rate Accelerator, which utilized a plastic slide descending over a page of print to force the reader to keep ahead. This was often frustrating to the reader and he'd attempt to stop the plastic shutter by hand and the shutter would break. The instructor needed to be a mechanic of sorts having to tighten screws and replace broken shutters. Other similar devices such as the rateometer and a less cumbersome accelerator were in use using the SRA books, level 1 thru 3. Tests of rate using the 1st article in the series were compared to tests of rate at the end of the series to graph and chart progress.

At the upper grade school and even the college level as early as 1936 the metronoscope, a triple shutter, short exposure device for controlled reading was used. It was a mechanical device that established reading in a rhythmical left-to-right sequence, and conditioned an accurate return sweep.

The reaction time was controlled by limiting the length of the exposure time, and, as the material could not be reread, regressive movement within the line was discouraged. Speed of reading was automatically controlled. In actual practice the instructor inserted a story roll in the instrument—similar to the roll in a player piano, and adjusted the speed dial. Phrases in the lines corresponding to shutter width were of varying lengths but were controlled and directed by the manufacturer.

This same concept was utilized in films by the California Test Bureau at that time to develop a series of films for this same purpose. They, however, did not pursue selling of this product though they had developed the films. Similar to this metronoscope presentation were the films produced by the

Iowa Reading Film Series. A bar of light highlighted the 2 or 3 word phrases in a line of print and moved inexorably to the end of the line with a return sweep to the next line. Again the span of recognition of print was controlled by the manufacturer not the reader. The Harvard Reading Film Series adopted a different approach and used a slanted bar of light moving across the line of print in an attempt to allow for individual spans of recognition. In those days, film projectors did use a rheostat to control the speed of film movement and so a variety of rates could be established by the instructor in addition to those established in the film series. Speed or rate of reading was the thing. A little later, Evelyn Wood's approach caused a stir because no equipment other than the book was used.

It wasn't until later that a focus on comprehension and study-type reading became apparent. Rachel Salisbury's doctoral dissertation on organization and outlining, resulting in her manual called *Better Work Habits* (World Book, 1936) became a useful tool in teaching. The work of the trainers in the air force using the 3R approach to study was implemented early in college adult work. The PQ RST by Stanton followed and later Robinson came up with his SQ3R approach, which many of us used in teaching.

And what was reading like in the elementary grades? We all know that the late forties and early fifties was the heyday of the basal reader. When Rudolph Flesch in 1955 produced his polemic *Why Johnny Can't Read,* his thesis was that "we were not teaching phonics." And I agreed with him! This may have been why he agreed to address the Reading Conference of some 4000 I arranged at Lehigh University at a later point when he was not accepting speech requests elsewhere. But it wasn't a difficult position to take because an examination of the Basal Readers of the day found what I called "fractionated phonics."

The Basal Reader was the ubiquitous tool to teach reading in the primary grades during the 40's and 50's and every major figure associated with a University, Gales, McKee, Betts, Grey, O'Donnell, Witty, Rowland, Dolch, etc., were also represented by a basal series produced separately by the many publishers that existed at that time. The odd part about these readers was that they all followed a pattern: a limited vocabulary, a formulaic agreement of so many new words per story, so many new words per page, and fractionated phonics. Phonics was not taught but discovered—the analytic approach, and began with consonants. Pronunciations of these were discovered first at the beginning of words, then the ends of words and finally the middle position of words. The rationale for this fractionated phonics discovery approach was not apparent in the literature and even though I asked many of the series "authors," I could get no good answer. The best I could find was the research of the tachistoscopic researchers like Tinker who showed us that when words were flashed at 1/100 of a second or less that adults recall consonants at the beginning of words most frequently, at the end next most frequently and then in the medial position. What adult behaviors had to do with children's abilities was not discussed and we know that discovery approaches were negated by later research.

The point of this was that essentially no one of the series "authors" believed in teaching phonics *directly* and thus Flesch's statement was correct.

Remember, too, that all of these series started their discovery approach to word recognition using consonants. When Open Court materials appeared on the scene, I received a number of calls decrying their use because they were teaching vowels first and long vowels at that. I pointed out to each caller that there was nothing more wrong with this approach than starting with consonants, that there was no law or rule about which to start with, just the convention of series authors. (That same convention negated using contractions, quotation marks, etc., in early readers as being too difficult a concept for children to deal with.)

If, in fact, we wanted a logical research approach to base our introduction of the 1 letter-sound correspondences, we needed look no farther than the work of cryptographers. They all recognized that the letter e is the most ubiquitous of letters in running print and you start with that in busting English based codes. While it's also true that the letter e represents the schwa sound most frequently, then the short sound, most of the schwa sounds relates to the word *the* which we would teach via look-say anyway.

The work of Godfrey Dewey (1923) on letter sound correspondence in running words could have guided us producing an entab *sridl* order of introduction of short vowel and consonants sounds. Later research found in our own journal updates this early knowledge.

But right now there's no rule, which requires that phonic elements be taught in any sequence and such current authors as Barbara Fox (2004) makes that point in her text *Word Identification Strategies*. I happened to be reading this earlier today to determine what current authors are writing and noted her comment "You may be surprised to learn that research does not support the use of any particular sequence over another. There is no prescribed order in which the letter-sound patterns must be taught, no immutable learning hierarchy and no sequence chiseled in stone. You are free to teach letter-sound patterns in any order whatsoever. . . " (116). And, of course, I agree with her.

Of interest, too, in this reading period was also a lack of recognition of early literacy development (now called emergent) and that as early as the age of 3, when scribbling was purposeful, that "literacy hunger" was shown among children. Reading in kindergarten (or earlier) was verboten and unheard of.

I recall participating in a panel discussion relating to issues of the day with Roma Gans, Helen Robinson and others in a huge session housed in an auditorium. It must have been Cobo Hall in Detroit where IRA met. In any case we as individuals were to respond to questions on current issues put to us. The question of reading in kindergarten was asked and none of the panel seemed to want to touch this "hot button" item since no one volunteered. Nothing loath, I took up the question and supported teaching reading in kindergarten offering a literacy hunger rationale. Roma Gans jumped on me, taking me to task, supported the opposite, and pointed out that kindergarten was a socialization play experience, etc., and that "If we taught them to read, Al, then what would they read." This I submit was kind of an embarrassing position to take since there were probably three or four hundred children's writers among the thousands in the audience. But it points up to the strong views people held against "feeding them when they're hungry" and even differentiating instruction, and reflected our early concerns or lack thereof.

Recall reveals that at each end of the reading spectrum certain characteristics were obvious. In the beginning, a timidity about providing differential literacy instruction prior to the first grade, and a sameness of instruction dominated by the "star" system established by publishers to edit their series all of which aped each other. At the other end, the high school/college/adult levels, there was an emphasis on the mechanical, relying on devices to diagnose, to provide motivation, or to control peripheral aspects of the act and art of reading.

References

Dewey, G. (1923). *Relative Frequency of English Speech Sounds*. Cambridge: Harvard University Press.

Flesch, R. (1955). *Why Johnny Can't Read: A New Look at the Scandal in Our Schools*. New York: Harper.

Fox, B. (2004). *Word Identification Strategies* (3rd ed.). Upper Saddle River, NJ: Merrill/ Prentice Hall.

Gates, A. (1952). Standardized Reading Tests–Their Uses and Abuses. *The Reading Teacher, 5*(5), 1-2.

RESEARCH
AWARDS

SHARING STORYBOOKS:
A STUDY WITH FAMILIES FROM
DIVERSE CULTURAL BACKGROUNDS

Dissertation Award

Jacqueline Lynch

University of British Columbia

Abstract

This study examined the ways in which families from diverse cultural backgrounds support their children's literacy development through storybook sharing. There were 35 parents videotaped while sharing a narrative with their 3- or 4-year-old children. The sample consisted of East Asian Canadians, South Asian Canadians, Mexican Canadians, European Canadians, and First Nations or Native American people. Videotapes were transcribed in their entirety and parent-child interactions were coded using a modified scheme by Shapiro, Anderson, and Anderson (1997). The types of gestures, statements, and questions by parents and children were used in the analysis. Many low level cognitive demands characterized the types of parent-child interactions. However, parents engaged in scaffolding to support their children's literacy development.

The purpose of this research was to describe the ways in which families from diverse cultural backgrounds interact with their children in storybook reading. The importance of parents reading to children has been heavily promoted by educators for some time. As early as 1908 in the United States, Huey suggested that children's literacy learning begins with parents reading to their child at home. It seems that no other single activity is regarded as important as the shared book experience between caregivers and children for children's early literacy development (Neuman, 1999). Despite the importance placed on storybook reading for children's literacy learning, there is little known about the quality of storybook interactions among diverse cultural groups (Anderson, Anderson, Lynch, & Shapiro, 2003). If educators continue to encourage parents from diverse cultural groups to read to their children, then it is important that there is awareness of the types of interactions that occur when parents are encouraged to do so. Parents' interaction with children in storybook reading has shown to relate to children's literacy knowledge (Leseman & de Jong, 1998).

During parent-child book sharing, certain types of questions place more cognitive demands on children than do others. As well, certain statements exemplify more or less cognitive distancing. Sigel (1970) defined distancing as "behavior or events that separate the child [individual] cognitively from the immediate behavioral environment" (pp. 111-112). It refers to the interposing of physical and/or psychological space between the person and the event (Sigel, 1993).

Torr and Clugston (1999) based their research on Sigel's (1970) distancing model. They claimed that questions that seek a *yes/no* response (that seek to confirm) or demand information about person, location, or time (e.g., who? what? where? when?) do not encourage children to engage in abstract reasoning, unlike questions (e.g., how? why?) that require some explanation about cause and effect, consequences, or processes. Moreover, ". . . questions which make 'higher order' cognitive demands on children . . . are thought to promote literacy understandings in terms of developing skills of hypothesizing, predicting, and understanding the relativity of one's own perspective relative to others" (p. 31). Haden, Reese, and Fivush (1996) claimed that prediction and print interactions are considered highly demanding for children while association interactions are considered moderately demanding, requiring some distancing from the present to relate the text to past or future experiences. Snow (1991) addressed the importance of certain types of talk about text for story comprehension. She suggested that talk that goes beyond the immediate text, such as predicting outcomes and evaluating parts of a story,— need fosters the type of cognitive skills necessary for higher-level comprehension. She emphasized the importance of such "decontexualized language" for children's literacy achievement.

Few studies have examined interactions in storybook reading among diverse cultural groups. One of the studies to include diverse cultural groups was conducted by Bus, Leseman, and Keultjes (2000). They studied how parents from different cultural groups living in the Netherlands mediated a simple narrative text to their 4-year-old children. Bus et al.'s study included 19 Surinamese-Dutch, 19 Turkish-Dutch, and 19 Dutch low SES mother-child dyads. Mothers from ethnic minorities were less inclined to deviate from text than were non-minority mothers. Interactions between dyads from ethnic minorities were characterized by low cognitive-demand behaviors such as naming details. Gunderson and Anderson's (2003) research combining interviewing and survey techniques to investigate beliefs about literacy learning and teaching held by Chinese Canadian, European Canadian, and Indo-Canadian parents, found that ethnic minorities were less inclined to deviate from text than were non-minority mothers. There were more interactions with text among non-minority families. European Canadian parents felt it was most important that children interrupt and ask questions when engaging in shared reading.

The research presented here is part of a larger, longitudinal study of multiliteracies which includes (a) interviews with parents about their literacy beliefs, (b) the videotaping of shared storybook reading, (c) engagement in mathematical tasks, and the assessment of children's language and literacy knowledge (Anderson, Anderson, & Shapiro, 1999). The results presented here on shared storybook reading represent one part of the analysis of the larger, longitudinal study.

Method

This study included 35 children and their parents living in an urban area of Western Canada. Thirteen boys and 22 girls participated and all of the children were involved in preschool programs. Children were 3 or 4 years of age. Mostly mothers (28 mothers and 7 fathers) were involved in this study. Parents were from diverse cultural backgrounds, which included East Asian Canadians, South Asian Canadians, Mexican Canadians, European Canadians, and First Nations or Native American people. The area where the study was conducted is composed of many families from diverse cultural backgrounds (Anderson, Anderson, Lynch, & Shapiro, 2003). Parents' education level ranged from a high school diploma to university graduate degrees.

Videotaped Storybook Reading

The researcher contacted preschools and daycares in neighborhoods with diverse populations. Preschool administrators were informed about the purpose of the study, i.e., to examine how parents from diverse cultural backgrounds support children's multiliteracy development, and the tasks involved in this study. Preschool administrators who agreed to participate were given permission letters and information about the study to distribute to parents. Parents returned the letter to the preschool and the researcher collected the returned forms. The researcher contacted by phone those parents who agreed to participate and arranged a time to meet with parents and children. Parents were asked to complete several tasks and to give permission for their children to complete several tasks, which were part of the larger, longitudinal study. One shared book reading activity for each family in the sample is focused on in the findings presented here. Only families who could complete the tasks in English were asked to participate. Nevertheless, in some instances parents reverted to another language while book sharing. In these instances, a research assistant was employed to transcribe these interactions and readings.

Parents were told that this study would examine how they support children's literacy through storybook reading. Parents were asked to share a storybook with their child, *Swimmy* (Lionni, 1991) or *Mr. McMouse* (Lionni, 1992) in their home or at the preschool, as they preferred. Approximately half of the participants chose to have the videotaping done in their home. When the dyads were videotaped in the home, parents were asked to choose a place they would like to share the storybook. Preschools often provided a quiet area for the videotaping of parents and children when parents chose to have the taping completed there. The video recorder was turned on and was placed at a distance of approximately 12-15 ft from the participants to keep the distraction at a minimum. Parents were given the narrative by the researcher and were asked to share the story with their children as they normally would to reveal how they interact with their children while book sharing. The researcher pretended to be busy in order to be less of a distraction. Two different narratives were used to help control book familiarity as these parents would be videotaped twice in a two-year period. The researcher maintained a record to assure that there was a balance of the books shared. Parents were thanked by the researcher after book sharing with their child and the families engaged in other activities as part of the larger study, such as playing a board game. An honorarium was given when the families completed all of the tasks.

Data Preparation

Videotapes were transcribed in their entirety in relation to parent and child interactions when book sharing and were used for coding. All gestures to the text and illustrations and all verbal interactions were recorded. Also, whether the parent or the child spoke during the interaction was recorded.

Data Analysis

Data from the videotaping were coded using a modified category scheme developed by Shapiro, Anderson, & Anderson (1997). This scheme was selected because of its focus on different levels of thinking skills associated with the various types of interactions. Certain types of interactions have been shown to relate to children's achievement (Leseman & de Jong, 1998). Shapiro et al.'s scheme was more specific than some others (e.g., Dickinson, DeTemple, Hirschler, & Smith, 1992; Sonnenschein & Munsterman, 2002) where interactions were grouped into broader categories. The focus of the analysis was also different for these studies. Haden et al.'s (1996) scheme was somewhat similar to Shapiro et al's (1997) scheme, however gestures where not included in their coding. Shapiro et al.'s coding scheme was based on the literature on interactions in shared book reading contexts (Anderson, 1987; Yaden, Smolkin, & Conlon, 1989) and most closely served the purpose of this study.

The researcher modified Shapiro et al.'s (1997) coding scheme in several ways. The most apparent of these were not including the attention to mathematics, and by including questioning as a category within each type of interaction rather than as a separate category. The "new knowledge" category was omitted from the original scheme and a category labeled "association" was added. These changes were made after the researcher transcribed the videotapes and reviewed the transcripts. This coding scheme was modified because of the need to focus on specific literacy events in the shared reading and to distinguish questions from statements because questions and statements produced different types of discourse (Kertoy, 1994). Procedural talk was not included in the data analysis because the purpose of the study was to examine interactions based on the print and content of the narrative.

The researcher reviewed all of the transcripts and coded all of the data according to the scheme described below. Each unit of meaning was coded. This usually included phrases or sentences, sometimes separated by a pause. All gestures were coded. Whether the parent or child spoke or gestured in the interaction was first recorded. Next, the type of interaction was recorded, such as clarification or confirmation. Finally, whether the unit of meaning was a statement or question was identified. An example of one of the coding recordings: p-conf-q. This meant that the parent asked a confirmation question. When gestures were used in the story sharing activity, they were recorded in a similar pattern: e.g., c-gest-i, which meant the child pointed to the illustration. The total number for each type of interaction was calculated and used in the analysis. The types of interactions coded and used in the analysis for this study can be viewed in Table 1. Figure 1 is a bar graph that depicts the mean score of the types of interactions in the shared reading activity.

The researcher coded all of the data and a graduate student specializing in literacy education independently coded 26% of the data that had been randomly selected by the researcher. On this set of data, an agreement of 81% was obtained before discussion and 89% after discussion of the disagreements. An independent samples *t*-test was used to examine differences in the categories of parent-child interactions based on the specific book shared. No significant differences were found.

Coding Scheme. A total of 27 categories, which included questions, statements, and gestures, were used in this study. Two categories (i.e., child print statements and child print questions) were combined into one category because there was only one child who asked a question about print and this child also made statements about print. The sum of the types of interactions was recorded.

Table 1. Total Number and Mean Scores of Parent-child Interactions

	Total	*M*	*SD*
	N = 35	*N* = 35	*N* = 35
Gesture 1	320	9.14	8.48
Gesture 2	223	6.37	6.06
Gesture 3	56	1.60	3.01
Gesture 4	14	.40	.91
Print 1	50	1.43	3.64
Print 2	34	.97	4.39
Print 3	30	.86	2.29
Confirmation 1	520	14.86	13.51
Confirmation 2	395	11.29	9.20
Confirmation 3	329	9.40	12.11
Confirmation 4	50	1.43	2.16
Clarification 1	193	5.51	5.23
Clarification 2	38	1.09	1.60
Clarification 3	47	1.34	2.09
Clarification 4	38	1.09	1.90
Elaboration 1	36	1.03	1.60
Elaboration 2	11	.31	.76
Elaboration 3	13	.37	1.09
Elaboration 4	2	.06	.24
Association 1	10	.29	.46
Association 2	5	.14	.36
Association 3	12	.34	.64
Association 4	2	.06	.24
Prediction 1	15	.43	.70
Prediction 2	3	.09	.28
Prediction 3	16	.46	.82
Prediction 4	2	.06	.24

Note. 1 = parent-statement; 2 = child-statement; 3 = parent-question; 4 = child-question.
Exception: Gesture 1 & 2 = point to illustration; Gesture 3 & 4 = point to print.

Categories were grouped based on whether the parent or the child spoke in the interaction. The following is a list of the types of interaction categories included in this study, an explanation of their meaning, and examples of the categories:

- Gesture 1 & 2: Parent/child points to the illustration with his/her finger.
- Gesture 3 & 4: Parent/child points to the print with his/her finger.
- Print/graphophonics: Parents and children make statements and ask questions about the print or the sound and name of individual letters.

Figure 1. Mean Score of Parent-Child Interactions in Storybook Reading.

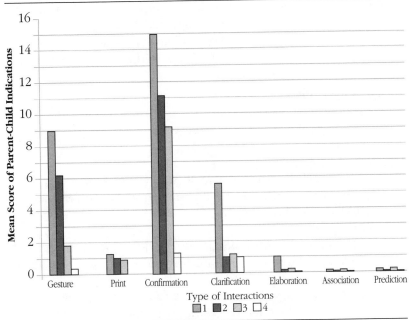

Note. 1 = parent-statement; 2 = child-statement; 3 = parent-question; 4 = child-question. Exception: Gesture 1 & 2 = point to illustration; Gesture 3 & 4 = point to print.

- Confirmation: Parents and children confirm that which is written in text by repeating the text exactly or by paraphrasing the text. Parents and children confirm what is in the illustrations by labeling what is seen in the illustration. Interactions involve basic comprehension of what has already occurred in the text, for example, by helping the child order story events. Confirmation also includes parents' and children's responses to one another (agreement or disagreement).

- Clarification: Parents and children explain the meaning of what is written in the text or that presented in the illustration. There is more of a connection made to help one understand what is happening in the text or illustrations than that which occurs in confirmation. The cause-effect relationship included here makes explicit many implicit connections in the story, for example, why a character performs a certain action.

- Elaboration: Parents and children expand on or extend what is in the text (not necessary for clarifying what is happening in the text but helps to create meaning). The elaboration of text sometimes occurs after clarification interactions.

- Association: Parents and children incorporate their own personal experiences in interactions with text and illustrations.
- Prediction: Parents and children make statements or ask questions about what will happen in the text or illustrations. That is, they predict future story events.

Examples of the Categories.

- Print/graphophonics
  P: Can you tell me what all those letters are?
  C: s m s m
- Confirmation
  ONLY ONE OF THEM WAS AS BLACK AS A MUSSEL SHELL.
  (Capitalization indicates that the parent read the text verbatim.)
  P: One of them was black.
- Clarification
  AN EEL WHOSE TAIL WAS ALMOST TOO FAR AWAY TO REMEMBER.
  P: Because the head of the fish is here and its tail is way down there.
- Elaboration
  BUT WHEN SPINNY WAS HALFWAY UP THE TRUNK, SPINNY SAW A BLACK CAT SLOWLY NEARING THE TREE.
  P: What do cats like to do? They like to eat mouse.
- Association
  BUT THE SEA WAS FULL OF WONDERFUL CREATURES AND. . . .
  P: Ooh, just like we saw at the Aquarium.
- Prediction
  ONLY TIMOTHY AND SPINNY WERE STILL RUNNING. THE CAT A FEW FEET BEHIND.
  P: She is going to run up these (steps) as fast as she can.

Limitations

The data analysis included here involves one observed interactive reading for each parent-child dyad, during a session arranged by the examiner. Sessions arranged by an examiner may be less realistic and not as valid a representation of its meaning and purposes in everyday experiences as a naturally occurring storybook reading event (Rogoff, Mistry, Goncu, & Mosier, 1993). However, parents were given the opportunity to have the shared reading taped in their home. It is expected that discomfort and atypical actions that may have been present at the initiation of parent-child book sharing would have become more natural and realistic as the taped session progressed. The video recorder was placed at a reasonable distance from the participants to reduce its distraction during this event. The researcher observed that after several minutes, the participants, in general, did not look at the camera, which may signify a focus on the book sharing. The results of this study reflect interactions around a narrative. The results may vary depending on which book genre is used.

Findings

The most common types of interactions between parents and children during story sharing were confirmation statements and questions. Just over 50% of the interactions (53%) were confirmation statements and questions, spoken by the parent and the child. Gesturing to illustrations was also common among the families in this study (22%) and this interaction often accompanied confirmation statements and questions. Therefore, 75% of the interactions were confirmation related and involved pointing to illustrations.

Clarification statements and questions by parents and children accounted for 13% of the interactions. Interactions around print, including talk and gestures, were 7% of the total interactions. Prediction, association, and elaboration statements and questions were less frequently used by parents and children in the shared reading activity. When these types of interactions were combined, they accounted for 5% of the total number of interactions in the shared reading activity.

Interactions by parents were 67% of the total number of interactions in storybook reading while 33% were by children. There was little extension of text, particularly by children. Approximately 70% of the elaboration statements were made by parents. There were few examples of parents creating meaning beyond the text. Parents, however, did make clarifying statements to help their child understand the meaning of the story. These accounted for 8% of all parent-child interactions. Some parents focused on print through talk and pointing to print (6%), and this interaction was slightly more common than parents' association, prediction, and elaboration statements and questions combined, which accounted for 4% of all parent-child interactions. Often, talk about print was accompanied by pointing to print.

Children mostly made confirmation statements when interacting with the text (48% of their total interactions), which often consisted of a comment about the illustration (27% of their interactions). Children asked almost as many clarification questions as confirmation questions. Clarification questions by the child accounted for 5% of their interactions and confirmation questions accounted for 6%. There was a much greater difference between the number of confirmation questions asked by parents and the number of clarification questions asked by them. Of the questions asked by parents, 20% were confirmation while 3% were clarification questions. There were more questions asked by parents than were asked by children overall. Parents asked 14% more questions than did children. A focus on print accounted for 4% of children's total interactions .

Discussion

It seems that confirmation or low level cognitive demand interactions (Hayden et al., 1996) were somewhat common in parent-child interactions with young children based on a number of related factors. Some factors proposed to relate to this type of interaction include parents' SES and children's book reading experiences. Research suggests that parents from low SES tend to interact with children in less cognitively challenging ways (Dickinson et al., 1992; Sonnenschein & Munsterman, 2002). Sonnenschein and Munsterman's (2002) research with mostly low-income African-American and European-American parents and their 5-year-old children found that talk about the immediate content was the most common type of discussion in shared book reading. Bus and van IJzendoorn (1995) suggested that children with little past experience in being read to are less competent and therefore need more support in communication of the pictures and the text. Bus et al.'s (2000) study with Dutch, Turkish-Dutch, and Surinamese-Dutch families, found that Dutch parents focused more attention on connections going beyond the text and on children's own experiences as opposed to the ethnic minorities in their study. Confirmation statements and questions dominated the discussion in shared book reading in the current study. Many of the families in the current study came from similar SES backgrounds, ranging from lower-to-upper middle class backgrounds. Because parents agreed to be videotaped while sharing a storybook, it was assumed that children had at least some experience in being read to by their parents. Parents' cultural background may relate to their focus on confirmation interactions. It was claimed that parents often interact and teach their children based on memories of how they learned to read (Evans, Barraball, & Eberle, 1998).

Prediction, association, and the elaboration of text are considered more cognitively challenging for children than are other types of storybook interactions, such as confirmation statements (Haden et al., 1996). However, parents and children seldom engaged in these types of interactions. It has been shown that some cultures do not agree with predicting when reading (Gunderson & Anderson, 2003), which may support the finding of few prediction interactions when book sharing. For some families, religion may influence the way in which they interact with text, in that there is little questioning of the text and more of a focus on learning the text verbatim (Heath, 1983). Anderson and Gunderson (1997) claimed that for some cultures accuracy is important from the beginning, rather than accuracy would evolve from practice. Perhaps cultural background may relate to the number of questions that could be answered directly from the text as well as the repetition of text in this study. Differences based on culture may also be the result of different views on how to interact with children. Parents may model what is interesting and important for their child to remember (Snow & Ninio, 1983). Association statements and questions, which involve linking new material to children's previous experiences, seemed to be an important tool for helping some children become literate (Taylor, 1998). Parents made few attempts to associate the text with children's personal experiences in the shared book reading in this study. It may have been the case that the narrative was different from many of the experiences of children in this study or that parents saw little benefit in relating the text to children's personal experiences. Bus et al. (2000) suggested that as parents are more responsive to children, conversations around the reading of the text go beyond the text and include discussion of children's own experiences related to the story.

Parents interacted more by using statements than questions. The use of questions may help to engage children in thinking about the text. When the parent explains what is happening in the text, he or she is not attempting to involve the child (Bus & van IJzendoorn, 1995). Heath's (1983) research showed cultural differences in question interactions in that low-SES African American caregivers did not use questions as much as low-SES White mothers. When parents asked questions in the current study, these were often confirmation questions. Asking questions that involve complex inferences may be more helpful for children's literacy development (Bus & van IJzendoorn, 1995). Parents asked few clarification questions in this study and more frequently made clarification statements. It may be that parents were sensitive to their children's literacy level and felt that children would not be able to answer these types of questions. There were few attempts to engage children's thinking in this way.

Children's use of questioning during story sharing suggests their interest in learning more about the story. Children in this study asked as many clarification questions as they made clarification statements. Flood (1977) found that questions asked by children in book sharing were the best predictor of children's success in pre-reading tasks. It may be the case that children ask questions before they make statements exemplifying their knowledge. More research has focused on parents' interaction with children in storybook reading than children's initiation of interactions.

Pointing out print in the shared reading activity played a small role in the total number of interactions. Sonnenschein and Munsterman (2002) found that parents and young children typically do not engage in talk relevant for increasing knowledge about print. It could be argued that some children may lose interest and the ability to follow the story when there is a focus on print rather than the story. Print is considered a high demand interaction because children have to treat the story and the text simultaneously (Hayden & Fagan, 1987). Some parents from diverse cultural backgrounds have strong skills-based beliefs about how children learn to read and to write, yet they do not focus on print in their shared reading with children (Lynch, 2003). Therefore, some parents consider learning about the mechanics of print important for children's literacy development, but they may not use the shared reading context to teach these skills. It may be the case that some cultural groups prefer to engage in the direct teaching of literacy skills outside of storybook reading. Senechal, LeFevre, Thomas, and Daley's (1998) research showed that oral language but not written language skills increased when parents shared a storybook with their child. "A program designed to enhance written-language skills through the use of storybooks may not be successful if it does not integrate instruction of print-specific skills during the book readings" (Senechal et al., 1998, p. 110).

With such an emphasis on book reading experience when children begin school, parents should be made aware that specific types of interactions have shown to relate to children's literacy achievement (Leseman & de Jong, 1998). It has been claimed that when children initiate a discussion in storybook reading, their discussion often involves low-cognitive-demand behaviors, such as discussion of pictures and character labeling, than when parents initiate the discussion (Bus et al., 2000). Hence, it is important for parents to scaffold for children statements and questions that place higher cognitive demands on children. Previous research has shown that when mothers used immediate talk or low cognitively demanding interactions, the children tended to do the same and when mothers used non-immediate talk, children tended to use it (DeTemple & Tabors, 1994). One example of this situation in this study involved the mother asking the following: "Ooh, what is happening?" The child, shortly after, asked: "Why is he out of breath?". An analysis of the transcript revealed that this type of question was not asked by the child previous to the initiation by the parent. This finding related to Vygotsky's (1978) zone of proximal development wherein parents help to scaffold children's learning (Bruner, 1986). When scaffolding, parents adjust their interactions based on children's responses to their interactions. The following is an example that shows that when a father notices a lack of his daughter's understanding of story plot and vocabulary, he does not make further attempts to ask what is happening, and he begins to confine the discussion to the illustrations, in particular, to labeling them. The father goes from making clarifying questions and statements, to confirmation questions and statements, to a focus on illustrations. The trend is from high demand interactions to less cognitively demanding interactions.

HE SWAM AWAY IN THE DEEP WET WORLD. HE WAS SCARED, LONELY AND VERY SAD.
F: Because the tuna fish ate all the red fish and Swimmy was left alone and he was very sad
C: Alone
HE SAW A MEDUSA MADE OF RAINBOW JELLY.
F: Why do they call it rainbow jelly?
C: (no response)
F: Because it was different colors, right?
AN EEL WHOSE TAIL WAS ALMOST TOO FAR AWAY TO REMEMBER
F: What it this? (refers to illustration)
C: Eel (makes shape with hands)
AND SEA ANEMONES WHO LOOKED LIKE PINK PALM TREES SWAYING IN THE WIND.
F: So what did he find . . . he found sea animals. What is this pink animal? (refers to illustration)
C: Sea animals

Previous research has shown that parents are sensitive to children's developmental level with text and adjust their interactions accordingly (Bus & van IJzendoorn, 1995). From the transcripts of storybook reading interactions, it was apparent that many parents tried to scaffold learning for their children. Some parents scaffolded children's learning by asking more difficult questions for children to see if children could answer them, and then proceeded to ask less challenging questions if their child had difficulty answering the question. Also, when children asked questions that demonstrated knowledge about the topic of the book, parents made more cognitively challenging statements about the text in further interactions with their children. This demonstrated that parents monitored children's level of understanding and made more challenging statements in relation to children's current literacy understanding. Storybook reading provides an optimal situation for parents to engage in scaffolding with their child (DeBaryshe, 1992). Scaffolding is important for helping to guide children's learning.

Although some parents from diverse cultural backgrounds in the current study used scaffolding in storybook reading to enhance children's understanding of text, low-level cognitive demands in storybook reading dominated the types of interactions. Children's literacy level may have influenced parents' interactions with children in shared reading. However, parents should continue to strive to challenge children's thinking level. It has been suggested that difficulties in reading and writing in school may be due to failure to develop abstract approaches and strategies (Sorsby & Martlew, 1991). Storybook sharing provides an opportunity to engage in abstract thinking.

Conclusion

As stated by Bus et al. (2000) "the potential role of book reading as a stimulus for early literacy may vary among culturally divergent groups" (p. 73). Indeed, storybook reading may be just one way in which children become literate but its important role in helping children become literate has not changed. Certain types of interactions in storybook reading have been shown to relate to children's literacy development and parents should be made aware that these types of interactions, when developmentally appropriate, may help their children's literacy development. Some parents may also require modeling of the interactions in order to incorporate them into shared reading with their child.

"Children from lower socioeconomic and nonmainstream cultural communities often exhibit somewhat poorer school achievement, and their less-extensive knowledge of literacy is evident even by the time they begin school" (Scarborough & Dobrich, 1994, p. 247). Perhaps early literacy activities, such as storybook reading, can provide an initiation into higher order thinking processes that can be built on in schools. Leseman and de Jong (1998) hypothesized that a focus on nonimmediate discourse was important for the development of reading comprehension.

Educators often tell parents that they should read to their child, but little is known about what occurs when parents from diverse cultural backgrounds are asked by educators to read to their children. Studies such as the present one with diverse cultural groups describes the type of knowledge children may be learning from interacting with their parents in specific ways in storybook reading. It may be important for both educators and researchers to ask parents about their reasons for engaging in particular literacy behaviors, including their interactions with children in storybook reading. This insight on reasons for parents' interactions with children may foster a better understanding between home and school of how best to support children's literacy learning.

References

Anderson, J. (1987). *Cognitive and social interactions in shared big book experiences.* Unpublished doctoral dissertation, University of Alberta, Canada.

Anderson, J., Anderson, A., Lynch, J., & Shapiro, J. (2003). Storybook reading in a multicultural society: Critical perspectives. In A. van Kleeck, S. Stahl, & E. Bauer (Eds.), *On reading to children: Parents and teachers* (pp. 203-230). Mahwah, NJ: Lawrence Erlbaum.

Anderson, J., Anderson, A., & Shapiro, J. (1999-2002). *The emergence and mediation of multiple literacies in young children from diverse backgrounds* [410-99-0200]. Ottawa, Ontario: Social Sciences and Humanities Research Council of Canada.

Anderson, J., & Gunderson, L. (1997). Literacy learning outside the classroom. *The Reading Teacher, 50,* 514-516.

Bruner, J. (1986). *Actual minds, possible worlds.* Cambridge, MA: Harvard University Press.

Bus, A., Leseman, P., & Keultjes, P. (2000). Joint book reading across cultures: A comparison of Surinamese-Dutch, Turkish-Dutch, and Dutch parent-child dyads. *Journal of Literacy Research, 32,* 53-76.

Bus, A., & van IJzendoorn, M. (1995). Mothers reading to their 3-year-olds: The role of mother-child attachment security in becoming literate. *Reading Research Quarterly, 30,* 998-1015.

DeBaryshe, B. (1992). *Early language and literacy activities in the home.* Greensboro, North Carolina: North Carolina University, Department of Human Development and Family Studies. (ERIC Document Reproduction Service No. ED 351 406)

DeTemple, J. & Tabors, P. (1994, December). *Styles of interaction during a book reading task: Implications for literacy intervention with low-income families.* Paper presented at the National Reading Conference Annual Meeting, San Diego, CA.

Dickinson, D., DeTemple, J., Hirschler, J., & Smith, M. (1992). Book reading with preschoolers: Coconstruction of text at home and at school. *Early Childhood Research Quarterly, 7,* 323-346.

Evans, M., Barraball, L., & Eberle, T. (1998). Parental responses to miscues during child-to-parent book reading. *Journal of Applied Developmental Psychology, 19,* 67-84.

Flood, J. (1977). Parental styles in reading episodes with young children. *The Reading Teacher, 30,* 864-867.

Gunderson, L., & Anderson, J. (2003). Multicultural views of literacy learning and teachings. In A. Willis, G. Garcia, R. Barrera, & V. Harris (Eds.), *Multicultural issues in literacy research and practice* (pp. 123-144). Mahwah, NJ: Lawrence Erlbaum.

Haden, C., Reese, E., & Fivush, R. (1996). Mothers' extratextual comments during storybook reading: Stylistic differences over time and across texts. *Discourse Processes, 21,* 135-169.

Hayden, H., & Fagan, W. (1987). Fathers and mothers reading familiar and unfamiliar stories to their children. *Reading-Canada-Lecture, 5,* 231-238.

Heath, S. (1983). *Ways with words.* United Kingdom: Cambridge. University Press.

Huey, E. (1908). *The psychology and pedagogy of reading.* New York: Macmillan.

Kertoy, M. (1994). Adult interactive strategies and the spontaneous comments of preschoolers during joint storybook readings. *Journal of Research in Childhood Education, 9,* 58-67.

Leseman, P., & de Jong, P. (1998). Home literacy: Opportunity, instruction, cooperation and social-emotional quality predicting early reading achievement. *Reading Research Quarterly, 33,* 294-318.

Lionni, L. (1991). *Swimmy.* Logan, IA: Perfection Learning.

Lionni, L. (1992). *Mr. McMouse.* New York: Knopf.

Lynch, J. (2003). *Shared storybook reading in families from diverse cultural backgrounds.* Unpublished doctoral dissertation, University of British Columbia, Canada.

Neuman, S. (1999). Books make a difference: A study of access to literacy. *Reading Research Quarterly, 34,* 286-311.

Phillips, G., & McNaughton, S. (1990). The practice of storybook reading to preschool children in mainstream New Zealand families. *Reading Research Quarterly, 25,* 196-212.

Rogoff, B., Mistry, J., Goncu, A., & Mosier, C. (1993). Guided participation in cultural activity by toddlers and caregivers. *Monographs of the Society for Research in Child Development, 58*, (Serial no. 236).

Scarborough, H., & Dobrich, W. (1994). On the efficacy of reading to preschoolers. *Developmental Review, 14*, 245-302.

Senechal, M., LeFevre, J., Thomas, E., & Daley, K. (1998). Differential effects of home literacy experiences on the development of oral and written language. *Reading Research Quarterly, 33*, 96-116.

Shapiro, J., Anderson, J., & Anderson, A. (1997). Diversity in parental storybook reading. *Early Child Development and Care, 127-128*, 47-59.

Sigel, I. (1970). The distancing hypothesis: A causal hypothesis for the acquisition of representational thought. In M. Jones (Ed.), *Miami symposium on the prediction of behavior, 1968: Effects of early experience* (pp. 99-118). Coral Gables, FL: University of Miami Press.

Sigel, I. (1993). The centrality of a distancing model for the development of representational competence. In R. Cocking & K. Renninger (Eds.), *The development and meaning of psychological distance* (pp.141-158). Hillsdale, NJ: Lawrence Erlbaum.

Snow, C. (1991). The theoretical basis of the home-school study of language and literacy development. *Journal of Research in Childhood Education, 6*, 1-8.

Sonnenschein, S., & Munsterman, K. (2002). The influence of home-based reading interactions on 5-year-olds' reading motivations and early literacy development. *Early Childhood Research Quarterly, 17*, 318-337.

Sorsby, A., & Martlew, M. (1991). Representational demands in mothers' talk to preschool children in two contexts: picture book reading and a modeling task. *Journal of Child Language, 18*, 373-395.

Taylor, D. (1998). *Family literacy: Young children learning to read and to write.* Portsmouth, NH: Heinemann.

Torr, J., & Clugston, L. (1999). A comparison between informational and narrative picture books as a context for reasoning between caregivers and 4-year-old children. *Early Child Development and Care, 159*, 25-41.

Vygotsky, L. (1978). *Mind in society: The development of higher psychological processes.* Cambridge, MA: Harvard University Press.

Yaden, D., Smolkin, L., & Conlon, A. (1989). Preschoolers' questions about pictures, print conventions and story texts during reading aloud at home. *Reading Research Quarterly, 24*, 189-214.

Author Note

My thanks to Dr. Jim Anderson, my doctoral supervisor, for his support of this research. This research was partially funded by a grant from the Social Sciences and Humanities Council of Canada, Award No. – 752-2002-1860.

THE EFFECTS OF VISUALIZATION INSTRUCTION ON FIRST GRADERS' STORY RETELLING

Master's Thesis Award

Tracy Zimmerman

SUNY Brockport College

Abstract

This study investigated the effects of visualization instruction on first graders' comprehension as shown in their retelling scores that preceded a running reading record. This study was based on the need to teach students how to actively engage in comprehending text while reading. Students were taught how to visualize stories with no print, stories without illustrations, and stories with illustrations and print. Journals and story maps were utilized to increase visualization usage and retelling abilities. Pre- and post-tests were given to identify students' use of visualization strategies and to measure the effects of this skill on their retelling scores. The results of this study showed a statistically significant improvement in students' retelling and visualization scores following the visualization instruction.

The purpose of this study was to determine if visualization instruction in a balanced literacy program adequately teaches first graders to independently use visualization strategies while reading to enhance their story retelling abilities. The first graders in this study were taught the importance and use of visualization and retelling strategies to aid, as well as to demonstrate, their comprehension of text.

Need for the Study

Primary students are taught a myriad of literacy skills and strategies to become effective decoders and fluent readers. These skills and strategies lay the groundwork for comprehending text, but they do not ensure it. Comprehension needs to be taught in order for students to understand and remember that they read (Bell, 1991). Comprehension strategies, such as inferring, predicting, asking questions, and summarizing, should become automatic and independent within each child. Visualization, or visual imagery, is another very important comprehension tool that students need to learn and use independently. When students form pictures in their minds of what they read, they are better able to remember and understand text (Gambrell & Jawitz, 1993).

Comprehension of text is a critical and active process; it is the reason why we read. Students need to be taught the importance of actively thinking while reading to comprehend text. Supported by their research, Brabham and Villaume (2002) define active readers as strategic readers who are thoughtful and skillful when they read. Brabham and Villaume believe that when we teach students how to become strategic readers, we also teach them that reading is empowering. They maintain that students who feel empowered by their own reading are, for example, more often compelled to visualize their understanding of what they read. Likewise, they are more apt to ask their own questions about literature, make connections with text, and make predictions about possible outcomes to enhance their comprehension.

Educators need to teach children how they can be successful, or empowered, when they read. Too often teachers spend time teaching children how to comprehend individual stories with skills that cannot be generalized to other text. Visualization is one way that readers can successfully achieve comprehension, as it is a skill that can be used with every story that a child reads; it is a realistic tool to help children comprehend text. Some research suggests that a major difference between students who are efficient at comprehending and those who are not is that the former are better able to develop visualizations during the reading process. Seeing the author's message, seeing "the movie," increases students' abilities to make connections, inferences, predictions, and commit their sense of the story to memory for recall (Ekwall & Shanker, 1998).

Further research that links greater student comprehension with increased visualization instruction in the classroom will be powerful to teachers seeking authentic ways to enhance their students' literacy skills. There is a need for research that exemplifies how students' visualizations can be brought from an automatic level to an enhanced conscious level allowing them to actively process what they "see" and ultimately help them to comprehend, retain, and make meaningful what they read.

Review of the Literature
The Importance of Visualization

When we choose visualization as a means to better understand a story, we make our reading and the voice of the author more personal (Goudvis & Harvey, 2000). The image or the "movie in our minds" engages us and, according to Bridge, Long, and Winograd (1989), it increases the effectiveness of our memory. Visual imagery functions as an "organizational tool for coding and storing meaning gained from the reading" (p. 370). Additionally, Gambrell and Jawitz (1993) support that mental images aid other processes used to comprehend text as well, such as constructing inferences, making predictions, and using schemata.

An effective reader is one who can gestalt images, or visualize the whole circumstance, that an author is describing. "Vivid gestalt imaging may even be considered a 'vicarious experience'" (Bell, 1991, p. 248). That is, as Goudvis and Harvey (2000) previously stated, the reader learns from the movie that is created in his or her mind, as opposed to actually living the events of the story. With strong visualizations that gestalt imaging allows, an individual is better able to predict and understand the sequence of events in a story, form relationships with the characters, learn new vocabulary, and ultimately store this information efficiently for later retrieval when he is called to demonstrate comprehension of the text (Bell, 1991).

Balanced Literacy

A balanced literacy program is ideal for teaching and learning visualization skills as it is based on research and provides different reading and writing experiences for children while giving them different levels of support. Skill instruction is meaningful as students acquire appropriate reading strategies and greater comprehension, rather than simply trying to complete a book or prescribed lessons. The teacher's role is to observe students while helping them to develop strategies, like visualization, which are necessary to become independent readers and writers (Blair-Larsen & Williams, 1999).

Some characteristics of balanced literacy that easily accommodate visualization instruction are that teachers read aloud to students to model the use of comprehension strategies and to expand students' vocabulary. Enlarged text is used for shared reading experiences to teach children critical reading strategies. Guided reading allows teachers to work with small groups of children who have the same literacy needs at a given point in time and supports the use of skills taught while children attempt to problem solve on their own. Lastly, independent reading provides students with opportunities to apply reading strategies independently. (Fountas & Pinnell, 1996). Again, these are only some of the aspects and qualities of a balanced reading and writing program that support visualization instruction and student practice so that skills may become purposeful and independent.

When beginning visualization instruction in a balanced literacy classroom, Ekwall and Shanker (1998) suggest that teachers initially read aloud to students to teach and model the use of visualization strategies. A teacher should begin by reading aloud, then think aloud to children about what he or she visualizes while reading. Students should be invited to express their visualizations so differences and similarities in mental images can be discussed. The remaining elements of a balanced literacy program should then follow.

The Design of the Study
Research Questions
1. Does the teaching of visualization strategies in a balanced literacy program significantly impact first graders' retellings during a running reading record?
2. Does the teaching of visualization strategies in a balanced literacy program significantly impact first graders' use of visualization during a running reading record?

Methodology
Subjects
The subjects in this study were twenty-two heterogeneously grouped first graders in a suburban elementary school. Eleven students were boys and eleven students were girls.

Materials
The materials that were used in this study were (a) leveled books designated by the school for conducting running reading records, (b) necessary forms the teacher filled in during each running reading record, (c) a teacher notebook to log answers to the three visualization questions students were asked during the running reading record, (d) post-it notes, (e) student journals, (f) read aloud books, (g) shared reading big books, and (h) leveled guided reading books. The following is a list of read aloud and shared reading books used to instruct students on visualization strategies:

Carl Goes to Daycare by Alexander Day (Green Tiger Press)
Dream Weaver by Jonathan London (Silver Whistle)
Mufaro's Beautiful Daughters by John Steptoe (Lothrop, Lee, and Shephard Books)
Hattie and the Fox by Mem Fox (Bradbury Press)
Everything Grows by Raffi (Crown)
The Berenstain Bear Scouts Save That Backscratcher by Stan and Jan Berenstain (Scholastic)

Procedures

The teacher conducted a running reading record on each student at the onset of this eight-week study as a pretest to determine his or her independent reading level and knowledge about visualization usage. Books used for these running reading records were designated by the school for the purpose of assessing students use of strategies and to determine their instructional reading levels. Halfway through the running reading record, the book was removed by the teacher and the student was asked three visualization related questions to set a baseline for his or her knowledge about this concept (see Appendix B). The questions were asked at this point to see if the child was creating images about the content of the story during the reading. The book was returned for the third question, and then the student completed the running reading record. After reading the book, each student was asked to retell the story in his or her own words to demonstrate comprehension of the story. An additional set of standard comprehension questions was asked after each student had read and retold the story. Scores for these questions were only used to help calculate each child's independent reading level and was not studied in relation to the visualization instruction.

During the six weeks that followed, students were taught the importance of visualization and how to use visualization strategies with books that have pictures and with books that do not, including wordless picture books. Students drew pictures and wrote in their journals about what they visualized in their minds, and they wrote about key words that triggered those visualizations. They were given time to verbalize their visualizations with peers. Students then learned how to use those images to produce an enhanced story retelling. The Story Face story map was introduced as a visual tool for retelling a story (see Appendix A). All instruction was done through teacher modeling in read alouds, group modeling and practice in shared reading, and individual refinement in guided reading groups.

The teacher conducted a posttest during the eighth week of the study by using running reading records the same way they were used for the pretest at the beginning of the study. This allowed the researcher to look for increased retelling scores and an increase in use of visualization while reading.

Analysis of Data

Points were earned on the retelling portion of the pre- and post-tests when a child verbally gave details relating to the main characters, setting, plot, and ending of the stories. More points were received when details were given in correct sequence. The school provided forms and standardized procedures for the retellings.

Students earned up to three points, one for each question, on the visualization portion of the pre- and post-tests. A point was earned for the first question if a student answered "yes" to making a picture in his or her mind. If the student said "no," then the questioning did not continue and the student did not receive any points.

If a student, for question number two, stated or described a picture in two or more words that was seen in the students' mind, and it was relevant to the context of the story, then that child received one point. A response might have begun with, "I saw. . . ." If a child was unable to state or describe a picture in his or her mind, the questioning stopped, and the child did not receive any points for the first or the second question. Therefore, the first two questions had to be answered satisfactorily to receive two points; otherwise no points were earned suggesting that visualization was not really used.

One point was earned for the third question if a child mentioned and located one or more words in the story that described the picture that was created in his or her mind. A student did not earn a point for this question if an answer was not given or if the words stated did not appear in the text. If the child did not earn a point for this question, the previous two points earned from questions one and two still remained.

Findings and Interpretations

A paired two-sample t test for the means of the pre and post retelling measures, and likewise for the pre and post visualization measures, was conducted to determine the statistical difference between the two means in each case.

The first research question was: Does the teaching of visualization strategies in a balanced literacy program significantly impact first graders' retellings during a running reading record? The data present in Table 1 show that the critical t was 2.08. The obtained t was -7.38. This demonstrates that there was a statistically significant difference between the pre and post retelling scores.

Table 1. *t* Test: Paired Two Sample for Means—Retelling

	Pre-test	Post-test
Mean	6.14	15.86
Standard Deviation	4.58	4.27
Observations	22	22
Hypothesized Mean Difference	0	
df	21	
t Stat	-7.38	
t Critical two-tail	2.08	

The second research question was: Does the teaching of visualization strategies in a balanced literacy program significantly impact first graders' use of visualization during a running reading record? The data present in Table 2 show that the critical t was 2.08. The obtained t was -3.81. This demonstrates that there was a statistically significant difference between the pre and post visualization scores.

Table 2. t Test: Paired Two Sample for Means—Visualization

	PRE-TEST	POST-TEST
Mean	0.91	2.36
Standard Deviation	1.27	1.18
Observations	22	22
Hypothesized Mean Difference	0	
df	21	
t Stat	-3.81	
t Critical two-tail	2.08	

Conclusions and Implications
Observations

Looking at the data and working with the students in this study, I observed that the range of scores for both the retelling and visualization measures decreased from the pre-tests to the post-tests. The scores of the lower achieving students increased the most which, in turn, decreased the ranges. Possibly these students gained the most because they had the most room to grow.

Sometimes during the visualization post-test, students gave responses stating that the pictures in the book, not just the words, helped them to visualize. A few students made inferences using the pictures they created in their minds. This suggested that more types of visualization skills than measured were used by the children.

Some of the higher achieving students did not use visualization during the posttest, even when they may have used it during the pretest. Their reading growth over the course of this study may have made the book levels for the post running reading records too easy for them. It is possible that students do not need to use or rely on visualization to comprehend text that is lower than their maximum independent reading levels. In a post hoc analysis, I found that statistically students' post visualization scores had no effect on their post retelling scores. Sometimes students showed growth on one post-test but not the other. An individual student in this study, for example, commented before his post retelling, "I am going to try to visualize it." His pre visualization score was zero, and his post visualization score increased greatly to a three out of three points. He was definitely successful using visualization. His pre retelling, however, was already a high number of 18. His post retelling only went up to 20 out of an infinite number of points. This does not prove that visualization helped him to gain those two points and certainly did not help him to achieve a proportionately greater post retelling score.

Implications

Implications for the Classroom

As the data in this study revealed, visualization instruction greatly increases students' use of the skill and, when combined with story retelling instruction, it also increases students' ability to demonstrate their comprehension through retellings.

Visualization instruction can be easily implemented by incorporating it into read alouds, shared reading instruction, journal writing, and guided reading instruction. Balanced literacy programs allow teachers to provide varying levels of support to teach this strategy. After modeling for students how to visualize and make pictures in one's mind or on paper, it's a matter of providing students with practice to use the skills taught. Students need many opportunities to visualize when listening to and reading stories. It is also very important to teach students the importance of visualization, and comprehension as well, so they understand why and when they should visualize to help them comprehend stories.

Today's education system encourages teachers to incorporate skills and content together as opposed to teaching them in isolation. Visualization instruction is ideal because it supports the use of other comprehension strategies, such as inferring, making connections, and making predictions. When students actively think about text with visual images in their minds, they are in a better position to think critically about what might happen next in the story, about why an event occurred in the story, and how events in the story relate to themselves, other stories, or the world.

Implications for Further Research

I would suggest asking students to stop reading to tell the researcher when they have visualized during a running reading record. Visualization can happen at any point during a story and further research should be sensitive to that. Also, allowing a child to stop and signify when a picture is made in his or her mind is more valid than asking a child to respond with yes or no. This would prevent a child from telling the researcher a perceived desirable response. Further research can investigate the impact of visualization instruction on students' retellings during a running reading record, but without instruction on using visualization to give a detailed retelling as in this study. This would show the significance of visualization instruction on its own.

A comparative study looking at the differences between high and low achieving students and differences between girls and boys could be developed. This will provide educators with more knowledge about how to meet the needs of different populations of students or specific children. Differentiated visualization instruction might prove to be more profitable for students at different skill levels.

A comparative study that surveys and investigates different school systems' methods for teaching visualization in or throughout the various grade levels might show the magnitude of its benefits. This type of research could show which methods are easier to implement and which methods provide districts with greater results. Knowledge can be gained about how to successfully build upon visualization instruction that has been introduced in the primary grades. All comparative research can be used to create ideas for future experimental research to further refine teaching strategies.

Final Statement

Visualization instruction in this study had a statistically significant impact on students' story retelling performance and visualization use. The interaction between story retelling and visualization instruction helped the students who participated to further comprehend the text they read. Techniques used in this study are recommended for all primary and intermediate educators to promote active thinking while reading to meet a goal of greater story comprehension for all students.

References

Bell, N. (1991). Gestalt imagery: A critical factor in language comprehension. *Annals of Dyslexia, 41,* 246-259.

Blair-Larsen, S. M., & Williams, K. A. (1999). *The Balanced Reading Program.* Newark, Delaware: International Reading Association.

Brabham, E. G., & Villaume, S. K. (2002). Comprehension instruction: Beyond strategies. (questions and answers). *The Reading Teacher, 55,* 672-676.

Bridge, C., Long, S., & Winograd, P. (1989). The effects of reader and text characteristics on imagery reported during and after reading. *Reading Research Quarterly, 24*(3), 353-371.

Ekwall, E. E., & Shanker, J. L. (1998). *Locating and correcting reading difficulties* (7th ed.). Upper Saddle River, New Jersey: Prentice-Hall.

Fountas, I. C., & Pinnell, G. S. (1996). *Guided reading: Good first teaching for all children.* Portsmouth, New Hampshire: Heinemann.

Gambrell, L. B., & Jawitz, P.B. (1993). Mental imagery, text illustrations, and children's story comprehension and recall. *Reading Research Quarterly, 28*(3), 265-273.

Goudvis, A., & Harvey S. (2000). *Strategies that work: Teaching comprehension to enhance understanding.* York, Maine: Stenhouse Publishers.

Staal, L. A. (2000). The Story Face: An adaptation of story mapping that incorporates visualization and discovery learning to enhance reading and writing. *The Reading Teacher, 54,* 26-31.

Appendix A

(This story face map has been revised for the purpose of this study.)

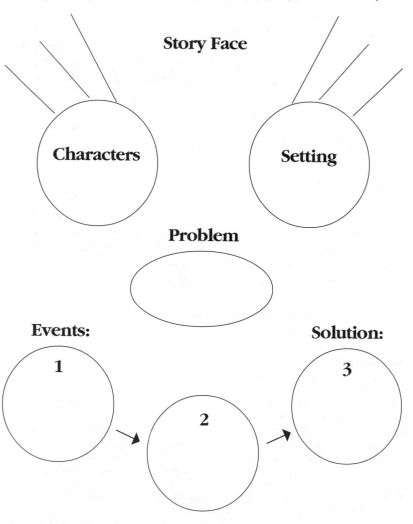

Adapted from Staal (2000)

Appendix B

Students will answer the following questions developed by Keene and Zimmerman (cited in Goudvis & Harvey, 2000, p. 191) to determine their knowledge and use of visualization strategies. The use of these questions have been adapted and revised for this study. Student responses will be logged during the pre-test and post-test running reading records.

(Teacher will remove the book.)
1. Were there places in the story where you made a picture in your mind?

2. What images or pictures did you see?

(Teacher will return the book to the student.)
3. What specific words helped you create that picture in your mind?

(Student may locate those words in the story.)

THE POWER OF MESHING
LITERACY PROCESSES
AND PRACTICES

Tuning into the Sounds of Language: Teaching Phonemic Awareness through Rhymes, Songs, Poetry and Children's Literature

JoAnn R. Dugan

Ohio University

Barrie A. Brancato
Jocelynn L. Smrekar

Clarion University

Abstract

Phonemic awareness is a conscious awareness that words consist of phonemes, the smallest units of sound, that are arranged in particular sequences and chunks. Instruction in phonemic awareness has been shown to improve a child's ability to decode words in the process of learning to read print. In this chapter, we suggest language-based activities that incorporate children's rhymes, songs, chants, and stories to help children tune into the sounds of the spoken language and to make connections between oral language and their written counterparts more explicit.

Sitting on the front porch,
Painted like new-
The farm's all in order,
There's not much to do.

"Take care of the farm,
We'll be back by two!"

Skip to my Lou, my darling!

Lou, Lou, skip to my Lou,
Lou, Lou, skip to my Lou,
Lou, Lou, skip to my Lou,
Skip to my Lou my darling!
                         (Westcott, 1989)

A familiar song *Skip to My Lou,* adapted and illustrated as a picture book by Nadine Bernard Westcott (1989), is a fun-filled, sing-song story that works great for identifying rhyming words with the long /oo/ vowel sound. After reading and discussing the story, the teacher rereads selected parts, pausing before the rhyming words, and prompting the students to fill in the blanks. For example,

The farm's all in order, there's not much to (pause) /do/.
"Take care of the farm. We'll be back by (pause) /two/!"
Skip to my (pause) /Lou/, my darling!

To call attention to the rhyme patterns, the teacher has students identify the rhyming words and say the part of the word that rhymes. For example, do /o/, two /wo/, Lou /ou/. Next, the teacher helps students attend to the individual phonemes by segmenting the initial sound or onset from the final rime /d/ -/o/, /t/-/wo/, /L/-/ou/. The children echo the sounds after the teacher, then blend the sounds to say the word.

Teachers can help students make connections between the sound of the words and their spellings by writing the rhyming words on chart paper, then calling attention to the different spelling patterns by highlighting or underlining the rime patterns with colored marker (d*o,* tw*o,* L*ou,* m*oo,* hulla-bal*oo,* y*ou,* cock-a-doodle-d*o,* n*ew,* Ph*ew*). Students learn to identify the rime, but also learn that words may be spelled differently even though they sound alike.

To further extend this activity to reading, read aloud *Owl Moon* by Jane Yolen (1987) and have the children listen for the *whoo-whoo-whoo-who-who-who-whooooo* of the owl. Children can participate in the reading by making the hooting sound of the owl during the reading. As an extension, children can apply this knowledge by listening to, creating, and representing other bird or animal sounds in their own stories or songs. This activity is one of several we are suggesting to develop phonemic awareness, an important linguistic knowledge that is useful in learning to read.

Phonemic Awareness
Defining Phonemic Awareness
Phonemic awareness is a conscious awareness that words consist of phonemes, the smallest units of sound, that are arranged in particular sequences and chunks (Stahl, & Murray, 1994). According to Williams, phone-

mic awareness is "the awareness of the sounds (phonemes) that make up spoken words. In alphabetic languages, letters (and letter clusters) represent phonemes, and in order to learn the correspondences between letters and sounds, one must have some understanding of the notion that words are made up of phonemes" (cited in Harris & Hodges, 1995, p. 185).

This linguistic knowledge is useful during reading an alphabetic language such as English. Application of this linguistic knowledge during oral language experiences involves listening to, identifying, and manipulating the individual phonemes in spoken words. Phonemic awareness develops as young children learn to speak through their conversations with others and through early reading experiences (Morrow, 2001). While children seem to naturally use this knowledge in their oral language, they may not consciously be aware how they do this. They may not realize how the sounds of the language can be intentionally manipulated to form new words. They also may not be aware of the connections between the sound patterns of words in their oral language and the patterns of words in written language. For some children, developing a conscious awareness of this knowledge requires explicit and intentional instruction to help them notice patterns and combine these sound patterns to form words. In Harris and Hodges (1995), Joanna Williams states that phonemic awareness instruction "is not simply phonics instruction but rather training that enhances concurrent or subsequent phonics instruction or other reading instruction." In addition to spelling and invented spelling activities, Williams suggests that teachers give children "literature that focuses on playing with sounds through rhyme, alliteration, and so on" (p. 186).

Levels of Phonemic Awareness

Levels of phonemic awareness include an awareness of individual and combined sounds in the spoken words, an ability to compare and contrast beginning, middle and ending sounds in spoken words, an ability to blend and split phonemes in words, an ability to isolate and segment individual phonemes in words, and an ability to manipulate phonemes by deleting and substituting phonemes to make new words (Treiman, & Zukowslo, 1991). These levels do not necessarily develop in a sequential or linear order, but may overlap and develop in the process of learning to read and write. While more than one level may be apparent in these phonemic awareness activities, teachers may choose to focus on a particular level to give children practice with skills and knowledge that they need most.

Research Basis for Phonemic Awareness in Learning to Read

Studies have identified phonemic awareness as a high predictor of a child's reading success during the first two years of formal instruction (Adams, Foorman, Lundberg, & Beeler, 1998; Bryant, MacLean, Bradley, & Crossland,

1990; Juel, Griffith, & Gough, 1986). A conscious awareness of the sound patterns in words is useful when a child is learning to read, spell and write words. Children without a conscious awareness of the sounds of words tend to be poor readers or have difficulty making the connections between speech and print. Instruction in phonemic awareness has been shown to improve a child's ability to decode words in the process of learning to read print (NICHD, 2000).

Children who have numerous opportunities to expand their language and linguistic experiences are better prepared to decode unknown words and make sense of what they read (Halliday, 1975; Morrow, 2001). "Alphabet knowledge is a byproduct of extensive early literacy experiences," (Strickland, 2002) not merely the result of teaching the alphabet alone (Ehri, 1983; Venesky, 1975). Like alphabet knowledge, phonemic awareness may be one of the best predictors of reading success (Stahl & Murray, 1994), yet it too develops best through a variety of rich literacy experiences (Moustafa, 1997).

Research shows that children who are learning to read, emergent readers, or beginning readers benefit from phonemic awareness instruction that includes visual manipulation of letters and words in print context. Castle, Riach, and Nicholson (1994) found that including phonemic awareness instruction in a whole language program helped kindergartners spell more words and decode more pseudo-words than the children who did not have phonemic awareness instruction. However, there were no differences between the phonemic awareness trained group and control groups in reading real words or connected text. Other studies also have shown that children benefit when alphabet letters are included in the phonemic awareness instruction especially when children manipulate letters as opposed to passively exposing them to the letters (Ball & Blachman, 1991; Ehri & Wilce, 1987; Kerstholt, van Bon, & Schreuder, 1994, 1997).

Williams (1979, 1980) developed a phonemic awareness program that taught learning disabled children to segment and blend speech sounds in spoken words using wooden squares printed with alphabet letters. Children were taught in small groups. Lessons began with an interesting read aloud of a story that featured the phonemic awareness skills being taught. In addition to segmenting and blending words, the children read sentences highlighting the meanings of words, completed worksheets, and played phonemic awareness games. Williams found that the children in the phonemic awareness program were able to decode more words than those in the control group. However, long-term effects showed no increased improvement, perhaps because teachers had reduced the amount of phonemic awareness instruction or because special needs students required remediation in other processes of reading.

Bradley and Bryant (1983, 1985) found that using plastic alphabet letters to teach sound categories and spellings of words resulted in significant effects on standardized reading and spelling tasks over phonemic awareness instruction without letters. Likewise, Blachman and colleagues (Ball & Blachman, 1991; Blachman, Ball, Black, & Tangel, 1994; Tangel & Blachman, 1992) found that kindergartners who were taught to segment words using blank tiles and letters outperformed children in the control group on reading and spelling words. These results suggest that phonemic awareness instruction should engage children in hands on activities that involve letter-sound manipulation in reading and spelling words such as word building and writing.

Other studies have shown a reciprocal relationship between phonemic awareness and learning to read. That is, learning to read and spell can enhance children's phonemic awareness and their ability to apply the alphabetic system to reading and spelling words. Letter-sound instruction, when combined with printed words, helps beginning readers detect phonemes in the medial position of words or consonant clusters (Ehri, 1984; Ehri & Wilce, 1980, 1986).

Based on these research findings, our goal is to suggest rich and meaningful language-based activities that incorporate children's rhymes, songs, chants, and stories. These activities are intended to help emergent readers and younger struggling readers tune into the sounds of the spoken language and to make connections between those and their written counterparts more explicit. We concur with educators (Halliday, 1975; Morrow, 2001; Moustafa, 1997; Strickland, 2002; and Williams, 1995) who recommend instruction that develops phonemic awareness in the context of language and literature experiences that actively engage children in numerous opportunities to manipulate the sounds of the language in connection with print.

An Instructional Routine for Scaffolding Phonemic Awareness

Our integrated and language-based activities consist of oral language experiences, focus activities and practice activities (LFP). In Figure 1, ideas which incorporate phonemic awareness for each level of this routine are summarized. Particular sound patterns are introduced first in oral language experiences using children's rhymes, songs, chants, poems and stories (Trachtenberg, 1990). These language experiences are collaborative to permit scaffolding in meaningful contexts and to engage children in singing, chanting, reading aloud and choral readings, and repeated readings with the teacher (Smith, 2000). Then the teacher focuses the children's attention toward individual phonemes and sound patterns, to intentionally and explicitly develop specific levels of phonemic awareness and to give the children opportunities to manipulate these sound patterns (Yopp, & Yopp, 2000). Following the focus activity, children are given opportunities to apply their linguistic knowledge in a context of creative and generative language experiences. Teachers with whom we've shared these activities have found them to be beneficial in their efforts to raise children's awareness of the sounds of our language.

**Figure 1. Language-based, Focus, and Practice Activities
0for Scaffolding Phonemic Awareness (LFP)**

ACTIVITY	LANGUAGE-BASED (L)	FOCUS ACTIVITIES (F)	PRACTICE (P)
Storybook reading	Read story, e.g., "We're Going on a Bear Hunt"	Hunt for words—single syllable words with specific onsets and rimes, stretching onset, blending rime, etc.	Children generate (may dictate) parallel story; Teacher helps children use sound spellings
Singing, chanting, rhyming	Teacher models singing song; Children sing song, clap and move to rhythm	Teacher models phonemes, matches letters with phonemes, separates and blends phonemes and syllables; Children echo, identify words and phrases that rhyme, clap syllables in words	Children substitute rhyming words in their song; Teacher writes lyrics on chart and highlights rhyming words, helps children notice similarities and differences in spelling patterns for sounds
Poetry reading	Read poem to children, listen and visualize; Dramatize parts of poem	Draw attention to rhyming names, clap syllables of rhyming words, word building, T-charts, Word walls	Children write or dictate poems with rhyming words, nonsense words, words for animal sounds and noises

Children appear to be better able to capture and gain control over larger units of sound before smaller units of sound (Stahl & Murray, 1994; Treiman & Zakowslo, 1991). Therefore, with preschoolers, or older children who have very little sensitivity to the sound structure of language, teachers first may wish to focus predominantly on rhyme (Bishop, Yopp, & Yopp, 2000).

As children acquire an ability to rhyme, instruction in phonemic awareness may focus on the largest sub-syllabic units in a word, or the onset and rime. The onset is the part of the syllable that precedes the vowel; the rime is the vowel and any consonants that follow it. In the following section, we describe how to develop phonemic awareness in the context of several language-based activities.

Language-Based Phonemic Awareness Activities
Stories for Developing Rhyme

Dr. Seuss stories are perfect for developing awareness of onsets and rimes in one-syllable words and substituting onsets to make new words using the same rime. For example, *Green Eggs and Ham* (Seuss, 1960) consists of repetitive text containing numerous phonograms with both long and short vowels. After reading and enjoying the story, the teacher rereads selected passages and allows the children to identify the rhyming words. Children listen for the words that rhyme, calling them out or clapping, snapping fingers or raising their arms when they hear them.

I could not, would not, on a boat.
I will not, will not, with a goat.
I will not eat them in the rain.
I will not eat them on a train.

(Seuss, 1960)

This story can serve as a source for developing connections between sounds and print, spelling patterns, word walls, word banks or word building activities. Words can be pulled from the story, written on cards, and posted in the classroom where children easily see and interact with them. Children can create new words by substituting different initial consonants as shown below.

b oat	r ain
g oat	tr ain
c oat	g ain
fl oat	p ain

An engaging story for utilizing onset and rime is *We're Going on a Bear Hunt* by Michael Rosen (1997). After reading and enjoying the story, propose to the children that you go on a word hunt. Have the children sit on the floor with their feet together and their knees bent. The teacher begins the chant and students echo. Everyone slaps their toes, then slaps their knees with the beat of the chant, keeping the rhythm going. Onsets and rimes are echoed and then blended to form words. Single syllable words such as *door, light, fix, ran, and can* work best. Words that begin with consonant sounds such as /f/, /l/, /m/, /n/, /r/, /s/, /v/, /w/, /y/, /z/, /th/, /sh/ may be stretched to highlight the onset as it is blended with the rime as in /nnnnnnnnnap/ while students slide their hands from toes to knees.

Teacher: *Going on a word hunt!*
Students: *Going on a word hunt!*
Teacher: *What's the word?*
Students: *What's the word?*
Teacher: /n/ (echo) /ap/ (echo) /nap/ (echo) /nnnnnnnnap/ (echo)

Rhyming activities may be followed by activities that focus on individual units of sound within words, the largest unit being the syllable. For example, in the word cupboard, there are two syllables: cup and board. The following activities can be used to develop students' ability to identify and manipulate syllables.

Tikki Tikki Tembo is a story by Arlene Mosel (1989) about a pair of Chinese brothers, one who had a very long name (Tikki Tikki Tembo No Sa Rembo Chari Bari Ruchi Pip Peri Pembo) and the other brother who had a very short name (Chang). After reading and discussing the story, teachers may encourage their students to say the names of the two boys. Then have them say the names again, but this time, clap each syllable as it is said. For instance, Tikki Tikki Tembo's name has 21 syllables, thus 21 claps. In contrast, Chang's name has only one syllable, thus one clap.

Students can gain additional practice with this activity by clapping the syllables in their own names. As a group, say each child's name and clap as you separate the syllables. The teacher can model this when taking attendance, clapping the number of syllables as she/he calls each child's name.

To apply this knowledge, the children might create pseudo-names for themselves, write them on cards, and sort them by the number of syllables. These can be posted on a bulletin board in the classroom as examples of single and multi-syllable words.

Sharing the book *Tingo Tango Mango Tree* by Marcia Vaughan (1995) is another way of incorporating syllable manipulation in the classroom. This particular story is about an iguana named Sambala Bombala Rombala Roh, a flamingo named Kokio Lokio Mokio Koh, a parrot named Dillaby Dallaby Doh, a turtle named Nanaba Panaba Tanaba Goh, and a bat named Bitteo Biteo. Again, students can clap the syllables, notice the rhyme, note the spelling patterns, and create new names for their favorite animals.

Songs, Chants, and Rhymes for Manipulating Sounds

Traditional nursery rhymes, finger rhymes, and chants can also be used to engage children in rhyming, manipulating small chunks of sounds, and isolating and substituting individual phonemes.

"Clap, Clap, Clap Your Hands" is a popular song sung in many classrooms across the U.S. and can be readily adapted to focus attention on the onsets and rimes in words (Yopp, 1992). Hand and body motions are combined with singing to make for a lively experience. The first two verses are provided below.

> Clap, clap, clap your hands,
> Clap your hands together.
> Clap, clap, clap your hands,
> Clap your hands together.
>
> Snap, snap, snap your fingers,
> Snap your fingers together.
> Snap, snap, snap your fingers,
> Snap your fingers together.

Teachers can add additional verses that the children create: for example, *wave, wave, wave your arms; shake, shake, shake your legs; bend, bend, bend your elbows; tap, tap, tap your toes.*

A word play song to the tune of "Someone's in the Kitchen with Dinah" (first verse) and "I've Been Working on the Railroad" (second verse) goes like this (Michado, 1995):

I have a song that we can sing
I have a song that we can sing
I have a song that we can sing
It goes something like this:

Fe-Fi-Fiddly-I-o
Fe-Fi-Fiddly-I-o-o-o-o
Fe-Fi-Fiddly-I-o
Now try it with the /m/ sound

Me-Mi-Middly-I-o
Me-Mi-Middly-I-o-o-o-o...

When substituting phonemes, teachers should be sure to model the sound rather than the letter name. As children learn the pattern, they can suggest phonemes to substitute in the song. This activity works well when teaching or reinforcing the sounds of the consonants in the English alphabet. While it is primarily a listening activity, teachers can help children make connections to the print by giving them the consonant letters and helping them match these with their phonemes as they sing the song.

Poetry: A Medium for Creative Sound Play

Poetry is ideal for developing phonemic awareness because of its rhyming language, short verse, and use of alliteration (words that begin with the same sound) and onomatopoeia (words that sound like the sounds they represent). When poetry is combined with role play and dramatization, children can respond actively and creatively to the sounds and rhythm of language. Rhyme, rhythm, and action are creatively combined in "The Birds' Square Dance" by Beverly McLoughland (1992), a poem featured in *Pterodactyls and Pizza* by Lee Bennett Hopkins (1992).

Swing your partner
Cockatoo
Bluefoot booby
Maraboo

Cassowary
Heel and toe
Toucan, noddy
Oriole

Chachalaca
To the right
Bobolink and
Hold her tight

Kittiwake and
Tap your feet
Loon and puffin
Parakeet

Flap your feathers
Curlew, crow
Pipit, tern and
Do-si-do.
                    (McLoughland, 1992, pp. 22-23)

After reading the poem, allow pairs or small groups of children to choose a bird. Ask them to create a dance for their bird. With children sitting in a circle on the floor, read the poem again in chorus, clapping the syllables and keeping the rhythm going. As each verse is read, the children stand and perform their bird dance.

As a follow-up, read the story *Barn Dance* (Martin & Archambault, 1986). Then have the children clap the rhythm and square dance with a partner as the text is read aloud.

Right hand! Left hand! Around you go!
Now back-to-back your partner in a do-si-do!
Mules to the center for a curtsey an' a bow!
An' hey there, skinny kid! Show the old cow how!

"Ode to a Cereal Box" is a poem by Fran Haraway featured in *Pterodactyls and Pizza* (Hopkins, 1992) that contains action words with similar initial consonants, consonant blends and diagraphs.

	Similar rimes	**Similar onsets**
I strike	b**ike**, h**ike**	**str**oke
I shred	h**ead**, b**ed**, **red**	**shr**ivel
I smash	h**ash**, b**ash**, c**ash**	**sm**ooth
I stab	d**ab**, c**ab**, l**ab**	**st**ing
I rip	s**ip**, l**ip**, d**ip**	**r**ole
I rend	b**end**, l**end**	**r**ant
I grip	**rip**, t**ip**, fl**ip**	**gr**in
I grab	j**ab**, n**ab**	**gr**asp

I jiggle,	w**iggle**	**j**oggle
Jostle,	b**ostle** (nonsense word)	**j**umble
Jolt, and jab	m**olt** and d**ab**	**j**ag and **j**erk

But—
Cannot
Budge
The "lift this tab."

(Hopkins, 1992, pp. 54-55)

After reciting and acting out the poem, teachers help students hear the similarities and differences in the onsets and rimes by separating and blending them. Students who are reading and writing but need more practice with consonant blends and diagraphs can make cereal box word walls that they keep on their desks. First, students cover an empty cereal box with construction paper. Next, copy action words found in the poem in T-charts drawn on the box, separating the onset from the rime as shown in the example below. Then, students generate new words using the same onset and rime for each action word and write these in the appropriate T-chart, again separating the onset from the rime. Finally, students use these new words to write their own poems right on their box.

> Sm | ash
> h | ash
> c | ash
> b | ash
> cr | ash

Stretching the sounds in words can help children blend individual phonemes and syllables into whole words. A fun way of stretching sounds is with a balloon. Blow up the balloon and pinch the neck while letting out just a bit of air to make it screech. Open and close the neck of the balloon in short or long bursts to stretch the sound. Students can practice doing this while reciting a poem, segmenting the onsets and rimes, separating and blending syllables, and elongating the ending sounds. "Balloons" by Fran Haraway in *Pterodactyls and Pizza* (Hopkins, 1992) is perfect for this activity.

> Twenty balloons in a cellophane sack—
> Wrinkled and withered, mishapen and slack,
> Limp, waiting rainbows at once promising
> Marvels of happiness, laughter, and spring—
> Bright hope for only a dollar a pack.
> (Hopkins, 1992, p. 67)

Teachers might also read "Eight Balloons" by Shel Silverstein (1981).

Students can clap during the "pop," screech their balloons for the "whoosh" sound, and then let their balloons fly away as the poem ends.

> Eight balloons no one was buyin'
> All broke loose one afternoon.
> Eight balloons with strings a flyin'
> Free to do what they wanted to.
> One flew up to touch the sun-POP!
> One thought highways might be fun-POP!
> One took a nap in a cactus pile-POP!
> One stayed to play with careless child-POP!
> One tried to taste some bacon fryin'-POP!
> One fell in love with a porcupine-POP!
> One looked close in a crocodile's mouth-POP!
> One sat around 'til his air ran out-WHOOSH!
> Eight balloons no one was buyin'—
> They broke loose and away they flew,
> Free to float and free to fly
> And free to pop where they wanted to.

(Silverstein, 1981, p. 58)

Poetry can also provide examples of made-up words that rhyme. Some of these featured in *Imagine That! Poems of Never-Was* (Prelutsky, 1998) include "The Land of the Bumbley Boo" and Multikertwigo by Spike Milligan, and "The Drum-Tummied Snumm" by Dr. Seuss. When reading poetry and stories with made-up names and nonsense words, students have opportunities to apply their phonemic awareness knowledge and abilities in creative and imaginative ways. Students can experiment with manipulating sounds, discovering new sound and spelling patterns, and engaging in creative language play to form new words and new texts. They learn that language is a constructive and creative process of stringing sounds together to form words with many meaningful combinations and variations.

Conclusion

In summary, our purpose has been to share phonemic awareness activities that are language–based, meaningful and interesting to children. We have shown how this knowledge can be developed using rhymes, songs, poetry and literature for children. These integrated activities are intended to serve as inspiration for teachers, not as prescriptive lessons. We encourage teachers to adapt the activities to suit the needs of their students. While some children need explicit instruction in phonemic awareness, *all children* need and benefit most from meaningful and interesting reading and writing.

References

Adams, M. J., Foorman, B. R., Lundberg, I., & Beeler, T. (1998). *Phonemic awareness in young children.* Baltimore, MD: Paul H. Brookes.

Ball, E., & Blachman, B. (1991). Does phoneme awareness training in kindergarten make a difference in early word recognition and developmental spelling? *Reading Research Quarterly, 26,* 49-66.

Bishop, A., Yopp, R. H., & Yopp, H. K. (2000). *Reading for reading: A handbook for parents of preschoolers.* Boston: Allyn & Bacon.

Blachman, B., Ball, E., Black, R., & Tangel, D. (1994). Kindergarten teachers develop phoneme awareness in low-income, inner-city classrooms: Does it make a difference? *Reading and Writing: An Interdisciplinary Journal, 6,* 1-18.

Bradley, L., & Bryant, P. (1983). Categorizing sounds and learning to read: A causal connection. *Nature, 30,* 419-421.

Bradely, L., & Bryant, P. (1985). *Rhyme and reason in reading and spelling.* Ann Arbor: University of Michigan Press.

Bryant, P. E., MacLean, M., Bradley, L. L., & Crossland, J. (1990). Rhyme and alliteration, phoneme detection, and learning to read. *Developmental Psychology, 26* (3), 429-438.

Castle, J., Riach, J., & Nicholson, T. (1994). Getting off to a better start in reading and spelling: The effects of phonemic awareness instruction within a whole language program. *Journal of Educational Psychology, 86,* 350-359.

Ehri, L. C. (1983). A critique of five studies related to letter name knowledge and learning to read. In L.M. Gentile, M. L. Kamil, & J.S. Blanchard (Eds.), *Reading research revisited* (pp. 143-153). Columbus, OH: Merrill.

Ehri, L.C. (1984). How orthography alters spoken language competencies in children learning to read and spell. In J. Downing & R. Valtin (Eds.), *Language awareness and learning to read* (pp. 119-147). New York: Springer Verlag.

Ehri, L. C., & Wilce, L. (1980). The influence of orthography on readers' conceptualization of the phonemic structure of words. *Applied Psycholinguistics, 1,* 371-385.

Ehri, L.C., & Wilce, L. (1986). The influence of spellings on speech: Are alveolar flaps /d/ or /t/? In D. Yaden & S. Templeton (Eds.), *Metalinguistic awareness and beginning literacy* (pp. 101-114). Portsmouth, NH: Heinemann.

Ehri, L. C., & Wilce, L. (1987). Does learning to spell help beginners learn to read words? *Reading Research Quarterly, 22,* 47-65.

Griffith, P. L. & Olson, M. W. (1992). Phonemic awareness helps beginning readers break the code. *The Reading Teacher, 45* (7), 516-525.

Halliday, M. (1975). *Learn how to mean.* London: Edward Arnold.

Harris, T. L., & Hodges, R. E. (Eds.). (1995). *The literacy dictionary: The vocabulary of reading and writing.* Newark, Delaware: International Reading Association.

Juel, C., Griffith, P. L., & Gough, P. B. (1986). Acquisition of literacy: A longitudinal study of children in first and second grade. *Journal of Educational Psychology, 78,* 243-255.

Kerstholt, M., van Bon, W., & Schreuder, R. (1994). Training in phonemic segmentation: The effects of visual support. *Reading and Writing: An Interdisciplinary Journal, 6,* 361-385.

Kerstholt, M., van Bon, W., & Schreuder, R. (1997). Using visual support in preschool phonemic segmentation training. *Reading and Writing: An Interdisciplinary Journal, 9,* 265-283.

Michado, J. (1995). *Early childhood experiences in language arts.* NY: Delmar.

Morrow, L. M. (2001). *Literacy development in the early years: Helping children read and write* (4th ed.). Needham Heights, MA: Allyn and Bacon.

Moustafa, M. (1997). Reconceptualizing phonics instruction. In C. Weaver (Ed.), *Reconsidering a balanced approach to reading* (pp. 135-157). Urbana, IL: National Council of Teachers of English.

National Institute of Child Health and Human Development (NICHD). (2000). *Report of* the National Reading Panel. Teaching children to read: An evidence-based assessment of the scientific research literature on reading and its implications for *reading instruction* (NIH Publication No. 00-4769). Washington, DC: U.S. Government Printing Office.

Smith, J. A. (2000). Singing and songwriting support early literacy instruction. *The Reading Teacher, 53,* 646-651.

Stahl, S. A., & Murray, B. A. (1994). Defining phonological awareness and its relationship to early reading. *Journal of Educational Psychology, 86,* 221-234.

Strickland, D. (2002). The importance of effective early intervention. In A. E. Farstrup & S. J. Samuels (Eds.), *What research has to say about reading instruction.* (pp. 69-86). Newark, Delaware: International Reading Association.

Tangle, D., & Blachman, B. (1992). Effect of phoneme awareness instruction on kindergarten children's invented spelling. *Journal of Reading Behavior, 24,* 233-261.

Trachtenberg, P. (1990). Using children's literature to enhance phonics instruction. *The Reading Teacher, 45,* 648-653.

Treiman, R., & Zukowslo, A. (1991). Levels of phonological awareness. In S. A. Brady & D. P. Shankweiler (Eds.), *Phonological processes in literacy* (pp 67-83). Hillsdale, NJ: Erlbaum.

Venezky, R. L. (1975). The curious role of letter names in reading instruction. *Visible Language, 9,* 7-23.

Williams, J. (1979). The ABD's of reading: A program for the learning disabled. In L. Resnick & P. Weaver (Eds.), *Theory and practice of early reading* (Vol. 3, pp. 179-195). Hillsdale, NJ: Erlbaum.

Williams, J. (1980). Teaching decoding with an emphasis on phoneme analysis and phoneme blending. *Journal of Educational Psychology, 72,* 1-15.

Williams, J. (1995). Phonemic awareness. In T. L. Harris & R. E. Hodges (Eds.), *The literacy dictionary* (pp. 185-186). Newark, Delaware: International Reading Association.

Yopp, H. K. (1992). Developing phonemic awareness in young children. *The Reading Teacher, 45,* 696-703.

Yopp, H. K., & Yopp, R. H. (2000). Supporting phonemic awareness development in the classroom. *The Reading Teacher, 54,* 130-143.

Children's Literature References

Hopkins, L.B. (Ed.) (1992). *Pterodactyls and pizza.* New York, NY: The Trumpet Club.

Martin, B., & Archambault, J. (1986). *Barn dance!* New York, NY: Henry Holt and Co.

McLoughland, B. (1992). Birds' square dance. In L.B. Hopkins (Ed.), *Pterodactyls and pizza* (pp. 22-23). New York, NY: The Trumpet Club.

Mosel, A. (1989). *Tikki Tikki Tembo.* New York: Henry Holt and Co.

Mulligan, S. (1998). Multikertwigo. In J. Prelutsky (Ed.), *Imagine that! Poems of never-was* (p. 34). New York, NY: Alfred A. Knopf.

Mulligan, S. (1998). The land of bumbley boo. In J. Prelutsky (Ed.), *Imagine that! Poems of never-was* (p. 38). New York, NY: Alfred A. Knopf.

Prelutsky, J. (1998). *Imagine that! Poems of never-was.* New York, NY: Alfred A. Knopf.
Rosen, M. (1997). *We're going on a bear hunt.* New York: Little Simon.
Seuss, Dr. (1960). *Green eggs and ham.* New York, NY: Beginner Books.
Seuss, Dr. (1956). *If I ran the zoo.* New York, NY: Random House.
Silverstein, S. (1981). *A light in the attic.* New York, NY: Harper Collins.
Vaughan, M. (1995). *Tingo tango mango tree.* Morristown, NJ: Silver Burdett.
Westcott, N.B. (1989). *Skip to My Lou.* New York, NY: The Trumpet Club.
Yolen, J. (1987). *Owl moon.* New York, NY: Scholastic.

Teaching Fluently: Exploring Teaching Practices in Divergent Certification Programs

Catherine Zeek
Lassell College

Carole Walker
Texas A&M University-Commerce

Abstract

Differences in teaching practices in divergent certification programs were investigated through transactional inquiries by the authors in collaboration with pre-service and in-service teachers. Narratives written by teachers trained through university coursework and intensive field experiences as well as those completing coursework for certification while teaching were analyzed. The process revealed striking commonalities including concern for students, integrated lessons built around strategies, active student involvement, and use of good children's literature. The differences, while subtle, suggested that the traditional teachers had slightly greater "teaching fluency" (the entry level subject matter knowledge currently equated with "highly qualified" as well as the skills which help teachers orchestrate a much wider variety of types of knowledge). An unanticipated benefit of transactional inquiry that emerged was its contribution to participants' ownership of their own professional development.

Mandates associated with the *No Child Left Behind Act* (NCLB) (Executive Summary, 2001) call for "highly qualified" teachers who have passed the appropriate certification exams and measure the success of districts, schools, teachers, and children by their scores on various standardized tests. Concurrent—but not in concert—with concerns about teacher quality, educational policy makers responded to a national teacher shortage by expanding the certification routes available to prospective teachers. In our state those who wish to teach can still seek traditional certification following a degree program. However, other options are also available to those who have degrees or skills in fields other than education, particularly high-need areas such as math, science, and bilingual education. These options include emergency certification, which allows an uncertified individual to teach while taking courses toward certification, and alternative certification, which allows an uncertified individual to teach while participating in a program combining classroom experience and university coursework or professional seminars. These options increase the flexibility school districts have in making assignments and may encourage dedicated individuals to enter teaching from other fields. Successful candidates from any program must pass the state certification examinations in pedagogy and subject areas, suggesting that newly certified teachers bring comparable knowledge bases. Questions remain, however, about the classroom effectiveness of teachers trained in traditional and alternative preparation programs.

As university teacher educators, we continue to explore how our teacher preparation programs can help candidates develop more effective literacy teaching practices. In our research, we look beyond content knowledge demonstrated on standardized tests to teaching practices and to events that affect them. We begin with teachers' narratives of practice and structure transactional inquiries (Zeek, Foote, & Walker, 2001) around those narratives to encourage teachers to articulate their understandings of effective literacy instruction. Our participants include candidates in traditional, emergency, and alternative certification programs supported by our two universities.

The current analysis began with our questioning whether candidates in divergent certification programs expressed different ideas of effective literacy teaching. To explore our question, we re-analyzed narratives that candidates had previously developed, looking specifically at differences and similarities among the various types of programs. Our reading of these narratives led us to our idea of *fluency* in teaching that we define as entry level subject matter knowledge, deep understandings of learning and learners, and the skill to orchestrate these types of knowledge to create successful learning environments. We assume that effective teachers are fluent teachers. We further assume, in line with research supporting professional development schools (Carnegie Forum, 1986; Goodlad, 1993; Holmes Group, 1990; Levine, 1992; National Commission on Excellence in Education, 1983; National Commission on Teaching and America's Future, 1996; Wise & Darling-Hammond, 1986), that novice teachers can learn from and with effective, experienced mentor teachers. In this article, we briefly set the context for our ongoing research, describe transactional inquiry, and report on our analysis of these narratives.

Context

Our two universities offer and support traditional, emergency, and alternative teacher certification programs. Table 1 presents an overview of our programs' features. Our traditional certification students have extensive field-based experiences during their junior and senior years, taking increasing responsibility for planning, teaching, and evaluating lessons in close contact with university professors and public school mentors. Their on-campus coursework, planned in conjunction with field experiences, leads them to connect practice and theory. Just as importantly, their coursework is designed to challenge students to articulate and reevaluate their beliefs about teaching and learning in light of their developing understanding of learning processes. Collaboration with peers and scaffolding by university and public school teacher educators "nudge" them to reflect on and resolve clashes between practice and theory as they occur, and to refine their ideas of effective teaching (Linek, Nelson, Sampson, Zeek, Mohr, & Hughes, 1999; Olson, 2000; Wold, 2003).

Table 1. Comparison of Types of Certification Programs.

	TRADITIONAL: *For candidates without baccalaureate degrees*	POST-BACCALAUREATE: *For candidates with baccalaureate degrees*	
		EMERGENCY	ALTERNATIVE
Level of coursework	Undergraduate Leads to baccalaureate degree	Undergraduate or graduate Determined by deficiency plan prepared by university	Graduate Includes professional development seminars Determined by certification entity
Length of program	Minimum of 124 credit hours	Generally 12-36 credit hours completed in 2-3 years	Varies; often completed in 1 year or less
Recommended for certification by	University	University	Certifying entity— school district, service center, university, other
Teaching experience during program	Field experiences, both teaching and observation, with final student teaching or internship	Employed as teacher during program	Employed as teacher during program
Mentoring and evaluation	University instructors (on-site), public school teachers Administrator may evaluate (per district guidelines)	Mentor teacher may be provided by school or district District provides new teacher induction Administrator evaluates according to state and district requirements	Mentor teacher and instructional specialist assigned by district District provides new teacher induction and professional development seminars Administrator evaluates according to state and district requirements

Students in our programs who are pursuing post-baccalaureate (emergency or alternative) certification are enrolled in university courses, but already have responsibility for a classroom. The in-class and field components of their university courses encourage them to examine their own instructional practices from a research/theory perspective. Because their teaching situations do not generally include time for structured reflection or on-site university support, and may also lack intentional mentoring by public school colleagues, they have little expert feedback during their teaching and little guidance when they confront contradictions between theory and practice. Reflection, particularly in collaboration with colleagues, has been shown to affect practice, often encouraging novices to adopt more effective practices (Linek et al., 1999; Olson, 2000; Rust, 2002; Wold, 2003; Zeichner & Liston, 1996). Because of these differences in program structure, we questioned whether we would see differences in teachers' descriptions of effective literacy teaching. To explore our question, we used transactional inquiry.

Transactional Inquiry

In Theory

As teacher educators in state universities with large educator preparation programs, we work with pre-service and in-service teachers in a variety of contexts: university-based undergraduate and graduate courses, field-based seminars, professional development in school districts, and induction academies for first-year teachers. In all these settings for most of a decade we have increasingly structured professional development sessions around the teachers' narratives about their experiences learning to teach and mentor, especially their "aha" moments. In the process, we developed the term "transactional inquiry" to describe the process of a group of readers responding to and reflecting on a text and on others' responses to the text for the purpose of informing and guiding further inquiry (Zeek, Foote, & Walker, 2001). Transactional inquiry engages teachers in a series of transactions with their own experiences and knowledge, the texts themselves, and the social context (Rosenblatt, 1978). The strategy begins with teachers' narratives of practice, making visible their thought processes (Connelly & Clandinin, 1990, 2000; Jalongo & Isenberg, 1995; Richert, 2002), encouraging reflection on beliefs and practices (Connelly & Clandinin, 1999, 2000; Jalongo & Isenberg, 1995; Ritchie & Wilson, 2000; Rust, 2002), and providing opportunities for interaction with colleagues (Jalongo & Isenberg, 1995; Richert, 2002; Rust, 2002). Transactional inquiry is based on a social constructivist theory of learning (Vygotsky, 1986; Wertsch, 1985), suggesting that knowledge is constructed through exploring one's own and others' ideas. Teachers critically examine their own beliefs, practices, and struggles through interaction with their colleagues. This productive messiness encourages each participant to move beyond her/his "starting point."

In Practice

Transactional inquiry involves interrelated processes. The first is using narratives as data sources. Teachers worked alongside us writing narratives using this prompt: *The story I want to tell is about a reading or writing lesson I taught [or observed] that turned out even better than I thought it would.* After the resulting narratives were transcribed we read them looking for initial "answers" to our question about differing literacy practices among teachers trained in divergent programs (Zeek & Walker, 2002). We then invited teachers in training to work with us to analyze a story from another site and/or program using this prompt to speculate on its meaning: *Now that I have read [someone else's story] I can see that. . . .*In the next step we used two prompts to elicit reflective insights on learning and personal professional development: (a) *Learning is a developmental process, and I suggest the next step for the teacher in this story would be. . . .*(b) *I suggest that my next professional step is. . . .*(Walker & Zeek, 2003; Zeek & Walker, 2003). The last step in the transactional inquiry process is making visible the answers and pursuing new questions emerging from the narratives and the process.

Our work with transactional inquiry confirms our assumption that teachers learn from their experiences and each other, although they may be in separate times and places (Fleener, Walker, Foote, & Zeek, 1998; Lyons & LaBoskey, 2002; Ritchie & Wilson, 2000; Zeek, Foote & Walker, 2001). In their narratives and responses to others' narratives, we find examples of connections with other teachers (I can *take her story and apply it to my own classroom.*), reflections on their own development as teachers (I can *ask questions and get feedback on what is what and what I can change to make what I'm doing better.*), and directions for their continuing development (The next step for me is *to encourage my students to believe and accept that learning is life long. That it doesn't stop when someone hands you a diploma.*).

Investigating Differences in Teaching Practices

As we develop effective coursework and professional development, we continue to turn to teachers' narratives as an indicator of the practices they choose. To explore whether the type of certification program leads to differences in teaching practices, we used transactional inquiry to reexamine and compare over 100 narratives written by teachers trained through traditional and alternative/emergency programs. Our analyses of their narratives revealed both commonalities and differences in their teaching practices and suggested to us the idea of fluency in teaching. Appendix A includes samples of the narratives we analyzed.

Commonalities and Differences

The *commonalities* across the certification programs were striking. The narratives were thoughtful, well developed, and reflective, suggesting that they enjoyed teaching, as well as writing about their lessons and students for a wider audience. Teachers trained in both programs were concerned for their students; taught extended, integrated lessons built around strategies rather than isolated skills; used active learning and transaction models rather than transmission; referred to methods and materials from their university coursework, including dialog journals and children's literature; and acknowledged other influences on their teaching, such as lessons from their own teachers. We were surprised to note that none of these teachers used the state-mandated high-stakes tests to evaluate their own effectiveness or their students' learning. Instead their measures of effectiveness included student involvement and teacher evaluation. Two traditionally trained teachers wrote,

This lesson was effective because it used literature and students could actually taste how hot the jalapeno and the ice were. This made their similes much more descriptive and meaningful to read.

This lesson was effective in that the students were allowed to be as creative as they wanted to be. It showed students that the way they view characters can help with reading skills including predictions, inferencing, generalizing, & cause & effect. It was motivational.

Two alternative/emergency candidates wrote,

Everybody participated in their groups showing that comprehension has taken place.

It was an effective literacy activity because all the students were actively engaged. They were all reading. The children were also demonstrating problem solving techniques to maser the material. The teacher was evaluating and making mental notes about the students' progress. The teacher later reflected from these observations. She evaluated her reading groups to make sure the students were properly placed.

The *differences* between the narratives of teachers from the two programs were less striking. The traditionally trained teachers generally wrote longer stories with more details; used more powerful literacy strategies, for instance basing their lessons on their observations of student needs; consistently included lesson assessment—or measures of effectiveness—in their stories; showed more evidence of collaboration; and believed they were using effective strategies. Assessing why their lesson turned out better than they thought it would five traditionally trained teachers demonstrated these attributes:

I allowed myself to be vulnerable and to learn from my mistakes as well as my students.

Things and learning moments occurred that I had not anticipated.

I used several sources for the lesson. Once I read one idea I incorporated my own ideas and activities according to the learners in the classroom. *All* of the students were engaged and excited about learning and being challenged.

I was excited with the students and their success, and they experienced a new way of writing.

The students were writing their own story, NOT a story that was structured and being checked for errors. They were motivated by knowing they could share their stories with the class.

Describing how they knew a literacy lesson was effective, the alternatively or emergency certified teachers tended to focus on characteristics of the lesson. Five of these teachers responded,

This plan was very effective because if students came to a word they didn't know when reading they would revert back (in their mind or from the chart display) and phonetically sound the word out. The students enjoyed the routine of going over the phonetic key charts. They liked the pictures and learned the words and spellings associated with each picture. The students also became excited about learning new words and becoming better readers.

I think this was an effective lesson plan because I used several strategies and many variated [sic] activities to start on the simple level of identifying phonics so that they can sound out unfamiliar words and moved up to learning to read whole new story.

I was being observed and during my evaluation conference, I was told that my liaison would want her child in my class. That let me know it was a good lesson, and I was a good teacher.

This was effective because it was a different type lesson being more hands on and away from the daily "basal reader" and reading curriculum set forth by the district. It made the children use their creativity and vocabulary knowledge. . . Also, I had fun teaching this lesson versus the daily strategies for the adopted reader.

I think it was effective because they were having fun and learning.

Teaching Fluency Revealed
Through reflections on lesson effectiveness. In further reflecting on these teachers' narratives, we found evidence of the attribute we call *teaching fluency*. Although the differences in the narratives across the divergent certification programs were subtle, they suggested a difference in teaching fluency. Those completing transactional inquiries with us did not cite their

subject matter knowledge as evidence of lesson effectiveness. Instead they mentioned aspects which when orchestrated result in fluent teaching: using a variety of types of knowledge; understanding the diverse needs of the learners in their classes; working with home, community, and colleagues; helping all children to succeed; and integrating technology as a learning tool for themselves and their students. Differences such as greater attention to detail, more powerful literacy strategies, and collaboration suggest those trained in the traditional programs were slightly more fluent teachers.

Through reflections on another teacher's narrative. The teachers' analyses of the narrative *Willis' Teacher's Story* (Appendix B), their ideas about the moral of the story, and their suggestions for next steps for this teacher and for themselves provided further support for the idea of teaching fluency. Those completing traditional programs suggested morals that were more expansive and more specific to the story (*As teachers we need to take time and effort to discover our students' problems so we may help them not punish them.* and *Don't assume that a student deficiency means they're not interested. Take time to get to the heart of the problem.*), as well more specific next steps for his teacher (*Publish Willis' work in a book and provide him with a copy. Give him many opportunities to use the computer*). Those teaching while completing coursework in alternative programs suggested pithier, generic morals (*Don't assume you know it all.* and *First impressions may be deceiving.*) and more general professional development ideas (*To attempt to have a more positive attitude and expectations for her students. To have an open mind before declaring an assignment a "disaster."*)

When suggesting next steps for themselves, the suggestions of traditionally trained teachers were longer and suggested more collegiality. *To ask questions and get feedback on what is right and what I can change to make what I am doing better. To familiarize myself with accommodations I can use in my classroom for students with learning disabilities.* Both groups suggested classroom applications. An alternatively trained teacher's next step was *take her story and apply it to my classroom and document my personal/professional growth*, while a traditionally trained teacher's next step was *learn from this story and apply it to my own students.* Teachers from each program made suggestions that showed them to be reflective practitioners open to further professional growth. One alternatively trained teacher's next step was to *keep a journal and share it with other teachers as positive growth* while another suggested *reflect on my own teaching and critique my own lesson in class to better facilitate their learning,* and a traditionally trained teacher recommended *workshops on writing for all learning styles and at-risk students.*

Extending Our Inquiry

Answers

The last phase of transactional inquiry allows initial questions to be *answered* and new questions to emerge. We used transactional inquiry to investigate differences in the literacy practices of teachers trained in traditional and alternative certification programs. We began our process expecting to see pronounced differences in their descriptions of effective literacy instruction. Through transactional inquiries, we found, instead, that the similarities between the groups were more visible than the differences. Both sets of narratives (a) included clear objectives and assessments in their literacy lessons, although none of them referred to the state-mandated knowledge and skills or the related high-stakes exams; (b) tended to be learner-centered; (c) emphasized integrated strategies rather than isolated skills; and (d) referred to elements of their university coursework, such as lesson structures and materials. The commonalities within these sets of narratives across certification areas are explained partially by the fact that all of the students are enrolled in university courses, rather than in service center-based or for-profit certification programs. They seem to be incorporating some of the habits of reflection and learner-centeredness that we intentionally provoke.

We found subtle differences. Traditionally trained teachers told somewhat longer stories, included more details, and described more powerful strategies. Such differences suggested the possibility that traditionally trained teachers are more fluent in their literacy practices—a possibility that could be telling over a year's worth of lessons and one that deserves further investigation. Through other transactional inquiries we will explore the links between fluent teaching and elements of our teacher preparation programs, particularly mentoring, reflection, and field-based experiences, through classroom observations, teacher reports, and students' test results.

New Questions

Transactional inquiry allows new possibilities to emerge. Our reflections on teachers' reflections about professional development suggested that an unanticipated benefit of transactional inquiry is its contribution to teachers' ownership of their own professional development. Engagement in transactional inquiry allows teachers to go beyond the passive trainee role they often play in college courses and formal staff development sessions: *This means I am still learning as I grow to be an effective teacher.* The format pushes them to critically examine their own practices and how they affect students' literacy learning to realize *the teacher possesses many techniques and strategies to reach all students.* Transactional inquirers struggle with their beliefs about teaching and learning and ask hard questions: *How do I help my students be success-*

ful? What will I use to help me teach? How do I use the community and school services? How do I work with my colleagues?

Through transactional inquiries teachers are encouraged to take responsibility for their own professional growth by identifying and discussing events that challenge them: *The student should be an **active** participant (whenever possible) in assessment as well as learning.* Our research suggests that preservice teachers value the support and collaboration that they find in these groups as they realize their peers face similar challenges and that in-service teachers value the connections with other teachers. *Inviting other teachers and community interaction into your classroom is always a great personal growth that will enhance your students' learning environment.* Because both groups have had opportunities to examine their practices and articulate their beliefs, we hypothesize they may be more likely to focus on the needs of the learners in their classes than teachers who have only been trained to use literacy programs. New questions emerging during the last phase of this inquiry included: (a) *Does transactional inquiry help teachers shape their own professional development?* (b) *Do transactional inquiries enhance teachers' feelings of ownership and value?*, and (c) *Will increased feelings of ownership and value lead to increased teacher retention?* Our conclusions at this point are based on the teachers' narratives and their analysis of others' narratives. We continue to explore our questions with the goal of better supporting candidates in each type of certification program.

References

Carnegie Forum on Education and the Economy, Task Force on Teaching as a Profession. (1986). *A nation prepared: Teachers for the 21st century.* New York: Author.

Connelly, F. M., & Clandinin, D. J. (1990). Stories of experience and narrative inquiry. *Educational Researcher, 19*(5), 2-14.

Connelly, F. M., & Clandinin, D. J. (Eds.). (1999). *Shaping a professional identity: Stories of educational practice.* New York: Teachers College Press.

Fleener, C., Walker, C., Foote, M., & Zeek, C. (1998, February). We thought you'd never ask: Mentor teachers tell their stories. Paper presented at the meeting of the American Association of Colleges for Teacher Education, New Orleans, LA.

Goodlad, J. I. (1993). School-university partnerships and partner schools. In P.G. Altback, H. G. Petrie, M. J. Shujaa, & L. Weis (Eds.), *Educational policy: Volume 7, Number 1. Professional development schools* (pp. 34-39). Newbury Park, CA.: Corwin Press.

Holmes Group. (1990). *Tomorrow's schools: Principles for the design of professional development schools.* East Lansing, MI: Author.

Jalongo, M. R., & Isenberg, J. P. (1995). *Teachers' stories: From personal narrative to professional insight.* San Francisco: Jossey-Bass.

Levine, M. (1992). A conceptual framework for professional schools. In M. Levine (Ed.), *Professional practice schools: Linking teacher education and school reform.* (pp. 8-24). New York: Teachers College Press.

Linek, W. M., Nelson, O. G., Sampson, M. B., Zeek, C. K., Mohr, K. A. J., & Hughes, L. (1999). Developing beliefs about literacy instruction: A cross-case analysis of current studies of preservice teachers. *Reading Research and Instruction, 38,* 371-386.

Lyons, N., & LaBoskey, V. K. (Eds.) (2002). *Narrative inquiry in practice: Advancing the knowledge of teaching.* New York: Teachers College Press.

National Commission on Excellence in Education. (1983). *A nation at risk: The imperative for education reform.* Washington, DC: U.S. Department of Education.

National Commission on Teaching and America's Future. (1996). *What matters most: Teaching for America's future.* New York: Author.

Olson, M. R. (2000). Linking personal and professional knowledge of teaching practice through narrative inquiry. *Teacher Educator, 35*(4), 109-127.

Richert, A. E. (2002). Narratives that teach: Learning about teaching from the stories teachers tell. In N. Lyons & V. K. LaBoskey (Eds.), *Narrative inquiry in practice: Advancing the knowledge of teaching* (pp. 48-62). New York: Teachers College Press.

Ritchie, J. S., & Wilson, D. E. (2000). *Teacher narrative as critical inquiry: Rewriting the script.* New York: Teachers College Press.

Rosenblatt, L. M. (1978). *The reader, the text, the poem: The transactional theory of the literary work.* Carbondale, IL: Southern Illinois University Press.

Rust, F. O. (2002). Professional conversations: New teachers explore teaching through conversation, story, and narrative. In N. Lyons & V. K. LaBoskey (Eds.), *Narrative inquiry in practice: Advancing the knowledge of teaching* (pp. 173-188). New York: Teachers College Press.

Vygotsky, L. (1986). *Thought and language* (A. Kozulin, Trans.). Cambridge MA: MIT Press.

Walker, C., & Zeek, C. K. (2003, January). *How do they describe effective literacy teaching? Exploring beliefs of teachers in divergent certification programs.* Paper presented at American Association of Colleges for Teacher Education, New Orleans, LA.

Wertsch, J. V. (Ed.). (1985). *Culture, communication, and cognition.* Cambridge, UK: Cambridge University Press.

Wise, A. E., & Darling-Hammond, L (1986). *Licensing teachers: Design for the teaching profession.* Santa Monica, CA: RAND Corporation.

Wold, L. S. (2003). An examination of teachers' "learning to act on reflection." *Reading Research and Instruction, 42*(3), 52-74.

Zeek, C. K., Foote, M., & Walker, C. (2001). Teacher stories and transactional inquiry: Hearing the voices of mentor teachers. *Journal of Teacher Education, 52,* 373-381.

Zeek, C. K., & Walker, C. (2002, April). *Literacy beliefs and practices of teachers in divergent certification programs.* Paper presented at the American Educational Research Association, New Orleans, LA.

Zeek, C. K., & Walker, C. (2003, October). *Orchestrating fluency: Exploring teaching practices in divergent certification programs.* Paper presented at College Reading Association, Corpus Christi, TX.

Zeichner, K.M., & Liston, D.P. (1996). *Reflective teaching: An introduction.* Mahwah, NJ: Lawrence Erlbaum Associates.

Appendix A. Sample Narratives

Prompt: Tell about an effective literacy lesson you have taught or observed. What made it effective?

Traditionally Trained Teachers
Narrative T1

An effective literacy lesson I have taught for several years focuses around the popular children's book, *The Napping House*. First, Audrey Wood is one of my favorite authors. I spotlight several authors each semester, and she always is a favorite of my students. When I spotlight an author, my intentions are not only to excite my students about reading and provide quality literature, but also to integrate skills through the use of these picture books. Since my students are eager to hear each new book by these authors, they become very involved in the lesson.

During this lesson (which occurs over a week), we discuss napping and even suggest synonyms (yes, my kids know that word) for the word nap. The children and I always take a picture walk through the books (esp. w/ a big book) before reading. The first time I read is for enjoyment. The next day, I read again while tracking the print. Afterwards we'll discuss the story, illustrations, & concepts about print. The third day is another read aloud – some kids are ready to chime in at parts. We'll get into discussing the sequence of events in the story beginning with the grandma napping to the flea waking the mouse. The fourth & fifth days are choral readings. I place flannel board characters in my language center so the children can retell the story to each other. I also use a storytelling apron on 1-2 of the days to tell the story orally (w/o using the illustrations) w/ Velcro characters.

What makes this lesson effective? Not only are my children hearing & interacting w/ a good piece of literature, but they learn about sequencing, synonyms & what a cumulative story is. The children become so confident they can read the story w/ me & classmates. Then they have the opportunity to read the story themselves in the reading center, as well as retell the story using a flannel board. All this plus my students learn more about a well-known author!

Narrative T2

Literacy Lesson—My "favorite" lesson was on Immigration. We read the chapter in the Social Studies book, but it wasn't enough. I designed a survey for my students to use when interviewing an immigrant (1/2 of my students are immigrants themselves). The survey asked several basic questions—what year did you come, etc. up to more detailed . . . "Tell the story of the day you came." The students then compiled the information in graphs and wrote a story about the particular person they interviewed and why they came to the United States. I published the stories in a book and gave each student a copy. It was a fantastic lesson—we wrote, read, graphed and shared. I felt, at the time, that I was the best teacher in the world. [I don't often feel remotely like the best teacher]

Why was it an effective lesson?
Integration of content area
Family stories
Publication
Readers' chair
Prior knowledge
High interest level

Narrative T3

Creepy Crawly Creatures

- Four days prior to lesson, I visited the school library and checked out approximately 30 books on bugs, spiders, bats, frogs, etc. Students spent four days browsing through the books. Students identified 3 to 4 favorite animals.
- I took students favorite animals list and assigned each student 1 animal. We went to the library where students were introduced to how to use the encyclopedia.
- Students copied 6 facts about their animal from the encyclopedia. I encouraged facts to be really creepy or a surprising fact.
- We went back to class where students wrote 1 paragraph about their creature. We did a short writing exercise about a "grabbing" introduction and transition words also & then students made a final copy of paragraph.
- I typed the paragraphs during lunch. That afternoon students illustrated for about 1 hour. I was shocked initially at the level of detail, but this *was* a creature they found interesting.
- We laminated the pages and put it in a book.
- I sent the book home nightly for parents to share & we have a copy of it in our library.

Effective

- Plenty of *time* to develop the research and writing.
- Subject of high interest to students
- Many components, reading, writing, research, science
- A final product to be shared with others—motivated some students to produce quality work
- Students had choice in what they study
- I gave students a model of the final product

Alternatively Trained Teachers

Narrative A1

Effective Literacy Lesson

We discussed alliteration and what alliteration is and reasons you might use alliteration in writing. I read *Animalia* (sp?) to the children after our brainstorming season, then we review the purpose of Alliteration. Then the children create an alliteration advertisement using their name. Example: Millionaire Mason makes money, Marvelous Melissa manipulates mathematics. The children also draw a picture to represent their advertisement which goes on the "All American Alliteration Advertisement" bulletin board to be shared with our learning community. This was effective because it was a different type lesson being more hands on and away from the daily "basal reader" and reading curriculum set forth by the district. It made the children use their creativity and vocabulary knowledge to create an advertisement slogan to represent their name. Also, I had fun teaching this lesson versus the daily strategies for the adopted reader.

Narrative A2

Students read to aloud [sic] various brothers Grimm stories. Then students had to compare stories and characters in story. Students created gingerbread houses, calculated the distance from one character's house to another. Students also had to create a gingerbread house. Students created big book of favorite story giving specific theme, plot, characters. Students created shoe prints and had to measure distance from class to another point and determine how many shoes—feet—inches were required.

I think it was effective because they were having fun and learning.

Narrative A3

The lesson was one that I observed of first graders in a guided reading group. When they sat down on the floor in a circle the teacher reviewed some reading strategies that the students used to figure out "tricky" words. Some examples were chunking, sounding out, and looking at the little word in the big word.

The teacher then did a picture walk with the students, stimulating there (sic) background knowledge about the book. The teacher took this time to make predictions and plant words that might be unknown to them in their knowledge base. The teacher would discuss the new word before reading so that the student would be successful.

The students then began reading aloud at different paces. The teacher observed as the students read and came across "tricky" words. When the student came across a word they did not know they would problem solve and the teacher would jump in if necessary.

At the end of the lesson the students would add the strategy they used to their learning log. The teacher ended the lesson by again reviewing reading strategies.

It was an effective literacy activity because all the students were actively engaged. They were all reading. The children were also demonstrating problem solving techniques to master the material. The teacher was evaluating and making mental notes about the students progress. The teacher later reflected from these observations. She evaluated her reading groups to make sure the students were properly placed.

Appendix B. Willis' Teacher's Story

It was towards the end of the year and my first year of teaching. After months of observation and experimentation with lesson plans, I decided to close the year by having my students write autobiographies. I noticed they were always talking, or bragging, about their young lives and this would be something they would do without hesitation. Also this would give me the opportunity to really learn more about them outside of school and to really see how much they had retained from previous writing assignments. . . .

The autobiography was divided into three parts. . .[covering] an area in their life: (1) birth to four years old, (2) kindergarten to sixth grade, and (3) their future. I provided questions to be answered and incorporated into their paper. It was also a tool to help my kids expand on their findings and to involve their parents and other family members. . . . I was impressed with myself as a teacher. My joy was soon stripped from me when Willis asked, "Miss, why you makin' us do this boring stuff?" . . . "It's the end of the year and we already did all the writin' stuff." I was not surprised that Willis would ask this. Instead I was fearful that my other students would follow suit and mutiny would occur. However . . . [t]hey were excited about placing their lives on paper and that other students and I were genuinely interested.

I devoted one week to each area of the autobiography. My kids and I proofread, edited, and critiqued everyday. As an incentive, I permitted each writer to type his or her work on the computer. My classroom was like a newspaper office with journalists buzzing around to meet a deadline. The kids were falling into my trap of writing and we were all enjoying it. All except Willis. . . . He did absolutely nothing and his defiant behavior got worse. Until we were into the second part of the autobiography.

It was a Tuesday, I think, when Willis turned in a rough, rough draft of the first part of his autobiography. . . . Mind you, Willis had only done the bare minimum, but I was happy. I could tell Willis was satisfied with his work and somewhat embarrassed that it took him long enough to come around. I didn't fully critique his work only because I was afraid he would get discouraged and stop. Instead I accommodated him and the rest of the class with extra days to finish, due to his late start. Soon Willis was begging to come to class during my planning period to finish his work on the computer. I allowed him to do this a few times. I couldn't believe the transformation. My aide said it was because he enjoyed computers but never was given the opportunity to really use one. I didn't care. I was just happy that he was participating in some kind of writing experience voluntarily. . . .

On the last day of school, Willis' mother came to volunteer for field day. Much to Willis' surprise, I had saved his work and printed it out for his mother. She remembered that Willis was asking a bunch of questions about himself as a baby, but she did not have time to sit down and talk. This explained why he didn't start on time. I felt ashamed and thought Willis was only being defiant because he didn't want to participate. In actuality, he did want to write. He just didn't have the information at the time that I had requested. Another lesson learned for Ms. Scott.

Reading and Auditory Processing: A Collaborative Project

Daniel H. Sisterhen
Martha J. Larkin
Cathleen Doheny
Donna M. Harkins

State University of West Georgia

Abstract

This chapter describes a broad, literacy-based collaboration project involving university faculty, general education teachers, special educators, speech-language pathologists, and public school administrators. It focuses on the application of a multi-tiered collaboration model designed to improve reading instruction and auditory processing disorder intervention. The chapter includes a discussion of the project planning, implementation, and ongoing observation.

Professional collaboration on literacy makes intuitive sense and is well supported in the literature (Friend & Cook, 2003; Harn, Bradshaw, & Ogletree, 1999). The well-known advantages of efficiency, consideration and socialization of diverse perspectives, and synergistic impact support the use of a team collaboration model whenever practical and available. Historically, the typical collaboration application has consisted of a single-tiered model where the participants are often closely related by discipline, organization, and/or proximity. This article describes a project currently in operation which exhibits a three-tiered collaboration approach by participants who are not all related by discipline, organization, or proximity.

Disorders involving central auditory processing, language development, and reading are developmental difficulties requiring the involvement of specialized support personnel in addition to the general education teacher (Vaughn et al, 2000). A substantial literature base indicates a strong conceptual and neurological relationship between these three disorders (Bradham,

2001; Chermack & Musiek, 1997; Flexer, 1999; Gillon, 2001; Hull, 2001; Jerger & Musiek, 2000). Given this close relationship, the central goal of the project is to assist the general education teacher, the special education teacher, and the speech-language pathologist in managing students with reading difficulties and central auditory processing disorders through collaboration and co-teaching. The model chosen to accomplish this involves the participation of three teams: (a) university faculty; (b) school-based educators; and (c) district public school administrators. The project is supported by a state improvement grant designed to improve the instruction of children with disorders in the regular classroom setting.

Conceptual Framework
Collaboration

Duchardt and colleagues (1999) noted that the organizational structure of higher education does not provide opportunities for interdisciplinary collaborative planning and teaching. They also stated that university educators are recognizing the benefits of teamwork and are exploring creative ways to co-plan and co-teach in order to address the diverse needs of university and public school students. Some university educators now may be attempting efforts to model collaboration in university settings in order to practice what they teach. Many educators in the public schools may not have had the opportunity to participate in co-taught university classes and thus, do not think that they have the knowledge or skills to begin collaborating with colleagues. Hudson and Glomb (1997) indicated that "Effective collaboration requires that teachers have knowledge and skills in how to effectively communicate and share their technical expertise for the purpose of solving classroom problems and providing continuity across instructional settings" (p. 442). Typically, general education and special education teacher preparation programs give each group of educators technical expertise for their respective disciplines, but little time is spent in the university programs teaching collaboration strategies and interpersonal communication skills. Hudson et al. (1997) suggested that university faculty co- teaching collaboration skills to general and special educators enrolled in the same class(es) gives the instructors an opportunity to model collaboration skills for the students.

Although special education—general education collaboration is becoming more prevalent in the public schools, other educators are participating in collaborative efforts, too. Harn et al. (1999) stated that collaborative service delivery models involving speech-language pathologists are replacing the traditional "pull out" approaches to speech-language pathology in many schools. In the new models, speech-language pathology interventions are becoming integrated into the classrooms, and some speech-language pathologists may provide services in the classroom. Such changes emphasize the importance of the speech-language pathologist in the school's literacy program.

Central Auditory Processing, Language, and Reading

The relationship between central auditory processing, language, and reading is both conceptual and neurological (Bradham, 2001; Chermack & Musiek, 1997; Gillon, 2001; Hull, 2001; Schow & Nerbonne, 2002; Zemlin, 1998). The human brain is neurologically organized to develop verbal language through the auditory channel. The auditory channel can be described in terms of two main divisions: the peripheral auditory system and the central auditory system. The peripheral system converts acoustic signals such as speech into neurological impulses. The central auditory pathways transmit these impulses to the auditory cortex, the hearing / language center of the brain. These pathways and the auditory cortex comprise the central auditory system. Further, the pathways involved in hearing are not limited to the auditory cortex. The auditory cortex is also connected to Wernicke's area, a nearby portion of the brain that mixes speech and visual signals from the occipital lobe, the vision center of the brain. This direct neurological connection between the auditory cortex and visual cortex is best demonstrated by the fact that Wernicke's area is most active when a child listens and when a child reads (Gilbertson & Bramlett, 1998).

So, it is important to note that the primary reading centers of the brain are located near the auditory portions of the brain (Chermack & Musiek, 1997; Flexer, 1999). This indicates that humans are neurologically wired to develop spoken language and reading skills through the central auditory system (Chermack & Musiek, 1997). Phonological or phonemic awareness, the explicit awareness of the speech sound structure of language units, forms the basis for the development of reading skills (Gilbertson & Bramlett, 1998). The relationship can be even more succinctly defined by noting that reading is a secondary linguistic function built on speaking (Collins & Cheek, 1999; Flexer, 1999; Simon, 1985). Finally, the National Reading Panel reports that the ability to manipulate the sounds in language is a strong predictor of later reading success (NICHD, 2000).

Children who have difficulty with listening, understanding speech, or language development in the absence of any other learning, cognitive, or emotional disorder are often diagnosed as exhibiting a Central Auditory Processing Disorder (CAPD) (Jerger & Musiek, 2000). The Task Force on Auditory Processing (1996) notes additional CAPD characteristics including difficulty with sound localization, auditory discrimination, auditory pattern recognition, and the temporal aspects of sound. While there is no universal agreement on the nature of CAPD, it is often considered a learning disorder and is often just one aspect of a more complex language-learning disorder (Jerger

& Musiek, 2000). This close relationship between central auditory processing, language, and reading may offer educators an additional tool to identify children at risk for future literacy problems which may result in earlier intervention.

The diagnosis of CAPD is occurring with rapidly increasing frequency in the elementary school-age population. The Individuals with Disabilities Education Act (IDEA) (1990) mandates that these children be served in the least restrictive environment, which often equates to the general education classroom. IDEA envisions close collaboration between the general education teacher and support personnel, such as speech-language pathologists and special educators. So, we have both a close developmental relationship between auditory processing, language, and reading disorders as well as legislation to treat them in an environment that, almost by definition, appears to mandate collaboration in some form.

Project Description

The project developed as a result of a Georgia Department of Education grant focused on the acceleration of collaboration and co-teaching among university faculty, public school educators, and public school administrators. The grant, *Reading and Auditory Processing (RAP)*, is a state improvement grant funded through the Georgia Learning Resources System (GLRS). GLRS, a teacher support system, is charged with preparing general education and special education teachers to serve students with disabilities in the general education classroom. The grant is approved for two years at $10,000 per year, beginning in 2002. It provides funding for such teacher development expenses as instructional material, professional seminars, staff development, salary supplement, travel, and office supplies (Sisterhen et. al, 2002).

The model chosen to assist the general education teacher, the special education teacher, and the speech-language pathologist in managing students with reading difficulties and central auditory processing disorders includes the development of three teams: (a) university faculty, representing the disciplines of reading, special education, and speech-language pathology; (b) school-based general education teachers, (c) special education teachers, and (d) speech-language pathologists; and (e) district public school administrators.

During the development of the grant proposal, the university team contacted local county public school administrators to generate interest in participating in a project to both promote collaboration and improve literacy and auditory processing skills. Upon approval by the public school administration and grant award, the university and administration teams identified and recruited educator participants including general education teachers, special education teachers, and speech-language pathologists (See Table 1).

Table 1. Reading and Auditory Processing (RAP) Participants

Year 1	Year 2
University Faculty 1 Special Education 1 Speech Language Pathology 2 Reading	University Faculty 1 Special Education 1 Speech Language Pathology 2 Reading
School District Administration Team 1 Special Education Director 1 Staff Development Coordinator 1 Primary School Principal	School District Administration Team 1 Special Education Director 1 Staff Development Coordinator 1 Primary School Principal 1 Elementary School Principal
School District Educators (Primary School) 1 General Education Teacher (K) 1 Special Education Teacher 1 Speech-Language Pathologist	School District Educators (Primary School) 1 General Education Teacher (K) 1 Special Education Teacher 1 Speech-Language Pathologist
	School District Educators (Elementary School) 1 General Education Teacher (4th grade) 1 Special Education Teacher 1 Speech-Language Pathologist
Total: 10 participants	Total: 14 participants

The county school district was chosen because of its proximity to the university (within one hour's drive), its commitment to reading improvement, and its willingness to participate in the Reading and Auditory Processing grant. The small, rural school district has a high rate of illiteracy and poverty. The literacy rate for the county in which the school district is located is about 40%, so many of the students come from families who are not literate. Approximately 50% of the school age students are eligible for free/reduced lunch and all of the schools in the district qualify for Title I. Therefore, a number of the students come from families of low socioeconomic status. The total school population consists of approximately 3,600 students with approximately 500 of those enrolled in the primary school who participated in the grant. Approximately 13% of the students in the district receive special education services.

The K-12 Educator Team

As noted earlier, one of the advantages of a collaboration model is that general education teachers, special education teachers, and speech-language pathologists bring different perspectives to teaching. An important responsibility of K-12 general educators is to plan, implement, and evaluate instruction that will help students grow as readers, writers, and communicators of language. Reading instruction is a daily activity for these teachers. The goal for students in the elementary grades is to become independent and strategic users of printed language so they will experience success in school and in life. Special educators in public schools modify instruction to address the individual needs of students with disabilities as outlined by their individual education plans (IEPs). Reading instruction may or may not be a daily activity for special education teachers, depending on the individual needs of their students. Speech-language pathologists provide therapy for students who have been identified with speech, language, and/or hearing problems. They treat a wide range of communicative disorders involving such areas as receptive language, expressive language, and articulation. In the majority of cases, the focus is on oral language which we identified earlier as directly related to future literacy skills.

So, it is clear that all three educators work with some of the same students on auditory skills; however, they teach the skills in isolated settings from three different perspectives. There is often little communication among the K-12 educators about how their goals for learners could be integrated to reinforce the skills they are teaching. For example, the reading teacher works with a student on phonemic awareness while the speech-language pathologist works with the same child on articulation. The special educator works on listening and following directions with the same child in the resource room. Phonemic awareness, articulation, listening, and following directions are interrelated auditory skills, and development in one skill area enhances development in the other areas (Bradham, 2001; Smith, Simmons, & Kameenui, 1995).

Based on conversations between the university team and the K-12 educators, the lack of coordination among the general education teacher, the special education teacher, and the speech-language pathologist results from four main areas of concern: (a) a lack of understanding of each other's goals, roles and techniques; (b) the lack of time during the day for discussion and coordination; (c) the lack of formal collaborative goals; (d) a fear that coordination may in some way result in a change in job descriptions. Anecdotal evidence gathered by the authors during implementation of this project suggests that speech-language pathologists feel unqualified to work in the field of 'literacy', while general educators and special educators have expressed similar fears of working in the field of 'speech problems'.

The University Faculty and District Public School Administration Teams

A key component to accomplishing the project's main goal of improving the coordination and collaboration among the three educators across three separate disciplines included collaboration and co-teaching by the university team. This team consisted of two faculty members from the Department of Special Education and Speech-Language Pathology, and two members from the Department of Curriculum and Instruction. Some of the faculty team's primary contributions include the development of a sequence of inter-departmental didactic courses for the participating K-12 educators, new practicum supervisory support provided in the field, and sponsorship of guest speakers for continuing education professional development.

The faculty team developed a new sequence of three content/collaboration courses including Reading Theory, Development, and Practices (READ 7271), Collaboration: Families, Professionals, and Students (SPED 7722), and Clinical Assessment and Instruction (READ 7285). (See Table 2 for a description of these courses). The courses were co-taught in varying degrees, with the highest level of faculty collaboration occurring in the Clinical Assessment and Instruction course. READ 7285 was developed specifically to address the relationship between auditory processing and reading-related concepts such as: (a) phonological and phonemic awareness; (b) the assessment of skills related to literacy; (c) teaching strategies for identified reading and CAP disorders; (d) development of instructional plans; and (e) field-based components to be completed at the school site. Specific course requirements include (a) a case study, (b) one research study, (c) formal and informal assessments to target reading focus areas, (d) management of assessment and planning data, (e) collaborative lesson plans, (f) observation notes, and (g) follow-up focus

Table 2. Reading and Auditory Processing (RAP) Courses

YEAR 1—PRIMARY SCHOOL DISTRICT EDUCATORS TEAM
YEAR 2—ELEMENTARY SCHOOL DISTRICT EDUCATORS TEAM

Summer
READ 7271   Reading Theory, Development, and Practices
A seminar/discussion course dealing with the teaching of reading at the primary level (PK-5), including an introduction to skills, approaches, materials, methods, and philosophies. Significant literature will be reviewed from a current and historical perspective.

SPED 7722   Collaboration: Families, Professionals & Students
This course assists in preparing educators to enter educational settings ready to operate within the new paradigm of collaboration rather than that of an isolated professional. There is a strong focus on respecting the roles various persons play, whether it is a professional, family member, or student, and how these roles support each other in the process of designing effective programs for students, particularly for those with disabilities. Much of the discussion will center on inclusive settings.

Fall
READ 7285   Clinical Assessment and Instruction
Special topics course to enhance the diagnosis and treatment of reading problems in a supervised clinical setting. Course content addresses the six dimensions of literacy as reported by the National Reading Panel.

group interviews. The initial planning included applications for both primary and elementary schools, grades PK-2 and 3-5, respectively. Focus on the PK-2 grades was directed toward planning, assessing, and co-teaching phonemic and phonological awareness. Planning, assessment, and co-teaching vocabulary development received the most emphasis in grades 3-5.

The field-based practicum component required the public school educators to administer a battery of assessments, analyze results, as well as plan and implement appropriate instruction. The university faculty observed the educators during this process and offered feedback through discussion of the benefits and challenges of engaging in collaborative planning and co-teaching in the public school. Additionally, the public school educators received material for facilitating planning, assessment, and instruction delivered via both the didactic courses and on-site at the public schools. The public school educators are encouraged to meet regularly during the week to plan, discuss, and evaluate collaborative activities, as well as teach in the same classroom whenever possible.

Approval and support from the district school administration team including the Special Education Director and School Principal was critical. Without the endorsement of senior administrators, the K-12 educators would be unable to dedicate any significant time to the project. As discussed shortly, time limitations emerged as a key factor.

Observations

Even though the grant is only in its second year, the university faculty has made a number of significant observations. Applying the theory of collaboration to the practical environments of the university and public school settings has been revealing. First, they found that the general educator, special educator and speech-language pathologist could all benefit from additional training in teaching literacy. For example, even though they were exposed to a wealth of literacy resources such as the informal phoneme awareness assessments available online, the school district primary team needed assistance from the university faculty in administering these instruments and recording the data from them. The three collaboration and literacy courses, together with the basic program requirements, were not sufficient to prepare the educators for either the challenge of collaboration or teaching literacy. While the educators demonstrated good learning outcomes, they could have benefited specifically from additional coursework in basic methodology. Beneficial learning outcomes included competence in administering a battery of basic assessment instruments and identifying reading difficulties. Further coursework in basic teaching strategies, curriculum, and instruction would have enhanced the educators' ability to match instruction to the individual needs of the students.

Positive learning outcomes were not limited to the public school educators. As the university faculty team improved their collaborative skills with each other, it became clear that they often used different terms when referring to the same developmental processes or disorders. Given that professionals often rely on their own unique terminology in communications, a common understanding across professions is critical. A specific example involved the learned ability to isolate and manipulate the sounds of spoken words. The reading and special education faculty tended to refer to this process as *phonemic awareness*, while the speech-language pathology faculty member often referred to this same process as *auditory processing*. During discussion and planning activities, the university team members and educators from three different disciplines gained a great deal of knowledge about the similarities and differences of reading, special education, and speech-language pathology.

An additional positive outcome included improvement in the incorporation of existing student information. As collaboration improved across disciplines, the identification and use of currently available assessment data (e.g., Basic Literacy Test) also improved. This information sharing improved the efficiency of administrative activities as well as avoiding duplicative testing. Two of the university faculty helped the school district educator team at the primary school administer informal Phoneme Awareness Assessment Tools (see http://teams.lacoe.edu/reading/assessments/assessments.html) such as Recognizing Rhyme Assessment, Phoneme Isolating and Phoneme Matching for Beginning Sounds, and Phoneme Blending. These assessments were given as pre- and post-tests to the class of kindergarten students who were co-taught by the school district educator team for years 1 and 2 of the grant. During year 2 of the grant, the school district educator team at the elementary school chose to give their own vocabulary assessments to their co-taught 4th graders to determine student progress. All of the data from the assessments are not accessible yet for final analysis, but preliminary observations of the available data indicate that most of the primary and elementary students co-taught by their respective teams did improve their literacy skills in the targeted area (i.e., phonemic awareness for kindergarten students, and vocabulary for 4th grade students).

The major challenge encountered was time constraints. There simply wasn't enough time to engage in as much collaboration or team-teaching as desired, regardless of whether the environment was administrative, university, or public school. Raywid noted in 1993 that lack of sufficient time was a primary area of concern in collaborative efforts. Time was an issue with basic needs such as planning meetings, as well as with specific needs such as faculty setting up appointments to model collaboration and instructional strategies for the public school educators. A primary positive learning outcome for both the educator and faculty and teams was a clear transition from 'hit or miss' planning to some structured planning and co-taught lessons. By the end of the first year, all teams had made gains in the effective use of collaborative opportunities. However, time constraints remained a challenge for all, both within and between teams.

The Future

Although the funding for the *Reading and Auditory Processing Project (RAP)* is complete, it is the intent of the university faculty, school district administrator team, and the school district primary and elementary school teams to continue the multi-tiered collaboration model. The school district received a Reading First Grant (2004) and several of the primary and elementary school team educators are attending training during summer 2004. The *RAP* participants anticipate that the collaborative interventions and activities begun during the *RAP* state improvement grant will continue and expand as part of the Reading First Grant. Also, the school district administration team has expressed an interest in working with the university faculty to begin additional collaborative teams at the middle and high school levels during the 2004-05 academic year.

All participants will continue to pursue the goals of the *RAP* project, meet the challenges, and expand collaboration activities wherever possible. The initial collaborative efforts have become somewhat contagious. Other educators in the primary and elementary schools have been curious about the RAP activities and have expressed an interest in joining the collaborative teams during the next school year. The original school district teams are committed not only to including new members, but also to improving collaboration and instructional methodology. The multi-tiered collaboration model embodies mutually beneficial collaboration within and between teams. Part of the focus in future efforts will be placed on the exploration and implementation of additional processes to address the time constraints across the board. Specific focus will be placed on the exploration of processes to increase the amount of on-site modeling and collaboration between the university team and the educators. Finally, supplemental coursework and/or staff development to address basic literacy instruction and methodology will be developed and implemented.

References

Bradham, T. S. (2001). *Auditory processing disorders in children.* Paper presented at the ASHA Convention, New Orleans, LA.

Chermak, G. D., & Musiek, F. E. (1997). *Central auditory processing disorders: New perspectives.* San Diego: Singular.

Collins, M. D., & Cheek, Jr., E. H. (1999). *Assessing and guiding reading instruction.* New York: McGraw-Hill.

Duchardt, B., Marlow, L., Inman, D., & Christensen, P. (1999). Collaboration and co-teaching: General and special education faculty. *Clearing House, 72*(3), 186-190.

Flexer, C. (1999). *Facilitating hearing and listening in young children* (2nd ed.). San Diego: Singular.

Friend, M., & Cook, L. (2003). *Interactions: Collaboration skills for school professionals* (4th ed.). Boston: Allyn & Bacon.

Georgia Department of Education. (2004). *Reading First State Grants.* Funded through the Georgia Department of Education, Atlanta, GA.

Gilbertson, M. & Bramlett, R. K. (1998). Phonological awareness screening to identify at-risk readers: Implications for at-risk readers. *Language, Speech and Hearing Services in Schools, 29*, 109-116.

Gillon, G. (2001). *Causal & correlative links between spoken and written language difficulties in children.* Paper presented at the ASHA Convention, New Orleans, LA.

Harn, W. E., Bradshaw, M. L., & Ogletree, B. T. (1999). The speech-language pathologist in the schools: Changing roles. *Intervention in School & Clinic, 34*(3), 163-169.

Hudson, P., & Glomb, N. (1997). If it takes two to tango, then why not teach both partners to dance? Collaboration instruction for all educators. *Journal of Learning Disabilities, 30*, 442-448.

Hull, R. H. (2001). *Aural rehabilitation: Serving children and adults* (4th ed.). San Diego: Singular.

Individuals with Disabilities Education Act. (IDEA), PL 101-476. (1990). Title 20, U.S.C. 1400 et seq: *US Statutes at Large, 104*, 1103-1151.

Jerger, J. and Musiek, F. E. (2000). Report on the consensus conference on diagnosis of auditory processing disorders in school-age children. *Journal of the American Academy of Audiology, 11*, 467-474.

National Institute of Child Health and Human Development (2000). *Report of the National Reading Panel. Teaching children to read: An evidence-based assessment of the scientific research literature on reading and its implications for reading instruction: Reports of the subgroups* (NIH Publication No. 00-4754). Washington, DC: U.S. Government Printing Office.

Raywid, M. A. (1993). Finding time for collaboration. *Educational Leadership, 51*(1), 30-34.

Schow, R. L., & Nerbonne, M. A. (2002). *Introduction to audiologic rehabilitation* (4th ed.). Needham Heights, MA: Allyn & Bacon.

Simon, C. S. (1985). *Communication skills and classroom success.* San Diego, CA: College-Hill Press.

Sisterhen, D. H., Larkin, M. J., Harkins, D. & Doheny, C. [Investigators]. (2002). *Reading and auditory processing (RAP).* State Improvement Grant from the Georgia Learning Resources System, Georgia Department of Education, Atlanta, GA.

Smith, S. B., Simmons, D. C., & Kameenui, E. J. (1995). *Synthesis of research on phonological awareness: Principles and implications for reading acquisition* (Technical Report no. 21, National Center to Improve the Tools of Education). Eugene: University of Oregon.

Task Force on Central Auditory Processing-ASHA. (1996). Central auditory processing: Current status of research and implications for clinical practice. *American Journal of Audiology, 5*(2), 41-54.

Vaughn, S., Bos, C., & Schumm, J. S. (2000). *Teaching exceptional, diverse, and at-risk students in the general education classroom* (2nd ed.). Boston, MA: Allyn & Bacon.

Zemlin, W. R. (1998). *Speech and hearing science: Anatomy and physiology* (4th ed.). Needham Heights, MA: Allyn & Bacon.

LEARNER-CENTERED TEACHERS' APPROACHES TO LITERACY INSTRUCTION: ARE THEY "BEST PRACTICE?"

Barbara Combs

University of North Dakota

Abstract

This chapter explores the question: to what extent do learner-centered teachers' described instructional practices correspond with the research on effective practices in literacy instruction? A descriptive definition of learner-centered teaching is offered followed by a review of the research related to effective practices in literacy. Next, findings related to literacy instruction practices drawn from an analysis of 16 in-depth interviews with learner-centered teachers are offered. Finally, these practices are compared to those presented in the literature on effective literacy instruction. The comparison reveals that teaches who describe themselves as learner-centered engage in effective literacy instruction. These teachers implement a variety of practices including theme and genre studies, investigations, workshops, and process oriented, collaborative approaches to reading and writing.

For the past two years, I have attended meetings at the state and local level where the words *No Child Left Behind* and *Reading First* have become mantras. Their repetition seeks to lull me into a lethargic belief that simply following the right reading prescription and disregarding the teacher, the child, the school or the community will ensure literacy success (and higher test scores). There is little mention of real teachers engaged in real practice with real students. Instead, talk centers on adhering to "the list" of accepted assessments, basalized literacy programs, and controlled training sessions, so that implementation of one size practice can be assured. I was at first uneasy, but now I find myself dismayed and alarmed. One size, whether we talk about trivial trappings like swimsuits and shoes or the critical, complex, and messy work that teachers do to ensure children's literacy growth, fits few.

The most important element in a child's successful literacy development is the teacher (Allington & Johnson, 2001; Gambrell & Mazzoni, 1999). Indeed, recent approaches to the study of best or effective literacy practice highlight what teachers do to promote their students' literacy achievement (Cantrell, 1999). By exploring the classrooms of successful teachers of literacy, we might better understand what processes and practices result in effective literacy learning for children.

In a related field of inquiry, research supports and illustrates the centrality of the teacher in the learning experience. Specifically, this body of research focuses on the beliefs and practices of learner-centered teachers and offers descriptive definitions of this concept (Paris & Combs, 2000, 2001). The collection of teachers' lengthy narratives represents a variety of pedagogical approaches and fall within a range of content areas, including literacy related instruction. The purpose of this study was to re-examine the interviews of teachers who espoused a learner-centered stance in order to compare their stated practices with existing research findings related to effective practice in literacy instruction

Related Literature

Two areas of research are drawn upon in this study: descriptive definitions of learner-centered practice and elements of effective/best practice in literacy instruction.

Learner-centered Practice

The definition of the term "learner-centered" used here is drawn from the work of Paris and Combs (2000, 2001). The authors, after conducting an extensive review of the literature on learner-centered teachers and teaching and analyzing teacher interviews, offered a descriptive definition of what it means to be learner-centered, grounded in teachers' daily practice. The key elements that comprise the definition are as follows:

- The teacher is focused on the learner,
- The teacher guides and facilitates the learning,
- The teacher promotes active engagement, and
- The teacher promotes learner ownership and responsibility.

Effective Teachers of Literacy

A review of recent literature in this area reveals that quality instruction is tied inextricably to the beliefs and abilities of quality instructors (Allington & Johnson, 2001; Block, Oak, & Hurt, 2002; Ruddell, 1995). Effective teachers of literacy share characteristics with effective teachers everywhere. In general they:

- are passionate/enthusiastic about the subjects they teach;
- are extremely knowledgeable about the subjects they teach and how to teach them;

- care about children and believe that each can and will learn;
- plan, implement and revise instruction based upon the assessed needs of learners; and
- work to promote the development of independence in learners through opportunities for choice and collaborative and scaffolded learning experiences.

A comparison of the characteristics of learner-centered teachers and effective teachers of literacy demonstrates their shared understandings (see Table 1) and reveals a grounding in the constructivist theory that holds the learner at the center and focuses on how learning occurs (Au, 2003; Fosnot, 1996; Marlow & Page, 1998).

Table 1. Comparison of Learner-Centered Teachers and Effective Teachers of Literacy

Characteristics of Teachers Who Are Learner-Centered	Related Characteristics from Effective Teachers of Literacy Literature
The teacher is focused on the learner	The teacher cares about children and believes that each can and will learn
The teacher guides and facilitates the learning	The teacher plans, implements and revises instruction based upon the assessed needs of learners
The teacher promotes active engagement, learner ownership and responsibility	The teacher works to promote the development of independence in learners through opportunities for choice and collaborative and scaffolded learning experiences

Effective Practices in Literacy Instruction

According to Stewart (2002), "[the] quest of effective practices is to discover what is best in terms of actual children in actual classrooms" (pp. 2-3). We look then to the research on effective teachers of literacy—those in whose classrooms children appear to flourish as readers and writers. What are the common literacy instruction practices of such teachers?

The approaches to literacy instruction that effective teachers of literacy employ are real, relevant, changeable, and social in nature (Gould, 1996). Such instruction involves process-oriented and balanced approaches to the teaching of reading and writing (Allington & Cunningham, 1996; Au, 2003; Gambrell & Mazzoni, 1999) that attends to the understanding of reading and writing as complex, active, and recursive in nature (Kutz & Roskelly, 1991). Reading is a meaning-making process consisting of actions in which children tap into prior knowledge, identify the words in the text and draw information from it, and integrate the new information with prior understandings (Fountas &

Pinnell, 2001). Writing is a process consisting of actions in which children pre-write, draft, revise, and edit. The writer moves back and forth from one stage to another in a non-linear way depending on "purpose, audience and personal writing habits" (Cramer, 2001, p. 36). Instructional approaches that support the concepts of process and balance include: reading and writing workshops, teacher read alouds, guided reading and writing, shared reading and writing, literature discussion groups, and sustained independent reading (Au, 2003; Cunningham & Allington, 1999; Fountas & Pinnell, 2001) In such approaches, skill instruction is not ignored but rather taught in conjunction with meaningful, extended language activities (Applebee, 2003). In addition, children are immersed in literate-rich environments (Wharton-McDonald & Hampton, 1998) and are provided with extended periods of time for learning where teacher modeling, scaffolding and feedback occur (Cantrell, 1999).

This review of literature related to successful teachers of reading and writing indicates a need for effective educators to provide a wide variety of balanced teaching and learning approaches. The purpose of the present study is to examine the literacy related instructional practices of teachers who espouse a learner-centered philosophy with an eye towards addressing the following question: To what extent are the literacy related instructional practices described by these learner-centered teachers congruent with the literature on effective (best) teaching of literacy?

Methods
Participants

This study builds upon the author's collaborative work related to the analysis of in-depth interviews detailing the perspectives and narrative histories of teachers throughout the United States (Paris & Combs, 2000). To date, nineteen educators have been interviewed. Two are male and seventeen are female. All are white. Ten are elementary school teachers (one working primarily with English language learners); four are secondary teachers in the areas of Drama and English; one works in a middle school setting in the area of English; one is a retired secondary English teacher currently an adjunct in a postsecondary College English & English Teacher Education program; two are teacher educators (and the researchers in this project) and one is an elementary school principal and former first grade teacher. All have taught a minimum of five years and some for over twenty.

The interview process has been conducted in two rounds. Early interviewees were selected because of their membership in Foxfire, a grassroots teacher organization noted for a culturally responsive, community focused, learner-centered approach to teaching (Starnes, 1999; Starnes & Paris, 2000). More recent participants have been chosen because the two researchers conducting the study have perceived their practice to be learner-centered based upon their conversations or by the recommendations of other interviewees.

Data Sources and Analysis

The sources of data were interviews and demographic information collected from participants. The initial interviews took place in the late summer of 1999 and the most recent one was conducted in November of 2003. In keeping with the notion of cultural interviewing (Rubin, H & Rubin, I, 1995), the goal of this research is to learn about the behaviors and understandings of people within a particular group. To do so questions were minimal and open-ended thus encouraging interviewees to provide narratives, stories, and examples for researchers to analyze. The interview process consisted of two phases. During the first, participants were asked to respond to the following questions:

- We're interviewing you because either you've identified yourself to be or you are someone perceived to be a learner-centered teacher. Could we begin by talking about what learner-centered means to you?

- Would you please tell the story of how you came to be the teacher you are today?

Most recently, two questions have been added to further focus the research (Only Carol, the most recent interviewee, has responded to these.):

- Given the current climate in assessment and accountability for teachers, how do you know and how do you demonstrate that your students are learning?

- Would you please describe your teaching and assessment in the area of literacy, specifically reading and writing?

During the second phase, interviewees were given a copy of their transcript and an audiotape. They were asked to read the interview and add or change information in response to this reading. Of the nineteen interviews, only five have completed these second reviews and most changes to the original transcripts have been minor.

Sixteen of the 19 interviews were analyzed for this study (see Table 2 for general demographic information of participants). The researchers' transcripts have worked as checks and balances to alert us to the ways our own perspectives might color how we listen to and understand others, and so have not been included here. Also, a review of the principals' transcript showed that most information given related to administrative rather than classroom practice, and so this interview transcript too is excluded.

Table 2. General Demographics of Study Participants

Teacher	Years Teaching	Grade	Location
Dan	14	High School Drama	Suburban, Deep Southeast
Doreen	11+	8th Grade Reading	Urban, Deep Southeast
Alice	16	4th Grade	Rural, Central Southeast
Cathy	18	High School English	Rural, Central Southeast
Debbie	16	4th, 5th grades (looping)	Suburban, Central Southeast
Olivia	13	4th grade	Suburban, Northwest Coast
Anna	11	3rd, 4th, 5th grades (combination)	Rural, Central Mid-West
Carol	22+	1st grade	Suburban, Upper Mid-West
David	20	High School English	Rural, Southwest Coast
Erin	20+	1st Grade	Suburban, Northeast
Lana	17	1st grade	Urban Northwest
Emily	27	1st grade ESL	Suburban, Northeast Coast
Nancy	12+	K-6 Math Specialist	Rural, Northeast
Nora	36	College English	Rural, Northeast
Rose	25	2nd Grade	Suburban, Northeast
Marge	24	High School English	Rural, Deep South

The remaining transcripts were analyzed in two stages. In the first stage, data related to participants' definitions and examples of learner-centered teaching were gathered and analyzed for emerging themes that would provide descriptive headings for participants' perspectives of the concept. Next, a review of the literature was done looking for explicit and implicit meanings of the term learner-centered. Core themes emerging from the literature and grounded in the teachers' narratives provided the descriptive definition of learner-centered teaching (Paris & Combs, 2000) that frame the results reported here.

In the second stage, data related to participants' practices in literacy instruction, primarily those text units related to reading and writing instruction were coded and categories that would hold participants' descriptions were developed. Finally, a review of the literature related to effective literacy practices was done in order to place teachers' stories within the broader context of "best" or effective practice in the field of literacy instruction.

Findings

Common patterns of literacy related practice emerged from an analysis of these interviews; although the manner in which teachers talked about each is unique. In addition, three concepts that seemed to encompass the work that went on in these classrooms were evident: establishing a community, knowing the learner, and identifying teacher and student roles and responsibilities. Because they seem to set the climate for learning in the classroom, information related to each these concepts will be presented first. Then, findings related to teachers' approaches to literacy instruction will be reported.

Classroom Climate

It was clearly important for all those interviewed to establish a strong community of learners and an expectation that all who were within that community would learn, teacher and children alike as demonstrated in the following excerpts:

I do say we because it is a "we" you know; we are doing this or that. And it's not the royal we. I mean there are 24 of us, 23 shorter people and me and we are making decisions together. (Olivia, excerpt 155-158)

I try to create an expectation in the classroom that we all will learn, we will all be reading, we will all be able to contribute, and then help them understand there are different ways to do this. (Lana, excerpt 224-226)

I think it's really central to build that community and have them feel comfortable and accepting of each other, what they know, what they don't know and what they need to know (Nora, excerpt 376-378)

Olivia, Lana, and Nora's words mirror Stewart's (2002) belief in the reciprocal nature of the role of teacher and student. Also, Au's (2003) concept of the importance of learning through social interaction is echoed in these excerpts. Indeed, most of the teachers interviewed expressed a belief in the importance of building a climate that would promote collaborative learning.

Even though teachers expected students to learn from and with each other, many spoke as well of the importance of the individuality of the learner within this collaborative framework. There was a belief that only through knowing each child well could appropriate, supportive instruction be designed:

I spend a lot of time learning about my children, learning where they are. I know the district has curriculum through our standards, our benchmarks, our critical knowledge, and I know that's what I'm expected to teach, but I have to start with the children themselves. (Carol, excerpt, 40-46)

As I deliberate about what specifically to teach and how to teach it, I am keeping in mind my students as individuals whose lives and prior experiences are part of the greater whole of who they are as learners at this particular moment. I need to take them from where they are to where I want them to be. (Doreen, excerpt, 1-7)

[W]hat you do is that you look for things in that child, places where that child can succeed in the classroom, and you adapt your curriculum and your lesson plan so that that child can be successful while at the same time you've increased his skills (Marge, excerpt 278-281)

Gambrell and Mazzoni (1999) state that "best practices involve a 'custom fit'—not a simple 'one size fits all' approach" (p. 12). Clearly, Carol, Doreen, and Marge acknowledge the need to discover that 'custom fit' for their students, given the school's curriculum and the children's ages and experiences. Carol's in-depth description of her classroom practices further revealed that she spent a good deal of time early on assessing her students seeking answers to questions like: *Where are they in their learning? Developmentally where are they? What factors impede or encourage their learning?* She then used this information to plan lessons that would guide them through the required curriculum, an important characteristic of effective literacy teachers (Ruddell, 1995).

The roles of the teacher and students, expected and enacted, had a profound impact on the sorts of literacy instruction that was described in the interviews. One primary component of the teacher's role was to create a match between what needed to be learned as mandated by the curriculum to the desires and interests of the learner. Throughout her interview, Olivia described her role as one of *engaging the learner, getting them going*, and *getting the ball rolling*. Nora provided a script when recalling her work with secondary English students:

> Well, I have tried to say, "This is the curriculum. This is what we have to do or this is what we need to cover. How do you want to go about it?" (Nora, excerpt, 371-372)

Dan expressed pride in and belief that his students would learn what they needed if he didn't get in their way:

> [I]f you take a stack of books and put it out to them and say, "Ok, what do you need to know out of this, and what do you want to learn?" that there's an almost ninety percent correlation of what's written in the curriculum, and it is totally fascinating to me. And they know how to get there. And if you tell them to go do it . . . they go do it with a great deal of integrity, a great deal of true ownership in the learning process, and a heck of a lot better than I can do it. It continually amazes me... (Dan, excerpt, 347-357)

For many of the interviewees, the match between student and curriculum was tied first and foremost to the requirements of the curriculum and then, as Nora and Dan noted, students were offered the opportunity to become the teacher through choices in texts, materials, learning tasks, and group work (e.g., small group, whole group, or individual). A similar idea of "managed choice" and distributed authority was noted by Allington and Johnston (2001) in their descriptive research of fourth grade teachers.

Effective teachers know how and when to step in and step out, when to be teacher, when to be learner, and when to be a partner in learning. They

play a multiplicity of roles (Block et al., 2002). Alice a 15+-year veteran aptly exemplified this perspective in her description of interactions with her students:
> . . . the magic word is facilitator. Sometimes I'm a general overseer; sometimes I'm a disputer manager. Sometimes I'm a keynote speaker; sometimes I'm the cheerleading section. I think my role changes as the students' needs change—what they need me to be. (Alice, excerpt, 433-436)

The students in the classrooms were described as active participants eagerly and fully engaged in the planning, implementation, and assessment of curriculum. They offered ideas and these ideas were considered seriously by the teachers with whom they worked. Students were expected to take on roles as independent, responsible learners; and teachers talked a good deal about the need to build independence in the learners whether it was with Lana's first graders: "I try to create an expectation in the classroom that we all will learn we all will be reading, we all will be able to contribute" (Lana, excerpt, 283-284) or Marge's high school students: "when you give a child responsibility for his own learning, then he, if he is a true student, is going to find a way to . . . get out of that class what he needs to get to go on" (Marge, excerpt, 377-379) (Combs, 2003). Such core elements were also found in the literature on exemplary literacy teachers (Allington & Johnston, 2001; Applebee, 2003; Wharton-McDonald & Hampton, 1998).

Literacy Related Instructional Practices

Teachers' interviews provided perspectives on and engagement in general pedagogical approaches to literacy instruction as well as specific reading and writing activities. (See Table 3 for a summary) A more detailed discussion of each category including examples from teachers' interviews follows.

Table 3. Instructional Approaches Implemented

APPROACHES	IMPLEMENTATIONS
Reading & writing workshops	
Genre studies	Biography, historical fiction, folktales, legends, and short story.
Inquiry/theme study	Celebrations, community, and weather
Special projects	Video tour, postcard development, play writing, cultural investigation.
Skill Development	Integrated phonics instruction, mini-lessons word walls, language experience, word study
Other writing instruction	Invented text, journal writing, pen-pal writing
Other reading instruction	Partner/buddy reading, independent reading of self-selected texts, literature circles.

Instructional Approaches

A wide variety of approaches were named by teachers interviewed in this study. The majority of those who gave explicit information on classroom practices, talked about using investigations and projects based upon curriculum requirements and children's interests in order to develop their students' literacy. These broad terms were often used to describe genre and theme studies as well as workshop-oriented approaches to reading and writing.

Carol was the only teacher who explicitly mentioned employing a workshop approach; most likely because she was asked to talk directly about her literacy instruction while others responded to the more general learner-centered question noted earlier: "I teach in a reader's and writer's workshop format. I believe so strongly in that that I just can not go any other way" (Carol, excerpt, 914-15).

Nora's narrative revealed that elements of workshop (mini-lesson, independent activity and conferring time, and share time (Calkins, 1994; Hagerty, 1992) had a real place in her classroom as well: "But we . . . they drafted and chose their own topics, and they held peer conferences." (Nora, excerpt, 406)

Seven teachers described projects and investigations. Olivia's investigations consisted mainly of genre studies ranging from biography to folklore. From the outset of the biography unit, her students became involved whether or not it was her original intention:

> I had two giant boxes of book . . . and I take them out, and I throw this big, huge pile on the floor because they need to be sorted by famous men, famous women, Native Americans, sports figures and stuff. . . . They see me getting into their books, and they're coming back to me saying, "What's this?" "Well, this is . . ." you know, "I think this one needs to go to famous men." . . . "This one goes here, this one goes there." And so then the books are all organized and I'm thinking, "Well, now they've seen them, so I'm not going to really put them back up on the shelf." So, I laid them out in the book corner, and they start[ed] digging through them. (Olivia, excerpt, 43-54)

Nora engaged her high school students in a study of the short story genre while Anna's class explored Native American legends as a way of helping her first graders attending a reservation school learn to read.

> [T]he difficult part is giving them enough guidance without being— without telling them. . . . I still have the notes on the short story, you know, what questions do we want to ask and how will we do this, and the writing about short stories, and the creation of short stories at the same time because they were reading and writing together. (Nora, excerpt 330-343)

We had one ratty version of an Indian legend book and we used that. And we went back to the pragmatic reading. I'd tell the legend, the kids would act it out. [W]e'd have to act it out for two or three days. Then, they would draw a storyboard. In Lakota tradition it goes around and around, and I'd check their sequencing, make sure they had the story down. [W]e'd act it out some more, and eventually they would write it out in their own words. And it worked. It worked awesome. (Anna, excerpt, 781-88)

Projects and investigations like those described by Olivia and Anna represent a shift away from de-contextualized skills approaches and seek to balance curriculum which teaches skills within a rich and extended framework where children explore important issues and ideas (Applebee, 2003).

Teacher's narratives also included a broad range of reading, writing, speaking, and listening activities. Erin's students wrote journal entries and learned how to keep flight logs after flying in an airplane that she herself piloted. The original focus of study was a unit about weather, but Erin allowed children's questions to direct where the study would take them and even she was surprised when flying became the real focus of exploration.

It went from learning about the weather, all the way to learning about the instruments in the airplane. And so the next thing they wanted to do was go up. They wanted to know, "Why can't you let us fly?" So, and these were boys. The girls said, "I'll take a ride" but the boys said, "I want to fly!" Yeah! Go up and fly! So, I put a request in to the board. (Erin, excerpt, 211-215)

Dan's eighth grade students decided to arrange, conduct, and transcribe interviews of a variety of people in their school to explore the skill of sequencing. They used the information to develop a twelve-minute video introducing their school to new students. Dan was particularly animated as he related how this activity helped his struggling learners develop a better understanding of sequencing.

And then it suddenly dawned on me. . . . Wow! There's the curriculum right there. There's writing inclusion, there's reading there's technical writing, there's reading skills. It was beyond me. (Dan, excerpt, 191-193)

Emily 's class, most of whom were from El Salvador and the Dominican Republic, explored their cultural histories and created a variety of authentic artifacts.

It looked, I guess, kind of free for anybody coming into my classrooms because they saw an array of activities being performed simultaneously by small groups of students. But . . . actually what they were doing can be identified as some of the standards that they needed to meet in both Social Studies and Careers, and Math, Science, and Technology, and also Language Arts. . . . A typical statement that I get from students who have never had me [and] come to my class is: "But Mrs. D., we haven't done any reading or any math." I turned to him and said, "We've been reading and doing math all day long." (Emily, excerpt, 312-20)

Block et al. (2002) stated that exemplary literacy teachers employ a philosophy of "disciplined eclecticism," a phrase coined by Baumann, Hoffman, Moon, and Duffy-Hester (1998, p. 647). Teachers know how to engage their students, maintain high expectations for learning, and monitor and alter approaches to meet the needs of individual learners. Clearly, Emily and Dan (as well as others as revealed in their narratives) can be described as disciplined eclecticists. They engaged their students in a multiplicity of approaches and were continually looking for ways to combine content and methods that enhanced their students' learning, supported their self-esteem and promoted students' roles as both architects and artists of their learning (Stewart, 2002).

For the seven teachers who described their approaches to learning in terms of investigations, explorations and projects, an instructional cycle beginning with community building and ending with demonstration and evaluation was common. The elements of that cycle are presented in Figure 1.

This cycle shares characteristics of the inquiry-learning model advanced by Short and Burke (1991) and Short, Schroeder, Laird, Kauffman, Ferguson, and Crawford (1996). Rather than covering content, children are encouraged

Figure 1. Cycle of Instruction

Building Community
Establishing routines
Getting to know and trust each other

Connecting to the Curriculum
Selecting a focus of study
Selecting the instructional approach

Sharing and Evaluating
Student Learning

Engaging the Students
Tapping student interest
Providing choice
Negotiating time and materials

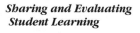

Active Learning
Through Group Work

to be problem posers and solvers. Rather than filling children's days with preplanned activities, children are encouraged to participate in the planning process much like Dan's students proposed to learn the skill of sequencing through conducting a project that would teach them and others more about their school.

There was little use of the term "skill" in the interviews. Specific skill development, when discussed, was embedded in talk about the larger approaches to instruction occurring in these classrooms (Au, 2003; Gambrell & Mazzoni, 1999; Taylor et al., 2002). Both Anna and Carol noted the use of word walls to build their students knowledge and quick recognition of words that children were learning to read and spell.

> [O]ur wall got covered with word strips, so we could have those words up there so we can see them all the time. Because a dictionary for them was, you know, they'd lose it. (Anna, excerpt, 422-424)

> [S]o they're doing self editing and the things they're editing for are capitalization, punctuation, does it make sense, how many sentences? It needs to be at least four to five sentences long, looking for word wall words for spelling. If it's on the word wall then they have to spell it that way. (Carol, excerpt 864-867)

Dan, as noted previously, talked about his students employing reading skills such as sequencing and questioning as they carried out their project. Cathy implied work related to fluency development as she described her high school reading class.

> I started a personal Reading class. . . . I'd like to see what happened if we'd just bring in the kids in and let them read for forty minutes. But also do some writing, there had to be some writing in there. And then I started documenting the research, you know, was there improvement? And almost always, almost always, except for some rare situation, there was dramatic improvement. (Cathy, excerpt, 299-302)

Finally, Rose understood the need to teach skills but was emphatic about putting them into the context of children following their own questions:

> [T]he child brings to the master [teacher] the questions that are floating in that child's mind and through an exploratory dialogue they go where the child needs to be and answer the questions in a way that the child needs answered. Now, I'm not naïve enough to think that through that you don't have real skills and curricular matters that need to be addressed . . . . you have to get involved with skills, there's no way you couldn't. You couldn't grow ideas if you didn't have skills. (Rose, excerpt, 601-06)

At least eight teachers noted other activities in reading and writing instruction. Journal writing was done for a variety of reasons. Erin's students kept journals related to their study of the weather while Olivia's students' journals were tied to a literature study on biography. In Olivia and Carol's classrooms students often engaged in buddy or partner reading to support each other:

> [W]e' d partner them up, you know, across their age, and sometimes out of the third grade book and, again, across age thing, and then they'd select their own book that was appropriate for their level. (Olivia, excerpt 779-781)

> I have a read aloud. There's some whole group reading, some shared reading, maybe we'll go off and partner read that same story. (Carol, excerpt 796-799)

Alice's young students decided that pen pal letters might be a good idea and she was enthusiastic in her support of it as an authentic way to develop their literacy:

> I remember one year when I was teaching first grade they decided they wanted to do pen pals—and they didn't think we could do that, of course, but we wrote to random post office addresses all over the country, one in every state. We heard from about twenty-two different schools. So instead of me saying, "Ok, we need to write neatly, we need to form our letters, we need to spell the words," they knew that they needed to do that because they were talking to real people in other states, and they wanted to represent themselves well. And, of course, when they're letters came in then they had all that reading in front of them, you know, and didn't even think about it. (Alice, excerpt, 484-92)

An additional theme related to effective literacy instruction ran through the majority of interviews, regardless of the instructional approach or activity employed. These teachers were not tied to particular texts to carry out their curriculum. In contrast they actively sought out a variety of materials including their local neighborhood. This can be seen in Anna's use of the native legend's book to teach reading or Erin's students' airplane ride as part of their weather investigation. The goal of improved literacy was the focus and teachers used whatever texts and materials helped them reach that goal.

Conclusion

This study set out to examine the interviews of learner-centered teachers in light of the literature related to the practices of effective teachers of literacy. In returning to the central question, to what extent are the literacy related instructional practices described by these learner-centered teachers congruent with the literature on effective (best) teaching of literacy, this study provides evidence that there is indeed a strong congruence as detailed in the findings section and outlined in the comparison in Table 4.

Table 4. Comparison Chart of Literacy Practices

CHARACTERISTICS OF EFFECTIVE LITERACY PRACTICES IN THE LITERATURE	COMPARATIVE LITERACY PRACTICES OF LEARNER-CENTERED TEACHERS
Literature-based instruction with eclectic use of materials (children's literature, basal anthologies, non-fiction) (Allington & Johnson, 2001; Block, Oaker & Hurt, 2002)	Genre Studies; Theme Studies; Literature Circles; Browsing Baskets (a collection of books at a variety of genre and interest levels)
Balanced instruction with skills instruction embedded in context of literature and language study that allows for extended engagement with ideas & issues (Applebee, 2003; Au, 2003; Block, Oaker & Hurt, 2002; Gambrell & Mazzoni, 1999; Stewart, 2002)	Process Writing; Reading/Writing Workshops; Genre Studies; Language Experience Approach
Student engagement in personally relevant process of intellectual discovery (Ruddell, 1995)	Cultural Investigations (Native legends & Cultural histories of children from the Dominican Republic and El Salvador); Local Community Investigations
Student engagement in authentic, meaningful, collaborative experiences (Applebee, 2003; Au, 2003; Gambrell & Mazzoni, 1999; Stewart, 2002)Partner/ buddy Reading; Postcard Project; Video Project; State to State Pen-Pals Literate Rich Environment (Wharton-McDonald &Hampton, 1998)	Word Walls; Genre Studies; Browsing Baskets

One important limitation of the study reported here deals with the nature of the questions asked of the participants in the first phase of the larger study. Because they were not expressly asked to describe their literacy related practices, as was Carol, a participant in the second round of interviews, an in-depth description of those practices and their relationship to "best practice" could not be reported here. As the second phase of the study progresses, more detailed information will become available. A second limitation may be related to the drawing of conclusions about teacher practices based upon interviews only with no confirming observational data. The purpose of this study was to understand the teachers' perspectives related to their practice. The full, complex, and multifaceted stories told by these teachers, comprising more than 500 pages of transcribed text over sixteen interviews, does accomplish this purpose.

The literacy related practices described by teachers who have adopted a learner-centered philosophy are strongly matched with those practices that research suggests are best practice for children's literacy development. The stories of these teachers support those who seek to engage in constructivist, balanced approaches that provide students with both the "skill and the will" to become proficient literacy learners (Gambrell & Mazzoni, 1999, p. 13). This support is of no small importance in a time when many are asked, none too gently, to return to a scope and sequenced, prescribed and scripted, literacy curriculum. The reflection on practice of the teachers interviewed for this study call for a very different curriculum, one that is varied and complex and adheres to a belief in the centrality of the learner:

> I think it's the children first. . . . The curriculum guides us, but I have to start with the children where they are, where their strengths are and then I can take them and lead them. (Carol, excerpt 63-66)

References

Allington, R., & Cunningham, P. (1996). *Schools that work: Where all children read and write*. New York: Harper Collins.

Allington R., & Johnston, P. (2001). What do we know about effective fourth grade teachers and their classrooms? In C. Roller (Ed.), *Learning to teach reading: Setting the research agenda* (pp. 150-165). Newark, DE: International Reading Association.

Applebee, A. (2003). Balancing the curriculum in the English language arts: Exploring the components of effective teaching and learning. In J. Flood, D. Lapp, J. Squire, & J. Jensen (Eds.), *Handbook of research on teaching the English language arts* (pp. 676-684). Hillsdale, NJ: Erlbaum.

Au, K. (2003). Balanced literacy instruction: Implications for students of diverse backgrounds. In J. Flood, D. Lapp, J. Squire, & J. Jensen (Eds.), *Handbook of research on teaching the English language arts* (pp. 955-964). Hillsdale, NJ: Erlbaum.

Baumann, J. F., Hoffman, J. V., Moon, J., & Duffy-Hester, A. (1998). Where are teachers' voices in the phonics/whole language debate: Results from a survey of U.S. elementary teachers. *The Reading Teacher, 50*, 636-651.

Block, C., Oaker, M., & Hurt, N. (2002). The expertise of literacy teachers: A continuum from preschool to grade 5. *Reading Research Quarterly, 37*(2), 178-197.

Cantrell, S. (1999). The effects of literacy instruction on primary students' reading and writing achievement. *Reading Research Instruction, 39*(1), 3-26.

Cramer, R. (2001). *Creative power: The nature and nurture of children's writing*. New York: Longman.

Cunningham, P., & Allington, R. (1999). *Classrooms that work: They can all read and write* (2nd ed.). New York: Longman.

Fosnot, C. T. (1996). Constructivism: A psychological theory of learning. In C.T. Fosnot (Ed.), *Constructivism: Theory, perspectives, and practice* (pp. 8-33). New York: Teachers College Press.

Fountas, I. C., & Pinnell, G. S. (2001). *Guided reading: Good first teaching for all children*. Portsmouth, NH: Heinemann.

Gambrell, L., & Mazzoni, S. A. (1999). Principles of best practice: Finding common ground. In L. Gambrell, L. Morrow, S. Neuman, & M. Pressley (Eds.), *Best practices in literacy instruction*. New York: The Guilford Press.

Gould, J. S. (1996). A constructivist perspective on teaching and learning in the language arts. In C.T. Fosnot (Ed.), *Constructivism: Theory, perspectives, and practice* (pp. 92-102). New York: Teachers College Press.

Kutz, E., & Roskelly, H. (1991). *An unquiet pedagogy: Transforming practice in the English classroom*. Portsmouth, NH: Heinemann.

Marlowe, B., & Page, M. (1998). *Creating and sustaining the constructivist classroom*. Thousand Oaks, CA: Corwin Press.

Paris, C., & Combs, B. (2000, April). *Teachers' perspectives on what it means to be learner-centered*. Paper presented at the meeting of the American Educational Research Association, New Orleans, LA.

Paris, C., & Combs, B. (2001, August). *What teachers mean when they say they are learner centered*. Paper presented at a meeting of the Association of Teacher Educators, Portland, OR.

Ruddell, R. (1995). Those influential literacy teachers: Meaning negotiators and motivation builders. *The Reading Teacher, 48*(6), 454-464.

Short, K., & Burke, C. (1991). *Creating curriculum: Teachers and students as a community of learners*. Portsmouth, NH: Heinemann.

Short, K., Schroeder, J., Laird, J., Kauffman, G., Ferguson, M., & Crawford, K. M. (1996). *Learning together through inquiry: From Columbus to integrated curriculum*. York, ME: Stenhouse.

Starnes, B. (1999). *The Foxfire approach to teaching and learning: John Dewey, experiential learning, and the core practices*. Charleston, VA: Appalachian Educational Laboratory. (ERIC Document Reproduction Service No. EDO-RC-98-6)

Starnes, B. & Paris, C. (2000). Choosing to learn. *Phi Delta Kappan, 81*, (5), 392-397.

Stewart, M. T. (2002). *Best practice? Insights on literacy instruction from an elementary classroom*. Newark, DE: International Reading Association.

Taylor, B., Pearson, D. P., Clark, K., & Walpole, S. (2002). Effective schools accomplished teachers. In C. Nichols (Ed.), *Evidence-based reading instruction: Putting the National Reading Panel Report into practice* (pp. 185-188). Newark, DE: International Reading Association.

Wharton-McDonald, R., & Hampton, J. M. (1998). Expert primary teaching of literacy is balanced teaching. In M. Pressley (Ed.), *Reading instruction that works: The case for balanced teaching* (pp. 151-191). New York: The Guilford Press.

Author Study Inquiry Promotes "Theory into Practice" for Teaching Literacies

Linda S. Wold

Purdue University Calumet

Abstract

This analysis of the Author Study Inquiry (ASI) describes what fifth graders learned about applying reading comprehension strategies during their study of favorite authors. The researcher used ethnographic methods to document comprehension strategy use embedded in ASI as students surveyed materials, read biographical texts, investigated Internet sources, and used PowerPoint to present studies. ASI was guided by deliberate integration of spoken, written and visual literacies (Standards for the English Language Arts, 1996) and by longstanding research that form follows function. Technology, as one form, supported literacy learning as students inquired about authors on the Internet. The function of ASI was to promote students' comprehension application as they internalized strategies to determine importance, used multiple literacies to develop ideas, and synthesized data. Students in this technology-limited classroom created a culture of more reading and enthusiasm for ASI; improved research and technology skills; applied comprehension strategies; and exhibited increased motivation to read.

Author Study Inquiry (ASI) is a curriculum strategy in which fifth graders investigate favorite authors through the study of trade books, Internet sources and use of multiple literacies to improve their use of comprehension strategies. This analysis of the students' inquiry process documents how ASI promotes enhanced comprehension and technology use. According to Begoray (2003), there is an urgent challenge for educators to provide multiple literacies for students to access routes to become more literate. In this study, the researcher incorporated multiple literacies, as embedded spoken, written, and visual literacies of the *Standards for the English Language Arts* (1996), to help children integrate languages in addition to reading and writing. The notion of multiple literacies included spoken language (to speak and listen), written language (to read and write), and visual language (to view and visually represent). The integration of these literacies promoted opportunities for student learning because reading, writing, thinking, researching, drafting, visually representing, and sharing ideas were set firmly in the inquiry process.

This study focused on ways in which the teachers used the form of technology to address the function of ASI (Hymes, 1972), which was to advance students' comprehension development. ASI embedded the inquiry processes of comprehension strategy use, research, and technology strategies to create author presentations (Wold, 2002).

Research Foundations

The purpose of this analysis of the ASI was to determine how an in-service teacher and her fifth graders learned to become more literate through the integration of spoken, written, and visual literacies, and the use of technology. Comprehension strategies were embedded in the tasks leading to the creation of student presentations. ASI centered on the study of biography in informational texts and on critical comprehension strategy use that helped students generate questions, determine importance, make connections, infer meanings, draw conclusions, evaluate information, and synthesize ideas (Keene & Zimmerman, 1997) in inquiry and technology formats.

Key research theories that ground the ASI method include research of best literacy practice, collaboration in learning, technology to enhance literacy instruction and engagement, and informational text in intermediate grades. The foundation between theory and practice is highlighted in the following studies.

Research of Best Literacy Practice

Literacy research indicates that multiple theories support best practice. The ASI is built on four theoretical strands of research in best literacy practice. First, best literacy practice (*Standards for the English Language Arts*, 1996; Gambrell, Morrow, Neuman, & Pressley, 1999; Keene & Zimmerman, 1997; Zelmelman, Daniels, & Hyde, 1998; Fielding & Pearson, 1994), includes the integration of spoken, written, and visual communications (Standards for the English Language Arts, 1996; Leu, 2000; Vygotsky, 1978) in the inquiry process. Second, the importance of direct comprehension instruction (Gambrell, Morrow, Neuman & Pressley, 1999) supports student development in making meaning from text readings. Third, determining importance and synthesizing ideas are best taught to students and applied during the inquiry process, based on critical comprehension research (Keene & Zimmerman, 1997). Fourth, choice in reading materials supports "best practice" (Worthy, 2000;

Zelmelman, Daniels, & Hyde, 1998), because of its positive impact on reading comprehension (Fielding & Pearson, 1994).

Collaboration in Learning

Collaboration plays a critical role in supporting students as they discuss how to use new technologies and apply important comprehension strategies. Vygotsky's (1978) theory of the social nature of learning emphasizes that students learn to grasp ideas from more expert others as they talk through ideas. Learning talk naturally evolves as students discover peer experts who can quickly help them edit their texts and solve technology problems.

Technology to Enhance Literacy Instruction and Engagement

The goal of the ASI was to advance students' comprehension while using technology as one form to support learning. Hymes (1972) has argued that form follows function, and his research has grounded the inquiry process. A review of literacy and technology research explains how the use of newer technologies often creates high levels of engagement and interest (Leu, 2000). Though technology was not selected primarily for this reason in this study, its use resulted in high levels of engagement. Internet technology provided student access to additional biographical details about authors that were not available in the school library. Students read about favorite authors both from Internet website publications and classroom text collections. Technology supplemented the classroom teacher's text sets of author biographies and published works. Mrs. Hart also collected extra materials about the selected authors and the books they had written to foster a culture of reading.

Informational Text in Intermediate Grades

Informational text reading is considered a part of intermediate grade curricula as students read to learn. Children's literature researchers have urged teachers to include integrated content literacy practices involving informational texts to expand text reading, even in the primary grades (Albright, deLara, & Davis, 2003; Duthie, 1996; Richgels, 2002), because learning about informational texts can also improve students' comprehension (Armbruster, Anderson, & Ostertag, 1989). To better understand informational text genre, Duthie (1996) has shown that biography and autobiography offer opportunities for students to discover the world as they read books about society, its varied social conditions, the complexities of life, and the significance of people in history.

In the ASI, choice was also key for supporting the development of positive student attitudes about reading (Worthy, 2000; Zelmelman et al., 1998), which in turn, supported exploration of their interests. Potential for student engagement was maximized by the opportunity for students to choose authors of interest.

Finally, researchers still need to investigate how the integration of multiple literacies in reading biographical texts benefits student comprehension development beyond the primary grades.

To focus the research study, these questions guided the analysis of the ASI:

1) Is there an impact on fifth graders' integration of literacies and their improved use of comprehension strategies due to their learning about and using technology and biographical texts to research selected authors?

2) If there is an impact from the ASI, what does the documentary evidence reveal about students reading informational texts that supported fifth graders in their discovery of new learning?

Methods

Participants and Setting

The research sample included one Caucasian teacher in her sixth year of teaching and 24 fifth graders, consisting of 56% Caucasian, 25% Hispanic, and 4% African-American. One student, who did not return her parental consent form, was not included in the study and moved during the second semester. Approximately 17 % of the students received free or reduced lunch.

Mrs. Hart (pseudonym) was certified in both elementary and special education and had spent three years as a case manager working with special needs high school students. Due to her diverse teaching experiences, she taught many of the special needs fifth graders. Of Mrs. Hart's five special needs students who had individual education plans, two attended only social studies classes in her room each day and were not included in the class enrollment or data collection.

Though quantitative data is not generally a part of ethnography, initial baseline data was collected to document student reading capacity: 44 % of the students were reading at fifth grade level or above, and 56 % were reading below grade level. Beginning of the year guided reading levels for the class indicated: eight at the second grade level; four at the third grade level; two at the fourth grade level; six at fifth grade level; and five students read beyond the fifth grade level. Student reading scores were administered at the beginning and end of the year based on running record scores and the results of the Gates-MacGinitie Reading Tests (2000) to determine reading achievement gains.

School Description

Larken School, a pseudonym for a Midwestern inner city K-5 elementary school near a large metropolitan area, had more than 35% student mobility. Almost half of the K-5 students were eligible for free or reduced meals. Student enrollment was 60% Caucasian, 25% Hispanic, 10% African-American, and 5% other. The school's faculty was 90% Caucasian, and 10% African-American and Hispanic. The faculty was involved in yearly Four Block training (Cunningham, Hall & Sigmon, 1999) that ensured professional development and literacy support for K-5 teachers.

This fifth grade class had limited technology experiences. These were also students at a school which offered minimal technology opportunities. At the beginning of the ASI, students gained access for the first time to 11 computers that were networked in the media center. In prior years, computers were not available for group work. The media center schedule for available classroom use included only one 45-minute weekly session. Students were not allowed to free-flow to the Media Center to use computers or check out books unless their teacher requested special permission to do so.

Author Study Inquiry Procedures

To begin the inquiry process, students learned to ask discovery questions about their authors. The scholastic website (http://teacher.scholastic.com/writewit/biograph) was frequently used as a resource for the class. This Internet site guided the development of inquiry questions about favorite authors. After brainstorming ideas, students selected questions that seemed to capture important aspects of their authors' lives. The final set of questions included the compiled list that was attached to the inside of students' ASI folders (see Table 1).

Table 1. Author Study Inquiry Questions

1. When was your author born?
2. What kind of background information about your author can you add?
3. When did your author start writing?
4. How long has your author been writing books?
5. What kinds of books has your author written?
6. How many books has your author written?
7. What contributions has your author made to our world?

Students also learned to skim and scan texts to investigate various resources such as the Internet and grade-appropriate texts. Then students conducted interviews of second graders to select authors for presentation. The follow-up to the interviews included fifth graders reading as many of the authors' books and reviews as were available (Darigan, Tunnell, & Jacobs, 2002).

Finally students searched the Internet to consider quality authors and texts. After choosing their favorite authors, students determined importance of materials collected, synthesized information based on planning and design of their presentations, and prepared oral PowerPoint presentations to share with peers and other audiences. The initial list of authors, created from the interviews of second graders, was revised after the first Internet search due to lack of source materials (see Table 2). Students also decided to add Jim Aylesworth, a visiting author to their school, to share their presentations with him at the end of the semester.

Table 2. Author Study Selections

Jim Aylesworth (author visit to school)

Eve Bunting (changed from Lois Ehlert)

Marc Brown

Tomie dePaola

Laura Numeroff

Dav Pilkey

Patricia Polacco

Jack Prelutsky (changed from Dr. Seuss)

Faith Ringgold (changed from Barbara Park)

Jon Scieszka

Ed Young

The Data Collection

During the five-month themed unit on ASI in the fall and spring terms, data collection occurred weekly. Data sources included field notes of instruction in the school media center, 45-minute video recordings each month, student artifacts and survey questions, self-reports of teacher and student learning, descriptive field notes, informal interviews, and copies of all related reading materials such as guided reading levels and class assessments. The researcher and an undergraduate student involved in the study wrote descriptive documentation to capture students' responses and the classroom teacher's instruction. The researcher also wrote additional field notes about highlighted learning events in the data collection for locating clustered patterns and themes during the analysis.

Four informal interviews occurred during the five-month inquiry. Students first responded to the "Know and Want to know" sections of the KWL strategy (Ogle, 1986) to write about what they knew about authors and technology and what they wanted to learn during the study. For the mid-year and year-end surveys, students were asked to report what they learned (L) from "KWL" in the ASI and to note if they read more books about their authors by using evidence from their reading logs. They were also asked to explain what they had learned about authors and how they felt about the

ASI in general. In April, a PowerPoint Technology survey was administered to each student to verify technology competency (Microsoft Office Specialist Objectives: Power Point 2002, n.d.).

Data Analysis

The purpose of the data analysis was to determine if patterns existed. Data analysis followed Miles and Huberman's (1994) interactive analysis model, a three-part analytical model for qualitative research. The data sources were analyzed for pattern regularity, and then consistent themes were coded, checked against outliers, and reduced to graphic organizers for determining patterns in multiple contexts and events. These themes became the major categories used to verify findings and draw conclusions.

Triangulation (Mathison, 1988) of data provided verification of findings. Specifically, triangulation occurred in multiple member checks with the classroom teacher, the researcher, the undergraduate researcher, and student self-reports; by multiple methods of data collection, including field notes, video taping, and summary documentation; and in multiple reading contexts involving comprehension instruction, creation of ASI projects, and use of critical reading comprehension strategies in other content areas. Findings were repeatedly verified in multiple contexts and data sources to confirm results (Miles & Huberman, 1994).

Findings

The ASI created novel opportunities for Mrs. Hart and the fifth grade students to learn new technology and specific comprehension strategies while engaged in personal discoveries. The analyses show that participation in the ASI impacted fifth graders' integration of literacies and resulted in several interesting and positive findings. Students demonstrated (a) a classroom culture of more reading; (b) enthusiasm for ASI; (c) improved research and technology strategies; (d) effective comprehension application; and (e) increased motivation to read. These findings are discussed in detail in the following sections.

A Classroom Culture of More Reading

At the close of the fall term, students responded to survey questions about reading volume. Twenty-one students participated in this self-reported survey on the effect of the ASI on their reading when asked (a) to report if they read more books, less books, or the same number of books they've always read since ASI began and to explain their responses; and (b) to provide evidence for their answers. They were also asked to describe their feelings about reading the ASI texts. Sixty-two percent of the students reported that they read more texts, 33% read the same amount of text, and 5% read less than they've always read. John explained that he read more because "Reading is a lot more powerful then it was to me," while Joseph mentioned, "I started to like reading more because I do not like reading the same books." Several students felt they read the same amount of books and based their responses on the fact that they read the same number of minutes during reading time. Rachel, one of the gifted students and the only one who claimed that she read less said, "I have been lazy about reading but I am trying to change." In the next term of the ASI data collection, an attempt will be made to quantify students' volume of reading in school and out of school.

Overall, students read author biographies, autobiographies, and trade books written by favorite authors, and informational resources on the Internet, from author study packets, and other reference materials that were added to the students' author book collection bins. Generally fifth graders read from 30 to 40 additional pages of print about their authors, and scanned much more text. Based on Mrs. Hart's observations and considering the added Internet readings, it could be inferred that all students read more Internet and trade book texts.

Though specific out-of-school student reading was logged each quarter, the classroom teacher could not easily determine if books read at home were specifically related to the author study project. Mrs. Hart commented that students read more and that comment evolved from her documentary notes in which she recorded student behaviors as they read author study books and related Internet materials during school time but not during the Author Study Project time.

In summary, the majority of fifth graders reported positive attitudes about enjoying reading more, feeling "accomplishment" in reading, and "liking how certain authors write." Although Rashida positively responded to reading the books, "I felt happy and smart. I feel this way because she write [sic] amazing story nothing is boring and she make [sic] no one feel dumb," Leigh was the one student who honestly remarked, "The books were good but it is not what I am interested in." During the second semester when students selected their own fifth grade authors, all students reported positive attitudes about their participation in the study.

Enthusiasm for Author Study Inquiry

The ASI created a culture for learning and presenting information that had not occurred in the early part of the semester. Initially fifth graders were excited about the study, but as they learned more about favorite authors and made connections to texts and books read in other classes, their enthusiasm became contagious. Students' conversations about learning enhanced further study about authors. The classroom teacher created a culture that honored students' talk and consistently encouraged them to become experts in all facets of the study. Some students became PowerPoint experts, supporting peers as they added slides to their presentations, while others taught categorization skills to those in need. All students became experts about their favorite authors. This enthusiasm emerged across the first term and lasted throughout the second term of the study.

Improved Technology and Research Strategies

At the beginning of the study, informal surveys, asking students to list what they already knew and what they wanted to learn about authors and technology, revealed that students had limited knowledge about authors and no knowledge of PowerPoint. The following the results are organized by frequency of responses related to both what students knew about authors and technology.

At first, students reported that they knew what an author was, a bit about their writings, and a few named book titles by specific authors. Six students were interested in authors' personal lives and questioned how long it took to write a book and publish a good story. When asked about technology, no one in the class knew how to use PowerPoint, though 15 students had minimal keyboarding skills and 20 students specifically wanted to learn to type faster. Thirteen students had used the Internet a couple of times and 12 had done a simple Internet search. Six students understood what was involved in e-mail and had played a computer game. Students also reported they wanted to learn more about: the Internet and research (n=10), E-mail (n=4), and how to improve their keyboarding skills (n=3).

By the beginning of the second term, students began their Author Study Inquiries with minimal teacher support. After two Internet sessions during the fall data collection, students were able to access various author sites with ease. In the spring term, they knew the appropriate Internet web sites and could easily search for information independently. Fifth graders self-assigned new authors even before the second inquiry began. Mrs. Hart claimed that she had difficulty waiting to start up the second term of the project because "the students were so anxious to begin." For example, during the December break, many of the students created research drafts for their Author Study PowerPoint slides and were begging to begin the next inquiry. To resolve this dilemma, Mrs. Hart asked the students to collect books written by these new authors and review all Internet findings to confirm their selections. In January, students read many Internet sources and a variety of texts to insure that their author selections were interesting and appropriate.

Overall, students read from both Internet sources and author study text sets, though it is not clear if they read more from specific sources because it was difficult to compare Internet and published texts. The font size of the Internet information was generally small and included 20- to 40 pages of biographical information on single authors whereas author text fonts in trade books varied greatly. When students selected authors who wrote lengthy novels, it was assumed that they read more from the author's books than from Internet sources. For example, the "Harry Potter" team read all of his books over vacation. Clearly they read more literary than Internet text.

The fall interview data indicated that none of the students or classroom teacher had ever used PowerPoint. In early April, a Microsoft PowerPoint 2002 (Microsoft Office Specialist Objectives: Power Point 2002, n.d.) competency list, which assessed only what students learned about PowerPoint during the ASI, was used to gauge students' technology progress. The results showed that all students demonstrated gains in creating slide shows and using multiple features to modify visual elements in their PowerPoint presentations. Because Mrs. Hart was providing student support during and after instruction, she felt less competent than her students in knowing and being able to use technology well, but still reported less intimidation in working with students on future PowerPoint investigations.

Effective Comprehension Application

Pre and post data collected on reading achievement included running records and the Gates-MacGinitie Reading Tests (2000) informal reading results. Though these assessments indicated improvement for most students, specific use of two comprehension strategies were coded in the documentary evidence as major themes in the student artifacts, field notes, videos, and informal interviews. These themes included students' demonstration of making connections and determining importance as they searched for information, collected written artifacts of each author, and created their ASI presentations.

In the first pattern, all research participants noted students consistently making connections about authors and their own personal lives. Initially, students did not make connections because they had limited knowledge about authors and their backgrounds. As the study progressed, students were observed discussing key details that they had discovered about their authors while engaged in spoken, written, and visual communications. For example, one researcher noted Sharina saying, "My author's poems sort of sound like Dr. Seuss's writing." Jarrod explained, "That author has the same birthday as me!" And, Carlos remarked, "Wow! He loves dogs. So do I." These connections were personal and became consistent and more strategic as students began to connect meanings about their authors' lives with their own.

As the second regular pattern noted in the data collection, initially students did not understand how to determine importance or prioritize their data to prepare their presentations. At first every student highlighted and selected numerous author details for their presentations, sometimes underlining an entire paragraph with translucent marker. At the conclusion of the data collection, 90 % of the class learned to determine importance in selecting key information and highlighting critical ideas from texts. Students' heightened awareness of how to determine importance in selecting critical ideas was documented in a follow-up social studies lesson at the end of the term. Mrs. Hart stated that every student was able to pinpoint critical information in the text and determine details to synthesize big ideas. This documentation suggests that students were beginning to demonstrate metacognitive knowledge (Baker & Brown, 1984) of comprehension strategies, the understanding of when and how to determine importance and the self-regulation to apply the strategy appropriately in different contexts.

During the study, Mrs. Hart learned along with her students and became more knowledgeable about teaching comprehension effectively. Often she would explain to her students that she had posed a bad question that didn't really support their learning. Then, she would remark, "I think I need to say that in a different way so that you understand what I mean."

Such thoughtful responses created a positive, risk-free environment for learning. From field notes taken during the implementation of ASI, Mrs. Hart described the excitement in the classroom when students continually asked to work on the project, even during self-selected reading time. Based on 24 students at the end of the fall term, 70% of her students were now reading on grade level or above (compared to 44% at the beginning of the term). In November, Mrs. Hart reviewed her students' reading progress and was certain that even her less successful students were making more sense of texts and had moved forward in their guided reading levels.

At year's end, assessment results indicated general comprehension improvement. Of the 21 students completing both pre and post Gates-MacGinitie Reading Tests (2000), 71% demonstrated increased reading achievement: three students showed average gains; three showed eight-month gains; eight showed 1.2 year gains; and one showed a 2.4 year gain. Twenty-nine percent of the students (six students) showed little or no gain (.2 month gain, static results, or slight regression). These were students who received special services or were determined to need special testing and support. Though quantitative gains in reading achievement were not evident for all students, other important changes were noted in the findings regarding reading attitude.

Based on the pre and post running record data, it was not possible to determine exact gains in comprehension achievement from students' leveled book readings and related retellings. The fifth grade basal reading series determined guided reading level growth in clustered assessment data. Consequently, students who began reading at level WXYZ and revealed the same results on the final assessments, WXYZ, did not reveal actual reading progress even when the classroom teacher noted growth in reading achievement. In future assessments, running records will be administered using benchmark texts to show individual reading progress.

Increased Motivation to Read

Throughout the fall semester, motivation was extremely high for all but four students who claimed that they didn't like their authors. The two dissatisfied partners complained that they could not find sufficient material on the Internet. In supporting their inquiries and providing additional resources, the researcher found their dilemma to be true. Students seemed to enjoy bragging about their Internet sources and trade book collections. The author Ed Young, as well as a few other authors, had limited Internet resources or literature texts available for students to read.

During the spring term, students began preplanning "next" authors to ensure that they would select a favorite. Students selected desired authors and all were motivated to research their chosen favorites. The difference in motivation between the first and second terms was clear. The first authors were selected for fifth graders' buddy readers who were in second grade. Though the fifth graders enjoyed discovering information about the second graders' favorite authors, they were not as interested in their authors or the picture book content of many of the primary texts. In the second term, student choice impacted the ASI because fifth graders were able to key into their own interests by selecting author favorites known to fifth graders, while they continued to improve their reading attitudes and achievement (Worthy, 2000).

Across the data collection, the documentary evidence reveals that there was an impact from the ASI. Fifth graders showed their success and enjoyment of reading informational text genre, particularly when the informational texts were self-selected. As the students engaged in multiple literacies to access author information and determine what would be most important to their audiences, they learned to make personal connections to their own lives and to determine the distinction between an interesting and important fact for engaging the audience.

A final informal survey asked students what they had learned about authors and technology. Their responses captured similar reports that were shared previously, but most important was their "All About Me" section that they added to their slides. The "All About Me" section shared their accomplishments during the ASI and confirmed that they had truly transformed into authors themselves. Here is Kerry's version of "All About Me," written by a student who had not been to school before grade five:

About the Author

Kerry has seven people in her family. She has a mom and a dad, two sisters, two brothers, and one nephew. She has two dogs and one cat. The cat's name is Haden, and the dogs' names are Boomer and Thunder.

Kerry learned about Author Study in fifth grade. First she checked websites to find information about Tomie dePaola. At this website, she read his biography. Then she read more information about Tomie's life and his books. Second, she used the website info to make this PowerPoint presentation.

Right now I am working on another book about Andrew Clements. I know how to do the research and how to write the book. I'm an author now!

Discussion

As Mrs. Hart learned with her students and became smarter about teaching comprehension strategies and using technology, she focused on how students might use these critical strategies in other content areas. She reported, "All of my students were able to determine importance of ideas and highlight key points in their social studies texts without my prompting." She was not asked to translate for students how to use comprehension strategies in other subjects but did that based on her understanding of strategy transfer. It made sense to her. Other teachers might not teach for learning transfer without explicit instruction to do so.

By the end of the first semester, all students were adept at using PowerPoint and the Internet to search for, create, and save information for future use and for presentation. The ASI PowerPoints were presented to their peers and second grade buddy readers as the culmination of the study. Students practiced their presentations from hard copy slides and then used the LCD projector to present to parent and student audiences. One group of students was able to share their Jim Aylesworth presentation with him when he came for an on-site author visit. The students were astonished when Aylesworth acknowledged that he didn't know how to use PowerPoint. Ryan, one of our fifth grade tech experts, quickly walked him through the steps explaining, "It's really easy."

Limitations

Limitations of this research study included the use of self-reported data, technology accessibility, time constraints, and access to quality nonfiction author study texts. Most of the limitations presented obstacles that were overcome by the flexibility and resourcefulness of the classroom teacher and students.

First, self-reported data may be less valid, particularly from young students. However, this problem was largely overcome by the triangulation of data from other sources.

Second, though technology accessibility was much improved from the previous year, the school was not wired for Internet use in classrooms and provided limited overall technology access. Consequently, the students were eager to learn about new technologies when the network computers became available in the fall of 2003. This focal classroom may be less representative of K-5 elementary schools in the 21st century. If this ASI were conducted in a school with a history of Internet and technology application, the findings might be less robust because Internet access might be commonplace. However, it is also possible that students who are initially more adept at technology use might use their own initiative to be even more productive when exposed to this approach.

As the study advanced into the second semester, technology accessibility became more limited due to the breakdown of many of the student computers. For several class sessions, only eight computers were usable for research investigations. This resulted in some students not being able to complete their online research or to practice their final presentations on the LCD projector since that was in repair for several months. This problem created significant issues, especially when several classes were cancelled because of field trips or school competitions.

Third, time constraints were common. The short 45-minute weekly sessions available for computer work were too brief. Consequently, the classroom teacher allowed students to work on preparing their PowerPoint slides during free time and when other class assignments were completed. The undergraduate researcher also provided bi-monthly classroom support for students to work on their ASIs. Then students used index cards to organize their data and plan for the slide sequences. Because of these time constraints and schedule changes, it was not possible for all students to complete their inquiry projects during the second term.

Finally, access to quality nonfiction author study texts and trade books was limited in the intermediate grades of this elementary school. Though the classroom teacher and the researchers spent time at local libraries finding additional resources, this mid-sized school did not have a wide range of developmentally appropriate nonfiction texts for intermediate students to read. A particular problem involved providing interesting and appropriate materials for the wide range of student reading levels. The International Reading Association (2004) position statement on classroom libraries states that students without sufficient access to books will not develop the habit of reading. It is clear that this critical issue of access to books should not be overlooked.

Summary

The ASI created opportunities for a wide range of fifth grade readers to read, write, think, create visual details, draft, and revise texts for presentation to others. The strength of the inquiry process was that students used multiple literacies in a theoretically-driven manner to represent research-based best practices. Students learned to use interconnected language systems, including technology, to create their author studies. They learned to use comprehension strategies and organize information collected from a variety of print and nonprint sources while they were integrating critical spoken, written, and visual communications.

As one possible framework for supporting the integration of multiple literacies and multiple access routes for intermediate learners to become engaged in authentic literacy tacks, the ASI offers options to readers. All of the findings suggest that improved literacy teaching and student learning require choice, strategic modeling, and a focus on critical comprehension strategies that support the development of reading competency. On behalf of some of Mrs. Hart's students who claimed they'd always hated to read, why not consider ASI as an option?

References

Albright, L. K., deLara, A. B., & Davis, K. (2003). Powerful possibilities for primary grades: Combining informational text with content literacy practice. *The New Advocate, 16*(1), 29-41.

Armbruster, B. B., Anderson, T. H., & Ostertag, J. (1989). Teaching text structure to improve reading and writing. *The Reading Teacher, 43*, 130-137.

Baker, L., & Brown, A. L. (1984). Metacognitive skills and reading. In P. D. Pearson, R. Barr, M. L. Kamil, & P. Mosenthal (Eds.), *Handbook of reading research* (pp. 353-394). New York: Longman.

Begoray, D. L. (2003). Sign, sign, everywhere a sign: Multiplying literacies in the preservice language arts curriculum. In C. M. Fairbanks, J. Worthy, B. Maloch, J. V. Hoffman, & D. L. Schallert (Eds.), *52nd yearbook of the National Reading Conference* (pp. 128-138). Oak Creek, WI: National Reading Conference.

Cunningham, P. M., Hall, D. P., & Sigmond, C. M. (1999). *The teachers' guide to the Four-Blocks: A multi-method, multi-level framework for grades 1-3*. Greensboro, NC: Carson-Dellosa.

Darigan, D. L., Tunnell, M.O., & Jacobs, J. S. (2002). *Children's literature: Engaging teachers and children in good books*. Upper Saddle River, NJ: Pearson Education.

Duthie, C. (1996). *True stories: Nonfiction literacy in the primary classroom*. York, ME: Stenhouse.

Fielding, L., & Pearson, D. (1994). Reading comprehension: What works. *Educational Leadership, 51*, 63-68.

Gambrell, L. G., Morrow, L. M., Neuman, S. B., & Pressley, M. (1999). *Best practices in literacy instruction*. New York: The Guilford Press.

Gates-MacGinitie Reading Tests. (2000). Level 5. Itasca, IL: Riverside Publishing.

Hymes, D. (1972). Introduction. In C. B. Cazden, V. P. Jones, & D. Hymes (Eds.), *Foundations in sociolinguistics: An ethnographic approach* (pp. xi-lvii). Philadelphia: University of Pennsylvania Press.

Keene, E., & Zimmerman, S. (1997). *Mosiac of thought: Teaching comprehension in a readers' workshop.* Portsmouth, NH: Heinemann.

International Reading Association (2004). Providing books and other print materials for classroom and school libraries. Retrieved on June 11, 2004 from http://www.reading.org/positions/media_center.html

Leu, D. J. (2000). Literacy and technology: Deictic consequences for literacy education in an information age. In M. L. Kamil, P. B. Mosenthal, P. D. Pearson, & R. Barr (Eds.), *Handbook of Reading Research*: Vol. III (pp. 743-770). Mahwah, NJ: Lawrence Erlbaum.

Mathison, S. (1988). Why triangulate? *Educational Researcher, 17*(2), 13-17.

Microsoft Office Specialist Objectives: PowerPoint 2002. Retrieved on September 11, 2004 from www.microsoft.com/learning/mcp/officespecialist/objectives/powerpoint2002.asp.

Miles, M. B., & Huberman, A. M. (1994). *Qualitative data analysis.* Thousand Oaks, CA: Sage.

Ogle, D. (1986). K-W-L: A teaching model that develops active reading of expository text. *The Reading Teacher, 39*, 564-570.

Richgels, D. J. (2002). Informational texts in kindergarten. *The Reading Teacher, 55*(6), 586-595.

Standards for the English Language Arts (1996). Newark, DE: The International Reading Association; Urbana, IL: The National Council of Teachers of English.

Vygotsky, L. S. (1978). *Mind in society: The development of higher psychological processes.* (M. Cole, Ed. and Trans.). Cambridge, MA: Harvard University Press. (Original work published in 1930)

Wold, L. S. (2002). Language arts instruction. In B. Guzzetti (Ed.), Literacy in American: An encyclopedia (pp. 277-281). Santa Barbara, CA: ABC-CLIO.

Worthy, J. (2000). Conducting research on topics of student interest. *The Reading Teacher, 54*(3), 298-299.

Zelmelman, S., Daniels, H., & Hyde, A. (1998). *Best practice: New standards for teaching and learning in America's schools.* Portsmouth, NH: Heinemann.

Author's Note

Linda Wold is grateful to Dr. Francine Johnston for broadening her vision about the study of authors and children's literature. She also thanks Dr. Edward Vockell for his useful comments on an earlier draft of this manuscript, and the research participants who were committed to helping fifth graders learn.

The Value of Interactive Writing as an Intervention for the Literacy Acquisition of Struggling First-Grade Students

Barbara K. O'Connor
University of Akron

Abstract

The purpose of this single-subject design research study, plus baseline and post-intervention testing, was to examine the effects of interactive writing on the phonological processing of six struggling first grade students, using an adapted form of interactive writing, in which students responded with independent writing samples. Three hundred seventy five daily independent writing samples were analyzed for phonemes and letters per word that were either correctly spelled or reasonable representations. The researcher-assisted intervention interactive writing was also analyzed for phonemes and letters per word. The data showed that each child presented a specific profile that differed from the others both before and after the intervention. Their responses differed as well. Both positive and negative responses resulted. The researcher-assisted intervention writing was analyzed at a higher level than the students' ability to independently write for the duration of the study, with the gap narrowing by the end of the intervention.

Both phonemic awareness, which is a necessary but insufficient component of learning how to read, and exposure to print, also necessary but insufficient, are essential for students to learn the spelling-sound correspondence rules of language, or the orthographic cipher (Juel, Griffith, and & Gough, 1986).

According to research over the last 30 years, phonemic awareness, specifically blending and segmenting of sounds in words, has been found to be of primary importance in learning to read (Ehri et. al., 2001; National Reading Panel, 2000). Students at the beginning of kindergarten, and of course first grade, who lack this understanding are potential recipients for training in phonemic awareness. Most phonemic awareness research programs consist of isolated skills and games that, although fun and entertaining, would not be considered balanced literacy curricula. Others, more literacy-based, are less structured and systematic, but may lack the explicit and direct instruction that poor readers need in order to learn how words work in English (Gaskins, Gaskins, & Gaskins, 1991). Moreover, the majority of phonemic awareness training programs are intended for the kindergarten year, in preparation for formal literacy acquisition in the first grade.

Longitudinal studies (Foorman, Francis, Beeler, Winikates, & Fletcher, 1997; Scanlon & Vellutino, 1996; Torgesen, Wagner, & Rashotte, 1997; Vellutino, Scanlon, & Tanzman, 1994) have provided preliminary data that indicates "that early direct instruction in phoneme awareness and sound-symbol knowledge (phonics), within a complete reading program, increases decoding skills, word recognition abilities, and to some extent, reading comprehension skills in many at-risk kindergarten, first-, and second-grade children" (Lyon & Moats, 1997, p. 580).

Endorsing balanced literacy, Pearson (2001) states that ". . . the most skilled readers are those who have both well-honed automatic word identification processes and rich stores of knowledge that they use to construct, monitor, and refine the models of meaning they construct as they read" (p. 79). Even so, some students need more focus on one element in the reading success story, and beginning readers especially need to learn how to identify words in order to access meaning. For these early readers, phonemic awareness appears to be an important precursor to the phonics understanding that is a major ingredient of word identification.

Balanced literacy instruction has become the solution to the "Reading Wars" in which skills and meaning were debated as the "best way to teach reading" (Vacca, 1996, p. 3). Reading is an interactive process in which the associations between reader, text, and context are continually renegotiated, each taking precedence at varying times during the reading process. In this "middle" model, skilled readers use both word identification and background knowledge to construct and monitor meaning during reading. The reader interacts with the text to make meaning, using phonics as an essential feature of building meaning. Phonics is a means to an end. Within this model, reading and writing are related synergistically, in that learning in each process benefits learning in the other. Balance, as in the "balance of nature," is a matter of accumulating an assortment of skills, strategies, processes, and practices to comprise a synergistic, comprehensive curriculum for all students (Pearson, 2001, p. 78).

Models of Literacy Development

One of the elements of balanced literacy instruction is the ability to read words using word identification strategies and phonics skills. In order to provide a window on what early skills might be, researchers have examined the developmental sequence of learning to read and have developed models of literacy acquisition, that have been classified into stage and non-stage models. These models focus on the student and what the student is actually learning or how the student relates to and constructs meaning of written communication. Non-stage models suggest that there is no difference between the beginning reader and the experienced one; that for both the goal is the search for meaning. Stage models on the other hand, propose that as time progresses, qualitative differences appear as the beginning reader gains experience and expertise in identifying written words. These differences are assumed to illustrate orthographic growth rather than semantic and syntactic development. Stage models reflect improved skill in ways to identify words and the "actual processes readers use, not just their control of these processes" (Juel, 1996, p. 762).

Whereas the construction of meaning in both paradigms is the ultimate objective of reading, non-stage models rely mostly on semantic and syntactic knowledge, with a minimal focus on orthographic knowledge, while stage models depend on the development of orthographic knowledge to achieve this fundamental goal of comprehension (Juel, 1996).

This study is based upon stage models of reading acquisition, assuming that the differences in beginning reading are dependent primarily upon the development of orthographic knowledge, with comprehension the paramount goal. Ehri and McCormick (1998) preferred the term *phases* to describe periods of development that may overlap but are not necessarily a prerequisite for movement to the next phase. Noting that phases merely highlight prominent characteristics of word learning, they described the following phases in the development of learning to read sight words: pre-alphabetic in which beginners do not use alphabetic knowledge to read words, partial-alphabetic with readers using partial letter-sound correspondence (namely beginning and ending sounds), full-alphabetic in which readers fully decode and blend, consolidated-alphabetic or orthographic with readers using familiar word families or patterns, and the automatic phase of mature proficient readers.

Stating that "spelling ability and word reading ability are highly correlated in the early primary grades (K-2)," Morris (1999, p. 33) identified developmental spelling stages with his Spelling (Phonemic Awareness) Task that is more precise than others at the beginning levels. Stages are labeled as semi-phonetic, representing one and two phonemes; letter-name with three and four phonemes; and within-word pattern showing five phonemes. This developmental spelling stage identification was used to evaluate the students' independent writing samples collected during throughout this entire study.

Because first graders come to school with varying levels of phonemic awareness, some come without any sense of sounds within words, and because little oral phonemic awareness training actually occurs in first grade, how can these students catch up in order to make sense of the phonics instruction they do receive in this most important year of literacy acquisition?

Interactive Writing

Interactive writing evolved from the language experience approach (Ashton-Warner, 1963; Stauffer, 1980) in which the teacher scribed for the children's dictated text. It is a form of shared writing (McKenzie, 1985) and is a part of the literacy lesson framework developed by The Ohio State University educators, Pinnell and McCarrier (1994). The goal of interactive writing is to "provide rich, educative experiences for young children, particularly those considered to be educationally at risk" (Button, Johnson, & Furgerson, 1996, p. 447).

Interactive writing is related to Reading Recovery (Clay, 1993), a successful one-on-one tutorial intervention program for the lowest 20% of first grade readers, and includes among other activities, a Hearing and Recording Sounds in Words task within a child's self-composed sentence. This task in the Reading Recovery lesson (Clay, 1993) is commensurate to interactive writing within the literacy lesson framework that was developed as an adaptation of Reading Recovery for classroom use (Pinnell & McCarrier, 1994).

According to Wasik and Slavin(1993), Reading Recovery does not provide a "systematic presentation of phonics, yet during the reading and writing activities, letter-sound relationships are taught as one of the basic strategies in solving problems" (p. 183). They also note the tutoring program considers intervention to be successful when students "reach the level performance of their classmates in the middle reading group" within 60 sessions (p. 181).

Interactive writing is a method of supported writing in which the teacher and students share the pen in creating conventionally spelled and punctuated text, focusing on sounds and the letters that represent them, as well as other concepts of print and writing conventions (McCarrier, Pinnell, & Fountas, 2000).

Using direct instruction and questioning, the teacher draws attention to and "demonstrates concepts of print, early strategies, and how words work." She "provides opportunities to hear sounds in words and connect with letters." She "helps children understand 'building up' and 'breaking down' processes in reading and writing [and] provides opportunities to plan and construct texts" (Button, Johnson, & Furgerson, 1996, p. 448).

The significance of this study was to determine if interactive writing, which implicitly combines four processes, how words work, language experience, reading, and writing could be used as a balanced literacy intervention to accelerate the learning of struggling first-grade students.

Most previous related research into the development of phonemic awareness tends to focus on large groups of quantitatively studied students, using direct, explicit, systematic, and sequential curriculums (Foorman, Francis, Fletcher, Schatschneider, & Mehta, 1998; Juel, 1988; Juel et al., 1986; Torgesen, Alexander, Wagner, Rashotte, Voeller, & Conway, 2001; Vellutino, Scanlon, Sipay, Small, Chen, & Pratt, et al., 1996).

These studies reveal very little about the actual process of teaching and learning on a daily basis, nor do they provide evidence of adapting to children's learning needs as they are presented. Therefore, this inquiry is best answered by a teaching method that is "recalibrated with each response of the child" (Gaffney, 1994, pp. 240-241) and a research method that allows for continuous monitoring of that process and evaluation of progress. Instead of following a scripted program of instruction, teaching in this study consisted of that which met the presented needs of the learner at his or her points of difficulty or confusion. This approach to teaching, known as constructivism, depends upon the demonstration of the student's knowledge and understandings as well as confusions and misunderstandings to which the teacher responds with experiences and opportunities to construct new understandings and learning. The learner is believed to construct knowledge, based upon prior knowledge and experiences as well as the new teaching and experiences presented by the teacher or encountered in daily living.

In order to meet the needs of daily interaction, instruction, and monitoring, while continually assessing the progress of the learners, as well as directing future instruction, single subject experimental research was chosen as the best method for this inquiry.

Single Subject Research in Literacy

Single subject research affords "the capacity to conduct experimental investigations with the single case, i.e., one subject" (Kazdin, 1982, p. 3). According to McCormick (1995), single subject experimental research is a method that is designed to clearly establish the effects of an intervention on a single individual or a small number of individuals. It is designed to guarantee that changes in responses of the individual are indeed attributable to the intervention and are not a result of consequence or other causes. Differing from group comparison experiments, single subject research assures that decisions are made as a result of changes in the individual during the study. This method can reveal important trends, although it is not undeniable proof of cause and effect

Single subject research includes (a) collection of baseline data before institution of the intervention, (b) manipulation of variables, (c) frequent collection of data over time, (d) use of control procedures rather than control groups, (e) collection of permanent products or use of observational recording that are examined by standard measurement approaches, (f) assessment of inter-observer agreement for both dependent and independent variables, (g) graphing of all data, (h) use of specific guidelines, (i) visual rather than statistical analysis of each individual's graphed data, (j) collection of maintenance and transfer data at post-intervention, and (k) controls in the interpretation of data to assure reliability and believability of conclusions. Data analysis is personalized, illustrating before, during, and after intervention data; graphed; and analyzed individually, providing important knowledge about individual subjects (McCormick, 1995).

Research Question

What effects does interactive writing, used as an intervention, have on the reading acquisition of small groups of struggling first grade students, who are deficient in or have not yet developed phonemic awareness, or the ability to identify sounds heard in words? This main research question comprises five sub-questions:

How does interactive writing influence (a) the phonemic awareness, (b) the alphabetic knowledge, (c) the phonological processing, (d) the developmental spelling, and (e) the reading ability of these struggling first grade students?

Method

The research question was intended to examine closely, and on an on-going basis, the responses of struggling first grade students, to interactive writing used as an early intervention for the acquisition of literacy. In order to follow the progress of these students, and be able to analyze their growth on a daily basis, single subject experimental research was chosen as the investigational tool.

Setting

The setting for this study was a suburban elementary school just outside a major urban area in the Midwest. Enrollment in the district that year was 40.7 % White, 51.7% Black, 2.9% Asian/Pacific Islander, 3.7% Multiracial, 1.1% Hispanic, and 0.04% Native American.

Participants

Although the researcher had intended to select the participants in the study from across the grade level, the principal selected the single regular first grade classroom and the classroom teacher selected six students, based on her normal beginning-of-the-year testing, and those that she considered needed extra attention, dividing them into two groups of three.

Normal beginning and end of the year testing known as the Common

Tools, consisted of fall and spring Letter Identification (Clay, 1993); fall and spring phonics, actually the Hearing and Recording Sounds in Words (Dictation) Task (Clay, 1993); beginning and spring spelling, consisting of 20 first grade spelling words; and fall and spring writing assessments, prompted with the title, *My Friend*, which was graded with a rubric ranging from zero to three.

Unbeknownst to the researcher, these same six students also began working with a reading tutor on a daily basis at the same time that baseline testing began for the first group and as was later revealed to the researcher, some of them also worked with weekly volunteer reading tutors from the community. One of the children in the first group had attended a post-kindergarten enrichment program over the previous summer, designed to teach phonemic awareness. One student from the second group moved and dropped from the study at winter break. Five students completed the full study.

Multiple Baseline Design

The six children were divided into two instructional groups of three, two girls and one boy in group one, and two boys and one girl in group two. In order to comply with the National Reading Panel's (2000) recommendations that small groups of students work for 20 hours or less, 25-30 minutes per day on phonemic awareness training was most effective, and to be able to study individuals within the groups, multiple baseline design was indicated.

The goal of single subject research has been to identify each individual's current ability, performance, or response levels at the start of the experiment, and then to examine the degree of change in the individual's responses that are induced by the intervention, followed by assessment of ability at post-intervention. Multiple baseline design has allowed the study of individuals within groups, with each child's responses examined and analyzed individually on a daily basis over time (McCormick, 1995).

Multiple baseline design has also required that groups begin intervention at differing times, dependent upon the data acquired from the earlier baseline phase, which must show stability before moving each group into intervention. Also required has been evidence of stable change for the earlier group due to the intervention before the second group has started into intervention (Kucera & Axelrod, 1995; M. Tankersley, personal communication, 2001). These requirements or control procedures, in this case stability of data, ensure that the intervention is responsible for the change in behavior and not a consequence of chance or some outside event.

Time Frame for Phases. For the first group, baseline lasted 20 days, followed by intervention. On day 14 of the first group's baseline phase, the second group began baseline, which lasted 16 days, also followed by intervention. This lag in starting the second group was done to avoid a more prolonged baseline experience for them. Baseline consisted of individual sessions with each child, and no groups were used. Within these individual sessions, pre-testing was administered and daily independent writing samples were obtained from each child. Baseline was not intended to last a specific number of days, but only until the data obtained becomes stable (Kucera & Axelrod, 1995).

Intervention lasted 40 days or 20 hours for each group. Group one was so reluctant to end the group sessions that they asked for an additional day of group intervention, resulting in 41 days. Individual children were absent on various days, but the groups progressed through the full complement of sessions. The instructional intervention was used initially for 16 days with group one and for 7 days with group two. As the intervention began and students were required to work in groups as opposed to singly, one of the students began to pout and refused to cooperate when she could not get her way. On various other occasions, some of the boys, especially Child F, acted out and talked out, in what appeared to be attempts to get attention focused back on them as in the one-on-one baseline sessions. Due to these inappropriate behaviors that began to interfere with the intervention, a second additional behavioral intervention was added to the instructional intervention. This double intervention phase lasted for the remaining 24 days for group one and for the remaining 33 days for group two.

Upon completion of the 40 or 41 sessions, groups were disbanded and post-intervention was begun on an individual basis. At approximately one-month intervals after completion of post-intervention testing, the researcher re-visited the school to gather more data. Post-intervention and follow-up totaled between 5 and 7 days per student.

Baseline and Post-Intervention Testing

Baseline and post-intervention testing was used to assess the overall value of the intervention on most of the measures or sub-questions specifically, the effect of interactive writing used as an intervention on the phonemic awareness, alphabet knowledge, developmental spelling, and reading ability of these struggling, first grade students. These questions relied on the effects of the intervention, but could be answered best by testing before and after the intervention took place. The final sub-question, the effect of interactive writing on the phonological processing of these students, required on-going evaluation of their performance in order to shape and direct the intervention and to collect the pertinent data, and was therefore the basis of the intervention portion of this single subject research study.

The baseline phase of the study consisted of individual work with students on a daily basis and included some form of pre-intervention testing and an independent writing sample requested with the direction to "write a story for me and say the words slowly that you want to write and put down the sounds you hear." These writing samples were also the data for the intervention component of the study and were obtained at every daily session during baseline, intervention, and post-intervention.

Measurement Tools. Table 1 illustrates that this baseline and post-intervention testing was comprised of the six subtests in the Observation Survey of Early Literacy Achievement (Clay, 1993), Letter Identification, the Ohio Word Test, Writing Vocabulary, Hearing and Recording Sounds in Words Dictation Task, Concepts About Print (replaced by an Emergent Reader Behavior Inventory obtained from a Reading Recovery trainer), and the Running Record of Reading Texts. The baseline and post-intervention testing also included two forms of Rapid Automatic Naming (Denckla & Rudel, 1974), the research team form from Neuhaus, Foorman, Francis, and Carlson (2001), which uses two commonly reversible and confusing letters for early learners, p and d, and an alternate form, using non-reversible letters, created by the researcher. The R.A.N. (Rapid Automatic Naming) task consists of 50 stimuli consisting of 5 familiar lower case letters randomly repeated 10 times over in five rows. The child is timed and asked to read the letters as rapidly as possible. Denckla and Rudel (1974, 1976) found that this naming speed differentiated dyslexic readers from average readers and also other learning disabled children. This discrimination was found to be apparent from the first day of kindergarten. Further studies have found that these differences remain apparent throughout the grades into adulthood and are especially true for letter naming. Torgesen suggested that these R.A.N. identified dyslexic readers might be "treatment resistant" (Wolf, 1999).

In addition, four different phonemic awareness tasks were administered, the Spelling (Phoneme Awareness) Task (Morris, 1999), the Lindamood Auditory Conceptualization Test (Lindamood & Lindamood, 1979), the Yopp-Singer Test of Phoneme Segmentation (Yopp, 1995), and the Classroom Phonemic Segmentation and Blending Test (Taylor & Pearson, 1988). These four phonemic awareness tasks assess the child's ability to correctly identify the sounds heard in words or to spell words reasonably or correctly. Other activities such as sequencing cards and stories were used to fill in the rest of baseline, preparing the structure for the students to work with the researcher for extended lengths of time, without providing any instruction in the goals of this study.

Dependent Variables. Dependent variables or target behaviors in the baseline and post-intervention testing differed with the question being addressed and the assessment used. Phonemic awareness was assessed with the four phonemic awareness tasks. Alphabet knowledge was assessed with the Letter Identification subtest of the Observation Survey of Early Literacy Achievement and the two Rapid Automatic Naming assessments.

Table 1. Baseline and Post-Intervention Testing

Test	Child A*		Child B		Child C		Child D**		Child E		Child F	
	Base	Post	Base	Post	Base	Post	Base	Post	Base	Post	Base	Post
Observation Survey of Early Literacy Achievement (Clay, 1993)												
Letter ID [Stanine 5=52-54]	46	52	50	54	51	53	53	–	52	54	48	52
Ohio Word [Stanine 5=10-11]	2	7	6	8	2	9	6	–	6	9	2	10
Writing Vocabulary [Stanine 5=20-24]	8	33	18	28	10	43	2	–	9	37	16	32
Dictation [Stanine 5=27-30]	17	34	23	33	23	32	29	–	30	34	18	31
Concepts About Print [Stanine 5= 16]	15	16	14	16	9	13	15	–	10	15	11	14
Running Record Level [Stanine 5=6-7]	2	5	4	7	3	5	2	–	3	5	2	5
Rapid Automatic Naming Tasks	Base	Post	Base	Post	Base	Post	Base	Post	Base	Post	Base	Post
RAN Assessment—Adaptation	53 s	~35 s	53 s	39 s	53 s	37 s	42 s	–	38 s	34 s	42 s	38 s
RAN Assessment—Neuhaus, et al., (2001) Norm<70 seconds	58 s	47 s	59 s	50 s	54 s	36 s	40 s	–	51 s	39 s	69 s	44 s
Phonemic Awareness Tests	Base	Post	Base	Post	Base	Post	Base	Post	Base	Post	Base	Post
1. Spelling (Phoneme Awareness) Task (Morris, 1999) [Scoring: 1-2 Semi-Phonetic, 3-4 Letter Name, 5 Within-Word Pattern	2.1	3.2	1.85	2.75	2.3	3.05	3.25	–	2.75	3.25	2.1	3.35
2. Lindamood Auditory Conceptualization Test (Lindamood & Lindamood, 1979) [Grade 1 norm=41-61]	31	30	27	21	24	22	21	–	37	40	36	40
3. Yopp-Singer Test of Phoneme Segmentation (1995) (22 total) [Norm 2nd sem. K=11-12]	22	18	7	20	20	20	7	–	16	17	6	18
4. Taylor-Pearson Classroom Phonemic Segmentation and Blending Test (1988) [Norm=8/12]	10	12	4	9	9	12	8	–	10	12	5	8

*Participated in summer phonemic awareness enrichment program. **Withdrew from school and intervention before completion.

Developmental spelling was assessed with the Spelling (Phoneme Awareness) Task, the Writing Vocabulary Task and the Hearing and Recording Sounds in Words Dictation Task of the Observation Survey of Early Literacy Achievement. Reading ability was assessed with the Running Record of Text Reading of the Observation Survey.

Procedures for Assessing. All baseline assessments were administered to each student individually, one assessment per day and repeated again in post-intervention. Data were compared for each student, baseline and post-intervention, to determine the overall value of the intervention separate from the intervention data. Writing samples were also obtained daily in both baseline and post-intervention and analyzed following the same procedures as was done throughout the intervention phase.

Intervention

The intervention consisted of interactive writing as described by McCarrier, et al. (2000), in the text, *Interactive writing: How language and literacy come together, K–2,* and adapted for the purposes of this study. Time constraints resulted in changes in the actual intervention regimen, so that the sessions did not follow the traditional interactive writing schedule of eight essential elements. A set curriculum evolved in order to fit as much actual interactive writing as possible into the daily 30-minute sessions. The resulting intervention contained four segments: daily re-reading of the previous day's interactive writing, a selection of children's literature read aloud by the researcher, a personal response time in which each child was able to discuss and compose a personal response to the reading and construct that response using interactive writing with group and researcher assistance, followed by an independently composed and constructed story (writing sample) by each child. This independent "story" writing was the permanent product used for daily data collection and analysis.

Measurement Tools. Each day the writing sample that was obtained from each student was read orally by the student into a tape recorder to store pronunciation and word usage, and to assist in translation of independent student writing. No reinforcement was given for the writing samples other than meaning-oriented responses. That is, no spelling or writing assistance was given during the independent writing time throughout the study. Occasionally, questioning occurred when the student reading did not match what was written. In addition, the researcher occasionally would pronounce a word for a student to assist in writing, but at no time was spelling assisted. This writing sample was obtained at every session during baseline, intervention, and post-intervention.

Dependent Variable. The dependent variable or target behavior in this intervention was the measurement of growth in the ability to correctly or reasonably represent phonemes in words. These words comprised the 375 daily "story" samples that were composed independently and written by each of the six students in the study that were used for analysis. Each daily independent writing sample was obtained by asking the students to write a story for the researcher, with the direction to "say the words slowly that you want to say and put down the sounds that you hear."

Procedures for Assessing. Figure 1 illustrates three composite measures that were collected and graphed each day from these samples. The first measure was a checklist of consonant and vowel phonemes developed from the *Lindamood phoneme sequencing program for reading, spelling, and speech: Teachers' manual for the classroom and clinic* (Lindamood & Lindamood, 1998). Each writing sample was assessed for the exact count of any phonemes correctly or reasonably represented in the students' spelling of words, and the total was graphed.

The second measure from the same writing sample consisted of data that were also collected on the number of occurrences of correct or reasonable 1, 2, and 3 phoneme representations as well as a third measure consisting of 4, 5, and 6 or more phoneme representations. Reasonable phoneme representations were considered by the researcher to be acceptable spellings of phonemes that were not correctly spelled, but could be sounded out correctly as represented. Data from these measures indicated growth in the ability to represent more complex phoneme sequences over time. These three measures of data were the basis of the following assessment, phoneme blending and sequencing accuracy checklist, which was used to compute the average phonemes per word per daily writing sample. It was this assessment that was used as a composite score to measure student growth over the length of the study. All measures had unlimited ceilings due to the fact that the children had control over the length of the writing samples, including number and choice of words resulting in possible multiple occurrences of individual phonemes within the single sample.

Additionally, this average phoneme per word composite score was evaluated according to six levels of phoneme sequences represented in spellings. These levels, equal to the 1, 2, and 3 phoneme "words", and 4, 5, and 6 phoneme "words" representations mentioned above, also represent two levels each of both semi-phonemic and letter-name spelling, and one level of within-word pattern spelling taken from Morris'(1999) developmental stages in young children's spelling, plus an additional level of 6 phoneme "words" that some of the children produced.

According to Morris (1999), semi-phonemic spelling consists of the beginning or ending consonant (1 point or phoneme) or beginning and ending consonants (2 points or phonemes). These stages reveal the student's inability to attend to the sequence of sounds in words, beyond beginning

Figure 1. Graphic Representation of Data

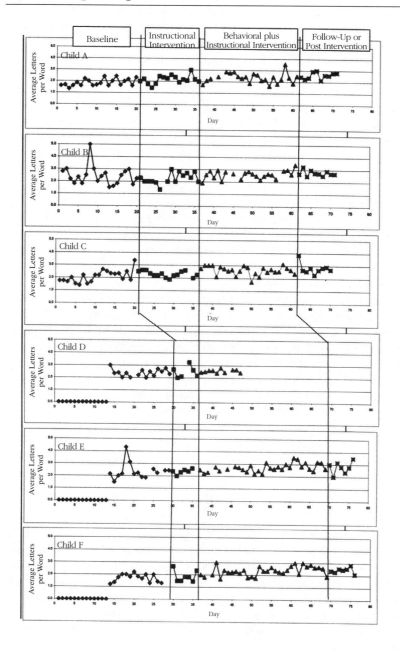

and ending phonemes. It is possible that two phonemes may be correctly or reasonably represented within a longer or multi-syllable word, or one of the two, or both sounds may be other than a beginning or ending consonant, perhaps a stressed interior consonant, or a vowel sound.

Letter-name spelling illustrates the student's ability to sound through words, making one-to-one letter-sound matches. These spellings consist of a single vowel spelling, correctly represented, in addition to the beginning and ending consonant sounds (3 points or phonemes). More complete representation of consonant blend sounds and digraphs in words would be worth another point (4 points or phonemes) (Morris, 1999). Again, three or four correctly or reasonably represented phonemes in longer words may also be possible.

Within-word pattern spelling (5 points or phonemes) includes correctly or reasonably represented marked long vowels, which include a second silent vowel or a diphthong containing two vowels representing one phoneme. These spellings reveal that the student has become aware of patterns that do not follow the fixed, one-to-one correspondence of the previous stage (Morris, 1999). Here, too, five correctly or reasonably represented phonemes in longer words may be found.

Some of the students were occasionally producing reasonable 6 phoneme representations, and so level 6 was added by the researcher. Words with 6 or more correctly or reasonably represented phonemes earned 6 points per word. The total points for all written words were combined for an average daily score of correctly or reasonably represented words.

Inter-Rater Reliability. There was a final total 93% agreement between the researcher and the rater evaluating the individual independent writing samples. 97% of consonant scores, 92% of vowel scores, and 91% of composite phonemes/letters per word scores which were derived from the 1, 2, 3, and 4, 5, 6 phoneme words, showed agreement. There was a 100% agreement between the researcher and the rater evaluating the group-composed writings.

Results

Although this study relied on the intervention to measure the effect of interactive writing on the phonological processing of the students, it could not answer the remaining sub-questions, concerning the effect of interactive writing on phonemic awareness, alphabet knowledge, developmental spelling, and reading ability. These were addressed with the baseline and post-intervention testing, using the Observation Survey of Early Literacy Achievement, Rapid Automatic Naming Tasks, and four phonemic awareness assessments listed in Table 1.

Testing

According to the testing: (a) phonemic awareness showed gains and losses, according to the four phonemic assessments used, the Spelling (Phoneme Awareness) Task (Morris, 1999), the Lindamood Auditory Conceptualization Test (Lindamood & Lindamood, 1979), the Yopp-Singer Test of Phoneme Segmentation (Yopp,1995), and the Taylor-Pearson Classroom Phonemic Segmentation and Blending Test (Taylor & Pearson,1988); (b) alphabetic knowledge improved for all students, using the Letter Identification (Clay, 1993) and the R.A.N. tasks (Neuhaus, et al., 2001 and researcher adaptation); (c) phonological processing, best shown by the daily collected intervention data, showed that all of the children improved in different ways. This was supported by baseline and post-intervention assessments; (d) developmental spelling improved for all students, shown by the Spelling (Phoneme Awareness) Task (Morris, 1999), the Writing Vocabulary and Hearing and Recording Sounds in Words Dictation Task (Clay, 1993); and (e) reading ability improved, illustrated by the Running Record of Text Reading (Clay, 1993). All of these improvements resulted from the children's involvement in their regular first grade classroom, the daily reading tutor, weekly reading tutors from the community for some of the students, both of whom were not revealed to the researcher until after the study began, and this daily interactive writing intervention. Baseline and post-intervention results are shown in Table 1 and graphic representation of intervention results are shown in Figure 1.

Comparing their post-intervention scores to the published year-end Ohio stanines revealed equal to better attainment for the children in the study on all measures except the Ohio Word Test. In comparing the children's scores with their class common tools year-end assessments, Letter Identification and the Dictation Task scores were equal to the class mean except for one student in each case who scored below the class mean. Comparison with their class means is more valid than with the stanine comparisons, because the children in the study were a subset of their class and unrelated to the stanine group, except by being urban mid-western first grade students in discrete years. Reading Recovery (Clay, 1993), with which this intervention is related, considers intervention to be successful when students reach their class means.

Intervention Data

Although all of the children progressed in various ways, there was little evidence of substantial, consistent change in any of the children due to the intervention in this study. However, visual analysis of the individual composite graphs of phonemes/letters per word for each child showed that there was progress for each child in varying degrees.

The average phoneme/letter per word composite graphs of daily independent writing provided information about the students' phonological processing abilities. The graphs showed a single daily score for each student comprised of weighting words bynumber of phonemes. Therefore, one-phoneme words were worth one point, two-phoneme words were worth two points, and so on through six or more phoneme words worth six points each. If a child wrote 30 two-phoneme words, his score for the sample would be 60. If another child were to write 10 six-phoneme words, his score would also be 60. In this way the quality of spelling development was more heavily weighted than quantity of words and actually favored improvement in developmental spelling over the number of words in the sample.

Means. The means, or average scores for the six children across four phases, show an increase for 88% of the phases. Children grew from semi-phonetic spellers able to represent from 1.70 to 2.44 phonemes per word in baseline; to approaching letter-name stage, able to represent from 2.34 to 2.72 phonemes per word in the final intervention phase in their independent daily writing. Follow-up averages ranged from 2.45 to 2.82 phonemes/letters per words.

Trends. Trends (progress during a phase, either ascending upward or descending downward) ascended 70% of the time, close to three quarters of the total phases for all of the children across four phases (a total of 23 phases). The behavioral plus instructional intervention was less positive than the instructional intervention alone.

Extrapolation of baseline data showed mixed results as well. All six students showed growth in phase means, but only four showed growth in phase trends. The baseline trends for two of the children show that the act of daily inventive writing was more effective than the intervention.

Immediacy of behavior change revealed abruptness between all phases for all students, but nearly every data point in the study also showed the same abruptness. The actual intervention can therefore not be assumed to be the cause of the changes in behaviors from one phase to another. Although all of the data for all of the children appear unstable, only three children showed variability over 50% beyond the mean or average score in a phase, and all of these were single points in baseline, therefore the data can be assumed to be stable except for these single outliers in three baselines. The intervention appeared to decrease variability in data points for three of the children, showing that it did have an effect. For the other three, intervention seemed to increase variability over that of baseline, showing that it did not. The number of data points was sufficient for each phase for each child. Overlapping data points indicate that the intervention was not powerful, and in fact had only slight effect in 12% of the comparisons.

A comparison of phase trends (researcher and computer-generated comparison of the trend lines for each child) revealed that the instructional intervention was stronger for four of the children, baseline was the strongest phase for one child, and follow-up was the strongest for another.

Analysis of Interactive Writing Sessions. In addition to the analysis of each child's daily independent writing samples, the permanent products from the interactive writing intervention sessions were also analyzed for phonemes per word and letters per word assessment. The mean phonemes per word for group one's compositions was 3.246 in the instructional intervention phase. For the behavioral plus instructional intervention sessions, the mean was 3.174 phonemes per word. The total intervention for group one produced a mean of 3.194 phonemes per word.

Group two had a mean of 3.429 phonemes per word for the instructional intervention phase. The behavioral plus instructional intervention phase resulted in a phoneme per word count of 3.114. The mean for the total intervention for group two resulted in 3.154.

In an effort to avoid comparing dissimilar data, the same intervention data was also analyzed for letters per word, as the students' daily writing samples eventually came to be assessed. Table 2 illustrates the analysis.

Table 2. Analysis of Interactive Writing Intervention Sessions

| | Mean Phonemes per Word Letter Name | | | Mean Letters per Word Within-Word | | |
Group	Instructional Intervention	Behavioral plus Instructional Intervention	Total Intervention	Instructional Intervention	Behavioral plus Instructional Intervention	Total Intervention
1	3.246	3.174	3.194	3.873	3.769	3.798
2	3.429	3.114	3.154	4.042	3.636	3.698

This data indicate that the actual intervention session group-assisted compositions were assessed at a much higher level that the students' individual independent writing performances throughout the study. In other words, the total intervention was evaluated as operating at a 3.7 to 3.8 letters per word composite score when the students were actually only operating from 2.45 to 2.82 phonemes/letters per word levels at the end of the study. The beginning of the study could be compared to their baseline means, ranging from 1.70 to 2.44 phonemes/letters per word. Clearly, this intervention, dependent upon the words chosen by the students, was in the upper ranges of, or even above their zones of proximal development, or the level of spelling that they "use but confuse" (Bear, Invernizzi, Templeton, & Johnston, 2000, p. 16), especially in the early days of the intervention. The "use but confuse" level of spelling consists of the spellings that they are incorrectly attempting, or those that they can construct correctly only with assistance from more capable others, and is just beyond what they are able to independently and correctly construct (see Table 3).

Table 3. Intervention vs. Independent Writing Samples

INTERVENTION WRITING ANALYSIS	INDEPENDENT WRITING ANALYSIS
Phonemes per word	Baseline
Group 1—3.194	1.70—2.44
Group 2—3.154	Instructional Intervention
	1.87—2.47
Letters per word	Behavioral + Instructional Intervention
Group 1—3.798	2.34—2.72
Group 2—3.698	Post-Intervention
	2.45—2.82

Intervention Summary. The intervention taken as a whole resulted in inconsistencies across children. Gains in mean levels ranged from a mild (14-19%) to a moderate (36-44%) increase in the children's ability to correctly or reasonably represent spellings of words during the course of the study. Individual trends were ascending or positive for 66% of the phases, indicating somewhat positive responses to instruction. The behavioral plus instructional intervention positively impacted only two of the children, and actually hindered the progress of the other four.

Extrapolation of the baseline trends showed that two of the children actually benefited more from the daily inventive writing than from the intervention itself and brings into question the value of the intervention. It is also evident that although the intervention, assisted by the researcher, operated at a higher level than the students' independent writing abilities throughout the study, it did contribute mild to moderate gains in their spelling abilities.

Analysis of Individual Summaries. The individual summaries reveal that each child began the intervention with a specific profile of strengths and weaknesses that differed from the others. Further, each child reacted to the intervention in different ways. For some of the children, the actual intervention appeared to contribute to furthering their abilities, whereas for others the simple act of daily independent writing seemed to be of more influence.

Further study may point to specific characteristics or markers that predict success. Child A appeared to be at a grapheme-phoneme match level of development and was perhaps not quite ready for the intervention, but made strong progress, nonetheless. Child B seemed to move from a strictly visual orientation to spelling to a more phonetic one, and showed moderate growth. Child C had a variety of personal and emotional needs that appeared to interfere, but also made strong improvement. Child D and Child E began the study with more phonemic skills than the others. Whereas Child E also made moderate progress, it would have been interesting to see what effect the complete intervention would have had with Child D, who moved before the study's completion. Child F also had behavioral interferences, but made powerful advances after the behavioral intervention was instituted, although he remained low at the conclusion of the study.

Discussion and Conclusions

External Validity. External validity pertains to generalizability. Single subject research provides generalizability through replication, in this case, repeating the same experiment with different subjects. A number of such replications producing the same results are necessary to assume generalizability (McCormick, 1995). Therefore, this study lacks external validity or generalizability because it is not a replication.

Additional threats would include generalizability across subjects because these children were all struggling, low socio-economic status (SES) African American children living in an affluent inner ring suburb of a large urban area. There is no transfer assumption of these results to other children in different circumstances. Generalizability across settings also is a consideration. Although the intervention took place in several places in the school at the beginning of the study, it was held completely outside of the regular classroom. There is also no assumption that these same results would occur in a classroom setting with a full first grade class or with groups within a class setting.

Internal validity. Internal validity was a limitation in this particular study because there is no assurance that only manipulation of the variables, or the actual intervention used, was solely responsible for the changes in behavior (Palincsar & Parecki, 1995). For five of the subjects, the simple act of daily writing combined with individual attention was enough to produce change in writing abilities, whether that change was positive or negative, shown as ascending or descending trends. Only Child D could be described as showing an almost level trend in baseline, and therefore supposedly no change in behavior in response to the baseline conditions.

A second threat to internal validity was the possibility of confounding of the testing procedures (Palincsar & Parecki, 1995). The children often used some of the same words from day to day in their daily independent writing samples that were not always spelled the same. It would be easy to reason that they might be on the lookout for how to spell those words, knowing that they were required to write independently every day.

A third very important threat to internal validity was that of maturation. The growth seen in the children in this study may be due to their maturation or increase in age as well as their skills resulting from being in first grade during the entire study.

An additional threat would be multiple-intervention interference. This can occur when more than one intervention is used in a study and the effects of the second intervention are attributed to the first (Palincsar & Parecki,

1995). In this study, the second intervention consisted of the first intervention plus a behavioral one. Therefore, this threat would not be considered operative. But the children also were involved in daily pull-out, small group reading tutoring, and five of them worked with reading tutors weekly. The curriculum director of the district had assured the researcher over the summer that the children selected for the study would be participating in no other intervention programs, when in fact they began working with the reading tutor on a daily basis at the same time the first baseline period began. Any or all of these unexpected interventions could also be responsible for, or contribute to the progress made by the children in the study.

With the exception of one child, none of the children claimed to feel frustrated with the repetition of the daily sessions, nor did they outwardly admit to being disinterested. However, it was a sense that the researcher felt was shared as the study continued, following the same pattern, day after day. Although the children did not verbalize their lack of interest, their behavior seemed to indicate it.

Finally, selection bias was a consideration. This study was designed to work with the lowest achieving first grade students in a school. The principal of the school decided that it would focus on one first grade classroom. The classroom teacher selected and grouped the children without consulting the researcher, so that the researcher had no say in the selection process. Although this study initially was designed for children lacking phonemic awareness, it became apparent during baseline testing that not all of the children lacked this skill. In fact two of the children, Child A and Child E, appeared to have a firm awareness across three phonemic awareness tests at the onset of the study.

If the expectation of participants lacking in phonemic awareness were absolute, the study would not have been able to be completed. The decision was made to go ahead with the study despite this limitation and others, and examine the results of the intervention.

In single subject research, stable baseline data is required before instituting the intervention phase. This requirement assures that the intervention is responsible for any change that occurs (Kazdin, 1982; Kucera & Alexrod, 1995). For all of the children, all of the data appeared unstable visually, but in actuality only three of the children had a single outlier apiece, in baseline. Group one was moved into baseline despite this instability because as baseline progressed, Child B was losing ground without instruction or reinforcement for his behavior. The intent of an intervention study is never to adversely affect a child's performance, even in baseline. Therefore, in order to interrupt his descending trend, the intervention was instituted despite the instability of his and another student's baseline data phases.

For group two, the same situation occurred, but less dramatically, with only one child in the group having an unstable baseline, indicated by data more than 50% away from the mean, and which resulted in a single outlier in the phase.

This study had many limitations that restricted the ability to draw firm conclusions. Although all of the children grew in their abilities of phonemic awareness, alphabet knowledge, phonological processing, developmental spelling, and reading ability, none of these areas of growth can be attributed solely to this intervention.

In addition to the mixed results gleaned from the assessments used in this study and the large number of limitations, other conclusions resulted from the data in this intervention study.

Individual Growth. It is obvious from both the intervention and baseline and post-intervention data that the children all grew in their reading and writing abilities. Each component of the research design served to supplement the other, each providing data in a way the other could not. From the baseline and post-intervention data, specifically the Morris Spelling (Phoneme Awareness) Task (Morris, 1999), it is clear that the students made gains in their ability to represent phonemes at a higher level when given specific words to spell, compared to what they demonstrated in their daily independent writing samples. On the other hand, the intervention data shows the growth that occurred, as well as the regressions. Together they form a more complete picture of the children's progress during the study. According to the Morris Spelling (Phoneme Awareness) Task (1999), four of the five students would be considered letter name spellers by the end of the study, whereas only one was letter-name at the onset. Generally the children would be classified as semi-phonetic 2 at the beginning of the study (see Table 1). Both stages could be considered appropriate for first grade, depending upon the time of the school year, the district, the school, and the particular class.

In addition to the improvement demonstrated by all of the children in the study, the data show that each child reacted differently to the intervention. No two children were the same at the beginning or at the end of the study, despite exposure to the same intervention. This indicates that "one size fits all" education might be inadequate and may easily be the most important finding of the study.

Behavioral Intervention

Adding the behavioral intervention to the existing instructional intervention did not benefit four of the students in the study, and actually restricted their progress. The addition of the behavioral intervention was necessary for Child F, who was regressing during the instructional intervention and resulted in gains in his learning and performance. It also improved Child C's decreasing instructional phase trend.

Intervention Writing Levels

The analysis of the intervention interactive writing shows that it operated well above the children's demonstrated ability levels or zones of proximal development for most of the study, with the gap narrowing at the end of intervention and follow up. This indicates that although much of the intervention interactive writing was above the children's zones of proximal development, their performance means steadily improved in most phases, showing that they did benefit from all the instruction they were receiving from the various sources.

Value of the Intervention

Although greater progress was hypothesized at the onset of this study, all of the children progressed well. The classroom teacher reported that all of the children passed the reading portion of the district end of year testing, though not necessarily the math portion. The effects of their classroom instruction, the daily reading tutor, the weekly reading tutor, and this study can be considered positive factors for such an accomplishment.

Recommendations

Interactive writing may be a valuable addition for teaching the writing process including the conventions of written language and connecting reading and writing in the kindergarten and first grade classroom, where there are multiple levels of ability. With the goal to develop a "focus on language and using language to learn" (McCarrier et al., 2000, p. 12), interactive writing can explicitly teach these concepts in ways other writing methods cannot. It can provide incidental or unsystematic, yet direct focus in a wide range of zones of proximal development. It can also be a "powerful demonstration" of "how words work" in our language, as well as how writing is accomplished for young learners (McCarrier et al., 2000, p. 12). However, despite these assertions, this current study implies that as it was practiced in this study, interactive writing may not be the optimum intervention for these children, who struggled with literacy acquisition.

In explaining developmental spelling theory (Henderson, 1990; Read, 1971), Invernizzi, Abouzeid, and Gill (1994) stated that the effectiveness of "incidental word study on the run" (p. 156) can be tentative and that direct instruction in spelling should be "timed and targeted to students' [developing] understanding [of how written words work]" (p. 158) or their zones of proximal development. They further stated that not all children need this type of concerted instruction, but for those who do not learn to spell easily, it is the task of the teacher to:

> reduce the variance between these students' orthographic awareness
> and conventional spelling forms . . . through a systematic study of word

features carefully selected to match the developmental word knowledge of the student, a proximal zone identified through interpreting the students' invented spellings. (p. 165)

Alternatively, the National Reading Panel (2000) reported that systematic synthetic phonics instruction has a more significant and positive effect on low SES children's alphabet knowledge and word reading skills than less focused instructional approaches. Although writing is generally considered a synthetic process using the process of building up words sound by sound, and sentences word by word (Clay, 1991), the word study focus of interactive writing could also be considered analytic, starting with spoken whole words and breaking them down into their constituent phonemes and letters, and as stated above, incidental, deriving the teaching sequence from the context of authentic experiences rather than a pre-planned program.

Interactive writing, as practiced in this study, may be too broad-based and diffused to produce the powerful results in phonemic awareness and phonological processing necessary for this type of learner to accelerate learning. Interactive writing has multiple key features, ranging from writing for authentic purposes, sharing the task of writing, using conversation or oral language to support the process, creating a common text, using the conventions of written language, and connecting reading and writing, as well as making letter-sound connections at various levels (McCarrier, et al., 2000). This acknowledged broad-based focus, and the results of this current study may indicate that a more focused intervention, operating closer to or especially within the children's zones of proximal development, may have enabled the children to make more progress.

Although the children in this study were not classified as having special needs, learners who lag behind need to accelerate their learning in order to catch up with their peers and their grade level. Reading Recovery, one prototype of interactive writing, considers successful "discontinuation" of tutoring to be reached by the student's ability to match the average level of his class and by his development of a "self-extending system" of reading and writing strategies (Clay, 1993).

In comparing the study participants' with their classmates' end of year scores on the "common tools" that are administered throughout the district, all of them equaled the mean of their class on letter identification, and four of the five equaled the means of their class year end scores on phonics (Hearing and Recording Sounds in Words Dictation Task), and writing. Only two equaled the spelling mean score at year-end. One child remained below the class means on the three of the four assessments. These would not necessarily be considered powerful results, because the means for self-extending systems at the end of first grade would include both reading and writing abilities.

Although these results were generally positive, there is no proof that this intervention alone could be credited with the students' success. It was at best, a contributor to the success that was shown throughout the study and at the end of year "common tools" testing.

In general, the data from this study indicated that interactive writing used as an intervention for struggling first graders in this particular research situation cannot be credited with powerful outcomes due to mixed results, multiple limitations, and diminished progress for most of the children in the behavioral plus instructional intervention phase. Since the supplementary behavioral intervention was beneficial to only two students' learning, and actually decreased the progress of the other four students in the study, one might imply that the addition of the behavioral component served to dilute the focus of the intervention and resulted in lowered progress for the four students.

An additional limitation, repetition and lack of motivation may imply that the intervention needed more variety from day to day to sustain student interest and engagement. The decreasing phase trends of some of the children may be indicative of this need for change or a possible mismatch between the child, the process, or the personalities involved.

The lack of success may also be due to the intervention lacking true balance. Research on effective early intervention programs has shown that they share specific characteristics. These programs consist of extensive reading, writing, and word study, in addition to other features. The current study could be considered a balanced literacy practice, but lacked extensive student reading in supportive text and coordination with classroom instruction (O'Connor, 1999), which are common features of these successful programs.

For the children in this study, a more balanced intervention program, including extensive student reading in supportive text; more systematic, sequential instruction that is more focused within their zones of proximal development; and intervention instruction coordinated with classroom instruction may have produced higher levels of growth. It may be that the progress demonstrated by these children exceeded their particular abilities and learning styles. It may be that they progressed much beyond where they would have, if they had not participated in this intervention. This study supports the premise that one size does not fit all in education or in intervention. To be most effective, intervention needs to be individualized, selected for exact needs and abilities, or at least tailored to particular needs and learning styles.

References

Ashton-Warner, S. (1963). *Teacher.* New York: Bantam Books.

Bear, D. R., Invernizzi, M., Templeton, S., & Johnston, F. (2000). *Words their way: Word study for phonics, vocabulary, and spelling instruction.* Upper Saddle River, NJ: Merrill/Prentice Hall.

Button, K., Johnson, M. J., & Furgerson, P. (1996). Interactive writing in a primary classroom. *The Reading Teacher, 49,* 446-454.

Clay, M. M. (1991). *Becoming literate: The construction of inner control.* Portsmouth, NH: Heinemann.

Clay, M. M. (1993). *An observation survey of early literacy achievement.* Portsmouth, NH: Heinemann.

Denckla, M. B., & Rudel, R. G. (1974). "Rapid automatized naming" of pictured objects, colors, letters, and numbers by normal children. *Cortex, 10,* 186-202.

Denckla, M. B., & Rudel, R. G. (1976). Rapid automatized naming (R.A.N.): Dyslexia differentiated from other learning disabilities. *Neuropsychologia, 14,* 471-479.

Ehri, L. C., & McCormick, S. (1998). Phases of word learning: Implications for instruction with delayed and disabled readers. *Reading & Writing Quarterly: Overcoming Learning Difficulties, 14,* 135-163.

Ehri, L. C., Nunes, S. R., Willows, D. M., Schuster, B. V., Yaghoub-Zadeh, A., & Shanahan, T. (2001). Phonemic awareness instruction helps children learn to read: Evidence from the National Reading Panel's meta-analysis. *Reading Research Quarterly, 36,* 250-287.

Foorman, B. R., Francis, D. J., Beeler, T., Winikates, D., & Fletcher, J. M. (1997). Early interventions for children with reading problems: Study designs and preliminary findings. *Learning Disabilities: A Multidisciplinary Journal, 8,* 63-71.

Foorman, B. R., Francis, D. J., Fletcher, J. M., Schatschneider, C., & Mehta, P. (1998). The role of instruction in learning to read: Preventing reading failure in at-risk children. *Journal of Educational Psychology, 90,* 37-55.

Gaffney, J. S. (1994). Reading Recovery: Widening the scope of prevention for children at risk of reading failure. In K. D. Wood & B. Algozzine (Eds.), *Teaching reading to high-risk learners: A unified perspective* (pp. 231-246). Boston: Allyn and Bacon.

Gaskins, R. W., Gaskins, J. C., & Gaskins, I. W. (1991). A decoding program for poor readers—and the rest of the class, too! *Language Arts, 68,* 213-225.

Henderson, E. H. (1990). *Teaching spelling* (2nd ed.). Boston: Houghton-Mifflin.

Invernizzi, M., Abouzeid, M., & Gill, J. T. (1994). Using students' invented spellings as a guide for spelling instruction that emphasizes word study. *The Elementary School Journal, 95,* 155-167.

Juel, C. (1988). Learning to read and write: A longitudinal study of fifty-four children from first through fourth grade. *Journal of Educational Psychology, 80,* 437-447.

Juel, C. (1996). Beginning reading. In R. Barr, M. L. Kamil, P. Mosenthal, & P. D. Pearson (Eds.), *Handbook of reading research: Vol. II* (pp. 759-788). Mahwah, NJ: Lawrence Erlbaum.

Juel, C., Griffith, P. L., & Gough, P. B. (1986). Acquisition of literacy: A longitudinal study of children in first and second grade. *Journal of Educational Psychology, 78,* 243-255.

Kazdin, A. E. (1982). *Single-case research designs: Methods for clinical and applied settings.* New York: Oxford University Press.

Kucera, J., & Axelrod, S. (1995). Multiple-baseline designs. In S. B. Neuman & S. McCormick (Eds.), *Single-subject experimental research: Applications for literacy* (pp. 47-63). Newark, DE: International Reading Association.

Lindamood, C., & Lindamood, P. (1979). *Lindamood auditory conceptualization test* (Revised). Chicago: Riverside.

Lindamood, P., & Lindamood, P. (1998). *The Lindamood phoneme sequencing program for reading, spelling, and speech: Teacher's manual for the classroom and clinic* (3rd ed.). Austin, TX: Pro-Ed.

Lyon, G. R., & Moats, L. C. (1997). Critical conceptual and methodological considerations in reading intervention research. *Journal of Learning Disabilities, 30*, 578-588.

McCarrier, A., Pinnell, G. S., & Fountas, I. C. (2000). *Interactive writing: How language and literacy come together, K-2*. Portsmouth, NH: Heinemann.

McCormick, S. (1995). What is single-subject experimental research? In S. B. Neuman & S. McCormick (Eds.), *Single-subject experimental research: Applications for literacy* (pp. 1-31). Newark, DE: International Reading Association.

McKenzie, M. G. (1985). *Journeys into literacy*. Hattersfield, England: Schofield and Sims.

Morris, D. (1999). *The Howard Street tutoring manual: Teaching at-risk readers in the primary grades*. New York: The Guilford Press.

O'Connor, B. K. (1999). *Early literacy intervention: What works? Research-based components of early literacy*. Unpublished manuscript, Kent State University.

National Reading Panel. (2000). *Teaching children to read: An evidence-based assessment of the scientific research literature on reading and its implications for reading instruction. Summary report*. Washington, DC: National Institutes of Health.

Neuhaus, G., Foorman, B. R., Francis, D. J., & Carlson, C. D. (2001). Measures of information processing in rapid automatized naming (RAN) and their relation to reading. *Journal of Experimental Child Psychology, 78*, 359-373.

Palincsar, A. S., & Parecki, A. D. (1995). Important issues related to single-subject experimental research. In S. B. Neuman & S. McCormick (Eds.), *Single-subject experimental research: Applications for literacy* (pp. 137-150). Newark, DE: International Reading Association.

Pearson, P. D. (2001). Life in the radical middle: A personal apology for a balanced view of reading. In R. F. Flippo (Ed.), *Reading researchers in search of common ground* (pp. 78-83). Newark, DE: The International Reading Association.

Pinnell, G. S., & McCarrier, A. (1994). Interactive writing: A transition tool for assisting children in learning to read and write. In E. H. Hiebert & B. M. Taylor (Eds.), *Getting reading right from the start: Effective early literacy interventions* (pp. 149-170). Boston: Allyn and Bacon.

Read, C. (1971). Pre-school children's knowledge of English phonology. *Harvard Educational Review, 41*(1), 1-34.

Scanlon, D. M., & Vellutino, F. R. (1996). Prerequisite skills, early instruction, and success in first grade reading: Selected results from a longitudinal study. *Mental Retardation and Development Disabilities, 2*, 54-63.

Stauffer, R. (1980). *The language experience approach to the teaching of reading* (2nd ed.). New York: Harper and Row.

Taylor, B. M., & Pearson, P. D. (1988). *Classroom phonemic segmentation and blending test*. Unpublished manuscript, University of Minnesota.

Torgesen, J. K., Alexander, A. W., Wagner, R. K., Rashotte, C. A., Voeller, K. K., & Conway, T. (2001). Intensive remedial instruction for children with severe reading disabilities: Immediate and long-term outcomes from two instructional approaches. *Journal of Learning Disabilities, 34*, 33-58.

Torgesen, J. K., Wagner, R. K., & Rashotte, C. A. (1997). Prevention and remediation of severe reading disabilities: Keeping the end in mind. *Scientific Studies of Reading, 1,* 217-234.

Vacca, R. T. (1996). The reading wars: Who will be the winners? Who will be the losers? *Reading Today, 14*(2), 3.

Vellutino, F. R., Scanlon, D. M., Sipay, E. R., Small, S. G., Chen, R. S., & Pratt, A., et al. (1996). Cognitive profiles of difficult-to-remediate and readily remediated poor readers: Early intervention as a vehicle for distinguishing between cognitive and experiential deficits as basic causes of specific reading disability. *Journal of Educational Psychology, 88,* 601-638.

Vellutino, F. R., Scanlon, D. M., & Tanzman, M. S. (1994). Components of reading ability: Issues and problems in operationalizing word identification, phonological coding, and orthographic coding. In G. R. Lyon (Ed.), *Frames of reference for the assessment of learning disabilities: New views on measurement issues* (pp. 279-324). Baltimore, MD: Paul H. Brookes.

Wasik, B. A., & Slavin, R. E. (1993). Preventing early reading failure with one-to-one tutoring: A review of five programs. *Reading Research Quarterly, 28,* 179-200.

Wolf, M. (1999). What time may tell: Towards a new conceptualization of developmental dyslexia. *Annals of Dyslexia, 49,* 3-28.

Yopp, H. K. (1995). A test for assessing phonemic awareness in young children. *The Reading Teacher, 49,* 20-29.

ENGAGING PRESERVICE TEACHERS IN READING, "STICKY NOTE" STYLE: AN ANALYSIS AND PRACTICAL IMPLICATIONS

Christine A. McKeon
Michelle L. Lenarz

Walsh University

Linda C. Burkey

Mount Union College

Abstract

Teacher educators need to study the practices they use to teach preservice teachers. In this chapter we describe a strategy in which preservice reading teachers wrote comments on sticky notes as they read a reading methods textbook. We also describe how one university professor engaged her students in learning about authentic assessment through the sticky note strategy. We analyze the sticky notes and suggest how this strategy helped us understand the connections teachers make as they read literacy related content. In addition, we suggest a way to teach preservice literacy educators about authentic assessment.

"Learning to read requires sharing, interaction, and collaboration." "I found the multicultural list useful!" "My daughter is beginning to make rhyming words!" This is a small sampling of comments written on sticky notes by undergraduate preservice teachers as they read about literacy topics in a developmental reading methods textbook (McKeon, Lenarz, & Burkey, 2003).

Although the number of reading courses required for teachers varies from state to state, we would surmise that typically preservice teachers are assigned textbook and/or article readings throughout their coursework as part of their knowledge base. While *in-service teachers* are encouraged to construct meaning as they read (Keene & Zimmerman, 1997), how preservice teachers respond to text-based information about reading has not been the focus of attention.

Pressley and colleagues found that college students were not selective or strategic when studying a text for a test; they failed in searching for information in a text; they did not monitor whether they knew the main idea of a passage; and they did not elaborate on the facts in the text (Pressely, El-Dinary, & Brown, 1992; Woloshyn, Willoughby, Wood, & Pressley, 1990). College students engage in reading that is unsophisticated, inefficient, and ineffective from an information-processing perspective (Pressley et al., 1992; Wood, Motz, & Willoughby, 1998).

Conversely, skilled adult readers apply multiple reading strategies in a purposeful manner. These include setting reading goals, varying reading style according to the relevance of the text to reading goals, making predictions, and constructing summaries and conclusions (Taraban, Rynearson, & Kerr, 2000). College students need to understand that "comprehension strategies are not intellectual crutches, but are very much a part of mature intellect" (Pressley, Brown, El-Dinary, & Afflerbach, 1995, p. 216). According to Taraban et al. (2000), teacher educators need to test the effects of strategy use in specific contexts, demand more expert-like strategic behavior, and situate comprehension strategies in everyday contexts.

We believe that preservice teachers typically learn strategies for teaching reading comprehension. How they learn to teach and assess comprehension, however, has not been the focus of extensive research. Preservice and inservice teachers in classes and workshops reported that they "seldom saw real strategy teaching either in their K-12 schooling or college reading methods classrooms" (Dowhower, 1999, p. 673). "There is a need for greater emphasis in teacher education on the teaching of reading comprehension. Such instruction should begin at the preservice level, and it should be extensive, especially with respect to teaching teachers how to teach comprehension" (Williams, 2002, p. 256). Teacher educators need to know how to clear up confusions that emerge as their students practice the modeled strategies. They also need to engage students in the reading process from the inside-out by using think-alouds to "unpack [their] brain and show kids all the things that go on in [their] heads" as they read (Villaume & Brabham, 2002, p. 674).

In an effort to teach preservice teachers a comprehension strategy, we provided them with an opportunity to practice it. In addition, we used the strategy to explore how preservice reading teachers process and comprehend text-based reading about literacy as part of their course requirements. We designed a reading assignment in hopes of engaging them in open-ended personal responses to the readings.

Our project evolved as a collaborative effort based on an idea adapted from Harvey and Goudvis (2000) in which sticky notes are used to help students express multiple levels of reading comprehension. One aspect of the strategy involves modeling for students via think-alouds, what the teacher is thinking, and coding responses to segments of the text reading as "text-to-text", "text-to-self", or "text-to-world". A text-to-text relationship might be another story that the student is reminded of during the reading; a text-to-self response would be one in which the student relates personally to the story or text; a text-to-world sticky note might be one in which the student recalls a global event associated with what is being read. In this paper we share our adaptation of using sticky notes as an *active* comprehension strategy that we taught our students, as well as one in which we gleaned "snapshots" of future teachers' understanding of literacy content as they read textbook chapters and used the strategy. In addition, we share how preservice teachers were taught to use sticky notes as a way to assess reading comprehension with children.

Related Literature
Teacher Preparation
Although teacher education has recently received unprecedented national attention, the public and political mindset has been to attack preservice preparation programs as failing to produce well-prepared teachers (Harmon et al., 2001). In particular, *reading* teachers have taken the forefront in the attack which resulted in the congressional mandate to create a National Reading Panel whose charge was to examine scientific reading research. The findings of the National Reading Panel (2000) became the impetus for the *No Child Left Behind Act of 2001,* part of the reauthorized Elementary and Secondary Education Act and part of which calls for improving the quality of teaching and "putting reading first" (U. S. Department of Education, n. d.).

Furthermore, accountability is a current issue that challenges universities and colleges nationwide, especially in teacher preparation programs of literacy education. National, state, and local standards that ensure preservice teachers are prepared and are experts in the teaching of reading tend to serve as key indicators today for core courses and content in reading education at the university/college level. The International Reading Association (n.d.), for example, has recently developed a revised framework for *Standards for Reading Professionals.*

Research on teacher education in reading, however, lags far behind other areas of reading research. According to a review of Anders et al. (2000) report, "in the past 30 years, 19,457 studies have been conducted on reading, and 140 studies have focused on preservice reading education" (p. 724). Although scant, the research that has been conducted regarding preservice teacher education in reading has focused on preservice teachers' reading skills, attitudes, habits, home and school experiences, performance on tests, and belief systems. Clearly, more research is needed on how preservice teachers obtain knowledge about reading. Anders et al. (2000) suggest that teacher educators need to study their own practices. Hoffman and Pearson (2000) highlight the importance of studying how we actually teach teachers to be teachers of reading.

One response to this gap in research was the establishment of The National Commission on Excellence in Elementary Teacher Preparation for Reading Instruction by the International Reading Association whose charge was to "describe current reading teacher education and identify program factors that lead to excellent reading instruction and reading achievement" (Maloch, Fine, & Flint, 2003, p. 348). A preliminary analysis of excellent teacher preparation programs revealed that *personalized* teaching by faculty is one of eight key elements. "Such personalized teaching includes attention to the individual student, scaffolding of learning, and the creation of a caring context for learning" (Harmon et al., 2001, p. 268). In the study reported here, the researchers suggest that when literacy professors respond to students' sticky note comments as they read text-related material about literacy, there is the potential for modeling a caring learning environment, providing preservice teachers with individual attention, and scaffolding learning.

Comprehension

Reading teachers know that comprehension is the essence of reading and that it involves multiple processes including decoding, knowing vocabulary, relating the text to prior knowledge, and conscious processing (Pressley, 2000). Early studies regarding the teaching of reading comprehension were typically characterized as direct instruction models in which the teacher would select a strategy, teach it, and often assess students' comprehension (Williams, 2002). As a result of these early studies, the field of reading embraced the importance of prior knowledge, question generation, summarization, story grammar, and mental imagery (Pressley, 2000).

During the mid 80s, with the introduction of reciprocal teaching (Palinscar & Brown, 1984), studies began to focus on teaching multiple comprehension strategies (Pressley, 2000). The studies led to a focus on teaching reading comprehension strategies with direct teacher explanation as a key component. Developed by Duffy, Roehler, and Mason (1984), the "direct explanation" approach to teaching reading comprehension was to *train* teachers to be explicit in their instruction and to help teachers learn how to explain to children that reading is a problem solving process. Although the results of several studies conducted by Duffy et al. (1986) did suggest that teacher explanation increases students' awareness of thinking while reading, the results were not conclusive regarding reading achievement (Williams, 2002).

Based on the work of Rosenblatt (1978), additional studies lead to approaches to teaching reading comprehension known as transactional strategies instruction. In addition to teacher explanations of strategies, this type of instruction includes the teacher's modeling the strategy, scaffolding or assisting students as needed, and collaboration among the readers as they talk about text (Pressley, 2000; Williams, 2002). Research on how teachers learn to teach these strategies, however, is limited (Williams, 2002).

Influenced by the work of Vygotsky (1978) and the social nature of learning, views of reading comprehension strategy instruction that include talk about text extend to reader response theory. A review of the literature on children's responses to literature by Martinez and Roser (2001) revealed three characteristics of instruction that focus on children's responses to literature: "(a) teachers can shape children's responses through the organization of literature study, (b) children's responses during literature discussion are best nurtured when teachers and students assume different roles, and (c) a variety of instructional tools have been found to sustain children's responses" (p. 412). Instructional tools include response journals, discussion frames, and literature prompts.

Although not included in Martinez and Roser's (2001) literature response review, in this study, the researchers view the work of Harvey and Goudvis (2000), as a significant contribution to strategy instruction in reading comprehension. Based on the seminal work, *Mosaic of Thought*, by Ellin Oliver Keene and Susan Zimmerman (1997), in which they teach teachers how to engage students in the process of reading comprehension as a "mosaic of thought," Harvey and Goudvis (2000) provide explicit teaching strategies with classroom examples that encompass what research shows good readers do when they read. Good readers make connections, ask questions, visualize, infer, distinguish between important and less important information, and synthesize. One reading comprehension strategy that supports strategic reading by making connections is the sticky note strategy described at the outset of this paper.

In this study, we share how preservice teachers used a variation of the strategy to make sense of their reading methods textbook over one semester. Not only did we get a snippet of how they connected with the text, but we also provided them with practice in using the strategy as a learning tool that fostered making connections and asking questions. We share this study in light of the limited research on how preservice teachers learn to teach comprehension strategies (Williams, 2002).

Reading Assessment

Public and political agendas have placed reading assessment at the forefront of educational reform. Reading proficiency tests have reached an unprecedented peak as a national agenda. In fact, "because assessment and literacy standards are policy tools that have emerged primarily from a political context, a growing number of reading professionals feel their discretionary instructional powers slipping away in the wake of systematic reform" (Vacca, 2001, p. 175).

In addition, there is a body of literature that suggests how teachers prepare students for what has come to be known as "high-stakes" testing (Guthrie, 2002; McAuliffe, 1993). On the other hand, there is considerable discourse that challenges "high stakes" assessments (Calkins, Montgomery, & Santman, 1998; Hoffman, Assaf, & Paris, 2001; International Reading Association, 1999; Toll, 2002). Alternative, authentic assessments that are meaningful, inquiry and student centered, however, are still a major focal point of assessment practices to which reading teachers are committed (Afflerbach, 1993; Afflerbach & Kapinus, 1993; Barrentine, 1999; Calfee & Perfumo, 1993; Guthrie, Van Meter, Mitchell & Reed, 1994; Johnston, 1992; Paris et al., 1992).

According to Serafini (2000), "when assessment becomes a process of inquiry, an interpretive activity rather than simply the 'objective' measure of predetermined behaviors, teachers will be able to use assessment to make informed decisions concerning curriculum and instruction in their classrooms" (p. 392). Tierney's (2000) commentary reflects a similar notion. "I see the new millennium as marking a more enduring shift toward learner-centered assessment, encompassing a shift in why assessments are pursued as well as how and who pursues them" (p. 244). In this study we suggest one way to engage preservice teachers in a discussion about authentic assessment by scaffolding its application using the sticky note strategy.

The Study

Participants and Setting

The researchers are two university professors and a college professsor who teach literacy courses in the Midwest. The students included 26 preservice teachers in two classes of *Methods of Teaching Developmental Reading* at the university and 38 preservice teachers in two sections of the class entitled, *Meeting Individual Needs in Reading*, at the college. All of the students were juniors or seniors.

The preservice teachers at the university enrolled in *Methods of Teaching Developmental Reading* had taken one or two other reading courses entitled *Principles and Practices of Teaching Phonics, Developmental Language Literacy*, and/or *Reading in the Content Area*. After *Methods of Teaching*

Developmental Reading, these preservice teachers enroll in one or two other reading courses entitled *Reading Assessment and Intervention* and/or *Clinical Practicum in Reading*. The preservice teachers at the college enrolled in *Meeting Individual Needs in Reading* had taken at least three other reading courses entitled *Phonics, Processes, and the Structure of Language, Content Area Reading, Integrated Language Arts for Emergent Readers and Writers*, and/or *Teaching Reading and Writing in the Middle School*.

The preservice teachers enrolled in *Methods of Teaching Developmental Reading* were in the middle of their reading series coursework while the students enrolled in *Meeting Individual Needs in Reading* were at the end of their reading series coursework. All of the preservice teachers at the college and university had been admitted to their respective education department or division's teacher preparation program.

Procedure

For several years, one of the researchers had implemented the sticky note strategy in her reading classes in order to provide the preservice teachers with a response vehicle as they read their reading methods textbook, *Reading and Learning to Read* (Vacca, Vacca, Gove, Burkey, Lenhart, & McKeon, 2003). Although the preservice teachers were invited to share open-ended thoughts and comments regarding information found in the text, they were encouraged to wonder and make personal connections as they read. When the researcher responded to the students' sticky notes, she often wrote lengthy sticky note responses that clarified information or pointed out the quality of the students thinking and personal observations. The researcher enjoyed providing the preservice teachers with the individual attention and, in turn, the students often wrote "thank you" sticky notes in response. After sharing the idea with the co-authors and explaining the satisfaction that seemed to emerge from the strategy, the three professors decided not only to use the sticky notes, but also to analyze the results, thus providing the impetus for this study.

The research questions which guided this qualitative study were: (a) how can college reading professors engage preservice teachers in multiple levels of comprehension?; (b) how can college reading professors engage preservice teachers in making text-to-text, text-to-self, and text-to-world responses?; and (c) what types of responses do preservice teachers make when engaging in "text-to-text," "text-to-self," and "text-to-world" responses? At the outset of the semester, the university professors introduced the students to Harvey and Goudvis' (2000) sticky note strategy for reading comprehension. One researcher required that, after reading each of fifteen chapters of the methods textbook throughout the semester, the students needed to respond with sticky notes and post them in a folder. The second researcher required that they respond to ten of the fifteen chapters. As they were completed, the professors collected, read, and responded to them with personal comments. The third researcher modeled the strategy as a form of assessment mid-semester during the *Meeting Individual Needs in Reading* course by having the students read the International Reading Association's *Position Statement: High-Stakes Testing* (International Reading Association, 1999) and respond with sticky notes. All of the students were encouraged to write reflections, comments, thoughts, or questions on the sticky notes. The sticky notes were collected at the end of the semester.

Data Analysis

The sticky notes from the university classes were analyzed using the constant comparative method of descriptive analysis (Glaser & Strauss, 1967). After discussion and recursive analysis by the researchers, five themes emerged and were subsequently coded. The themes, categorical definitions, and codes are presented in Table 1. An outside reader, a university professor in the behavioral sciences, coded 20% of the data in order to provide for interrater reliability. He was in agreement with 90% of the previously coded sticky notes.

The third researcher involved her *preservice teachers* in the analysis and used the activity as a way to model sticky notes as a form of assessment. After reading the position statement and responding with the sticky notes, each theme that had been defined by the researchers was explained and placed as a title on pieces of chart paper. The preservice teachers were then instructed to take their sticky notes and place them on the theme-labeled chart paper that best characterized the note. After observing the number of sticky notes in each category, small group discussion took place regarding the content of the notes and how classroom teachers could use the strategy for assessment purposes.

Results and Discussion

Table 1 presents the themes, categorical definitions of the themes, their codes, and some examples of preservice teacher responses. The five types of themes were declaratory statements, affective statements, realization comments, content questions, and mentoring questions. Declaratory statements (DS) were non-judgmental comments that restated a thought or an idea that was explained in the chapter. An example of a student's declaratory statement is "Predictable books not only help with fluency but are a way for children to feel success at reading." Affective statements (AS) were comments that reflected a personal response like "I love the idea of having learning centers." Realization comments (RC) were comments that reflected an "aha" moment about an issue, term, phrase, or concept. An example of a preservice teacher's realization comment is "I think it is amazing how early children begin imitating written language." Content questions (CQ) were questions about content

Table 1. Data Analysis: Themes, Definitions, Codes, and Examples

Theme	Categorical Definition	Code	Examples
Declaratory Statements	Non-judgmental comments that restated a thought or an idea that was explained in the chapter.	DS	"Predictable books not only help with fluency but are a way for children to feel success at reading."
Affective Comments	Comments that reflected a personal response.	AC	"I love the idea of having learning centers."
Realization Comments	Comments that reflected an "aha" moment about an issue, term, phrase, or concept.	RC	"I think it is amazing how early children begin imitating written language."
Content Questions	Questions about content in the textbook.	CQ	"Better explain automaticity. I was confused."
Mentoring Questions	The preservice teachers asked for advice or elaboration beyond the text-based information.	MQ	"Are there certain comprehension strategies that you recommend more for a content book versus a storybook?"

in the textbook. Content questions included student responses like "Better explain automaticity. I was confused." Mentoring questions (MQ) were questions in which the preservice teachers asked for advice or elaboration beyond the text-based information like "Are there certain comprehension strategies that you recommend more for a content book versus a storybook?"

Table 2 presents the frequencies and percentages of sticky note responses for each class and is organized by professors and categories. There are several observations that the researchers glean from the findings. First, the preservice teachers in the second and third researchers' classes wrote more declaratory statements. It appears that these teacher preparation students viewed the task as an opportunity to reiterate information they deemed important in the reading. For example, in the *Methods of Teaching Developmental Reading* class, students wrote comments such as "Reading Recovery focuses on low-ability readers in the program receiving daily individual instruction for 15 minutes" and "Predictable texts are good for developing fluency because the kids can rely on the pattern of the book to read." One student decided to list the words he thought were important, "story frames, story map, KWL, think alouds, discussion webs." In the *Meeting Individual Needs in Reading* class, preservice teachers wrote comments such as, "The primary purpose of assessment is to help students by providing information about how instruction can be improved" and "It is unlikely that high-stakes assessments will ever be abandoned." These types of responses are on a literal level and appear to reflect a note-taking stance. While the researchers did not intend the preservice teachers to use the sticky note strategy as a vehicle for writing literal level information, the researchers do not think it is necessarily negative.

Table 2. Frequencies and Percentages of the Sticky Note Responses

PROFESSORS	N	DECLARATORY STATEMENTS	AFFECTIVE COMMENTS	REALIZATION COMMENTS	CONTENT QUESTIONS	MENTORING QUESTIONS	TOTAL
[McKeon] Required student responses to 15 chapters of *Reading and Learning to Read* (Vacca, Vacca, Gove, Burkey, Lenhart, & McKeon, 2003)	13	6 (3%)	42 (18%)	24 (10%)	68 (30%)	90 (39%)	230 (100%)
[Lenarz] Required student responses to 10 of the 15 chapters of *Reading and Learning to Read* (Vacca, Vacca, Gove, Burkey, Lenhart, & McKeon, 2003)	13	44 (30%)	38 (26%)	35 (24%)	9 (6%)	21 (14%)	147 (100%)
[Burkey] Required student responses to *Position Statement: High-Stakes Testing* (International Reading Association, 1999)	38	79 (43%)	40 (21%)	8 (4%)	61 (32%)	0 (0%)	188 (100%)

The students' declaratory responses identified key concepts and ideas from *Reading and Learning to Read* (Vacca et al., 2003) and *Position Statement: High-Stakes Testing* (International Reading Association, 1999) on their sticky notes. The students did need to read and decide what they viewed as significant information. Good readers know how to distinguish important information from less important information. "The ability to determine importance in text often requires us to use related comprehension strategies such as drawing inferences and summarizing information" (Harvey & Goudvis, 2000, p. 24). As we reflect on why the initial researcher's students did not tend to write declaratory statements, we speculate that, because she had used the strategy for several years, she tended to encourage the students to respond in a more personal manner and she wrote lengthy sticky note responses to the students. Furthermore, the researchers surmise that the preservice teachers in the third researcher's courses wrote declaratory statements, because they were trying to pinpoint important points in the position statement.

Another observation garnered from Table 2 is that preservice teachers in all of the classes wrote comments that were affective or personal in nature. For example in the *Methods of Teaching Developmental Reading* classes, students wrote such comments as: "I have no idea what method I learned to read by–Dad's not sure either–Books have filled my life for as long as I can remember–I learned somehow!"; "I hate standardized tests. I was terrible at them as a young student, even though I got excellent grades. I've never felt comfortable taking them and probably won't like teaching them."; and "I love the 'Have-a-Go' strategy. The idea of trying without worrying about right and wrong would have appealed to me as a child." Comments from the *Meeting Individual Needs in Reading* preservice teachers included: "Politicians out . . . Teachers in!!"; and "I often feel it is frustrating that politicians, school board members, and test publishers usually not educators make major decisions about schools and classrooms." As opposed to the declaratory statements and the questions, these comments demonstrated that the preservice teachers used the sticky notes as a way to associate what they were reading to personal experiences and/or opinions. On the one hand, they provided the students with a way to document schema; on the other hand, they served as a sounding board. They, in essence, were making connections. Good readers tap their prior experiences, knowledge, emotions and understandings when they read (Harvey & Goudvis, 2000; Keene & Zimmerman, 1997; Pressley, 2000).

Still another observation gleaned from Table 2 is that, although there were fewer realization comments written by the second researcher's preservice teachers, all of the classes did use the sticky notes to express an "aha" moment or thought that emerged based on the reading. Examples from two of the researchers' classes included: "I'm amazed as to how independent writing has become a big part of students' classroom time."; "I now know that my vocabulary is better today, because of all the reading I did as a kid!"; "Reading and writing connect!"; "I found the sections about scribbling to be very interesting. I think it is amazing how early children begin imitating written language."; and "I thought that the term automaticity was pretty interesting. I never really associated the word before with reading. I also liked the analogy to driving a car!" A realization comment written by a presevice teacher in the third researcher's class was: "I did not realize students scoring low on a test could lower my salary, but after thinking about it, I see that many things could affect it." These comments reveal that, indeed, the students realized they were gaining new information from reading. Harvey and Goudvis (2000) would characterize this as synthesizing. "Synthesizing information involves combining new information with existing knowledge to form an original idea, a new line of thinking, or a new creation" (p. 25).

Table 2 also reveals that the preservice teachers used the sticky notes to ask questions. Content questions were those in which the students wanted clarification or elaboration about a topic in the book or the position statement. For example, one *Methods of Teaching Developmental Reading* student wrote, "I'm confused about double-entry journals. Are they the same as response journals?" Another asked, "What's the difference between a basal and an anthology?" A preservice teacher in the *Meeting Individual Needs in Reading* class wanted to know, "How much has high-stakes testing increased in recent years?" And another student asked, "Why don't policy makers take into account other assessments?" In addition to content questions, two of the researchers' preservice teachers asked numerous mentoring questions. These were questions in which the students went beyond the text with thoughtful queries. Quite often these questions were practical in nature, and they were not addressed in the text. Some examples include: "Are the methods identified in the chapter appropriate if adapted to ISE older students?"; "Do readability formulas take into account diversity of students? If not, how do students from diverse factors fit it?"; "How common is it to come across a principal who has a different teaching philosophy than you do? How do you fix this without butting heads?"; and "What are some good approaches for teaching children with speech problems? Like if they are learning the word 'yellow' and they say 'lellow.' Do you correct them or what? What is the best strategy?" These types of questions seem to document that the students were thinking on a higher level about the content of the text; they were actually going beyond the text and responding in a "what if" frame of mind, much like questioning the author. "Proficient readers ask questions before, during, and after reading. They question the content, the author, the events, the issues, and the ideas in the text" (Harvey & Goudvis, 2000, p. 22). Although the second researcher's preservice teachers did not ask questions on a mentoring level, the researchers surmise that because the sticky note activity was a one-time event and due to the nature of the reading assignment, the opportunity for this type of response was not evident.

In addition to the content of the sticky notes, which was the researchers' primary source of data, our discussion now turns to the process of learning about sticky notes as an assessment tool that occurred with the third researcher's preservice teachers in the *Meeting Individual Needs in Reading* class.

To learn about the developmental nature of comprehension teachers are more likely to rely upon tools that authentically assess (Barrentine, 1999; International Reading Association, 1995). They will collect performance samples in relation to the student's success on a particular task or a set of reading tasks (Guthrie et al., 1994). Assessment does not have to be formal (Paris et al., 1992). At times the most informal type of assessment can provide the teacher with a wealth of information about the development of comprehension. A particular informal assessment utilized to assess comprehension development is through the use of sticky notes.

In this project, after having her students place their sticky notes on the posters that indicated the initial categories, the third researcher then proceeded to ask, "What can we learn from the number of sticky notes on each poster?" The preservice teachers then made comments such as, "we are focusing more on what is in the context of the article than thinking about it." Another preservice teacher said, "Even though we read the article, we still have a quite a few questions about the content." Someone else volunteered, "It looks like we had opinions about the article." The third researcher and her preservice teachers then continued the conversation by discussing how the teacher can learn information about students' comprehension by looking at the overall number of responses when using the sticky note strategy. Effective assessment is interpretive and social; therefore, teachers need to be reflective assessors (Johnston, 1992).

The next discussion focused on the content of the sticky notes. The third researcher explained that to get more information about the students' comprehension development, the content of the sticky notes had to be read. The class of preservice teachers was then divided up into four groups. Each group analyzed the content of a specific themed poster. The researcher asked each group to answer the following question: "What can I learn?" Discussions then focused on the content of the posters. The preservice teachers that analyzed the declaratory statement information pointed out that the comments were either restatements from the text or were directly copied from the article. As pointed out earlier, distinguishing important information from the less important is a skill strategic readers use (Harvey & Goudvis, 2000). The preservice teachers analyzing the affective comments reported that most of the comments were "I like . . ." or "I don't agree with." One preservice teacher explained that there were a large number of responses, because the article itself was written so the reader would generate an opinion and that, even though it involves higher order thinking skills, it was easy for the reader to affectively respond. The discussion then turned toward the realization comments. The preservice teachers acknowledged that both the affective and realization themes depended on higher-order thinking skills and that they required different levels of engagement. They pointed out that for a reader to make an "aha" connection, it requires a more advanced level of thinking which is a more complex process. Making connections and synthesizing information to formulate new ideas are characteristics of good readers (Harvey & Goudvis, 2000). Finally, content questions were analyzed. The preservice teachers believed that the themed chart paper really contained important information. The questions on the poster related to specific information from the article as well as additional related questions. The preservice teachers discussed that the different types of questions demonstrate the different levels of reading engagement and understanding. Questioning is another strategy that good readers use (Harvey & Goudvis, 2000).

The final discussion focused on the overall usage of sticky notes. When asked, "What can we learn from sticky notes about comprehension development?" overwhelmingly the preservice teachers were amazed. They had a *realization* about the amount of comprehension information teachers can learn from this authentic instructional activity. They learned that, by shifting the focus from an instructional activity to an assessment tool by asking oneself, "What can I learn from the students sticky notes?", teachers can tap into the process of reading comprehension for individual children. Balancing literacy assessment practices is important (Afflerbach & Kapinus 1993). The preservice teachers also acknowledged the value of authentic literacy assessments, such as the sticky note activity, "Because the students would not know they were being assessed. It was a fun activity."

Teachers today want to know more about factors that contribute to their students' comprehension development and about how the students think while reading. Providing preservice teachers with the sticky note activity and having them analyze it as an assessment tool seemed to assist these future teachers in understanding the literacy-instructional-assessment process. Professors of future literacy teachers need to document effective strategies for teaching preservice teachers (Hoffman & Pearson, 2000). This approach to scaffolding teacher preparation students into viewing teaching and assessment as reciprocal tasks seemed to work with this group of students quite well.

Limitations and Implications

We acknowledge that this study is limited. Although we made the initial attempt to code the sticky notes, our analysis can be taken further. Researchers need to look beyond categories when analyzing text (Silverman, 2000). Our next steps might be to look more closely at the the nature of the preservice teachers' declaratory statements and ask the question, "As teacher-preparation students read a literacy methods textbook, do certain themes emerge as topics of importance to them as they read?" What about their questions about the content presented in the text? We might examine the question: "How does one characterize preservice teachers' questions after reading text information about literacy? Is it literal information they don't understand? Is it inferential information? Is it practical information?" These questions would focus on the nature of teacher preparation studies that are sorely needed (Hoffman & Pearson, 2000; Williams, 2002). Tapping into the literature on the role of text learning in classrooms might be an avenue that would help us understand how teachers learn (Wade & Moje, 2000).

There are other questions that arise from the researchers' data that are unanswered. In what areas do students have mentoring questions that are unanswered in the text? Do age and experience influence the type of affective comments they construct using sticky notes? Needless to say, the researchers understand that this study only touches on a small bit of information about a strategy that the researchers used in their university classrooms. In addition, the informal discussions by the preservice teachers who were learning an assessment strategy might have been crafted to reflect more analytic data. The researchers might have conducted interviews, done follow-ups as students tutored children throughout the course, and investigated whether or not they used the strategy and how they interpreted the results. The researchers agree that following teachers as they implement strategies is important and that assessing children's knowledge following the teaching of a strategy is crucial (Williams, 2000).

Preservice reading teacher programs, however, typically involve multiple experiences including self-evaluations, coursework, field experiences, and examinations (Anders, Hoffman, & Duffy, 2000). What seems to be lacking in the field of teacher preparation are studies that more closely examine the nature of preservice teacher experiences in which they actually construct knowledge about reading and assessment. In this study, the researchers began to examine one strategy in which preservice teachers were first taught a comprehension strategy in two sections of a reading methods class, and then were asked to use it as a *proactive* way to express their thinking and learning as they read a reading methods textbook. The researchers responded to the sticky notes with thoughtful and often caring comments, and they provided the preservice teachers with individual attention as part of the process. In addition, two classes at the college learned an authentic assessment tool by encountering the process first-hand. All of the professors scaffolded learning on some level. In addition to other characteristics, quality teacher preparation programs foster caring, individual attention, and scaffold learning (Harmon et al., 2001).

A Closing Comment

Teacher preparation programs are under scrutiny; research strategies for teaching teachers how to teach reading comprehension are nebulous; and assessment practices on all levels of education are "under fire." Our hope is that we have motivated literacy professors to consider adapting the strategies we have tried; we also hope they will investigate, study, and analyze the nature of learning experiences in which they engage *their* preservice teachers. According to Hoffman and Pearson (2000), "[it] is becoming increasing clear that if reading teacher educators don't take initiative and responsibility for setting research goals, someone else will" (p. 41).

References

Afflerbach, P. (1993). STAIR: A system for recording and using what we observe and know about our students. *The Reading Teacher, 47*(3) 260-263.

Afflerbach, P., & Kapinus, B. (1993). The balancing act. *The Reading Teacher, 47*(1), 62-64.

Anders, P. L., Hoffman, J. V., & Duffy, G. G. (2000). Teaching teachers to teach reading: Paradigm shifts, persistent problems, and challenges. In M. L. Kamil, P. B. Mosenthal, P. D. Pearson, & R. Barr (Eds.), *Handbook of reading research: Vol. 3* (pp.719-742). Mahwah, NJ: Lawrence Erlbaum Associates.

Barrentine, S. J. (Ed.). (1999). *Reading assessment: Principles and practices for elementary teachers*. Newark, DE: International Reading Association.

Calfee, R. C., & Perfumo, P. (1993). Student portfolios: Opportunities for a revolution of assessment. *The Journal of Reading, 36*, 532-537.

Calkins, L., Montgomery, K., & Santman, D. (1998). *A teacher's guide to standardized reading tests: Knowledge is power*. Portsmouth, NH: Heinemann.

Dowhower, S. L. (1999). Supporting a strategic stance in the classroom: A comprehension framework for helping teachers help students to be strategic. *The Reading Teacher, 52*(7), 672-689.

Duffy, G. G., Roehler, L. R., & Mason, J. (Eds.) (1984). *Comprehension instruction: Perspectives and suggestions*. New York: Longman.

Duffy, G. G., Roehler, L. R., Meloth, M.S., Vavrus, L. G., Book, C., Putnam, J., et al. (1986). The relationship between explicit verbal explanations during reading skill instruction and student awareness and achievement: A study of reading teacher effects. *Reading Research Quarterly, 21*, 237-252.

Glaser, B. G., & Strauss, A. L. (1967). *The discovery of grounded theory: Strategies for qualitative research*. New York: Aldine de Gruyter.

Guthrie, J. T. (2002). Preparing students for high-stakes test taking in reading. In A.

E. Farstrup & S. J. Samuels (Eds.), *What research has to say about reading instruction* (pp. 370-391). Newark, DE: International Reading Association.

Guthrie, J. T., Van Meter, P., Mitchell, A, & Reed, C. T. (1994). Performance assessments in reading and language arts. *The Reading Teacher, 48*(3), 266-271.

Harmon, J., Hedrick, W., Martinez, M., Perez, B., Keehn, S., Fine, J. C. et al. (2001). Features of excellence of reading teacher preparation programs. In J. V. Hoffman, D. L. Schallert, C. M. Fairbanks, J. Worthy, & B. Maloch (Eds.), *50th yearbook of the National Reading Conference* (pp. 262-274). Chicago: National Reading Conference.

Harvey, S., & Goudvis, A. (2000). *Strategies that work: Teaching comprehension to enhance understanding.* York, ME: Stenhouse.

Hoffman, J. V., Assaf, L. C., & Paris, S. G. (2001). High-stakes testing in reading: Today in Texas, tomorrow? *The Reading Teacher, 54*(5), 482-492.

Hoffman, J., & Pearson, P. D. (2000). Reading teacher education in the next millennium: What your grandmother's teacher didn't know that your granddaughter's teacher should. *Reading Research Quarterly, 35*(1), 28-44.

International Reading Association. (n.d.). *Standards for reading professionals.* Retrieved January 5, 2004, from http://www.reading.org/advocacy/standards/introduction.html

International Reading Association (1995). *Reading assessment in practice.* Newark, DE: Author.

International Reading Association (1999). High-stakes assessment in reading: A position statement of the International Reading Association. *The Reading Teacher, 53*(3), 257-264.

Johnston, P. H. (1992). Nontechnical assessment. *The Reading Teacher, 46*(1), 60-62.

Keene, E. O., & Zimmerman, S. (1997). *Mosaic of thought: Teaching comprehension in a reader's workshop.* Portsmouth, NH: Heinemann.

Maloch, B., Fine, J., & Flint, A. S. (2002). 'I just feel like I'm ready': Exploring the influence of quality teacher preparation on beginning teachers. *The Reading Teacher, 56*(4), 348-350.

Martinez, M. G., & Roser, N. L. (2001). A review of research on children's responses to literature. In J. V. Hoffman, D. L. Schallert, C. M. Fairbanks, J. Worthy, & B. Maloch (Eds.), *50th yearbook of the National Reading Conference* (pp. 409-418). Chicago: National Reading Conference.

McAuliffe, S. (1993). A study of the differences between instructional practice and test preparation. *The Journal of Reading, 36,* 524-530.

National Reading Panel. (2000). *Teaching children to read: An evidence-based assessment of the scientific research literature on reading and its implications for reading instruction.* Washington, DC: Author.

No Child Left Behind Act of 2001, Pub. L. No. 107-110.

Palincsar, A. S., & Brown, A. L. (1984). Reciprocal teaching of comprehension-fostering and monitoring activities. *Cognition and Instruction, 1,* 117-175.

Paris, S. G., Calfee, R. C., Filby, N., Hiebert E. H., Pearson, P. D., Valencia, S. W., & Wolf, K. P. (1992). A framework for authentic literacy assessment. *The Reading Teacher, 46*(2), 88-98.

Pressley, M. (2000). What should comprehension instruction be the instruction of? In M. L. Kamil, P. B. Mosenthal, P. D. Pearson, & R. Barr (Eds.), *Handbook of reading research: Vol. 3* (pp. 545-561). Mahwah, NJ: Lawrence Erlbaum Associates.

Pressley, M., Brown, R., El-Dinary, P. B., & Afflerbach, P. (1995). The comprehension instruction that students need: Instruction fostering constructively responsive reading. *Learning Disabilities Research and Practice, 10,* 215-224.

Pressley, M., El-Dinary, P., & Brown, R. (1992). Skilled and not-so-skilled reading: Good information processing and not-so-good information processing. In M. Pressley, K. Harris, & J. Guthrie (Eds.), *Promoting academic competence and literacy in school* (pp. 91-127). San Diego, CA: Academic Press.

Rosenblatt, L. M. (1978). *The reader, the text, the poem: The transactional theory of the literary work.* Carbondale, IL: Southern Illinois University Press.

Serafini, F. (2000). Three paradigms of assessment: Measurement, procedure, and inquiry. *The Reading Teacher, 54*(4), 384-393.

Silverman, D. (2000). Analyzing talk and text. In N. Denzin & Y. S. Lincoln (Eds.), *Handbook of qualitative research* (pp. 821-834). London: Sage Publications.

Taraban, R., Rynearson, K., & Kerr, M. (2000). College students' academic performance and self-reports of comprehension strategy use. *Reading Psychology, 21,* 283-308.

Tierney, R. J. (2000). How will literacy be assessed in the next millennium? *Reading Research Quarterly, 35*(2), 244-245.

U. S. Department of Education. (n. d.). *Elementary & secondary education: Table of contents.* Retrieved January 5, 2004, from http://www.ed.gov/policy/elsec/leg/esea02/index.html

Vacca, J. L., Vacca, R. T., Gove, M. K., Burkey, L. C., Lenhart, L. A., & McKeon, C. A. (2003). *Reading and learning to read* (5th ed.). Boston: Allyn & Bacon.

Vacca, R. T. (2001). A focus on the media, policy-driven literacy practices, and the work of reading professionals. In R. Flippo (Ed.), *Reading researchers: In search of common ground* (p. 175). Newark, DE: International Reading Association.

Villaume, S. K., & Brabham, E. G. (2002). Comprehension instruction: Beyond strategies. *The Reading Teacher, 55*(7), 672-676.

Vygotsky, L. (1978). *Mind in society: The development of higher psychological processes.* Cambridge, MA: MIT Press.

Wade, S. E., & Moje, E. B. (2000). The role of text in classroom learning, In M. L. Kamil, P. B. Mosenthal, P. D. Pearson, & R. Barr (Eds.), *Handbook of reading research: Vol. 3* (pp.609-627). Mahwah, NJ: Lawrence Erlbaum Associates.

Williams, J. P. (2002). Reading comprehension strategies and teacher preparation. In A. E. Farstrup & S. J. Samuels (Eds.), *What research has to say about reading instruction.* Newark, DE: International Reading Association.

Woloshyn, V., Willoughby, T., Wood, E., & Pressley, M. (1990). Elaborative interrogation and representational imagery facilitate adult learning of facts presented in paragraphs. *Journal of Educational Psychology, 82,* 513-524.

Wood, E., Motz, M., & Willoughby, T. (1998). Examining students' retrospective memories of strategy development. *Journal of Educational Psychology, 90,* 698-704.

THE POWER OF PROFESSIONAL DEVELOPMENT AND POLITICS IN LITERACY TEACHER EDUCATION

Impacting Literacy Politics, Policies, and Legislation: Moving from Inactive Idlers and Reactive Regretters to Proactive Professionals

Francine Falk-Ross
Northern Illinois University

Mona W. Matthews
Georgia State University

Mary Beth Sampson
Texas A&M University-Commerce

Barbara J. Fox
North Carolina State University

Jill Lewis
New Jersey City University

Maryann Mraz
University of North Carolina

Jill Reddish
University of West Georgia

D. Ray Reutzel
Utah State University

Loraine T. Pace
Utah House of Representatives
Co-chair of the House Education Committee

Abstract

This chapter summarizes and extends the expert knowledge provided by five politically active literacy educators and a state representative. The written reflections are a follow-up to their formal presentations at the annual CRA conference's Teacher Education Division meeting. Each writer reflects on a different area in which literacy professionals can focus their energies toward becoming more involved in the political arena in order to influence national literacy issues. The topics of focus include review of historical mandates, suggestions for initial communications and contacts, knowledge of influential factors, and increases in political awareness. The overlap in the presenters' interests and the power of their suggestions are important for literacy educators to consider closely.

Traditionally, most educators have not viewed politics as an integral component of their professional lives. Yet, in today's world, politics and education are intertwined as decisions concerning curriculum, budgets, and assessment made at the state and national levels affect the work of literacy professionals. Consequently, many of us now realize that our past inattentiveness to the political world is an untenable posture. As educators with responsibility for preparing preservice and inservice teachers to create effective classroom literacy environments, we have a professional obligation to advocate for literacy issues in political arenas. Our knowledge of and experiences with literacy could inform the political debates and perhaps effect policy decisions in positive ways. However, a desire to contribute is not sufficient, for we must do so in ways that invite others to listen. Because this is a discourse for many of us, we often might find ourselves feeling unsure as to the best way to proceed in order to positively impact opinions, policies, and legislation and wondering if it is possible for an individual to "make a difference."

All of the above were among the concerns that were voiced at the 2002 College Reading Association Teacher Education Division meeting exploring five "hot topics": Decision Making, Policy and Legislation, Professionalism, Technology, and Teacher Shortages and Alternative Certification Programs. A survey was given at the conclusion of the 2002 session asking the attendees what the Teacher Education Division should focus on during the 2003 meeting. When the results were tallied, 91% of the 110 attendees had selected Policy and Legislation as their number one choice. Written comments verified that the participants wanted an information session sharing the perspectives and experiences of individual educators who had positively interacted with public officials and impacted policy and legislation.

In order to meet these definitive requests, the decision was made that the 2002 Teacher Education Division session should consist of a panel that included both educators who had been politically active for many years and those who were relatively new to political proactiveness. It was important that panel members had experiences that enabled them to share how they had individually proactively increased their political awareness, effectively communicated issues and perspectives, developed allies in the political system, and positively impacted the educational environment for children.

This article is a result of that session. Five politically astute CRA members and one state representative share their perspectives and experiences. Each has worked to influence the political process for the benefit of literacy education. Taken together, these individuals begin to assist us in creating a basic understanding of the register for communicating politically within the genre of politics.

Of Professors and Politics Effectively Shaping Public Literacy Policy: A Collaborative Perspective

In this first section, D. Ray Reutzel with Loraine T. Pace describe their collaboration. First, Ray provides background for viewing current literacy issues, and then he and Loraine offer suggestions for literacy educators interested in collaborating with policy makers in the political process.

Background on Current Literacy Issues

The pendulum of literacy instructional practice has swung back and forth between pedagogical and philosophical extremes for more than 200 years in U.S. educational history. During these years, debates about literacy policy and practice were largely confined to persons within the educational establishment. Not until the past decade have politicians seized upon "literacy" as both a national political tool and an objective for reform.

In the mid-1990s, President Clinton began an effort to make operational the plans of the meetings of the National Governor's Conventions as embodied in the legislation called *Goals 2000: Educate America Act* (U.S. Department of Education, 1994). Along with a focus on increased professional development in literacy education, President Clinton strongly supported and urged nationwide testing in reading and mathematics. Simultaneously from within the congressionally funded testing service, the *National Assessment of Education Progress (NAEP)*, 1994 data were released in May of 1995 showing that the literacy establishment's curricular flirtations with "whole language" had resulted in measurably significant national and local declines in fourth grade reading scores. Taken together, these events converged at a point in history where "literacy education" attracted the attention of national politicians and policymakers.

Data from across the nation were amassed not only showing the failure of "whole language" to deliver a more literate public, but also that failure to learn to read on grade level at an early age, by third-grade, was clearly correlated with nearly every undesirable social, political, and economic malady (Fielding, Kerr, & Rosier, 1998). Add to the drama of declining national reading achievement in 1995, contentious "reading wars," and a professional declaration of war on "quantitative" research methodology as inadequate and unenlightened. Furthermore, fascination among literacy researchers with researching teacher attitudes and beliefs about literacy instruction as well as a perceived penchant in the literacy research community for regarding student motivation over literacy achievement were portrayed in the press and in the U.S. Congress as misguided since student reading achievement among those in the lowest 10th percentile was slipping across the nation (Fourth Grade Reading Highlights: The Nation's Report Card, NAEP, 2000). As a consequence, literacy researchers and their research were characterized by the press and politicians as unscientific and focused on tertiary issues unrelated to the concerns of the American public. In the late 1990s, literacy instruction was thought to be in dire need of reform. Reading reform as policy reform was first to take the shape of *The Reading Excellence Act.*

The Reading Excellence Act national legislation consisted of federal funding targeted to underachieving and poverty schools where lagging reading achievement needed immediate attention. Furthermore, the research to be used to "reform" literacy education in these underachieving schools was to meet the high bar of "scientific" standards accepted within other highly regarded professional fields such as engineering, business, nursing, and medicine. No longer would something as socially, politically, and economically powerful as literacy is left to the "educationists."

With the election of George W. Bush in 2000 to the U.S. Presidency, the literacy policy direction, already well ensconced in bi-partisan efforts within the U.S. Congress, was furthered with the reauthorization of the *Elementary and Secondary Education Act of 1964* into the sweeping legislative reform of public education known as *No Child Left Behind.* Within this legislation, the scientific reading research agenda and the assurance that early reading instruction would include attention to early, intensive, explicit phonics instruction was made law. It is important to note that *No Child Left Behind* is not Democrat or Republican law, but American law. It represents the will of the people as manifested in the acts of their elected representatives from 435 congressional districts and 50 states. This significant new federal intervention into state or local education provided federal funds to states for *Reading First* grants to cement the reading reforms begun in the mid-to-late1990s.

Only now, with the proverbial political wolf not only at its door, but also sitting within its parlor and warming itself by the fire, did the literacy profession awake from its deep political apathy, even antipathy, to an awareness of its state. Having previously ignored the unrelenting criticisms of the press, the mounting public outcry, and the gradual but steady gaze of politicians, the world of literacy education is now in a state of a "hostile" take over.

Predictably, some among us have continued down the well-worn academic path of bemoaning the interference and ignorance of public representatives interjecting themselves and their ill-begotten policies into literacy education where they have no expertise. Such individuals continue to operate as if they believe they still have power to coerce change through their expert knowledge of the field seemingly unaware that the contentions of the "reading and research paradigm wars" of the 1990s had stripped them of nearly all of their credibility with the public and the politicians.

Still others, during this same period, have become tacitly aware of the potentially dangerous waters that lay ahead if the literacy profession were to continue its flirtations with fringe research topics, advocacy of untested curricular innovations, and philosophical flights of fancy that snubbed the public's declared desire to focus on evidence-based literacy instruction that clearly and positively affect literacy achievement. This group of literacy professionals aligned themselves with a professional movement in the mid to late 1990s known as "balanced literacy" seeing not too far off the signs of political interest that could result in a substantial loss of power, voice, and presence related to the future of literacy education.

Nonetheless, we find ourselves as a profession now in a deep political and policy abyss looking up without a ladder. How did the literacy profession, one so deeply committed to democratic values as integral to schooling and education, so distance itself from the very product of that democratic process itself by ignoring, even failing to acknowledge the desires of the public and its elected representatives in our debates, research, and dialog? Have we, as a profession, failed to learn one critical civics lesson taught so eloquently and well by Edmund Burke (Bartlett, 1919) in his Speech on the Conciliation of America. He said, "All government,—indeed, every human benefit and enjoyment, every virtue and every prudent act,—is founded on compromise . . ." As a literacy profession, we can ill afford to continue living in the Burger King fantasy world where we think can have it our way! We must learn now, before it is everlastingly too late, the art of compromise and political engagement.

Having said this, I have endeavored since 2001 to become very much involved in local political matters potentially affecting education, but in particular early childhood education and literacy education. I have contacted my local legislative representatives and maintain a continuing personal contact. Furthermore, I have tried to involve myself with my local representative in literacy and educational issues in the state, and much to my surprise and pleasure, my local representative has made valiant efforts to keep me involved and informed as well. Together, Representative Loraine Pace of the Utah Legislature and I have fashioned a list of suggestions that we shared at the past 2003 Teacher Education Division meeting at the CRA Conference in Corpus Christi, TX. Stemming from our joint efforts, we offer the list below to those who want not only to become engaged in the political process but who honestly want to learn the art of "compromise" and succeed, at least to some degree, in having a voice to shape the literacy policy of their local, state, and national governments.

Suggestions for Successfully Engaging in the Political Process as Literacy Educators

1. Get to know your local, state, and national representatives. Obtain their contact information including e-mail, phone number, and business address.
2. Learn how to make positive constituent contacts with legislators. Invite a

legislator to lunch to offer your expertise, insights, and involvement. Help them see you as a resource to which they may turn when in need of information.

3. Do not offend your legislators. Respect their time and intelligence. Inform yourself about issues and be prepared to offered informed opinions that show a balance of interests. Come prepared to listen as well as to advocate your position.

4. Become familiar with the legislative process (sequence of events) so that your contacts can be timely.

5. Be a credible, non-partisan lobbyist that a legislator can trust. Always, always, always tell the truth and be absolutely trustworthy. Get your facts straight and be able to document your assertions. Offer to make available an *executive summary* of factual information for the use of your legislator on demand.

6. Legislators are not miracle workers. Do not present problems without simultaneously presenting potential solutions and ideas.

7. Legislators are bound by laws and ethics. Do not offer gifts, services, etc. that would compromise their integrity.

8. Legislators do not only deal with educational issues. Many legislators deal with a wide range of issues including zoning, plumbing codes, natural resources, transportation, etc. You are the expert on education and must narrow the many issues to a concise list of only two or three priority issues for discussion and action.

9. Put a face on the effects of legislation. Bring children, teachers, parents who are affected by legislation (positive or negative) to advocate for your position on the issues. When asked to testify the same is also true, put a real face on the effects of legislation.

10. Remain in regular contact with elected representatives. Go out of your way to keep communications constant and positive. A "thank you" note goes a long way when a legislator has put in many long hours of service without adequate remuneration much like those of us who work in education! Ask to be put on their mailing or e-mail distribution list for upcoming issues, reports, and legislation that may impact educational funding, policy, or practices (See Appendix for electronic mailing list information).

Advocacy for the Literacy Professional: A Federal Perspective

In this section, Barbara Fox presents information for readers interested in advocacy at a federal level. She provides a description of three requirements for successful advocacy: knowing whom to contact, knowing how to frame messages, and knowing when to speak out on issues.

Literacy educators engage in many different advocacy activities from speaking out on behalf of effective literacy programs to championing quality teacher education. The skills literacy educators bring to advocacy at the community and state levels are the same abilities needed to be a successful literacy advocate in the United States House of Representatives and the Senate. My interest in the federal legislative process goes back to the 1980s when I worked on the Senate Education Arts and Humanities Subcommittee (now known as the Subcommittee on Children and Families). My perspective was further shaped when I chaired committees on government relations and social issues for the International Reading Association, the College Reading Association, and the North Carolina Reading Association. Based on these experiences, it is my perspective that successful advocacy depends in large part on knowing whom to contact, how to frame messages and when to speak out on issues. First and foremost, it is important to make the right contacts on Capitol Hill.

Whom to Contact

By far and away, literacy educators are most likely to affect legislation by contacting the legislators who represent them in Congress. While it is obvious that legislators depend on the votes of their constituents for reelection, what may not be so obvious is that legislators take their constituents very seriously. The best place to be heard and the first point of contact is a legislator's personal office. Personal offices are staffed by many legislative assistants, one of whom is responsible for tracking education legislation. Legislative assistants are an important link in the advocacy chain. If an advocate cannot meet face-to-face with a Representative or Senator, the education legislative assistant is the next best contact. A second advocacy channel consists of legislators who serve on the Senate Subcommittee on Children and Families, the House Subcommittee on Education Reform (preschool through high school) and the House Subcommittee on Education and the Workforce (adult issues). Each subcommittee has its own staff that assist in crafting legislation and gathering information relevant to issues. It is therefore important to contact not only the legislators on the subcommittees, but also the subcommittee staff. Staffs in personal offices and on subcommittees are potentially influential front line contacts when busy legislative agendas preclude a face-to-face meeting with a Representative or Senator.

How to Craft the Messages

Success rests on the content of the message, to be sure, but success also depends on how the message is crafted. A high-impact message is concise, factual and clear. It addresses only one issue or bill. Effective letters are one page long and ask for a reply or action. Whether writing letters, sending faxes or visiting legislators, an effective message explains how the issue or bill will impact the legislator's district, offers solutions and is stated in terms everyone understands. In delivering messages, it is important for the advocate to know the member's district and voting history. This enables the literacy educator to contextualize the issue or bill in a framework that is not only personally relevant to the legislator, but also important for the literacy community. Personal efforts also may be combined with the advocacy activities of professional associations who have a constant presence on Capitol Hill, such as the International Reading Association or the American Library Association.

When to Advocate

The most effective time to advocate for literacy is just before or just after a bill has been introduced. The time to influence a new bill, legislation under consideration for first time, is before the bill is introduced. For the reauthorization of legislation, the best time to have an effect is before the bill is marked-up, a process whereby initial changes are made to the introduced bill. It is important to deliver an advocacy message before mark-up so that changes will be in the version that each body, House and Senate, use as a working draft. The budget cycle is another consideration. If an advocate is requesting resources, it is important to make the request before the budget is crafted and agreed on.

It is commonly accepted practice for literacy educators to champion sound literacy practices and programs in schools and communities. The clear federal focus on reforming education in general, and literacy in particular, makes the early twenty-first century a critical time to advocate for sound literacy policy. Members of the House of Representatives, Senators and their staffs are interested in what literacy educators have to say, and literacy educators, based on their activities advocating at the school, community and state levels, have the knowledge and experience to affect national policy through advocacy.

Working as an Education Advocate: A State Perspective

Jill Lewis provides information for those interested in advocacy at the state level. She uses examples from her own experience to inform readers about how to increase political awareness, how to communicate opinions about issues effectively, and how to develop political allies.

Although as educators, we are surely tired of being beaten up and told what a bad job we are doing; we confidently assure each other that our critics are wrong. It is the 'each other' part of our responses that gets us into trouble. Yes, we do complain to colleagues about how misunderstood teachers are and how much we really know about how to help struggling readers. But we speak only to ourselves, to our cronies in the teachers' room, to our faculty at department meetings and to members of our inbred listserv. What we need is to be heard outside our circle. We need to be on the frontline fighting. I share examples from the 10-15 years of my own advocacy work to illustrate how to increase political awareness, how to effectively communicate views on issues, and how to develop allies in the political system.

How to increase your political awareness

My approach has been to learn different points of view and the arguments opponents have used. I share my own reform ideas with others for feedback and I make a concerted effort to read between the lines when new proposals for school reform are made. This enables me to know who might win and to predict both the intended and unintended consequences of these proposals. I use public opinion poll results, newspaper commentaries, and letters to the editor to identify and be able to anticipate changing or emerging education policies.

I rely on a wide array of sources and strategies to remain aware of education politics. This includes reading newspapers very carefully, tracking state and federal legislation at such websites as congress.org and those of my state legislature and state department of education. I join listservs that provide information which lead to research documents and which present different stances. I visit think tanks, mayors and governor websites, attend professional conferences, and develop collaborations for literacy projects to obtain different perspective. (Some useful URL's appear at the end of this paper in the Appendix.)

The information flow is overwhelming, especially since the Reading Excellence Act and No Child Left Behind (NCLB) legislation. Almost every organization has something to say about how children are learning (or not learning) to read, even those who have never taught offer solutions. While some ideas have merit, others are ill conceived. Education advocates need to discern both and need to be armed with information to support or counter ideas. Without this knowledge, we cannot be proactive.

How to communicate effectively about issues

Education advocates are not always sure their communication is effective. I use different methods for different audiences. However, in each instance, whether working alone or with a professional organization, I had to know to whom I was talking, and what I wanted. I also had to be prepared to put this in writing as part of the public record. The communication strategies I have used include (a) writing position papers in collaboration with others from my own state reading association and, sometimes, with other organizations; (b) writing commentaries and letters to the editor; (c) editing a themed journal on advocacy for our state reading association; (d) testifying at hearings of my state's Board of Education, Assembly Education Committee, and other policymaking groups; (e) writing/disseminating New Jersey Literacy Initiative Mission Statement in collaboration with other groups; and (f) speaking about advocacy and collaboration at state and national conferences.

As chair since 1986 of our state reading association's Legislation Committee, I call upon members to advocate for or against policy. I also encourage my own college students to become involved by reinforcing the belief that each of us can be an education advocate if we have information and understand why it is important.

How to develop allies in the political system

To develop allies in the political system, I had to first get organized. This included (a) understanding the relationship between the different policy bodies in the state, (b) familiarizing myself with current education policies and determining the positive and detrimental effects they could have on literacy programs and instruction, (c) learning how to access federal and state documents, and (d) identifying and joining listservs that offered up-to-date information. I also learned who the influential education policy makers were. Allies cannot be developed unless you know who shares your point of view and thus, might work with you, and you must also know who the powerful individuals are with whom you need to cultivate relationships.

Soon after I began my work as New Jersey Reading Association's (NJRAs) Legislation committee chair, I realized that not much would happen if I limited my sphere of influence to only other educators. To broaden this sphere, we developed an Advisory Board to the NJRA Legislation Committee. By including others in the advocacy work of our state reading association, we felt we would strengthen NJRA's position and reach a wider and more diverse audience. Representatives include stakeholders from the State Department of Education, business, the media, and the New Jersey Legislature. This Advisory Board works with NJRA's Legislation committee to write position papers and plan conferences.

The Advisory Board has helped enormously in our association's ability to develop allies in the political system. It has led to invitations to join committees or boards, including the New Jersey Business and Industry Association Education Committee and the Community Advisory Board for our state's major public television network. Board members have been asked to serve on statewide Task Forces to develop literacy policies and to assist with statewide literacy initiatives. Our participation in these activities has introduced us to individuals who influence state education policy, including directors of the state's Chamber of Commerce, State Library Association, Literacy Volunteers of America, and the State Department of Education, as well as members of the State Legislature and the State Board of Education. As a consequence of these efforts, state policymakers know they can call on us—and they do.

Each year our organization gives a Legislator of the Year award to profile a policymaker with whom we have worked or whose interests and legislation have been congruent with ours. Building allies in the system also means that when our association has concerns about pending legislation, we can call on influential individuals for assistance and support. By knowing what is happening and by working with others, I have contributed to getting bills defeated or passed; to making a difference in our state's new Administrative Code for teacher licensure; and to affecting the content and dissemination of our state standards for language arts literacy.

What is important, however, is to remember the bottom line; it is not about any one individual, rather education advocates need to help others develop their advocacy skills and be willing to share knowledge and strategies. Advocating for the profession and students should be viewed as a critical part of our professional responsibilities. In this way, we build the critical mass necessary for impacting education policy.

Teaching Teachers to be Politically Proactive: A Researcher to Practice Perspective

In this section, Maryann Mraz describes how insights from her dissertation about factors which are more likely to influence policy makers' decisions can be used to inform work with preservice and inservice teachers.

Identifying the factors that influence policy makers' decisions can contribute to a better understanding of how communication between policy makers and policy informants can occur most effectively (Roller, 2001). My interest in this led to the development of my doctoral research that examined the factors that influenced policy decisions in literacy education.

Both literacy professionals and policy makers who participated in the study agreed that public sentiment as communicated through constituency groups, individuals, and the media do influence policy decisions in literacy. These two participant groups, however, disagreed about the extent to which professional literacy educators and the organizations that represent them had been successful in communicating their views on literacy issues to policy makers.

One explanation given for literacy professionals' perceived lack of influence on the policy making process was the belief that literacy professionals were not, generally, prepared to communicate with policy makers. For example, literacy professionals tend to give complex, circuitous answers to questions about effective literacy practices, rather than concise summaries and solutions that busy policy makers seek.

The findings of the study suggest a need for educators to become informed about the policy-making process and knowledgeable about how to effectively communicate information about literacy learning to both community constituents, who influence policy makers, as well as to the policy makers themselves. Creating an awareness of the importance of communicating effectively and giving educators resources to do so can help to develop proactive professionals. One forum for presenting this information to preservice and inservice teachers is their coursework. At the undergraduate level, professors of reading methods courses can utilize resources such as on-line position statements from professional literacy organizations and state department documents that present current expectations for literacy instruction and issues under review. Class discussions and collaborative assignments can address the content of these sources and their potential use to convey to families and community constituents not only *what* is being done in classroom literacy instruction but also *why* particular practices are effective.

Graduate coursework can cover policy issues in greater depth, focusing on students' independent exploration of literacy policy topics. Multiple perspectives of issues (for example, high-stakes testing, the standards movement, models of reading instruction, and historical perspectives of literacy instruction) can be investigated by students. Government reports and documents, such as *The Report of the National Reading Panel* and the *No Child Left Behind Act* can be incorporated into class discussions and independent investigations. Listed at the end of this paper are sample sources that can inform preservice and in-service educators about policy issues in literacy education and suggest effective ways for educators to participate in the policymaking process. My research suggests, although, as literacy educators we think our views are important, unless we communicate these views in informed and concise ways policy makers will not perceive them as useful.

Helping Educators Proactively Increase Their Political Awareness Through Empowering Graduate Courses: A Curricular Perspective

Jill Reddish continues a higher education focus of advocacy and presents ideas for building political awareness in graduate courses.

For the past five years, I have worked with educators pursuing their Master's and Specialist degrees in Education. Despite being well-educated, competent individuals, in the arena of politics, the graduate students who enter my classes are generally not well informed about many of the state and federal policies affecting them. Furthermore, they often feel disempowered to change the political state of affairs in their state, county, or even in their schools. As one who strongly believes in democracy and the importance of the educators' voice in the formation of educational policies, I have made it an integral part of my courses to increase my students' political awareness and to empower them to take action to impact their educational environment for the benefit of children and themselves. When it comes to shaping policies on the state and national level, educators do not have to be a voiceless body.

Across the country in colleges of education, teachers are learning how to provide effective instruction, manage students better, and align curriculum and assessment in new and innovative ways. Yet, what impacts the content teachers teach and how teachers assess performance are not found in the graduate curriculum. Today, perhaps more than ever, education is very political and school curriculums are highly politicized (Ornstein and Hunkins, 2004). If our goal is to help educators shape their educational environments for the benefit of student learning, empowering educators with a political voice is critical. Empowerment of teachers involves elevating their professional knowledge and engaging teachers in decision making (Blase and Blase, 1994).

Graduate courses are practical settings for increasing educators' political awareness. Teachers enroll in graduate courses to learn and that includes learning about the politics and policies that impact their profession. In graduate courses, educators have more time and to think beyond managing day-to-day responsibilities and to consider broader issues. Generally, graduate courses include teachers from several schools with different ethnic and social backgrounds. This diversity presents an opportunity for rich political discussions.

There are many ways to increase political awareness in graduate courses. One is to share websites designed to inform educators about the political front. Most national and state professional education organizations have websites that contain information about current educational policies. Another way to increase political awareness among graduate students is to have them find and present to fellow educators websites related to educational policy. This is an excellent way to develop their ability to analyze and utilize the Internet and the political information available on it. State departments of education websites are also rich sources of information on state policies. Often information related to legislative decisions, Power Point presentations, and video taped press releases can be found on state department websites (See Appendix).

A third way to develop educators' understandings of the political process is to invite guest speakers to your class. Guest speakers afford students the opportunity to ask questions and engage in dialogue with someone who is directly involved in local, state, or federal politics. Guest speakers who have first-hand knowledge about how legislators arrive at decisions and who or what played a key role in the adoption of a given policy are not always available to the general public. If bringing guest speakers to campus is not practical, students can be asked to interview someone involved in local or state politics.

Understanding what happens behind the scenes in policy making is an important part of being a politically savvy educator. The benefits of helping educators increase their political awareness through graduate courses are immense. From a democratic perspective, this action creates more knowledgeable voters who can use their votes to achieve desired outcomes for the entire citizenry. From the educators' perspective, there is an increased sense of empowerment and a discovery of ways to be proactive versus reactive towards education policy making. For children, the inclusion of educators' voices in policymaking leads to the improvement of schools and student achievement (Shannon, 2001). Assisting educators to increase their political awareness should be an important outcome for teacher educators and college courses are excellent venues for accomplishing that goal.

Concluding Thoughts

During the past decade, the teaching and learning of reading have become a prominent topic in the political debates. Logic would suggest that those trained to understand the complexity of these issues would be influential and necessary participants in such discussions. However, in reality literacy educators are frequently passed over when these issues are considered, and are often viewed as ineffective participants in the debates. Consequently, frustration has intensified among literacy educators as decisions made in the political arena are affecting the day-to-day lives of literacy professionals and their students. This frustration was evident in the 2002 Teacher Education Division meeting as the members identified educational policy and legislation as their number one concern. The consistency in their survey rankings and the tenor of their comments during the meeting provided the impetus for planning the program for the 2003 meeting. As a result, representative politically active literacy professionals were invited to share information and recommendations of how to engage in the political process. Six of those professionals shared their ideas in this paper.

In summary, D. Ray Reutzel and Loraine T. Pace provided importance historical background to explain recent legislative moves and the differences in perspectives between policy makers and literacy educators. They suggested the use of compromise to gain access to, and credibility with, policy makers. Barbara Fox and Jill Lewis spoke of the importance of identifying those who are players in the political process and who, therefore, have the potential to influence federal and state policy. However, knowing whom to talk with is not sufficient. Both emphasized that we must also become knowledgeable about the issues, concise in our political communications, and collaborative in our work. Maryann Mraz and Jill Reddish discussed the importance of making political advocacy a focus of our work as teacher educators. They provide ideas for how to assist college students to develop their ability to participate in political debates and underscore the importance of knowing the facts and communicating effectively. Taken together, these leaders' ideas can serve as models to motivate and support the actions of all literacy educators for advocacy of political issues at national, state, and university forums. Suggestions for appropriate actions at the local levels of governance are not discussed in this article; instead this area is left to the discretion of educators to move forward with their special knowledge of the immediate political environments to gain rights and equity for literacy education, such as through passing school levies or collaborating with local politicians on projects that benefit literacy education efforts. Attention to the important topic of local politics is an excellent extension of this article.

Through the ideas presented in this paper, we hope to make some contribution to increasing our understanding of how to become proactive professionals in order to impact literacy politics, policies, and legislation. The TED plans to continue this focus during the 2004 meeting, and we hope through these efforts we can assist literacy professionals to develop a deeper awareness of how to communicate in a forum many of us have ignored during our professional tenures. These political arenas have their own audience, form, and functions and to be effective, we must learn what these are and how to present our views in ways that create a dialogue with our political partners rather than a diatribe that we share only among ourselves.

Reference

Bartlett, J. (1919). *Edmund Burke: Speech on the Conciliation of America, Vol. II, p. 169.* New York: Columbia Encyclopedia.

Blase. J. & Blase, J. R. (1994). *Empowering teachers: What successful principals do.* Thousand Oaks, CA: Corwin Press, Inc.

Fielding, L., Kerr, N., & Rosier, P. (1998). *The 90% reading goal: 90% of our students will read at or above grade level by the end of third grade.* Kennewick, WA: National Reading Foundation.

Fourth-Grade Reading Highlights 2000: The Nation's Report Card. Washington, D.C.: National Center for Educational Statistics, NCES 2001-513/National Assessment of Educational Progress.

Goals 2000: Educate America Act (1994). Washington, DC: U.S. Department of Education.

Mraz, M. (2003). Factors that influence policy decisions in literacy education: Perspectives of key policy informants. (Doctoral dissertation, Kent State University, 2002). *ProQuest Digital Dissertations.*

National Reading Panel (2000). *Report of the National Reading Panel: Teaching children* to read, an evidence-based assessment of the scientific research literature on *reading and its implications for reading instruction.* Washington, DC: National Institute of Child Health and Human Development.

NAEP 1994 Reading: A first look—Findings from the National Assessment of Educational Progress (revised edition). (1995). Washington, DC: U.S. Government Printing Office.

No Child Left Behind: Reauthorization of the Elementary and Secondary Education Act—1964. (2001). Washington, DC: U.S. Department of Education.

Ornstein, A. & Hunkins, F. (2004). *Curriculum foundations, principals, and issues(4th Ed)*. New York, NY: Pearson, Allyn and Bacon.

Reading First: No Child Left Behind. (2001). Washington, DC: U.S. Department of Education.

Report of the National Reading Panel: Teaching Children to Read. (2000). Washington, DC: National Institute for Child Health and Human Development.

Roller, C.M. (2001). A proposed research agenda for teacher preparation in reading. In Roller, C. M. (Ed.), *Learning to teach reading: Setting the research agenda*. Newark, DE: IRA.

Shannon, P. (2001). *Becoming political, too: new readings and writings on the politics of literacy education*. Portsmouth, NH : Heinemann.

Snow, C.E., Burns, M.S., & Griffin, P. (1998). *Preventing Reading Failure in Young Children*. Washington, D.C.: National Academy Press.

Title VIII - Reading Excellence Act. (1999). Washington, DC: U.S. Department of Education.

Appendix. Annotated Electronic Mailing Lists/Newsletters

International Reading Association web-site
The IRA website contains an continually updated government relations report, a slide presentation on evidence-based reading instruction, information specific to the *Reading First/No Child Left Behind* legislation and the *Reading First* application process, position statements on reading instruction and assessment, information on state and local councils involved in advocacy efforts, and links to government web-sites.

National Middle School Association (NMSA)
This website publishes a concise document titled, *No Child Left Behind: Implications for middle level learners.* This publication summaries the NCLB legislation, outlines implications for middle school teachers and students, and suggests a series of "action steps" that can be taken by schools to respond to the requirements of NCLB.

Center for the Improvement of Early Reading Achievement (CIERA)
This website offers current and archived reports on an assortment of literacy education and literacy policy issues.

Education Commission of the States (ECS)
This website provides information on policy issues and decisions specific to particular states, as well as aggregate information on state education initiatives and policies nationwide. Information related to NAEP scores, reading programs, and legislative initiatives are also available here.

State Department of Education web-sites:

California Department of Education	www.cde.ca.gov
Colorado Department of Education	www.cde.state.co.us
Florida Department of Education	www.firn.edu/doe
Georgia Department of Education	www.doe.k12.ga.us
Illinois State Board of Education	www.isbe.state.il.us
Texas Education Agency	www.tea.state.tx.us
Massachusetts Department of Education	www.doe.mass.edu
New Jersey Department of Education	www.state.nj.us/education
New York State Department of Education	www.nysed.gov

The information found at each of the above URL's for state departments of education is representative of that for most states in that it provides access to specific policy initiatives, policy decisions, standards, and assessment procedures for representative states. Links to additional professional resources are typically listed on these sites.

New Jersey Literacy Initiative Mission Statement
This site provides details of the Mission Statement and the evidence supporting the Mission Statement.

An Intervention Program for Helping Pre-certified Teachers Succeed on the Teacher Licensing Exams

Agnes Marie Imburgin Stryker

Texas A&M University-Commerce

Abstract

The role of testing in American education is increasing. Examinations are now used to determine if pre-certified teachers are "highly qualified." A test preparation program was developed to teach critical reading and test-taking skills, to stimulate metacognition, and to provide additional skills to pass these examinations.

Data were collected from 79 pre-certified teachers. Qualitative analysis included (a) analysis of questionnaires given prior to and after taking the intervention program and (b) correspondence from the participants. Quantitative analysis included paired sample t-Tests and individual sample t-Tests of pre-certified teacher's previous and current Exam scores. The results showed, at the .05 level, a significant increase in scores with a mean improvement of 8.24. It is concluded that the intervention program is effective in improving certification examination scores by increasing problem solving and critical thinking skills.

There is a crisis in education today. Not only is there a shortage of highly qualified teachers, but there is controversy concerning how to determine if a teacher is *highly qualified.* The current method is a teacher certification examination. This has branded teacher certification examinations as high stakes tests.

These examinations have put pressure on the pre-certified teacher as well as colleges of education. If a teacher training institution finds its students scoring too low on these licensing tests, their accreditation is at risk

(Abt-Perkins, 2002). The anxiety concerning certification examination pre-occupies those who are studying to be educators. Those who find standard-ized tests especially challenging now find their apprehension increases as their vocation of choice balances on the results of a test.

Historical Perspective

Teacher licensing based on the results of standardized testing began in the early 1920s. In 1933, the National Survey of the Education of Teachers Bulletin No. 10 explored "The concept of proficiency" and the "Need for more accurate measurement of teaching merit." The '50s and '60s saw many debates about educational reform. When the Elementary and Secondary Education Act (Title I) (*NCLB*, 2001) was ratified, congress demanded accountability for the funds spent, thus evaluation on a governmental level began. In the 1970s educators heard a public outcry concerning the quality of education. The public concluded that people went into education because they lacked the academic abilities for other professions. Americans viewed the public school system as producing graduates who were incapable of meeting the increas-ingly complex demands of employment. Concern over quality education laid the groundwork for the education reform movement of the '80s. The quality of America's education became media propaganda and a political issue, thus spur-ring the National Commission on Excellence in Education (Wakefield, 2003).

Galluzzo (1996) explained that the excellence movement evolved into a standards movement. If standards are established, it is presumed that quality can be assured. Standards could then define content knowledge and skills along with the quality of instruction. Standards could also ensure that school programs, including teacher education, would help make the transfer out of the age of industrialization into the age of information. Thus, throughout the nation, assessments on local and state levels were being refined and endorsed.

Legislation's major objective for teacher assessment was to improve the quality of entry-level teachers by regulating and monitoring the teacher licens-ing process, thus eliminating educators who were not competent in basic knowledge and skills (Pearlman & Gitomer, 2000). The Federal government affirmed and encouraged licensure testing in order to determine teacher qualification. Today, we are in the midst of the new political reform *No Child Left Behind* (*NCLB*), stating that each child should be educated by a *highly qualified teacher.*

The major question facing colleges and asked by students is, "Can assess-ment determine 'highly qualified'?" Is assessment for teacher licensing really needed?" The truth is, assessment is here to stay. The general public thinks of assessment as the yardstick of educational quality (Linn, 2000). The government looks at assessment as an assurance that quality exists. State teacher examinations provide the public with a sense of confidence and quality in those who work with their children (Ananda & Rabinowitz, 2001). Society further believes that teacher assessment will assure continued progress (Pullin, 2001). To assure parents that qualified educators teach their children, Texas requires that all educators pass two state licensing exams. Since 1986 the Examination for Certification of Educators in Texas (ExCET) (NES, 1999) had been required. In 2003, Texas instated the Texas Examination of Educator Standards (TExES) (NES, 2002).

Pre-certified teacher examinations are similar to examinations that many professionals take before becoming fully licensed. However other professional examinations have commercial books and programs that explain the tests, include practice tests, and teach the specialized test-taking skills needed. These books and programs focus on knowing oneself as a student and as a skilled confident professional (Hoefler, 2000; Nugent & Vitale, 2000). Finally these preparation programs help improve professional problem-solving and critical thinking skills. Books and programs about ExCET/TExES and some other educator examinations have not had this component. This information is usually not included in teacher education programs.

Can certification tests determine if pre-certified teachers are highly qualified in background knowledge and skills as well as professional knowledge? Studies suggest that certified teachers have comparable or even slightly better academic skills than the overall population. There is an indication that the verbal ability of teachers, as measured by standardized tests, is positively related to their students' test scores. Therefore standardized tests *could* indicate *qualified*. However does *highly qualified* mean *highly effective?*

Unfortunately there have been no studies to show that these academically adept teachers are effective teachers (Blair, 2001; Darling-Hammond, 1996,1997b). Experts report that little evidence exists to show that the teacher licensure tests can determine if a candidate is competent to teach (Tellez, 2003). Bransford, Brown, and Cocking (1999) remind us, "Expertise in a particular domain does not guarantee that one is good at helping others learn it (p. 32)."

Most standardized tests, including teachers' examinations, have been accused of being racially and culturally biased (HtmlResAnchor Wayne, 2003). Many studies have found that candidates from different races and cultures have scored less than their white peers (Dounay, 2000; Justice & Hardy, 2001). Educators express their concern that minorities' low scores lead to questions about the reliability and validity of the examinations (Watras, 2003). National Evaluation Systems (NES), the private testing company developing and publishing ExCET/TExES, admits that validity can be a problem (Gorth & Chernoff, 1986).

Teacher certification examinations have been challenged in court. Although the courts' opinions have favored the states and the governmental agencies rather than the plaintiffs, the courts have demanded that the reliability and validity of the tests be established. Court decisions have also required that reasonable steps for accommodations be inaugurated (Watras, 2003). If the result of a standardized test is the only critical factor states and school districts rely upon to hire teachers, these tests are then considered employment tests (Pullin, 2001).

Teacher licensing exams are shrouded in controversy. Critics contend that it is almost impossible for standardized tests to measure a teacher's caring, perseverance, and creativity. Other intangibles such as higher-order capabilities and student rapport are also ignored. Furthermore, critics maintain that the tests fail to measure critical knowledge and skills adequately and effectively (Zirkel, 2000). They argue that testing may deny opportunities to potentially good teachers because of their poor test-taking skills.

Pre-certified Teachers' Response

Many would-be qualified teachers question their test-taking abilities. They seem to have little confidence in their skills and abilities. Consequently they question their intelligence even though their grades and class work are usually above average (Cohen, 1997). Could these students benefit from an intervention program that helps them realize their strengths and weaknesses (metacognition), increase knowledge of the test-taking skills, and change their attitude toward the test? Could teaching test-taking skills also result in a sense of empowerment, increased self-efficacy, and a sense of control over the testing situation? Could teaching test-taking skills counter the many factors that influence the tester, such as personal factors and environmental conditions?

There has been much speculation but not much research to determine how much a test taker can gain on teacher certification examinations if test-taking strategies are taught. Studies have been done with elementary and high school students showing that children receiving formal instruction in test-taking did increase their scores (Berendt & Koski, 1999). Nursing schools, reporting similar problems with students passing their licensing examination, developed strategies to assist nursing students to successfully pass their exams (Oermann, Truesdell, & Ziolkowski, 2000). If teaching test-taking strategies works with other students and other professions, it could be beneficial to pre-certified teachers.

It has been demonstrated that a positive academic self-efficacy promotes exam performance (Schunk, 1994). Intervention can also affect self-efficacy. Krieshok, Ulven, Hecox, and Wettersten (2000) have seen intervention increase vocational student's self-knowledge and self-efficacy. Higgins' (2000) work with high school students noted the relationship between self-efficacy, achievement, and lower test anxiety after instruction and intervention. Elementary students' intervention and guidance increased self-efficacy and awareness of metacognition. What and where are the cognitive resources and course of action to help pre-certified teachers?

Often students are not aware of how to identify what problems they are having. Many times students' self-efficacy is so low that they will think other students are smarter because they perceive other students being successful in testing situations. Even though students may learn new test-taking strategies, they are not beneficial unless students are able to transfer those strategies to the testing situation (Flippo & Borthwick, 1981). Metacognition can monitor and facilitate this transfer.

Most authorities in educational measurement recognize the impact of test-taking skills. Flippo and Borthwick (1981) have described teaching test-taking strategies as a "bona fide entity" that deserves attention. The following study was conducted to determine if teaching test-taking strategies would impact metacognition, increase self-efficacy, and increase test scores of pre-certified teachers.

Research Design

The methodology chosen was a quasi-experimental design combining qualitative and quantitative components. The first qualitative portion of the study describes the procedure to help pre-certified teachers realize their strengths and abilities in taking standardized tests. The method used was Interactive Qualitative Analysis (IQA), developed by Dr. Norvill Northcutt at the University of Texas. IQA is a systematic approach using a group process procedure to produce and analyze qualitative data. The IQA methodology consists of inductive and deductive group processing that produces a theory of action from what the participants actually experience or perceive (Northcutt, Miles, Robins, and Ellis, 1998). The main issue during the IQA portion of the study was discovering what pre-certified teachers perceive as their abilities to pass standardized tests, and what they perceived as stumbling blocks to passing the ExCET.

The second qualitative portion describes the test-taking strategies that provide additional skills needed to pass the ExCET. The third qualitative portion looks at the researcher's notes that were taken during the test-taking skills sessions. The final qualitative portion reports pre-certified teachers' perspective of the test-taking skills program. It also determines if the participants consider the strategies they learned to be instrumental in increasing their critical reading/thinking skills and helping them succeed on the ExCET. This qualitative portion was accomplished by analyzing and coding all the participants' e-mail correspondence with the researcher.

To support the qualitative data, the quantitative portion of the study descriptively analyzes the data from different sources. First, the pre-certified teacher's previous ExCET scores and current ExCET scores are analyzed by using paired sample t-Tests and individual sample t-Tests. This determined if the intervention program resulted in additional problem solving and critical thinking skills as indicated by improved ExCET scores. Second, a quantitative analysis of their pre-intervention and post-intervention responses on the *Skills Questionnaire* determines the pre-certified teacher's perceptions of test-taking skills versus the required skills needed for the ExCET. The researcher used the same *Skills Questionnaire* as both a pre-intervention and a post-intervention survey. By comparing the pre-intervention and post-intervention survey, any change in the participant's self-efficacy and metacognition could be noted.

The study was conducted at the ExCET review sessions in April 2002 (prior to the May 4th ExCET) and in July 2002 (prior to July 13th ExCET).

Purpose

The purpose of the study was threefold. First, it answers the following question: Which factors do pre-certified teachers perceive as stumbling blocks to successfully completing the licensing examination? Second, it determines if pre-certified teachers consider that they have increased the skills needed to pass the ExCET after participating in an intervention program. Third, it evaluates if the program designed to develop critical reading/thinking skills would successfully increase pre-certified teacher's self-efficacy and confidence in taking the examination, thus reducing stress toward testing.

Participants

The participants are described in Table 1 (n=79). Since the participants voluntarily attended the sessions, there was no deliberate attempt to equalize gender, ethnicity, age, educational background, or teacher training program. All participants were repeat test takers since a previous failure placed them as a "high risk" for passing the examinations. In a personal interview at the Texas State Board for Educator Certification in Austin, TX (March 15, 2002), Marilyn Cook indicated that when a person retakes ExCET he/she usually scores lower on the retake than on the first ExCET exam. She has found that the more often a person takes the ExCET the less likely it is that they will pass.

Table 1. Description of Participants

	AFRICAN AMERICAN	ASIAN	HISPANIC	WHITE
Male	2	0	2	6
Female	11	3	1	54
Total	13	3	3	60

Note: For the purpose of this study, the test-taking strategies program held in April and July are combined and treated as one session for qualitative analysis.

Description of the Program

The ExCET/TExES Test Taking Skills Program is a one day, five hour long intervention program, especially designed for pre-certified teachers who do not intuitively pick up the study and test-taking skills needed to pass standardized certification tests. The program focuses on the participants knowing their assets as students and as skilled professionals (a form of metacognition), and changing their attitude toward these tests by increasing their problem-solving and critical thinking skills. During the session the facilitator explains the test configuration, teaches the specialized skills needed by utilizing five specific steps to answer sample test questions, and guides students while they practice the new skills. This process not only helps with passing the certification exams, but also assists the student in becoming a better and more confident professional (Hoefler, 2000; Nugent & Vitale, 2000). Since 2002, over 900 pre-certified teachers have attended the program; 96.5% have passed the ExCET/TExES. This manuscript however details the study of the original 79 at-risk test takers.

The pre-certified teachers who participated in the study knew what testing attributes were needed, which skills they already had, and which ones they needed to develop to pass the ExCET. They identified the following six stumbling blocks to successfully passing the certification tests:

- knowing which details were important and which were not;
- understanding what the question was asking;
- being able to relate the details of the stem to the question;
- being able to relate the question to the material already learned;
- being able to read and understand the vocabulary used; and
- working with multilevel answers.

They also decided that just practicing answering questions would not overcome those stumbling blocks. With all the practice they had, they still did not feel prepared to take the ExCET. In their opinion, they needed instruction in **how** to answer the questions and **how** to think through the answers. To help the test takers overcome those stumbling blocks and decode the ExCET questions, five steps were developed.

The five steps are:

- **Step 1**—Circle the grade or student's age involved in the situation. This is important to help them remember the age/grade in order to select the appropriate related response.
- **Step 2**—Underline details to assist in *Knowing which details were and were not important.* The participants are reminded that what is a detail for one person is not necessarily a detail for another. For example, one question contains the statement: *She uses a multi-sensory presentation including a lot of manipulatives, visual aids, and*

verbal support. Some test-takers consider **multisensory presenta-tion** an important detail, while others consider **a lot of mani-pulatives, visual aids, and verbal support** as an important de-tail. Either phrase is correct. The test-takers are warned that "less is more" and that selecting both as details was unneeded.

- **Step 3**—Box in the question. This step isolates the question and defines the details in them, thus helping to *know what the question is asking.*

- **Step 4**—Restate the question in their own words. Substituting com-mon words for education jargon is part of this step. This not only activates prior knowledge but also aids in *being able to relate the important details of the stem to the question.* The test-takers discover that this step helps put the details into perspective and aids in their determining which competency the question is addressing.

- **Step 5**—Read the answers and eliminate those that are not correct. If they need to, test takers should repeat step 4 to reaffirm the ques-tion and its relationship to the stem of the question.

The researcher developed a total of 20 questions that used these five steps to decode the question. Each question also reinforced one or more of the skills the groups deemed necessary to overcome the stumbling blocks of ExCET. For example, the following question addressed the factor *knowing which details were important and which were not:*

Lisa is the youngest child in Ms. Lei's kindergarten. Lisa finds particu-larly frustrating her inability to read books as some of the older chil-dren in her class. How could Ms. Lei best adapt the classroom to mini-mize this source of frustration for Lisa?

A. *removing books for a few weeks.*

B. *introducing some new wordless picture books and encouraging her to tell a story from those pictures.*

C. *providing a new center with magazines from which Lisa can cut out pictures.*

D. *creating templates that Lisa can use to trace outlines of words.*

To explain how to discern important details from unimportant details, the parts of the question were carefully assessed. The test-taker located the stem of the question and evaluated important nouns and verbs and their relationships. In this example, the words that needed careful attention are bolded and underlined.

Lisa is the **youngest child** *in Ms. Lei's* **kindergarten**. *Lisa finds par-ticularly* **frustrating her inability to read books** *as some of the older children in her class.*

In the question's stem, the underlined bolded words describe a discouraging situation in a 5-year-old child's life.

Another factor needing attention "knew what the question was asking. " Here the learners isolated the question and decided exactly what the question asked. Attention was directed to details, qualifiers, and noticing the verb's relationship to the stem of the question.

How could Ms. Lei **best adapt the classroom** *to* **minimize** *this* **source** *of frustration for Lisa?*

The underlined bolded words indicate that the question asks to adapt the classroom (not the child) to minimize (not remove) the source of frustration.

In looking at a third factor, *being able to relate the question to the details of the stem,* the learners were guided to combine the critical parts of stem with the question. The critical parts are identified below.

A. **removing books** *for a few weeks*
B. *introducing some new picture* **wordless books** *and encouraging her to tell a story from those pictures*
C. *providing a* **new center** *with magazines from which Lisa can* **cut out pictures**.
D. *creating templates for* **Lisa's use** *to trace outlines of words*

Being able to relate the question to the material already learned, a fourth factor, was one involving recall and evaluation of information previously learned. The test taker had to conjoin the concepts learned on an educational topic and apply them to the scenario presented, then examine and evaluate the answers in the following manner:

A. *This is not applicable in Texas; since Texas has the reading initiative program this is not a good choice.*
B. *This would be an adaptation of the classroom library. Emergent literacy begins with handling books and gleaning a story from its pages.*
C. *This would be an adaptation of the classroom, but it would not support Lisa and her early literacy.*
D. *This would not adapt the classroom.*

The learners chose their answer as B. The answer of B fulfilled all the details in the question and the qualifications.

To aid in *being able to read and understand the vocabulary,* and *working with multilevel answers, a* different question was authored. In this question the techniques of "phrasing" and "translation" were used. "Phrasing" breaks apart long involved sentences found the in stem of the questions into smaller phrases in order to make reading and comprehension easier. The students were also encouraged to substitute common words for more difficult words or "educational" jargon into common language. One question used to teach these skills was:

Because of PL 94-142, the Education for All Handicapped Children Act and the 504 provisions, Ms. Ascon has three identified slow learners in her 4th grade social studies class. They are studying the chronicles of the Caddo Indians. Ms. Ascon uses a multi-sensory presentation including a lot of visual aids, manipulatives, and verbal support. Which of the following best describes the results she can expect from the students in the learning process?

I. *Learning study skills and study strategies.*

II. *Slow students will be able to keep up with the pace of the other* average students.

III. *Increased visual components will help learners with analysis and application of the information.*

IV. *Abstract information will be facilitated more easily.*

V. *Instructions for summative projects will not need to be repeated.*

A. I, II, IV

B. III, V

C. I, III, V

D. IV, V,

Below is one way to rewrite the question. The words substituted or "translated" are bolded and underlined below.

*Because of the **national law**, Ms. Ascon has three identified slow learners in her **4th grade** social studies class. The class is currently **studying the history** of the Caddo Indians. She uses a multi-sensory presentation including a lot of **hands on things**, **things to look at**, and **discussion**. Which of the following best describes the results she can* expect from the students in the learning process?

I. *Learning study skills and study strategies.*

II. *Slow students will be able to keep up with the pace of other average students.*

III. **More seeing things** *will help learners with* **taking apart and using** *the information.*

IV. *Abstract information will be **learned** more easily.*

V. *Instructions for **the ending** projects will not need to be repeated.*

Once the test-taker understands the stem of the question, hints for answering multilevel questions were given. The technique included finding one answer they thought was the correct answer and one answer they were sure was the incorrect answer. This procedure would help them to eliminate incorrect choices and simplify selecting the actual answer. By using these skills, the test-taker could examine the stem of the question and select the answer in the following manner:

    I.   *Might be right.*

    II. *Might be right*

    III. **This is correct.**

    IV. *Might be incorrect*

    V. **Not correct**

    A. *I, II, I*—NOT the correct answer; it does not have a III

    B. *III, V*—NOT the answer; it has a V

    C. *I, III, IV*—The CORRECT answer; it has a III and does not have a V

    D. *IV, V*—NOT the answer; it does not have a III and does have a V

Each participant was presented with ExCET style questions to answer. While answering the questions the pre-certified teachers were encouraged to think aloud and explain why they answered each question the way they did. When a question was answered incorrectly, that question was explained so the pre-certified teacher could learn from his mistakes.

Results

The results were first analyzed quantitatively. The *Skills Questionnaire* was given preceding the session to ascertain each individual's attitude prior to their group work. After the test-taking skills session, the participants repeated the *Skills Questionnaire*. Quantitatively analyzing the difference between the pre- and post-session questionnaire would determine if the pre-certified teachers felt they could use newly learned test-taking skills, techniques, and information to answer the ExCET questions correctly (see Table 2). All of them (100%) agreed they now had the ability to find the correct answers on most ExCET questions and 95% believed they were prepared to successfully take the ExCET.

Examining the post-session *Skills Questionnaire* responses, those that agreed to the factors of *knowing what the question was asking* and *being able to relate the question to the stem of the question* increased to an average of 94%. Those that reported having difficulty selecting the correct answers on the ExCET decreased from 80% to 42% and those who had difficulty with *multi-level questions* decreased from 65% to 15%. Comparing the pre- and post- questionnaire about *knowing which details were important and which were not,* the average response of those who agreed that they **could** differentiate between important and unimportant details increased to over 95%.

Examining the factor of *being able to relate the question to the material already learned* in the post-session *Skills Questionnaire,* the researcher found that instead of 65% agreeing that they had the information needed on the

Table 2. Comparative Results Pre-session and Post-session Skills Questionnaire [Skills Questionnaire]

QUESTION	PRE-SESSION		POST-SESSION	
	AGREE	DISAGREE	AGREE	DISAGREE
I have the ability to find the correct answer on most ExCET questions.	76	25	100	0
I can recognize the organization (main ideas and details) of ExCET questions	76	23	95	5
I have enough techniques to answer ExCET questions correctly.	63	37	95	5
It is simple to select the answers in multilevel questions.	35	65	85	15
I am prepared to take ExCET.	59	41	95	5
I understand the underlying concepts of domains and competencies required to complete the test.	86	14	99	1
I can delete the unimportant statements and understand the main ideas in ExCET questions.	75	25	96	4
I find answering questions on ExCET difficult.	85	15	57	43
I can separate the answer apart from the distracter.	58	42	94	6
I can determine the specific information needed to answer ExCET questions correctly.	65	35	95	5
I can summarize the ExCET question in my own words.	68	32	95	5
I have difficulty selecting the correct answers on ExCET.	80	20	42	58
When I read the stem of the ExCET question, I can recognize important details.	77	23	95	5
I can pick out the specific information in each question needed to answer it correctly.	67	33	87	3
I have had the opportunity to practice with and efficiently analyze ExCET questions before I take the test.	81	19	91	9
I am effective in analyzing the structure of ExCET questions.	65	35	96	4
I am confident in using my academic skills to answer ExCET questions.	73	27	94	6
I have the information I need to be successful on ExCET.	45	55	94	6
I can notice most of the distracters in the list of answers.	76	24	97	3

ExCET, 94% now agreed. Ninety-five percent agreed that they could now recognize the basic concepts of the test and 99% could now understand the underlying organization of the domains and competencies.

The final quantitative data focused on comparing the participants' previous ExCET scores with their post-remediation scores. The differences between the groups' scores were statistically different with a minimum improvement of -13, a maximum improvement of +27 and a mean improvement of +8.24 (standard deviation, 9.05). The Difference between the participants' prior scores and post-remediation scores was calculated by using a Paired Samples t-Test (see Tables 3, 4, 5).

Table 3. Difference between Prior Scores-Post-remediation Scores

SCORES	N	MEAN	STD. DEVIATION	T	SIG: 2-TAILED
Prior	79	68.51	11.23	-8.09	.000
Current	79	76.75	10.07		

Table 4. Difference between Prior Scores and Post-remediation Scores of the Professional Development ExCET

		PAIRED SAMPLES t-TEST			
TEST SCORE	N	MEAN	STD. DEVIATION	t	SIG: 2-TAILED
Prior	37	71.80	11.49	-3.138	.003
Current	37	76.83	10.20		

Table 5. Difference between Prior Scores and Post-remediation Scores of the Comprehensive ExCET

		PAIRED SAMPLES t-TEST			
TEST SCORE	N	MEAN	STD. DEVIATION	t	SIG: 2-TAILED
Prior	42	65.61	10.28	-9.668	.000
Current	42	76.69	10.08		

Comparing the two tests taken, the Professional Development and the Elementary Comprehensive, results of the t-Test indicated that there exists a statistically significant difference at the .003 alpha level (see Table 6). This supported the idea that the review/test-taking skills session was effective for either test.

Table 6. Comparing the Professional Development ExCET and the Comprehensive ExCET

		Independent Samples t-Test			
Test Score	N	Mean	Std. Deviation	t	Sig: 2-tailed
P.D.	37	5.03	9.74	-3.086	.003
Comp	4 2	11.07	7.42		

Note: Comparing the results of the ExCET test taken in May and in July revealed that there was no significant difference as to when the test was taken.

The data in this study from the IQA procedure were analyzed qualitatively to describe the perceptions of the participants. The data showed that all the pre-certified teachers who participated identified that they had the following strengths and abilities to pass standardized exams: Test-taking strategies and skills, knowledge, organization, stress management, preparation and study skills. The IQA procedure confirmed that in order to pass the ExCET test-takers must have specific skills to process the ExCET questions and to determine the correct answer.

Qualitatively analyzing data compiled from 47 E-mails determined that the newly learned strategies were perceived as beneficial. Nineteen participants reported feeling prepared, more skillful, and confident when taking the test. Fourteen participants commented on having a sense of pride in their accomplishment. These feelings of efficacy are important to note because, as eight participants commented, they can be extended to other ExCET tests they have to complete for certification (see Appendix).

The qualitative and quantitative analysis, when looked at collectively, confirmed that the described intervention program teaching test-taking and critical reading/thinking skills helped pre-certified teachers become more confident test-takers who could increase their scores on the ExCET.

Findings

The overall findings indicated that pre-certified teachers can reflect on their abilities and know their own learning needs. They possess the metacognitive powers to not only know about their own test-taking skills but also which skills they lack. Since the pre-certified teachers did consider themselves capable of taking tests and able to learn, they could learn additional skills that would help them be successful on the teacher certification test. After attending the review/test-taking skills session where critical reading/thinking skills and test-taking techniques were learned, the pre-certified teachers' scores on the ExCET improved. The study found that the intervention procedure did succeed, with 86% of the participants increasing their ExCET scores by a mean of 8.24 points. Of the 79 examinees, 68 passed their test.

Discussion

The steps and techniques that were taught have been adapted for Texas' teacher certification test, but they could be adapted for any teacher certification examination.

Prior to the review/test-taking skills session, 73% of the pre-certified teachers agreed that they had mastered some test-taking skills which were useful for correctly answering some ExCET questions. Yet they also perceived that they didn't have enough test-taking techniques or skills to find the correct answer on most ExCET questions. In their eyes, memorizing facts would not help them on the ExCET. Something more was needed.

Would answering practice ExCET questions be that "something more?" On the pre-session *Skills Questionnaire*, 81% of the participants said they had the opportunity to practice with and analyze the ExCET questions. Yet even with all the practice, they did not feel prepared to take the ExCET. In their opinion, they needed instruction in **how** to answer the questions and **how** to think through the answers. These skills were not found in available references on ExCET. Nor has there been study that deals with helping ExCET/TExES test takers prepare for the examination.

Between 76% and 86% agreed to *understanding the underlying concepts* and as well as *recognizing the organization of the domains and competencies of the ExCET.* Yet with all that background information, approximately 80% still thought finding the correct answer on the ExCET was difficult.

After the review/test-taking skills session, well over 90% felt they could find *the correct answer on most ExCET questions.* E-mails recount that they had confidence in using their new skills and now felt prepared (see Appendix). It wasn't just answering additional questions that extended their self-efficacy, but the instruction in the procedural knowledge on how to "think logically" on ExCET/TExES.

While progressing through the questions that emphasized the test-taking techniques and critical reading-thinking skills, the participants' approaches to answering the questions changed remarkably. This was evident by watching them think aloud during the test-taking skills portion of the review session. The researcher also noticed that the participants' attitude was evolving from a sense of discouragement to one of accomplishment and confidence. When test-takers feel confident about their skills and their self-efficacy increases, they perceive less stress (see Appendix), and the test becomes "an inconvenience" rather than a stressful situation (see Appendix).

The participants' comments demonstrated that they had a new confidence in their abilities. One participant came up to the researcher and said "I can teach this to my class for Texas Assessment of Academic Skills [Texas' achievement test] preparation." That statement depicted the real increase of self-efficacy and the value the participant placed upon their new accomplishment. As the post-session *Skills Questionnaire* and e-mails show, this increase of self-efficacy not only counteracts discouragement, but also instills a feeling that the test taker can use their knowledge and skills to be successful on other standardized tests.

Answering multilevel questions is another example of the participants' increase in skills producing an increase in self-efficacy. The participants were asked to respond to *it is simple to select the answers in multilevel questions* on the *Skills Questionnaire.* Sixty-five percent thought multilevel questions were difficult to answer. Once a test taker "got the hang" of answering multilevel questions, the questions became less stressful and "almost fun" (see Appendix). This is confirmed by the fact that after learning how to answer multilevel test questions, 85% agreed on the post-session questionnaire that they were easily answered.

One by-product of the review/test-taking skills session was the participant's decision to take a proactive approach toward the testing situation. The July group decided that distractions from other test-takers, noise from air conditioning units, poor facilities, location and the time of day the test was taken, etc. could not be remedied by any test-taking strategy or review session. The July group contended that a letter to the State Board for Educator Certification would be their best course of action. The researcher looked upon this assertiveness as a reflection of positive attitudes in those test takers. Test-takers were not only analyzing where their difficulties lay in successfully taking a test, but they were also realizing what would or would not correct those difficulties.

Implications

When teachers contend with the stress and anxiety of standardized tests, they may have more empathy for their students who have the same feelings. By realizing that stress and anxiety can be relieved, pre-certified teachers may try to help their own students reduce the amount of tension felt prior to taking tests. The teachers who had opportunities to reflect on and use their skills could be more willing to guide their students' similar reflection. As this study shows, this form of metacognition would be excellent to increase self-esteem and self-efficacy toward test taking.

Often teachers model their instructive techniques after the way they have been taught. If pre-certified teachers are taught with the emphasis on a certification test, they will follow that lead. These future teachers will be influenced to teach to the current assessment test. Students need more than being taught to get ready to take a test. This is as unproductive as the recitation methods of the mid-1900s (Darling-Hammond, 1997a). If students are taught in an effective and creative manner, taught to problem solve, and taught to think critically, the content knowledge will be there from which they can draw upon when taking any standardized test. These qualities of critical thinking and problem solving will also extend to acquiring test-taking skills. Test-taking techniques should be taught, but neither the skills nor the test should be the focus of any curriculum.

Conclusions

The significance of this study is threefold. First, an intervention program that directly teaches test-taking skills in a limited time **does** develop test-taking skills that enhance problem solving and critical reading/thinking skills. A by-product of developing these skills for some participants is the reduction of stress and anxiety toward taking the ExCET, or any other standardized test.

A second significance is that the information concerning the success of the intervention skills program can spread to other colleges of education and teacher training institutes. This information would encourage universities and teacher training institutes to develop an effective and creative teacher education program that will produce effective, creative teachers who know the value of problem solving and critical reading/thinking skills.

A third significance is the far reaching yet unseen effect it has on children taught by teachers who know the value of creative teaching, critical thinking, and methods to teach test-taking skills without teaching to the test.

References

Abt-Perkins, D. (2002). HtmlResAnchor Reports from the States: Illinois—Cheap Tests and Standardized Education Programs. *English Education, 34*(2), 156.

Ananda, S., and Rabinowitz, S. (2001). The high stakes of high-stakes testing. Policy Brief. (Report No. EDO-TM-90-3). Washington, DC: American Institutes for Research. (ERIC Document Reproduction Service No. ED455254)

Berendt, P. R., & Koski, B. (1999). No shortcuts to success. *Educational Leadership, 56*(6), 45-47.

Blair, J. (2001). Threatened Texas college preserves its right to prepare teachers. *Education Week, 21*(15), 19-21.

Bransford, J. D., Brown, A. L., & Cocking, R. R., (Eds.). (1999*). How people learn: Brain, mind, experience, and school.* Washington, DC: National Academy Press.

Cohen, L. R. (1997). I ain't so smart and you ain't so dumb: Personal reassessment in transformative learning. *New Directions for Adult and Continuing Education, 74*(2), 61-68.

Darling-Hammond, L. (1996). What matters most: A competent teacher for each child. *Phi Delta Kappan, 78*, 193-200.

Darling-Hammond, L. (1997a). Doing what matters most: Investing in quality teaching. In *What matters most: Teaching for America's future.* New York: National Commission on Teaching and America's Future.

Darling-Hammond, L. (1997b). *The right to learn: A blueprint for creating schools that work.* San Francisco, CA: Jossey-Bass.

Dounay, J. (2000). High-stakes testing is high-stress, too. *Education Digest, 65*(9), 9-13.

Flippo, R. F., & Borthwick, P. (1981, December). Should test-wiseness curriculum be part of undergraduate teacher education? Paper presented at the Annual Meeting of the American Reading Forum, Sarasota, FL. (ERIC Document Reproduction Service No. ED218591)

Galluzzo, G. R. (1996). The standards have come. *Journal of Industrial Teacher Education, 34*(1), 11-18.

Gorth, W. P., & Chernoff, M. L. (Eds.). (1986). *Testing for teacher certification.* Hillsdale, NJ: Lawrence Erlbaum Associates.

Higgins, B. A. (2000). *An analysis of the effects of instruction of metacognitive and study skills upon the self-efficacy and achievement of male and female students.* Oxford, Ohio: Miami University. (ERIC Document Reproduction Service No. ED447152)

Hoefler, P. (2000). *Successful problem solving and test taking for beginning nursing students* (3rd ed.). Bartonsville, MD: Medical Education Development Service (MEDS) Publishing.

Justice, M., & Hardy, J. C. (2001). Minority students and the Examination for the Certification of Educators in Texas (ExCET). *Education (Chula Vista, CA), 121*, 592-596.

Krieshok, T. S., Ulven, J. C., Hecox, J. L., Wettersten, K. (2000). Resume therapy and vocational test feedback: Tailoring interventions to self-efficacy outcomes. *Journal of Career Assessment, 8*, 267-281.

Linn, R. (2000). Assessment and accountability. *Educational Researcher, 29*(2), 4-15.

National Survey of the Education of Teachers Bulletin No. 10, Vol. III, V, III (1933). Washington, DC: Us Government Printing Office.

National evaluation systems (NES), Inc. (1999) Examination for the Certification of Teachers in Texas (ExCET) Amherst, MA: National Evaluation Systems.

National evaluation systems (NES), Inc. (2002) Texas Examination of Educators Standards (TExES). Amherst, MA: National Evaluation Systems.

No Child Left Behind Act of 2001, Pub. L. No. 107-110.

Northcutt, N., Miles, C., Robins, L., & Ellis, L. (1998). Innovations 1998. Learning Center Course #6: Making "hard decisions" with "soft data": Strategic group planning and evaluation tools. Paper presented at the meeting of the League for Innovations in Community Colleges, Dallas, TX.

Nugent, P. M., & Vitale, B. A. (2000). *Test success: Test-taking techniques for beginning nursing students.* Philadelphia, PA: F. A. Davis.

Oermann, M., Truesdell, S., & Ziolkowski, L. (2000). Strategy to assess, develop, and evaluate critical thinking. *The Journal of Continuing Education in Nursing, 31*, 155-160.

Pearlman, M. A., & Gitomer, D. H. (2000). Policies for teacher improvement. *Educational Horizons, 78*, 129-130.

Pullin, D. C. (2001). Key questions in implementing teacher testing and licensing. *Journal of Law & Education, 30*, 383-439.

Schunk, D. H. (1994). Self-regulation of self-efficacy and attributions in academic settings. In D. H. Schunk and B. J. Zimmerman (Eds.) *Self-regulation of Learning and Performance: Issues and educational Applications (pp. 75-100).* Hillsdale, NJ: Lawrence Erlbaum Associates.

Tellez, K. (2003). Three Themes on Standards in Teacher Education: Legislative Expediency, the Role of External Review, and Test Bias in the Assessment of Pedagogical Knowledge. *Teacher Education Quarterly, 30*(1), 9-18.

Wakefield, D. (2003). Screening Teacher Candidates: Problems with High-Stakes Testing *The Educational Forum, 67*, 380-8.

Watras, J. (2003). Can Teacher Qualifying Exams Improve Education? *Educational Foundations, 17*(2), 71-85.

Wayne, A. J. (2003). Teacher Inequality: New Evidence on Disparities in Teachers' Academic Skills. *Review of Educational Research,* 73(1), 89-122

Zirkel, P. S. (2000). Tests on trial. *Phi Delta Kappan, 81,* 793-794.

Appendix

E#-01

Subject: PD
Date: Sun, 11 Aug 2002 11:18:18 -0400 (EDT)
From:XXXX@aol.com

I just want to thank you for all your help during this learning process. I passed the PD test, I had a feeling that I did. You know sometimes you just feel you did. Well 1 down and 1 to go. I'm going to sign-up for the Comp test that is offered in October. I know I can do good on that one too.

E-#02

Subject: Good News
Date: Mon, 12 Aug 2002 07:16:21 -0400 (EDT)

Just wanted to let you know that I received my comp scores on Friday.

I am finally official. In May I got an 84 on the PD, and now I got an 84 on the Comp as well. It was and is a great feeling. I couldn't have done it without you. Hope your summer is going well . . . and again thank you . . . I hope to keep in touch.

E-#03

Date: Wed, 14 Aug 2002 18:57:03 -0700 (PDT)
From:XXXXX@yahoo.com>

I made a 67 on the test the first time I took the test, but. I did better on this one. I passed . . .

I will e-mail you again in the fall about some other workshop for the Professional Development. Now I'm not so stressed out and am motivated to pass it the first time.

Thanks

E-#04

Subject: Hey!
Date: Thu, 15 Aug 2002 08:35:42 -0500
From:XXXXX@community.isd.tenet.edu>

Hey!
I just wanted to tell you thanks for everything last Spring. I made an 86 on my eled comp after failing it three times before. WOW! Now all I have to do is the PD and I know I can do it. Have a great year. XXXXX

E-#05

Subject: ExCET
Date: Sat, 10 Aug 2002 18:03:29 -0500
From:XXXX@prodigy.net

You were right. I passed. I knew more about taking a test than I thought. I felt I passed the test when I left but then I talked to everyone else and I began to have second thoughts.I don't mind taking the next one. I think it is more of an inconvenience than anything else.

Thanks for your help. Couldn't have done it without the review session.

E-#06

Date: Tue, 23 Jul 2002 16:33:39 -0500
From: xxxxx@stjohnsschool.org>

Wow! What a test . . . The strategies you taught us for answering multi-level questions (I, II, III, IV, etc.) was very helpful. I was very familiar with that format and the way to read the scenarios and pull out the important parts along with making sure I found the qualifiers before answering the questions. I just felt like the content of some of the questions was repetitious and it wasn't necessarily what I studied. Your workshop prepared me well—I couldn't have done it without you! I just didn't always feel real confident in my abilities before.

Thanks again for all of your help!

E-#07

Subject: ExCET
Date: Mon, 05 Aug 2002 16:12:32 +0000

. . . I'm glad it the test is over. I did just what you said with the multilevel questions. They weren't a problem at all, they even got to be sort of fun. I feel very confident that I passed. Thanks for all your help and techniques. I wouldn't have been able to do it without you.

E-#08

Date: Sat, 27 Jul 2002 19:36:47 -0500

. . . Everything that you taught us in the workshop were lifesavers; especially the test taking strategies and Blooms (the levels and vocabulary).

Thank you for all of your help . . .

PREPARING PRESERVICE TEACHERS TO SHOW EVIDENCE OF P-12 PUPIL LEARNING

Jane F. Rudden
Lillie S. West

Millersville University of Pennsylvania

Abstract

Teacher education institutions are responding to the call to show that they are preparing teacher candidates to show reasonable evidence of their teaching's impact on P-12 pupil learning. In the process of identifying a reliable instrument that fulfills the requirement for data-driven evidence without compromising authenticity, colleges and universities have engaged in curriculum changes, faculty training, and collaboration with practicing teachers and Arts and Sciences faculty. In this chapter the authors describe a custom-designed mentoring process that is used by one university to support teacher candidates throughout the Teacher Work Sample (TWS) process. First, the authors describe the differences between past practice and the new expectations as defined by the TWS. Second, the mentoring process is described including the training of mentors. The authors provide a detailed description of the TWS paradigm that includes implementation issues supported by related research and theory.

The rallying call to restructure teacher candidate evaluation measures has been sounded by accrediting bodies, education reformers, researchers, and professional education associations. No longer is it sufficient that teacher candidates be evaluated on content knowledge and pedagogical content knowledge. It is now incumbent upon teacher preparation institutions to prepare candidates to show evidence of the impact of their teaching on P-12 pupil learning. This is a tall order and one that departs distinctly from previous standards.

Cochran-Smith (2000) stated, "As we enter the 21st century, the future of teacher education is at best uncertain. The standards movement now dominates discussions about teaching and learning, curriculum, assessment, as well as all aspects of teacher learning, teacher assessment, and teacher certification" (p. 163). This sentiment was echoed in a report released by The American Federation of Teachers (AFT) (2000). In the report, the AFT called for more rigorous standards in the preparation and evaluation of new teachers. One of the recommendations made was the institution of a rigorous exit/licensure test that "aim[s] for a level of rigor that is consistent with what entry-level teachers in other high-performing countries are expected to know" (p. 36).

In addition to the AFT, The National Council for Accreditation of Teacher Education (NCATE) (2001) has weighed in with modified standards that include a requirement to show evidence that teacher candidates can connect theory to practice and impact learning in P-12 classrooms. Among the recommended evidentiary documentation forms are portfolios, video taped practice, exhibits of pupil products, and reflective essays. One recognized framework for documenting the measure of impact of teaching on learning is the Teacher Work Sample (TWS) model.

Teacher Work Sample (TWS) Model

It has been suggested that the TWS can be used "as credible evidence of [prospective teachers'] effectiveness in *fostering student learning*" (McConney, Schalock, & Schalock, 1998, p. 343). Teacher Work Sample Methodology (TWSM) is an outgrowth of education reform in Oregon beginning in 1991 at Western Oregon University. It is built on 30 years of conceptual development focusing on cognitive and contextual considerations. The developers at Western Oregon have devoted ten years to extensive research and development establishing a database of more than 1,000 student teachers and the data they collected on the learning gains of more than 20,000 K-12 pupils. It is "based on a design for instructing and assessing teachers that reflects what the professional literature indicates are effective planning, instruction, assessment, and reflective teaching strategies" (Girod, 2002, p. ix). The two underlying principles of TWSM as stated by Girod are to help improve the learning of school children and to prepare teachers to independently judge their own effectiveness and to know how to improve their ability to do so. The explicit purpose of the TWSM is "to focus on the effects of teaching and to provide a direct link between teaching and learning" (Stronge & Tucker, 2000, p. 39).

Recent studies were conducted on the validity, reliability, and alignment of TWSM standards and tasks with national standards. Findings indicated that face validity (Stronge & Tucker, 2000) and content and construct validity (Denner, Norman, Pankratz, & Salzman, 2003; Salzman, Denner, Bangert, &

Harris, 2001; Stronge & Tucker, 2000) were encouraging. Strong agreement of inter-rater reliability was found when raters received focused training (Denner et al., 2003; Salzman et al., 2001; Stronge & Tucker, 2000). Girod (2002) reported a direct correspondence between TWS tasks and several of the National Council for Accreditation of Teacher Education Standards (NCATE), and Denner et al. (2003) reported that TWS tasks corresponded with seven of ten standards as defined in the Interstate New Teacher Assessment and Support Consortium (INTASC).

Although TWSM has been modified for use in various states and at various institutions of higher education, several underlying components remain the same. TWSM relies on authentic classroom assessment to document student learning (Blacklock & Cartwright, 2003; Girod, 2002; Stronge & Tucker, 2000; The Renaissance Partnership for Improving Teacher Quality, 2001). It provides a contextually grounded portrayal of teaching; all teaching, goals, and assessments are linked to specific contextual factors (Blacklock & Cartwright, 2003; Girod, 2002; Stronge & Tucker, 2000; The Renaissance Partnership for Improving Teacher Quality, 2001); and it emphasizes teacher reflection to improve teaching and professional development (The Renaissance Partnership for Improving Teacher Quality, 2001). Several states have adopted TWSM as part of their initial licensure criteria (Girod, 2002; Salzman et al., 2001). A modification of TWSM has been chosen by Oklahoma Title II Teacher Enhancement Program because "it is the most authentic assessment currently available to measure the teachers' ability to impact student learning in the classroom, not only according to NCATE standards, but also according to Oklahoma's fifteen teaching competencies" (Fredman, 2002, p.6).

Blacklock and Cartwright (2003) reported positive results for struggling elementary readers as well as teacher candidates when using the Teacher Work Samples (TWS) paradigm. Fifty-five teacher candidates were assigned to work with fifty-five elementary students identified as struggling readers for twelve weeks using the following components of TWS: (a) alignment of intervention strategies with unit goals, (b) student needs, and (c) pre- post- and formative assessments. A comparison of pre- and post-assessment scores indicated positive results for all K-6 subjects in almost all literacy goals. Teacher candidates also showed positive changes in the following dispositions: (a) responsibility of the classroom teacher to teach struggling readers, (b) self-efficacy toward teaching struggling readers, and (c) responsiveness and persistence toward teaching struggling readers.

Distinguishing Features of the TWS

Specific components of the TWS that represent a different way of thinking about planning for instruction are:

- *Connecting learning goals to state and local standards.* This refers to state and local standards in the P-12 schools. Candidates are expected to link every instructional goal to a relevant state or local goal. Over the course of their studies, candidates design multiple lesson plans and learning centers suitable for P-12 pupils. This helps ensure their increased expertise in matching teaching objectives with appropriate standards.
- *Modifying instruction based on pre-assessment data.* Unlike past practice, the TWS does not allow for instructional planning without pre-assessment data. Candidates learn to conduct a knowledge probe, assess students' level of understanding, and modify instructional plans to accommodate individual learning needs as indicated by those data.
- *Analyzing post-assessment data and reflecting on teaching relevant to the impact on pupil learning.* Post-teaching assessment data are used to determine the effect of teaching on student learning. This step goes beyond an isolated posttest and creates a link between one teaching event and subsequent tutorials or instructional plans for individual learners.

Findings from a study of the Renaissance Teacher Work Sample Project support the TWS as "a method for providing credible evidence of teacher candidate performance with respect to state and institutional teaching standards and for instruction-embedded evidence of their impact on student learning" (Denner, Norman, Pankratz, & Salzman, 2003, p. 20). The components discussed above contribute to making the TWS a workable format for teacher candidates to use in achieving the goal of demonstrating not only what they know and can do, but also what impact their teaching has on P-12 pupil learning.

Implementation of the TWS Approach

As a member of The Renaissance Group, Millersville University of Pennsylvania had the unique opportunity to participate in a 5-year Title II grant, "Improving Teacher Quality through Partnerships that Connect Teacher Performance to Student Learning," (The Renaissance Partnership for Improving Teacher Quality, 2001) specifically aimed at the process of institutionalizing the TWS paradigm. Throughout the project, we were challenged to set reasonably achievable goals at each stage of the program of studies, and provide our candidates with the support and guidance to ensure their success. As we evaluated which approach would best serve our teacher candidates, we reaped the rewards of change in program curricula, practice, and a renewed appreciation for the value of collaboration.

Collaboration took place at various levels: (a) between Education and Arts and Sciences faculty; (b) between candidates and faculty; and (c) among faculty, candidate, and classroom practitioner. These collaborations provided a foundation to support candidates as they worked to design a unit of instruction that reflected the integration of assessment and planning. For example, professors from the school of Arts and Sciences acted as mentors to elementary education majors who were designing units of instruction in specialized science areas, music, or social sciences.

At the outset of this project, candidates expressed a lot of anxiety about being prepared for the summative TWS they were expected to complete during their student teaching semester. We addressed this concern by implementing TWS first with a small pilot group. The size of the group gradually expanded until, four years later, every teacher candidate was prepared to independently design a unit of instruction that met the TWS guidelines. Not only did the pilot group gradually expand, we also established a logical plan for implementation that showed candidates each course in their program that would address components of the TWS. Each component of the TWS that is covered in a specific course is listed and designated with a level of expectation: (a) Introduced (I), (b) Practiced (P), or (c) Mastered (M). This scaffolding of the instruction and the expectations of the candidates is illustrated in Figure 1. Every teacher candidate receives a program timeline in ElEd 100: Introduction to Elementary Education. Seeing the whole picture manages their expectations and calms their anxieties about being prepared to successfully design a TWS on their own.

The cornerstone of the successful implementation of the TWS paradigm is a mentoring process that provides expert guidance to the candidates through the formative stages of developing a TWS. The mentoring model is designed to be an integral part of the process of implementing the TWS, functioning as a bridge between past practice and the TWS expectations.

Figure 1: Course Program timeline for TWS component instruction

Millersville University of Pennsylvania
Elementary/Early Childhood Undergraduate Education Major
Teacher Work Sample (TWS) Timeline

Course in the Major	Component of TWS	I: Introduced P: Practiced M: Mastered
Introductory Block		
ELED 100: Introduction to Elem Ed	Contextual Factors	I, P
	Learning Goals	I, P
SPED 101: Introduction to Spec Educ	Contextual Factors	I, P
Foundations Block *(formative modified-TWS)*		
EDFN 211: Foundations of	Contextual Factors	P
Modern Education	N/A	
EDFN 241: Psychological	Learning Goals	P
Fndatns of Teaching	Assessment Plan	I
EDUC 220: Foundations of Reading	Design for	I
	Instruction	I, P
	Instructional	I
	Decision Making	I, P
	Analysis of Learning	
	Reflection & Self-evaluation	
Required		
EDUC 333: Children's Literature	N/A	
EDFN 320: Instructional Technology	Analysis of Student	I, P
in Elem Educ	Learning	
ELED 376: Assessment for Instructional	Contextual Factors	P
Planning	Learning Goals	P
	Assessment Plan	P, M
	Design for Instruction	P
	Instructional	P
	Decision Making	P, M
	Analysis of Student Learning	P
	Reflection & Self-evaluation	
Early Childhood Certification		
ELED 312: Seminar: Pre-Kindergarten	Contextual Factors	M
	Learning goals	P
	Assessment Plan	I
	Design for Instruction	P
	Instructional Decision Making	P
	Analysis of Student Learning	I
	Reflection & Self-evaluation	P
ELED 313: Seminar: Kindergarten	Learning Goals	P
	Assessment Plan	P
	Design for Instruction	P
	Reflection & Evaluation	P

Professional Block
*(formative TWS during field experience based
on mini-unit of 3-5 lessons)*

ELED 325: Teaching of Literacy	Contextual Factors	P
ELED 340: Teaching of Social Studies	Learning Goals	P
ELED 351: Teaching of Mathematics	Assessment Plan	P
ELED 361: Teaching of Science	Design for Instruction	P
EDUC 305: Field Experience	Instructional Decision Making	P
	Analysis of Student	P
	Learning	P
	Reflection & Self-evaluation	

ELED 461 and ELED 462: Student Teaching: Summative TWS
1st placement: written version
2nd placement: oral version

Compiled & designed by Rudden 2003

Connecting Teacher Preparation
To P-12 Student Learning

Then and Now

One way to appreciate the challenge of the TWS and offer a rationale for its serving as a credible source of evidence of the impact of teaching on learning is to look at a side-by-side comparison of the typical Unit of Instruction expected of teacher candidates in the past at this institution and the expectations of the TWS. Figure 2 depicts a simple comparison between those expectations.

The components connected by dotted lines reveal the gaps between past practice and the expectations of the TWS. It is clear to see that past practice sanctioned the pre-determined planning of instruction without attention to contextual factors or pre-assessment data. Further, the analysis of learning results rested solely on post testing in the past versus the TWS expectation to analyze learning results (pre and post) and disaggregate data to determine which learners require further adaptations to instruction.

Figure 3 shows an elaborated comparison between the expectations for the Unit of Instruction following the guidelines of past practice and the TWS. The primary distinctions between past practice and the TWS can be summed up by looking at the impact of contextual factors and pre-assessment data on the design for instruction. In terms of contextual factors past practice features

Figure 2. Simple Comparison of the Components of a Traditional Unit of Instruction and the Teacher Work Sample

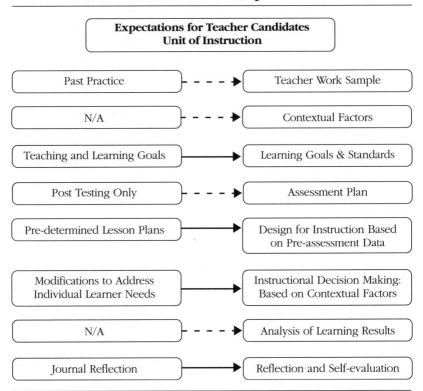

pre-determined lessons written and delivered like a neat little package of one-size-fits-all instruction. In the TWS, attention to the contextual factors provokes thinking about instruction in terms of possible adaptations that are called for to facilitate learning. For example, a classroom of 25 that includes 7 students who are English Language Learners (ELL) requires thinking about teaching in a way that predicts adaptations for individual differences and needs. Other contextual factors that might influence adaptations to instruction include (a) learning styles, (b) learning disabilities, (c) giftedness, (d) reading levels, (e)socio-economic status, and (f)cultural/ethnic influences on attitude toward learning, etc. Students do not learn in isolation from their environment, so teachers need to consider the possible impact of these factors on the teaching/learning process.

The impact of pre-assessment data on the design for instruction supports the practice of activating students' prior knowledge of the concept and

Figure 3. Elaborated Comparison of the Components of a Traditional Unit of Instruction and the TWS

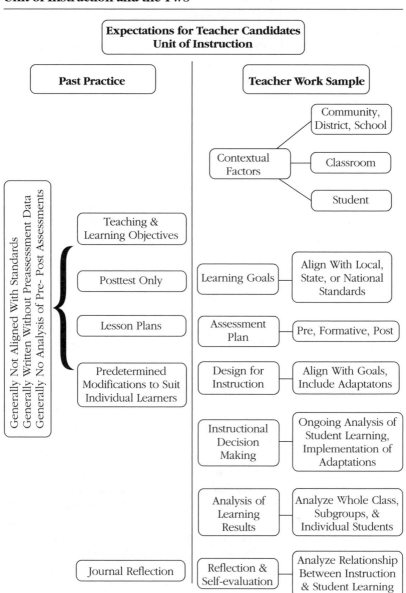

assessing whether they have sufficient prior knowledge to continue with the instruction or need further instruction before advancing to the next level of understanding. For example, if pre-assessment data indicate that the majority of the students have the prior knowledge necessary to comprehend an advanced understanding of the concept, the teacher can plan to continue with the lesson with embedded adaptations to bring the rest of the class up to the same level of understanding. Adaptations are generally implemented *during* instruction and comprehension is checked frequently with formative measures to ensure all students are on track. The teacher's reflection and self-evaluation should include an analysis of the relationship between the adaptations made to instruction and the level of student learning.

Teacher candidates complete two TWS units of study during student teaching, one for each 7-week placement. In addition to compiling and teaching the unit of study, the teacher candidate writes a 20-page narrative plus attachments that describes each of the seven TWS performance standards during the first placement. During the second placement, the teacher candidate meets several times with the mentors to orally describe each of the TWS performance standards.

The Bridge to New Habits of Mind

The goal of mentoring is to help teacher candidates change their perception of teaching from delivering pre-planned instruction to instruction that is based on learner needs, abilities, and prior knowledge. To accomplish this goal using the TWS, candidates must achieve expertise in three areas: (a) content knowledge, (b) pedagogical content knowledge, and (c) the influence of the school culture on learning. Recognizing the complexity of this task, a mentoring component has been developed as the way to model and enable teacher candidates to practice this new way of thinking. Members of the Renaissance Partnership developed the *Manual for Mentors: Coaching Teacher Candidates Through the Teacher Work Sample* and the *Manual for Teacher Candidates: Tips for Preparing the Teacher Work Sample* that have been used for training of faculty and school practitioners and as an additional tool for teacher candidates (The Renaissance Partnership for Improving Teacher Quality, 2001).

The mentoring component is linked to Cognitive Coaching (Costa & Garmston, 2002) and to Vygotsky's notion of the developmental stages of the cognitive domain: specifically, the Zone of Proximal Development, defined as that level of cognitive understanding that requires the support of a more capable other to be successful (Colton & Sparks-Langer, 1992). The mentor provides scaffolding to enable the candidate to move from what he or she already knows about teaching and the school culture to new understandings and skills. This scaffolding occurs on a continuum within the teacher candidate's Zone of Proximal Development (Colton & Sparks-Langer, 1992).

Direct and Indirect Mentoring

The focus of the mentoring process is always on helping teacher candidates become expert planners, reflective thinkers, problem solvers, and decision makers. The underlying purpose is to enhance the teacher candidate's self-directed learning, the ability to be self-managing, self-monitoring, and self-modifying (Costa & Garmston, 2002). Although self-directedness is the goal, there are times when teacher candidates need the mentor to be direct and to give specific suggestions and advice. Mentors must continually assess the level of functioning of the candidate and know when to take a direct approach or an indirect approach.

Cognitive coaching emphasizes the use of verbal and nonverbal language cues to communicate and to direct. These techniques include paraphrasing, probing, pausing, and reflective questioning (Costa & Garmston, 2002). Examples of verbal and nonverbal communication used in the direct and indirect approaches are described in Table 1.

Table 1. Continuum of Mentoring

Direct (Consulting) (MENTOR – teacher Candidate)*	Less-Direct (Coaching) (mentor/TEACHER CANDIDATE)*
Purpose: To provide information, skills, resources, or knowledge	**Purpose:** To improve decision making and reflective analytical thinking
Actions: Model and teach Provide directions Give examples Provide resources	**Actions:** Acknowledge and listen (assess what pre-service teacher should consider or re-think) Paraphrase ideas stated by pre-service teacher Probe for other ideas, perspectives, approaches, or interpretations Prompt analysis and reflection Brainstorm ideas or approaches
Language: You should . . . It is important to remember . . . Here is an example of . . . Always keep in mind. . . . Let's review what we know about alternative assessment.	**Language:** You mentioned that you wanted students to. . . . Tell me your thinking about. . . . What might be going on here? What might be a different approach to . . . ? How might this affect the students?

*Note: Words in all capital letters denote who does the most talking and analyzing.

When to Mentor

Mentoring occurs throughout the teacher education program, beginning in the freshman year and continuing through the senior student teaching practicum. Education faculty members who have been trained in the TWS prompts and scoring rubrics and in the mentoring process assume the role of mentor during the freshman to senior year, modeling and explaining the components of the TWS. They guide the candidates in the formative stages of developing the skills required. Opportunities to practice these skills in classroom settings are systematic and sequenced throughout the program of study. This ensures repetition and application to meaningful use that is supported by feedback throughout the process. (see Figure 1 for a reference to courses where specific TWS components are introduced, practiced, and mastered)

The mentoring team approach during student teaching that replaces the traditional supervisor/practitioner model enables all shareholders a place in the process: (a) Education faculty, (b) Arts and Science faculty, (c) university supervisors, and (d) school practitioners. Training sessions are provided on how to effectively use the TWS prompts and scoring rubrics. Mentoring training includes Arts and Science faculty, supervisors, and classroom practitioners. Training sessions have been held on campus and in public schools with varying times of two to six hours. Arts and Science faculty have been invited and encouraged to participate in mentoring elementary education students in the design of their units of instruction. Some of these faculty members have attended the formal trainings; others have participated in informal discussions. Arts and Sciences faculty support candidates primarily with content knowledge, making sure that the academic content is accurate and that misconceptions have been clarified. Arts and Sciences faculty and student teachers meet one or two times, usually in the faculty member's office, to review and assess the accuracy of the academic content and to develop appropriate activities and authentic assessments. Education faculty and university supervisors support the candidate primarily with pedagogical content knowledge. Formative support is provided during the semester prior to student teaching in the professional block classes. Student teachers are expected to complete the TWS independently; however, supervisors provide support as needed. Classroom practitioners who are most qualified to help the candidates understand the influence of the school culture on teaching and learning assist teacher candidates during the professional block field experience and student teaching. Table 2 shows a typical distribution of responsibilities across all constituents.

Table 2. Responsibility and Role of the Mentor

RESPONSIBILITY/ROLES/MENTORING TASKS	WHO DOES IT
Model, explain and provide feedback on the skills and expertise required to do TWS	Education faculty Field Supervisor School Practitioner
Assess and coach the teacher candidate's analytical and reflective thinking and writing	Education faculty Field Supervisor School Practitioner
Help the teacher candidate to move from naïve concepts (or lack of knowledge) to a new skill or understanding.	Content (Arts & Sciences) Faculty Education faculty Field Supervisor School Practitioner

The Importance of Mentoring

The need for mentoring throughout the formative stages of the candidate's development is especially important in their understanding how to modify instruction and assessment based on contextual factors, and how to narrate an analysis of student learning. Mentoring teams concentrate their efforts on guiding the candidates in their understanding of these components.

The mentoring model followed in the implementation of the TWS enables teacher candidates to focus on student learning. We have seen evidence of this in the way they reflect on and self-evaluate after teaching. The impact of their teaching on learning is prominently featured, rather than a preponderance of affective comments about how much the children seemed to enjoy a lesson. The personal and professional goals expressed in their reflections are directly related to improving their abilities to affect student learning. This trend supports a reasonable presumption that teacher candidates are developing new habits of mind relative to planning instruction. Holding to a high standard of reflective thinking, they are becoming better planners, problem solvers, and decision makers.

Discussion

In this chapter, we first described the differences between past practice and the new expectations as defined by the TWS; then, we described the support system of mentoring developed to ensure candidate success. The objectives of the TWS are echoed in the expectations for teacher candidates outlined by NCATE (2001) and the International Reading Association's *Standards for Reading Professionals-Revised 2003* (2004). *NCATE Standard 1: Knowledge, Skills, and Dispositions* explicitly states the requirement that schools of education provide evidence that they are preparing teacher candidates who can demonstrate the effect of their teaching on P-12 pupil learning. The Renaissance Group Project has been informally cited as an example of efforts that will address this component of the standard. The International Reading Association (2004) revised their 1998 Standards for Reading Professionals to include specific and measurable criteria for teacher candidates in the following categories: (a) foundational knowledge; (b) instructional strategies and curriculum materials; (c) assessment, (d) diagnosis, and evaluation; (e) creating a literate environment; and (f) professional development. Teacher preparation programs use these standards to guide curriculum planning and evaluate their candidates. The standards closely track the NCATE standards in expectation levels to the degree that, if a teacher preparation program meets these Specialized Program Association (SPA) standards, NCATE considers this endorsement as evidence of having met the NCATE standard for candidate knowledge, skills, and dispositions.

The Teacher Work Sample model represents a new paradigm for evaluating teacher candidates and we suggest it as one example of a framework to guide teacher candidates in planning instruction based on data, modifying instruction based on individual learner needs, and reflecting on their teaching and its effects on pupil learning.

In this chapter, a comparison was drawn between past practice and the expectations of the TWS to illustrate the high expectations set for teacher candidates. Though the TWS model imposes a rigor that requires focus on contextual factors, analysis of learning, and self-evaluation relevant to pupil progress, the unexpected benefits of using this model include a refining of abstract dispositions and habits of mind that are not easily taught.

The notion of mentoring the teacher candidate through the process of planning for instruction and analyzing pupil progress is not taken lightly. Mentoring training for practicing teachers and university supervisors is a major part of implementing the TWS paradigm. By its very nature, mentoring requires participation by all stakeholders. Repeated trials and pilot studies of the mentoring model have added a level of confidence in its validity.

The scope of this chapter was limited to the call from accrediting agencies to show evidence of impact of teaching on learning; the response to that call by one university; and the mentoring process that supports the candidate from the beginning to end of the process.

References

American Federation of Teachers (2000, April). *Building a profession: Strengthening teacher preparation and induction*. (Report of the K-16 Teacher Education Task Force). Washington, DC.

Blacklock, K. K., & Cartwright, D. (2003, February). *Teacher Work Samples and struggling readers: Impacting student performance and candidate dispositions.* Paper presented at the annual meeting of the American Association of Colleges for Teacher Education, New Orleans, LA. (ERIC Document Reproduction Service No. ED472395)

Cochran-Smith, M. (2000). Teacher education at the turn of the century. *Journal of Teacher Education, 51,* 163-165.

Colton, A. and Sparks-Langer, G. M. (1992). Restructuring student teaching experiences. In C. Glickman (Ed.) *Supervision in transition.* Alexandria, VA: Association of Supervision and Curriculum Development (ASCD).

Costa, A. L. and Garmston, R. J. (2002). *Cognitive coaching: A foundation for Renaissance schools.* Norwood, MA: Christopher-Gordon Publishers.

Denner, P. R., Norman, A. D., Pankratz, R. S., & Salzman, S. A. (2003, February). *Connecting teaching performance to student achievement: A generalizability and validity study of the Renaissance Teacher Work Sample assessment.* Paper presented at the annual meeting of the Association of Teacher Educators, Jacksonville, FL. (ERIC Document Reproduction Service No. ED474079)

Fredman, T. (2002, February). *The TWSM: An essential component in the assessment of teacher performance and student learning.* Paper presented at the annual meeting of the American Association of Colleges for Teacher Education, New York. (ERIC Document Reproduction Service No. ED464046)

Girod, G. R. (2002). *Connecting teaching and learning: A handbook for teacher educators on Teacher Work Sample Methodology.* Washington, DC: American Association of Colleges for Teacher Education. (ERIC Document Reproduction Service No. ED463282)

Lipton, L. & Wellman, B. (2002) *Mentoring Matters.* Sherman, CT: Miravia.

McConney, A. A., Schalock, M. D., & Schalock, H. D. (1998) Focusing improvement and quality assurance: Work samples as authentic performance measures of prospective teachers' effectiveness. *Journal of Personnel Evaluation in Education, 11,* 343-363.

National Council for Accreditation of Teacher Education (2001). Professional standards for the accreditation of schools, colleges, and departments of education. Washington, D.C.: NCATE.

Professional Standards and Ethics Committee, International Reading Association. (2004). Standards for reading professionals-revised 2003. Newark, DE: International Reading Association. Retrieved on June 30, 2004, from http://www.reading.org/advocacy/standards/standards03_revised/.

Salzman, S. A., Denner, P. R., Bangert, A. W., & Harris, L. B. (2001, March). *Connecting teacher performance to the learning of all students: Ethical dimensions of shared responsibility.* Paper presented at the annual meeting of the American Association of Colleges for Teacher Education, Dallas, TX. (ERIC Document Reproduction Service No. ED451182)

Stronge, J. H. & Tucker, P. D. (2000). *Assessing teacher performance with student work: The Oregon Teacher Work Sample Methodology.* Washington, DC: National Education Association.

The Renaissance Partnership for Improving Teacher Quality. (2001).*Improving Teacher Quality through Partnerships that Connect Teacher Performance to Student Learning.* Retrieved July 19, 2004, from http://fp.uni.edu/itqProjectActivities/index.htm

How Preservice Teachers Score an Informal Reading Inventory: Strengths and Weaknesses

Jerry L. Johns
Susan K. L'Allier

Northern Illinois University

Abstract

This study examined how reliably preservice teachers scored and interpreted data regarding three aspects of an informal reading inventory: word recognition, oral miscues, and reading comprehension. Subjects (N=49) enrolled in their second undergraduate reading course received instruction in the administration, scoring, and interpretation of the Basic Reading Inventory *(Johns, 2001). After instruction, participants completed four scoring and interpretation tasks. Their responses were compared to those of an expert in the area of informal reading inventories. Results indicated that the participants were highly reliable with the work related to word lists and total miscues. They had some difficulty scoring and interpreting unexpected comprehension responses. However, they demonstrated the most difficulty with identifying significant miscues. The investigators take the demonstrated weaknesses into consideration when providing recommendations for improving instruction that will enable preservice teachers to enter their own classrooms with the skills needed to more reliably score and interpret informal reading inventories.*

In a previous study, these researchers found that practicing teachers were, based on an analysis of their accuracy in completing summary sheets and interpreting those results to determine the three reading levels for three different students, highly reliable in their scoring of the *Basic Reading Inventory* (Johns, 2001). In this study, the researchers focused on the reliability of preservice teachers to score and determine reading levels for word lists, oral reading passages, and comprehension questions.

Framework for the Study

Student progress in reading is at the forefront of today's educational agenda, and one of the multiple indicators often used to demonstrate that progress is the informal reading inventory (Ackland, 1994; Harris & Lalik, 1987; Margolis & McCabe, 1988; Paris & Carpenter, 2003; Searls, 1988). Used over time, such inventories can present a clear picture of a student's progress in several critical areas of reading: word identification, oral reading accuracy and rate, reading comprehension, and listening comprehension (Ackland, 1994; Ediger, 2000; VanLeirsburg & Johns, 1995).

As informal reading inventories were developed and used in the middle and latter part of the 20th century, researchers mainly focused on internal aspects of the inventories. Attention was given to (a) the specific components that should be included in an inventory (Johnson, Kress, & Pikulski, 1987); (b) the scoring guidelines that should be used to determine the independent, instruction, and frustration reading levels (Anderson & Joels, 1986; Betts, 1946; Davis & Ekwall, 1976; Homan & Klesius, 1985; Johns & Magliari, 1989); (c) the definition of a miscue (Anderson & Joels, 1986; Ekwall, 1974) and of significant miscues (Goodman, 1973); and (d) reliable methods for determining comprehension including an examination of the use of questions and retelling (Allen & Swearingen, 1991; Helgren-Lempesis and Mangrum, 1986), and the addition of a prior-knowledge assessment (Caldwell, 1985) and look-back procedure (Cardarelli, 1988; Kender & Rubenstein, 1977, Leslie & Caldwell, 2001).

The more recent recognition of the informal reading inventory as an appropriate assessment tool to determine if students are progressing toward the achievement of state and national reading standards has focused attention on the need for practicing and preservice teachers to be proficient administrators, scorers, and interpreters of such inventories. Concerns over teacher reliability in these areas (Harris & Lalik, 1987; Kelly, 1970; Klesius & Homan, 1985; Paris, Paris, & Carpenter, 2001) have led to a small number of studies.

Practicing teachers who were enrolled in graduate reading courses were the subjects of studies by Roberts (1974) and Johns and L'Allier (2003). Roberts' study compared the effectiveness of two types of instruction related to the identification of oral reading errors and the assignment of a corresponding reading level. Participants in the experimental group received basic instruction about the procedures and scoring plus practice sessions with instructor feedback, while participants in the control group only received the basic instruction. The results indicated that the experimental group was significantly better at identifying oral reading errors but not at determining the corresponding reading level.

Johns and L'Allier's (2003) study examined the reliability of practicing teachers to score the summary sheet data of an informal reading inventory after they had received about two hours of classroom instruction that included both lecture and practice completing student assessment samples. When all of the data were considered, agreement was 96% when compared to the consensus scoring of three experts. When the subjects' determination of the reading levels was compared to that of the experts, the average agreement percentage was 89%. Thus, both studies indicated that, when instruction included practice sessions with sample assessments, practicing teachers enrolled in graduate reading courses were highly reliable in their ability to score and interpret informal reading inventories.

Because of their undergraduate coursework, their years of experience in the classroom, and their participation in on-going professional development activities, it may be that practicing teachers have a more developed understanding about the reading process and informal assessments than do preservice teachers who have had much less coursework and time in the classroom interacting with students. These experiences, as well as the instruction, may enable practicing teachers to be more reliable in their scoring of an informal reading inventory. However, with the increased emphasis on assessment by the classroom teacher, it is important that today's preservice teachers be ready to administer, score, and interpret an informal reading inventory when they enter their classrooms. A few studies have focused on the relationship between instruction and scoring proficiency of preservice teachers (Traynelis-Yurek & Strong, 2000; Wedman, Hughes, & Robinson, 1993; Windell, 1975). Windell (1975) developed a module that included a manual and practice sessions linked to audiotapes to teach about the informal reading inventory. The results of his study found that preservice special education teachers who went through the module were significantly better at determining a student's instructional level than similar preservice teachers who had received no instruction about informal reading inventories. Thus, this study seems to support the basic supposition that some instruction is better than no instruction.

Wedman, Hughes, and Robinson's study (1993) examined the effectiveness of two types of instruction. Preservice teachers in the systematic cooperative learning group received nine hours of instruction that included lectures, small group coding of several audio-taped student samples, and feedback from the instructor regarding the coding. Preservice teachers in the direct instruction group also received nine hours of instruction; however, all of their instruction was lecture in format. On a multiple-choice test related to the administration and scoring of informal reading inventories, the systematic cooperative learning group scored significantly better than the lecture-only group. However, it should be noted that the participants in the systematic cooperative learning group reported on an after-instruction perception survey that the lectures contributed to their understanding of the procedures almost as much as the group work. The results of this study suggest that lecture and guided practice are both important components of instruction for preservice teachers.

Traynelis-Yurek and Strong (2000) examined the difficulties preservice teachers had in scoring a simulated informal reading inventory. Even though they had received instruction about the administration and scoring prior to the simulation activity, these preservice teachers, who came from three different teacher-training programs, still had difficulty accurately scoring miscues and comprehension responses. The results of this study suggest that these two aspects need more attention during instruction.

To provide additional information regarding the reliability of scoring informal reading inventories by preservice teachers, this study's design incorporated several of the implications from the earlier studies. First, the instruction provided to the preservice teachers included both lecture and guided practice using examples from actual elementary students. Second, the individual tasks were designed to provide more specific information concerning the difficulties preservice teachers would likely encounter when scoring and interpreting various aspects of an informal reading inventory. Thus, the results should lead to further suggestions to assist teacher educators in helping preservice teachers enter their classrooms with the skills needed to reliably score and interpret informal reading inventories.

Method
Sample
Forty-nine students enrolled in an undergraduate reading course titled "Organizing for Effective Elementary Reading Instruction" were asked to complete four tasks commonly undertaken when administering and scoring any informal reading inventory. All of the students were majoring in elementary education, and "Organizing for Effective Elementary Reading Instruction" was their second course in reading. In their first reading course, informal reading inventories were briefly described during a lecture/discussion on various reading assessments. During the second reading course, students read the manual for the *Basic Reading Inventory* (Johns, 2001) and viewed a video depicting a sample administration of that inventory. Class time was spent scoring and determining reading levels for a variety of student samples and discussing any aspects of administration and scoring that the preservice teachers found confusing. The instructor, who was not one of the researchers, has extensive experience using informal reading inventories with elementary students and, prior to this study, had taught the administration, scoring,

and interpretation of the *Basic Reading Inventory* (Johns, 2001) to several classes of preservice teachers.

Materials and Procedures for the Study

The subjects in this study completed four separate tasks. The first task (see Appendix A) was based on the actual responses made by a student on the seventh and eighth grade word lists from Form A of the *Basic Reading Inventory* (Johns, 2001). The preservice teachers calculated the sight, analysis, and total scores and then used the scoring guidelines to determine the corresponding reading level for each word list. The second task (see Appendix B) focused on a coded sample of a student's oral reading of the fourth-grade passage from Form A of the *Basic Reading Inventory* (Johns, 2001). The preservice teachers counted the total number of miscues, determined the number of significant miscues, and used the scoring guides to determine the corresponding reading level. The third task (see Appendix C) was related to a student's actual responses to the comprehension questions for the fourth-grade passage from Form A of the *Basic Reading Inventory* (Johns, 2001). The preservice teachers scored each response, totaled the number of incorrect responses, and used the scoring guide to determine the corresponding reading level.

The final task was the most authentic and complex. The preservice teachers listened to the fourth-grade passage from Form B of the *Basic Reading Inventory* (Johns, 2001) that was read aloud by their instructor; moreover, it represented the actual reading of an elementary student. The instructor also read the student's actual responses to the corresponding comprehension questions. The preservice teachers, as they listened, coded the passage for miscues and wrote down the responses to the comprehension questions. After listening, they counted the total number of miscues, determined the number of significant miscues, scored the comprehension questions, totaled the number of incorrect responses, and used the scoring guidelines to determine whether the scores placed the oral reading and comprehension at the independent, instruction, or frustration level.

After the students had completed all of the tasks, the materials were returned to the researchers for scoring. Each completed summary sheet was compared to the master sheet that represented the responses of the main researcher, who was considered an expert because he has developed informal reading inventories and also presented workshops throughout the country on the administration and scoring of such inventories. For each word list, the agreement percentage was based on how well the subjects and the expert agreed on the sight, analysis, and total scores, and on the corresponding reading level. For the coded miscue passage, an agreement percentage was determined for the total number of miscues and its corresponding reading level as well as for the number of significant miscues and its corresponding reading level. The agreement percentage for the comprehension task was based on the total number of correct responses and the corresponding reading level. For the final multi-task example based on an elementary student's performance, an agreement percentage was computed for three aspects: the number of total miscues and its corresponding reading level; the number of significant miscues and its corresponding reading level, and the number of correct comprehension responses and its corresponding reading level.

Based on the researchers' previous study with practicing teachers and the estimated difficulty of the various tasks in this study, it was expected that these preservice teachers would have a high degree of agreement with the expert on the word lists, the total number of miscues/corresponding reading level on the coded oral reading passage, and the comprehension responses. However, it was expected that they would have a lower degree of agreement with the expert on the number of significant miscues/corresponding reading level on the coded oral reading passage and on the final multi-task sample. Since the determination of significant miscues requires an understanding of syntactic and semantic appropriateness, this task would appear to necessitate an increased number of higher-level judgments than are needed for the simpler counting requirements of the word list task and the determination of total miscues from the coded passage. In addition, on the final task, it was believed that the need for the subjects to actually code the miscues from the oral reading passage would likely result in more inaccuracies than the counting of miscues in an already-coded passage.

Results
Word List Task

When the results for the two word lists were combined, the total overall agreement with the expert was 92%, indicating that the preservice teachers were able to reliably score and determine corresponding reading levels for this relatively simple task. The agreement for the seventh-grade word list (96%) was higher than for the eighth-grade word list (88%). A close examination of the responses revealed that the coding of the response for the word "custody" on the eighth-grade list may have been confusing; some subjects scored it as incorrect under analysis because the student gave an incorrect pronunciation of the word before finally giving the correct pronunciation. It is possible that the subjects inaccurately scored this word because similar examples had not been encountered and discussed during the instructional portion of the course.

Total and Significant Miscues on the Coded Oral Reading Passage

For the task of counting total miscues, the subjects' agreement with the expert was 86%. An examination of the individual responses indicated that most of the errors were due to an undercounting or over counting of miscues, rather than to an inability to accurately use the scoring guides to determine the corresponding reading level. As expected, the subjects had more difficulty counting significant miscues. For this aspect of the task, the subject/expert agreement was 72%. Analysis of the errors indicated that some subjects counted self-corrected miscues as significant miscues and others found it difficult to determine when a miscue did and did not create a change in meaning.

Comprehension Responses

The agreement between the preservice teachers and the expert on the comprehension task was 79%. As was the case with the word lists and total miscues, some subjects simply added incorrectly. However, other errors could be pinpointed to those responses where greater judgment was required. In these cases, some subjects failed to give partial credit to a response that deserved such credit, and others gave partial credit to a response that deserved none. For example, with the question, "What colors were the leaves in this story?", the correct response needed to include two of the following: yellow, orange, red. The student's response was "red and green." That response deserved partial credit; however, some subjects gave the response total credit while others gave it no credit.

Multi-task Passage

Table 1 shows the agreement percentage for the various tasks in the fourth-grade passage that was coded and scored by the preservice teachers. When coding and counting the miscues from an oral reading passage, subjects were much more accurate in their scoring of total miscues (93%) than of significant miscues (68%). This pattern was consistent with results from the earlier passage on which the miscues had already been coded. In both tasks, these preservice teachers appeared to have considerable difficulty determining whether or not a miscue caused a change in meaning. However, they appeared to have less difficulty scoring comprehension questions, and their agreement percentage on the comprehension portion of the multi-task passage (81%) was consistent with the agreement percentage on the earlier comprehension task (79%). In order to determine a student's overall reading level on an oral reading passage, it is necessary to consider the data related to oral miscues and to comprehension. The results of this study indicate that preservice teachers would determine a student's reading level most reliably using total miscues and comprehension (87% agreement).

Table 1. Percentages of Agreement with the Expert for the Multi-task Passage

	Agreement percentage
Total and significant miscues	80%
Total miscues	93%
Significant miscues	68%
Comprehension	81%
Total miscues and comprehension	87%

Conclusions

The various tasks in this study provided a consistent picture of preservice teachers' strengths and weaknesses in scoring an informal reading inventory. Their strengths included the ability to reliably score word lists (92% agreement with the expert) and total number of miscues from an oral reading passage (86% and 90% agreement on the two different tasks). They were less reliable in their scoring of comprehension responses (79% and 81% agreement on the two different tasks). Their main weakness lay in their lack of higher-level decision-making ability to determine the significant miscues from an oral reading passage (72% and 68% on the two different tasks).

While the results in this study were internally consistent, it should be noted that the study was limited to one informal reading inventory and to students from one university who had been presented with instruction about that reading inventory that included the reading of the manual, the viewing of a video depicting a sample administration of the inventory, and the completion/discussion of sample inventory responses during at least one class period. Thus, the implications of the results should be restricted to similar teachers who had engaged in similar reading, video viewing, and teacher-guided practice. However, the results were consistent with the results from at least one previous study (Traynelis-Yurek & Strong, 2000). In both studies, even after instruction, preservice teachers had difficulty with some aspect of miscue coding and comprehension scoring. Thus, across populations, there do appear to be some common problems that need attention.

Helping Preservice Teachers Achieve Higher Levels of Scoring Expertise

The reliability results and an examination of the subjects' errors on the various tasks provided data to the researchers concerning practices that instructors might employ to help preservice teachers achieve higher levels of scoring expertise with the *Basic Reading Inventory* (Johns, 2001). The investigators believe these recommendations are applicable for instruction about other informal reading inventories as well.

First, it is recommended that more time be spent on the areas of significant miscues and self-corrected miscues. While preservice teachers appeared competent in coding, counting, and determining the corresponding reading level for total miscues, they had difficulty determining whether a given miscue was significant or not. These researchers suggest that further work on significant miscues be included in the in-class coding/discussion of actual student samples. Such activities would (a) allow the instructor to specify how a variety of significant miscues cause changes in meaning, (b) give the preservice teachers opportunities to ask questions about specific miscues, and (c) give the preservice teachers practice in orally explaining their reasoning for classifying a miscue as significant or not significant. Prior to whole class discussions, having pairs of preservice teachers compare their miscue scoring would afford increased opportunities to orally present their rationales for various scoring decisions. These activities should provide the instruction and guided practice in the higher-level thinking needed to improve the reliability of scoring significant miscues. In addition to a focus on significant miscues, it is recommended that the instructor clarify the role of self-corrections. Some informal reading inventories include self-corrections in the count of total miscues; others do not. Specific mention of how the inventory being used deals with self-corrections should prevent preservice teachers from making errors in this area.

Some attention also needs to be given to the scoring of comprehension questions. Preservice teachers need more practice with the scoring of responses that may be (a) accurate in terms of the general topic but were not specifically mentioned in the passage, and (b) worthy of partial credit instead of total credit or no credit. Once again, it would seem that such guided practice should be part of the in-class work with actual student samples.

In order to appropriately determine a student's three reading levels and thus provide appropriate recreational and instructional reading materials for that student, it is necessary to consider the student's oral miscues and comprehension. Since the results of this study indicate that preservice teachers are highly reliable in scoring total miscues and quite reliable in scoring comprehension, these researchers would recommend that for their work with students during early clinical experiences and student teaching, preservice teachers use those two measures to determine a student's reading levels. However, preservice teachers should not ignore the issue of significant miscues. It is recommended that cooperating teachers review the results of any informal reading inventories given by preservice teachers and provide specific feedback about their scoring of significant miscues. With this feedback, the preservice teachers can use the significant miscue data to help determine instructional needs for individual students.

Finally, it is recommended that preservice teachers be reminded to refer to the manual frequently when scoring informal reading inventories. These researchers have frequently seen student teachers score inventories without once looking at the manual. Perhaps instructors could point out specific pages that would be most helpful; these pages could then be bookmarked in some fashion or removed and placed in protective sleeves for easy access. Such pages might include the following: a summary of the administration and scoring procedures (e.g., page 48 in the *Basic Reading Inventory*, [Johns, 2001]); an explanation of significant miscues (e.g., pages 30, 33, 45, and 46 in the *Basic Reading Inventory* [Johns, 2001]); and an overview of how to score comprehension responses that may deviate from those given in the inventory (e.g., pages 27 and 28 in the *Basic Reading Inventory*, [Johns, 2001]).

References

Ackland, R. T. (1994). Let's look at reading: Interactive professional development using informal reading inventories. *Dissertation Abstracts International, 55*(11), 3477.

Allen, D. D., & Swearingen, R. A. (1991, May). *Informal reading inventories: What are they really asking?* Paper presented at the annual meeting of the International Reading Association, Las Vegas, NV.

Anderson, B., & Joels, R. W. (1986). Informal reading inventories. *Reading Improvement, 23*, 299-302.

Betts, E. A. (1946). *Foundations of reading instruction.* New York: American Book Company.

Caldwell, J. (1985). A new look at the old informal reading inventory. *The Reading Teacher, 39*, 168-173.

Cardarelli, A. F. (1988). The influence of reinspection on students' IRI results. *The Reading Teacher, 41*, 664-667.

Davis, E. E., & Ekwall, E. E. (1976). Mode of perception and frustration in reading. *Journal of Learning Disabilities, 9*(7), 53-59.

Ediger, M. (2000). *Appraising reading achievement.* Missouri, U.S. (ERIC Document Reproduction Service No. ED441217)

Ekwall, E. E. (1974). Should repetitions be counted as errors? *The Reading Teacher, 27*, 365-367.

Goodman, K. S. (1973). Analysis of oral reading miscues: Applied psycholinguistics. In F. Smith (Ed.), *Psycholinguistics and reading* (pp. 158-176). New York: Holt, Rinehart and Winston.

Harris, L. A., & Lalik, R. M. (1987). Teacher's use of informal reading inventories: An example of school constraints. *The Reading Teacher, 40*, 624-630.

Helgren-Lempesis, V. A., & Mangrum, C. T., II. (1986). An analysis of alternate-form reliability of three commercially-prepared informal reading inventories. *Reading Research Quarterly, 21*, 209-215.

Homan, S. P., & Klesius, J. P. (1985). A re-examination of the IRI: Word recognition criteria. *Reading Horizons, 26*(1) 54-61.

Johns, J. L. (2001). *Basic reading inventory* (8th ed.). Dubuque, IA: Kendall/Hunt.

Johns, J. L., & L'Allier, S. K. (2003). How well can teachers score an informal reading inventory? In M.B. Sampson, P. E. Linder, J. R. Dugan, & B. Brancato (Eds.), *The College Reading Association yearbook: Vol. 25: Celebrating the freedom of literacy* (pp. 251-264). Commerce, TX: College Reading Association.

Johns, J. L., & Magliari, A. M. (1989). Informal reading inventories: Are the Betts criteria the best criteria? *Reading Improvement, 26*, 124-132.

Johnson, M. S., Kress, R. A., & Pikulski, J. J. (1987). *Informal reading inventories* (2nd ed.). Newark, DE: International Reading Association.

Kelly, D. (1970). Using an informal reading inventory to place children in instructional materials. In W. K. Durr (Ed.), *Reading difficulties: Diagnosis, correction, and remediation* (pp. 111-119). Newark, DE: International Reading Association.

Kender, J. P., & Rubenstein, H. (1977). Recall versus reinspection in IRI comprehension tests. *The Reading Teacher, 30*, 776-779.

Klesius, J. P., & Homan, S. P. (1985). A validity and reliability update on the informal reading inventory with suggestions for improvement. *Journal of Learning Disabilities, 18*(2), 71-76.

Leslie, L., & Caldwell, J. (2001). *Qualitative reading inventory.* New York: Longman.

Margolis, H., & McCabe, P. (1988). The use of test results by elementary school teachers to place students in basal and content materials. *Ohio Reading Teacher, 22*, 6-14.

Paris, S. G., & Carpenter, R. D. (2003). FAQs about IRIs. *The Reading Teacher, 56*, 578-580.

Paris, S. G., Paris, A. H., & Carpenter, R. D. (2001). *Effective practices for assessing young readers* (Report No. CIERA-3-013). Ann Arbor, MI: Center for the Improvement of Early Reading Achievement.

Roberts, J. D. (1974). Identification of oral reading errors and functional reading levels on informal reading inventories. *Dissertation Abstracts International, 35*(9), 5994.

Searls, E. F. (1988). What's the value of an IRI? Is it being used? *Reading Horizons, 28*(2), 92-101.

Traynelis-Yurek, E., & Strong, M. W. (2000). Preservice teachers' ability to determine miscues and comprehension response errors of elementary students. *Journal of Reading Education, 26*(1), 15-22.

VanLeirsburg, P., & Johns, J. L. (1995). Portfolios: Teachers' perceptions and practices. *Michigan Reading Journal, 29*(1), 14-23.

Wedman, J. M., Hughes, J. A., & Robinson, R. R. (1993). The effect of using a systematic cooperative learning approach to help preservice teachers learn informal reading inventory procedures. *Innovative Higher Education, 17*, 231-241.

Windell, I. (1975). *Development and evaluation of a module to train special education teacher trainees to determine a pupil's instructional reading level.* Bloomington: Indiana University. (ERIC Document Reproduction Service No. ED111142)

Appendix A. Word List Task

List A 3717 (Grade 7)	Sight	Analysis	List A 8183 (Grade 8)	Sight	Analysis
1. dwell			1. quote	quotation	+
2. slogan			2. ventilate		
3. knapsack			3. surgeon		
4. administration			4. analyze		
5. gangster			5. masterpiece		
6. flatter	flutter	+	6. pollute		
7. incredible			7. extradorinary	camo	
8. algebra			8. camouflage	camoflag	+
9. bachelor	backalor	+	9. ruthless		
10. vocabulary			10. perpendicular		
11. longitude			11. juvenile		
12. salvia			12. vacancy	văcancy	D.K.
13. peninsula			13. dictator		
14. monarch	mon/arch	+	14. negative		
15. feminine			15. honorary	honor	+
16. quench			16. custody	custŏdy	custŏdy +
17. competition			17. maneuver		
18. disinfectant			18. faculty		
19. ambitious			19. pneumonia	D.K.	D.K.
20. orchid	orchard	orchard	20. embassy		
Number Correct			Number Correct		
Total			Total		

Level: Ind.   Inst.   Frust.   **Level: Ind.   Inst.   Frust.**

Key	Scoring Guide for Graded Word Lists		
+ = corrected	Independent	Instructional	Frustration
D.K. = didn't know	20 19	18 17 16 15 14	13 or less

Appendix B. Miscue Task on Coded Oral Reading Passage

A 5414 (Grade 4) Activating Background: Read the tile to yourself; then tell me what you think will happen.

Background: Low |———————+———————| High

Fire and Animals

saw ⊚
The summer was a dry one, ~~unusual~~
for this area. Trees and bushes in the forest
P   dried
wilted and died. One afternoon a storm
and
came to the forest↓ Thunder was heard and
begun ⊚
lightning was seen. Then it began to
rain. <u>A spark</u> touched the leaves and a
very
fire began. The fire spread↓quickly. The
animals warned each other as they hurried
to escape the flames. As the fire came
fall ⊚
closer, <u>trees fell</u> to the ground. Their
branches were yellow, orange, and red.
The smoke was so thick, ~~that~~ the animals
could hardly breathe. Many couldn't
Escape the danger of the flames.

Word Recognitions Scoring Guide

Total Miscues	Level	Significant Miscues
0-1	Independent	0-1
2-4	Ind./Inst.	2
5	Instructional	3
6-9	Inst./Frust.	4
10+	Frustration	5+

1. Count the *total* miscues made in the passage. All of the following are included when counting miscues:

   - Substitutions (e.g., the for a; shown as the on the passage)
     a
   - Omissions
     Words (e.g., the ~~big~~ bear)
     Punctuation (e.g., the dog↓)
   - Additions (arrow indicates where the word was inserted)
   - Self-corrections(e.g., that ⊚)
   - Examiner aid (P over the word)

   Do *not* count repetitions—noted by underlining of the word(s).

   Write the number of total miscues in the Total Miscues box at the bottom of the page. Use the scoring guide and indicate the level on the line provided.

2. Determine *significant* miscues using the following criteria:
   - Examine each miscue.
   - A miscue that is corrected is *not* counted as significant.
   - A miscue that does not result in a significant change in meaning is *not* counted as significant.
   - Examiner aid (P) *is* a significant miscue.

   Write the number of significant miscues in the Significant Miscues box at the bottom of the page. Use the scoring guide and indicate the level on the line provided.

Total Miscues [   ]   Significant Miscues [   ]

Level: _____   Level: _____

Appendix C. Comprehension Task

A 5414 (Grade 4) Comprehension Questions

T 1.___ What is this story about"
(a forest fire)

F 2.___ What did the animals try to do?
(escape; warn each other)
run to save their lives

F 3.___ What was unusual about this summer?
(it had been a dry one)
hot and wet

F 4.___ What was heard and seen in the
woods before the fire began?
(thunder and lightning)

F 5.___ What started the fire?
(a spark; lightning)
from the

F 6.___ What colors were the trees in this story?
(yellow, orange, and red [any 2])
red and green

F 7.___ Why was it difficult for the animals
to breathe?
(smoke filled the air; the fire)
from all the smoke

I 8.___ Why do you think the fire spread
quickly?
(any logical response; it had been
a dry summer) **lightning**

E 9.___ What problems do you think the
animals that survived the fire might
have? (any logical response)
try to find another home

V 10.___ What does "escape" mean?
(get away; any logical response)
to get out quickly

☐ Questions
Missed

Level: _____

Comprehension Scoring Guide	
Questions Missed	Level
0 to 1	Independent
1 to 1/2–2	Ind./Inst.
2 to 1/2	Instructional
3 to 4-1/2	Inst./Frust.
5+	Frustration

Scoring the Responses

1. Refer to the passage as needed.

2. Write your score of full credit (+), half
credit (1/2), or no credit(-) on the line
next to the question.

3. A line under words indicated the
student's response.

4. Words or phrases that have been printed
on the form also indicate the student's
response.

5. Determine the number of questions
missed. Write this number in the Questions Missed box.

6. Use the scoring guide and indicate the
level on the line provided.

Remember,
you can give a response
- full credit (+),
- half credit (1/2),
- no credit (-).

Becoming Teachers of Writing: A Model of Professional Development for Primary Teachers

Ruth A. Oswald
Kristine Lynn Still

The University of Akron

Abstract

The No Child Left behind Act of 2001 (NCLB) *is very clear about the qualifications for teachers of core academic subjects. Therefore school districts are in need of quality professional development for their teachers. Research demonstrates that the reading and writing processes are symbiotic, so it is important that teachers attend to writing as well as reading instruction. Unfortunately with time an increasing concern in the school day, writing has been pushed aside in favor of reading and other subjects. This article shares the collaboration of one rural school district and a university professor, and their yearlong effort to provide professional development for primary teachers in writing instruction. Discussion includes a summary of recent literature on effective professional development as well as a review of the overall project. Finally, a summary of participant feedback is provided as well as the implications of these outcomes for future professional development.*

This article represents a collaborative effort between a university educator and a doctoral candidate in literacy at the same university. The purpose of this effort is to provide a program description of professional development. The university educator planned and delivered a series of professional development sessions over the course of a year for primary teachers in a rural school district on the topic of writing instruction. Feedback from the participants was collected in the form of evaluations and a questionnaire at the conclusion of the sessions, and this feedback was then used to plan future in-service sessions. A review of recent literature was also conducted on the topic of professional development, including recent trends that affect this development and essential components of effective professional development that impact classroom practices. A summary of the outcomes, based on the authors' evaluation of this program, as well as implications for future professional development are also included.

Background

The *No Child Left Behind Act of 2001* (*NCLB*) requires that teachers of core academic subjects be highly qualified. Therefore, school districts are seeking professional development for their teachers to support this requirement. This legislation is designed to support teachers by giving them the very best tools including the research-based lessons and materials as well as the best training to ensure that no child is left behind. The *NCLB* legislation has very specific guidelines that can be summarized into eight key elements of professional development which include the following:

1. All activities are referenced to student learning.
2. Schools use data to make decisions about the content and type of activities that constitute professional development.
3. Professional development activities are based on research-validated practices.
4. Subject matter mastery for all teachers is a top priority.
5. There is a long-term plan that provides focused and ongoing professional development with time well allocated.
6. Professional development activities match the content that is being instructed.
7. All professional development activities are fully evaluated.
8. Professional development is aligned with state standards, assessment, and the local school curriculum ("Strategies for", 2004, p.1).

The writing process is an essential skill that learners of all ages need to master in order to become functional and literate members of society. Research demonstrates that the reading and writing process are symbiotic, so it is important that in light of the *NCLB*, we attend to writing as well as reading instruction. Graves (2002) explained,

> We forget that writing is the making of reading. Children who write apply phonics, construct syntax, and experience the full range of skills inherent in authoring a text. Writers are more assertive readers and are less likely to accept the ideas and texts of others without question, since they are in the reading-construction business themselves. But writing is very expensive to assess and, unlike reading, seldom evaluated (p. 2).

Unfortunately with time an increasing concern in the school day, writing has been pushed to one side in favor of reading and those other subjects that can easily be tested.

The current emphasis on scientifically-based reading research (SBRR) does not support the importance of a process approach to writing instruction since research in this area has been qualitative in nature, often focusing on individual children. The findings of the National Reading Panel (2000) do not include writing as one of the "five essential components" of reading instruction because of this lack of SBRR in the area of writing instruction.

However, a recent report by the National Commission on Writing in America's Schools and Colleges (*Report Calls,* 2003) calls for an immediate launch of an implementation campaign, *The Writing Challenge to the Nation*, a five-year effort to be led by former Senator Bob Kerrey, current President of New School University in New York City. The report calls writing "The Neglected R" and cites National Assessment of Educational Progress (NAEP) research to support the inadequate progress of students from grade four through twelve to support its recommendations. According to this NAEP research, approximately 50% of the students at grades 4, 8, and 12, meet "basic" requirements and only one in five can be labeled "proficient." Commission Vice-Chair Arlene Ackerman, San Francisco Superintendent of Schools states, "Very few things are more important to improving student achievement than restoring writing to its proper place in the classroom" ("Report Calls," 2003, p. 4). The report announces that the amount of time and money devoted to student writing must be dramatically increased in school districts throughout the United States, and recommends that state and local curriculum guidelines must require writing in every curriculum at all grade levels.

Another current national and state educational trend that supports the emphasis on writing instruction is the standards-based movement. Ohio's state language arts content standards include three standards focusing on writing development. For this reason, the first author was invited by a rural school district to develop and provide yearlong professional development for their primary teachers on the topic of standards-based writing instruction. The teachers from the district had requested this training.

Review of Recent Literature on Effective Professional Development
What are the goals of professional development?
There are three major goals guiding professional development efforts (Robinson & Carrington, 2002). First, is the knowledge base of the teachers for whom the experience is specifically designed in which facilitators hope to see growth. Second, when teachers realize they have gained new information, they are encouraged to take this new information and transform it into manageable forms that come alive in their practice. The third and ultimate goal is for the professional development to positively change student outcomes. If *serious* teachers can see the connection between learning some-

thing new and valuable that will increase student achievement, professional development facilitators are more than likely welcomed with open arms by participating teachers. Teachers are more likely to accept change if it helps their students learn more efficiently and effectively (Guskey, 1986).

Guskey (1986) states:

> Clearly, teachers are attracted to staff development programs because they believe these activities can potentially expand their knowledge and skills, contribute to their growth, and enhance their effectiveness with students. But it is also clear that teachers carry with them to staff development programs a very pragmatic orientation. What they hope to gain through staff development programs are specific, concrete, and practical ideas that directly relate to the day-to-day operation of their classrooms (p. 6).

What are the most effective models of professional development?

The most effective models of teacher professional development must move beyond the traditional model based on the transmission of information from someone in authority. Research indicates that adults learn best in situations that reflect a constructivist view of learning (Sandholtz, 2002). Zepeda (1999) believes that learning is much more than the transfer of knowledge from one who is knowledgeable to one who is not. Her perception of the learning process is a personal experience whereby the reflection and transformation of ideas, experiences, and points of view integrate with each other to create knowledge. Zepeda (1999) further claims that when a constructivist perspective is applied to teacher learning, the focus shifts to teachers' abilities to make critically reflective judgments in active environments and how their subsequent reactions change in response to new insights. The ultimate model of professional development will result in the formulation of learning communities among staff members involved in the professional development experience. Kinnucan-Welsh & Jenlink (1998) conclude that learning communities become the necessary support system for the construction of meaning and knowledge for individuals as well as their collective groups. Recent research conducted by Robinson and Carrington (2002) resulted in a list of three effective models for professional development. Their list included the following:

- A focus that is based on "active involvement" of staff and administration;

- A model that is both extensive and progressive in nature; and

- A series of professional development experiences that are undertaken in a climate of school reculturing and collaboration which prove to enhance teacher ownership and relevance of the in-service.

What skills are essential in guiding effective professional development?

Many essential skills are needed when guiding effective professional development. Inter-group skills are necessary for bringing teams of professionals together to work in pursuit of common goals related to staff development. According to Baldwin and Keating (1998):

> . . . building a level of trust within a group, working specifically on communication and conflict resolution skills, and developing a sense of team prior to focusing on a specific task has clear advantages in predicting more successful outcomes. In any situation where collaborative team work is essential to meeting specific goals, students can benefit from the use of a similar team building process which includes identifying the intended outcomes of team building, breaking down the essential participant skills needed, and then teaching these skills in the workshop. Through this process any collaborative project can build an appropriate foundation for success (p. 304).

As mentioned in the previous quote, students can also benefit from team building. If the staff development is presented in this format, then the learning of participants could potentially be two-fold, with the primary content information being presented in a unique and engaging format that will result in an added technique that teachers could use in their classroom settings.

What is the role of reflection in professional development?

Reflection can be defined as thinking about practice to improve teaching and student learning. According to Reilley (1999), "Although there are different conceptions regarding reflection, there generally is agreement on the importance of actively and carefully examining one's thoughts in order to improve one's teaching" (p. 896). Dewey's (1933) notion of reflection centered on the idea of giving a subject serious consideration by mentally turning it over. Dewey claimed that doing this would enable one to act deliberately and intentionally. Reilley (1999) states, "The recent movement towards developing reflective practitioners has led to a body of research which focuses on the teacher as researcher, an inquirer into her own practice" (p. 897). Schon (1987) believes that due to reflection, teachers are able to participate in their own professional growth and development in ways that are both creative and conscious. Reflection can potentially be a valuable role for both preservice and in-service teachers alike. It can also be a powerful venue for those who "actively" think about their practice. Ultimately, the goal of reflection is that it will lead to improved teaching and learning.

How can professional development support the pursuit of professional standards?

Over the past decade, teacher associations have demonstrated that our profession has the ability to reach a consensus on teaching standards without imposing uniformity and style. There is an emerging system for professional development based on profession-defined standards and values. According to Ingvarson, (1998) professional development should be viewed as a "system" aiming to provide answers to the following questions:

- Who determines what teachers should get better at? In other words, who determines what the goals and purposes of professional development will be? Who governs allocation of resources to these various purposes?

- What is the basis for determining what teachers should get better at, or what teachers should know and be able to do? How is this knowledge determined? Who is assumed to have the expertise to do this?

- Who decides how teachers will learn and what is the basis for their credibility and legitimacy? Who provides the infrastructure for professional learning? Who provides the professional development activities and who designs and runs them? Who accredits the providers? How are they funded? Who pays for the courses?

- Who evaluates whether teachers have developed and improved the quality of their practice? On what basis and how is this assessment of performance conducted?

- What are the incentives and rewards for teachers to invest their time and energy in professional development? What is the relationship between evidence of professional development and career development? What status is placed on high-quality teaching in comparison, say, with career paths in school administration? (p. 129).

It is evident that in recent times, there has been an influx of standards that teachers are encouraged to meet in their teaching efforts, which are present at both state and national levels. Professional development if structured accordingly can aid teachers in familiarizing themselves with the knowledge-base necessary to help their students master these critical standards. Ingvarson (1998) further claims that, "A standards-based professional development overturns old assumptions about who provides 'in-service' education and how and where professional development takes place" (p.135). Furthermore, "Teachers and their professional bodies are more likely to set up their own support networks within and across schools to help each other implement teaching standards and prepare for the next career stage. They can work toward attaining profession-defined standards in multiple ways" (p.135).

Project Design

As a university literacy educator with twenty-five years of teaching experience in primary classrooms, the first author was invited by a rural school district to present a series of professional sessions on the topic of standards-based writing instruction. This author holds a constructivist viewpoint and agrees with Gould (1996) and Graves (1983) about the implications of this theory for the instruction of the language arts, in that social activities integrated into the language arts processes can actually lead to better writing, reading, and spelling. This author had spent years incorporating the writer's workshop approach to writing instruction in her classroom based on the format explained by Calkins (1994) and Graves (1983). This approach includes daily, interactive time for writing, with young writers generating their own topics, a mini-lesson format for direct instruction, and always includes a time for writers to share their writing with an audience at the conclusion of the workshop. During her doctoral studies, she had assumed the role of teacher-researcher to conduct action research in her classroom examining the effects of a variety of audiences on young children's writing development.

Focusing on the writing process approach to writing instruction during this yearlong professional development project clearly supported the standards-based movement and this district's goal to provide a series of professional sessions on the topic of standards-based writing instruction for their primary teachers. Ohio's Academic Language Arts Content Standards (2002) include three standards that focus on writing (K-12): 1) Writing Process Standard, 2) Writing Applications Standard, and 3) Writing Conventions Standard. Some of the benchmarks by the end of the K-2 program focus on (a) generating ideas for written compositions; (b) developing audience and purpose for self-selected and assigned writing tasks; (c) using organizers to clarify ideas for writing assignments; (d) using revision strategies and resources to improve ideas and content organization, (e) word choice and detail; (f) editing to improve sentence fluency, grammar, and usage; (g) applying tools to judge the quality of writing; and (h) publishing writing samples for display or sharing with others.

Prior to developing concrete plans for the project, the first author met with the superintendent, elementary principals and the curriculum director from the district. At this session, the superintendent explained the district goals that related to this professional development project. The administrators wanted to support their teachers as they were attempting to align their language arts instruction with the new state content standards. They had polled their primary teachers concerning their greatest professional development need relating to these standards, and there was a strong request for assistance with their writing instruction. Many of these teachers did not feel confident about their current approach to writing instruction. By involving the teachers from the beginning of this project, these administrators followed the guidelines for effective professional development suggested by Baldwin and Keating (1998) and Ingvarson (1998) relating to team building and the empowerment of teachers. The first author asked for the district's goals in relation to this project which included the following:

- For teachers to understand that every student reads and writes at different developmental levels.
- For a framework and consistency in writing instruction to be established across the district.
- For professional development time to be used wisely and effectively.
- For phonics instruction to be consistent throughout the district.

The first author then used these goals as well as the academic content standards for writing instruction to plan the first professional development session as well as incorporated her own goals based on her beliefs about children's writing development. Her goals for this first session included the following:

- To consider participants' prior knowledge (schema).
- To consider participants' setting (Amish/Mennonite community/conservative philosophies, etc.).
- To offer professional development that supports consistency across the district but also respects teachers' differences and allows them ownership, this in turn empowers them to be decision makers.
- To provide a deep understanding of the process approach to writing instruction.
- To connect this theory to practice.
- To link the process approach to writing instruction with Ohio's Academic Language Arts Content Standards (2002).

Session One

The combination of these two sets of goals determined the format of the first in-service session. The session began with a brief introduction and an opportunity for the participants to complete the K&W sections of a KWL graphic organizer which focused on the topic of writing instruction. The participants were asked to reflect on what they knew (K) and what they wanted to learn (W). By doing this, the presenter could informally assess the current working knowledge base of her participants to plan an appropriate and meaningful experience. The presenter began with a formal presentation of Writing Workshop which introduced the concept of writing as a process and how the teachers could get this started in their own contexts. The presenter shared the concept of using writing as an assessment tool and incorporated the idea of using developmental continuums and rubrics to assist in this process. The presenter involved the session participants in an activity which required using actual writing samples from early, emergent, and transitional writers. During this activity, participants determined the developmental stage, strengths, and needs of their students who wrote the samples, and they went on to plan appropriately for their writing instruction. This particular activity supported the current curriculum model proposed by the state of Ohio which involves instruction based on the academic content standards and requires teachers to engage in a continuous cycle involving assessment, revision, and instruction. Linking to the *Ohio Academic English Language Arts Standards* (2002), the participants also worked with writing standards in grade level groups to determine which grade level indicators they introduce and are responsible for teaching to mastery. The presenter ended this first session by providing an assignment that the participants needed to complete before the next in-service. The assignment encouraged these teachers to slowly begin implementing writer's workshop in their own classrooms. They were encouraged to collect student writing samples, assess these samples, and bring one to share in the second session. In addition, they were asked to keep a reflective journal about the process they had begun. The presenter was mindful of guidelines of *NCLB Act* (2001) and the standards-based movement while planning this session such as the idea that professional development should be aligned with state standards, assessment, and the local school curriculum. Another guiding principle throughout this project was the goal to help these teachers and this school district manage current state and federal accountability measures.

The overall plan for this yearlong project included three in-services for all the K-2 teachers in the district as well as some classroom visits by the presenter to model writing lessons for individual teachers. The first session was entitled: Introduction to Writing Workshop/Assessing Children's Writing; the second: Implementing Writing Workshop; and the third: Writing in a Comprehensive Literacy Program. At the time this article was written, the presenter had completed the first two in-services and one class visit. The participants completed an evaluation at the conclusion of the first session. This evaluation required them to note what they learned, liked, and plan to use. The following is a summary of their comments:

I learned the key components of writer's workshop and how to organize.

Thank you for bringing the children's writing samples and allowing us to work with partners; I learned where students may be on the continuum and how to use their writing to plan instruction.

I liked and plan to use a lot of the resources the presenter gave us (child-friendly checklists, graphic organizers, ideas like "write the room").

I learned that I can ask my kindergarten students to do more writing activities even if they are not able to actually write the ABC's.

I liked the presenter's easygoing manner, not at all stressful (Oswald, & Still, 2004)

The evaluation also asked them to comment on what they felt they needed more of and the following is a summary of their feedback:

- Help with time management of writing workshop
- How much editing and when to do it?
- How much to help in spelling unknown words when they want to know?
- More on mini-lessons; see a mini-lesson demonstrated
- More on how to get kids to want to write
- How to move children from one level to the next?

Session Two

This feedback and the assignments given at the conclusion of the first in-service were used to plan the second professional development session. The second session began with the participants presenting their "homework" which allowed these teachers to share writing samples from their own students and their insights gained by evaluating these samples. As the participants presented their "homework" at the beginning of this session of the in-service, important discussions took place based on their reflections and questions. There were many comments about the effect of their reflective journaling on their thinking and understanding of the process approach to writing instruction. Several participants commented that they plan on continuing this kind of journaling. This sharing time also helped build collegiality amongst these teachers as they supported each other during these informal presentations. The presenter offered an in-depth presentation on each aspect of writer's workshop which involved the following topics; mini-lessons, invented spelling, and interactive writing for K-1 students. To further illustrate these topics, video clips of an interactive writing session in a kindergarten classroom and writer's workshop in a 3rd grade classroom were shared and then discussed. The video clips that were shared came from two videos entitled, *Inside Reading & Writing Workshop* by Joanne Hindley (1998) and *The Four Blocks* by Patricia Cunningham and Dottie Hall (1996). To culminate this second session, the presenter involved the participants in a strategy called "T.A.G." (Sharing Strategies, 2003) which encouraged the teachers to tell, ask, and give suggestions about the ideas of process writing and implementing the writing workshop in their classrooms. Ideas generated included using the author's chair, microphone, peer editing, and publishing. During the "T.A.G." strategy, a key highlight of the session occurred after the presenter shared a variety of ideas to help young writers generate their own topics. They especially liked the idea of having children draw a heart on a sheet of paper and then drawing or writing things or people that are very important to them or "dear to their heart" in the middle of the heart. This strategy helps children understand that authors write about their own experiences, memories and people that are dear to them.

The evaluation at the end of this second session required the participants to again comment about what they learned, liked, and planned to implement. The following is a list highlighting their collective thoughts about this second session:

I learned more about interactive writing and what a mini-lesson looks like. I plan to use all the examples of mini-lessons and link them to the standards and benchmarks for my grade level.

The videos really helped to make it clear, what it looks like in a real classroom.

I liked all the ideas: the "heart", author's chair, microphone, using correction tape when editing.

This second session evaluation also asked them to comment on what they needed more of and their ideas included the following:

- When to edit students' spelling and how often? When is **too much** that would discourage them?
- Ideas for book extensions in writing to replace standard book reports.
- Time! Daily writing routines and help with mini-lessons.
- Ideas for publishing.
- Taking a writing lesson from the very beginning to publishing.

This feedback made it abundantly clear that while these teachers had increased their understanding of writer's workshop, this approach to writing instruction is complex and requires ongoing training and support for teachers.

A First/Second Grade Scenario

After the second in-service session, the first presenter was invited by one of the teachers to visit her 1st/2nd grade classroom to demonstrate a writer's workshop session. This was an Amish public school with no electricity and the children walked to school. The presenter used a big book, *Pig in the Pond* by Martin Waddell (1992), to conduct a shared reading. This book supported the focus of the mini-lesson on "onomatopoeia", the formation of a word by imitation of a sound such as boom, cuckoo, etc. It also connected to these children's knowledge of farm animals. Following the shared reading, the presenter led a brainstorming session of sounds they hear in their daily life. Next, the children began to write their stories using this device— "onomatopoeia." The students wrote their stories with enthusiasm and enjoyed sharing them with the whole group. The teacher was also enthusiastic about her students' writing and said, "Now I understand writer's workshop!" (Oswald & Still, 2004)

Planning for Future Professional Development Sessions

The first author is returning to this district in the near future to conduct another in-service on "Writing in a Comprehensive Literacy Program." The planning of this session will again be based on the feedback from the participants as well as the initial goals guiding this project based on *NCLB* and the state standards. A questionnaire was mailed to these teachers by the presenter to determine what they have implemented from past sessions into their classroom practice. The following is a summary of their comments:

- Process approach to writing instruction;
- Interactive writing;
- Using children's writing as an assessment tool;
- Linking mini-lessons to state language arts content standards;
- Setting up a writing center and daily routines to support children's writing;
- Allowing students to generate their own topics; and
- Encouraging children to share more of their writing and to support one another.

The questionnaire also asked for the participants to generate questions they still may have had about effective writing instruction. Their questions focused on time and management of writer's workshop, especially with editing students' writing. The final portion of the questionnaire asked the participants to evaluate the structure of the in-services in terms of what was most and least helpful. Again, they reiterated that they liked (a) the informal format that required them to be active participants, (b) the expertise of the presenter, (c) use of actual children's writing samples, (d) ongoing sessions with "homework" that allowed them to practice what they had learned and come back with remaining questions, (e)the videos and demonstrations, (f) the strategies and graphic organizers, (g) the positive approach to children's writing instruction and (h) the alignment to the state content standards.

Based on this participant feedback and the review of the literature presented previously in this article, future sessions for this district will focus on:

- Providing in-services on more book extension ideas.
- Providing in-services on how to establish writing routines in the classroom.
- Providing in-services on how to teach "mini lessons" that focus on the writing process.

- Providing continued in-service on "the writing process.
- Providing in-service on how to incorporate all that they are learning into professional development portfolios which could potentially reflect upon their mastery of the Ohio Content Standards for writing.

Why is Writing Instruction an Important Topic for Professional Development Sessions?

The discussion of the project design implemented in the professional development sessions described in this article clearly supports and illustrates suggestions taken from relevant research related to writing instruction. In the description of the project design, the presenter stressed the importance of the professional development sessions in relation to the standards-based movement. Its importance is validated in a study undertaken by Isaacson (2004). He states:

> A survey of state standards reveals that students should know the writing process and be able to produce personal narratives, expository reports, letters, persuasive essays, imaginative stories, and occasionally other forms of writing. Mastery of conventions is also important in almost every state, suggesting that teachers should not overlook the teaching of spelling, punctuation, and grammar (p. 51).

In the abstract for this article, the term "symbiotic" was used in relation to the processes of reading and writing. Calkins (1983) illustrates this concept in her book, *Lessons from A Child: On the Teaching and Learning of Writing*. Calkins describes this process in detail as if present in the mind of a child while reading and writing. She states:

> While composing, children read continually. They read to savor the sounds of their language, they read to see what they had written, they read to regain momentum, they read to reorient themselves, they read to avoid writing. They read to find gaps in their work, they read to evaluate whether the piece was working, they read to edit. And they read to share the work of their hands (p. 153).

The presenter described how she involved the teacher participants in many activities related to their own classroom contexts. At the culmination of the first session, she described a task that invited the teachers to collect and assess writing samples of their current students. Her hope was that they would read their children's writing through new and refreshed lenses much like the following scenario described by Calkins (1983):

> We were learning to read children's writing in a new way, seeing the printed words as the tip of the iceberg and speculating what might lie under the surface. Sometimes I'd dismiss a piece of writing and then Mrs. Howard would see things in it; sometimes it was the other way around.

For both of us, looking for what it revealed about the writer. Sometimes there seemed to be no pattern at all to children's errors (p. 21).

Throughout the discussion of two professional development sessions, the presenter offered numerous strategies allowing the teacher participants to give their students choice in choosing topics for writing. Calkins (1983) supports this idea of teacher flexibility by stating:

> I had expected that when children chose their own topics, they would become more invested in writing. But I hadn't expected the changes which became apparent in their written products. Now that the children were writing about everyday events in their lives, they used telling details and with specific concrete information (p. 28).

The presenter devoted a great deal of the second session to the writer's workshop and even after this second session, teacher participants still wanted more insight on how to go about establishing routines for writer's workshop in their own classrooms. The presenter will use their suggestion as she plans future development sessions. Calkins (1983) supports the establishment of flexible yet consistent routines in the following statement:

> It is significant to realize the most creative environments in our society are not the ever changing ones. The artist's studio, the researcher's laboratory, and the scholar's library are each deliberately kept simple so as to support the complexities of the work-in-progress. They are deliberately kept predictable, so the unpredictable can happen (p. 32).

After the first and second sessions, the presenter was invited into a first/second grade classroom to demonstrate the writer's workshop in action. Her decision to follow up by acting as a guest teacher in this particular classroom supports the importance of demonstration in the consultation process. According to Troia & Graham (2003):

> One way that consultants can foster such confidence is by demonstrating in the classroom how to use effective writing instructional tactics…It is much more powerful and affirming to model how to provide effective instruction than to simply describe it (p. 85).

After careful consideration of the teacher participants' comments, the presenter realizes the need for teachers to be supported in motivating their young writers. The presenter will incorporate ideas suggested by Bruning & Horn (2000) as she plans future sessions. They suggest the following ways in which to develop motivation for writing:

> We see a number of keys to developing motivation to write, all related to intrinsic motivation. We first need to build student beliefs about writing's nature and potential. These include not only a sense of writing's power, but also a realistic appraisal of its difficulty. Students need to

see writing's value as an intellectual and social tool, as well as develop confidence in their writing ability. Second, authentic writing goals and contexts are likely to provide motivational support. Real purposes and audiences clearly convey writing's pragmatic purposes and help students develop a sense of their own writing voice. Third, developing writers need to experience writing task conditions supportive of motivation. These would include encountering complex writing tasks in manageable parts; being helped to set specific, proximal goals; receiving feedback on progress toward goals; and learning writing strategies and when to use them. Fourth, because of writing's complexity and students' prior experiences in many classrooms, many students will have negative feelings about writing and have unproductive writing habits. Approaches are needed that help students deal with negative affect and establish new, productive writing approaches (p. 34).

Finally, Bruning & Horn (2000) state that, "Programs that develop student motivation for writing are most likely to be designed and implemented by those who understand, implicitly, the power and pleasure of writing" (p. 35). As is evident in this article's discussion of the professional development sessions provided, the presenter clearly epitomizes this belief system and possesses the knowledge and passion that Bruning & Horn (2000) hold in high regard.

Discussion

The planning and implementation of this yearlong professional development project was an important learning experience for the presenter as well as the participants. The presenter learned that effective professional development begins with goals and good communication amongst the presenter, district administrators and most importantly, teachers. The teachers' perceived needs were the impetus for this project. Presenters need to consider participants' prior knowledge and scaffold their learning of new approaches to instruction. It is important to consider teachers' ideas, concerns, approaches to teaching and goals.

Teachers' understanding is enhanced when strong connections are made between theory and practice with demonstration, videos of actual classrooms, and active participation in practicing strategies. Teachers want ideas and materials that they can implement immediately into their classrooms. Professional development sessions should include a balance of lecture, demonstration, and participant involvement. Teachers' understanding is enhanced by multiple sessions on the same topic with time in between to practice what they have learned and opportunities to reflect, question, and discuss.

Finally, the presenter learned that actual classroom demonstration is powerful. When she used the opportunity to visit a classroom and allowed the teacher to watch her demonstrate a writer's workshop session with the teacher's own students, the teacher responded with, "Now I understand writer's workshop!" It is unfortunate that time and financial resources limit this approach to professional development for classroom teachers.

How has the presenter in this study incorporated research-based principles of effective professional development in her in-service sessions?

Sandholtz, (2002) states, "School/university partnerships can create opportunities for teachers to increase their professional interactions with colleagues" (p. 817). The presenter in this study has clearly created a partnership that aligns with the current research findings on effective professional development for teachers. As research indicates, serious teachers can see the connection between their growth as professionals and the success of their students in the classroom. Two of the important outcomes apparent in the evaluation of this project relate to the positive attitudes and commitment of the participants within the project. The presenter actively involved the participants by allowing them to initially choose what they wanted to learn more about and then further encouraged them to use artifacts from their individual classrooms for study. Many opportunities were provided for the participants to reflect on their development by completing evaluations and a questionnaire, which guided the development of future sessions.

Implications for Future Professional Development

A good first step for developing more effective instructional programs is to have a long-range plan. Allington (2001) explained that, "school districts have five-year plans for replacing roofs, for upgrading athletic fields, for purchasing buses and new textbooks. But the same districts with these longer-term plans for buildings, grounds, textbooks, and transportation rarely have a five-year professional development plan—even for new teachers" (p. 112).

And finally, perhaps the most important concept relating to effective professional development is that individual differences in teachers must be considered and valued. The teachers who participated in this project were involved in the decision making from the beginning. Their ideas were valued, and their voices were heard. Allington (2001) supports this respect for teachers and states, "When teachers work under conditions of low autonomy they do not seem to develop the very expertise that will be necessary to teach expertly" (p. 116).

Moore (2000) believes that the most effective professional development is one that is an ongoing process. Key features of a successful process involve appropriate well-thought-out training and provide opportunities for individual follow-up through supportive observation, feedback, dialogue, and peer coaching. Further, Little (1993) believes that the most influential professional development opportunities are those offered with frequency over a significant duration of time. Little (1993) states, "Professional development must be constructed in ways that deepen the discussion, open up the debates, and enrich the array of possibilities for action" (p. 148).

The model for ongoing professional development described in this article can set the stage for collegial discussions and active involvement. This ongoing project based on principles of the *NCLB Act* and standards-driven professional development has exciting possibilities to impact the continuing growth of these primary teachers of writing. Valuing teachers as professionals empowers them to become highly effective instructors, which is our best hope for elevating the achievement of students.

References

Academic content standards: K-12 English language arts. *(2002). OH: The State Board of* Education and the Ohio Department of Education.

Allington, R. (2001). *What really matters to struggling readers: Designing research-based programs.* New York: Longman.

Baldwin, M. D., & Keating, J. F. (1998). Innovative team building practices for professionals: developing inter-group skills to enhance effective performance. *Innovative Higher Education, 22,* 291-309. Retrieved September 1, 2003, from http://journals.ohio link.edu:20080/cgibin/sciserv.pl?collection=journals&journal =0742562.

Bruning, R., & Horn, C. (2000). Developing motivation to write. *Educational Psychologist, 35*(1), 25-37. Retrieved July 22, 2004 from http://www.leaonline.com/doi/pdf/10.1207/s15326985ep3501_4.

Calkins, L. (1994). *The art of teaching writing* (Rev. ed.). Portsmouth, NH: Heinemann Educational Books.

Calkins, L. (1983). *Lessons from a child: On the teaching and learning of writing.* Portsmouth, NH: Heinemann Educational Books

Carson Dellosa (Producer) & Cunningham, P. (Writer). (2000). *The four blocks literacy model: Writer's workshop [Motion Picture].* (Available from Carson -Dellosa Publishing Co., Inc., 4321 Piedmont Parkway, High Point, NC 27260)

Cunningham, P. & Hall, D. (1996). *The four blocks: A framework for reading and writing in classrooms that work* [Videotape Recording]. Clemmons, NC: Windward Productions; [distributed by IESS].

Dewey, J. (1933). *How we think a restatement of the relation of reflective thinking to the educative process.* New York: Heath and Company.

Gould, J. S. (1996). A constructivist perspective on teaching and learning in the language arts. In Fosnot, C. T. (Ed.) *Constructivism: Theory, perspectives, and practice.* New York: Teachers College Press.

Graves, D. H. (1983). *Writing: Teachers and children at work.* Portsmouth, NH: Heinemann Educational Books.

Graves, D. H. (2002). *Testing is not teaching.* Portsmouth, NH: Heinemann.

Guskey, T.R. (1986). Staff development and the process of teacher change. *Educational Researcher, 15*(5), 5-12.

Hindley, J. (1998). *Inside reading and writing workshops* (Videotape Recording No. 1-57110-071-7). Milwaukee, WI: Stenhouse Publishers.

Ingvarson, L. (1998). Professional development as a pursuit of professional standards: The standards-based professional development system. *Teaching and Teacher Education, 14,* 127-140. Retrieved September 1, 2003, from http://journals. ohiolink.edu:20080/cgibin/sciserv.pl?collection=journals&journal=0742051.

Isaacson, S. (2004). Instruction that helps students meet state standards in writing. *Exceptionality, 12*(1), 39-54. Retrieved July 22, 2004 from http://www.leaonline .com/doi/pdf/10.1207/s15327035ex1201_4.

Kinnucan-Welsch, K., & Jenlink, P. (1998). Challenging assumptions about teaching and learning: Three case studies in constructivist pedagogy. *Teaching and Teacher Education, 14,* 413-427.

Little, J. W. (1993). Teacher's professional development in a climate of educational reform. *Educational Evaluation and Policy Analysis, 15*(2), 129-151.

Moore, K. (2000). Successful and effective professional development. *Early Childhood Today, 15*(3), 14-17.

National Reading Panel. (2000). Teaching children to read: An evidence-based assessment of the scientific research literature on reading and its implications for reading instruction: Reports of the subgroups. Washington, DC: National Institute of Child Health and Human Development.

No Child Left Behind Act of 2001, Pub. L. No. 107-110, 20 U.S.C. § 6301, 115 Stat. 1425. (2002). Retrieved December 6, 2004 from http://edworkforce.house.gov/issues/ 107th/education/nclb/nclb.htm.

Oswald, R. (2001). The influence of audience awareness in children's writing of different genres: A case study of a second-grade class. *Celebrating the Voices of Literacy: The Twenty-Third Yearbook,* 35-54. Commerce, Texas: Texas A&M University: The College Reading Association.

Reilley, A. F. (1999). The role of reflection on preservice teachers' development in the context of a professional development school. *Teaching and Teacher Education, 15,* 895-909. Retrieved September 1, 2003, from http://journals.ohiolink. edu:20080/ cgibin/sciserv.pl?collection=journals&journal=0742051.

Report calls for "a writing revolution". (2003, June/July). *Reading Today, 20*(6), 4.

Robinson, R. & Carrington, S. (2002). Professional development for inclusive schooling. *The International Journal of Educational Management, 16,* 239-247. Retrieved September 1, 2003, from http://journals.ohiolink.edu:20080/cgi-bin/ sciserv.pl?collection=journals&journal-0951354.

Sandholtz, J. H. (2002). Inservice training or professional development: contrasting opportunities in a school/university partnership. *Teaching and Teacher Education, 18,* 815-830. Retrieved September 1, 2003, from http://journals.ohiolink. edu:20080/cgibin/sciserv.pl?collection=journals&journal=0742051.

Schon, D. A. (1987). *Educating the reflective practitioner.* San Francisco: Jossey Bass.

Strategies for improving teacher quality by ED.gov. (October, 2002). Retrieved January 17, 2004, from http://www.ed.gov/admins/tchrqual/learn/tqstr/edlite-slide 008.html.

Sharing Strategies. (Allyn & Bacon, 2003). Chapter 13: Facilitating Writing. Retrieved December, 2004, from http://www.d.umn.edu/~thughes/sped4210/documents/ vaughppt.13.ppt

StrayLight Media (Producer), & Williams, S. (Producer/Director). (1998). Reading *conferences; A video presentation with Joanne Hindley* [Motion picture]. (Available from Stenhouse Publishers, 477 Congress Street Suite 4B, Portland, ME 04101)

Troia, G. A., & Graham, S. (2003). Effective writing instruction across the grades: What every educational consultant should know. *Journal of Educational and Psychological Consultation, 14(1),* 75-89. Retrieved July 22, 2004 from http://www.leaonline .com/doi/pdf/10.1207/s1532768xjepc1401_04.

Waddell, M. (1992). *The pig in the pond.* Cambridge, MA: Candlewick Press.

Zepeda, S. J. (1999). *Staff development: Practices that promote leadership in learning communities.* Larchmont, NY: Eye on Education.

EARLY CHILDHOOD TEACHERS' BELIEFS AND PRACTICES TOWARD CHILDREN'S SUBVOCALIZATIONS DURING READING

Carla Baker Deniz

George Mason University

Abstract

This chapter explores the results of a study completed in the spring of 2003. Thirteen teachers were interviewed about their beliefs and practices toward children's subvocalizations during reading. All of the teachers in the study indicated a belief that young children naturally subvocalize while reading. However, teachers' practices varied greatly from "We encourage them to do that" to "[We have] to teach them that your eyes are moving and your . . . lips are still". Additionally, teachers appeared to have inconsistent views of the importance of subvocalizing during reading. Previous research shows that such vocalizations are often an effective tool students use when working through problems (Azmitia, 1992; Bivens & Berk, 1990; Lee, 1999) and can be used by teachers to monitor student growth and to assist in scaffolding a child's learning (White & Manning, 1994; Winsler, Diaz, & Montero, 1997).

The behavior of subvocalizing during reading is well documented in the literature (Dickie, 1973; Hardyck & Petrinovich, 1970; Sokolov, 1969). More recent studies in the field of private speech indicates that such vocalizations are often a necessary tool students have for working through problems (Azmitia, 1992; Bivens & Berk, 1990; Lee, 1999), and also can be used as an effective tool teachers can use to monitor student growth and ability and to assist in scaffolding a child's learning (White & Manning, 1994; Winsler et al., 1997). Some researchers have suggested that preventing a child from using private speech can negatively affect a child's task success (Lee, 1999;

Vygotsky, 1935/1978). For example, Lee's 1999 experiment the differences in children's use of private speech in two different settings. In the first setting, children were discouraged from using private speech; in the second setting they were encouraged to use private speech. Lee found that children in the encouraging condition "produced more than double" the amount of task-relevant private speech than did their discouraging condition counterparts. She also found that the children in the discouraging condition produced triple the amount of task-irrelevant private speech than their encouraging condition counterparts.

Overall, there is evidence that task-related private speech might be an important factor in task performance and future achievement in reading. In fact, Pechman's 1978 study found a positive correlation (0.87) between the amount of private speech used during a reading task and later reading achievement. Additionally, Hardyck and Petrinovich (1970) found that as the difficulty of reading passages increases, a reader will engage in more subvocal speech. Hardyck and Petrinovich also found that readers who were allowed to engage in subvocalized speech were able to comprehend more of the text than those readers who suppressed the speech.

Although many researchers have discussed the implications of children's subvocalizations for early childhood educators (Berk & Winsler, 1995; White & Manning, 1994; Winsler et al., 1997), and it is now clear from naturalistic studies that young children engage in considerable amounts of subvocalizations in early childhood classrooms (Berk, 1986; Deniz, 2003; Winsler, Carlton, & Barry, 2000; Winsler & Diaz, 1995), research is lacking at present about what teachers beliefs and practices are toward such speech. Anecdotal reports suggest that there is much variance among early childhood educators in attitudes toward children's subvocalizations, with occasional reports appearing that some teachers actively discourage such speech by children in their classrooms. Such a practice would be inconsistent with suggestions from the research literature to encourage and monitor such subvocalizations.

Literature on Early Childhood Teacher Beliefs

The act of reading aloud to oneself for the purpose of self-communication is considered to be a form of private speech. The speech is intended for the self, not for others. Research shows that a child's use of private speech peaks around the time the child is four to five years old, after which her use of private speech begins to decrease in frequency and duration (Azmitia, 1992; Berk & Spuhl, 1995; Bivens & Berk, 1990; Kohlberg, Yaeger, & Hjertholm, 1968; Winsler et al., 1997). The current study investigated the beliefs of early childhood teachers about children's private speech.

There is evidence in the literature that teachers' beliefs do influence their practices (Charlesworth et al., 1993; McCarty, Abbott-Shim, & Lambert, 2001; Stipek & Byler, 1997; Vartuli, 1999; Wing, 1989). Wing (1989) studied the relationship between teachers' beliefs, instructional decisions, and children's conceptions of reading and writing. Her study included interviews of the directors of two nursery schools and observations and interviews of the children who attended those schools. She found that the directors' beliefs were highly consistent with their philosophies and practices, and that the children's conceptions of reading and writing reflected the beliefs of the directors. In her 1999 study, Vartuli investigated teachers' self-reported beliefs and practices and their relation to actual practices. She surveyed 137 teachers and observed each of their classrooms. Vartuli found that teachers' self-reported beliefs had a positive moderate correlation with the observed practices. McCarty et al. (2001) studied the relationship between teachers' self-reported beliefs and self-reported and actual practices. Like Vartuli, they found moderate correlations between self-reported beliefs and self-reported practices as well as between self-reported beliefs and observed practices.

The Current Study
Purpose of the Study
Teachers' beliefs and self-reported practices toward children's subvocalizations during reading have not been explored in the literature discussed previously. The current study was part of a larger study that examined teachers' beliefs and practices toward several different kinds of private speech during various academic tasks. The current study focuses on children's use of private speech during reading. The following questions were explored: What are teachers' beliefs about children's subvocalizations during reading? What practices do teachers report adopting when they encounter a child engaging in subvocalizations during reading?

Methodology
This study focused on early childhood teachers of children five to seven years old. The sample consisted of 13 early childhood teachers: Five kindergarten teachers, five first-grade teachers, and three multiage kindergarten/first-grade teachers in three suburban public schools in Northern Virginia. From early October through mid- November, 2002, each classroom was observed for teacher/child interactions in the context of children's private speech use for a minimum of three hours. Within three weeks after the observations were completed, each of the teachers was interviewed for 60 to 90 minutes about their beliefs and practices related to children engaging in various forms of private speech. The current study focuses on the teachers' responses relevant to children's use of private speech during reading.

The interviews were analyzed using Qualres (Baker Research, Ltd.) qualitative data analysis software. For this initial analysis, the interviews were examined for themes. These themes were then coded and then further examined for commonalities and differences (Miles & Huberman, 1994). An outside analyst also examined the interview data at different stages of the analysis. This analyst was selected for her unfamiliarity with the subject, as recommended by Maxwell (1996).

Observation data was used as a means of triangulation. Observation data was examined for evidence of themes that appeared to emerge from the interview data. It was also used to get "at tacit understandings . . . as well as aspects of the participants' perspective that they are reluctant to state directly in interviews" (Maxwell, 1996, p. 76).

Throughout the analysis, the researcher wrote memos, as suggested by Miles and Huberman (1994). They suggest Glaser's (1978) definition of a memo: "the theorizing write-up of ideas about codes and their relationships as they strike the analyst while coding . . . it can be a sentence, a paragraph, or a few pages. . . it exhausts the analyst's momentary ideation based on data with perhaps a little conceptual elaboration. (p. 83-84)."

Results

The participating teachers' responses to questions regarding reading aloud private speech were examined and several themes emerged. These themes were grouped into two overarching themes: "Teachers' beliefs about subvocalizing during reading" and "teachers' practices toward children's subvocalizing during reading."

Teachers' Beliefs About Subvocalizing During Reading
Subvocalizing Is "Beneficial."

Many of the teachers who participated in this study indicated a belief that children are "not ready to close their lips and do it only with their own brain power" (Louise, kindergarten teacher). Additionally, many of the teachers indicated that subvocalizing during reading is beneficial "when you're using it to work out a problem, when you're talking about, um, stretching out words and going back and rereading you're writing, when you're trying to– to talk through your story before you write it. . . " (Cindy, multiage k/1 teacher). Teachers noted that subvocalizing aids children in thinking through the process and problem solving.

"Children's Concept of Reading Is Hearing It."

Some of the teachers in this study indicated a belief that children's conception of reading is "hearing it". They attributed this conception to the fact that teachers and parents model reading aloud behavior to children from a very young age: "For the ones who are just learning to read, in their minds that's what reading is" (Sid, multiage k/1 teacher.) For example, Jackie (kindergarten teacher) stated that:

> I think they associate a story with hearing it. So, because at their age, that's the only way they've ever had a story. I mean– maybe I have one or two kids who can read a little, but in general, at this age, the only way that they can get into that story is if someone has read it. So that's how they see right now, reading a book. They have to do it orally.

Teachers noted that children do imitate parents and teachers as a way of learning, and that novice readers will pretend to read a book out loud using the same expressions they have heard their parents or teacher use.

Advanced Readers do not Subvocalize During Reading.

Some of the teachers noted that if a child is an advanced reader, the child would tend not to engage in subvocalization during reading: "As a matter of fact as I think about it now, I'm thinking of all of my advanced readers, they're sitting quietly reading, they're not . . . They– sometimes I see lips moving but I don't hear anything . . ." (Miriam, multiage k/1 teacher). In fact, Sid (multiage k/1 teacher) added that the subvocalizations of more advanced students are quieter, more private.

In contrast to the idea of a more natural progression, several of the teachers noted that children who engage in subvocalizing "have not been taught silent reading, so they all pretty much read. . . talking out loud to themselves. . .You know, you gotta teach them that your eyes are moving and your mouth, your lips are still. . . " (Betty, kindergarten teacher) These teachers noted that it "takes time" to be able to learn to "speak in their brain."

Teachers' Practices Toward Children's Subvocalizing During Reading.

Teachers indicated several practices they engage in regarding children who are subvocalizing during reading. These practices were instance-specific. That is, the practice depended upon the situation at the time, and the volume of the subvocalizations. The teachers would either encourage, ignore, or discourage the behavior.

Encouraging Subvocalizations During Reading.

Several of the teachers who participated in this study indicated that they encourage children to subvocalize during reading. For example, Louise (kindergarten teacher) said "I would encourage it, because I think they need to hear these sounds to work out the problem so with their reading." Nada (first grade teacher) also indicated that she encourages children to subvocalize so that she can monitor their progress: "Once in a while a kid will not read out loud, and I'll say 'I need to hear it. Show me your finger and let's point to the word and I want to hear you read it."' Debbie also noted that she "ask[s] them to use the low voice when they're reading so. . . the people that are here to help them can hear them read to see if they're making mistakes or not." Only two of the teachers who participated in this study indicated that they monitor children's progress by listening to children's subvocalizations.

Discouraging Subvocalizations During Reading.

Most of the teachers who participated in this study stated that they generally ignore children's subvocalizations during reading. However, teachers noted two situations in which they would discourage a child from subvocalizing during reading. These situations included when a child was too loud and during testing.

Child's Subvocalizations are too Loud. Several of the teachers noted that children's subvocalizations during reading may be distracting to those seated near the child. For example, although she does encourage children to subvocalize during reading, Debbie indicated that if a child becomes too loud, she will ask the child to lower his voice. She spoke specifically about one child, Oggi:

> Oggi– he's a loud reader . . . and he's a bright boy. I have to speak to him many times to lower his voice because he gets so excited and enthused at what he's reading that he really gets into it. . . I just try to [say] "Oggi you need to lower your voice a little bit, you– you're disturbing the group over here." Just to bring to his attention that he's a little too loud. . .

Testing Situations. Some of the teachers also indicated testing situations as being a time they would discourage children from subvocalizing. During the regular school day, Miriam (multiage k/1 teacher) and Sid (multiage k/1 teacher) allow the children in their classes to talk freely as they work or play. However, both Miriam and Sid talked about quieting their children during testing situations:

> If we're having a test, I do ask for quiet. And it is hard for them then, because then they're still wanting to talk. We have to teach them how to take these standardized tests, and so, every now and then we say okay "we're having a test, this is serious, you cannot talk," and it's very hard for them to think without talking. They just want to say the answer or. . . they want to talk about it out loud to rethink it, it's hard for them to not say it. (Miriam)

Both Miriam and Sid talked about the need for being quiet during standardized testing and the mismatch of testing situations with children of this age:

Which is why, when we have to take tests, it's so uncomfortable, because they have to be quiet, and they're not used to being quiet. We don't make them be quiet, because we don't value that. (Sid)

Discussion

It is encouraging that the teachers in this study generally found subvocalizing to be beneficial to children, and that teachers, in general, encourage children to subvocalize. However, although the practice of using children's subvocalizations as a means to monitor children's progress has been suggested in the literature (Berk & Winsler, 1995; White & Manning, 1994; Winsler et al., 1997), few of the teachers in the current study indicated that they did so.

This study brings attention to the relationship between traditional testing environments and children's subvocalizations. A few of the teachers in this study indicated that they noticed a mismatch between naturally occurring subvocalizations and the artificial testing environment. In the case of standardized testing, children are required to remain quiet during the exam. Children who engage in subvocalizing during problem solving are quieted at these times when they potentially need it the most. Further examination of the relationship between different testing environments and subvocalizing is recommended.

Additionally, the testing methods used in these early grades should be reconsidered with subvocalizing in mind. Young children should be allowed to use this valuable tool. Of particular importance are the findings from the research of the potential harm of preventing a child from engaging in this speech. Vygotsky (1978) noted that: ". . . our experiments demonstrate that . . . the more complex the action demanded by the situation and the less direct its solution, the greater the importance played by speech in the operation as a whole. Sometimes speech becomes of such vital importance that, if not permitted to use it, young children cannot accomplish the given task" (p. 26).

Testing policy-makers are encouraged to investigate other possible environments that may allow for subvocalizations during testing. Additionally, researchers are encouraged to examine the impact of current testing environments on achievement.

References

Azmitia, M. (1992). Expertise, private speech, and self-regulation. In R. M. Diaz & L. E. Berk (Eds.), *Private speech: From social interaction to self-regulation* (pp. 101-122). Hillsdale, NJ: Erlbaum.

Baker Research, Ltd. (2002). *Qualres: Qualitative data analysis software* [Computer software]. Alexandria, VA: Author.

Berk, L. E. (1986). Relationship of elementary school children's private speech to behavioral accompaniment to task attention and task performance. *Developmental Psychology, 22,* 671-680.

Berk, L. E., & Spuhl, S. T. (1995). Maternal interaction, private speech, and task performance in preschool children. *Early Childhood Research Quarterly, 10,* 145-169.

Berk, L. E., & Winsler, A. (1995). *Scaffolding children's learning: Vygotsky and early childhood education.* Washington, DC: National Association for the Education of Young Children.

Bivens, J. A., & Berk, L. E. (1990). A longitudinal study of the development of elementary school children's private speech. *Merrill Palmer Quarterly, 36,* 443- 463.

Charlesworth, R., Hart, C., Burts, D., Thomasson, R., Mosley, J., & Fleege, P. (1993). Measuring the developmental appropriateness of kindergarten teachers' beliefs and practices. *Early Childhood Research Quarterly, 8,* 255-276.

Deniz, C. B. (2003). Early childhood teachers' beliefs about and self-reported practices toward children's private speech (Doctoral dissertation, George Mason University, 2003). *Dissertation Abstracts International, 64,* 09A 192.

Dickie, J. (1973). Private speech: The effect of presence of others, task and intrapersonal variables. *Dissertation Abstracts International, 34,* 03B. (UMI No. 04192-001).

Glaser, B. (1978). *Theoretical sensitivity: Advances in the methodology of grounded theory.* Mill Valley, CA: Sociology Press.

Hardyck, C. D., & Petrinovich, L. F. (1970). Subvocal speech and comprehension level as a function of the difficulty level of reading material. *Jounal of Verbal Learning and Verbal Behavior, 9,* 647-652.

Kohlberg, L., Yaeger, J., & Hjertholm, E. (1968). Private speech: Four studies and a review of theories. *Child Development, 39,* 691-736.

Lee, J. (1999). The effects of 5-year-old preschoolers' use of private speech on performance and attention for two kinds of problem solving tasks. *Dissertation Abstracts International, 60,* 06A. (UMI No. AAG99-32671).

Maxwell, J. (1996). *Qualitative research design.* Thousand Oaks, CA: Sage Publications.

McCarty, F., Abbott-Shim, M., & Lambert, R. (2001). The relationship between teacher beliefs and practices, and Head Start classroom quality. *Early Education & Development, 12,* 225-238.

Miles, M., & Huberman, A. (1994). *Qualitative data analysis: An expanded sourcebook* (2nd ed.). Thousand Oaks, CA: Sage.

Pechman, E. (1978). Spontaneous verbalization and motor accompaniment to children's task, orientation in elementary classrooms. *Dissertation Abstracts International, 39,* 786A. (UMI No. DDK78-05964).

Sokolov, A. (1969). Studies of the speech mechanisms of thinking. In M. Cole & I.Maltzman (Eds.), *A handbook of contemporary Soviet psychology* (pp. 531–573). New York: Basic Books.

Stipek, D., & Byler, P. (1997). Early childhood education teachers: Do they practice what they preach? *Early Childhood Research Quarterly, 12,* 305-325.

Vartuli, S. (1999). How early childhood teacher beliefs vary across grade level. *Early Childhood Research Quarterly, 14,* 489-514.

Vygotsky, L. S. (1978). *Mind in society: The development of higher mental processes* (M. Cole, V. John-Steiner, S. Scribner, & E. Souberman, Trans.). Cambridge, MA: Harvard University Press. (Original work published 1935)

White, C. S., & Manning, B. H. (1994). The effects of verbal scaffolding instruction on young children's private speech and problem- solving capabilities. Instructional *Science, 22*(1), 39-59.

Wing, L. (1989). The influence of preschool teachers' beliefs on young children's conceptions of reading and writing. *Early Childhood Research Quarterly, 4*(1), 61-74.

Winsler, A., Carlton, M. P., & Barry, M. J. (2000). Age-related changes in preschool children's systematic use of private speech in a natural setting. *Journal of Child Language, 27*, 665-687.

Winsler, A., & Diaz, R. M. (1995). Private speech in the classroom: The effects of activity type, presence of others, classroom context, and mixed-age grouping. *International Journal of Behavioral Development, 18*, 463-487.

Winsler, A., Diaz, R. M., & Montero, I. (1997). The role of private speech in the transition from collaborative to independent task performance in young children. *Early Childhood Research Quarterly, 12*(1), 59-79.

THE POWER OF
ACCOMMODATING LITERACY
DIVERSITY AND SPECIAL NEEDS

SOMEPLACE SPECIAL: IMAGES OF THE LIBRARY EXPERIENCE IN CHILDREN'S LITERATURE

Suzanne S. Monroe

West Texas A&M University

Abstract

This exploration of children's literature features contemporary and historical images of libraries as settings for empowering diversity and literacy. Featured selections focus on personal, family, and community literacy experiences and events. Representation includes protagonists of racial, ethnic, and language diversity. Images are included of both women and men as librarians, and both girls and boys are featured as library patrons. These publications represent a variety of genre: realistic and historical fiction, fantasy, and nonfiction; they provide empowering images and positive messages about literacy, specifically within the context of the community library.

According to novelist Pete Hamill in *D'Artaganan on Ninth Street*, "The library is a place where most of the things I came to value as an adult had their beginnings." (Griliches, 1996, p. 67). Hamill's reflection is reminiscent of the influence of libraries and librarians in the lives of several outstanding authors of children's literature: Patricia McKissack, Gary Paulsen, Katherine Paterson and Christopher Paul Curtis, among others.

According to Patricia McKissack (2001), prolific author of both fiction and nonfiction, the public library in Nashville, Tennessee provided intellectual stimulation as well as a safe haven from the 1950s world of segregation and discrimination. In McKissack's *Goin' Someplace Special* (2001), with beautiful illustrations created by equally prolific and well-known illustrator Jerry Pinkney, we see evidence of the power and influence of the public library in the life of a young African American living in a southern town in the 1950s. There's a place in this town where all are welcome, no matter what their skin color; and protagonist Tricia Ann knows exactly how to get there. To her, it's someplace special and she's bursting to go by herself. She hurries to catch the bus heading downtown, but unlike the white passengers, she must sit in the back behind the Jim Crow sign wondering why life is so unfair. In her Author's Note, McKissack explains,

> Nashville, like most southern cities in the 1950s, was segregated. The doors of hotels, restaurants, churches and amusement parks were posted with Jim Crow segregation signs that barred African Americans, who also had to endure the further indignities of riding in the backs of buses, attending separate schools, sitting in the last rows of the balcony, and drinking from separate water fountains. But, in the late 1950s, Nashville's public library board of directors quietly voted to integrate all their facilities. The downtown branch was one of the few places where there were no Jim Crow signs and blacks were treated with some respect. (McKissack, 2001, p.32)

> I was almost twelve when my parents trusted me to make the trek to the library by myself . . . Along the way, I had to face all kinds of racial bigotry and discrimination. But, for me, the library was always filled with a specialness that made the effort worthwhile. Since I felt welcome there, I checked out books more often. And the more I read, the better I understood why my grandmother believed the library was someplace more exciting, more interesting, and more informative than hotels, movies, restaurants, and amusement parks. She, like Andrew Carnegie, whose great wealth helped to build the library, knew that "reading is the door to freedom." (McKissack, 2001, p. 32)

Noted author of *Hatchet* (Paulsen, 1987) and other popular survival stories, Gary Paulsen was first influenced and empowered by a librarian in a small town in Minnesota. She issued Paulsen his first library card, and encouraged his reading preferences coupled with her own recommendations for new reading adventures (Peters, 1999).

> It would take him more than a month to read the book the librarian had given him. But from that moment on, books were a part of his life. After the first volume, he read another. That took him two weeks. But the pace picked up soon after, until he was reading nearly two books a week. Westerns, science fiction, and even the occasional classic . . . Gary read them all, and through his reading he escaped from the difficulties of everyday life. But reading was more than an escape. He learned from books, learned that there was more in the world than what his life so far taught him. That was a lesson he never forgot. (pp. 6-7)

Katherine Paterson, winner of the Hans Christian Anderson Award for her entire body of work, has related stories of her early childhood experience as a daughter of missionaries. Challenged by frequent moves, she found excitement and adventure in books as well as solace and security at various local libraries (Trumpet Video Visits, 1993).

More recently, Christopher Paul Curtis acknowledged that he created both of his Newbery award-winning titles of historical fiction in the nurturing and supportive environment of the Windsor Public Library in Ontario, Canada (Podell, 2000). It is obvious from these testimonials that libraries serve a purpose far beyond the access to information. For many readers, young and old, the library has represented a dependable sense of place—a place of safety and consistency as well as excitement and discovery, a place of welcoming familiarity combined with an underlying reserve and formality, and always, a place supporting equitable access to information and the interaction between people and books!

The Many Faces and Places of the Library Experience

Recently there have been significant changes in themes of trade book publications as well as an increase in the publication of both picture books and chapter books about libraries, librarians and library patrons. In the 1980s, there were two notable selections available to young readers: *How My Library Grew by Dinah* (1983), realistic fiction by Martha Alexander, and *Check It Out! The Book about Libraries* (1985), nonfiction by Gail Gibbons. In contrast to these earlier limited publications, there are currently available a wide variety of quality children's books, representing different genre, and portraying unique images of libraries as well as empowering images of librarians and library patrons.

The following selections focus on personal, family, and community literacy experiences and events. Representation includes protagonists of racial, ethnic, and language diversity; and family contexts range from single parent to extended families. Images are included of both male and female protagonists as librarians and library patrons. The publications also represent a variety of genre: nonfiction—biographical and informational, historical fiction, realistic fiction, and modern fantasy. These diverse selections of children's literature provide empowering images and strong messages about literacy, within the historical or contemporary context of the public library.

Nonfiction–Biographical and Informational

Nonfiction is currently the largest growing genre in children's literature, with more than 2,000 new titles being published each year. Given that nonfiction is so very popular with children and that more high quality publications continue to flood the market, it is not surprising that in many school libraries more than half of the titles are nonfiction (Tomlinson & Lynch-Brown, 2002). The following selections are representative of the current variety in both content and format.

Through simple text and illustration, Gail Gibbons details the history of books and libraries in *Check It Out! The Book about Libraries* (1985), a picture book of nonfiction for young readers. She also describes various kinds and sizes of collections, different sources of information and services, as well as additional services through audio-visual media, computers, bookmobiles, special collections for the handicapped, and planned programs for author/ illustrator visits. Gibbons uses unbiased illustrations to promote equity of gender, age, race, and exceptionality.

In *My Hometown Library* (1994), William Jaspersohn introduces young readers to the many aspects of the library while highlighting its influence on his own life and career. The realistic color photographs and unique layout make for a visually appealing tour of a local library in Guilford, Connecticut. Jaspersohn suggests,

> Joining a library is easy. At my hometown library, all you have to do is show that you are a citizen of the town and fill out a form. Then a librarian types your name and address into a computer and gives you a library card with your name on it. Presto! You may start borrowing books and other materials immediately. (Jaspersohn, 1994, p. 10)

The Inside-Outside Book of Libraries (1996) by Julie Cummins includes informational text and large, colorful illustrations by Roxie Munro. The author highlights the variety of collections in bookmobiles, school and public libraries, as well as the vast public holdings of the Library of Congress and the more unconventional collections at Folsom State Prison and aboard the U.S. Naval carriers. Cummins comments on the value of home libraries:

> Your own library needn't be fancy or neatly organized. It can be a simple shelf or even a trunk. What matters is that you have chosen the books that are there. Some people keep books in their libraries that they haven't yet read—to look forward to reading. Others look fondly upon their libraries for the favorite characters and scenes, authors and ideas they've already enjoyed and will enjoy again. Few things offer the lifelong pleasures that books do. From spellbinding stories to true adventure, from humorous poetry to mathematics and biography, books enable us to laugh, to dream, to hope–and to envision the future. (Cummins, 1996, pp.31-32)

Ms. Davison, Our Librarian (1996) by Alice K. Flanagan is a colorful photo essay based on the daily responsibilities of an African-American librarian in the St. George Library Center of the New York Public Library. The text is simple and concise with excellent photographs intended for emergent readers. Although brief in format, this book provides a solid introduction to the duties of a librarian as well as the daily operation of a library.

In *Librarians* (1998), author Dee Ready provides younger readers with informative and colorful photographs accompanied by simple text, a glossary, suggested web sites, and related picture book selections. Ready describes these librarians as community helpers in school and public libraries and bookmobiles, and includes images of men and women of diverse racial and ethnic backgrounds as librarians.

Two recent publications designed for emergent readers are *We Need Librarians* (2000) by Jane Scoggins Bauld and *A Day with a Librarian* (2000) by Jan Kottke. In the first selection by Bauld, the text is formatted in single sentences on each page with an adjacent photograph of male or female librarians of diverse background. This selection may be easily held by small hands; and includes an index and word list, a simple glossary, related book titles and a list of suggested web sites. In the second selection by Kottke, the text is simple with a maximum of three sentences per page, and photographs of a local school librarian. This small book includes an index, a glossary of new words, recommended web sites, and a list of books on the same topic.

Other Nonfiction: Historical Perspectives and Changing Images

In *Books and Libraries* (1991), Jack Knowlton provides a historical overview of symbol systems, technology, and storage as related to the development of writing, books, and libraries. The author describes books and libraries in the context of various cultures: Babylon, Egypt, China, Greece, the Roman Empire, Europe during the Middle Ages and Renaissance, Germany, Colonial America, and the American western frontier. Each historical sketch is complemented by a colorful illustration of the period. Knowlton concludes with this reflection:

> From the clay tablets of ancient Sumeria to the computers in modern libraries, the purpose of books and libraries hasn't changed at all. Books and libraries are the memory of mankind. They are the storehouses of human thought and imagination. Nothing is hidden from you in the library. Books contain wisdom and wit, facts and fantasy, for young and old alike. With a book in your hand you can look into the past and even catch glimpses of the future. (Knowlton, 1991, p. 36)

A unique nonfiction picture book is *The Librarian Who Measured the Earth* (1994) by Kathryn Lasky. For this biography, the author completed research on the life of Eratosthenes, a Greek student of math, science, and philosophy, who later became a chronologist and author of books.

Eratosthenes was appointed chief librarian of the Alexandria Library in Egypt, where he helped readers and writers with their research while supervising forty librarians who organized and maintained seven hundred thousand papyrus scrolls. Double-spread illustrations by Kevin Hawkes extend Lasky's imaginative text, lending credibility to the images of larger-than-life libraries of the ancient world.

Two publications which are appropriate for young adult as well as adult readers are excellent black and white photo essays: *Cultural Gems: An Eclectic Look at Unique United States Libraries* (1996) written by Mary and Richard Maturi and *Library: The Drama Within* (1996) by Diane Asseo Griliches.

In *Cultural Gems: An Eclectic Look at Unique United States Libraries (1996)*, author Mary Buckingham Maturi collaborates with her husband and photographer Richard Maturi in a visual presentation of unique libraries by geographic region, from coast to coast, across the United States. The creators include a panorama of civic buildings from metropolitan cities, small towns and farm communities. Their work emphasizes architectural detail and includes historical and anecdotal narratives for each library site. This publication is a handy reference for every student of libraries as well as a significant work in popular culture.

In *Library: The Drama Within* (1996), photographer Diane Asseo Griliches includes unusual photographs of historical and geographic diversity coupled with brief anecdotes of famous and unusual libraries. She has also included an extensive essay as well as outstanding quotes from well-known literary giants. Griliches comments in the Preface and Acknowledgments:

> I am frequently asked how I happened on the idea of photographing libraries...The path was opened by my love of books and my great fondness for libraries, one of the very few institutions on earth where any soul may walk through its doors free, and depart enriched. I was also moved by the beauty of libraries. In contrast to many recently built ones, most libraries built in years past had artistic significance. They were symbols of optimism and civic pride. With their inspiring architecture, fine woodwork, walls lined with books, bronze lamps, sculpture, and murals, one was surrounded by greatness, a greatness matching the collection of intellectual treasures within. (Griliches, 1996, p. vii)

Another nonfiction publication for sophisticated young adult readers is *Libraries through the Ages* (1999) by Fred Lerner. Although intended for a younger audience, much of the material is based on his earlier adult nonfiction publication, *The Story of Libraries: from the Invention of Writing to the Computer Age* (Lerner, 1998). The 1998 publication was the first book of its kind in years to chronicle the crucial role of libraries throughout history. More concise and with nearly twice as many illustrations as its predecessor, the

1999 young adult publication will appeal to the reader looking for an international overview of book collections, from the early invention of writing to the challenges of the computer age. From ancient Egypt to the great Alexandria Library, Lerner describes the libraries of Han-dynasty China, India, the Middle East, Medieval and Renaissance Europe, and the formation of the United States Library of Congress. The author includes easy-to-read yet well-researched information regarding the historical background of public libraries as contemporary technological developments. In excellent narrative style, Lerner presents the development of symbol, books, and libraries in the context of larger global cultures and events.

In *Library: from Ancient Scrolls to the World Wide Web* (2000), John Malam introduces an inviting picture book format which includes essential information about contemporary libraries. This colorful trade book includes text intended for the accomplished reader with detailed illustrations of a lending library, special needs library, bookmobile, children's library, audiovisual and multimedia library, reference library, local studies library, business library, rare book library, and the library bindery. Malam has also included a unique time line of library history, snapshots of famous libraries, and an extensive glossary of library terminology.

Historical Fiction

Historical fiction brings history to life by placing appealing characters in accurately described historical settings. The works of this genre represent the authors' in-depth research efforts combined with a bent toward the imaginative. By sharing stories of these characters' everyday lives as well as presenting their successes and failures, authors of historical fiction provide readers with the human side of history, making it more real and memorable.

A unique story that is based on the true account of the country's first traveling bookwagon is *Clara and the Bookwagon* (1988) by Nancy Smiler Levinson. Soon after Mary L. Titcomb becomes the public librarian in Hagerstown, Maryland, she decides to make books available to many people who live far from the city. She first establishes small book stations in general stores, churches and homes throughout the area; and in 1905, she designs the first horse-drawn "bookmobile" to be driven by library janitor Joshua Thomas, who routinely covered 500 square miles of back-road territory. Author Levinson portrays the local librarian as an influential mentor of a young girl who wants to read, but is discouraged by her father's preconceived notions about the value of reading: "Our farm is not the right place for a bookwagon . . . we are too busy here." (Levinson, 1988, pp. 54-55). But the librarian is persistent, and eventually teaches Clara to read.

Also emphasizing the empowerment possible with a library card is

Richard Wright and the Library Card (1997) by William Miller. This picture book addresses one of the social issues of the 1920s in the still-segregated South: access to literacy. Although a fictionalized account, the story is based on an important literacy event in the life of Richard Wright, who was born in Mississippi and later moved to Memphis, where he gained access to the library and use of a library card only through the assistance of a white co-worker. Wright read many books during his years in Memphis; and was inspired to become a writer himself, becoming internationally famous for his publications of the 1940s. Haunting illustrations by Gregory Christie extend the mood of fear and limitation perpetuated by racism and exclusion in the South prior to the 1960s and the Civil Rights Movement. Wright used books, libraries and reading as his ticket to freedom!

Another example of empowerment through literacy is the story of an Iowa librarian and patron mentor in *Tomas and the Library Lady* (1997) by Pat Mora. In this picture book selection, the author has re-created the early literacy experiences of the late Tomas Rivera. Growing up in a Mexican-American family of migrant workers, Rivera later became an established writer, college professor, and the Chancellor of the University of California at Riverside. This wonderful story supports the idea that individual librarians do influence young readers through their impact on reading values and abilities. During a summer in Iowa, Tomas is encouraged by a local librarian to read, obtain a library card, and check out books. In exchange, he tutors the librarian in Spanish. Mora's narrative, enhanced by the warm and imaginative illustrations of Raul Colon, portrays the power of literacy in the life of a child, a family, and a community.

Realistic Fiction

Realistic fiction refers to stories that are within the realm of possibility. The protagonists of these stories are fictitious characters created by the author, but their actions and reactions are quite believable. In some instances, the fictional characters are based on a real person or event.

In contrast to the historical setting of rural Maryland in *Clara and the Bookwagon* (Levinson, 1988), Cari Best provides an urban setting for a very contemporary African American protagonist in *Red Light, Green Light, Mama and Me* (1995). In this delightful picture book, Lizzie accompanies her mother, a children's librarian, to her place of employment: the public library. Illustrator Niki Daly extends the text with colorful depictions of literacy events both inside and outside the library walls. The young protagonist reflects:

> My mama must be the most important person in the whole city . . . Inside Mama's library there is a Reading Room . . . It is so quiet that I can hear my shoes clicking across the floor. And there are millions of books.

High, low and in the middle, too. No wonder Mama is so smart . . . If
I had Mama's job, I'd look at books all day, smell them, and take home
all the ones with new covers. (Best, 1995, p.14)

A publication which describes the impact of books in the life of a librarian is *The Library* (1995), a family collaboration by author, Sarah Stewart,
and illustrator, David Small. This unusual picture book is based on the biographical sketch of Elizabeth Brown, a librarian who bonded with books
very early in her life and relished the adventure of reading.

She manufactured library cards
And checked out books to friends,
Then shocked them with her midnight raids
To collect the books again. (Stewart, 1995, p. 8).

Later as an adult, Brown accumulated so many books that she ran out
of storage space, and eventually donated her entire collection to the local
community library, which became known as the Elizabeth Brown Free Library. Small's humorous and light-hearted illustrations are a perfect match
with Stewart's poetic format. The couple dedicated this creative work to the
memory of "the real Mary Elizabeth Brown . . . Librarian, Reader,
Friend . . . 1920-1991" (Stewart, 1995, p. 1).

In *The Library Card* (1997), author Jerry Spinelli includes four intriguing
stories about the influence of a library card in the lives of young adults who
belatedly become hooked on reading. One of the protagonists in this chapter book is April Mendez, recently transplanted from New York City to the
country. April acknowledges the importance of a library card in her life,

I loved my library card. It was all creased and smudged and spilled on,
and the corners were rounded and furry. But it was the only official
card I have ever had, and the reason it was so beat-up was because I
carried it with me everywhere, because I never knew when I might
need it. My mother said it was a good thing I had it too, letting me
bring books home, because otherwise I would never leave the library,
because I couldn't stop reading . . . I still have the card. (Spinelli, 1997,
pp. 125-126)

Modern Fantasy

In contrast to these very possible stories are several improbable modern
fantasies that will capture the reader's imagination. In this genre, authors create
stories that are highly imaginative, yet believable.

In *Nicholas at the Library* (1990), author Hutchins portrays an imaginative young boy who encounters a chimpanzee hiding behind some books in
the children's collection. Nicholas requests assistance from the head librar-

ian, who joins him in the fantasy world of children's literature. Together, they search for a book that will provide the best home for the chimpanzee. This novel adventure through the fantasy world of children's books is enhanced by delightful illustrations by Ruth Ohi.

In a fantasy about life without libraries, *Aunt Chip and the Great Triple Creek Dam Affair* (1996), Patricia Polacco creates a future world in which books are used as . . . "doorstops, to hold up roofs, to sit on, to eat off, to sleep under, to mend fences, to stuff potholes, to prop up sagging buildings, and even to shore up the dam" (Polacco, 1996, p.9) . . . but never to be read. Protagonist Eli and his reclusive Aunt Chip visit almost everyday. He loves going to her home and listening to her great stories. One day in conversation, Eli discovers from his aunt that the town once had a library. It had been closed long ago, and replaced by television in every home.

> "Do you want to know what glory used to be on the corner of Cedar and Oak?"
> "What, Aunt Chip?" Eli climbed up next to her.
> "That's where the library used to be," she said.
> "What's a library?" Eli asked.
> "It's a place where books used to be kept, a long time ago," she answered wistfully.
> "Why did they keep books in a building?" Eli asked.
> "They kept them there for folks to borrow and take home to read. Look, child," and she went to a cabinet covered with cobwebs, took out a book, and opened it for him. Dust fluttered out of its pages. "Now look at this. Those are words. They tell about ideas, dreams, and feelings. They take you to places far from here. They show you how to be fair and just, and sometimes show you what happens when you're not. Books are a treasure. All you need is the key."
> "The key?" Eli asked.
> "The key! Knowin' these words and their meanings," she answered softly.
> "It's called readin'." (Polacco 1996, p.11)

The wild contemporary tall tale of *Library Lil* (1997) is written by Suzanne Williams, veteran children's librarian of twenty years, and illustrated by Steven Kellogg. Reminiscent of Polacco's protagonist "Aunt Chip," William's "Library Lil" has her work cut out for her. In Chesterville, as in Triple Creek, people prefer watching television to reading. But one stormy night, the wind blows down all the power lines and cuts off the usual television viewing. Lil finally has her chance to turn the townsfolk, as well as a visiting motorcycle gang, into readers.

When she'd cleared the parking lot, Lil drove the bookmobile on it.

Then she climbed down and headed toward the library's front door. "All right, boys," she called out. "I'm open for business." . . . It wasn't long before every man in Bill's gang was reading away. 'Course some of them hadn't learned too well in school, so Lil gave 'em some easier books to begin on . . . Last time I was over to Chesterville, they'd added a new wing to the town library. Seems Lil's been busier than ever. She's had to take on a library assistant to help out. The new assistant's a big fellow. The townspeople call him Bookworm Bill. (Williams, 1997, p. 30)

Each fantasy features a strong female protagonist as the librarian who mentors developing readers and mediates the literacy experience. Humorous, with serious underlying messages, these contemporary publications provide insights into the importance of literacy within families and communities, and the continuing influence of libraries, librarians, and library cards in children's lives. These publications are excellent examples of the kind of librarians described by Melvil Dewey in *Libraries in America:*

To my thinking, a great librarian must have a clear head, a strong hand, and above all, a great heart . . . and I am inclined to think that most of the men who will achieve this greatness will be women. (Gilriches, 1996, p. 111)

Conclusion

Speaking of great women, a recent publication in the genre of nonfiction is *A Library for Juana: The World of Sor Juana Ines* (2002) by Pat Mora, and illustrated by Beatriz Vidal. This is a wonderful biography of a seventeenth-century child prodigy, born in the rural village of San Miquel de Nepantla when colonial Mexico was ruled by a viceroy appointed by Spain. At an early age, Juana Ramirez de Asbaje revealed a deep love of knowledge and an inquiring mind. When she was three years old, Juana Ines followed her sister to school and peeked in the window, then begged the teacher to be allowed to stay so she could learn how to read. Soon she was making up stories, songs, and poems—she loved learning and reading, and couldn't wait to develop her own collection of books. Eventually, Juana became Sor Juan Ines de la Cruz, a nun, and devoted her life to writing. Though she died in 1695, Sor Juan Ines is still considered one of the most brilliant writers in Mexico's history. Her poetry is recited by school children throughout Mexico and is studied at schools and universities around the world. What an inspiring story!

Recognizing the power of words and pictures to influence our ideas about reading, I have continued in the exploration and research of children's literature for empowering images of literacy, specifically in the context of the community library. It is my hope that both children and adults will recognize themselves and others in the various literacy events and experiences depicted in these selections. With consistent exposure to positive images of literacy, young readers will be encouraged to identify with literate protagonists—those who enjoy stories, read and write books, visit the library, and regularly use their library cards. Hopefully, they will also identify with those adult models, mentors, and mediators of literacy known as librarians.

Through our continuing support of strong literacy images in quality publications, we have the opportunity to influence young readers and writers and also empower developing authors and illustrators. As parents, teachers, and librarians, we can ensure that these wonderful creations of authors, illustrators, and publishers are accessible to the children in our care. What better return on our investment than a new generation of enthusiastic readers, writers, and librarians who would all agree that, indeed, the library is "Someplace Special."

References

Alexander, M. (1983). *How my library grew by Dinah*. New York: H.W. Wilson Co.

Bauld, J. S. (2000). *We need librarians*. Mankato, MN: Capstone Press.

Best, C. (1995). *Red light, green light, mama and me*. New York: Scholastic.

Cummins, J. (1996). *The inside-outside book of libraries*. New York: Dutton Children's Books.

Flanagan. A. K. (1996). *Ms. Davis, our librarian*. Danbury, CN: Children's Press.

Gibbons, G. (1985). *Check it out!* New York: Harcourt Brace Javanovich.

Griliches, D. A. (1996). *Library: The drama within*. Albuquerque: University of New Mexico Press.

Hutchins, H. (1990). *Nicholas at the library*. North York, Ontario: Annick Press.

Jaspersohn, W. (1994). *My hometown library*. New York: Houghton Mifflin.

Knowlton, J. (1991). *Books and libraries*. New York: Harper Collins.

Kottke, J. (2000). *A day with a librarian*. Danbury, CN: Children's Press.

Lasky, K. (1994). *The librarian who measured the earth*. Boston: Little, Brown, and Co.

Lerner, F. (1998). *The story of libraries: From the invention of writing to the computer age*. New York: The Continuum Publishing Company.

Lerner, F. (1999). *Libraries through the ages*. New York: The Continuim Publishing Company.

Levinson, N. S. (1988). *Clara and the bookwagon*. New York: Harper Trophy.

Malam, J. (2000). *Library: From ancient scrolls to the World Wide Web*. Lincolnwood, IL: Peter Bedrick Books.

Maturi, M. B. (1996). *Cultural gems: An eclectic look at unique United States libraries*. Cheyenne, WY: 21st Century Publishers.

McKissack, P. (2001). *Goin' someplace special*. New York: Atheneum Books for Young Readers.

Miller, W. (1997). *Richard Wright and the library card*. New York: Alfred A. Knopf.

Mora, P. (1997). *Tomas and the library lady*. New York: Alfred A. Knopf.

Mora, P. (2002). *A Library for Juana: The world of Sor Juana Ines.* New York: Alfred A. Knopf.

Paulsen, G. (1987). *Hatchet.* New York: Puffin Books.

Peters, S. T. (1999). *Gary Paulsen.* Santa Barbara, CA: The Learning Works.

Podell, T. (2000). *Good conversations! A talk with Christopher Paul Curtis* [video]. Scarborough, NY: Tim Podell Productions.

Polacco, P. (1996). *Aunt Chip and the great Triple Creek Dam affair.* New York: Scholastic.

Ready, D. (1998). *Librarians.* Mankato, MN: Bridgestone Books.

Spinelli, J. (1997). *The library card.* New York: Scholastic.

Stewart, S. (1995). *The library.* New York: Farrar Straus Giroux.

Tomlinson, C. & Lynch-Brown, C. (2002). *Essentials of children's literature.* Boston: Allyn and Bacon.

Trumpet Video Visits. (1993). *Katherine Paterson.* New York: The Trumpet Club.

Williams, S. (1997). *Library Lil.* New York: Dial Books for Young Readers.

SOLVE: An Innovative Assessment Tool for Facilitating Mathematics and Reading Literacy Among Diverse Learners

Rosalind Duplechain
Jill Reddish
Elaine Roberts
State University of West Georgia

Abstract

Over a three-year period, an assessment and teaching tool was developed through collaboration and used with 300 preservice teachers in reading and mathematics courses. This innovative tool provided opportunities for professional reflection, decision-making, authentic assessments, conferences, and collaboration between preservice teachers and students, classroom teachers, university instructors, peers, and parents. Preservice teachers evaluated this tool as a viable method of assessing and meeting the needs of their students in a culturally responsive way. Preservice teachers reported: increased awareness of the complexities involved in the diagnosis and remediation process, understanding of the need for modeling specific strategies based on students' needs, heightened awareness of the dangers of making hasty judgments regarding what students know and do not know, confidence in their learning, and a deeper appreciation of the need to be culturally responsive educators. This innovative tool is counter to the current assessment culture based on traditional practices.

Learning is an innovative, complex, and constructivist process that should influence the nature of instruction and the role of assessment in classrooms (International Reading Association and National Council of Teachers of English, 1996; Morrow, Pressley, Smith, & Smith, 1997; National Council of Teachers of Mathematics, 2000). Just as learning is an innovative, complex, and constructivist process, assessment should be as well. Assessments that take into consideration these facets of learning provide a mechanism for understanding students' academic, social, and environmental needs and become a tool that helps the educator to more effectively meet the assessment challenges facing students (IRA/NCTE, 1996; Moon & Schulman, 1995).

Traditional Assessment Practices in Reading and Mathematics

In today's assessment culture, the idea that assessments need to be culturally responsive is relatively foreign. In fact, the traditional assessment practices of favoring and relying on standardized assessments as a primary indicator of student learning are quite culturally insensitive. Standardized tests, by their very nature, do not take student diversity (i.e., differences in their academic, social, and environmental needs and experiences) into account. According to Valencia (1997), standardized assessment results may not reflect valid results for students who perform below grade level. Also, because these types of tests are only administered once or twice during the school year, they may not indicate the intricacies of student progress. Lastly, standardized assessments are limited in the ways they can be adapted to meet the needs of special education students (Valencia, 1997).

Also foreign to today's assessment culture is the idea that assessments need to be designed and utilized with the purpose of informing instruction. Instead, the traditional assessment practice is to use assessment solely as an evaluation tool for student learning. The types of assessments that are typically used by teachers, such as student workbooks and chapter tests, frequently do not reflect current conceptualizations of literacy and mathematics (NCTM, 2000; Winograd, Paris, & Bridge, 1991). They tend to inform educators of what is not known more readily than they inform on what is known (Van de Walle, 2004). Lastly, traditional assessments tend to be one dimensional, in that the range of knowledge and skill that students are expected to learn is "extremely limited" (Danielson & Hansen, 1999, p. 12).

Traditional assessment practices are problematic. The practices of not designing and using assessments as a mechanism for understanding student diversity and informing instruction do not take into consideration the innovative, complex, and constructivist nature of learning. Consequently, traditional assessment practices cannot help educators meet the assessment challenges that today's students face. These ineffective assessment practices must give way to better practices otherwise we risk jeopardizing the success of teachers and students.

Moving Towards Better Assessment Practices in Reading and Mathematics

The first step in moving towards assessment practices is to know what good assessment should look like. Professional organizations such as the National Council of Teachers of Mathematics (NCTM) and the International Reading Association (IRA) provide principles and recommendations for educators regarding assessment. NCTM (1995) states that assessment should comprise six principles: focus on what students need to know and be able to do, enhance the learning of mathematics, promote equity and valid inferences about student learning, and be an open and coherent process. IRA (1991) recommends that literacy assessments . . .

- "must be based in current research and theory, not limited by traditional psychometric concepts, and must reflect the complex and dynamic interrelationship of reading, writing, and language abilities critical to human communications; . . .
- must incorporate a variety of observations, taking into account the complex nature of reading, writing, and language, and must also include high quality text, a variety of genre, and a range of authentic literacy tasks; . . .
- must reflect a broad based consensus about age appropriate literacy tasks for students taking into account the learning opportunities that have been provided for children in schools and communities; . . .
- need to reveal change over time at the level of the individual child; . . . and
- must be designed to eliminate bias toward students whose language, cultural, social, and ethnic backgrounds may be different from those of the majority population." (pp. 3-5)

The second step in moving towards better assessment practices is to have the tools and resources that reflect current theory and practice as delineated in the above principles and recommendations. The purpose of this paper is to provide teacher educators with an assessment tool that embodies the principles and recommendations set forth by NCTM (2000) and IRA (1991). This assessment tool is entitled SOLVE, an innovative assessment tool for facilitating mathematics and reading literacy among diverse learners (Ellis, Larkin, Roberts, Mizell, & Duplechain, 2001; Ellis, Larkin & Roberts, 2001; Ellis, 1995).

What is SOLVE?

SOLVE is an acronym for the process involved in collecting assessment data and planning appropriate instruction for mathematics and reading literacy (S=Student plus environment; O=Outline solutions; L=List goals for instruction; V=Visualize barriers, E=Evaluate the success of the plan). It is a flexible, organizational, assessment tool that facilitates the compilation of information from a variety of data sources into a comprehensive profile about students as learners. SOLVE is a reflective, case study approach that can serve preservice teachers, or teachers at any level of professional development, as they learn to strategically determine and address the needs of diverse learners.

The Organizational Structure of SOLVE

The first section of the SOLVE framework addresses three elements of SOLVE: (S) the student plus environment, (L) lists for goals for instruction, and (V) visualize and ascertaining barriers. This section of SOLVE requires teachers to analyze a variety of assessment data. Student work samples are gathered and observations and interviews are conducted. Students, classroom teachers, and caretakers are also interviewed in order to list individual and environmental factors that affect student learning. From all of these data sources, multiple concerns are formulated and learning goals are set. The

Figure 1. Solve Sheet #1 (Reading)

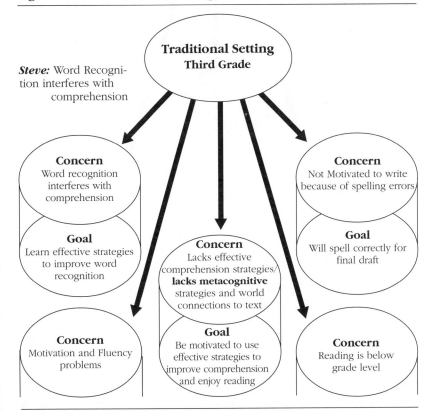

graphic organizer for this section of SOLVE is intended to provide a quick and comprehensive overview of the target student, that is, a student profile (see Figure 1 and Figure 2) that can be altered as concerns and learning goals change to ensure that students move from their zone of proximal development to higher levels of learning. Ideally, preservice teachers are expected to prioritize these instructional goals and to work towards accomplishing all of them.

Figure 2. Solve Sheet #1 (Mathematics)

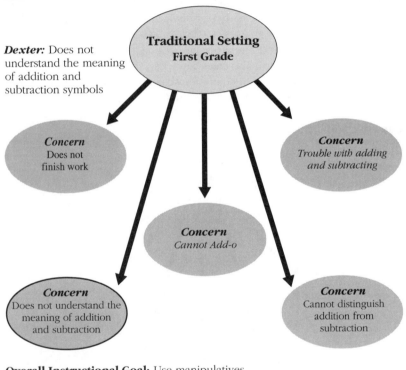

Overall Instructional Goal: Use manipulatives to teach algorithms step-by-step.

The second section of the SOLVE framework addresses one element of SOLVE: (O) outline solutions. This section of SOLVE includes solutions to the instructional goals identified is section one. These solutions are based on a balanced approach to teaching and learning. A balanced approach to reading includes the following: a) working with words, b) guided reading/reader response, c) self-selected reading, and d) writing (Cunningham & Hall, 1999; Fountas & Pinnell, 2001). A balanced approach in mathematics includes addressing both conceptual and procedural aspects for student learning

(Ashlock, 2002). Each element of the specified balanced approach is addressed when deciding on instructional strategies for each instructional goal. The graphic organizer for this section of SOLVE is intended to serve as a guide for teachers in their selection of instructional strategies when attempting to meet identified instructional goals (see Figure 3 and Figure 4). It is recommended that the instructional strategies implemented for both reading and mathematics case studies include constructivist teaching and learning methodologies that incorporate direct instruction/modeling. It is also recommended that technology, cooperative learning, and independent student inquiry be included in these instructional strategies whenever appropriate.

The third section of the SOLVE framework addresses the final element of SOLVE: (E) evaluate. This section of SOLVE requires preservice teachers, students, and caretakers if possible, evaluate student learning. Preservice teachers learn to self-evaluate their progress at diagnosing and remediating student concerns while being culturally responsive to their target student. Being culturally responsive means understanding student differences in academic, social, and environmental areas and taking these differences into

Figure 3. Solve Sheet #2 (Reading)

List steps to best solution

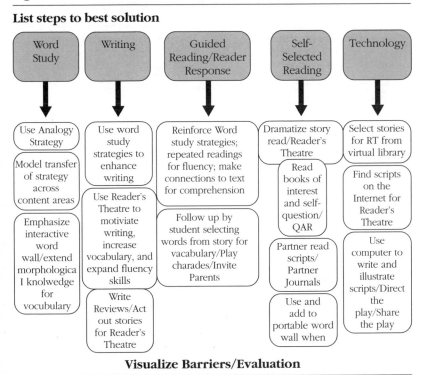

Visualize Barriers/Evaluation

Figure 4. Solve Sheet #2 (Mathematics)

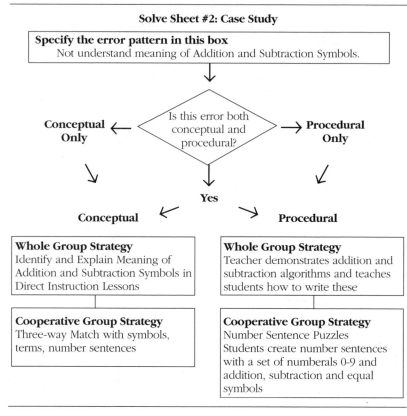

Solve Sheet #2: Case Study

Specify the error pattern in this box
Not understand meaning of Addition and Subtraction Symbols.

Conceptual Only

Is this error both conceptual and procedural?

Procedural Only

Yes

Conceptual

Procedural

Whole Group Strategy
Identify and Explain Meaning of Addition and Subtraction Symbols in Direct Instruction Lessons

Whole Group Strategy
Teacher demonstrates addition and subtraction algorithms and teaches students how to write these

Cooperative Group Strategy
Three-way Match with symbols, terms, number sentences

Cooperative Group Strategy
Number Sentence Puzzles
Students create number sentences with a set of numberals 0-9 and addition, subtraction and equal symbols

account when planning and implementing instruction. Students learn to self-evaluate their progress and help set new learning goals to increase their learning and self-esteem. Thus, SOLVE's design for assessment and learning helps preservice teachers evaluate the effectiveness of their instruction, understand their students more fully, and make decisions about future instruction and needed scaffolding and it helps students use what they know to become independent, motivated learners.

Using SOLVE as a Problem-Solving Tool With Preservice Teachers
Participants and Description
SOLVE was designed, refined, and used as an assessment, teaching, and instructional tool with preservice teachers at a southeastern state university (Ellis, Larkin, Roberts, Mizell, & Duplechain, 2001; Ellis, Larkin & Roberts,

2001; Ellis, 1995). For three years, university instructors used SOLVE when working with preservice teachers in diagnosis courses designed for teaching mathematics and reading assessment. More than three hundred preservice educators completed SOLVE case studies.

In general, preservice teachers were asked to use a case study approach as they engaged in numerous activities in order to diagnose and to correct student problems with mathematics and reading. Preservice teachers were to administer a pre-assessment and to use this assessment to identify concerns and instructional goals for a target student and to conduct interviews and observations of the target student. These interviews and observations served two purposes: to gather information of the student's needs in order to compile a comprehensive student profile and to either verify or modify the identified problem in mathematics and reading. Preservice teachers were also asked to research remediation strategies based on these concerns and goals, to write lesson plans that describe which strategies were carried out and how these were carried out, to provide a post assessment, and to evaluate pre-and post-data assessments in order to determine effectiveness of correction strategies.

Preservice teachers were also asked to engage in an extensive reflection process. By responding to specified reflection questions, preservice teachers were asked to reflect on the decisions they made as they diagnosed and remediated the identified concerns of their target student and then to write about these decisions and to engage in the process of bridging what they had learned in the field classroom to what they were learning in the university classroom about research, theory, and best practices. Preservice teachers were also asked to reflect upon how they would transfer the use of the SOLVE format to actual classroom practices and to evaluate the SOLVE process as a vehicle for their own learning. The specific reflection questions for reading and mathematics case studies are presented in Appendix A and B respectively.

As a result of engaging in these reflections, preservice teachers reported:

- "It helped me understand and develop balanced and integrated lessons for students with similar skills needs."
- "SOLVE helped me save time and yet organize my thinking while I worked with the student for my case study."
- "It is a great way for students to understand what they know and what they need to know."
- "I learned more about the student because we conferenced and discussed her progress using SOLVE as a guide."
- "Students understood purposes for learning and weren't as frustrated."
- "I hope to use it when I teach."
- "I will use it in student portfolios to help students learn to use strategies on their own."

Written responses to these reflection questions, as well as specific data sources, provided university instructors with data that were useful in determining the extent to which our preservice teachers were able to implement the SOLVE framework successfully. Other than these written reflections, these data sources included pre- and post-assessment data, plans for remediating concerns/instructional goals, and SOLVE frameworks (sections one and two– also referred to as SOLVE Sheet #1 and SOLVE Sheet #2, see Figures 1, 2, 3, & 4). For grading rubrics associated with these criteria, see Appendix C and D.

Conclusion: A Case for SOLVE

The traditional assessment practices employed by the majority of today's educators do not have the ability to help teachers to effectively meet the challenges of today's students because these practices do not reflect the nature of learning. Consequently, traditional assessment practices are ineffective.

In particular, traditional assessment practices are culturally insensitive because of their over-reliance on standardized tests that are only administered once or twice during the school year and do not take student diversity into account (Valencia, 1997). Also, traditional assessment practices do not typically use assessments to inform instruction. In sum, traditional assessment practices are incongruent with current conceptualizations of mathematics and reading literacy (NCTM, 2000; Winograd, Paris, & Bridge, 1991).

Unless we move our preservice teachers towards better assessment practices in mathematics and reading, we risk jeopardizing the success of teachers and students. Moving towards better assessment practices will require us to provide our preservice teachers with information, tools, and resources that are consistent with the recommendations set forth by professional organizations such as NCTM and IRA. One such tool is SOLVE (Ellis, Larkin, Roberts, Mizell, & Duplechain, 2001; Ellis, Larkin & Roberts, 2001; Ellis, 1995).

The comprehensive nature of SOLVE facilitates the efforts of preservice teachers, or teachers at any stage of development, towards meeting the assessment standards set forth by professional organizations. For example, SOLVE is consistent with National Council of Teachers of Mathematics (NCTM, 2000) in that it is an assessment tool that requires knowledge and understanding of all ten NCTM standards, supports the learning of mathematics, promotes equity and the making of valid inferences, and is an open and coherent process. SOLVE is also consistent with a number of the resolutions set forth by International Reading Association (IRA, 1991) in that it is an assessment tool that is based on current research and theory on literacy, reflects the complex and dynamic interrelationships of literacy, incorporates a variety of assessment practices, and requires the engagement of age-appropriate tasks. It is designed to be used in the improvement of instruction and learning over time and to allow the teacher to investigate the impact that students' language, cultural, social, and ethnic backgrounds may have on their learning.

Preservice teachers who used SOLVE reported numerous benefits. Among the most pertinent to this discussion were the benefits of increased awareness of the complexities involved in the diagnosis and remediation process, increased understanding of the need for describing and modeling specific strategies based on students' needs, enhanced recognition of the importance of scaffolding instruction, heightened awareness of the dangers of making hasty judgments regarding what students know and do not know based solely on standardized test data, and most importantly, preservice teachers gained a deeper appreciation of the need to be culturally responsive educators. Other reported benefits involved benefits to the target students themselves such as increased student confidence in their learning and other professional benefits to the preservice teacher such as providing them with opportunities for collaborative problem solving.

The SOLVE process encourages conferences and collaborative discussions between preservice teachers and students, classroom teachers, university instructors, peers, and sometimes parents. These conferences focused on the following: determining the needs of individual classroom students who were the subjects of the case studies, understanding the environmental effects and academic strengths and problems in reading and mathematics, and identifying and analyzing assessment results, teaching strategies, and learning outcomes to address the individual needs.

Thus, SOLVE is a viable assessment tool because it fulfills the principles and recommendations set forth by leading professional organizations, such as NCTM and IRA, who are responsible for gathering, interpreting, and informing educators about the current research and theory in the disciplines of mathematics and reading literacy. As a mechanism for understanding students holistically and for informing instruction, SOLVE guides the refinement of instruction by linking assessment with pedagogy and learning in a culturally responsive way. For these reasons, the SOLVE framework is an effective tool that has the ability to help teachers to effectively meet the assessment challenges of their students.

However, as beneficial as SOLVE can be, comprehensive assessment practices are counter to the current assessment culture based on traditional practices. Therefore, if teachers and administrators want to provide quality literacy education that meets the needs of individual students, they have to make a choice. Educators will need to "swim against the current" and follow a new vision.

References

Ashlock, R. (2002). *Error patterns in computation.* Columbus, OH: Merrill.

Bear, D. R., Invernizzi, M., & Templeton, S. (1996). *Words their way: Word study for phonics, vocabulary, and spelling instruction.* Englewood Cliffs, NJ: Prentice-Hall.

Cunningham, P., & Hall, D. (1999). *The teacher's guide to the four blocks.* Greensboro, NC: Carson-Dellosa Publishing Company.

Danielson, C., & Hansen, P. (1999). *A collection of performance tasks and rubrics: Primary school mathematics.* Larchmont, NY: Eye on Education.

Ehri, L. C. (1989). The development of spelling knowledge and its role in reading acquisition and reading disability. *Journal of Learning Disabilities, 22,* 356-365.

Ellis, E. S. (1995). *SOLVE: A collaborative problem solving strategy* [Masterminds Software]. Tuscaloosa, AL: Masterminds, LLC.

Ellis, E., Larkin, M., & Roberts. (2001, October). *SOLVE: A reading assessment tool.* Paper presented at the annual meeting of the Council for Learning Disabilities, Charlotte, NC.

Ellis, E., Larkin, M., Roberts, Mizell, & Duplechain. (2001). *SOLVE: A mathematics assessment tool.* Unpublished manuscript, State University of West Georgia.

Fountas, I., & Pinnell, G. (2001). *Guiding readers and writers, grades 3-6: Teaching comprehension, genre, and content literacy.* Westport, CT: Heinemann.

International Reading Association. (1991). *A board resolution of the International Reading Association on literacy assessment.* Retrieved on July 13, 2004, from HtmlResAnchor http://www.reading.org/positions/lit_assess.html.

International Reading Association and National Council of Teachers of English. (1996). Standards for the English Language Arts. Newark, DE and Urbana, IL: Author.

May, L. (1990). *Math with May: Trouble spots in learning mathematics.* Prospect Heights, IL: L. May.

Mizell, J.A., & Duplechain, R. (2002). *Diagnosing and correcting mathematical errors: Number sense and numeration.* North Chelmsford, MA: Erudition Books.

Moon, J., & Schulman, L. (1995). *Finding the connections: Linking assessment, instruction, and curriculum in elementary mathematics.* Portsmouth, NH: Heinemann.

Morrow, L. M., Pressley, M., Smith, J. K., & Smith, M. (1997). The effect of a literature-based program integrated into literacy and science instruction with children from diverse backgrounds. *Reading Research Quarterly, 32*(1), 54-76.

National Council of Teacher of Mathematics. (1995). *Assessment standards for school mathematics.* Reston, VA: Author.

National Council of Teacher of Mathematics. (2000). *Principles and standards for school mathematics.* Reston, VA: Author.

Roberts, E. (2004, in press). *Filling in the gaps: An integrated approach to literacy assessment, instruction, and learning.* Upper Saddle River, NJ: Merrill, Prentice Hall.

Stiggins, R. J. (1992*). In teacher's hands: Investigating the practices of classroom assessment.* Albany, N.Y.: State University of New York Press.

Valencia, S. (1997). Authentic classroom assessment of early reading: Alternatives to standardized tests. *Preventing School Failure, 41*(2), 63-70.

Van de Walle, J. (2004). *Elementary and middle school mathematics: Teaching developmentally.* Boston: Pearson Education.

Winograd, P., Paris, S., & Bridge, C. (1991). Improving the assessment of literacy. *The Reading Teacher, 45*(2), 108-112.

Appendix A. SOLVE Reflection Questions for Reading Case Study (Roberts, 2004)

Briefly answer the following SOLVE reflection questions for each area. Remember to include the literacy/technology connection and a balanced, integrated approach.

A. **Step 1 of SOLVE: Student and Environment**—Based on a holistic approach, after observing and interviewing the student about their environment what strengths and weaknesses did you notice? List these on SOLVE Sheet #1. What authentic assessments did you administer? What are the results?

1. **Informal Reading Inventory Example** —I administered the Informal Reading Inventory word lists and determined that the student was independent at the _____level, instructional at the _____level, and frustrated at the ___level for word recognition.

   Follow the same procedure for the miscues from the running record for the appropriate passage at the student's instructional level.

   After reading, include the comprehension level based on the answers for the comprehension questions and briefly reflect and write about the students' retelling of the story. What are your main concerns about the student? Why?

2. **Spelling Test Example**—I administered the Bear Spelling Test (Bear, Invernizzi, & Templeton, 1996). The results indicated that the student was at the ___spelling stage that correlates to Ehri's (1989) ___word recognition phase (i.e., pre-alphabetic, partial alphabetic, full alphabetic). This means that the student needs help with_____. Additional thoughts:

3. **Writing Sample Example**—Upon examination of the writing sample, I noticed that the student made _____type of spelling errors. The student has _____, punctuation knowledge, sequencing skills, etc.

   Does the student use vocabulary words that are appropriate for their age or avoid multi-syllabic words? How does the spelling impact the student writing? Additional thoughts:

   Do similar reflections about other tests administered and analyzed.

4. **Reading Strategy Knowledge Example**—Ask, record, reflect, and discuss the students' responses to the following:
   a. What do you do if you come to a word and you can't pronounce (say) it? Does the student have effective word recognition strategies? Remember to find out **specifically how** the student sounds out the word.

b. What do you do if you are reading and it doesn't make sense? Does the student have effective comprehension strategies? Does the student read fluently? Does the student have problems with vocabulary? Does the student have problems with phonemic awareness? (After administering assessments for phonemic awareness for young children)

5. **Motivation/Affect Example**—Does the student have an interest in reading? (After attitude survey)

B. **Step 2 of SOLVE: Outline and List Steps to Best Solution**—Using bulleted points to develop an instructional plan based on Cunningham and Hall's (1999) four blocks (use the following headings: Word Study, Writing, Self-Selected Reading at independent level, and Guided Reading/Reader Response (i.e., guided reading or content area reading strategy mini lessons, literature circles). Connect the solutions to technology.

Use observation notes and conferences with the student and caretakers to reflect upon instructional and learning progress and needs.

From the bulleted points you have developed, decide upon the best solution and list these on the second page of Solve (SOLVE Sheet #2) using four blocks lessons that include technology.

Remember to interconnect the four blocks to reinforce and integrate learning strategies.

C. **Step 3 of SOLVE: Employ and Evaluate** - Write a brief paragraph relating to the evaluations:
1. How will SOLVE be used as part of the student portfolio?
2. Are the parent and student reflections included?
3. What goals are met?
4. What new goals should be set?
5. Is the student independently transferring what is being learned to other authentic tasks?
6. Is the student increasing self-confidence in learning?
7. Other thoughts?

Appendix B. SOLVE Reflection Questions for Mathematics Case Study

A. Reflection: Post-Correction Diagnosing of Error

   1. Check Ashlock's (2002) textbook. What does he say about each of the problems that have incorrect answers?

   2. Check May's (1990) handout. What does she say about each of the problems that have incorrect answers?

   3. Check Mizell and Duplechain's textbook (2002). What do they say about each of the problems that have incorrect answers?

B. Reflection: Post-Correction Research of Concepts Related to Error

   1. List the procedural and conceptual knowledge that a student needs in order to successfully complete the work sample assignment

   2. Using either an encyclopedia or a textbook such as Van de Walle, find what is written about the major concepts related to your student's error. Copy this information, read and highlight any important ideas about this concept. Make APA citation.

   3. Using Ashlock's (2002) textbook, an article from any math journal, and/ or any teacher's manual in mathematics, identify any three teaching ideas related to your error. Make an APA citation.

   4. Make a list of any terms that would be helpful in teaching this error in the future. Using a math textbook such as Van de Walle or a dictionary, look up these terms. Type definitions for these terms in your own word—words that your case student would understand. Make an APA citation.

C. Reflection: Diagnosing and Correcting Process

   1. To what degree was your corrective strategy effective? Explain how does the post-test data support this?

   2. What did this student teach you about the . . .

     a. diagnosing process? What would you do differently?

     b. correcting process? What would you do differently?

     c. evaluation process? What would you do differently?

     d. reflection process? What would you do differently?

     e. error you chose to correct? How did post-correction research help you?

D. Reflection: Developing Sensitivity of Student's Needs
1. Describe the target student in terms of personal and environmental strengths and concerns (i.e., age, grade level, stage of cognitive development, cognitive style/learning style, performance level, special/ regular needs, attitudes towards subject area, list home support, and list school support)?
2. Briefly discuss how knowing about your student helped you design an age-appropriate and culturally sensitive correctional strategy. That is, when choosing examples of problems to solve, teaching aids/strategies, assignments for practice, and so on, how did you tailor these choices to meet the individual needs of this particular student?

Appendix C. Instructor's Rubric for Evaluating Literacy Case Study

Case Study Requirement	Percent of Case Study Grade
1. S—Statement of the Problem	15%
2. Selection and Administration of Authentic Assessments	15%
3. O—Solution of the Problem	20%
4. L—Instructional Plan	20%
5. V—Barrier and How to Overcome Barriers	10%
6. E—Reflections	20%
Total Score	100%

Comments (Preservice Teacher and Instructor)

_____

_____

_____

Appendix D. Instructor's Rubric for
Evaluating Mathematics Case Study

Case Study Requirements	Point Scale
Pre-data	**Scale:** 0–1–2–3–4–5

1. Data is present, child's identity protected, and assessment is marked for incorrect responses
2. Pre-diagnosed some errors
3. Pre-diagnosed each error
4. Correctly pre-diagnosed some errors
5. Correctly pre-diagnosed all errors

Observation Data　　　　　　　　　　**Scale:** 0–1–2

1. Present
2. Data focused specifically on what was seen and heard

Interview Data　　　　　　　　　　**Scale:** 0–1–2–3–4

1. Present
2. Data provided the intro question asked and child's response.
3. Data provided specific questions about the error pattern, beyond the intro question.
4. Data provided child's responses to the specific questions that were asked

Correction Strategy (Part 1)　　　　**Scale:** 0–1–2–3–4–5

1. Present
2. Correction strategy is consistent with error(s) from pre-test.
3. Conceptual, Intermediate, and Procedural steps of strategy are labeled ***and*** are consistent with type of error.
4. Independent practice (IP) was provided for child and child's answers from IP showed signs of being ready for the post-test.

Corrective Strategy (Part 2)　　　　**Scale:** 0–1–2–3–4–5

1. Used correct models, manipulatives, and/or drawings to represent concepts and operations
2. Provided an explanation for how manipulatives were used
3. Strategy included an emphasis on ideas needed to correct errors
4. Correct terms and information were used in strategy

Post-Data　　　　　　　　　　　**Scale:** 0–1–2–3–4–5

1. Present, child's identity protected, and marked for incorrect responses
2. Post-test items are consistent with error(s) from pre-test and not identical to pre-test or correction items
3. Pre-diagnosed some errors
4. Pre-diagnosed each error
5. Correctly pre-diagnosed some errors
6. Correctly pre-diagnosed all errors

Post-Correction Diagnosing   **Scale:** 0–1–2–3–4–5
1. Present
2. All of the appropriate texts were used.
3. Some of the appropriate information from texts was present.
4. All appropriate information from texts was present.

Post-Correction Research   **Scale:** 0–1–2–3–4–5
1. Present
2. Some of the required items were addressed.
3. All of the required items were addressed.
4. Some of the research results appear questionable.
5. All of the research results appear reasonable and directions were followed.

Diagnosing and Correcting Process   **Scale:** 0–1–2–3–4–5
1. Present
2. Some required items were addressed.
3. All required items were addressed.
4. All responses are reasonable but not completely consistent with diagnosing and/or correction steps.
5. All responses to the required items were consistent with diagnosing and correction steps and reasonable

Sensitivity to Student Needs   **Scale:** 0–1–2–3–4–5
1. Present
2. Some required items were addressed.
3. All required items were addressed.
4. All responses are reasonable but not completely consistent with student needs as identified in observational and interview data.
5. All responses to the required items were consistent with student needs as identified in observational and interview data

Deductions: Grammar, Punctuation, APA citations
Final Grade on Assignment

STUDENT LED LITERATURE DISCUSSION GROUPS WITH HIGH SCHOOL ESL STUDENTS IN KOREA: THE JOURNEY

Donald D. Pottorff

Grand Valley State University

Abstract

The purpose of this chapter is to examine a yearlong process of developing successful student led literature discussion groups in an international ESL high school in South Korea. Because limited English speaking students are often hesitant, or lack the skills necessary to carry on meaningful student led discussions in a second language, the Question-Answer-Relationship (QAR) strategy was introduced to help them understand the nature of questions that tend to elicit good discussion. In the chapter, the author describes the holistic literacy methods used in the classroom and the preparation, modeling and adjustments required to sustain successful discussion groups.

Student led discussion groups commonly referred to as literature circles (Daniels, 2002; Noe & Johnson, 1999; Hill, Johnson & Noe, 1995) or book clubs (Raphael, Kehus & Damphousse, 2001) are a relatively new phenomenon in school classrooms. Daniels (1994) traces them back to two independent classroom projects, one in Chicago in 1981, the second in Phoenix in 1982. Since that time, they have blossomed in popularity across the nation.

The underlying premise behind these student centered cooperative groups is that students can learn to initiate, conduct and manage their own discussions of common text in greater depth and sophistication than is possible with teacher led whole class discussions. According to Noe and Johnson (1999), these groups provide students with choice in what they read; give them more responsibility for dynamic discussions; and provide an opportunity for greater personal response, since group size is typically limited to four to six students. Raphael et al. (2001) talk about the defining characteristic of a book club as being the "transformation of the traditional classroom into a literate community" (p.2). They suggest that goals for these clubs should be to engage students in lively discussions, to assist them in taking responsibility for their own study of literature, and to help them become confident and eager readers.

Finally, Short (1995) believes that the heart of the curriculum is inquiry, and that literature circles contribute to the idea of an inquiry-based classroom. She believes that through inquiry students are able to search for questions that are significant in their lives. They can then become problem posers as well as problem solvers.

An Opportunity

Recently, I was granted a leave of absence to serve as ESL Department Chair at Taejon Christian International School in Taejon, South Korea, and to teach secondary ESL courses. The school was a small college prep school with a secondary enrollment of approximately 350 mostly Asian students, although twenty nationalities were represented. Approximately one-third of these students was limited English speaking and required to enroll in at least one ESL literacy course. The goal of these students and their parents was college attendance in an English speaking country, typically a country where they had lived with their parents for a period of two or more years at some point.

Purpose and Participants

The purpose of this article is to examine a yearlong process of developing successful student led literature discussion groups in an international high school ESL classroom in South Korea. Although I taught several secondary courses, the focus of this report will be on one class of 9th–11th graders with an enrollment of 16 students. The class contained five female and eleven male students who were of either Korean, Chinese or Japanese descent. Standardized achievement test scores in September revealed that their English reading abilities ranged from third to sixth grade.

Although I had read the research on literature circles, observed students taking part in them, and even participated in a discussion group myself, I had limited experience with the actual organization and planning necessary for successful implementation. Furthermore, other than the two act play article by MacGillivray, Tse and McQuillan (1995) and Dupuy's (1997) project with English-as-a-Foreign Language students, I found limited literature about using literature circles with high school ESL students, even though Daniels (1994) has role sheets in Spanish in his book. Nevertheless, I arrived at the school enthusiastic about the opportunity to experiment with literature circles in my courses. However, after meeting my students the first week of school my enthusiasm was somewhat dampened. The students soon informed me that they neither liked reading nor liked writing, and attempts to initiate a discussion on any topic, even one involving teen views and opinions was met with indifference. Quickly, I realized that I would have to put literature circles on hold in order to first address issues of motivating my students to read, to write, and to become active discussion participants.

Planning My Curriculum

Since the students in my courses had already progressed through a minimum of three of four levels of linguistic instruction, I was expected to focus my teaching on the improvement of reading comprehension, vocabulary development, and written and oral communication. For this, the highest level of ESL, there was no standard curriculum, but a respectable number of teaching materials had been collected. These included short stories, plays, and articles that were appropriate for their reading abilities. There was, however, a shortage of trade book collections and anthologies of short stories, and there were no records to inform me about what materials had been taught to which students in the past. I did have a generous budget to purchase new materials.

Reading Instruction

I first began by making decisions about the reading portion of my curriculum, keeping in mind Cambourne's (1988) advice on immersion in multiple kinds of texts. I decided that I would teach a short story, short play, or a teen article during each 80-minute block session, and that I would teach a reading comprehension or vocabulary strategy to go with it. Since there are so many creative strategies that serve a similar purpose, I would vary them in attempt to motivate my students. I would also vary their reading material to include famous short stories, traditional short stories, modern short stories, and teen stories such as those found in *Chicken Soup for the Teenage Soul* (Canfield, 1997). I would not over-teach, or over-analyze these stories.

To show my students that I valued reading, my only homework assignment was the reading of whole texts. I visited the library and checked out a sizeable collection of intermediate and junior high, grade level books and brought them to class. I set the homework assignment at 100 pages per week. By selecting more challenging books, students could actually cut the number of pages in half and earn two points per page. In addition, the pages read in class would count toward their assignment, and we would begin each class with ten minutes of sustained silent reading (SSR). They could either sign out books from me that I had obtained from the library, or they could visit the library themselves and make their own selections. There were also at least two large book stores in the area with sizeable juvenile and young adult collections in English.

Writing Instruction

Since I had made the decision that all homework would involve the reading of trade books, writing would need to be completed in class. The computer lab was not available, because other classes were already scheduled to use it during my class time. I decided that my writing program would be related to the material that we read in class. I would include a variety of writing genre in my curriculum that was geared toward interesting my students in writing. I penciled in personal response writing, RAFT (role, audience, format, and topic) a form of point-of-view writing (Santa,1988), autobiographical writing (Hamann, Schultz, Smith & White,1991), creative writing, poetry, advice column type responses to character conflict, predict-o-grams (Blachowicz,1986), and occasional summary writing. Research writing would be left to content area classrooms where it is typically used in abundance.

I decided to adopt and adapt the John Collins Method (Collins, 1997) as my instructional model for teaching writing. This method relies heavily on "focus correction areas" being emphasized in each piece of writing and has up to five types of writing. The first three types could easily be performed in a classroom setting without homework. Essentially this program emphasizes teaching a few writing skills at a time, and then correcting only those designated areas. I thought that this was important because judging from the writing samples I had collected, their writing tended to be developmentally at about a fourth or fifth grade level. I would give them ten points for writing ten lines, would have them "buddy check" each other's papers, and then turn them in to me. I would read through the papers, use a highlighter to mark focus correction errors, and then return them to students the next time we met. Students could then make their own corrections, meet with other students in class for corrections, or ask me for hints as I circulated the room. Papers would again be turned in to me, and students would receive up to ten additional points for a perfectly corrected paper.

I decided to offer students one further option. I would ask for two volunteers each time first drafts were turned in. The papers of the volunteers would then be made into transparencies, and would be corrected by the class on an overhead projector. The benefit to volunteers was that they would receive full credit for a corrected paper.

These decisions were consistent with Cambourne's (1988) theory that given plenty of opportunities to practice writing in authentic, nonpunitive ways, a student's writing will grow in sophistication. He refers to this as natural learning in a variety of contexts.

Oral Communication

Getting limited English speaking students to carry on meaningful discussions can be a difficult task. Often these students are more comfortable with short answer questions that are literal, rather than higher level, more thought provoking questions. If my students were ever going to be able to engage in student led literature circle discussions, then we would have to seriously address this issue.

In keeping with a holistic philosophy, I decided to center my discussions on the literature we read, and around the writing we did in response to that reading. After we had read Kate Chopin's "Story of an Hour,"(Draper, 1993) for example, I would ask them to think about Lucille, the main character, and her somewhat tragic life. I would then ask them to write about what they hoped their lives would be like. Would they marry, would they have children, where would they live, etc.? Next, I would ask them to assemble in their small share groups and take turns reading what they had written. Finally, I would lead a group discussion with "What if?" type questions to get them thinking about how unpredictable life can be.

It seemed important to me to teach students about the nature of inquiry and the discussions that can reasonably be expect when different types of questions are posed. I decided that Raphael's (1986) Question-Answer-Relationship (QAR) strategy might well serve that purpose.

The QAR was developed to improve reading comprehension (Ezell, Hunsicker & Quinque, 1996) by getting students to think about both product (the correct answer), and process (how the answer was determined). It has two main categories, "In the book," and "In my head." The first category deals with literal questions and has two sub-categories, "right there," and "think and search." "Right there" answers typically are brief, and can be found in one location on a page of the text. In contrast, "think and search" answers can be located in the text, but may be found in adjacent sentences, or even paragraphs (Raphael, 1986).

The "In my head" category also has two sub-categories, "Between the author and you," and "On my own" (Raphael, 1986). The first requires higher-level inferential thinking skills which entail analysis and synthesis, while the second is evaluative in nature and leads students to make value judgments, to form conclusions and to express relevant opinions. Although the QAR was developed specifically to improve reading comprehension, I reasoned that it might also serve the purpose of improving the quality of student led discussions once students witnessed the increased interaction that occurs when higher level questions are framed.

Student Responses to Implementation

As it turned out, I was more enthusiastic about the curriculum than my students. One bold tenth grader perhaps expressed the feelings of the class best when he confronted me with, "This is crazy! No one reads one hundred pages per week. It is impossible, and besides, we told you that we don't like to read!" (Kijun, personal communication, n.d.).

At first they barely tolerated the idea of reading short stories and materials in class, but as the days passed, they slowly began to sigh and moan less when I would introduce a story to be read. I allowed them to read silently, in pairs, in groups, or I invited those who wished to join me in a corner of the room to read together. If I managed to select something that they didn't particularly enjoy, or understand, however, body language and heads on the desks adequately conveyed their displeasure to me.

Then there was the problem of dialogue. At the end of the first month of classes, I still felt that we had never had an engaging discussion. Too frequently my questions were rebuffed with, *I don't know,* or with a silent shrug of the shoulders. When I asked if they had questions, or if they had strong feelings about what they had read, they never did. It appeared that the problem was deeper than just not knowing how to carry on a discussion. They clearly did not feel a need to do so. I decided to postpone using the QAR until they were more motivated to read.

I began to see more positive results in writing, however. At first they sought assurance that they would receive ten points for ten lines, and then would number down the sides of their pages and end their responses with exactly ten lines. As I journaled back to them in non-judgmental, personal responses, they began to pay less attention to the number of lines. Some responses began to continue onto the backside of the page. I also took note that some students who barely acknowledged my presence, actually began to carry on whole conversations with me in writing.

Tackling the Problem Head-On

Since discussions in the classroom seemed to go nowhere, I decided to seek a more neutral venue. My apartment was two blocks from school, so I asked for, and received, permission from the principal to take the students there for cokes and snacks, and to talk about unresolved class issues. The invitation was met with surprising enthusiasm, the most that I had witnessed with the class. I planned the event carefully.

Upon settling in over food, I was not surprised to find that these teenagers had no difficulty carrying on discussions and debates; they just weren't interested in talking about material that we read in class. I began our dialogue by asking them how they felt about ESL courses in general, and this course specifically. I soon learned more than I could have imagined. They held many negative feelings, and there was much mythology about ESL. Some students believed incorrectly that they were doing all of "this" work, but were not receiving high school credit for it. Others believed that to have an ESL course listed on your high school transcript would mean that no quality university would accept you as a student. Most felt that being in high school ESL was a stigma similar to that of being enrolled in high school special education, and that they would never be able to transition. I learned that a few of the students had been enrolled in ESL for up to five years. There was a great deal of discouragement and negativity.

I asked the students what they wanted to gain from my ESL course, and they agreed that they wanted to be able to pass the reading test and to improve their writing skills to the point where they could transition. I asked them how they proposed to do that when they expressed to me the fact that they neither liked to read nor write. They had no answers.

I had brought along a copy of a page from an article by Jacobs (2001). On the second page of the article, she quotes Stephen Krashen (1993) as saying, "Reading is the only way, the only way we become good readers, develop a good writing style, an adequate vocabulary, advanced grammar, and the only way we become good spellers" (p. 23). I had made a copy for each of the students, and highlighted Krashen's quote. I passed them out, and asked students to read the highlighted part. There was dead silence after they had read. Several students reread the quote. Suddenly a male student spoke out saying, "Why didn't anyone ever tell us this before? We didn't know this!"(Chae, personal communication, n.d.). Heads began nodding, and several students began talking at once. A vigorous discussion followed. The result was a significant epiphany that began to turn our year around.

The most immediate result in the classroom, was that students began to absorb themselves in reading. True, a couple of them were reading Dr. Seuss books, and another was reading Garfield comic anthologies, but all were reading. Within a short time, most were reading the required 100 pages per week without complaint, and were keeping up with their response journals. They began to ask me for suggestions for other "good books" like the ones they had just read, and the SSR time at the beginning of the class became valued. I now felt that we were ready to take on the problem of discussion.

Learning and Internalizing the QAR Strategy

In order to fully internalize the QAR, I reasoned that students would need to be taken through a series of graduated steps over a period of weeks. I began by developing colorful charts with library pockets and magazine cutouts for each of the four sub-categories of the strategy. It seemed logical that initially providing a visual prop would help to seal the categories in their minds. We studied the chart, then talked about each category, and about the concept of *product versus process* type answers. Next we read a short story, assembled into groups of three, and responded to twelve questions which I had written about the story. Their task was first to provide product answers for the questions. With that task finished, they were to talk about how they arrived at the answers, cut the questions into strips, and then place each in one of the four pockets. When they were finished, they were to combine with a second group, and compare results.

For the first time, lively discussions ensued. They soon found that most of their product answers were similar, especially for the lower level questions, but that there wasn't always agreement on how they had reached their conclusions. This especially troubled the concrete sequential students who demanded to know what the *real answers* were. We spent the rest of the period exploring the concept of how people arrive at understandings about issues differently in the world outside of the classroom, and how we often don't agree on matters because our own beliefs and experiences enter into our answers. We also talked about how these disagreements can lead to good discussions; and ultimately while listening to divergent opinions, our understandings are expanded. We continued to use the charts through three short stories.

Stage two was to remove the charts while continuing to think about both product and process. Thus, when I wrote questions for material we had read, students wrote down product answers, and then circled one of the four process categories that I had listed after each question. Discussion followed, and initially we were able to observe which types of questions engaged the class in greater reaction. From there, we moved to student prepared questions. After reading, they were instructed to work in pairs to construct eight questions, two for each category. They then combined with another pair to exchange questions and to compare and discuss results. This was quite popular and again discussions were lively.

Next we played *stump the teacher.* After reading, students again prepared a variety of questions, this time to query me. The catch was that after reading the question, they had to identify its sub-category before I answered it. Again, this activity caused them to reflect on types of questions and to seal in their minds the sub-categories. They also found great humor in the fact that I was able to answer only about 60% of their questions satisfactorily.

Finally, I asked them to write two quality questions that they felt would generate good discussion after they had read. We put those questions in a hat, and had someone draw them out. We would discuss a question, and then explore whether it had initiated interesting discussion. In this way, students gradually came to understand what was involved in posing good discussion questions.

Introducing Literature Circles

From the various student led discussion models, I chose Daniels' (1994) for implementation because it provides the most structure. I reasoned that this would be helpful with this group of students. Daniels identified eight possible roles students might assume when discussing fiction. These included "discussion director, literary luminary, illustrator, connector, summarizer, vocabulary enricher, travel tracer and investigator"(Daniel, 1994). A more recent edition of the book (Daniels, 2002) also identifies eight roles, but several have either been renamed, or reconfigured.

The day arrived when I asked my students how they would feel about conducting their own small group discussions of materials we read in class. There was immediate enthusiasm for the idea, but also some concern about whether it would work. I produced packets of specially prepared, color coded role sheets, and confessed to them that this was a new experience for me as well, but that we would work through it together. I then walked them through the concept of discussion roles and what each role would entail. The discussion director, for example, would prepare four, or five "Author and you," or "On my own," type questions, and the vocabulary enricher would select no more than five, or six words or phrases which the group might not fully understand (Raphael, 1986).

Afterward, we formed four groups of four, and each member was instructed to select one of the eight roles. The only required role was that of discussion leader. When they were finished, I gave them thirty minutes to read, "Thank You, Ma'am," by Langston Hughes (Osborne & Ahern, 1996), and to develop their role sheets. We then got back into our groups, to discuss the story. The initial results were disappointing. Most roles were performed in lecture style, i.e., *I chose these five words, and here is what each of them means*. The discussion leaders did no better. They wrote questions, which tended to have discussion potential, but typically would ask the first question to a single member of the group, and then move on to another question. All groups were finished in five to seven minutes. Cambourne (1988) wrote about the need for learners "to receive many demonstrations of how texts are constructed and used" (p.33). If this was going to work, much more modeling would have to be done. Most students clearly didn't understand the concept of initiating a discussion.

Extended Modeling

At the end of the class period, I asked for five volunteers to meet with me after school to prepare a model discussion demonstration. We would use the same story that we had read earlier in the day. We decided on the roles of discussion director, illustrator, vocabulary enricher, connector and literary luminary. I explained that the director was like the conductor of a fine orchestra who skillfully weaves in all of the roles and keeps the discussion going. He/she was not to settle for a single answer from one group member, for example, but would ask for agreement, disagreement, and the opinions of all of the members. The discussion director was not solely responsible for discussion, however. All members were responsible for leading discussion. When the illustrator held up her illustration, she was to ask the group if they could figure out what visual message she was trying to convey, and to what part of the story it was connected. The vocabulary enricher was to ask the group to turn to a specified page, find a certain paragraph, and then to locate a specific word. When the word was located, he would ask someone to read the sentence around it. He would then ask the members what they thought that the word meant. The connector was to make a connection between something in the story and something in her own life, but after she was finished, she was to ask whether anyone else in the group thought of connections. In this way, every member would contribute to the discussion to make it more authentic.

In class during the next block, the discussion went so well that I had to call a halt to the discussions after 20 minutes. Students were both encouraged and impressed, and we were able to talk about the potential for the various roles. We then got back into our groups, kept our previous roles and read Mona Gardner's, "The Dinner Party" (Osborne & Ahearn, 1996). This time discussion was much improved. In the coming days we went on to read two more short stories in preparation for whole books.

From Practice to Whole Novels

On a Monday afternoon, I arrived in class with a plastic tub containing twelve sets of novels. Students spent time passing books around, reading the jacket summaries, and asking questions about various books. When they had finished, I suggested that I would like to begin with four groups of four, and asked them how they wanted to form the groups. They were given the choice of forming groups by interest in novels, by assignment, or by selecting their own groups. The consensus was that they wanted to form their own groups. Three groups formed quickly. Suddenly I was left to question my wisdom with using this method when I found that there were four students who had hesitated, and now were left to work together. I went to them and asked if this was a problem. They rather unenthusiastically responded that it was okay, that they would give it a try. I was especially concerned about this group, because two of the boys were extremely shy, the third was a student with emotional problems who rarely completed his schoolwork, and the fourth was a girl who had to baby-sit her younger sister after school, and thus was rarely involved in extra curricular activities.

The next task was for students to decide on books, and to select roles for the first discussion. For this purpose they met in their groups to negotiate agreements. As it turned out, each group selected a different novel. The four books selected were *Sign of the Beaver* (Speare, 1983), *Julie of the Wolves* (George, 1972), *Night of the Twisters* (Ruckman, 1984), and *Call It Courage* (Sperry, 1940). Roles were arrived at rather quickly and easily, perhaps because there were only four roles to be chosen from the eight possibilities.

While they were making decisions, I also had decisions to make with regard to frequency, pacing and length of discussions. Fearing monotony if the technique were overused, I decided that we would use it only during alternate instructional blocks. This would give students adequate time to read the section of the book assigned, and to prepare their role sheets. In between, I would continue with short stories, comprehension and vocabulary strategies, and now we would have time to concentrate on all of the stages of the writing process. In terms of pacing, I decided to give them control of the number of pages they would read each time, but encouraged them to look for natural breaks somewhere between 20 and 30 pages. Discussions would be limited to 20 minutes, or as it turned out, expanded to 20 minutes with one group, and then 10 minutes would be given to redefining roles and marking the next passage to be read.

Implementation

As we worked our way through the first set of novels, it soon became apparent that some things were going well, while other aspects were problematic. Two groups blossomed, especially the group for whom I had had the most concern. The female student in that group was a deep thinker, exceptionally well organized and also very considerate. She became an unofficial leader and made sure that everyone's point of view was heard and that all were included in decision-making. Respect for one another began to grow day by day. For example, the boy with an emotional problem was a talented artist, and no one seemed to have had knowledge of his abilities. His first assignment was that of illustrator, and when he came with a beautiful drawing, the other three members of the group were astounded. Over the classroom the girl was heard to say, "My goodness! I could never do anything like that if I worked on it for a whole year!"(Meehee, personal communication, n.d.). This was a turning point for this young man. He never came unprepared for his discussion group the rest of the semester.

The third and fourth groups were not working so well. Group three had two very conscientious students who were eager to discuss, a 10th grade boy diagnosed with Attention Deficit Hyperactivity Disorder (ADHD) who had difficulty getting to class with the work he had completed, and a girl who often forgot to complete her homework. This regularly caused significant disruption because there might be three members ready for the discussion, sometimes all four, and upon occasion only two. To make matters worse, the two who tended to be unprepared (even though they usually had read the story) would try to complete their role sheets instead of participating. I was able over the weeks to help the student with ADHD with organization, but the group never quite jelled.

The fourth group was even worse. Each member would typically come prepared for discussion, but there was very little leadership emerging from the group. Thus, interaction would be concluded in minutes. No amount of modeling and encouragement on my part seemed to significantly help. Our frustration was mutual.

Restructuring the groups

The first novel took approximately four weeks. At the end of that period of time, I decided to restructure the four groups into three groups. The members of "the partially functional group" were divided among the other three groups. This increased the group memberships to five, five and six. The result was that the two groups that were functioning well accepted the new members and continued to flourish. This gave me time to concentrate my energies on the last group, which now contained five boys. I essentially joined their discussion group and took an active role in their discussions. As we worked, a strong bond grew among the boys. Successful discussions continued to be dependent upon my being in the group, but they fervently resisted a second group restructuring. We eventually read five novels in the semester, and I had to conclude that there wasn't a good conversationalist among the five boys. Nevertheless, they came prepared and were enthusiastic about the process.

Reflections

As I reflected on the project at the end of the year, I felt as if we had accomplished a great deal, although much of the evidence of success was in the form of anecdotal records and observations. For example, it was evident that a number of the students had developed a love of reading, and that they had learned something about the art of discussion. The wind of change had also occurred with regard to motivation. They arrived in class ready to go to work with attitudes that were more positive. One day in the spring, a student bounced in the door and announced to the class as she sat down, "I just love this class and our discussion group. It makes my day" (Pia, personal communication, n.d.). Several students nodded their heads, and made comments in agreement. I pursued the issue by inquiring about what they liked most. General consensus was that they had *choice* in novel selection and that they were able to carry on discussions in small groups that were much more interesting than teacher led discussions. One student replied, "We know how to ask questions that are better than most teachers" (Chi, personal communication, n.d.). The issue, I think, was that they were much more involved in their own learning. This is consistent with the findings of Cambourne (1988) when students are allowed to take charge of their own learning.

There was also a positive change in attitude toward the writing that we did. Much of our writing revolved around prompts that caused them to reflect on a problem in the story and to relate it to their own experiences. At other times the prompts had them giving advice to a character, or taking a point of view. At one point when we had read a story about identical twins, and I had asked them to write about what it might feel like to be an identical twin, one of the boys said to me, "You can't wait to get our writing and read it, can you?"(Higa, personal communication, n.d.). I had to admit that he was correct. Just as they had come to enjoy writing, I had come to enjoy reading, correcting and responding to their writing. I no longer viewed their papers as burdens hanging over my head to be graded into the night. Although no formal assessment was administered, samples of their writing were kept throughout the year, and there was ample evidence that many of them had made dramatic progress.

The area where the most tangible progress was made was that of comprehension and vocabulary development. The school tested ESL students twice per year, each time with alternate forms of the Gates-McGinite Reading Tests (2000). When August test results were compared with May results, the sixteen students showed a median improvement of 4.4 years, and a mean improvement of 5.3 years in comprehension. The range of improvement was from 2.4 to 8.9 years. On the vocabulary test, a test with which ESL students typically have difficulty because of vocabulary words being tested in isolation with multiple-choice answers, there was a median improvement of 1.8 years, and a mean increase of 2.5 years growth respectively. The range of improvement was from 0 to 8.9 years. These scores were sufficiently high to transition thirteen of the sixteen students out of ESL classes since the school policy was that reading comprehension had to be within two years of the student's chronological grade placement before he/she could transition. Three of the students who transitioned had received ESL assistance for up to five years.

It is important to recognize that it would be problematic to attribute these literacy gains solely to the instruction in my ESL course. All of these students were mainstreamed throughout the day in other content courses including a sheltered English class. In many respects it was a group effort to increase their literacy. In addition, attitudes toward taking the test began to change from that of frequent intense anxiety to one of confidence. Test anxiety, of course, can negatively affect scores. One student who had received instruction in ESL classes for four years, for example, said to me, "I'm ready for this test. This time I will pass it and transition out." When I asked him why he felt that way, he replied, "Now I know what you have to do to get better. You have to read, and I didn't understand that before" (Hahn, personal communication, n,d,).

Finally, the test used to measure reading achievement itself has some limitations. First of all, it is a group test, and group tests are generally considered not to measure achievement as precisely as individualized reading tests such as the Woodcock Reading Mastery Tests (Woodcock, 1998), or the Peabody Individualized Achievement Test (Markwardt, 1998). Secondly, the Gates-McGinite has only two sub-tests, i.e., vocabulary and comprehension, and vocabulary words are tested in isolation while comprehension is tested with only short passages with multiple-choice questions. Even so, the test is widely employed for reading screening around the U.S., and enjoys a reasonably good reputation.

Conclusions

The purpose of this article was to describe *the journey* toward successful student led book discussions in a high school ESL classroom where instruction was holistic in nature. The setting was in an international school in South Korea. With respect to student led discussion groups, I found few articles on this topic involving limited English speaking students, and I wanted to describe the year-long process, warts and all, as it unfolded. Too often conference presentations and articles leave the impression that secondary teachers can just jump right into literature circles and have instant success. A recent graduate course I taught in adolescent literature shed light on that issue. Of the twenty-four secondary English/language arts teachers enrolled only five had tried these discussion groups. Of the five, four had discontinued their use after a brief time. When asked why they no longer used literature circles, reasons were given that included such things as "they were too difficult to manage," "students wouldn't consistently come prepared," "the quality of the discussions were not adequate," and "students were unable to formulate good questions." It is hoped that this article will give the reader a positive example of the preparation, modeling, and instructional adjustment that may be required to reach a level where both students and teacher feel successful with literature circles.

Even after a year, there were adjustments that needed to be made. More thought needed to be put into how the groups were formed in the beginning. The intensive instruction that I gave after school on how all members of a group needed to take an active role in initiating discussion, needed to be given to all of the students early on. Much more modeling needed to have taken place, and finally, something would have to be done about a group that was unable to adequately function alone for a whole semester without my having to sit in on their discussions. Even so, it was an exciting year as together my students and I worked through multiple problems to achieve success.

References

Blachowicz, C. L. Z. (1986). Making connections: Alternatives to the vocabulary notebook. *Journal of Reading, 29*(7), 643-649.

Cambourne, B. (1988). *The whole story: Natural learning and the acquisition of literacy in the classroom.* Auckland, New Zealand: Scholastic.

Canfield, J. (Ed.) (1997). *Chicken soup for the teenage soul.* Deerfield, Florida: Health Communications.

Collins, J. J. (1997). *Selecting and teaching focus correction areas: A planning guide.* Rowley, MA: The Network.

Daniels, H. (2002). *Literature circles: Voice and choice in book clubs and reading groups.* Portland, ME: Stenhouse.

Daniels, H. (1994). *Literature Circles: Voice and choice in the student-centered Classroom.* Portland, ME: Stenhouse.

Draper, C. G. (Ed.). (1993). *Great American Stories I,* 2nd ed. Engle Cliffs, N.J.: Prentice Hall Regents, pp. 30-35.

Dupuy, B. C. (1997). Literature circles: An alternative framework for increasing Intermediate FL student's comprehension and enjoyment of texts in the target language. *Mosai,c, 5*(1), 13-16.

Ezell, H., Hunsicker, S., Quinque, M., & Randolph, E. (1996). Maintenance and generalization of QAR reading comprehsion strategies. *Reading Research and Instruction, 36*(2), 64-81.

Gates-McGinite Reading Tests (4th ed.). (2000). Itasca, IL: Riverside Publishing.

George, J. C. (1972). *Julie of the wolves.* New York: Scholastic.

Hamann, L. S., Schultz, L., Smith, M. W. & White, B. (1991). Making connections: The power of autobiographical writing before reading. *Journal of Reading, 35*(1), 24-28.

Hill, B. C., Johnson, N. J. and Noe, K. L. (1995). *Literature circles and response.* Norwood, MA: Christopher-Gordon.

Jacobs, C. L. (2001). Those kids can't read this book–it's too thick. *English Journal, 90*(6), 33-37.

Krashen, S. (1993). *The power of reading.* Littleton, CO: Libraries Unlimited.

MacGillivray, L., Tse, L. & McQuillan, J. (1995). Second language and literacy teachers considering literature circles: A play. *Journal of Adolescent & Adult Literacy, 39*(1), 36-44.

Markwardt, F. C., Jr. (1998). *Peabody individual achievement test-revised.* Circle Pines, MN: American Guidance Service.

Noe, K. L. and Johnson, N. J. (1999). *Getting started with literature circles.* Norwood, MA: Christopher-Gordon.

Osborne, J. & Ahearn, S. (Eds.). (1996). *Impact: Fifty short, short stories,* 2nd ed. (pp.166-169; 126-127) Austin, Texas: Holt, Rinehart & Winston.

Raphael, T. (1986). Teaching question-answer relationships, revisited. *The Reading Teacher, 39,* 517-519.

Raphael, T. E., Kehus, M. and Damphousse, K. (2001). *Book club for middle school.* Lawrence, MA: Small Planet Communications.

Ruckman, I. (1984). *Night of the twisters.* New York: Harper-Collins.

Santa, C. (1988). *Content reading including study systems.* Dubuque, IA: Kendall/Hunt.

Short, K. G. (Ed.). (1995). *Research and professional resources in children's literature: Piecing a patchwork quilt.* Newark, DE: International Reading Association.

Speare, E. G. (1983). *Sign of the beaver.* Boston: Houghton-Mifflin.

Sperry, A. (1940). *Call it courage.* New York: The Macmillan Company.

Woodcock, R. W. (1998). *Woodcock reading mastery tests-revised.* Circle Pines, MN: American Guidance Service.

DIALOGUE WITH CAREGIVERS:
PERCEPTIONS OF A READING CLINIC

Donna M. Harkins
Ronald S. Reigner
John M. Ponder
Gary O. Gregg
State University of West Georgia

Abstract

Caregivers' perceptions of reading clinic practices and the effects of these practices on their children were investigated through the use of pre- and post-involvement surveys, one-on-one interviews, and focus group discussions. Data were collected and analyzed for trends and themes within these caregivers' perceptions. Results indicated that caregivers enrolled their children in the clinic for a variety of reasons and that they were generally satisfied with the clinic's ability to fulfill these expectations. Issues specifically addressed in this study included: reasons why caregivers enrolled their children, home literacy environment of the clients, caregivers' expectations of the services provided, and perceived benefits of their children's participation in the clinic program.

Reading clinics have long been a part of many university programs in teacher literacy education. Traditionally these clinics have operated within the framework of a practicum experience for graduate and undergraduate students (Carr, 2003; Fitzgerald, 2001; Michael & Dougherty, 1999). The emphasis of these programs has been on assessment of clients' reading problems and the development of instructional plans to remediate those weaknesses (Allen, Swearingen, & Kostelnik, 1993; Kibby & Barr, 1999; Klenk & Kibby, 2000).

Only recently has some attention has been given to caregivers' (e.g., parents, grandparents, guardians, etc.) motivations for enrolling children in a clinic program. After a search for related literature, it appears that still less consideration has been given to caregivers' perceptions of the effectiveness of the assessment and instruction given in a clinic setting.

Research studies across several disciplines, including adult literacy, emergent literacy, child development, and systems analysis, suggest that family literacy programs build a sense of self-efficacy in family members (Rasinski & Padak, 2004). Key among those indicators is parental involvement which is an important aspect of children's literacy growth (Routman, 1996). Nistler and Maiers (2000) found that parents' values and beliefs and their involvement in literacy programs impacted their children's success in school. Parental involvement in literacy programs seems to benefit both children and parents (Rasinski & Padak, 2004). Landerholm, Karr, and Mushi (2000) found that early, on-going, and systematic evaluation can be used to identify a program's strengths and weaknesses. A continuous, evolving model of feedback evaluation made it possible to reach a program's goals.

This paper presents results of a study of caregivers' motivations for enrolling their children in and their perceptions of a reading clinic program. The purpose of the study was to ascertain caregivers' motivations for enrolling their children in a reading clinic program. A second purpose was to determine their perceptions of the effectiveness of the program.

Method
Participants
The participants in the study consisted of a sample of adult volunteers whose children were enrolled in a university reading clinic. The university is located in the southeastern United States and serves a semi-rural socioeconomic population in close proximity to a major southern city. The reading clinic enrollment is open to kindergartners through adults. School-age clients may be referred by parents, teachers, or counselors. Participants were recruited from the caregivers of school-age children attending the clinic in the 2001-2002 and 2002-2003 school years. Approximately twenty to twenty-five clients were served during each clinic session. For the purpose of this study, a clinic session is defined as approximately sixteen weeks of tutoring where clients come to the clinic weekly for ninety minutes. Data were collected at the beginning and the end of each clinic session. Weekly tutoring was composed of listening, reading, and writing activities. These meetings were planned and conducted by undergraduate students who were supervised by graduate students and university faculty.

Caregiver participants were recruited from those individuals who responded "Yes" to a question on the clinic's intake survey regarding their willingness to be involved in this research study. Participants agreed that information given to the researchers could be included in further studies and presentations at learned society meetings.

Over the course of the study, sixty-one caregivers returned the pre-involvement survey, while fourteen returned the post-involvement survey. This difference will be discussed later in the paper. Eighty-nine percent of those returning surveys were female; 63% were married. Thirteen percent of the caregivers returning surveys were African-American; the remaining participants were White. See Table 1 for a further breakdown of caregiver demographics.

Table 1. Caregiver Demographics

GENDER		MARITAL STATUS		INCOME		ETHNICITY	
Female	89%	Single	12%	Below $15,000	29%	African-American	13%
Male	11%	Married	63%	$15,000-24,999	9%	White	87%
		Divorced	19%	$25,000-34,999	21%		
		Separated	6%	$35,000-49,999	6%		
				$50,000-74,999	27%		
				Over $75,000	8%		

Note. Percentages include caregiver demographics from 2001 – 2003 school years.

Data Collection

Caregiver involvement consisted of pre- and post-involvement surveys, a voluntary one-on-one personal interview with a trained member of the research team, and voluntary participation in a focus group session upon completion of all personal interviews.

Analysis

Data from the pre- and post-involvement surveys were compiled and analyzed by graduate assistants and university faculty for emerging themes (Merriam, 1998; Stake, 1995). As suggested by the work of Kamil, Langer, and Shanahan (1985), our survey questions were designed to ". . . tap attitudes, opinions, and feelings—phenomena not easily observed" (p. 48). Interviews were conducted at the end of each clinic session and were followed by focus group meetings. Interview data as well as focus group meetings were recorded, transcribed, and analyzed. Graduate assistants transcribed the data; analysis was done by university faculty.

The process of coding the data involved the consideration and refinement of initial codes. One method of coding suggested by Miles and Huberman (1994) is to attach descriptive codes to data that initially require little interpretation. Caregivers' responses were analyzed first to limit the possibility of researcher bias. Initially identifying "themes" allowed the researchers to differentiate and cluster information from the data. Following this procedure, codes were created and attached to data to begin the process of assigning meaning to the information collected. Initial coding of data involved coding for categories suggested by the questions on the surveys. These codes were replaced by code terms that emerged from reading, transcribing, and analyzing the data.

Pre- and post-involvement survey questions (see Appendices A and B) addressed the reading habits of children and adults in the home, the kinds of materials that were read, and the time and location of reading in the home. The surveys included both a multiple-choice format and open-ended questions. For the multiple-choice questions, a prompt was given followed by four possible answer choices. With each question, respondents were asked to select the choice that best matched their opinion. The pre-involvement survey was given to all caregivers during the first clinic meeting of the semester. A post-involvement survey was also given to the caregivers during a meeting at the conclusion of each clinic session. Typically, this meeting coincided with the end of the semester. Many questions on the pre-involvement surveys were included on the post-involvement survey. On the post-involvement survey, additional questions asked for feedback about the client's literacy growth and attitude toward reading by the completion of the session.

Interview and focus group questions targeted caregivers' reasons for enrolling children in the clinic, perceptions of the strengths and weaknesses of the program, the impact of the program on their children, and suggestions for its improvement. Also solicited were any other issues that impacted reading clinic operations and effectiveness.

Data from caregivers pertaining to the reading clinic as well as other important elements of their children's reading development were gathered by means of carefully designed surveys, personal interviews, and focus group meetings. The data was regarded as informative and qualitative in nature rather than a quantitative measure of results. As such, this information was recognized as perceptual, and is considered important (Merriam, 1998; Stake, 1995) in planning future operations of the reading clinic.

Results

In the following section, the results of the caregiver surveys, personal interviews, and focus group data will be reported. Since consistent categories emerged from all three sources, results will be reported as a combination of data gathered from surveys, interviews, and focus group meetings. Because numbers were rounded to the nearest tenth, percentages reported may not equal 100%.

Over a two-year period, sixty-one caregivers completed pre-involvement surveys. Fewer of these participants (N = 14) completed post-involvement surveys at the end of each session due to any number of reasons. This lower response may have been due to the fact that clients did not finish out the clinic session and, therefore, caregivers were unavailable to complete post-involvement surveys. Some caregivers may have simply chosen not to complete the surveys.

On the pre-involvement survey, caregivers were asked how they had initially heard about the reading clinic. Approximately half (49.2 %) of this group reported that they had received clinic information from a friend or colleague. Approximately one-third of the caregivers who responded (33.8 %) selected the choice *other* for this question. Few caregivers selected the *teacher* (8.2 %) or the *school counselor* (6.6 %) choices. When asked about the degree of importance of reading in the home, almost all caregivers responded that reading was either *very important* (42.6%) or *extremely important* (55.7%). One participant chose a response that indicated reading was not valued in the home.

Caregivers reported that they held a very strong conviction that reading ought to take place in the home. When asked how often they personally read in the home, caregivers selected the following responses: *frequently* (64.0%), *daily* (18.0%), or *seldom* (18.0%). Central to this question is the notion that children who see their parents/caregivers reading in the home will be encouraged to read themselves (Purcell-Gates, 2000). When asked what they read, caregivers responded that *newspapers, magazines,* and *educational/ academic texts* were chosen. They indicated that this reading most often took place in the *evening, late at night,* or in the *morning.*

From these responses, it is not apparent if reading by the caregivers took place while the children were present, for these children would likely have been attending school or in bed during those times.

Data regarding *reading to* and *with* children in the home indicated that while caregivers responded that they believed reading at home was important, this belief did not always manifest itself in practice. When asked how often they read to their child and how often they listened to their child read, over half (60.7%) of the caregivers responded that they only read to their child *occasionally.* The choice f*requently* received 29.5% of the responses while *every day* received 9.8% of the responses. With regard to *listening to* their children read, 47.5% of the caregivers responded with *occasionally,* 37.3% responded with *frequently,* and 15.3% responded with *every day.*

Caregivers were asked about their children's level of interest in reading. While a majority (71%) selected that their children exhibited *moderate interest* or were *very interested,* special note was taken of the percentage of caregivers who selected the *little interest* and *no interest* choices, which were 25.4% and 3.3%, respectively.

When asked about their perception of their children's reading ability, a majority of the caregivers who responded felt that their children were reading *below grade level* (64.0%). Interestingly, however, 22% responded that their children were reading on grade level while 11.5% of the caregivers believed that their children were reading above grade level. One caregiver responded that she was not sure at what level her child was reading. Based on their perception of their children's reading ability, caregivers whose children were reading below grade level gave the following reasons for enrolling their children in the reading clinic: "low test scores," "poor word recognition," and "poor reading comprehension." Those caregivers whose children were reading at or above grade level enrolled them for reasons such as "more challenges," "continued school success," and "maintaining positive attitudes."

Caregivers' responses indicated that it took approximately one year from becoming aware of the need for intervention to enrolling their children in the clinic. During the year prior to enrollment, caregivers indicated that they "tried to provide help for their children themselves," hoped the children would "outgrow the problem," believed that "their children's teacher did not provide the help needed," or denied their children had a reading problem.

Caregivers enrolled their children in the clinic hoping to help improve their children's reading abilities. Among the expectations cited by caregivers were: "increasing their children's reading comprehension," "strengthening their children's desire to read," "giving their children more experience and practice with reading skills and concepts," "boosting their children's self-confidence when reading," and "providing literacy enrichment for them."

Near the end of each session, data were collected which examined caregivers' perceptions of whether their expectations were met. Specifically, data were collected as to what degree expectations were met, and how their children's abilities, attitudes, or interests with regard to reading changed. Caregivers were also asked if they would recommend the reading clinic to others.

Caregivers overwhelmingly indicated that their expectations were met or exceeded. Fifty percent of the caregivers who responded noted that the clinic experience *exceeded expectations*; 42.9% responded that it *met expectations*, while 7.1% responded with *less than expected*. When asked about the overall effectiveness of the reading clinic program, caregivers noted that they believed the program was generally effective. Approximately one-third (35.7%) responded that the program was *extremely effective,* 42.9% responded with *very effective*, and 21.4% responded that the program was *somewhat effective.*

When asked about their perceptions of how their children's reading ability had changed, most caregivers responded that they believed their children were "better readers" and "able to work more independently." Well over two-thirds of the caregivers responded that they believed their children showed improvement of some sort: *vast improvement* (14.3%), *moderate improvement* (57.1%), and *slight improvement* (14.3%). Approximately one-seventh (14.3%) of the caregivers who responded noted that they believed their children's reading ability did not improve.

Caregivers noted that their children's attitudes toward and interest in reading had changed positively. They specifically noted such affective attributes as "increased interest" and "more engagement." Almost half of the participants (42.9%) noted that their children had *much more interest*. Approximately a third (35.7%) of the caregivers responded that their children had *a little more interest*. About one-fifth (21.4%) of the respondents said there was *no change* in their children's attitude or interest toward reading.

In spite of the level to which caregivers believed their expectations had been met or whether they believed there were changes in their children's reading abilities or attitudes toward reading, 100% of the caregivers responded that they *would recommend* the reading clinic to others. Their reasons for recommending the program included elements of the program itself such as the "one-on-one instruction," tutors' "positive attitudes," and the introduction of "new reading strategies." Other reasons cited the positive effects on their children: "increased self-confidence" when reading, "meeting individual needs," and helping children become more engaged and strategic readers.

Discussion

Data were collected as part of an on-going study of caregivers' motivations for enrolling their children in a reading clinic and their perceptions of the clinic's effectiveness. Since the data reported here represents only the first two years of information gathering, this study presents an initial analysis of on-going data collection and research.

Although some tentative conclusions are drawn from this preliminary study, three limitations need to be addressed. The first limitation concerns the small number of post-involvement surveys completed and returned by caregivers. While there was a strong response from caregivers returning the pre-involvement survey, the number of caregivers who completed the post-involvement survey fell dramatically. Since the post-involvement survey was given on the final day of tutoring, only those caregivers whose children were in attendance completed that form of the survey. In general, it was found that caregivers were eager to participate in other forms of data gathering such as pre-involvement surveys, interviews, and focus group discussions. However, since the post-involvement survey was given to caregivers at the conclusion of the tutoring, caregivers might not have seen their participation as important. In that the caregivers had had on-going informal conversations with their children's tutors over the course of the clinic sessions, they possibly believed their voices had already been heard concerning their expectations and satisfaction with clinic services. Further, it is plausible to suggest that some caregivers believed their participation in focus groups and interviews made the information received through the post-involvement survey redundant.

Another limitation of this study involved the fact that the children served by the reading clinic might not accurately represent the school population in our geographic region, thus making our ability to generalize caregivers' perceptions to a broader spectrum somewhat limited. Caregivers responded that they received information about the reading clinic most often from other caregivers. Information concerning the clinic seemed to be communicated by caregivers whose children participated in the reading clinic sessions rather than from school personnel, such as teachers or counselors. Though a member of the reading clinic staff regularly made presentations to school faculties and administrations regarding the reading clinic and its services to the schools in our region, few clinic clients were referred directly from schools. Quite possibly, this low number of referrals may be due to the fact that many schools offer remedial programs of their own for students who are struggling readers. Schools may want to exhaust all district resources before referring students to an outside agency for help. School districts might possibly feel that they have failed students if they have to refer them to outside agencies. Thus, the clients who were served by the reading clinic were simply those whose parents took the initiative to seek additional help outside the resources of their children's schools.

The final limitation centers on one of the questions asked on the post-involvement survey. When caregivers were asked if reading took place in their homes, and if so, what types of materials are read, most caregivers indicated that reading did take place and that it consisted primarily of newspapers, magazines, and academic texts. With respect to these answers, we did not probe further to ascertain if the clients witnessed this reading by their caregivers in the home. Obviously, if the caregivers read while the child was present, it would have had greater impact than reading after the child had gone to bed or had left for school.

Most client referrals came from caregivers who told friends and colleagues about the services offered by the reading clinic. The fact that information concerning the clinic was spread by word of mouth throughout the community is encouraging and suggests that the clinic is having positive results on the children served for caregivers to be recommending it to others. While caregiver referrals are a valuable means of informing the community, this finding points out a need to build a more collaborative partnership with area schools so that more children who are struggling with reading can be served.

One clear finding from the study is that most caregivers had a strong position on the importance of reading in the home. These results seem to indicate a healthy desire to support the literacy development of their children at home. However, in terms of modeling this behavior for their children, caregivers seemed to read at times when their children were not present, for example, in the *evening, late at night,* or in the *morning* after children had left for school. Since one-third of caregivers responded that their children had *little or no interest* in reading, this suggests that caregiver reading practices influenced the reading attitudes of their children. In spite of a belief that reading is important, when there is little or no modeling of reading at home, children's attitudes may be negatively affected.

Most caregivers indicated that their reading consisted primarily of *newspapers, magazines,* and *educational texts.* One type of reading missing from this response was recreational reading, such as novels. This finding may suggest that caregivers saw reading as a functional activity rather than as a pleasurable one. This factor may have also affected children's attitudes towards reading.

While responses indicated that caregivers believed there was value in reading at home, when asked how often they read to or listened to their children read, most responded that this activity took place only occasionally. This finding may indicate the level of other activities that took place in the home, involvement in outside or after-school activities, the need to care for multiple children in the home, job demands, or a feeling of inadequacy when trying to help their children with school work.

Most caregivers enrolled their children in the reading clinic because their children were reading below grade level. However, almost a third of the children enrolled in the clinic were reading at or above grade level. This finding seems to suggest that all caregivers saw a value in the type of activities that took place in the reading clinic. When their children were reading below grade level, the tutoring that took place was valued because it helped children's literacy growth. For those children who read at or above grade level, clinic activities seemed to be equally valued by caregivers because they extended, enriched, and refined their children's literacy. Caregivers whose children were reading at or above grade level are interested in maintaining their children's progress and success in school as well as maintaining their children's positive attitudes toward reading.

Regardless of the reason for enrolling their children in the reading clinic, caregivers overwhelmingly responded that their expectations of the program were met or exceeded. A possible explanation for this response may be that caregivers believed that their children had experienced success in a number of ways. For example, caregivers reported that their children's reading ability had improved, that their attitudes toward reading had changed positively, and that the tutors had taught a variety of reading strategies which improved their children's confidence in themselves as readers. However, a number of caregivers responded that their expectations had not been fully met. These responses may have come from caregivers who had unrealistic expectations about the results they could expect in one clinic session. Some caregivers indicated in interviews and focus group sessions that they believed there would be "magic solutions" for their children's reading difficulties. Helping caregivers set realistic expectations for their children's literacy growth is an on-going goal for clinic tutors and administrators.

Most caregivers also indicated that they believed the clinic program was effective. Caregiver feedback indicating that the program was less than effective referred to the limited number of hours of clinic operation per week, the absence of a weekly written progress report, and/or the desire for more activities that they and their children could work on at home. Although most expectations were met, program effectiveness seemed to be a concern for some caregivers.

Conclusion

In light of the data collected from this study, it is evident that caregivers who enrolled their children in this clinic have genuine concerns about the literacy growth of their children. Caregivers have valuable insights into their children's abilities and attitudes and thus can provide needed input into the shaping of the reading clinic program. Continued collection of data from caregivers will help to inform clinic practices, leading to a more positive experience for clients and their caregivers. Future data collection and analysis will surely benefit the main audience of the clinic, the children, both in terms of fostering literacy development and positive attitudes.

References

Allen, D. D., Swearingen, R. A., & Kostelnik, J. L. (1993). University reading clinics: Changing focus for changing needs. In T. V. Rasinski & N. D. Padak (Eds.), *Inquiries in literacy learning and instruction*. Pittsburg, KS: College Reading Association.

Carr, K. C. (2003). Today's reading clinic: How relevant is the graduate reading practicum? *The Reading Teacher, 57,* 256-268.

Fitzgerald, J. (2001). Can minimally trained college student volunteers help young at-risk children read better? *Reading Research Quarterly, 36*(1), 28-46.

Kamil, M. L., Langer, J. A., & Shanahan, T. (1985). *Understanding reading and writing research*. Boston: Allyn and Bacon.

Kibby, M. W., & Barr, R. (1999). The education of reading clinicians. In P. Mosenthal & D. H. Everson (Eds.), *Advances in reading/language research, Volume 6: Researching the role of the reading clinic in a new age of literacy* (pp. 3-40). Greenwich, CT: JAI Press.

Klenk, L., & Kibby, M. W. (2000). Re-mediating reading difficulties: Appraising the past, reconciling the present, constructing the future. In M. L. Kamil, P. B. Mosenthal, P. D. Pearson, & R. Barr (Eds.), *Handbook of reading research: Volume III.* (pp. 667-690). Mahwah, NJ: Lawrence Erlbaum.

Landerholm, E., Karr, J. A., & Mushi, S. (2000). A collaborative approach to family literacy evaluation strategies. *Early Childhood Development and Care, 162,* 65-79.

Merriam, S. (1998). *Qualitative research and case study applications in education: Revised and expanded from Case Study Research in Education.* San Francisco: Jossey-Bass.

Michael, P. A., & Dougherty, C. (1999). Reading clinic: Past, present and . . . future? In D. H. Evensen, & P. B. Mosenthal (Eds.), *Advances in reading/language research, Volume 6: Reconsidering the role of the reading clinic in a new age of literacy* (pp. 365-384). Greenwich, CT: JAI Press.

Miles, M., & Huberman, M. A. (1994). *Qualitative data analysis* (2nd ed.). Thousand Oaks, CA: Sage.

Nistler, R. J., & Maiers, A. (2000). Stopping the silence: Hearing parents' voices in an urban first-grade family literacy program. *The Reading Teacher, 53,* 670-680.

Purcell-Gates, V. (2000). Family literacy. In M. L. Kamil, P. B. Mosenthal, P. D. Pearson, & R. Barr (Eds.), *Handbook of reading research: Volume III* (pp. 853-870). Mahwah, NJ: Lawrence Erlbaum.

Rasinski, T. V., & Padak, N. D. (2004). *Effective reading strategies: Teaching children who find reading difficult* (3rd ed.). Upper Saddle River, NJ: Pearson Merrill Prentice Hall.

Routman, R. (1996). *Literacy at the crossroads: Crucial talk about reading, writing, and other teaching dilemmas.* Portsmouth, NH: Heinemann.

Stake, R. E. (1995). *The art of case study research.* Thousand Oaks, CA: Sage.

Appendix A. Pre-Involvement Survey

Motivation:

1. What is (are) your reason(s) for enrolling your child in a reading program?

2. When did you see a need for intervention?

3. How did you determine your child's need for additional reading instruction?

4. How did you first learn about the Developmental and Diagnostic Reading Clinic?

   _____ Teacher   _____ School counselor   _____ Friend
   _____ Other (please specify) _____

5. What do you expect your child to gain from the Reading Clinic experience? (Check all that apply.)

   _____ Increase grade level in reading   _____ Better comprehension
   _____ More time spent reading at home   _____ Increased speed in reading
   _____ Better grades in Reading/Lang. Arts   _____ Reading aloud with expression
   _____ Higher standardized test scores   _____ Better word-attack skills
   _____ More interest in reading   (strategies to pronounce
   _____ More confidence in reading   unfamiliar words)
   _____ Better vocabulary   _____ Other _____

Personal Reading Habits:

1. How important is reading to you?

   _____ Not important   _____ Somewhat important
   _____ Very important   _____ Extremely important

2. How often do you read at home?

   _____ Never   _____ Seldom   _____ Frequently   _____ Daily

3. When do you read at home? (Check all that apply.)

   _____ Morning   _____ Afternoon   _____ Evening   _____ Late at night

4. Where do you read at home? (Check all that apply.)

   _____ Living room   _____ Dining room   _____ Kitchen   _____ Bedroom
   Other _____

5. What type of material do you read at home? (Check all that apply.)

   _____ Newspapers   _____ Magazines   _____ Books/novels
   _____ Educational Texts   _____ Other _____

Child's Reading:

1. Which of the following best describes your child's level of interest in reading at this time?

   _____ No interest   _____ Little interest   _____ Moderate interest
   _____ Very interested

2. How would you describe your child's reading ability at this time?

   _____ Below grade level   _____ On grade level   _____ Above grade level

3. How often do you read to your child?

_____ Never _____ Seldom _____ Frequently _____ Daily

4. How often do you listen to your child read?

_____ Never _____ Seldom _____ Frequently _____ Daily

Demographics:

1. Gender: _____ Male _____ Female

2. Marital status: _____ Single _____ Married

  _____ Divorced _____ Widowed

3. What is your yearly household income?

_____ Less than $10,000 _____ $10,000–14,999 _____ $15,000–24,999

_____ $25,000–34,999 _____ $35,000–49,999 _____ $50,000–74,999

_____ $75,000–99,999 _____ $100,000–149,999 _____ $150,000–199,999

_____ $200,000 or more

4. Ethnic background: _____ African-American _____ Asian

  _____ Hispanic/Latino _____ American Indian

  _____ White _____ Other _____

5. What is the primary language spoken in the home?

_____ English _____ Spanish _____ Other _____

6. What other language(s) is (are) spoken in the home?

_____ English _____ Spanish _____ Other _____

7. How many years of formal education have you had?

  1 2 3 4 5 6 7 8 9 10 11 12 13 14 15 16 More than 16

8. What is the highest diploma or degree you have earned?

_____ None _____ High school _____ GED

_____ Technical school _____ College _____ Post graduate

9. What is your relationship to the child participating in the Reading Clinic?

_____ Mother _____ Father _____ Grandmother _____ Grandfather

_____ Other (please specify) _____

Appendix C. Post-Involvement Survey

Reading Habits:

1. How have your personal reading habits changed since your child has been enrolled in the Reading Clinic?

_____ No change   _____ Less interested

_____ Somewhat more interested   _____ Much more interested

2. To what extent has your child's interest in reading changed since participating in the program?

_____ No change   _____ Less interested

_____ Somewhat more interested   _____ Much more interested

3. In your opinion, how much has your child's reading ability improved since participating in the program?

_____ No change   _____ Slight improvement

_____ Reasonable improvement   _____ Vast improvement

Reading Clinic:

1. How would you describe the overall effectiveness of the program?

_____ Counter productive   _____ Somewhat effective

_____ Reasonably effective   _____ Very effective

2. What is your level of satisfaction with the performance of your child's instructor/tutor during the program?

_____ Not satisfied   _____ Somewhat satisfied

_____ Reasonably satisfied   _____ Very satisfied

3. How often did the instructor/tutor discuss your child's progress with you?

_____ Never _____ Rarely _____ Occasionally _____ Weekly

4. To what extent do you believe your child enjoyed the program?

_____ Did not enjoy   _____ Moderately enjoyed

_____ Very much enjoyed   _____ Don't know

5. Overall, were your expectations for your child met?

_____ Less than expected   _____ Improved as expected

_____ Exceeded expectations

6. Overall, what is your level of satisfaction with your child's progress?

_____ Not satisfied   _____ Somewhat satisfied

_____ Reasonably satisfied   _____ Very satisfied

Please provide short answers to the following questions.

1. In what way(s) was the Reading Clinic experience helpful to or effective for your child?

   _____

   _____

2. In what way(s) was the experience NOT helpful or effective for your child?

   _____

   _____

3. What do you believe are the strengths of the Reading Clinic program?

   _____

   _____

4. What do you believe are the weaknesses of the Reading Clinic program?

   _____

   _____

5. What do you think can be done to improve the Reading Clinic program?

   _____

   _____

6. Other comments.

   _____

   _____

7. Would you recommend the Reading Clinic program to others?
   _____ Yes   _____ No

FOLLOW THE READER:
WHAT HAPPENS TO STUDENTS
WHO HAVE BEEN TUTORED IN A
UNIVERSITY READING CLINIC?

Nancy G. Kennedy
Rita M. Bean

University of Pittsburgh

Abstract

In this chapter, we present results of a descriptive study discussing students, and their reading habits, attitudes, and achievements after they have received tutoring at a university reading center. Clinic records at the university were analyzed to determine the extent of improvement made by students attending the clinic. Also, a follow-up questionnaire was sent to parents and children to determine their perceptions of their experience several years after they received reading instruction. Parents were also asked to respond to questions about student grades in reading and other subjects, outside reading and homework.

Reading clinics, or centers, exist in many colleges or universities that offer reading specialist certification or master's degrees in reading education (Hanes & Bader, 1985; Johns, 1992). They generally provide opportunities for students working towards certification to work with struggling readers, either one-on-one or in small groups (Bates, 1984) The rationale for such experience is that those learning to become reading specialists have opportunities to practice and apply what they are learning in a situation where they have maximum support and feedback. Clinical experiences also enable candidates to reflect on the teaching and learning processes for small groups of students or individual students, without the distraction that occurs in a classroom setting. Although the reading clinic can be found in many institutions with reading specialist programs, some clinics were discontinued because of lack of funding and resources, lack of faculty to advocate for the clinic, and some concern about the isolation of reading clinic experiences from mainstream academic programs (Schumm, Cuevas, Cas, & Pilonieta, 2003). Nevertheless, there are large numbers of institutions that still provide some type of practicum experience for their students. Hoffman and Topping (2001), for example, indicate that in Pennsylvania there are at least 15 state or state-related colleges or universities that provide reading clinics for their communities. In the Schumm, et al. (2003) survey of higher education institutions, seventy-four (56%) had reading clinics on campus; the remainder had what was described as satellite reading clinics, or school based classrooms, including candidate's own classroom. Institutions providing reading clinics tend to do so for two purposes: to provide specialized preparation experiences for reading teachers and to provide help for struggling readers.

Over the years, there has been much discussion about reading clinics, with supporters highlighting the value that occurs when teachers experience intensive, individual work with children, accompanied by coaching and feedback (Carr, 2003). On the other hand, there are those who believe that experiences in the reading clinic are too isolated from the classroom work that future reading specialists will need to do (Allen, Swearingen, & Kostelnik, 1993; Johns, 1992; Sanacore, 1991). Moreover, the reading clinic is often an expensive enterprise for universities, with low teacher-student ratios and space needs that may be difficult to achieve. Yet, teachers who have participated in a reading clinic indicate that they value those experiences and continue to use instructional procedures in their classrooms (Bean & Quatroche, 1989-90; Carr, 2003). The power of working with individual children, one-on-one, is also one that can benefit teachers, helping them to understand the process of learning to read without the distractions of working with many children (Hedrick, McGee & Mittag, 2000).

Reading clinics, however, have had more than one goal. In addition to providing graduate students with practice in assessing and instructing students with reading difficulties, they fulfill one of the major responsibilities of a university, that is, to serve the community in which it exists (Hanes & Bader, 1985; Hoffman & Topping, 2001). Parents bring students to the reading clinic with the expectation that the experiences there will make a difference in their children's reading performance. Yet, there is little research that relates to the effect of the reading clinic on student performance. Wilson (1960) studied the effect of one university reading clinic by conducting follow-up case studies of students who had attended the clinic. The program followed a diagnostic-prescriptive model of analyzing the reading problem and providing remediation. Wilson found that students who successfully completed a remedial reading program usually improved their scholastic performance and continued to develop new skills in the years that follow. Vurdien (1993) examined the effectiveness of a remedial reading summer school conducted by a suburban college. Teachers in the practicum course worked with sixteen students for four half-days a week for seven weeks. Methods used were Visual-Auditory-Kinesthetic-Tactile (VAKT), Directed Reading Activity (DRA) or Language Experience Approach (LEA), and students were read to for 20 minutes daily. Results indicated that students' mean independent reading level rose from of 2.5 to 3.8.

In this descriptive study, we attempted to analyze three evaluation questions: a) what were the measurable academic effects on students who attended the reading clinic?, b) What were parent's attitudes and opinions about the clinic?, and c) what were student's attitudes toward school and reading after attending the clinic. We analyzed student data to determine the performance of students who had attended tutoring sessions at the university reading clinic. We also sent questionnaires or called parents of students two or three years after tutoring to get their perspectives about the tutoring that their children had received and to obtain up-to-date information about how these children were performing in the school. Our rationale was that the information would be useful for decision making and for improving the clinical experience. In the following sections, we describe the reading clinic and its operation; we then go on to discuss the instruments used for the study; and finally, we discuss the results.

The Reading Clinic

The reading clinic serves as the focal point for a number of experiences provided for graduate students seeking reading specialist certification. Students are offered options for their practicum experience. These options include working in a local school district in a summer reading program, serving as a full-time reading specialist intern in a local school, or completing the practicum requirement in a traditional on-campus reading clinic site.

The clinic is directed by a university professor who provides the structure and guidance for the overall-program. There is a coordinator who handles all responsibilities related to its operation, i.e., recruiting children for tutoring, scheduling assessment, managing materials, and supervising graduate students who are enrolled in the practicum experience.

In this article, we focus on the on-campus reading practicum experience in which struggling readers are tutored by reading specialist candidates at the university; therefore, we describe the reading clinic only as it functions for this particular activity. The on-campus course was offered in the spring and summer terms. In the spring term, tutoring was on Saturday mornings over twelve weeks; each tutoring session was 75 minutes long. Likewise, in the summer, students received 75 minutes of tutoring for 12 sessions (three days a week for four weeks). Some students received one-to-one tutoring because of need or parent request, while others were placed in small groups of two or three. In both spring and summer terms, teachers attended seminars and workshops where they received help in planning lessons, assessing and using test data, and had opportunities to reflect on their teaching practices.

The practicum is generally one of the final experiences for the reading specialist candidates. They have completed, or are close to completing 18 to 21 hours of coursework in reading education before tutoring. IRA Standards (2003) recommend a minimum of 24 graduate credit hours in reading and language arts for reading specialist certification, including a six-credit hour supervised practicum experience. Our practicum is credited as a three-hour course, but students are required to spend approximately 72 hours on site, with additional time required for preparation, study, and report writing.

The instructor in this mentor-apprenticeship model monitored the program by observing and discussing students with teachers and parents. She provided a review of assessment tests to be used and also served in a supervisory capacity. The instructor observed and offered suggestions as to how teachers might improve their work with the children. She maintained a close working relationship with each teacher and discussed student progress weekly in a seminar. The instructor was the same for all four sessions, during the 1999-2000 academic year. The instructional procedure for tutoring used in the clinic is described below.

Teachers were instructed to develop lessons that included the following: a) warming up with a familiar re-read, b) word work, c) reading to develop and practice strategies skills, and d) writing. The purpose of the warm-up was to build fluency and improve self-esteem. Word work included at least one of the following: phonemic awareness activities, phonics, or structural analysis, depending on student need. Students then participated in a guided reading lesson where comprehension strategies were practiced and developed. Other daily activities were journal writing or written responses to literature. Teachers developed lesson plans based on each student's needs. They kept a daily reflection sheet on what they did and how it affected the children as a group and as individuals. ((Dr. Rae Tucker, personal communication, January 14 2003).

All teachers followed the format described above using materials that were appropriate for students. Students' achievements were measured using the following: curriculum based measures, the Qualitative Reading Inventory (QRI) (Leslie & Caldwell, 1995), and the Word Analysis section of the Woodcock Reading Mastery Test (Woodcock, 1987). In addition, the teacher and instructor monitored progress by examining running records, writing samples, and reflections kept by the teacher.

Initial testing of students took about one hour with children coming to the clinic to be assessed by the reading specialist candidates a week before tutoring began. Teachers summarized the results of the assessments as part of their class work, and they received feedback from the instructor. Results were used to plan instruction and to form small groups of students. Teachers were required throughout the term to monitor progress, give exit assessments, and write a final report.

A Parent's Day was held by the supervisor to inform parents of ways they could work with their children at home. In this session parents were able to view their child's tutoring session briefly, learn various ways by which they can help their child, receive a book list to guide their reading selections for their children, and socialize.

Another special program for the students was Poetry Day. Children were encouraged to write their own poem, or copy a favorite on chart paper. After practicing for several weeks the children came together to read their poems for the other children and teachers. This practice promoted fluency through repeated readings.

Methods

Students

Data from 87 students on whom we had complete information, and who attended sessions in either spring or summer 1999 or 2000, were collected. Of these students, 54 were male, and 33 were female. They included 48 primary students, 25 intermediate and 14 Junior/Senior High students. Seven of the 87 students were not included in the analysis because they were either emergent readers or were attending to receive specific instruction in writing only.

Two specific data sources were used to obtain information: test data from the students' files kept at the reading clinic and questionnaires for both parents and their children to follow-up. In this section, we discuss each of these data sources more fully.

Assessment Data From Files

We used test data from students' files kept in the reading clinic to address the question about student performance. The following instruments, used by teachers to assess performance of students when they attended the Clinic, provided us with pre and post test data for students;

Qualitative Reading Inventory-II (QRI). (Leslie & Coldwell, 1995)

Woodcock Reading Mastery Test (Woodcock, 1987). Word Analysis Section

Fluency rate (from either the QRI or curriculum based measures developed by teachers.)

A writing assessment and a reading attitude survey, *Attitudes Toward Reading and Writing* (Bean, R.M, n.d.), were also administered but these data were not used in this study since they were not administered to all children.

Questionnaires to Parents and Their Children

Two questionnaires were developed to obtain information about student and parent perceptions of experiences at the reading clinic, current performance of students in reading, attitude towards reading, and extent to which students were reading independently. The parent questionnaire was a fifteen-item survey that included Likert scale items, multiple choice items with numerical responses, and several open-ended questions (see Appendix A). The student questionnaire consisted of two multiple responses, three yes/no items and two open-ended questions (see Appendix B). Both questionnaires were developed from items that had been asked of parents and students at the end of their session at the reading clinic. Other questions were added that would give us a better picture of student's attitudes and skills several years after the clinic experience. Both instruments were reviewed by a faculty member with expertise in evaluation and the director of the clinic. Student questionnaires were attached to the parent questionnaire and mailed with the parent questionnaire.

Addresses for students who attended in the years 1999 and 2000 were obtained from clinic files and questionnaires were sent to 67 families in January, 2003. There is a difference in the number of students tutored (87) and the number of families because some families had more than one child attending, and some students came for more than one semester. Seven questionnaires were returned as undeliverable. Because we received only four replies in the mail, we then proceeded to do telephone interviews. We were able to make contact with 25 of the 60 parents who received the questionnaires, a 42% response rate. Given the time between tutoring and the survey, we knew we would have difficulty, not only locating families, but getting them to respond. We believe the detailed responses we received from those with whom we talked provided us with important information that can be useful for those involved in directing or coordinating clinical experiences.

Results

What Were the Measurable Academic Effects on Students Who Attended the Reading Center?

For each of the three tests used to determine progress, we defined gain as follows: for the QRI (Leslie & Coldwell, 1995), we categorized student progress on the QRI (n = 80) as follows: no change (no improvement); gain of one level or year (some improvement); gain of more than one level or year (great improvement). Analysis indicated that 50% of the students showed

Figure 1. Percentage of Students Who Improved

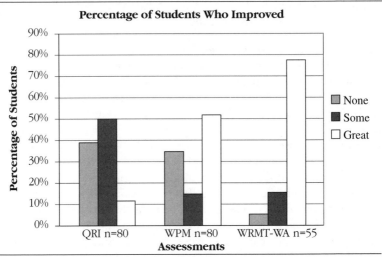

some improvement and 11% of the students showed great improvement, with 39% of the students showing no improvement on the *Qualitative Reading Inventory* (QRI) (see Figure 1). A breakdown by grade level indicates that 50% of the primary students, 56% of the intermediate students, and 64% of the junior /senior high students showed improvement on the QRI.

On the fluency rate, words per minute (WPM), a gain of one to five words was categorized as some improvement, a gain of more than 5 words great improvement. Results indicated that 15% of the students (n=80) showed some improvement in fluency while 51% showed great improvement. Thirty-four percent of the students showed no improvement on the fluency measure. Of the primary students 71% showed some or great improvement in fluency, 40% of the intermediate students showed some or great improvement, and 71% of the junior/senior high students showed improvement in their fluency rate.

On the W*oodcock Reading Mastery Test Word Analysis* section results were categorized as follows: some improvement, one to two months; great improvement, three or more months (Woodcock, 1987). Sixteen percent of the students (n=55) showed some improvement, and 78% showed great improvement on the Word Analysis Section. We have data for only 55 students on this measure because tutors were not required to administer the Woodcock Word analysis post-test when pretest results did not reveal any word attack difficulty.

It is interesting to note that 96% of the students made progress in at least one of the three areas that were assessed. Two students who did not make progress were already working at grade level. Only one student made no progress in any area. Twenty-four percent of the students improved in one area, 51% improved in two areas, and 21% improved in all three areas, while 4% showed no improvement.

What Were Parent's Attitudes and Opinions About the Center?

The results from the 25 of 60 parents whom we were able to contact indicate that parents felt the tutoring at the center was helpful (see Table 1). The answers, Agree and Strongly Agree, and Disagree and Strongly Disagree, were combined from the questionnaire when we reported it in Table 1. Parents and students with whom we conversed were very helpful in giving their insights and opinions of the tutoring at the reading clinic and how it helped their children. Eighty-six percent of the parents agreed that the tutoring received was helpful to their child's learning. Two parents (9%) disagreed, and one was undecided. Sixty-four percent of parents reported that their children's reading grades and other grades have improved since attending the clinic; 36 of parents disagreed, or were undecided. Seventy-six percent of the parents felt that their children evidenced greater interest in school with two parents disagreeing, and three undecided.

Table 1. Parents' Response to Follow-up Questions

Questions for Parents	Disagree n (%)	Undecided n (%)	Agree n (%)
1. My child is still receiving help after attending the clinic.	13(52)	-	12(48)
2. The tutoring given my child was helpful to his/her learning.	2(8)	1(4)	22(88)
3. My child's reading grades improved since attending the center.	6(24)	3(12)	16(64)
4. My child's grades in other subjects have improved since attending the center.	5(20)	4(16)	16(64)
5. My child shows a greater interest in reading since attending the center.	9(36)	6(24)	10(40)
6. My child shows a greater interest in school generally.	3(12)	3(12)	19(76)
7. My child is working as well as he can in reading at the present time.	3(12)	3(12)	19(76)
8. The reading center teacher talked to me about what she was teaching my child.	0	1(5)	24(96)
9. The reading center teacher gave advice about what to do at home to help my child.	0	3(12)	22(88)

Note. n=25
Note 2. Items from Appendix A were combined for this table. Agree and Strongly Agree were combined, as well as Disagree and Strongly Disagree.

Overall, parents believed that the tutoring helped their children, in terms of better learning, reading grade improvement, and improvement in grades in other subjects. Parents were divided on whether their child showed a greater interest in reading with 40% agreeing, 36% disagreeing, and 24% undecided.

Most of the parents had positive views of the tutors at the reading clinic. Ninety-six percent of parents indicated that the tutor talked to them about what she was teaching the child, with one undecided. Eighty-six percent of the parents felt that the tutor gave advice about how to help their child at home, with three parents undecided (see Table 1).

In the questionnaire, we asked parents to indicate the extent to which their children read for pleasure. Ten of the children did not spend any time reading for pleasure, ten children only spent from one to two hours weekly, four children spent three to four hours, and one child spent seven or more hours in pleasure reading weekly.

Even though 96% of students showed progress in at least one area of reading at the end of the clinic experience, almost half of the parents indicated that their children still needed help. Fifty-two percent of the parents indicated that their child was receiving reading help from private tutors, special reading and Titles I programs in schools, or by using commercial programs (i.e., Hooked on Phonics). It appears as though children with reading problems may continue to need support as they move through the grades. Moreover, forty-eight percent of parents indicated that their child had problems in other school subjects. They cited reading or all subjects as being the main difficulty (38.1%) with English (16%) and Science (12%) also listed. One parent indicated that anything that had a lot of reading or memorization was a stumbling block for her child.

Parent Responses to Open-Ended Questions

When given an opportunity to share other pertinent information, parents made some positive comments. One parent related that her child was just one grade below grade level; another said her child understands things now, one child is in the gifted program, and three students had more self-confidence. One parent responded that his child was "not afraid of it" any longer. Another parent employed the clinic teacher to continue working with her child. Some parents recommended that the clinic provide a more extensive evaluation protocol, while several voiced the desire to have more tutoring sessions or sessions throughout the year.

Parents indicated that it was difficult to get help for their child, and that the distance to the tutoring site was a problem. One single working mom said that she had to leave work in the summer to get her child to tutoring. Six parents related that their child had special needs or an attention deficit disorder, was learning disabled, and was either in special education or a learning support classroom.

Parents remembered that the clinic personnel were friendly and helpful, and that their children enjoyed coming. Parents evidenced strong support for the clinic. Some of the reasons mentioned for this were as follows: small class size (This allowed their child to get the help they needed.), parents' day, the instructor, their tutor, and a report for their child's teacher. Parents also appreciated receiving ideas to help their child at home after the tutoring was finished.

What Were Students' Attitudes Toward School and Reading After Attending the Center?

Of the 23 surveys completed by students (two students' surveys were not returned with the parent survey), 61% felt that they read more often since coming to the center, with 39% saying they did not. Sixty-one percent also felt that they enjoyed reading more, with 35% dissenting, and one student reported that his reading "was about the same" (see Table 2).

Table 2. Student Questionnaire on Attitudes Toward Reading

Questions for Students	Yes	No	Same
	n (%)	n (%)	n (%)
1. Do you read more often since coming to the center?	14(61)	9(39)	0
2. Do you enjoy reading more since coming to the center?	14(61)	8(35)	1(4)
	Yes	No	No answer
3. Do you have a library card?	21(91)	1(4)	1(4)

Note. n=23
Note 2. Two students did not return questionnaires with their parents' questionnaire.

To further determine attitude toward reading, we asked the students how often they used the school or public library. Ninety-one percent of the children had their own library card, and 48% of the students went to the school or public library to get books on a weekly or bi-weekly basis. Twenty-two percent of the students did not get books from the library, and another 22% did so only when they had to write a book report. Nine percent of the students indicated that they had an extensive library at home and did not need to take books from the library. All of the students who returned their surveys discussed their schoolwork with their parents at least weekly, with 74% discussing schoolwork at home daily.

Conclusions

Based on data from clinic files we concluded that the clinical experience was effective; that is, reading performance of most students did improve. There seemed to be more improvement in the area of word attack or skill development than in overall reading. A large percentage of students also improved in fluency. The lack of large gains on the QRI may reflect the more global aspect of instructional level, and the need for more instructional time to have an impact on these scores. We make no causal inference about the gain, especially for those students who attended during the school year (n= 27), given the instruction received in school. Nonetheless, the data provide information that we can share with current and future reading tutors to help them think more critically about how they can affect student performance. The results also indicate the importance of standard measures so that the impact of the clinical experience can be assessed, not only to determine whether instruction is effective, but to provide information for those in leadership positions who fund the clinical practice. Fiscal support for the clinic may be dependent on data such as these.

The gains made by students most likely reflect variability in student problems, age, and motivation to learn, including attendance. Wilson (1960) found that attending fewer than eleven sessions did not allow for permanent reading improvement. Most students in this study attended regularly with one or two absences. Completing this study made us appreciate the importance of a) encouraging students to attend on a regular basis, and b) keeping accurate attendance data. Also, one's motivation to learn is an issue and we are beginning to think of ways to address this, especially for the adolescents who need help.

Questionnaire results indicate that parents seem to have a positive view of the effects of the clinic, believing that their children had made progress by attending even though many continued to need help. Parents appreciated the many aspects of the clinic, including the help provided for their children, individualized attention, and the support given to parents by the instructor.

Students continued to have mixed attitudes toward reading and school after leaving the clinic. These struggling readers did not read for pleasure. Students, however, had positive memories of their nice teachers. They also remembered that the activities were fun, although some did not appreciate having to attend in the summer. Several remembered special treat days, and one remembered the fact that the home plate for a former major league baseball park is in the first floor of the building.

Limitations

Any follow-up study, especially one conducted two or more years after the intervention, is going to experience problems with locating participants and obtaining an adequate response rate. This was certainly true in this study. Not only did we experience difficulty in locating families, but after receiving only a few replies to our mail survey, we felt a need to conduct telephone interviews. Parents were very willing to talk about their experiences at the clinic by answering questions on improvement of the center. Some conversations were extremely long, as parents explained the difficulties of finding help for their struggling readers, how they had to drive long distances several times a week to obtain help, and the impact this had on their evening family time. The thoughtfulness and consistency of responses gave us confidence in the accuracy and trustworthiness of the data.

Recommendations
Programmatic

Selecting appropriate and standard measures that can be administered to all students as a means of determining progress is an important issue for reading clinic directors. Although tutors may not see the need for certain measures, given student reading abilities, the availability of such data can be useful as a means of documenting the success of the clinic experience, providing data that can support the existence of the clinic, and provide information useful for research purposes. Based on our findings, we believe the following should be administered to all students receiving instruction: an informal reading inventory, a fluency measure, a writing measure, and a reading attitude survey. A standardized measure of word attack skills would also be useful.

Given the positive responses of parents to the reading clinic experience, and because of the comments and questions they raise, it is recommended that clinics incorporate activities for parents. These could include: workshops for parents, observations of tutoring of their children, and opportunities for parents to network.

Clinics should also attempt to interact to the degree possible with the school from which the students come. Such interaction may help students as they transition from their work in the clinic to the classroom.

Because many students indicated that they did not enjoy reading, we suggest that those working with struggling readers in the clinic do more with helping these students gain an appreciation and joy of reading. This is not an easy task, but one that demands attention. The free selection of books, use of incentive programs, reading to students, and using the student's interests as a theme can also help to promote interest in reading.

Research

Clinics need to maintain a computerized database with test records and parental information recorded to expedite record retrieval and to keep track of students. Research into the progress of students would be facilitated with a database. This database system would enable several reading clinics to work together to collect data on their students. This is extremely important, given the small numbers of students generally served in a reading clinic setting.

Conclusion

In summary, this study describes an attempt by one reading clinic to take an in-depth look at what it does and whether students who receive instruction there have benefited from their participation. The study caused us to think more critically about the assessment tools we use, our data collection and record keeping, and our interactions with parents. The results are ones that should be useful to others interested in the clinical experience, not only as a means of preparing reading specialists, but as a source of support for struggling readers.

References

Allen, D. D., Swearingen, R. A. & Kostelnik, J. L. (1993). University reading clinics: Changing focus for changing needs. In T. V. Rasinski & N. D. Padak (Eds.), *Inquiries in literacy learning and instruction* (pp. 73-79). Pittsburg, KS: College Reading Association,

Bates, G. (1984). Profile of University based reading clinics: Results of a U.S. survey. *Journal of Reading,* 27(6), 524-529.

Bean, R. M. (n.d.). *Attitudes Toward Reading and Writing.* Pittsburgh, PA: University of Pittsburgh.

Bean, R. M. & Quatroche, D. (1989-1990). Preparation of Reading Specialists: Ready for the real world? *Journal of Clinical Reading,* 3(2), 1-4.

Carr, K. C. (2003). Today's reading clinic: How relevant is the graduate reading practicum? *The Reading Teacher,* 57(3), 256-268.

Hanes, M. L. & Bader, L. A. (Eds.). (1985). Standards and indicators of quality for clinical preparation in reading and the operation of reading clinics and clinics with reading components. [Clinical Division-CRA monograph] Columbia: University of South Carolina.

Hedrick,W. B., McGee, P. & Mittag, K. (2000). Pre-service teacher learning through one-on-one tutoring: Reporting perceptions through e-mail. *Teaching and Teacher Education,* 16(1), 47-63.

Hoffman, S. & Topping, D. (2001). Reading clinics: Same goals but many different paths. *Pennsylvania Reads: Journal of the Keystone State Reading Association.* 2(2), 10-26.

International Reading Association. (2003). *Standards for Reading Professionals.* Newark, DE: International Reading Association.

Johns, J. (1992). *From traditional reading clinics to wellness centers.* (Literacy Research Report No. 16). Dekalb: Northern Illinois University Curriculum and Instruction Reading Clinic. (ERIC Document Reproduction Service No. ED349544)

Leslie, L., & Caldwell, J. (1995). Qualitative Reading Inventory-II. New York: Harper Collins.

Sanacore, J. (1991). *Needed: private and university-based reading clinics with an updated perspective.* New York: Hofstra University Department of Reading, Language, and Cognition. (ERIC Document Reproduction Service No. ED329954)

Schumm, J., Cuevas, P., Cash, M. & Pilonieta, P. (2003, December). Reading Clinics in the U.S. a national survey of present practice. Paper presented at the annual meeting of the National Reading Conference, Scottsdale, AZ.

Tucker, R. (2003). Personal conversation, January, 14, 2003. Pittsburgh, PA: University of Pittsburgh.

Vurdien, R. (1993, January). *The effectiveness of reading centers attached to university reading programs.* Hempstead: New York University Institute for Education and Social Policy. (ERIC Document Reproduction Service No. ED 380772)

Wilson, R. M. (1960). *The scholastic improvement of successful remedial reading students.* Unpublished Doctoral Thesis, University of Pittsburgh, Pittsburgh, PA.

Woodcock, R. W. (1987). *Woodcock reading mastery test, word analysis section.* Circle Pines, MN: American Guidance Service.

Appendix A. Did The Reading Center Program Make A Difference?

Student _____ Current Grade _____

Directions: Circle the number which most clearly describes the way you feel about each statement.

1. The tutoring given my child was helpful to his/her learning.

Disagree strongly	Disagree	Undecided	Agree	Strongly agree
0	2	1	13	9

2. My child's reading grades improved since attending the center.

Disagree strongly	Disagree	Undecided	Agree	Strongly agree
1	5	3	8	8

3. My child's grades in other subjects have improved since attending the center.

Disagree strongly	Disagree	Undecided	Agree	Strongly agree
0	5	4	12	4

4. My child shows a greater interest in reading since attending the center.

Disagree strongly	Disagree	Undecided	Agree	Strongly agree
0	9	6	7	3

5. My child shows a greater interest in school generally.

Disagree strongly	Disagree	Undecided	Agree	Strongly agree
1	2	3	13	6

6. The reading center teacher talked to me about what she was teaching my child.

Disagree strongly	Disagree	Undecided	Agree	Strongly agree
0	0	1	15	9

7. The reading center teacher gave advice about what to do at home to help my child.

Disagree strongly	Disagree	Undecided	Agree	Strongly agree
0	0	3	13	9

8. My child is working as well as he can in reading at the present time.

Disagree strongly	Disagree	Undecided	Agree	Strongly agree
1	2	3	8	11

   Why do you think so? Grades-5, Doing as much as he can-2, Not afraid of it-1, special program 1, honors, Above 90%, spends lots of time, he can do better, tutoring continued.

9. Is your child still getting reading help? Yes 13   No 12
   How often? Weekly 2   Twice a Week 3   Daily 4   3x a week 2
   3-4 days a week 2
   Where?
   Chapter 1 -4, Public Schools Spec. Ed-2, Masonic Temple-2, Classroom Plus-2, Tutor 2, Private tutor during school hours-1, Modes Program-1, Sylvan-1, Huntington-1, Baldwin H.S.-1,

10. Does your child have problems in other school subjects? Yes 13   No 12
    Which ones?   Reading-6, Science-3, Engish-4, Writing-2, All-2,
    Spelling-2, Social Studies-1, Math-1

11. How much time does your child spend each week reading for fun?
    None 10   1-2 hours 10   3-4 hours 4   5-6 hours 0   7 or more 1

12. How much time does your child spend doing homework on a weekly basis?
    One hour or less 2   1-2 hours 7   3-4 hours 3   5-6 hours 8
    7 or more 4   Graduated 1

13. Is there anything else you want to share about your child and his/her reading difficulties and successes?

Confident with himself-3	Doesn't use time wisely	We work with him-2
Looks up words now	Never got phonics	Frustration comes out
Understands now	Gives up after a bit	with other subjects
In learning support	Just one grade below	Other siblings say
Vocabulary better	Stress-2	I like him better,
Spelling improved	Can't comprehend	since he gets so
Reads 25 books for school-1		much attention
Success due to excellent		In gifted program-2
reading background		2 nights to travel
		Distance-2

14. What do you remember most of all about the university reading center?

Enjoyed coming-6	Director	Tutor very positive influence
Friendly and helpful-4	Worked 1 on 1	Felt strange being with little kids
Intensive program-2	Individualized-1	Did not like Sat. AM
Got attention needed-2	Classes were fun	Guy teacher
Really cared -2	Parent day	Gave lots of things to work on
Helped with phonics	Proud of reading aloud	at home
Journal writing	Campus	
Gave report for teacher	Loved the games	

15. How should we change or improve the program at the reading center?

Excellent job	Give books/material list to parents
Creative teaching	Be able to tell if child has a disability-2
Sat. am was hard	Schedule difficult for working mom
Parking-3	Have more sessions
More extensive evaluation process	Needed phonics, but did not get in group
Parent packet on causes of reading	Great to have in summer
difficulties	
Needed more writing	
Need a place for teens, not put in with younger kids	
Teachers young, couldn't pick out things like experienced teacher	

Appendix B. Student Questions

1. Do you read more often since coming to the center?   Yes_15_ No_7_
2. Do you enjoy reading more since coming to the center?   Yes_14_ No_5_
3. How often do you talk about your school work at home?
   Not at all_0_   Daily_15_   Once or twice a week_4_   Weekly_2_
4. How often do you take books out of the school or public library?
   Not at all_5_   Twice a Week_0_   Weekly_10_
   When I have a school report_3_   Every 2 weeks_1_
   Use my home library_2_
5. Do you have a library card?   Yes_16_ No_1_
6. What do you remember most about the center?

The teacher-1	It was at Pitt-2	Pop
Bingo	It was fun-1	Donuts
Speed read time	Busy place	Home plate
Read aloud time	Confusing place	Nothing
Flashcards	Had to go in the summer	
Lots of books		

7. What do you remember about your center reading teacher?

Nice-6	Free candy	Doesn't remember much
Liked teacher -1		Nothing
Kept the teacher-1		NA-1
Enjoyed at time		

* Students did not answer all questions.
N=23 Two student surveys were not returned with the parent surveys.

THE POWER OF ADOLESCENT AND
YOUNG ADULT LITERACY

READING BETWEEN THE LINES: MIDDLE SCHOOL READERS UNCOVER MESSAGES IN MAGAZINE ADVERTISEMENTS

Roberta Linder
Francine Falk-Ross

Northern Illinois University

Abstract

The authors describe one teacher's experience with integrating critical media literacy into an existing middle school curriculum. Seventh grade students in five general education reading classes completed individual and group activities and participated in class discussions related to understanding the purposes and influences of magazine advertising. The results indicated that critical media literacy was a valuable addition to this middle school language arts curriculum, these students gained insight into the persuasive nature of advertising, and teens' genders affected the ways they responded to advertising. Additionally, the study of critical media literacy created expanded opportunities for dialogue in this seventh grade classroom.

Language arts teachers in middle schools are faced with the formidable challenge of implementing an extensive curriculum to develop in young adolescents the literacy strategies and competencies needed for an array of purposes including interpreting the messages in the myriad texts present in their daily lives. In fact, this role is specified in the *Standards for Reading Professionals* (IRA, 2003) that mandate the use of a wide range of instructional practices and curriculum materials (2.2, 2.3) and the creation of a diverse literate environment (4.2). Similarly, the *Standards for the English Language Arts* (NCTE/IRA, 1996) states that students should utilize their knowledge of language and media in order to "create, critique, and discuss print and nonprint texts" (p.25). The students' understanding of texts used to develop their literacy is mediated by assigned and self-selected textual resources and is heavily influenced by their developing social relationships and cultural affiliations. Guided by concerned voices that warn of commercial culture oozing into educational curriculum (Giroux, 1988) and of pedagogical responsibilities to (re)mediate adolescent literacies (Elkins & Luke, 2000), teachers need to develop student-empowering practices through the infusion of critical approaches to reading and writing competencies into the curriculum and through the refinement of the critical thinking skills of these impressionable consumers. That is, teachers need to "disrupt the commonplace" (Lewison, Flint, & Van Sluys, 2002, p. 382) as they confront adolescents with the realities of persuasive tactics and challenge them to see the media "through new lenses" (p. 383). This process of learning to critically and carefully evaluate print and non-print texts with respect to students' own sociocultural perspectives has been referred to in recent research as critical media literacy (Alvermann, Moon, & Hagood, 1999; Luke, 1999).

The purpose of this article is to present the process and outcomes of specific critical media literacy activities with magazine advertisements that were incorporated into 5 seventh-grade reading classes. The following questions guided this study: How can teachers introduce and integrate critical media literacy activities into classroom instruction, incorporating text from students' popular culture? What insights about media as a persuasive influence would students gain as a result of learning about advertising in familiar magazines? What role, if any, does gender play in middle school students' interpretations of messages in media forms? Using new foci of research and a pedagogy of multiliteracies to develop and integrate critical literacy activities (New London Group, 2000), we describe changes in young adolescents' responses to message portrayed in popular magazine advertisements.

Frameworks for Understanding Critical Media Literacy

In order to gain a clearer understanding of students' vulnerabilities and teachers' responsibilities in clarifying the content and intent of media forms, the researchers examined critical literacy within the context of a pedagogy of multiliteracies and applied this model to instruction for young adolescents, addressing the advertising trends in the present market. To provide insight into the new language and foci of pedagogical approaches, three areas of research review provide a conceptual framework.

A New Conceptualization of Literacy

The concept of literacy is changing significantly during the twenty-first century with the development of global technology. The current view of literacy is extending its boundaries, acknowledging that readers derive meaning from various types of text in print, visual, and auditory formats (Luke,

2003); that communication is expressed through speaking, listening, writing, reading, and viewing and representing information visually; and that literacies are personal, tied to home, school, community, and global influences (Alvermann & Hagood, 2000b; Hagood, 2000). The implication is that language arts instruction for middle school students should address the 'multiliteracies' existing in the popular culture, home, community, and school of the adolescent learner (New London Group, 2000). That is, educators can learn more about these different forms of print and language-based communication that young adolescents choose to represent and extend their thinking. By acknowledging and investigating the deeper meanings of media literacies, educators may gain greater insight into ways to facilitate learning (Gee, 2003).

A New Model for Instruction

Middle school literacy educators have the opportunity to intercede and mediate, or (re)mediate, the deeper (i.e., socially and politically charged) thinking and understanding of text by all students, including those marginalized by language and/or literacy learning differences (Luke & Freebody, 1997; Moje, Young, Readence, & Moore, 2000). The integration of critical media literacy strategies can be accomplished using overlapping approaches such as the pedagogy of multiliteracies suggested by the New London Group (2000). In this model, literacy learning, both in school and outside of school, is facilitated in the following contexts:

- *situated practice*—engages students in authentic, experience-based activities utilizing their prior and present cultural practices as well as their outside-of-school relationships and discourses, taking into account their affective and sociocultural needs and identities;
- *overt instruction*—provides active interventions designed to support the students as they focus on important elements of their learning activities, gain explicit information, and develop the necessary metalanguage;
- *critical framing*—helps students stand back from what they are studying and view it critically in relation to its social and cultural contexts; and
- *transformed practice*—requires students to demonstrate their new understandings by applying and revising what they learned, juxtaposing and integrating different discourses, social identities, or 'interests.'

Educators can use these contexts to develop students' deepening understanding of their idiosyncratic communication forms, also referred to as popular culture (Alvermann, Moon, & Hagood, 1999).

As students and teachers develop more critical understanding through their use of these contexts, their reading practices are transformed. In their studies involving critical media literacy, a series of researchers acknowledged the individual nature of students' assessment and understanding of everyday print and non-print texts, and how these influence students' knowledge of the world in social, economic, and political ways (Luke & Freebody, 1997). They recognized that issues related to culture and positioning within society, and of ideology, power, and gendered identities need to be addressed when considering media and artifacts of popular culture (Buckingham, 1998). Another concern was that the emotional engagement of the students with the media should be acknowledged and explored (Alvermann & Hagood, 2000a; Hobbs, 1998), and that students use this knowledge to build their access to resources for social discourse and literacy practices.

Vulnerabilities of Young Adolescents in New Times

Recognizing the empowering nature of critical media literacy activities as well as the cognitive, social, emotional, and physiological changes in young adolescents, these strategies optimally provide the core of middle school literacy programs. Specifically, the intellect of middle school students is characterized by their early attempts to use abstract reasoning (Piaget, 1972). They are eager to learn and want answers but are sometimes unable to discern between what is reliable or unreliable information. Socially, middle school students are striving to define themselves as individuals while at the same time they are heavily influenced by peer approval (Lesko, 2001). The emotional development of young teens is often rooted in self-consciousness or lowered self-esteem based on differences they perceive between themselves and others (Harter, 1990). In terms of physical development, middle school girls enter puberty about two years earlier than the boys, and all youngsters experience irregular periods of rapid growth (Erb, 2001). Middle school has always been challenging for students in the midst of these changes, but especially so in new times when young adolescents are subjected to additional influences, such as race, class, and gender (Lesko, 2001), and stronger pressures from political ideology (Cole & Griffin, 1986) and business organizations (Gee, 2000).

Advertisement organizations are aware of these emerging competencies and environmental pressures affecting young adolescents, and in targeting this audience they have relied on their knowledge of the developmental characteristics and sociocultural practices of adolescents. These shrewd marketing specialists are aware that the items purchased by teens reflect what they think of themselves and how they wish others to perceive them. Realizing that both physical attractiveness and socialization are important to teens, persuasive advertisements depict attractive individuals with desirable lifestyles and exciting social lives (Kelly & Edwards, 1998). This use of image advertising can attract adolescent consumers, but it can also present an ideal that leaves many teens feeling unattractive and dissatisfied with their bodies (Field,

Camargo, Taylor, Berkey, Roberts, & Colditz, 2001; Martin & Gentry, 1997). With some products, such as tobacco and alcohol, there have been accusations of marketing aimed at underage consumers (Chung, Garfield, Rathouz, Lauderdale, Best, & Lantos, 2002; Kelly & Edwards, 1998; Portner, 1997). There is a new, less stable form of capitalism that directs an increased focus on characteristics of the consumer audience (Gee, 2000). Young adolescents in middle school classrooms must be made aware of these subtle tricks of the trade which exploit their need for beauty or acceptance.

In summary, as young adolescents are drawn to and by the language and images of media messages, literacy educators can find ways to intervene to mediate deeper understandings of the persuasive tactics of a new capitalistic (print) environment. It is important to support middle school students' inquiry into how the advertising industry is utilizing information about adolescents' characteristics and culture in order to create ads that attract these diverse consumers. Then middle school literacy educators can draw upon their knowledge of adolescent characteristics and sociocultural practices by teaching critical media literacy techniques to improve young adolescents' scrutiny of media's social and political subtexts, challenging students to examine these texts through more critical lenses.

Methodology
Participants
Two teacher-researchers collaborated to develop the project and pilot it in the school classroom. The school-based researcher, a seventh grade teacher with 22 years of experience within the district, was responsible for implementation of the project, one of her first experiences with media literacy instruction at the middle school. The university-based researcher assisted in aligning the study with scientifically-based research practices and in data analysis. Although not a direct observer of classroom activities, the university-based researcher collaborated with the instructor on analysis of students' writing samples and anecdotal records. During the one-semester period of this study, 125 students attended the five reading classes and participated in the media literacy activities. There was no random selection of students utilized for this project; rather, the sample that was studied represented those 56 students who provided parental consent and student assent for participation. This latter group represented a wide range of sociocultural and educational backgrounds.

Context of the Study
The school day consisted of eight 40-minute periods containing the five academic classes (i.e., math, English, reading, science, and social studies), two periods of exploratory classes, and physical education. Attending the reading

classes of this seventh grade team were students enrolled in the general education program. The classroom under study was situated within a middle school serving approximately 800 students, located in a suburban public school district in northern Illinois. The student population included children that were White/non-Hispanic (91%), Black/non-Hispanic (2%), Hispanic (4%), Asian/Pacific Islander (2%), and Native American (less than 1%).

Data Collection and Analysis

Employing the principles of a basic qualitative study (Merriam, 1998), the seventh grade reading teacher assumed the role of participant observer in order to respond to the study's initial questions regarding the introduction of critical media literacy activities on the persuasive influences of advertising into her classroom instruction. Data were collected from materials at different points throughout the study: pre- and post-test administrations of a teacher-made assessment to capture students' recognition and judgments regarding advertising's influence and techniques; written and verbal responses that connected students' knowledge about advertising to their roles as consumers; and critical analysis activities focusing on the social and political stance of text in media. Materials for analysis included the results of the pre-and post-tests, artifacts from students' working folders (i.e., individual written responses to questions, group responses recorded during an examination of advertising in magazines, and redesigned ads), and anecdotal records of student interaction and classroom discussions by the teacher-researcher collected as a part of ongoing field notes and reflections.

The individual and group responses were first examined using open coding to determine recurring themes in the students' understandings, such as differences related to peer group versus individual reactions to ads and differences derived from students' need for superiority versus a need for belonging. The themes were then reassessed through axial coding to determine relationships between categories (Strauss & Corbin, 1990). Results of axial coding revealed connections between the gender and/or self-perception of the teen and the advertising technique selected for the response. Analyses were conducted independently by each of the two researchers followed by a meeting in order to discuss results and reach a high level of inter-rater agreement.

Project Activities

Magazine advertisements were chosen from among the wide variety of media texts (e.g., television programs and commercials, printed articles and newspapers, movies, and popular music) as the focus of this study because they serve as a major source of information and advice for adolescent girls and provide information and entertainment for male readers (Zollo, 1999). The students were challenged to view magazine ads from multiple new perspectives as they engaged in activities requiring them to develop skills as critical readers. The series of activities consisted of introductory lessons to spark students' prior knowledge about advertising and provide them with new information, opportunities to expand and apply their knowledge, critical examinations of magazine advertisements and the magazines in which they appeared, and the deconstruction and reconstruction of messages in existing ads. These activities, more fully explained in the following paragraphs, were aligned with the framework for effective critical literacy pedagogy outlined by the New London Group (2000), appearing in parentheses at the beginning of each description.

Pre- and post-tests. Students viewed a series of overhead transparencies representing five common topics in magazine advertisements (cars, food, jeans, cigarettes, and shoes) and were asked to write one or two sentences describing the message in each ad. The instructor scored each response on a scale of zero to four, based on the number of advertising elements identified in each response (type of item, brand name, information from visual or print design, method of persuasion). Responses received no points if they stated incorrect or insufficient information, failed to find a message, or stated that the ad contained no message.

Building awareness of persuasive nature of advertising (situated practice). Small groups of students selected appealing ads from magazines and used a T-chart to record ad "Techniques" that grabbed their attention and describe specific "Examples" from their chosen ads.

Learning about basic advertising techniques (overt instruction). Students completed a viewing guide for the video "Why We Buy What We Buy" (Cambridge Research Group, 2001). The magazine ads and viewing guide were placed into students' advertising folders.

Examining ads more closely (overt instruction/situated practice). Students were given a sheet summarizing the findings from their T-charts and listing vocabulary related to advertising techniques (see Appendix), and this information guided students as they identified the advertising techniques used for three ads selected from their folders.

Focusing on the Linguistic and Visual Designs (New London Group, 2000) of an advertisement (overt instruction/situated practice). Students selected another ad and wrote three questions related to its printed text (i.e., Linguistic Design) and one question related to its illustration (i.e., Visual Design). Questions and advertisements were exchanged and answered by the students.

Examining information about consumerism (overt instruction/situated practice). Students read an article entitled "Types of Teenage Consumers" (Berger, 2000, pp. 94-96) which contained statistics related to teenage spending; described four categories of teenage consumers identified by Teenage Research Unlimited (Zollo, 1999) as the Influencers, Conformers,

Edge Group, and Passives; and presented a list of teenage budget expenditures with corresponding percentages. Class discussions centered around questions based on the article: (a) Which type of consumer are you?; (b) What are the top two things on which you would spend your own money?; and (c) What are the top two things on which you would spend your parents' money?

Viewing information related to advertising (overt instruction). Students completed a viewing guide and discussed the video "Sexual Stereotypes" (Cambridge Research Group, 2002) which described stereotypes found in different media, discussed the media's role in developing teens' sexual awareness, and explained the importance of consumers being able to see through stereotypes.

Making personal connections between knowledge about advertising and life experiences (situated practice). Students provided written responses to any two of these four questions: (a) What advertising technique is most likely to appeal to teens? Explain and give examples; (b) What advertising technique is most likely to persuade you to buy a product? Explain and give examples: (c) What male stereotypes are used in magazine ads? Explain and give examples; and (d) The media (TV, movies, and magazines) give females mixed messages. They show women as sex objects and as thinking people. Do you think this is a confusing thing for girls? Explain.

Critically examining magazines and their advertisements (critical framing). Small groups were provided with three magazines that appealed to diverse audiences (e.g., *Time*, *Car and Driver*, *Glamour*). They recorded responses for information relating to the *types of ads in each magazine* (e.g., cosmetics, technology, alcohol), *types of people in ads of each magazine* (e.g., race, age, income, handicap, gender), the *amount of ads in each magazine*, and *things learned and remaining questions*.

Redesigning an ad (transformed practice). A point made in the video "Why We Buy What We Buy" (Cambridge Research Group, 2001) was that advertising depends on the suppression of information, and this activity challenged students to uncover this unstated information. Beginning with only the picture of a selected product, students redesigned the ads using "truthful" words or phrases, stripping away the "hype" that had been created by advertisers.

Results

The first outcome of this study, in response to the initial research question, was a confirmation that pedagogical approaches similar to those suggested by the New London Group (2000) can provide a structure for the introduction and integration of media literacy activities into middle level classroom instruction. Within the framework of a pedagogy of multiliteracies, the instructor was able to incorporate a variety of reading, writing, listening, and speaking activities which engaged students in a form of text from their popular culture and also provided them with practice on skills specified by middle school language arts curricula or state standards. This is consistent with recent research which demonstrated that critical media literacy can be used effectively within traditional programs (Hobbs & Frost, 2003).

The next set of results, related to the second research question, provided evidence that these seventh graders gained many insights into advertising and consumerism. The researchers analyzed data from pre- and post-tests, field notes about young adolescents as consumers, students' written responses, and comments from students' explorations of magazines.

Pre- and Post-tests

The results of the pre- and post-tests indicated that students had shown some improvement in their ability to detect messages in magazine advertisements. The pre-test mean score of 8.98 increased to 10.86 on the post-tests (20 points possible). The measured increase in these writing samples was not as large as had been anticipated based on students' oral discussion in class. This may be explained in part by the students' difficulty with providing written answers to open-ended questions. This group of students had not had experience with media-related activities and critical writing assignments, thereby limiting the depth of their written responses as compared to oral responses. Also, these numbers represent findings from a three-week long thematic unit, which narrowed the students' opportunity for growth.

Further analysis of pre- and post-test results revealed that students increased their ability to recognize the messages contained in advertisements, with a decrease from 25 responses receiving no points in the pre-test to only 10 responses in the post-test. In addition, there was a dramatic decrease in the number of "no message" responses from the students (pretest: n=13; post-test: n=1). The "no message" responses had all been written for ads that lacked any printed text besides the brand name, which had been initially interpreted by students as containing no message. However, students were able to discern messages from the visual designs in the ads upon completion of the project activities.

Young Adolescents as Consumers

Teacher field notes taken during class discussions on the article "Types of Teenage Consumers" (Berger, 2000) provided data about the spending habits of these seventh graders. When asked to identify the category of consumer that most closely described them, students were observed glancing at others in the room before raising their hands to respond and several refused to participate, behaviors indicating that their responses were mediated by the acceptance of their peers. The participating students identified themselves as 58% Passives, 37% Conformers, 3% Influencers, and 2%Edge Group. These results contradict the information in the article which stated that most teens identify themselves as Conformers. Although these students would not publicly acknowledge their need for conformity, their efforts to provide answers "acceptable" to other members of the class reinforced their desire to fit in.

In the second part of this discussion, students were originally asked to identify how they spent their money, but an additional question about spending parents' money was suggested by the students, and this distinction exposed an interesting pattern. Throughout the discussions, students provided twice as many responses about spending their parents' money, indicating that they spent it mostly on products meeting their *basic needs* (e.g., 34% clothing, 22% food) with lesser amounts spent on products for their *recreational activities* (e.g., 17% entertainment, 15% hobbies). However, a reversal of this pattern emerged when students discussed spending most of their own money on items related to *recreational activities*, 33% hobbies and 21% entertainment. The students' next expenditures, 18% clothing and 11% food, represented products meeting their *basic needs*. These responses described teens that participated as consumers of recreational activities/goods and influenced their parents' purchases of items providing for their basic needs.

Students' Written Responses

An analysis of students' advertising technique selections revealed a distinction between techniques that appealed to teens in general and those that appealed to them personally. These middle school students felt that teens are influenced by the concept of group conformity depicted in *Everyone Else Has One* (see Advertising Techniques in Appendix), writing about it twice as often as *Appeal to Excellence* or *Snob Appeal*. However, as individuals they failed to see themselves as being persuaded by this technique, claiming to be attracted by *Appeal to Excellence* or *Appeal to Authority* instead. This reluctance to publicly acknowledge their desire to fit in had also been evident in field notes of discussions involving types of teen consumers.

Coding of responses revealed several themes in the students' choices and opinions. First, students' comments indicated that they were especially sensitive to ads for brand-name products, particularly clothing and shoes. Some students expressed in their writing (pseudonyms used for all names) that wearing apparel displaying popular brand names and logos provided a sense of belonging, as appears below:

> For some teens it's easy to fit in. For others it is hard. Brand names help a lot with that issue. (Sue)

> For example many teens think they need to have the same thing to be like everyone else who has one. Teenagers want to be comfortable and feel like they are a part of the group. (Sheila)

Other students indicated that owning brand-name products helped those who wanted to feel superior to their peers:

> I want the best products for me. Looking cool and having something someone elese [sic] doesn't have is another reason. (Jason)

> The "Snob Appeal" technique appeals to teens because some of them want to be better than other students or they are concerned about their popularity. (Cassie)

As these teens pointed out, the manufacturer of the product is frequently of greater significance than the cost or quality.

Second, teens' written responses revealed an attraction to products with celebrity endorsements. Because young teens view these high-profile individuals as role models, some readers wanted to emulate the celebrities' styles of fashion or felt that they could trust stars' judgments about products, as they comment below:

> First of all, if I saw my favorite celebrity wearing a certain brand of clothes, I would want to wear them. (Elaine)

> One reason is when I know that a celebrity I know is in an ad, I think that I can look up to them and trust them (Brenda)

> I'm attracted to products used by pro athletes. (Mark)

Third, it was somewhat surprising that only two students wrote about *Sex Appeal,* even though young adolescents are becoming attracted to members of the opposite sex. This would suggest that perhaps *Sex Appeal* is more persuasive with older teens or is not acknowledged within the discourse of the classroom. However, these students offered their insights regarding the use of *Sex Appeal* in magazine advertisements:

> To begin with teens might think they will look better. Second, teens might feel more mature. (Mike)

> "Sex Appeal" is the advertising technique that is most likely to appeal to teens because you see it in videos today. (Stephanie)

Fourth, the fact that only six students wrote about the issue of sexual stereotypes in advertising suggests that this was a more challenging topic for seventh graders. Boys' responses identified strength, youth, athleticism, and dominance as characteristics frequently depicted by the models in ads for cigarettes, men's cologne, and designer clothes. The girls' comments noted that female models were often dressed revealingly or "being nasty," perpetuating the image of women as sex objects.

> If the young teen girls grow up to be just like the women they see dressing revealingly they will get a bad reputation towards them. (Sarah)

> They (magazines) show some teens in nothing but sexy clothes. They

show them pretty much what to wear in order to be sexy or be sex objects. (Cassie)

Apparently, stereotyping may have been a difficult topic due to students' reluctance to discuss sexual matters within the classroom context, their lack of attention to ads with sexual overtones, or perhaps their discomfort with critiquing images on which they have based their own identities.

Students' Explorations of Magazines

Analysis of group responses indicated that students had gained insights regarding audience, biases within ads, prevalence of advertising, and techniques used by advertisers.

Audience. Many groups noted that "magazines use different types of ads depending on who is reading them." Some observed that ads for cosmetics were prevalent in women's and girls' magazines, and that car magazine ads featured primarily vehicles and accessories with few, if any, people visible, focusing readers' attention on the automotive products.

Bias. Groups made frequent references to the lack of cultural diversity depicted in advertisements and listed several magazines that ran ads containing predominantly white people. One student expressed displeasure that most athletes featured in his sports magazine were black, but the ads generally contained white males. Other biases noted by groups related to the absence of older people, persons with disabilities, and individuals who were not model-perfect in their appearance.

Prevalence. Although some remarks overstated the amount of ads in magazines (e.g., more ads than articles, almost half the magazine was ads), a few groups noted that the largest number of ads appeared in the teen girls' magazines.

Techniques. Although sex appeal and celebrities were noted most frequently, some groups mentioned the use of bright colors in ads, and one group noticed that cigarette ads often extended over two full pages.

The questions generated by the students at the end of the magazine activity were also related to the four concepts of audience, bias, prevalence, and techniques (see Table 1). These students' comments and questions indicated they had gained new insights into the hidden messages of magazine advertisements by stepping outside their usual perspectives in order to examine magazines and ads through a more critical lens and pose some tough, thought-provoking questions.

Table 1. Student Questions about Magazine Advertising

AUDIENCE
Why aren't there cigarette ads in *CosmoGirl*?
Why does the magazine sell tobacco products even if minors read it?
Why do they put alcohol ads in a celebrity magazine like *Premiere*?

BIASES
Why don't the ads have handicapped people, old people, or African Americans?
Why are there always girls in shampoo ads?
Why do some ads have different races and some don't? Why can't they all be mixed races?
Why do people in ads always look good and make us jealous?

PREVALENCE
Why are there so many ads?
How come there are barely any ads in some magazines?

TECHNIQUES
How do they make people look good in the ads?
Are there really any other techniques?

In response to the third research question, this study concludes that teens' gender affects the way they are influenced by advertising. An equal number of male students' responses expressed that *Appeal to Excellence, Everyone Else Has One*, or *Appeal to Authority* were most persuasive to teens. These boys often commented on the outstanding quality of the products or the appeal of the celebrities, mostly professional athletes. In contrast, half of the females' responses were written about *Everyone Else Has One*, and all but three of the remaining paragraphs were about *Snob Appeal*. In their writing, the females communicated their impressions that teens were influenced by techniques that helped them position themselves as either a part of a group or superior to the group. The girls also associated feelings of happiness and self-confidence with their chosen techniques. In the paragraphs describing techniques that influenced them personally, students of both genders wrote most frequently about being persuaded by *Appeal to Excellence* and *Appeal to Authority*. However, several boys revealed a more practical perspective by choosing *Something for Nothing* or *Appeal to Tradition*, techniques ignored in the girls' responses.

One of the unintended results that emerged from this study was the inclusion of a different form of classroom discourse with critical media literacy experiences. Through a variety of classroom activities, students engaged in structured and unstructured opportunities for student-student and student-teacher interactions which provided a forum to openly discuss issues important to them. This type of frank, nonjudgmental communication enhanced the climate of the middle school reading classroom, validating the ideas and opinions of the teens and encouraging them to begin looking at their world through a more critical lens. In addition, the students appeared to take a great deal of pleasure in engaging with the magazines during the activities, and several asked to keep the magazines they had used in class. A number of students donated their old magazines or those of their parents, and many selected magazines they wanted to keep at the conclusion of the project. Finally, the reading teacher familiarized herself with teens' popular magazines as she purchased issues on a wide variety of topics. As a result, she became more knowledgeable about the lifeworlds of her students and the media messages surrounding them.

Discussion and Implications

This project involving critical media literacy is important for middle school language arts practitioners and their students based on the intended and unintended results. The study documented that critical media literacy could be successfully integrated into a seventh grade reading classroom without compromising instruction related to curriculum goals or state standards. Evidence of student learning was shown at the conclusion of their engagement with activities based on the pedagogical designs of situated practice, overt instruction, critical framing, and transformed practice (New London Group, 2000). These seventh grade students learned to read the messages in both the linguistic and visual designs of magazine ads, identified how their spending is influenced by advertising in combination with their positions within their peer groups, and discovered how magazines and their ads target some populations while ignoring others. The importance of peer group status was reinforced many times during this study, and the students also demonstrated gendered interpretations of textual messages. In addition, the middle school instructor found she could enhance the learning opportunities for students by opening lessons to discussions of relevant issues, including magazines and other forms of popular media, and she also familiarized herself with forms of text important to the teen culture.

The valuable insights gained by the instructor will guide future implementation of units involving critical media literacy. First, it may be necessary to utilize more written responses in order to elicit personal, rather than peer mediated, thoughts on sensitive issues. Incorporating written reflections at various points throughout the unit would permit students to record their feelings and reactions during the learning process. Second, more lessons focusing on sexual stereotypes and gendered identities may be beneficial for the students. Activities requiring students to explore the messages within stereotypes and to examine their responses to these messages would enable them to begin making connections between images projected by the media and their own behaviors. Third, the questions generated by students following the group magazine activity would serve as the basis for further inquiry or as an impetus for action. The transformation of the students would continue as they pursued answers for their questions about magazines and the advertisement industry and as they took action based on information they had discovered (e.g., letters to magazine editors, school displays about advertising, etc.).

The results of the study suggest a number of future directions for middle school language arts classrooms. First, the use of text from students' popular culture, such as magazines, is highly motivating to middle school students and encourages them to read more widely. Students in this study willingly interacted with many different types of magazines and took great pleasure in borrowing or receiving magazines related to their individual interests. Critical media literacy has the potential to enhance middle school reading programs because it encourages teens to view texts through different lenses, and it recognizes literacy materials that have meaning and relevance for teens.

Second, students would benefit from activities requiring them to develop a more critical perspective in viewing other types of media. This group of teens took their first steps toward uncovering media's hidden messages regarding stereotyping, privileging or ignoring segments of society, suppressing product information, and influencing consumer behavior, characteristics of the new capitalism (Gee, 2000). With the rapid expansion of technology providing adolescent readers with an ever-increasing number of messages, today's students must be prepared to make sound judgments regarding the authenticity and legitimacy of the print and visual images around them. Teachers and students can begin with critical examinations of media forms present within their schools, uncovering biases previously unnoticed in internet sources, social studies documentary videos, feature films used in classrooms, or the textbooks themselves.

In order to mediate teens' responses to the constant barrage of media messages, it is suggested that middle school language arts teachers become aware of the new directions and research in critical media literacy. Teachers can facilitate this type of literacy only when they transform their own practice after viewing their students, materials, and pedagogy through new lenses. Recent research, however, has indicated that perhaps practicing teachers find it difficult to begin implementing critical media literacy activities due to low comfort levels with media studies (Hobbs & Frost, 2003). (Re)introduction to critical media literacy theories and applications should become a component of preservice and in-service teacher education programs, providing support for the implementation of critical media literacy in middle school language arts classes.

References

Alvermann, D. E., & Hagood, M. (2000a). Critical media literacy: Research, theory, and practice in 'new times'. *Journal of Educational Research, 91*(3), 193-205.

Alvermann, D. E., & Hagood, M. (2000b). Fandom and critical media literacy. *Journal of Adolescent & Adult Literacy, 43*(5), 36-46.

Alvermann, D. E., Moon, J. S., & Hagood, M. C. (1999). *Popular culture in the classroom: Teaching and researching critical media literacy.* Newark, DE: International Reading Association.

Berger, A. A. (2000). *Ads, fads, and consumer culture: Advertising's impact on American character and society.* Lanham, MD: Rowman & Littlefield.

Buckingham, D. (Ed.) (1998). *Teaching popular culture.* London: University College London Press.

Cambridge Research Group, Ltd. (Producer). (2001). *Why we buy what we buy* [Motion picture]. (Available from Cambridge Educational, P.O. Box 931, Monmouth Junction, NJ 08852-0931)

Cambridge Research Group, Ltd. (Producer). (2002). *Sexual stereotypes* [Motion picture]. (Available from Cambridge Educational, P.O. Box 931, Monmouth Junction, NJ 08852-0931)

Chung, P. J., Garfield, C. F., Rathouz, P. J., Lauderdale, D. S., Best, D., & Lantos, J. (2002, March/April). Youth targeting by tobacco manufacturers since the master settlement agreement: The first study to document violations of the youth-targeting ban in magazine ads by the three top U.S. tobacco companies. *Health Affairs 21*(2): 254-263.

Cole, M., & Griffin, P. (1986). A sociohistorical approach to remediation. In S. deCastell, A. Luke, & K. Egan (Eds.), *Literacy, society and schooling* (pp. 87-109). Cambridge, England: Cambridge University Press.

Elkins, J., & Luke, A. (2000). Special themed issue: Re/mediating adolescent literacies [Editorial]. *Journal of Adolescent & Adult Literacy, 43* (5), 1-3.

Erb, T. O. (Ed.) (2001). *This we believe . . . And now we must act.* Columbus, OH: National Middle School Association.

Field, A. E., Camargo, C. A., Jr., Taylor, B., Berkey, C. S., Roberts, S. B., & Colditz, G. A. (2001). Peer, parent, and media influences on the development of weight concerns and frequent dieting among preadolescent and adolescent boys and girls. *Pediatrics, 107*(1), 54-60.

Gee, J. P. (2000). New people in new worlds: networks, the new capitalism and schools. In B. Cope & M. Kalantzis (Eds.), *Multiliteracies: Literacy learning and the design of social futures* (pp. 43-68). London: Routledge Falmer.

Gee, J. P. (2003). *What video games have to teach us about learning and literacy.* New York, NY: Palgrave Macmillan.

Giroux, H. (1988). *Schooling and struggle for pedagogies: Critical and feminist discourses as regimes of truth.* London: Routledge.

Hagood, M. C. (2000). New times, new millennium, new literacies. *Reading Research and Instruction, 39*(4), 311-328.

Harter, S. (1990). Self and identity development. In S. Feldman & G. Eliot. *At the threshold: The developing adolescent* (pp. 352-387). Cambridge, MA: Harvard University Press.

Hobbs, R. (1998). The seven great debates in the media literacy movement. *Journal of Communication, 48*(1), 16-29.

Hobbs, R., & Frost, R. (2003). Measuring the acquisition of media literacy skills. *Reading Research Quarterly, 38*(3), 330-355.

International Reading Association. (2003). *Standards for reading professionals.* Newark, DE: Author.

Kelly, K. J., & Edwards, R. W. (1998). Image advertisements for alcohol products: Is their appeal associated with adolescents' intention to consume alcohol? *Adolescence, 33*(129), 47-59.

Lesko, N. (2001). *Act your age! A cultural construction of adolescence.* London: Routledge Falmer.

Lewison, M., Flint, A. S., & Van Sluys, K. (2002). Taking on critical literacy: The journey of newcomers and novices. *Language Arts, 79*(5), 382-392.

Luke, A., & Freebody, P. (1997). The social practices of reading. In S. Muspratt, A. Luke, & P. Freebody (Eds.), *Constructing critical literacies* (pp. 185-225). Creskill, NJ: Hampton Press.

Luke, C. (1999). Media and cultural studies in Australia. *Journal of Adolescent & Adult Literacy, 42*(8), 622-626.

Luke, C. (2003). Pedagogy, connectivity, multimodality, and interdisciplinarity. *Reading Research Quarterly, 38*(3), 397-403.

Martin, M. C., & Gentry, J. W. (1997). Stuck in the model trap: The effects of beautiful models in ads on female pre-adolescents and adolescents. *Journal of Advertising, 26*(2), 19-33.

Merriam, S. (1998). *Qualitative research and case study applications in education.* San Francisco, CA: Jossey-Bass Publishers.

Moje, E. B., Young, J. P., Readence, J. E., & Moore, D. W. (2000). Reinventing adolescent literacy for new times: Perennial and millennial issues. *Journal of Adolescent & Adult Literacy, 43*(5), 4-14.

National Council of Teachers of English/International Reading Association. (1996). *Standards for the English language arts.* Urbana, IL: National Council of Teachers of English.

New London Group. (2000) A pedagogy of multiliteracies: Designing social futures. In B. Cope & M. Kalantzis (Eds.), *Multiliteracies: Literacy learning and the design of social futures* (pp. 9-37). London: Routledge Falmer.

Piaget, J. (1972). Intellectual evolution from adolescence to adulthood. *Human Development, 15*(1), 1-12.

Portner, J. (1997, June 4). Joe Camel illegally targets minors, FTC charges [Electronic version]. *Education Week.* Retrieved November 3, 2004, from http://www.edweek.org/ew/articles/1997/06/04/36camel.h16.html?querystring=Joe%20camel

Rudasill, L. (1986). Advertising gimmicks: Teaching critical thinking. In J. Golub (Chair) and the Committee on Classroom Practices (Eds.), *Activities to promote critical thinking: Classroom practices in teaching English,* (pp. 127-129). Urbana, IL: National Council of Teachers of English.

Strauss, A. L., & Corbin, J. (1990). *Basics of qualitative research: Grounded theory procedures and techniques.* Newbury Park, CA: Sage Publications.

Zollo, P. (1999). *Wise up to teens: Insights into marketing and advertising to teenagers* (2nd ed.). Ithaca, NY: New Strategist Publications.

Appendix.

1) *Snob appeal:* consumer will be considered better than others who don't buy the product
2) *Sex appeal:* use of sex to sell a product
3) *Appeal to Tradition:* "We have made the best product for over 100 years." Experience of the company is the key.
4) *Appeal to Authority:* This depends on a spokesperson, TV star, athlete, or celebrity to endorse an item. Using the product will make the consumer as wealthy, talented, or beautiful as the spokesperson.
5) *Plain Folks:* "Good ol' boys like us believe in plain, good-quality items, nothing fancy."
6) *Something for Nothing* or *More for Less:* This suggests that a cheaper product is of better quality than its higher-priced competitors.
7) *Appeal to Excellence:* This is almost like snob appeal. "Only the best is good enough for me."
8) *Everyone Else Has One:* This appeals to consumers who don't want to stand out by being different.

(adapted from Rudasill, 1986)

Recommended Procedures for Reading Mathematics in Current and Past Content/Secondary Reading Textbooks

Daniel L. Pearce
Nancy G. Reynolds

Texas A&M University-Corpus Christi

Abstract

This study investigated what is being recommended in content/secondary reading books for teaching students how to read mathematics. The researchers analyzed current and past content/secondary reading textbooks for reading ideas for mathematics in general and word problems in particular. This chapter provides a description and comparison of what was found in the textbooks. The analysis found that the texts written thirty years ago had more information on teaching students how to read word problems and mathematics in general than the current textbooks.

The reading process has been described by Stothard and Hulme (1996) as the interaction of two distinct processes: decoding and comprehension. These skills are necessary in the reading class and in the content areas. In mathematics it is necessary to decode (recognize) and comprehend not only words and sentences, but also numbers, symbols, graphs, drawings, lengthy descriptions, the shorthand used in equations, and word problems. Students must also be able to read critically and be able to distinguish between relevant and irrelevant information (Helwig, Almond, Rozek-Tedesco, Tindal, & Heath, 1999). Being able to read effectively in the mathematics class requires different skills than those employed in the other content areas and these skills must be taught (Cassidy, 1991).

Mathematics textbooks are attempting to address this problem by making mathematics more meaningful, by relating math to the real world, and helping students understand that math is all around them and is not a foreign language. The math textbooks of today have a new format. There are more words on the page and fewer pages of "math problems." This format requires students to apply their math skills to word problems reflecting real life situations rather than rely on pure computational abilities. This new format also requires more reading. In the past, students who were poor readers could sometimes shine in math class because reading is not a major requirement for pure computational mathematics. However, word problems do require reading ability and a student's success at word problems may be affected by his reading ability (Clarkson, 1983; Clements, 1980). Teachers are witnessing poor readers struggling in their mathematics courses because of their disabilities, limited English proficiency, or lack of reading skills (Hoff, 2001). In a teacher survey, nearly 80% agreed that poor reading skills contributed to student difficulty with word problems, and 88% agreed that students lacked the abilities to use the proper strategies (Benko, Loaiza, Long, Scharski, & Winkler, 1995).

There is limited research on what exactly causes the problems in solving word problems (Muth, 1992). The findings from the most recent research are not much different than decades ago when Vanderlinde (1964) suggested that the difficulties in solving problems could be contributed to reading deficiencies, careless reading, poor teaching, lack of computation skills, lack of strategies, and/or inadequate knowledge of vocabulary. However, Vanderlinde believed that the key to problem solving success was vocabulary instruction. He found that students who were exposed to more vocabulary words achieved higher scores than the students who were not exposed to vocabulary instruction. Recent research by Maikos-Diegnan (2003) substantiates this finding. Schell (1982) described mathematics as being the most difficult reading material among the content areas, contributing this difficulty to the vocabulary that can be ambiguous and sometimes alien to the child. Panchyshyn and Monroe (1992) found that more than 50% of the words used in an elementary mathematics textbook are not those most commonly used in the student's reading material. Because the words used in mathematics are usually abstract and are rarely used outside the classroom, low ability readers are at a disadvantage (O'Mara, 1981). Just as there are many facets to reading ability, so there are as many theories as to why children have difficulty reading mathematics. Muth (1991) states that there is mounting evidence that student's difficulties with word problems stem more from their lack of comprehension skills than from their lack of computational skills.

While we may be unsure as to what aspect of reading may be the culprit, research has shown us that ineffective reading skills are responsible for a significant number of errors in solving word problems (Clements, 1980) and that reading errors significantly contribute to lower performance on mathematics tests (Clarkson, 1983; Newman, 1977). In a review of research,

Aiken (1972) reported correlations between mathematical problem solving and reading comprehension ranged between .40 and .86.

These findings are critical due to the high verbal context found in today's textbooks. Teachers need to teach not only the mathematics curriculum, but also reading and learning strategies (Barton, Heidema, & Jordan, 2002). Many teachers are finding themselves unprepared for this new role as a quasi-reading teacher (Maikos-Diegnan, 2003). However, for students to be successful in mathematics, they must be taught how to "read" a word problem. So, where do the teachers and the many preservice teachers in our universities gain this knowledge? One source would be content/secondary-reading textbooks. However, this source of information was not as helpful as one would expect. Teachers, as well as administrators, asking for ideas to help their students read and understand mathematics better have approached the researchers of this study. Both teachers and administrators also commented on the shortage/difficulty of finding information in textbooks on these topics.

Unsuccessful quests for information by mathematics teachers prompted the present study. The researchers decided to investigate the extent to which the reading of mathematics was being addressed in content/secondary reading textbooks, what was being recommended, and whether or not the extent of coverage on reading and mathematics had changed in the last 20 plus years. The objective of this study was to find out the amount and kinds of information on reading and mathematics existing in content reading/secondary reading textbooks. An assumption underlying the study was that information had to explicitly exist in the textbooks and be available to a reader without the expert assistance of a professor or consultant.

The Study

The study had two parts. The first was a content analysis of recent content reading and secondary reading textbooks to determine what the textbooks contained on reading and mathematics. The second part of the study was an analysis of content/secondary reading textbooks published on or before 1980 to determine what they recommended.

Part I

Content analysis (Monaghan & Hartman, 2002) is a methodology that makes the text itself the object of study. In a content analysis, textual material is identified, apriori categories are established, two or more readers independently examine the texts looking for the apriori categories, findings are recorded, and results are compared. As a research tool, content analysis goes back to the 13th century (Smith, 2000) where it was used to study historical texts. In literacy research, content analysis methods have been used to study the motivational content of basal readers (Blom, Waite, & Zimet,

1970), the comprehension activities in basal readers (Durkin, 1981), and the writing activities in mathematics basals (Davison & Pearce, 1988).

Nine content/secondary reading textbooks were identified and examined for information on reading and mathematics. Each of the nine content books had a 2000 or later publication date. In addition, each had been mentioned in a survey of reading professors to identify significant books in the reading field (Pearce & Bader, 2001). The most recent edition of the book available to the researchers was the book that was analyzed. The nine content/secondary reading books evaluated were: Alverman and Phelps (2002), Brozo and Simpson (2003), Manzo, Manzo, and Estes (2001), Readence, Bean, and Baldwin (2000), Richardson and Morgan (2003), Roe, Stoodt, and Burns (2001), Ruddell (2001), Ryder and Graves (2003), and Vacca and Vacca (2002).

Initially, the researchers intended to analyze the textbooks for information on reading and solving word problems. Research into the topic led to the creation of a two-category system for ideas on solving word problems: teacher directed and student directed activities. The researchers independently analyzed one of the books from the identified texts (Richardson & Morgan, 2003). The purpose was to identify and code each reference to mathematical word problems in that text and compare results. During the coding the researchers felt that the categories did not adequately capture what was in the textbook.

The researchers decided to expand the analysis beyond word problems to reading and mathematics. While solving word problems would remain a factor in the analysis there were additional factors relating to mathematics and reading included in the analysis. Just focusing on word problems underrepresented the information on mathematics and reading in a textbook. This was especially true when considering one of the assumptions of the study, to identify reading and mathematics ideas in a book that a teacher could identify and use without expert assistance. The researchers devised a nine category system based upon what they thought was important. The researchers then went into the same textbook and tried to code the findings using the nine categories. The nine-category system, in turn, was collapsed into seven categories.

The seven categories of information were: (a) whether or not mathematics was included in the textbook's table of contents; (b) the number of times that mathematics was mentioned in the textbook's index; (c) whether or not the textbook had an identifiable section on reading mathematics materials; (d) whether or not the textbook discussed the difficulties encountered in reading mathematics materials; (e) whether or not the textbook contained any ideas for reading and solving word problems; (f) whether or not recommendations/examples were given to help students master mathematics vocabulary; and (g) any ideas suggested for reading mathematical text in general.

One of the assumptions, determining what an unassisted teacher looking in a text for information would find, helped form three of the categories: (a) whether or not mathematics was included in the textbook's table of contents; (b) the number of times that mathematics was mentioned in the textbook's index; and (c) whether or not the textbook had an identifiable section on reading mathematics materials. These three categories addressed the ease or difficulty a person picking up that textbook would have in finding and identifying information on reading and mathematics. The second category, the number of times that mathematics was mentioned in the index, needs clarification. While some textbooks might list one example in the index and other texts list pages (and in fact did), the number of mentions in an index was a measure of the amount of attention a textbook gave to reading and mathematics. Plus, it was discrete data that could be counted without attempting to interpret what it meant beyond the presence or absence in an index.

For the analysis, the researchers decided to code for "mathematically related reading ideas." "Mathematically related reading ideas" were defined as any reference to mathematics, either by itself or in conjunction with reading. Using these criteria, if a textbook presented an example of a strategy (i.e., KWL) by itself with no specific mention of mathematics it was not coded as a one of the seven categories. But if a strategy was explained and then a specific example on using it to solve a mathematics problem was presented then it would be coded as mathematics related. While a strict criteria might eliminate data because there are strategies that can be adopted across the subject areas, it was felt that a literal interpretation of the criteria would be more accurate.

The two researchers independently went through each of the nine content/secondary reading textbooks noting where any mention of reading and/or mathematics, recording what was found, and coding using the seven category system. The researchers then compared their codings, went back into the textbooks, and resolved their differences. All differences were resolved and the final interrelated agreement between the researchers was 100%.

Part II

The researchers identified eight content/secondary reading textbooks published in 1980 or earlier. Each of these textbooks had been mentioned in an earlier survey of reading professors to determine significant books in the field (Pearce & Bader, 1980). Plus, copies of the identified texts were available to the researchers. The "older" textbooks analyzed were: Aukerman, 1972; Hafner, 1977; Herber, 1970; Karlin, 1977; Lamberg and Lamb, 1980; Robinson, 1975; Shepherd, 1973; and Thomas and Robinson, 1977.

The researchers examined each of the "older" content/secondary reading books using the same procedures used when examining the "current" textbooks. Each of the textbooks was independently read and mathematical related examples were noted using the seven-category system. The same operational definition of mathematically related ideas used in the first part of the study was used. The researchers then compared results. The researchers examined differences and obtained 100% inter-rater reliability.

Findings

Part I

Listed in Table 1 are the findings from the analysis of the nine recent content/secondary reading textbooks.

As seen in Table 1, the content/secondary reading textbooks differed in the emphasis and coverage placed on mathematically related topics. Only Roe, Stoodt, and Burns (2001) listed mathematics in the table of contents. The textbooks varied in the amount of coverage given to the topic of reading and mathematics. Two texts (Manzo, Manzo, & Estes, 2001; Roe, Stoodt, & Burns, 2001) had specific sections that dealt with the difficulty involved in reading mathematical materials. The listing of mathematics related topics in the indexes also varied greatly, ranging from 12 times to none. Four of the texts did not mention mathematics or word problems in the index.

All of the texts examined had at least one recommendation on how to help students read and understand mathematical material. However, the depth and breadth of the coverage differed greatly. Two of the texts (Readence, Bean, & Baldwin, 2000; Ryder & Graves, 2003) offered a few scattered ideas on how students could be helped to read mathematics text more effectively.

Six of the texts (Alverman & Phelps, 2002; Brozo & Simpson, 2003; Manzo, Manzo, & Estes, 2001; Richardson & Morgan, 2003; Ruddell, 2001; Vacca & Vacca, 2002) contained examples that were embedded in discussions on specific topics. They were also in different parts of the text and consequently difficult to find. For that matter, the textbooks that did not mention mathematics in the index required a systematic search to find ideas dealing with mathematics in general or word problems in particular.

Concerning recommended procedures for helping students read and solve word problems, eleven different recommendations/ideas were identified that specifically mentioned word problems. The different ideas found are listed in Table 2.

As can be seen in Table 2, differences existed between the textbooks in recommended procedures for helping students read, understand, and solve word problems. Among the recommendations, only five of the nine books analyzed covered step procedures. In all total, seven different step procedures were identified.

Brozo & Simpson (2003). The seven step procedure (Brozo & Simpson, 2003) related an example of "talk through" strategy: (a) read the problem carefully underlining key words or phrases, (b) reword the problem, (c) identify

Table 1. Summary or Recommendations of Current Textbooks

	Math Mentioned in Table of Contents	# of Times Math in Index	Section on Reading & Math	Discussion on Difficulties in Word Problems	Ideas on Word Problems	Vocabulary Ideas for Math	Other Math Ideas not Specifically Dealing with Word Problems
Alverman & Phelps (2002)	No	0	No	No	Yes	Yes	1) anticipation reading guide 2) QAR
Brozo & Simpson (2003)	No	12	No	No	Yes	Yes	1) literature 2) writing
Manzo, Manzo, & Estes (2001)	No	3	Yes	Yes	Yes	Yes	1) math informal inventory 2) use real world artifacts
Readence, Bean, & Baldwin (2000)	No	0	No	No	Yes	Yes	1) background knowledge 2) margin gloss
Richardson & Morgan (2003)	No	0	No	No	Yes	Yes	2) literature 3) writing
Roe, Stoodt, & Burns (2001)	Yes	8	Yes	Yes	Yes	Yes	1) parphrase 2) real world problems 3) adjust rate 4) DRL 5) advanced organizers 6) reading guides
Ruddell (2001)	No	5	No	No	Yes	Yes	1) 3 level guides 2) QAR 3) ReQuest
Ryder & Graves (2003)	No	0	No	No	Yes	No	1) contrasting scenarios
Vacca & Vacca (2002)	No	10	No	Yes	Yes	Yes	1) literature 2) web resources 3) reading guides,

Table 2. Specific Suggested Ideas for Improving the Reading and Solving of Word Problems in Current Textbooks

SUGGESTED IDEAS	TEXT SUGGESTING IDEAS
Charting	Brozo & Simpson (2003)
Cooperative Grouping	Richardson & Morgan (2003)
	Roe, Stoodt, & Burns (2001)
Diagramming Problems	Roe, Stoodt & Burns (2001)
Discussion Web	Vacca & Vacca (2002)
Language Experience	Roe, Stoodt, & Burns (2001)
Modeling (talk throughs)	Brozo & Simpson (2003)
	Roe, Stoodt, & Burns (2001)
Reading Guide	Alverman & Phelps (2002)
Request	Richardson & Morgan (2003)
Reread (read twice)	Roe, Stoodt, & Burns (2001)
Step Procedures	Brozo & Simpson (2003)
	Manzo, Manzo, & Estes (2001)
	Richardson & Morgan (2003)
	Roe, Stoodt, & Burns (2001)
	Ryder & Graves(2003)

the problem to be solved, (d) rewrite as an equation, (e) solve, (f) check, and (g) state the answer.

Manzo, Manzo, & Estes (2001). The Dahmus method (Dahmus, 1970): (a) translate verbal statements into mathematical statements, (b) do no mathematical operations until all translation is complete, (c) read slowly, (d) state all facts mathematically, and (e) work.

Richardson & Morgan (2003). Problem solving procedure (Richardson & Morgan, 2003): (a) gather ideas/information, (b) define the problem, (c) form tentative conclusions,(d) test conclusions, and (e) make a decision.

Roe, Stoodt, & Burns (2001). This text presents three separate step process for reading, understanding, and solving word problems: Kress's 5-step procedure (Kress, 1989): (a) survey (read out loud), (b) question (what is being asked), (c) question (what is the process/operation), (d) read (reread out loud again), (e) work; Earle's 6-step procedure (Earle, 1976): (a) read problem quickly, (b) examine problem, (c) reread problem, (d) analyze the problem, (e) compute the problem, and (f) examine the answer; and SQRSCG (The six steps in the SQRQCQ procedure spell the acronym name) (Roe, Stoodt, & Burns, 2001): (a) survey, (b) question, (c) read, (d) question, (e) compute, and (f) question.

Ryder & Graves (2003). IDEAL is a problem solving strategy that stands for the following steps (Bransford & Stein, 1984): (a) identify the problem, (b) define the problem, (c) explore alternative approaches, (d) acting on the plan, and (e) looking at the effects. While not originally designed as a mathematics word problem strategy but instead as a problem solving/creative thinking protocol, this was presented as a means to solve a word problem in the text.

As can be seen from the listing above, not only did the five textbooks differ in which step procedure was being recommended, there were also major differences between the operations in the steps themselves.

Table 2 also shows that textbooks differed in the ideas presented for dealing with word problems. Two of the texts gave specific examples of using reading guides to help students with word problems. Three of the texts recommended having students write or create their own problems. Two of the texts recommended having the students work in collaborative groups.

Part II

The findings from the analysis of the eight "earlier" content/secondary reading textbooks are listed in Table 3.

As can be seen from Table 3, the "older" textbooks differed in the emphasis and coverage placed on mathematically related topics, and they tended to feature mathematics as an important aspect of content reading. Only one of these textbooks did not list mathematics in the table of contents (Karlin, 1977). Herber (1970) listed "Reading and Reasoning Guides: Mathematics" in the table of contents. The remaining six textbooks devoted at least a chapter to reading and mathematics. Hafner (1977) had two chapters on mathematics and reading. The listing of mathematics' related topics in the indexes also varied greatly, ranging from 12 times to none. However, two of the books (Aukerman, 1972; Lamberg & Lamb, 1980) that listed mathematics once in the index also had a chapter on reading and mathematics.

All nine texts examined included at least one recommendation on how to help students read and understand mathematical text. The depth and breadth of the ideas covered in the texts differed greatly. Herber (1970) did not approach reading mathematics as being unique from reading in other subject areas. He presented ideas and offered examples of mathematics related activities embedded in discussions on inferential reading, vocabulary activities, and reading guides. Karlin (1977) makes a vocabulary suggestion for mathematics and offers an example of how students can set their own purposes for reading mathematics. Interestingly, he does offer extended examples and ideas for the other content areas.

The rest of the "earlier" textbooks analyzed (Aukerman, 1972; Hafner, 1977; Lamberg & Lamb, 1980; Robinson, 1975; Shepherd, 1973; Thomas & Robinson, 1977), gave examples and elaborations of how teachers could help their students read mathematics using the ideas presented in that book. All six of these books included excerpts from lessons to illustrate what a teacher could do using the approaches suggested. While the majority of the ideas were teacher directed

Table 3. A Summary of the Findings of the Analysis of Older Textbooks

	Math Mentioned in Table of Contents	# of Times Math in Index	Section on Reading & Math	Discussion on Difficulties in Reading Math	Ideas on Word Problems	Vocabulary Ideas for Math	Other Math Ideas Not Specifically Dealing With Word Problems
Aukerman (1972)	Yes	1	Yes	Yes	Yes	Yes	1) involve students 2) DRL 3) survey reading; 4) questioning 5) adjust rate 6) "comic stripping"
Hafner (1977)	Yes	4	Yes	Yes	Yes	Yes	1) DRL 2) graphing 3) translating numbers into words 4) adjust rate 5) diagnostic test
Herber (1970)	Yes	0	Yes	No	No	Yes	1) reading guides
Karlin (1977)	No	0	No	No	No	Yes	1) diagnosing 2) surveying to establish a purpose
Lamberg & Lamb (1980)	Yes	1	Yes	Yes	Yes	Yes	1) DRL 2) writing 3) survey 4) adjust purpose and rate
Robinson (1975)	Yes	17	Yes	Yes	Yes	Yes	1) concept reading 2) principle reading 3) purposeful & slow
Shepherd (1973)	Yes	8	Yes	Yes	Yes	Yes	1) instructional Reading Guide for mathematics 2) adjust rate 3) reread 4) metacognitive awareness of what to do 5) translate English into numbers 6) DRL
Thomas & Robinson (1977)	Yes	15	Yes	Yes	Yes	Yes	1) instructional Reading Guide for mathematics 2) adjust rate 3) metacognitive awareness of what to do 4) teacher modeling/minilessons on how to read book

ideas, three of the texts (Robinson, 1975; Shepherd, 1973; Thomas & Robinson, 1977) gave examples of ways to make students aware of what to do on their own. While each of the textbooks called it something different, each of these ideas could be classified as metacognitive awareness activities.

Table 4. Specific Suggested Ideas for Improving the Reading and Solving of Word Problems in Older Textbooks

Suggested Ideas	Text Suggesting Ideas
Data diagramming/drawing representation	Aukerman (1972) Thomas & Robinson (1977)
Directed reading lesson	Aukerman (1972) Hafner (1977) Lamberg & Lamb (1980) Shepherd (1973)
Flow chart showing students what to do when reading a problem	Robinson (1975)
Handout instructing students how to read mathematics	Thomas & Robinson (1977)
Practice with different kinds of problems (including numberless, irrelevant fact, and real life problems	Aukerman (1972) Shepherd (1973)
Read problem orally Reading Guides	Thomas & Robinson (1977) Hafner (1977) Herber (1970)
Reread the problem (read at least twice)	Lamberg & Lamb (1980) Robinson (1975) Thomas & Robinson (1977) Shepherd (1973)
Reword/verbalize the problem	Shepherd (1973) Thomas & Robinson (1977)
Reword problem and eliminate non-important words	Aukerman (1972)
Reword problem and change numbers to "easy numbers"	Thomas & Robinson (1977)
Step procedures	Aukerman (1972) Hafner (1977) Lamberg & Lamb (1980) Robinson (1975) Shepherd (1973) Thomas & Robinson (1977)
Teacher Modeling (similar to think alouds)	Thomas & Robinson (1977)
Visualize the problem	Shepherd (1973)
Writing problems (creating own problems)	Lamberg & Lamb (1980) Shepherd (1973)

Fifteen different ideas and procedures for helping students read and solve word problems were identified. These are listed and summarized in Table 4.

As can be seen in Table 4, there were differences in what was recommended for helping students read, understand, and solve word problems. Among the recommendations, five of the books included some form of step procedures. The texts that included step procedures included:

Aukerman (1972). Reading-Study approach (Aukerman, 1972) is a series of steps that the teacher takes the student through. Aukerman gives two different sequences. The first was: (a) read problem to get main idea, (b) question self, (c) reread problem, (d) teacher questions students, and (e) estimate answer. The second sequence is: (a) read the problem to get main idea, (b) question self, (c) teacher questions students on facts, and (d) make number equations or open sentences.

Hafner (1977). Steps in Solving Problems (Hafner, 1977): (a) Read the problem accurately, (b) use mathematical symbols to set up the problem, (c) if possible set up in equation form, (d) perform operations, and (e) check.

Lamberg & Lamb (1980). This text offers four distinct steps to follow when working with word problems: Earle's (1976) 6-step procedure: (a) read problem quickly, (b) examine problem, (c) reread problem, (d) analyze the problem, (e) compute the problem, and (f) examine the answer; Polya's (1957) problem solving procedure: (a) understand the problem, (b) devise a plan, (c) try out the plan, and (d) reflect on the solution; Shepherd's (1973) 5-step procedure: (a) read the problem slowly, (b) reread the last sentence, (c) reread the entire problem, (d) decide processes to use, and (e) compute: and Thomas & Robinson's (1972) step procedure: (a) read the problem slowly, (b) reread the problem, (c) identify given facts, (d) plan attack, (e) estimate the answer, (f) compute, and (g) check.

Robinson (1977). There are two word problem step procedures provided in this text: Thomas & Robinson's step procedure (1972): (a) read the problem slowly, (b) reread the problem, (c) identify given facts, (d) plan attack, (e) estimate the answer, (f) compute, and (g) check; and Shepherd's 5-step procedure (1973): (a) read the problem slowly, (b) reread the last sentence, (c) reread the entire problem, (d) decide processes to use, and (e) compute.

Shepherd (1973). Shepherd 's 5-step procedure (1973): (a) read the problem slowly, (b) reread the last sentence, (c) reread the entire problem, (d) decide processes to use, and (e) compute.

Thomas & Robinson (1977). Thomas & Robinson's step procedure (1977): (a) read the problem slowly, (b) reread the problem, (c) identify given facts, (d) plan attack, (e) estimate the answer, (f) compute, and (g) check.

As can be seen from the listing above there were differences in the step procedures recommended. There were also differences in the suggested reading rate and purpose of the steps.

Beyond the emphasizing step procedures, Table 4 also shows that six of the textbooks contained instructions/recommendations for students to read the problem at least twice, vary rate of reading, and to verbalize what the problem is asking in their own words.

Discussion

The content analysis of the nine current content/secondary reading textbooks identified that the amount of attention given to reading and mathematics in today's textbooks varies between books. In none of the textbooks examined could the discussion on reading mathematical text be classified as being comprehensive. In fact, in places it seemed almost incidental. Given the emphasis placed on mathematics and science in state and federally funded programs, the researchers had expected to find more information about reading mathematics aimed at classroom teachers.

The amount of information devoted to reading word problems also varied between the books. The differences between textbooks on what was recommended ranged from some ideas to almost none. There was not a clear consensus across the textbooks on what would be effective for helping students read and solve word problems. There were also not many citations of research supporting the effectiveness of the different ideas that were presented. Given the over 50 years of history on word problems, the amount of research on them, and the emphasis placed on being able to read them in today's test structured schools, the researchers had expected to find more information and recommendations on reading word problems.

Comparing the "older" textbooks with today's textbooks, there appears to have been an overall decline in the amount of emphasis placed on reading and mathematics. Six of the "earlier" textbooks had extensive multi-page sections on reading and mathematics. In contrast, the majority of today's textbooks tend to follow Herber's (1970) approach and embed mathematics examples in other discussions of other topics. This overall difference between the "old and the new" can be seen by comparing the "other" columns in Tables 1 and 3. The older textbooks offer more ideas and suggestions on reading and mathematics. This might be the result of some ideas and suggestions being discredited over time.

Other differences exist between today's textbooks and the "older" textbooks. The first is the treatment of word problems. An examination of Tables 2 and 4 shows that a larger number of ideas were recommended in the older texts. Five of the older textbooks (Aukerman, 1972; Lamberg & Lamb, 1980; Robinson, 1975; Shepherd, 1973; Thomas & Robinson, 1977) presented multiple ideas for helping students read and solve word problems. In contrast, although six of the current textbooks mentioned problem solving, the number of ideas presented for word problems is not as numerous as the ideas presented in the textbooks from twenty years ago. This is especially true if Roe, Stoodt, and Burns (2001) was removed from the list of current textbooks.

Some ideas were more popular in the 1970s than now. One of these was the Directed Reading Lesson (DRL). Six of the "older" textbooks presented adaptations of the DRL for mathematics, along with an example of how it could be done. Four of these texts gave examples of the DRL for word problems. Only one of today's textbooks mentioned the DRL for reading mathematics.

Another idea that seems to wane is the importance of having students either vary their rate or reread a word problem. While today's textbooks all contained mention of the importance of readers varying rates of reading depending upon the purpose for reading, only Roe, Stoodt, and Burns (2001) mentioned the importance of rate variation for reading word problems. In contrast, six of the "older" textbooks mentioned varying rate and four recommended rereading a problem at least twice. Of the current textbooks, only Roe, Stoodt, and Burns (2001) specifically directed students to reread a word problem. The older textbooks also tended to give more of a rationale on why reading mathematics' material was difficult and needed to be read carefully.

An idea that still appears popular is the multi-step procedure for problem solving. Six of the "older" textbooks presented step procedures. Five of today's texts presented steps or variations of step procedures. Three of the five step procedures recommended by the current textbooks are different than the procedures mentioned in the "older" books. Two of the newer textbooks presented generic problem solving procedures and applied them to mathematics as opposed to procedures developed specifically for word problems. Step procedures have been recommended by the National Council of Teachers of Mathematics (NCTM, 2000) as being a critical skill necessary for success in problem solving. Beyond the observation that NCTM recommends step procedures and that the procedures have different recommended operations, generalizations are difficult. No text gave a rationale for why it chose that particular step procedure.

One aspect that made comparisons of the textbooks difficult is the changing vocabulary. In the 1970s, certain terms were used such as "Data Diagrams," "figures," and "showing how." Today these terms are called "charting," "graphic organizers," and "think alouds." Two recommendations that have remained constant are the importance of modeling for students and developing metacognitive knowledge in the students on how to read. Despite the changing terminology in the field, the older textbooks stressed both aspects. Today's textbooks also stress both. However, today's textbooks tend not to focus these aspects on mathematics. Instead they focus on these topics as desired traits in general.

Among the new recommendations contained in today's textbooks for helping students read and solve word problems were cooperative grouping, ReQuest (Richardson & Morgan, 2003), and use of the Web. Writing is also recommended and stressed more by today's texts than their predecessors.

The change in the organization of text became very clear to both of the researchers. Yesterday's textbooks tended to be easier to find and identify specific suggestions for reading mathematics and word problems. In contrast, today's texts, even those that mention mathematics in the index, require a degree of effort to find specific ideas on how to help students read mathematics and solve story problems.

The differences that have been found between current textbooks and those of 20 plus years ago could be explained by the shift from a skills approach to a more process orientation or increased knowledge base (although none of the current textbooks addressed that issue). In a more generic strategies approach to content literacy, the differences in the specific content areas are minor and reading processes/strategies exist that can be adapted to all or most content areas. In a more skills oriented approach, subject areas have their own skills and demands are placed on the reader in each unique area. Teachers' roles are to determine how they can assist their students in those subject areas. To the researchers, this dichotomy seems artificial because it is not an "either/or" situation. There can be generic processes that exist across disciplines and still have specific demands placed on a student in a specific discipline. Reading mathematics is not the same as reading a poem because the textual material being read is so different.

One of the purposes of this study was to determine what was available to a person who read a textbook searching for ideas to aid him/herself in a classroom setting. The older textbooks offered more specific information for the teacher. Even if a more generic process approach is accepted, given the demands mathematics places on reading, additional mathematical examples would be a useful addition.

The differences between the older and the newer textbooks could also be a function of the textbooks analyzed. Using different textbooks or a wider more comprehensive selection of textbooks could have resulted in different results. Finally, the web sites and CD Rom discs that accompanied the current textbooks were not examined. All or any of these variables might explain or change the outcomes of this study and the interpretation of the data.

This study attempted to answer two basic questions: what is being recommended in recent content/secondary reading texts for reading and mathematics; and what was recommended in older textbooks. What was found during the analysis supplied data to answer these questions. In addition, the analysis showed a shift in the information presented in the current textbooks to a more process generic approach to content literacy. While the role of this analysis was not to delve into or mediate the skills versus process approaches to content reading, we feel that the topic of reading and mathematics is worthy of addressing either explicitly or through examples and textbooks need to do that regardless of the textbook authors' philosophies. This is something some of the current textbooks did not do in a clear systematic manner.

The study also raised multiple questions that cannot be answered with the existing data. These questions include: (a) does the development in the reading textbooks of a more generic approach to strategies parallel or differ from the development in the mathematics textbooks; (b) why have some ideas, such as step procedures, continued to be presented (in several different permutations) and others, such as Directed Reading Lessons (DLR), almost vanished; (c) are there any "ideas" that are being promoted in mathematics that have not appeared in any of the content reading textbooks; and (d) out of all of the ideas on reading and mathematics presented in the different textbooks is there a research base for some ideas more than others? While the researchers cannot answer these questions with the data from this study, these are areas that need to be investigated. Especially important is the question about the applicability and validity of the ideas presented for reading mathematics, what works and what does not. Perhaps reading and mathematics is an area whose time has come to be rediscovered.

References

Aiken, L. R. (1972). Language factors in learning mathematics. *Review of Educational Research, 42,* 459-385.

Alverman, D. E., & Phelps, S. F. (2002). *Content reading and literacy: Succeeding in today's classrooms* (3rd ed.). Boston: Allyn & Bacon.

Aukerman, R. C. (1972). *Reading in the secondary school classroom.* New York: McGraw Hill.

Barton, M. L., Heidema, C., & Jordan, D. (2002). Teaching reading in mathematics and science. *Educational Leadership, 60*(3), 24-28.

Benko, A., Loaiza, R., Long, R., Sacharski, M., and Winkler, J. (1999). *Math word problem remediation with elementary students.* (Masters Thesis) Chicago: Saint Xavier University. (ERIC Document Reproduction Service No. ED434015)

Blom, G. E., Waite, R. R., Zimet, S. G. (1970). A motivational content analysis of children's primers. In H. Levin & J. P. Williams (Eds.), *Basic studies on reading* (pp.188-221). New York: Basic Books.

Bransford, J. D., & Stein, B. S. (1984). *The ideal problem solver: A guide for improving thinking, learning, and creativity.* New York: W. H. Freeman.

Brozo, W., & Simpson, M. (2003). *Readers, teachers, and learners: Expanding literacy across the content areas* (4th ed.). Upper Saddle River, NJ: Merrill/Prentice Hall.

Cassidy, J. (1991, February). Word problem wizardry. *Learning, 961-63.*

Clarkson, P. (1983). Types of errors made by Papua New Guinean students. *Educational Studies in Mathematics, 14,* 355-367.

Clements, M. A. (1980). Analyzing children's errors on written mathematics tasks. *Educational Studies in Mathematics, 11*(7), 1-21.

Dahmus, M. E. (1970). How to teach verbal problems. *School Science and Mathematics, 70*(4), 121-138.

Davison, D. M. & Pearce, D. L. (1988). The writing activities contained in mathematics basals. *School Science and Mathematics, 88* (6), 493-499.

Durkin, D. (1981). Reading comprehension instruction in five basal reader series. *Reading Research Quarterly, 16* (4), 515-544.

Earle, R. A. (1976). *Teaching reading and mathematics.* Newark, DE: International Reading Association.

Hafner, L. E. (1977). *Developmental reading in middle and secondary schools: Foundations, strategies, and skills for teaching.* New York: Macmillan.

Heelwig, R., Almond, P. J., Rozek-Tedesco, M. A., Tindal, G., & Heath, B. (1999). Reading as an access to mathematics problem solving on multiple-choice tests for sixth-grade students. *Journal of Educational Research, 93*(2), 102-124.

Herber, H. L. (1970). *Teaching reading in content areas.* Englewood Cliffs, NJ: Prentice Hall.

Hoff, D. J. (2001). Reading mastery is new requisite for solving math. *Education Week, 21*(14), 1-2.

Karlin, R. (1977). *Teaching reading in high school; Improving reading in content areas.* Indianapolis, IN: Bobbs-Merrill.

Kress, R. A. (1989). Trends in remedial instruction. *Journal of Reading, 32*(5), 370-372.

Lamburg, W. J., & Lamb, C. E. (1980). *Reading instruction in the content areas.* Boston: Houghton Mifflin.

Maikos-Diegnan, J. (2003). *Mathematical word problem comprehension.* (Masters Thesis) Union, NJ: Kean University. (ERIC Document Reproduction Service No. ED451481)

Manzo, A. V., Manzo, U. C., & Estes, T.H. (2001). *Content area literacy: Interactive teaching for active learning* (3rd ed.). New York: John Wiley.

Monaghan, E. J., & Hartman, D. K. (2002). In M. L. Kamil, P. B. Mosenthal, P. D. Pearson, & R. Barr (Eds.), *Methods of literacy research: The methodology chapters from the Handbook of Reading Research* (vol. III, pp. 33-48). Mahwah, NJ: Lawrence Erlbaum.

Muth, K. D. (1991). The effects of cuing on middle school students' performance on word problems containing extraneous information. *Journal of Educational Psychology, 83*(1), 173-174.

Muth,, K. D. (1992). Extraneous information and extra steps in arithmetic word problems. *Contemporary Educational Psychology, 17*(3), 278-285

National Council of Teachers of Mathematics. (2000). *Principles and standards for school mathematics.* Weston, VA: The National Council of Teachers of Mathematics, Inc.

Newman, M. A. (1977). An analysis of sixth-grade pupil's errors on written mathematics tasks. In M. A. Clements & J. Foyster (Eds.), *Research in mathematics education in Australia* (vol. 2, pp. 239-258). Melbourne: Swineburne.

O'Mara, D. (1981). The process of reading mathematics. *Journal of Reading, 25*(1), 22-30.

Panchyshyn, R. & Monroe, E. (1992, July). *Vocabulary considerations in mathematics instruction.* Paper presented at the fourteenth World Congress on Reading, Maui, HI.

Pearce, D. L., & Bader, L. A. (1980). Reading about reading: A survey. *Reading World,* *19* (4), 369-374.

Pearce, D. L. & Bader, L. A. (2001, October). Reading about reading: A survey revisited. Paper presented at the meeting of the College Reading Association, Orlando, FL.

Polya, G. (1957). *How to solve it: A new aspect of mathematical method.* Princeton, NJ: Princeton University Press.

Readence, J. E., Bean, T. W., & Baldwin, R. S. (2000). *Content area literacy: An integrated approach* (7th ed.). Dubuque, IA: Kendall/Hunt.

Richardson, J. S., & Morgan, R. F. (2003). *Reading to learn in the content areas* (5th ed.). Belmont, CA: Wadsworth.

Robinson, H. A. (1975). *Teaching reading and study strategies: The content areas.* Boston, MA: Allyn & Bacon.

Roe, B. D., Stoodt, D., & Burns, P. C. (2001). *Secondary school literacy instruction: The content areas* (7th ed.). Boston: Houghton Mifflin.

Ruddell, M. R. (2001). *Teaching content reading and writing* (3rd ed.). New York: John Wiley.

Ryder, R. J., & Graves, M. F. (2003). *Reading and learning in content areas* (3rd ed.). New York, NY: John Wiley.

Schell, V. (1982). Learning partners: Reading and mathematics. *The Reading Teacher,* *35* (5), 544-548.

Shepherd, D. L. (1973). *Comprehensive high school reading methods.* Columbus, OH: Charles E. Merrill.

Smith, C. P. (2000). Content analysis and narrative analysis. In H. F. Reis & M. Judd (Eds.), *Handbook of research methods in social and personality psychology* (pp. 313-338). New York: Cambridge University Press.

Stothard, S. E., & Hulme, C. (1996) A comparison of reading comprehension and decoding difficulties in children. In C. Carnoldi & J. Oakhill, (Eds.), *Reading comprehension difficulties: Processes and intervention* (pp. 93-112). Mahwah, NJ: Erlbaum.

Thomas, E. L., & Robinson, H. A. (1977). *Improving reading in every class: A sourcebook for teachers* (2nd ed.). Boston: Allyn & Bacon.

Vacca, R. T., & Vacca, J. L. (2002). *Content area reading: Literacy and learning across the curriculum* (7th ed.). Boston: Allyn & Bacon.

Vanderlinde, L. F. (1964). Does the study of quantitative vocabulary improve problem solving? *The Elementary School Journal, 65* (3), 143.

Struggling Adolescent Readers: Just Because They're in a Developmental Reading Class Doesn't Mean They Need Phonics

Carol D. Wickstrom

University of North Texas

Abstract

When adolescent readers are unsuccessful on reading tests in middle school, they are often placed in developmental reading classes in high school. The goal of these classes is to help the students improve their reading ability so that they can be successful in their coursework. Sometimes school administrators mandate programs to assist the students and to ensure that the teachers are addressing the students' needs. However, these programs often do not match the students' needs or the teachers' style of teaching. This chapter reveals how one effective teacher addressed this issue in her ninth grade developmental reading class.

When adolescents are placed in a developmental reading course, they have probably been struggling with reading for quite some time. For various reasons, they have moved from one grade to the next (Tovani, 2000). Some of these students may have been tested, and they may have received some kind of assistance along the way. Others may have gotten through the system because their classroom behavior was such that they were not noticed, they used other student's work, or they were deemed as doing their best. It is hoped that through placement in developmental classes the students will become proficient enough with reading so that they can be successful in their coursework.

In districts with low test scores and high drop out rates, high-ranking officials often think they know what programs will address students' needs in reading. These programs are brought into the district and teachers are forced to use them whether or not they are beneficial to the students. Programs using some form of computer-assisted instruction (e. g., Accelerated Reader, Read 180) are used because students can work at their own pace and because using a computer may increase student engagement. Other programs (e.g., Corrective Reading) place a strong emphasis on phonics because of the perception that students cannot read because they do not know phonics. Thus, once an individual is armed with knowledge of decoding skills, the individual's reading will greatly improve. For students at all levels, and even adults, lack of this knowledge can be the problem, so a phonics program is appropriate. While these programs are used with adolescents, research (Pavonetti, Brimmer, & Cipielewski, 2002; Peterson, Burke, & Segura, 1999) does not attest to their effectiveness.

Research has shown that when students have multiple opportunities to read a wide variety of material their reading improves (Krashen & McQuillan, 1996; Meyer, 2002). Allington (2000) indicated that struggling readers need to: read a lot, read books that they can read, read fluently, and develop thoughtful literacy practices. Additionally, researchers (Allen, 2000; Alvermann, 2002; Atwell, 2002; Beers, 2002) advocate literacy instruction that is varied enough to meet the students' needs and interests. Further, Fisher (2001) suggested that to increase student literacy, "school structures and sustained professional development are necessary" (p. 100). So it is more beneficial to the students to identify a program/method that focuses on multiple aspects of reading rather than on a single aspect.

The focus of this study was on the reading abilities of seventy-eight ninth grade students in a developmental reading class in which the teacher was mandated to use a phonics program rather than the comprehensive program that she was using. In this article the researcher demonstrates that a teacher using effective practices and knowledge of her students' abilities is more appropriate than a program mandated by someone without knowledge of the students.

Setting the Context

During the 2001-2002 school year the researcher spent five to six days a month working with Dottie (a pseudonym), a ninth grade reading teacher in a large urban school district in Texas. We began the year thinking that I would come to her class one to two days a week to help facilitate her comprehensive reading program. Over the past few years she had developed a large library of adolescent literature. Besides representing a wide range of genres, interests, and abilities, there were book sets for whole classes and small groups, books on tape, and books that accompanied a computer program. Additionally, she completed her advanced degree in reading, so she was knowledgeable of how to organize her classroom and schedule for a comprehensive program. Through her studies she had become well versed in the reading and writing workshop formats promoted by Nancie Atwell (1998) and Janet Allen (1995, 2002) so we were both excited about how the year would evolve.

When she started teaching in the district in 1995, the curriculum had been left up to the teachers. Since that time the district had provided other materials to be used with the students, but had left their usage to the discretion of the teacher. Thus, we assumed that this year would be the same, which would give us the opportunity to develop coursework that would fit the needs of her students. Unfortunately, despite all of her preparation and expertise, the school district mandated the use of a phonics based reading program for all students in the developmental reading courses. From the start, we both knew that the program was inappropriate for most of the students because the students had different problems and the program was treating them like they were all the same. Dottie was adamant that she was not going to use the program but was unsure as to how to make this happen. From her own classroom experiences with mandated programs, the researcher felt like the best plan of action was to demonstrate that the students did not need a phonics program. So, Dottie and the researcher agreed that the Qualitative Reading Inventory–3 (Leslie & Caldwell, 2001) would be administered by the researcher to all of the students in the classroom.

The Students and Classes

The majority of the students attending this high school were Hispanic and African American. During the 2001-2002 school year the school was 89% Hispanic, 10% African American, and 1% other. The students in Dottie's classes were representative of this configuration. Although the majority of the students had come from the "feeder" middle schools, many of the Hispanic students still spoke Spanish as their first language. Students were placed in the developmental reading class on the basis of their low performance on a reading test administered in eighth grade.

Classes at this high school were blocked, so class length was an hour and a half. The classes met every other day (i.e., A day and B day). Lunch occurred during fourth period, and in this case the students went to class for a half hour, then to lunch, and then back to reading class. On A days Dottie met with first, second, and third periods. On B day she met with fifth, sixth, and seventh periods.

While all students were enrolled in a ninth grade reading class, there were two levels, Reading I and Reading II. For Reading I students, it was the first time that they had taken the course and they were freshmen. The Reading II students were taking the course for the second time. The majority of these students had not received credit for the class due to absences or not completing the assignments. These students were in Dottie's sixth period class. For the purpose of this paper the sixth period class will not be included.

Use of the Informal Reading Inventory

The Qualitative Reading Inventory –3 (QRI) (Leslie and Caldwell, 2001) is an informal reading inventory given to individual students. It is designed to provide diagnostic information about "(1) conditions under which students can identify words and comprehend text successfully, and (2) conditions that appear to result in unsuccessful word identification, decoding, and/or comprehension" (p. 1). Since the results provide estimates of a student's independent, instructional, and frustration reading level, teachers can use these results to make decisions about student groupings and appropriate book levels. The inventory is neither norm-referenced nor standardized, so the results should be used solely to look at the individual student's abilities and growth.

After reading a passage the student was asked to retell as much of the passage as s/he could remember. If the retelling was insufficient, the researcher used the questions to ascertain the individual's level of comprehension. While the retelling format allows the individual to demonstrate their personal knowledge and understandings, many students have more experience with the questioning format so it gives a more accurate measure of their comprehension. From these readings the researcher determined each student's highest independent reading level. Because of the number of students and because it was the beginning of the year the researcher decided that the independent reading level for silent and oral reading would be sufficient enough to provide a starting point for book choices in both of these areas. Because Dottie practiced flexible grouping, changes could be made once the students began to complete assignments and make decisions about the books that they wanted to read.

During the oral reading the researcher recorded miscues and analyzed them later. The analysis allowed the researcher to identify areas of need with regard to phonics. Also, notes were made about each student's prior knowledge about the passage, vocabulary understanding, and fluency. By asking the students about various words in the passage (especially if some type of miscue occurred) the researcher checked vocabulary knowledge. The researcher considered the student to be fluent if punctuation was noted and a smooth pace was kept throughout the reading. Since many of the students first language was Spanish, syllabication and accent discrepancies that were the result of the language difference were noted.

Results of the QRI - 3

Table 1 represents the results of the students' silent reading ability at the independent level. For all of the classes there is a wide range of levels, grade 2 through high school, with the majority of students falling in the fifth and sixth grade level. For ninth graders, this indicates that the majority of the students read below grade level, but that they were able to read with some proficiency.

Table 1. Silent Reading—Independent Level

Class Period	2ND	3RD	4TH	5TH	6TH	UMS	HS	Total in Class
1st	0	1	2	6	6	1	1	17
2nd	1	1	1	6	8	1	0	18
3rd	1	1	5	4	6	0	0	17
5th	0	1	2	6	4	0	0	13
7th	1	2	1	3	4	2	0	13

Table 2 represents the results of the students' oral reading ability at the independent level. For all of the classes there was a wide range, grade two through high school, represented. However, for oral reading the students were clustered in grades four, five and six. According to the results nine students were below this range and four were above this range. Thus, for both oral and silent reading many of the students had similar abilities.

Table 2. Oral Reading–Independent Level

Class Period	2ND	3RD	4TH	5TH	6TH	UMS	HS	Total in Class
1st	0	0	6	5	6	0	0	17
2nd	0	2	2	3	8	3	0	18
3rd	1	4	1	4	6	1	0	17
5th	0	0	4	4	5	0	0	13
7th	1	1	1	5	5	0	0	13

Table 3 provides information about more specific aspects of their reading. Overall, the majority of students had difficulty with syllabication. When words were longer, the Spanish-speaking students tended to apply the Spanish rules for accents and pronunciation when the Spanish word was similar to the English word. With regard to word meaning knowledge (vocabulary) the students needed assistance. Often during the readings the students would ask the researcher about meanings of words. Or sometimes when they finished reading, they would say that they did not know a number of the words.

The words were often specific to a topic or were words that are not used in everyday conversations. Examples of these words included homogenized, ammonium, incinerator, tumultuous, emulate, and skirmish.

Table 3. Students with Word Related Difficulties

Class Period	Syllabication	Vocabulary	Fluency	Word Parts	Letter Needs	Total in Class
1st	16	10	9	10	1	17
2nd	12	14	9	10	2	18
3rd	13	16	5	10	1	17
5th	12	13	6	3	0	13
7th	10	12	4	6	1	13

The fluency column in Table 3 represents those students who needed assistance with fluency. While there are a number in each class, 58% of the students read fluently. In fact, it was often surprising that the students could read the passages fluently, yet score poorly on the comprehension. Students in all classes needed help with word parts with suffixes, prefixes, -ing and -ed representing the bulk of the needs. Students needing letter assistance represented a very small group. These students knew individual letters, but had difficulty with blends, digraphs, and diphthongs.

Table 4 represents the students and their comprehension of the readings. They were given the opportunity to retell first, and then if they did not recall very much information, the researcher gave them questions. The table indicates the manner in which they comprehended rather than the score on each reading. In general, students did much better when they answered questions about the readings rather than the retelling. The prior knowledge column indicates how many of the students were reading passages which they had limited prior knowledge. Although the researcher allowed students to choose the readings from the appropriate levels, they often indicated that they did not know about the topic. Their decision was often a matter of which of the choices was the shortest or had the most interesting title.

Table 4. Student Comprehension

Class Period	Direct Questions	Retelling	· Limited Prior Knowledge	Total in Class
1st	15	2	16	17
2nd	10	8	12	18
3rd	11	6	13	17
5th	11	2	11	13
7th	9	4	8	13

The Phonics Program and Dottie's Classroom

The format of the program provided forty-five minute lessons at several different ability levels. Table 5 indicates all of the components of the program. The areas of emphasis include word pronunciation, comprehension, and fluency. From this information it would seem that the program would work for Dottie's students. The researcher's administration of the informal reading inventory demonstrated that these were her students' areas of need.

Table 5. Focus Elements of the Upper Level of the Scripted Phonics Program

Element	Description
Word Pronunciation	• Emphasizes saying the word correctly • Provides assistance with vocabulary development • Application of affixes • Calls attention to word discrimination • Polysyllabic words emphasized
Comprehension	• Comprehension questions • Informational reading
Fluency	• Accurate reading of words • Rate building

Although the mandated program looks appropriate, there are a number of factors, which kept it from being the one for these students. First of all, the program was the only one that was supported by the district, which means that it was the only one that the teachers were supposed to use. This meant all students were expected to be doing the same thing and to progress through the program in a step-by-step manner. Due to the nature of human organisms everyone is different with different needs. An effective reading program is multidimensional. The report of the National Reading Panel (1999) determined that balance was a critical aspect of any reading program. Students need to engage in interesting books from various genres. There is a need for different types of reading—independent reading, shared reading, and reading aloud. While attention needs to be given to phonics and vocabulary, both should be done within context.

Using the word per minute format supplied by the program the researcher tested the students to determine their placement into the appropriate level of the program. The program was to be the sole means of reading instruction, so every student had to "fit" into one of the levels. Since the school used a block schedule, there were to be two lessons per period. Thus, there was neither room for other reading nor for differences that might occur in the students themselves.

While the program focused on word concepts and vocabulary, much of the practice was on words in isolation and the vocabulary was not meaningful to the students. Researchers (Allen, 2002; Nagy, 1988) have stressed the importance of word study within the context of the relevant material. Teachers need to help students make connections between these words and their personal knowledge and experience.

Even though there was a more in-depth comprehension component of the program, the district did not purchase that component so that the teaching of comprehension had to rely on the vignettes that accompanied the word work. The vignettes were often contrived stories that forced the usage of the vocabulary about topics that did not match the students' interests. Questions followed the vignettes, but the questions were at the literal level of comprehension. Thus, the students could answer the questions without reading the passages.

Last of all, the program had a scripted format that was to be followed rigorously by all teachers. These formats make it easy for teachers to follow and to know what to do next. But most teachers prefer their own style of teaching, as well as determining what they will use to teach. Nagel (1998) and Bullock (1998) support this concept because they believe that teachers will be more satisfied with their teaching, thus they will stay with the profession longer. Moreover, not only was the program an unsatisfactory fit for Dottie's style when she did try to use it, the students were insulted by the teaching format and by the content of the vignettes. Several of the students asked Dottie if she thought that they were "stupid." Allen (2000) emphasized the importance of gaining the necessary expertise to meet the challenges of the students, and the researcher believes that these students were telling Dottie the same thing.

What Did Dottie Do?

After a few days of attempting to use the program, Dottie gave up. She knew this was not a program that met her needs as a teacher and it certainly did not meet the needs of her students. Her knowledge of reading and teaching reading extended beyond reading and following a script, so she was offended by the program's format. Through the use of the data and the hands-on experiences with her students, she was aware of their strengths and needs. She was prepared to make decisions based on this information. Additionally, attitude was paramount to her decision because many of the students expressed a negative attitude about reading and about being in this class. According to her students they "knew how to read." In this regard Dottie believed that the program's phonics focused lessons accompanied by stories with decodable text that were not meant to engage the reader would do more harm than good. Postman and Weingartner (1969) maintain, "There is no learning without a learner. And there is no meaning without a meaning maker" (p. 81).

As a result, Dottie's mission became to create the learning environment and "program" that her students needed. Using her extensive library of adolescent literature she divided the students into literature groups. Knowing that matching students to appropriate books is critical (Routman, 1996), she made book choices based on the results of the informal reading inventory and interest surveys that the students completed. Comprehension was addressed in a variety of ways. Although the students were more accustomed to the direct questioning approach, the small group oral discussions provided students with different perspectives. Dottie also used open-ended questioning with writer's response as a means to cause students to think at different levels. During the group meetings Dottie focused students on main points, modeled effective reading strategies, used think aloud, and monitored their progress.

Besides working with their novel, students completed word work regularly. Some of the word work was done as a whole class and some was completed in groups so that they were able to work on specific needs. Although Dottie understood that reading is the most important factor that can increase student vocabulary (Bauman & Kameenui, 1991; Nagy, 1988), from the results of the informal reading assessment she realized that the students needed assistance in this area. The students needed vocabulary work to increase comprehension, to write more clearly, to communicate well, and to have a more in-depth understanding of words. The words came from various places, content areas, student choice, and the books read in literature groups. A strong emphasis was given to word parts (e.g., base words and affixes). There was work with the dictionary and thesaurus, but the goal was for students to be able to understand and use the words within a given context, not give meaningless definitions. The students who performed at the third grade level or lower on the informal reading inventory were involved with word work related to more basic elements of phonics (e.g., word chunks and sight words). They worked with a computer related program, which emphasized this type of word work and provided reading material at this level.

At the end of the year when students took the district tests, of the 78 students 69 passed the test. Of the nine that did not pass, four did not bother to come to the exam. With regard to final grades given by the teacher, 67 of the 78 students received passing grades. Five of these students did not pass because of their attendance. The four students that did not come to the exam are included in this number. Three of the remaining students that failed had tested at the second grade level on the informal reading test. Besides starting with a lower reading ability, these students were still learning English. Therefore, the test was not appropriate for them. So despite the fact that Dottie did not follow the program, the majority of her students succeeded in her class.

Additionally, many of the students had found books that they liked to read so they were reading for their own purposes, not just because they were required to read for a class.

While the findings and results of this study are positive, there are limitations. Due to the nature of a high school schedule and the number of students seen by each teacher, it is not always feasible for the teacher to administer an informal reading inventory. The sample size is small; therefore the results cannot be generalized. The principal knew Dottie's abilities and trusted her judgment to do what was best for the students. Not all teachers have this relationship, so Dottie's case is more the exception than the rule. Also, not all teachers have Dottie's knowledge base or conviction so her actions may not work for all teachers.

Final Thoughts

When school districts opt to have developmental reading classes at the secondary level, they must be mindful of the decisions that they make about the curriculum. Students at this level have already experienced lack of success. Adolescents are at the age where they are more conscious of what others think about them. Thus, the curriculum that is used must meet their learning needs while promoting their self-esteem. The individual that is closest to them, their teacher, must make decisions about the curriculum.

In this instance, Dottie made decisions about the curriculum that were appropriate for her students. She used methods that matched her beliefs about teaching and that adhered to effective teaching practices. Her students were fortunate to have a knowledgeable teacher who was willing to defy a district mandate.

References

Allen, J. (1995). *It's never too late: Leading adolescents to lifelong literacy.* Portsmouth, NH: Heinemann.

Allen, J. (2000). *Yellow brick roads: Shared and guided paths to independent reading 412.* Portland, ME: Stenhouse.

Allen, J. (2002). *On the same page: Shared reading beyond the primary grades.* Portland, ME: Stenhouse.Allington, R. L. (2000). *What really matters for struggling readers: Designing research-based programs.* Menlo Park, CA: Longman.

Alvermann, D. (2002). Effective literacy instruction for adolescents. *Journal of Literacy Research, 34,* 189-208.

Atwell, N. (2002)*In the middle: New understanding about writing, reading, and Learning* (2nd ed.). Portsmouth, NH: Boynton/Cook.

Baumann, J. F., & Kameenui, E. J. (1991). Research on vocabulary instruction: Ode to

Voltaire. In J. Flood, J. M. Jensen, D. Lapp, & J. R. Squire (Eds.), *Handbook on teaching the English language arts* (pp. 604-32). Hillsdale, NJ: Erlbaum.

Beers, K. (2002). *When kids can't read, what teachers can do: A guide for teachers 6-12.* Portsmouth, NH: Heinemann.

Bullock, R. (Ed.). (1998). *Why workshop? Changing course in 7-12 English.* York, ME: Stenhouse.

Fisher, D. (2001). "We're moving on up": Creating a schoolwide literacy effort in an urban high school. *Journal of Adolescent & Adult Literacy, 45*(2), 92- 101.

Krashen, S., & McQuillan, J. (1996). *The case of later intervention: Once a good reader, always a good reader.* Culver City, CA: Language Education Associates.

Leslie, L., & Caldwell, J. (2001). *Qualitative reading inventory-3.* New York: Longman.

Meyer, R. J. (2002). *Phonics exposed.* Mahwah, NJ: Lawrence Erlbaum Associates.

Nagel, G. K. (1998). *The Tao of Teaching: The special meaning of the Tao Te Ching as relating to the art of teaching.* Pomona, CA: Plume.

Nagy, W. (1988). *Teaching vocabulary to improve reading comprehension.* Newark, DE: International Reading Association.

National Reading Panel. (1999). *Report of the National Reading Panel: Teaching children to read. Report of the subgroups.* Washington, DC: National Institute of Child Health and Human Development.

Pavonetti, L. M., Brimmer, K. M., & Cipielewski, J. F. (2002). Accelerated Reader: What are the lasting effects on the reading habits of middle school students exposed to Accelerated Reader in elementary grades? *Journal of Adolescent & Adult Literacy, 46,* 300–311.

Peterson, C. L., Burke, M. K., & Segura, D. (1999). Computer-based practice for developmental reading: Medium and message. *Journal of Developmental Education, 22*(3), 12-14.

Postman, N., & Weingartner, C. (1969). *Teaching as a subversive activity.* New York: Dell.

Routman, R. (1996). *Literacy at the crossroads: Crucial talk about reading, writing, and other teaching dilemmas.* Portsmouth, NH: Heinemann.

Tovani, C. (2000). *I read it, but I don't get it: Comprehension strategies for adolescents.* Portland, ME: Stenhouse Publishers.

SUMMER READING PROGRAMS: PERCEPTIONS OF A UNIVERSITY FRESHMAN READING EXPERIENCE

Staci Stone
Bonnie Higginson
Laura Liljequist

Murray State University

Abstract

Summer reading programs for college freshmen have a number of benefits, including introducing students to academic life in higher education and conveying the importance of reading. Despite the proliferation of such programs on college campuses in the United States, there is little empirical evidence regarding the actual benefits to students. This chapter provides a brief history of summer reading programs and describes the planning, implementation, and assessment of such a program at a regional public university. Based on the assessment of the inaugural year of the program, this study suggests criteria for success of similar summer reading programs.

Many campuses have implemented common book or common reading experiences for students in recent years, but research on these programs at the university level is deficient. While we do see current events articles, such as the extensive coverage of the controversy about the University of North Carolina's summer reading program (debate about text selection that occurred on that campus for two consecutive years) in publications such as the *Chronicle of Higher Education* and *USA Today*, scholarly articles are lacking (Marklin, 2002; O'Connor, 2003). This article will help fill that gap by providing information about the history of summer reading programs, describing such a program at Murray State University, and explaining the assessment of that program's inaugural year.

Summer Reading Programs

The absence of research on this topic belies the popularity of summer reading programs. These reading programs began at private institutions, where they have been used for decades. Miami University in Ohio implemented a reading program twenty-three years ago, and other public institutions then adopted similar programs (Stanfield, 1999). According to the list available from the National Resource Center for the First-Year Experience and Students in Transition, 42 colleges and universities nationwide have summer reading programs (*Institutions reporting first-year summer reading programs*, 2004). This list was last updated in October 2004, but the list available previously included 77 institutions, so it is likely that there is not a reliable source about the number of schools that feature common readings. However, since colleges and universities have become increasingly interested in assisting students with the transition from high school to college and in retaining those students, it is likely that more than 42 institutions have implemented summer reading programs.

A major reason for the adoption of summer reading programs is that administrators are interested in the way that common reading programs establish learning communities, which help improve retention. As Gabelnick, MacGregor, Matthews, & Smith (1990), point out, "At the developmental level or as part of an honors program, learning communities can become a delivery system for academic excellence. Students rise to the occasion of learning communities: they perform better, accomplish more, drop out less" (p. 90). A few institutions, like California Polytechnic University, have campus-wide programs, in which all students, faculty, and staff are encouraged to read and discuss a common text (*PREFACE*, 2004). Many institutions, however, use summer reading programs that target first year students so that they are immediately members of a learning community when they step onto campus. For example, at Penn State Capital College, the purpose of the summer reading program is to "encourage intellectual interaction among students" (Jones, 2004). The primary purpose of summer reading programs at most universities and colleges is to provide a common experience, the foundation for a learning community. (e.g., *About the summer reading program*, n.d.; *Carolina summer reading program*, 2004; *NAU summer reading program*, 2004; *Summer reading 2004*, 2004; *The summer reading program*, n.d.; *Summer reading program*, 2004).

Summer reading programs are multipurpose. In addition to providing a common reading experience, thereby creating a common academic community, summer reading programs may be used to

- introduce students to college academics;
- improve reading ability;
- provide the opportunity for interaction with an author;
- assess reading and writing ability;

- encourage interaction among students, faculty, and staff; and
- promote habits of life-long reading and learning (*The 2004 summer reading program*, 2004; *Champlain College summer reading program*, 2003; Campbell, 2002; *Freshman summer reading project*, 2003; *Summer reading program*, 2004).

Klein (2002) stated that summer reading programs "introduce students to the behaviors and expectations of college, increase the interaction between student and faculty and among students to enhance community, integrate students into the larger campus culture, and set an academic tone for new students" (p. 11). Additionally, common reading experiences convey the importance of reading and the social dimensions of literacy.

Program Assessment

Most of the research on summer reading concerns programs for elementary and secondary students. That research recommends summer reading programs because they can increase vocabulary test scores and enhance reading achievement (Heyns, 1978; Miltenberger, Phillips, MacDonald, & Triplett, 2002; Paris, 2001). The proliferation of summer reading programs at colleges and universities in the last decade indicates that such programs must also be successful for college students. However, only one report provides empirical data about the assessment of a university's summer reading program.

According to the Policy Center on the First Year of College, the New Student Reading Initiative at Cornell University has been assessed (*New student reading initiative*, 2003). This program, begun in 2001, required all incoming students (freshmen and transfer students) to read a common book (Jared Diamond's *Guns, Germs, and Steel: The Fates of Human Societies*, 1999). The purpose of this program was to "provide new students with a shared purpose for academic exchange with each other, returning students, and faculty; provide a more intellectual basis for interaction outside the classroom; and provide a common intellectual experience" (par. 3). Students were also encouraged to attend events such as Diamond's public lecture, a community panel discussion, and small group discussions. The New Student Reading Initiative was assessed through three surveys: the Student Questionnaire, the Facilitator Questionnaire, and the First-Year Writing Seminar Instructor Questionnaire (2003). These questionnaires are not available in the report. According to the program's organizers, the results of this assessment revealed "in the main, the goals of the program were achieved and results encouraging" (par. 16).

Apparently, Texas Tech University has also assessed its summer reading program, which is part of the university's First Year Experience program (*Summer reading program*, 2004). Information describing these programs offers data about student satisfaction: in 2003, 72% of students "said they would recommend SRP [summer reading program] to other first year students" (par. 7). The assessment data from these universities indicate that, perhaps, institutions are beginning to assess summer reading programs; however, the assessment methods and results should be made available publicly.

The Freshman Reading Experience at Murray State University

In 2002, Murray State University initiated its Freshman Reading Experience, a summer reading program that encourages all freshmen to read the selected text prior to arrival on campus for Fall semester. The Freshman Reading Experience was implemented in order to

- provide a common academic experience for incoming freshmen;
- introduce students to intellectual life at Murray State University;
- create a greater sense of community among students, faculty, and staff;
- emphasize the value of reading; and
- establish the connection between reading and other cultural events on campus (*Freshman reading experience*, 2004).

The text was selected by a committee comprising faculty from various academic disciplines; this committee identified several possible books that would address the characteristics and needs of Murray State University's freshman student population that included succeeding in the face of obstacles, having a southern/rural heritage, coming from troubled family situations, being first generation college students, finding inspiration and appropriate positive role models, setting goals, adapting to new places and people, and recognizing and dealing with issues created by diversity. The committee ultimately chose *All Over But the Shoutin'* by Rick Bragg (1997), a former journalist for the *New York Times*. This memoir describes Bragg's experiences of growing up in an impoverished family in the South and his personal and professional struggles to succeed as a journalist.

In addition to reading the selected text, freshmen were encouraged to participate in activities related to the book, such as, the small group discussions with First Year Leaders (upperclassmen who work with a group of freshmen). These discussions were prior to the convocation for all new students; it featured Rick Bragg and was held during Great Beginnings, a three-day program that introduces freshmen to college life, especially the academic and social dimensions. After his address, Rick Bragg dined with a select group of freshmen and held a book-signing. During the Fall and Spring semesters, many instructors of freshman English courses incorporated ideas from the book into their writing assignments for students. The Provost's Office also sponsored a campus-wide essay contest—advertised under the tagline, "All Over but the Writin'"—featuring five categories with monetary awards. Additionally, several campus-wide programs addressed themes in the book. For example, Cinema International opened its fall season with the Coen brothers' *O Brother Where Art Thou?* (2000), featuring gospel music similar to that described by Bragg;, and the Women's Center sponsored a lecture by Mary Angela Shaughnessy, an author of *Sisters in Pain: Battered Women Fight Back* (2000), focusing on domestic abuse, an issue raised in Bragg's book.

While comments by faculty and students seemed to indicate that the inaugural Freshman Reading Experience was well received, empirical data about students' perceptions of this program were needed. Our assessment documents student participation in and perception of the Freshman Reading Experience, but it does not directly address students' literacy learning progress.

Purpose of the Present Study

Freshman reading programs are growing in popularity and number across the United States, yet little research on their effectiveness or value for students exists. Therefore, the purpose of this study was to investigate student perceptions of a freshman reading program, in order to improve future programs.

Method

Materials

The researchers developed a questionnaire designed to tap students' opinions concerning their experiences with the Freshman Reading Experience (see Appendix). Items addressed topics such as whether or not the book was required reading for one or more courses, the overall value of the Freshman Reading Experience, student opinions concerning the author's speech, and the perceived difficulty level of the book. Eighteen items asked participants to respond to questions concerning their overall experience or general opinions concerning the book or speaker. The questionnaire contained eighteen additional items (to which participants responded on a six-point Likert scale), which provided quantitative data on satisfaction.

Procedure

Near the end of the spring semester in the pilot year of the program, instructors teaching freshman composition courses were contacted by the researchers and asked to allow ten minutes of class time for the administration of the questionnaire; 6 of the 27 instructors of English 101–Composition, English 102–Composition and Research, and English 104–Honors Composition and Research participated. The researchers followed scripted instructions and student participation was both voluntary and anonymous. In ten sections of English 101, English 102, and English 104, completed questionnaires were collected from 210 students, a vast majority of whom were freshmen, representing approximately 15% of the freshman class, the target percentage set by the researchers.

Results
Descriptive Statistics
Only ten percent of those surveyed indicated that they did not know about the Freshman Reading Experience. Most (62%) found out about the Freshman Reading Experience when they attended Summer Orientation and many (49%) learned about the project from an informational letter sent to incoming students. Eighty percent of the participants indicated that they had read the book, and 67% read it during the summer. Eighty-two percent of those who read the book stated that *All Over But the Shoutin'* was at the right reading level, and 75% percent felt that the length of the book was appropriate.

When asked if the book had been required reading for a course during the academic year, 72% of the participants stated that it was required. Of those for whom the book was required reading, 95% said that the book was discussed in class, and 98% were given assignments related to the book.

Several campus-wide events were planned during the fall semester of the pilot year and were designed to connect to the primary themes of the book. Participants were asked about their attendance at these events. Fewer than 23% attended any of the four events on campus.

One question asked participants to identify persons with whom they had discussed the book. As expected, the most common group identified for discussion was faculty at 55%. However, 47% of participants discussed the book with other students, 30% with friends, and 27% with family members.

Open-ended Questions
Fifty percent of the participants heard Rick Bragg, the author, speak in August. The 110 who heard him speak were asked three open-ended questions. These qualitative responses were recorded on index cards and sorted independently by the three researchers to establish categories and to provide interrater reliability. Consensus among the three researchers was high and yielded seven categories. The most prevalent category was "good speaker/ interesting" (46 responses). Other categories were as follows: "connecting author to book" (22 responses), "seeing an author" (13), "neutral, unimpressed" (10), "inspiring/life experiences" (9), "funny" (7), and "miscellaneous" (3). Examples of written responses were: "Excellent speaker, very entertaining and enjoyable," "It was really a cool idea to have all freshmen read the book and then see the author," and "I loved the book, so seeing the author in person talk about his experiences was a great opportunity."

When asked about the perceived purpose of the Freshman Reading Experience through another open-ended question, responses reflected both positive and negative reactions to the program. Of the 182 qualitative responses, 45 stated that the purpose was to "give students a shared experience" while 34 stated that it was to "enhance reading." Other positive perceptions included "prepare students for college life" (31) and "prepare students for academics" (8). However, some respondents indicated that the purpose was to "waste time" (10) or to "raise money" (3). Perhaps the most surprising result to this question was that 31 participants wrote "don't know." One participant commented that "the purpose is to give all freshmen something in common for them to start conversations that might lead to friendships" while another stated that the purpose was "to open our minds to new reading and new material we probably wouldn't read on our own."

Thirty-eight percent of the participants indicated that the Freshman Reading Experience was of value to them while 62% percent found little or no value in the experience. When asked to elaborate, 140 provided a reason. These were again categorized and coded by the researchers in similar fashion to that described above. Those who found the experience to be of value fell into four primary categories: "liked the book/like to read" (26), "learned a lot/personal growth" (13), "helped with classes" (11), and "common experience" (6). Negative reactions fell into three primary categories: "did not participate" (27), "didn't like book/don't like to read" (25), and "didn't use in class/waste of time" (15). Written responses by participants included the following comments: "I didn't enjoy the book or feel that it gave me a similar experience with my fellow freshmen. In my English class we discussed it very little and I was frustrated" and "I learned that there are many people less fortunate than me and Rick Bragg overcame that to become an amazing writer."

Satisfaction Measure

Further study of students' satisfaction with the Freshman Reading Experience was based on the 18-item Likert-scaled satisfaction measure developed for this questionnaire. The satisfaction measure demonstrated acceptable internal consistency reliability (Cronbach's alpha = 0.81). Based on psychometric analysis, three items were deleted; two due to poor item-total correlations and a third as it did not contribute to any of the scale's four factors. Factor analysis using oblique rotation yielded four factors from the final 15 items. Oblique rotation was selected as it was expected that the factors would be correlated. The final four factors were as follows: (a) program/experience factor (7 items such as "This program should be continued next year", "More teachers should have used the book in class"), (b) book factor (3 items such as "I would never suggest this book to anyone"), (c) author factor (3 items such as "Seeing the author speak was the best part of the reading experience"), and (d) discussion factor (2 items such as "My Freshman Year Leader read the book and talked about it.").

Total satisfaction scores were then calculated as the sum of the final 15 items. Four factor scores were also derived by taking the mean of the subset of items on each factor. Total satisfaction and factor scores were then correlated with other variables of interest.

Based on these correlational analyses, there were several interesting relationships uncovered. For example, satisfaction was negatively correlated with both reading level ($r = -.32$, $p < .05$) and length ($r = -.35$, $p < .01$), such that satisfaction increased as book length and reading level decreased. This finding suggests that students enjoy the experience more when they do not find the material too challenging.

Satisfaction was positively correlated with the book having been required for at least one class ($r = .29$, $p < .05$), and respondents were more likely to value the experience if the book had been required for a class ($r = .19$, $p < .05$). Participants who reported that they valued the experience also reported overall higher satisfaction ($r = .69$, $p < .0001$). This result indicates that having professors actively incorporate the selected text into their courses is positively associated with the participants seeing the relevance of this experience.

Higher scores on the "book factor" of the satisfaction scale were correlated with having seen the author speak ($r = .36$, $p < .0001$) as well as with valuing the experience ($r = .51$, $p < .0001$). This correlation suggests that bringing the author to campus is related to the success of such programs.

Discussion

Although the current study provides insights into student perceptions of only one book and author, it does suggest criteria for success of summer reading programs similar to the Freshman Reading Experience. Based on the results of the study, the following factors appear to be critical components associated with summer reading programs:

1. Make the purpose of the program clear to incoming students as well as to campus stakeholders. If students are uncertain about the purpose or if they feel burdened by the request to read a book during the summer, then it will be difficult for the program to be considered successful. Only 38% of the respondents found the Freshman Reading Experience to be of value to them. Negative attitudes toward reading, inexperience in reading a book without guidance from a teacher, and confusion concerning the purpose of the program may have been contributing factors. To be truly successful, summer reading programs must become part of the overall culture of the campus community, and the purpose of such programs needs to be very clear from the outset.

2. Consider both length and readability of potential choices. The book used for the present study appears to have been appropriate for the vast majority of respondents. Moreover, the correlational finding that satisfaction increased as book length and difficulty decreased indicates that shorter, easier book selections will result in more successful programs.

3. Insure that instructors in freshman-level courses use the book for course assignments and class discussions. Results from the present study indicate that students were more satisfied with the Freshman Reading Experience if one or more of their instructors actually used the book in class. From our perspective, it is understandable that students would consider the Freshman Reading Experience a "waste of time" if they read the book during the summer and were never asked to discuss or write about it in a class, particularly since they were led to believe through letters and other communications that reading the book was required. Involving faculty from appropriate academic areas in the selection process is the first step in this process. Providing faculty with instructional resources such as discussion questions and assignments may also facilitate widespread use of the book.

4. If financial resources permit, bring the author of the chosen book to campus to speak to all incoming students. The vast majority of respondents who heard Rick Bragg speak had positive reactions to the experience. Many commented on the value of seeing a "real" author. His humor and ability to connect with the students helped make the inaugural year of the Freshman Reading Experience a success and is evidenced by the strong correlation between respondent's satisfaction and valuing of the experience with having heard the author speak. Therefore, prior to choosing the reading, book selection committees should learn as much as possible about potential authors and their ability to engage an audience.

Several limitations to the current study should be described. First, although all instructors of freshman composition courses were contacted and asked to permit the researchers to administer the questionnaire, only six volunteered to do so. The research was conducted near the end of the Spring semester, and many instructors may have been reluctant to participate because of course demands. Also, it is possible that those instructors who volunteered were more likely to have used the book for discussion and assignments during the semester, thus skewing the results more positively. Therefore, results should be interpreted with caution. Second, some of the students who participated in the study were not freshmen; thus, these upperclassmen enrolled in freshman composition were less likely to be familiar with the Freshman Reading Experience and its purposes. This may account for the relatively high number of "don't know" responses to the question pertaining to the purpose of the program. Finally, some items yielded conflicting responses from participants. For instance, when asked about the value of the Freshman Reading Experience (item #18), a number of respondents indicated that they enjoyed the book or hearing the author speak, but that the experience itself was not of value.

Implementing a summer reading program is a rather daunting task. Such programs require university-wide involvement, both in the book selection process and in the implementation phase. The study described here provides insights regarding student perceptions of one program, yet more research is needed to truly evaluate the effectiveness of summer reading programs in terms of student achievement and retention. Do these programs increase and enhance interaction between students and faculty? Do they set an academic tone for new students? Finally, do summer reading programs truly convey the importance of reading and the social dimensions of literacy? We certainly hope so, but future studies will need to address these issues before we can determine the real value of summer reading programs.

References

The 2004 summer reading program, (2004, August 30). Retrieved October 16, 2004 from Keene State College, Diversity and Multiculturalism Web site: http://www.keene.edu/dc/summerreading.cfm.

About the summer reading program, (n.d.). Retrieved October 16, 2004 from Miami University Web site: http://www.units.muohio.edu/srp/aboutsrp.html.

Beattie. L. E., Shaughnessy, M. A., & Beattie, E. L. (2000). *Sisters in pain: Battered women fight back.* Lexington, KY: University Press of Kentucky.

Bragg, R. (1997). *All over but the shoutin'.* New York: Vintage Books.

Campbell, K. (2002, July). *First year seminar.* Retrieved October 16, 2004 from Hamline University, College of Liberal Arts Web site: http://web.hamline.edu/cla/academics/firstyear/2001summerreading.htm.

Carolina summer reading program, (2004, August 26). Retrieved October 16, 2004 from University of North Carolina at Chapel Hill Web site: http://www.unc.edu/srp/index.html.

Champlain College summer reading program, (2003). Retrieved October 16, 2004 from Champlain College Web site: http://www.champlain.edu/summerbook/index.php.

Coen, J., & Coen, E. (Producers). (2000). *O brother, where art thou?* [Motion picture]. United States: Touchstone Video.

Database of program/strategy summaries for the support of first-year students at *doctoral/research-extensive universities,* (2003). Retrieved October 16, 2004 from Brevard College, Policy Center on the First Year of College Web site: http://www.brevard.edu/fyc/ruproject/data.htm.

Diamond, J. (1999). *Guns, germs, and steel: The fates of human societies.* New York: W. W. Norton Publishing.

Gabelnick, F., MacGregor, J., Matthews, R. S., & Smith, B. L. (1990). Learning communities: Creating connections among students, faculty, and disciplines. *New Directions for Teaching and Learning, 41,* 95-102.

Freshman reading experience, (2004). Retrieved October 16, 2004 from Murray State University Web site: http://www.murraystate.edu/fre/program.htm.

Freshman summer reading project, (2002). Retrieved October 16, 2004 from Temple University Web site: http://www.temple.edu/summerreading/.

Heyns, B. (1978). Summer *learning and the effects of schooling.* New York: Academic Press.

Jones, B. (2004, April 28). *Capital College's summer reading program 2004 presents.* Retrieved October 16, 2004 from Penn State Capital College, Summer Reading Program Web site: http://www.cl.psu.edu/sreads/pact/index.htm.

Institutions reporting first-year summer reading programs, (2004, October). Retrieved October 16, 2004 from University of South Carolina, National Resource Center for the First-Year Experience and Students in Transition Web site: http://www.sc.edu/fye/resources/fyr/reading/read01.html.

Klein, T. (2002). The search for a college commons. *About Campus, 7,* 9-16.

Marklin, M. B. (2002, August 5). Assigned reading of book on the Koran spurs rights lawsuit against UNC. *USA Today,* p. D-6.

Miltenberger, M. W., Phillips, R. H., McDonald, B. P. & Triplett, S. K. (2002). Small groups and mentors foster relationships during summer reading program—A qualitative analysis. *Journal of Higher Education Outreach and Engagement, 7,* 101-110.

NAU summer reading program, (2004, October 15). Retrieved October 16, 2004 from Northern Arizona University, Office of the Vice Provost for Undergraduate Studies Web site: http://jan.ucc.nau.edu/~d-ugstdy/uc101/student/srp.html.

New student reading initiative, (2003). Retrieved October 16, 2004 from Brevard College, Policy Center on the First Year of College Web site: http://www.brevard.edu/fyc/ruproject/cornelluniv/newstudentreading.htm.

Nist, S. L., & Simpson, M. L. (2000). College studying. In M. L. Kamil, P. B. Mosenthal, P. D. Pearson, & R. Barr (Eds.), *Handbook of Reading Research, Volume III.* (pp. 645-666). Mahwah, NJ: Erlbaum Associates.

O'Connor, E. (2003). Misreading what reading is for [Electronic version]. *Chronicle of Higher Education, 50* (2), B-20.

Paris, S. (2001). Designing and assessing summer reading programs. Paper presented at the 2001 CIERA Summer Institute. Paper retrieved October 16, 2004 from http://www.ciera.org/library/presos/2001/index.html.

PREFACE, (2004, September 22). Retrieved October 16, 2004 from California Polytechnic State University Web site: http://www.preface.calpoly.edu/.

Stanfield, D. (1999, August 13). From Homer to Krakauer. *Chronicle of Higher Education, 45,* A 43-44.

Summer reading 2004, (2004, June 17). Retrieved October 16, 2004 from Connecticut College Web site: http://www.conncoll.edu/academics/summer-reading/list.html.

The summer reading program, (n.d.). Retrieved October 16, 2004 from Meredith College, First Year Experience Web site: http://www.meredith.edu/students/fye/srp.htm.I

Summer reading program, (2004, January 7). Retrieved October 16, 2004 from Saint Francis University Web site: http://www.francis.edu/academic/GenEd/summerreading.shtm.

Summer reading program, (2004, April 12). Retrieved October 16, 2004 from University of Akron, New Student Orientation Web site: http://www.uakron.edu/college/univcoll/depts/orientation/reading.php.

Summer reading program, (2004, September 15). Retrieved October 16, 2004 from Texas Tech University, First Year Experience Web site: http://www.fye.ttu.edu/summer_reading_program.asp.

Appendix. Freshman Reading Survey

I. Respond to the following questions:

1. How did you find out about the Freshman Reading Experience? (Check all that apply.)

   ____ Letter sent during the summer

   ____ Summer Orientation

   ____ Great Beginnings

   ____ My Freshman Year Leader

   ____ I did not know about the Freshman Reading Experience

   ____ Other – Please explain

2. Did you read *All Over But the Shoutin'*?

   ____ No, I did not read the book. (If no, skip to #6)

   ____ Yes (If yes, answer #3, #4, #5)

   3. When did you read the book?

      ____ During the summer

      ____ During Great Beginnings

      ____ During the fall semester on my own

      ____ During the fall semester as required reading for a class

   4. The reading level of the book was

      ____ too difficult for me

      ____ at the right level for me

      ____ too easy for me

   5. The book's length was

      ____ too long

      ____ appropriate

      ____ too short

6. Has the book been required reading for a course you have taken (either last semester or this semester)?

   ____ No (If no, skip to #10)

   ____ Yes (If yes, answer #7, #8, #9)

   7. Prefix and course number or course name:

   8. Was the book discussed in class? ____ Yes ____ No

   9. Were you given assignments related to the book? ____ Yes ____ No

10. Where did you purchase the book?

    ____ MSU Bookstore

    ____ Online

    ____ Other bookstore

    ____ I have not purchased the book

    ____ I borrowed or shared the book

11. Were you aware that students in financial need could get a free copy of the book?

_____ No (If no, skip to #13)

_____ Yes (If yes, answer #12)

12. Did you take advantage of this and get a free copy of the book?

_____ Yes _____ No

13. Did you hear Rick Bragg, the author of *All Over But the Shoutin'* speak on Monday, August 19th?

_____ No (If no, skip to #15)

_____ Yes (If yes, answer #14)

14. What was your reaction?

15. Indicate whether you have attended other events during the semester that are connected to the book. (Check all that apply.)

_____ Film: "O Brother, Where Art Thou?"

_____ Play: "Our Town"

_____ Art Exhibit: "Behind the Walls"

_____ Lecture: "Sisters in Pain: Domestic Abuse"

_____ Other

16. Indicate with whom you have discussed the book.

(Check all that apply.)

_____ Your Freshman Year Leader

_____ MSU students

_____ Faculty members

_____ Your friends

_____ Your family

_____ Other

17. In your opinion, what is the purpose of the Freshman Reading Experience?

18. Was the Freshman Reading Experience of value to you?

_____ No. (Please explain.)

_____ Yes. (Please explain.)

II. Circle the number that most closely represents your opinion:

Strongly DISAGREE		Neither Agree nor Disagree		Strongly AGREE		N/A

a. Expecting students to read a book before starting classes is unfair.

1	2	3	4	5	6	7

b. Seeing the author speak was the best part of the reading experience.

1	2	3	4	5	6	7

c. One or more faculty members discussed the book in class.

1   2   3   4   5   6   7

d. I did not like the book.

1   2   3   4   5   6   7

e. My Freshman Year Leader said reading the book was not important.

1   2   3   4   5   6   7

f. Listening to the author helped me to understand the book.

1   2   3   4   5   6   7

g. Being asked to read a book before starting college helped me understand expectations as a college student.

1   2   3   4   5   6   7

h. I found the book interesting.

1   2   3   4   5   6   7

i. This program should be continued next year.

1   2   3   4   5   6   7

j. My Freshman Year Leader read the book and talked about it.

1   2   3   4   5   6   7

k. More teachers should have used the book in class.

1   2   3   4   5   6   7

l. I found the book difficult to read.

1   2   3   4   5   6   7

m. There is no need for the author to come to campus.

1   2   3   4   5   6   7

n. My Freshman Year Leader helped me be interested in the book.

1   2   3   4   5   6   7

o. There should have been more events that related to the book.

1   2   3   4   5   6   7

p. My family enjoyed the book.

1   2   3   4   5   6   7

q. I would never suggest this book to anyone.

1   2   3   4   5   6   7

r. Talking about this book was a way for me to meet people during Great Beginnings.

1   2   3   4   5   6   7

THE POWER OF
TECHNOLOGY AND LITERACY

READING PROFESSIONALS LEARN ON-LINE: USING THREADED DISCUSSIONS TO LEARN ABOUT THREADED DISCUSSIONS

Judy S. Richardson
Virginia Commonwealth University

Charlene Fleener
Old Dominion University

Linda Thistlewaite
Western Illinois University

Abstract

This project is a joint venture ABOUT using threaded discussions for teachers studying about reading instruction by USING threaded discussions in an on-line environment. The threaded discussions, using the course authoring system, Blackboard, generated five threads over three months, and involved instructional examples at three different state universities. The three colleagues learned from one another in a distance-learning environment and applied what they learned to their technology-based teaching. The purpose is to describe and provide commentary on discoveries made for instruction and communication during the project. Threaded discussions are presented as part of the act of communication, set in the context of transactional distance theory and social constructivism. The power of adult learning theory (Knowles, 1990) where adults learn from each other about something they have purposefully selected, construct their own learning environment, and consider each other as equal partners in the learning is supported by the outcomes of this collaborative exploration.

Literature Review
The Nature of Communication and Threaded Discussions

Threaded discussions are a series of responses to a topic, conducted in an online environment. Typically, they occur in conjunction with a distance learning community where learners do not meet in synchronous—"real"—

time, but communicate asynchronously–at different times. Knowlton and Knowlton (2001) define such discussions as "the asynchronous (out of time) exchange of messages using a bulletin board or email software" (p. 39). Course authoring systems such as Web CT and Blackboard build such threaded discussion opportunities into their software and many instructors have begun to make use of them for student interchange. Course authoring systems provide electronic structure and a format for a variety of instructional applications and for using instructional media such as text files, online examinations, gradebook files, audio and video files, and threaded discussion sessions. Threaded discussions are a relatively new form of communication in instructional settings. The traditional view of communication and collaboration assumes face-to-face encounters. Online communication, however, is gaining in popularity. Learners are beginning to seek learning environments where they can work collaboratively over time and space in a variety of settings (Hanley, 2001). Threaded discussions provide such an environment.

All communication is considered to be a social act. According to Mead (1934),

> A social act may be defined as one in which the occasion or stimulus which sets free an impulse is found in the character or conduct of a living form that belongs to the proper environment of the living form whose impulse it is . . . [It belongs] to the class of acts which involves the co-operation of more than one individual, and whose object as defined by the act . . . [or] social object . . . A social object [is] one that answers to all the parts of the complex act, though these parts are found in the conduct of different individuals. The object of the acts is then found in the life-process of the group, not in those of the separate individuals alone (p. 7).

Mead implies that a social act is something that originates from one individual, but requires the reflection and recognition by others that this act is indeed social. A social act is dependent upon a receptive group as well as the actions of individuals within that group. Mead's definition applies to threaded discussions. One person presents the topic in an online forum, and, if others accept and respond to it in that online forum, communication has occurred.

Transactional Distance and Threaded Discussions

Despite the arguments provided by some researchers (Roszak, 1986) contending that Internet interactions are not social and do not fit the requirements and definition of social interactions, many researchers (McDonald, 2002; McComb, 1993; Jonassen, Carr, & Yueh, 1998) believe otherwise. They feel that emotional responses and gestures can be experienced online and that social interactions can actually occur more easily in an online situation. For instance, one researcher conducted surveys of focus groups in both online and face-to-face situations and found that electronic discussions allow for a more open discussion and a higher comfort level within the groups, leading to more openness in the expression of individual opinions, in particular those regarding sensitive subjects. He also noted that participants who tend to be more passive in face-to-face interactions tend to take a more active role in electronic discussions (Tse, 1999). McDonald pointed out in her study that "In addition to facilitating the construction of new knowledge, online education supports social negotiation of ideas, providing multiple perspectives on any given topic and access to a vast array of information"(p. 13). Moore (1972, 1980) defined transactional distance as the psychological and communications space that occurs when teachers and learners are separated by distance. This separation can profoundly affect both teaching and learning. A psychological and communications space now has to be crossed, a space of potential misunderstanding between the inputs of the instructor and those of the learner.

The Theory of Transactional Distance (Moore, 1980) was a seminal theory in distance education. Before the existence of distance education, people took physical proximity between the learner and teacher for granted; as long as the students were in the same room as the teacher, they assumed the students were learning. However, with the emergence of distance educational forms such as the correspondence school, and radio and TV courses, physical distance between the teacher and students grew, and with that distance came challenges as well as opportunities. Did the physical distance between the teacher and learners mean the quality of the learning program was worse? Moore's theory examined the nature of 'distance' and suggested that physical distance was an indication of a barrier to communication and understanding, but did not always have to be. Especially in programs where physical distance could be overcome by means of communication technology, obstacles to learning came from other sources. The theory implies that learning does not necessarily take place when learners are gathered in the same place, nor is it necessarily true that learning cannot take place when people are physically apart (Moore, 1980). In fact the social distance that occurs within an online threaded discussion may provide a greater sense of democracy for a discussion by reducing access to potential prejudicial triggers that can arise related to physical appearance, race, gender, and even tone of voice (McComb, 1993). Moore found that the transactional distance that existed in a learner's situation is what determined the outcome.

Moore (1991) recognized that there are three kinds of interaction: (a) student-student, (b) student-teacher, and (c) student-content. In our study, the interaction was essentially student-student, with each of the three investigators learning from each other without teacher-like authority; each taught the others and learned about the content of threaded discussions and their possibilities as well. Knowlton and Knowlton (2001) also discuss the interactive nature of this interaction when they suggest that threaded discussions are "more than one-way communication from teacher to student or even a conversation between teacher and students. Instead, we are suggesting a conversation among a classroom community where the contributions of both teachers and students are valued and treated as a viable contribution to an educational dialogue" (p. 39).

Threaded Discussions as a Constructivist Way of Communicating and Learning

Components of a constructivist environment include: (a) shared knowledge; (b) authentic, (c) real world tasks; (d) scaffolding; (e) cognitive apprenticeship; (f) learner control; and (g) non-linear instruction (Hanley, 2001). Constructivism is a term used to explain what happens as a learner processes information (Pearson & Stephens, 1994). Applefield, Huber, and Moallem (2000) stated "The field of education has undergone a significant shift in thinking about the nature of human learning and the conditions that best promote the varied dimensions of human learning. As in psychology, there has been a paradigm shift in designed instruction; from behaviorism to cognitivism and now to constructivism" (p. 36). The researchers call constructivism one of the most influential views of learning during the last two decades. Fosnot (1996) also called constructivism "the most current psychology of learning" (p. 65). In a constructivist model, knowledge is transmitted to learners who are building information with help from many sources (Weaver, 1994). The learner must actively construct meaning by relating new material to the known, using reasoning and developing concepts. The process is not only individual but also social, because "by articulating ideas and experience through writing, speaking, and/or visually representing, students deepen their thinking and construct and organize their understanding of new material" (Gill & Dupree, 1998, p. 95).

The Nature of Collaboration and Threaded Discussions— The New Face of Cooperative and Collaborative Learning

Constructivism, then, leads to communication and collaboration, as experienced by the three participants in this study. Forerunners in the field of cooperative learning suggested that students be assigned to teams to learn new material, with each team representing a cross-ability section of the class. Key elements were (a) face-to-face interaction, (b) positive goal interdependence, (c) individual accountability, and (d) demonstration of interpersonal and small group skills (Slavin, 1994; Johnson & Johnson, 1991). Today cooperative learning has a number of new faces: (a) teaching life skills through group activities (Williams, 1996), (b) collaborating by consulting and discussing with classmates, (c) helping one another, and seeing what others are doing with students as experts and teachers as co-learners (Turner & Dipinto, 1997), (d) preparing learners for the workplace via cooperative problems with a business frame of reference focusing on using technology (Goldsworthy, 2000), and (e) learning through service and converting classrooms into caring communities (Turner, 2003).

One other exciting face of cooperative learning is the use of online discussion groups where topics are posted and participants are invited to respond (Holt, Kleiber, Swenson, Rees, & Milton, 1998; George, 2002; Greenlaw & DeLoach, 2003; Pappas, 2002). To facilitate student learning in an online environment, the discussion moderator must create the environment, guide the process, provide points of departure, moderate the process, manage the content and create community. Facilitators need to establish ground rules and expectations, use introductions and icebreakers, and involve participants directly in the process of community creation by inviting their ideas on ways to make this happen. This computer-mediated communication is a powerful discussion tool with opportunities for broader participation, more dynamic interaction, and the creation of a sense of virtual community (Holt, et al., 1998). Electronic discussions capture the two best features of critical thinking, traditional writing assignments and in-class discussions (Greenlaw & DeLoach, 2003) and allow for organizing responses and critically looking at patterns of engagement with participant-to-participant interaction viewed as one index of individual learning. However, teachers using this format must deal with a variety of issues, including the use of prompts, quality vs. quantity of submissions, and student concern that the ideas they had wanted to share had already been posted by someone else (Wickstrom, 2003).

Both the older and the newer directions for cooperative learning have two important concepts in common. First, students take greater charge of their own learning and analyze the opinions of others as well as their own. Second, the creation and maintenance of the learning community is important and is the responsibility of both teachers and students.

Several instructors have used forms of asynchronous and synchronous communication online to facilitate constructivist discussions. Wickstrom (2003) investigated what the effects of using a threaded discussion were for her pre-service teachers. Would their discourse improve? Would their reflection increase about course topics? She found that, while a discussion board provides a different opportunity for discourse and reflection than does a class discussion, it does not necessarily ensure it. Sotillo (2002) explored the advantages of using conferencing software for discussion and critique of peer writing. The participants found many benefits in talking to each other online; they had more control over the timing of their responses, the control over organizing and tracking changes, and general levels of engagement.

Summary of the Literature Review

The literature supporting the use of threaded discussions as an instructional tool on a variety of levels brings together elements of four domains of research: (a) communication, wherein Meade's (1934) definition of communication as a social act involves at least two conversants; (b) transactional distance, wherein interaction can take place face-to-face or from a distance; (c) constructivism, wherein learners build an information base through communication in a distance environment; and (d) cooperative learning, wherein learners rely on each other in the distance environment. As a way of sharing and responding to information, threaded discussions provide a venue for the type of social interaction that occurs when communication happens between individuals and groups. As communication and ensuing social interaction takes place over time and space, the distance between participants is bridged. Both students and instructors use the discoveries and affirmations found within the interactive discussions to reshape or build understandings; and as each depends upon the others for adding to and enriching their own learning, a cooperative process is developed.

Description of the Collaboration

A threaded discussion took place in a Blackboard on-line community where each participant could enter and react to five discussion threads over a period of three months. Blackboard is one of two dominant course authoring tools used for on-line teaching—the other is WebCT. Blackboard allows teachers to provide course instructional material, on-line, that enables students and teachers to discuss important issues with one another. The participants also "visited" one on-line course being taught by one of the authors at the time of this project.

How it started

As a result of a College Reading Association (CRA) conference session presented in fall 2002 for providing a venue for collaboration among colleagues on writing projects, the three participants for this study began a discussion about how to create effective on-line discussions. The conversation between the authors showed us that we each had some information and experiences but none of us had as much knowledge and as many experiences as all three of us could generate together. It seemed logical that we create a context to frame a discussion from which each of us could learn, transcending time and distance (Knowlton & Knowlton, 2001).

The Purpose of this Collaboration

Online courses and regularly taught courses with an online component are becoming more popular at the university level. Instructors find themselves being encouraged to use a course authoring tool such as Blackboard. They find that posting information online (syllabus, project descriptions, handouts, etc.) may be the easiest component to use, but providing for online threaded discussions is more difficult. The purpose of this project was to address this more difficult component. How could instructors successfully use each other's expertise to become more proficient at creating successful threaded discussions that built constructivist learning situations for their students? The collaboration was intended to provide an avenue for collegial commentary about instructional use of online discussions.

The Collaborative Design

Five discussion topics were proposed to stimulate the on-line conversation (see Figure 1 for a view of the actual threaded discussion). The discussion topics were generated in an initial face-to-face conversation and then posted on-line where each participant entered thoughts about the discussion prompt. The five discussion topics were:

- Pros and cons of threaded discussions,
- Characteristics of a good discussion,
- Lessons we have learned,
- Issues in developing threaded discussions, and
- Tips of the trade.

Over three months, each participant was expected to visit and respond to each thread, and to the comments made by the other two participants. The focus for comments was the experience of teaching reading courses using on-line components, especially threaded discussions within those courses. (see Figure 2 for a view of one thread)

Figure 1. A View of the Threaded Discussions Site

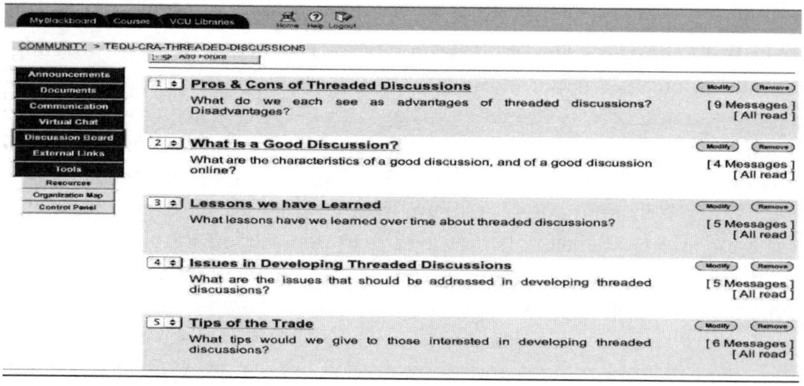

Figure 2: A View of One Discussion Thread

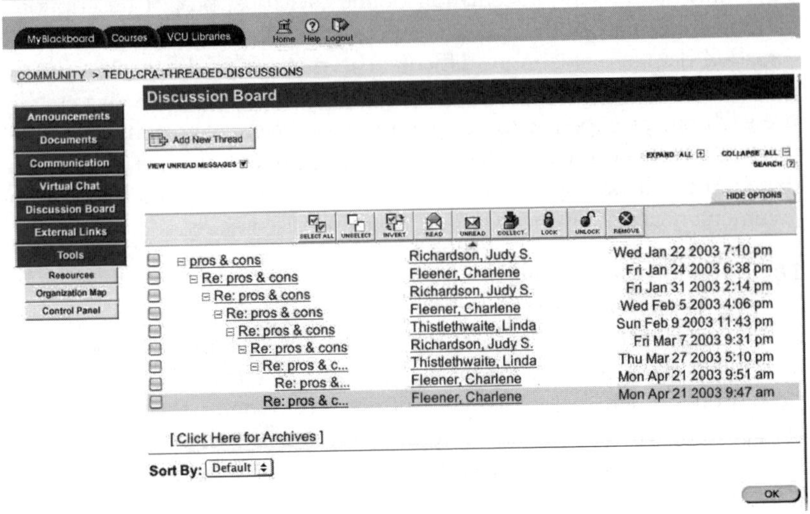

Personal Perspectives at the start of the study

These perspectives are presented as first person accounts to retain the personal and adult-to-adult relationship of the participant-learners.

Judy Richardson: I had been teaching in on-line and partially on-line environments for several years. All of the reading courses I now teach on-line or partially on-line are derived from the face-to-face versions I had taught in previous years. I have never developed a course specifically for on-line use before teaching it face-to-face; I pioneered on-line and partially on-line courses in my School of Education, but was never directed to do so—I just wanted to try this medium! I began using threaded discussions and other on-line components in my course, *Reading Instruction in the Content Areas*, over five years ago. Threaded discussions complimented course meetings because there was never enough time to discuss the many issues that occurred as content was discussed. I have since—two years ago—gone to a completely on-line environment to teach *Reading Instruction in the Content Areas*. In some discussions, students described strategies and activities with each other and commented on them. In other discussions, they commented on impressions of materials they had read and gained insights from each other. In other courses I teach (*Diagnostic Teaching of Reading in the Secondary Schools* and *Clinical Reading*), students read and react to proposed plans before face-to-face class sessions. These threaded discussions facilitate the face-to-face seminars and observations, which are crucial in clinical courses. A completely on-line environment has not worked for me in such courses. However, the asynchronous, partially on-line format has helped to prepare all students and the instructor to better use the seminar experience.

I already knew that threaded discussions can be a wonderful way to encourage interaction in an on-line course, but I was also frustrated that some discussions did not "catch on" nor did some students "catch the enthusiasm" of other students. I wanted to discover new techniques and understand how to offer my students a more effective on-line experience.

Charlene Fleener: Since entering the teaching arena at the university level six years ago as an assistant professor of reading I have found the work exciting and challenging but have experienced a steep learning curve related to technology implementation within my courses. It is my belief that the growth and widespread use of technology within our society makes the inclusion of electronic components in reading education courses a necessity. Although I had experienced teaching a televised course (*Developmental Teaching of Reading*) with auditory interaction, as well as some with both video and auditory interaction (*Survey of Reading Instruction* and *Reading to Learn Across the Curriculum*), as of the fall of 2002 I had not taught an asynchronous course. I was scheduled to teach my first one during the spring of 2003. Thus, I was very interested to ask questions and entertain suggestions my colleagues offered at the 2002 CRA conference in Florida. The course I was slated to teach, *Language Acquisition and Reading for Students with Diverse Learning Needs*, was one that I had not previously taught. I, along with my colleague, Jane Hager, wrote the curriculum for this course as an asynchronous offering. I had many questions and concerns considering both the course and the asynchronous teaching environment. I welcomed the opportunity to continue the conversation with Judy and Linda over the ensuing months narrowing our focus to a common concern, threaded discussions.

In the televised courses I had taught, e-mailing was a common venue for teacher-student interaction; however, there was no written forum for student-student interaction. Discussions in these "real-time" classes were cumbersome because of the types of technology delays that often interfere with synchronous instruction. Class size was also a factor because the one-way interaction courses often include 150 or more students located among as many as 40 sites. With such large enrollments it is not feasible for all to share ideas and opinions over the air within a class period. Threaded discussions appealed to me as a promising solution for allowing more learning to take place through social interaction in televised and traditional, as well as online courses. I also felt that my being a participant in threaded discussions might provide first-hand information and insight that would prove useful for me for helping my students deal with a new environment for learning.

Linda Thistlethwaite: Prior to participating in this project, I had taught three sections of a totally online course, *Language and Reading*, over a period of several years. This was a K-12 course (though taught once as a K-6 course for a group of teachers participating in a grant). Issues addressed included language development (including theory, expectations, and activities for both native and non-native speakers and readers of English) and language learning as it relates to reading difficulties (focusing on special populations). The course was one I developed as an online course, and, thus, I didn't have the preconception of "This is how I used to do it." In this course I had utilized online discussions by having students post messages to a discussion board. Students were directed to make the following kinds of submissions for each module of the course, choosing three different types of responses for each module: (a) a review of an Internet site, (b) a reflection on an issue/question of their choice from the course readings that had not been addressed in discussion questions that each participant answered individually but did not post for group review, (c) a reflection on a language activity they had developed and implemented for another of the course assignments, and (d) a response to the submission of another class member. Beyond the three required responses, students were encouraged to respond to the ideas presented by other class members.

By participating in this project I hoped to learn more effective ways of using online forums for discussion and learning. Internet teaching is still new enough to make collegial support imperative for success. I was in the process of developing another online course for adult educators teaching Adult Basic Education (ABE)/General Educational Development (GED) students and wanted to make it as effective as I could. Although I did have support from staff at my own university as I prepared to teach the *Language and Reading* course, I believed it would be even more helpful to interact with those from other institutions. I was also drawn to the discussion board approach for this interaction. I wondered if this type of discussion board interaction should be required of professors before they taught their first online course. Seeing how this worked from the teacher-as-learner perspective might greatly decrease concerns of educators who find themselves in the position of teaching via a medium they have never experienced as a student.

Collaborative Discoveries

Discussions occurred over three months, from January 22, 2003 to April 23, 2003. In that time, there were 29 reactions within the five discussion topics. For discussion one, nine responses were generated; for discussion two, four responses were generated; for discussion three, five responses were generated; for discussion four, five responses were generated; and for discussion five, six responses were generated. At the end of the spring 2003 semester, the conversation was ended and the three participants reviewed the five discussion topics to determine what each had learned as a result, and what themes seemed to emerge. They shared their impressions with each other and compared them to derive a common set of themes. This process is somewhat similar to triangulation (Lincoln & Guba, 1985) in that it promoted a "consistency" for the qualitative nature of this project.

Themes Generated

Five themes emerged from the five discussions, with themes overlapping the various discussions. Figure 3 shows these themes in outline form. The first was the *types of information posted* by the teacher and students on the bulletin board will influence communication generated. The instructors posted prompts for major discussion issues, provided feedback and responded to students through email and in such features as "To Sum it all Up." The students posted responses to teacher prompts, discussed their own issues, and shared practical activities and web sites in the course of their conversations.

The second theme was *responsibilities—the four "Cs."* It seemed imperative that discussion prompts and requirements for postings were *clear* (C #1). Instructions for site navigation and "how tos" were necessary. The value of discussion assignments had to be clearly explained to encourage investment. The feedback between instructor and student, and between students, had to *be communicated* (C #2) in a *timely* manner—a discussion had to maintain the immediacy that a face-to-face discussion naturally has. In addition to feedback on student responses, the announcement board tied to the threaded bulletin board can be an effective avenue for providing timely responses regarding questions about postings. To *create a community* (C #3), every participant needed to be part of the community of learners, accomplished through biographical sketches; and the audience needed to be the students rather than the instructor, with the instructor viewed as a member of this community rather than a "leader." This is supportive of the claim by Knowlton and Knowlton (2001) regarding valuing student contributions to the educational dialogue. *Creativity* (C #4) was essential in maintaining interest and viability for the discussions. This was accomplished with graphics, audio and video.

Theme three was *growth* for both students and instructors. As Tse (1999) has commented, participants are more active in electronic discussions. Discussions naturally grew better as students became more comfortable with the new discussion format; they took more responsibility for their own learning. The instructors learned to give more detailed feedback and summarize discussions to facilitate greater collective understanding. These features also helped the instructors grow in awareness of creating better face-to-face discussions and providing more support to students. This theme is consistent

Figure 3: Themes Generated

1. Types of Information
Types of information posted by the teacher on the bulletin board
a. Prompts for major discussion issues
b. Feedback about student responses—To Sum It All Up
c. Responses to points raised by class members during the discussion
d. Individual e-mails to students who raised a point that no one responded to

Types of information posted by the students on the bulletin board
a. Responses to teacher prompts
b. Student-chosen issues to discuss
c. Evaluations of web sites
d. Sharing of practical activities—projects completed with students

2. Instructor Responsibilities: 4 Cs
Clarity
a. Clarity of discussion prompts
b. Clarity of discussion requirements—of when postings are due, when the instructor will be grading, etc.
c. Clarity of relative value of various web sites
d. Clarity of the process of site navigation—need an initial face-to-face meeting with students, even those who have taken an online course in the past
e. Clarity of the "how to" of participating in bulletin boards

Communication
a. More timely feedback from the instructor—don't have to wait until next week
b. Announcements can be posted on the announcement board, responses can be made to student responses, e-mails can be sent to individual students who posted responses.

Creating Community (Making those participating in the threaded bulletin board feel like a community of learners)
a. Submission of biographical sketches at the beginning of the course
b. Availability of so many written responses
c. A focus on student-student responses rather than student-teacher ones
d. The teacher as a member of the community rather than the leader of the community

Creativity (Making the content interesting via having a deeper interactive quality)
a. Graphics—Seeing
b. Audio—Listening to
c. Video—Listening to and seeing

3. Growth—for both students and teachers
Students
a. Discussions just naturally getting better as students become more comfortable with online discussions
b. Students taking more responsibility for own learning
c. Students getting to read other students' responses—learning from peers—as more individual written work is available to all
— learning from the responses of others to discussion prompts
— learning from the web site evaluations completed by others

Teachers
  a. Teachers giving more detailed feedback (one types more than one hand-writes)
  b. Instructor "recaps" of the responses to a discussion prompt put organization to what is often a disorganized class discussion. The instructor has time to construct the recap instead of doing this "off the cuff" in a classroom situation.
  c Awareness that what has been done to enhance the threaded discussions (clarity; deeper interactive quality) can be used to enhance face-to-face class discussions
  d. Support and enthusiasm for what the other two shared
    1) Methods
    2) Resources—books, database of ideas from journals
    3) Worries and concerns

4. Advantage of online discussions over face-to-face classroom discussions
  a. Students sharing more than they typically would—everyone gets to talk
    — Having the processing time they need to think before they share without having to worry that the discussion will move to a new topic if they don't speak up right away—encouraging reticent students to share more (or are the students who are reticent to discuss face-to-face also reticent to share in online discussions?)
    — Having more time for discussion of an issue before the instructor has to move on to cover the next one—class is extended
  b. Students write responses more helpful than those they might make verbally
    — Input is more specific—name of journal, name of researcher
    — It's possible to easily print responses rather than taking notes or rather than not taking notes and then not remembering
  c. More efficient use of time for both students and teachers—perhaps because of greater clarity of assignments and discussion prompts

5. Concerns
  a. Teachers not being well prepared to teach online courses
  b. Teachers who effectively teach in the milieu spending much more time with the threaded bulletin boards than with in-class discussion and activities
  c. The ineffectiveness of threaded bulletin boards for some students, either because of their discomfort with technology or their tendency to be passive and wait for others to do the majority of the critical thinking
  d. The possible lack of effectiveness of the threaded bulletin board as a vehicle for delivering reading content, especially in practice-based courses in diagnosis and remediation as opposed to more theoretical courses

---

with the comments of Greenlaw and DeLoach (2003), who noted that online discussions capture the best features of organizing one's thoughts, critical thinking and reactions, and better discussions.

Theme four was concerned with enumerating the *advantages* of online discussions over face-to-face discussions. Students seemed to share more because they had more opportunity to "talk" online without one or two students dominating a discussion. This complements McDonald's (2002) contention that although some personalities may dominate a discussion by submitting lengthy responses or multiple responses the competition for "airtime" is eliminated and thus provides equal opportunity for submitting responses and sharing viewpoints. Time to process thoughts and discuss an issue without the "press of real time" was valuable. Students could locate and provide specific resources and use their time efficiently. In support of Moore's (1993) theory that physical distance did not have be a barrier to communication, physical distance was found to support and perhaps even encourage detailed and accurate communication. Perhaps this is because an increase in physical distance from one's classmates resulted in a decrease in physical distance from the learner's personal resources. There is not just one type of physical distance! These advantages also mirror Hanley's (2001) components of a constructivist environment, as well as the process of communicating as articulated by Gill and Dupree (1998).

However, there were *concerns* (theme 5). Were we—and other instructors—prepared to teach online courses and use threaded discussions before we needed to start using this medium? Do instructors need to spend even more time with the threaded discussions than they would spend in a face-to-face class? If so, are the advantages (see theme four) worth the disadvantage of expenditure of time? Would students remain passive, waiting for other students to "go first" and then simply react rather than being proactive? Is this system really effective for delivering the reading content?

Reflections of the three instructors

In this section, the themes are reflected upon and presented within a personal context by each of the three participants.

Judy Richardson: Related to the theme of *responsibilities*, I think I have become a *clearer* instructor because of the technology. I must make my assignments and discussion prompts very clear because I cannot embellish with comments just as I think of them. So, the technology has "forced" me to be very clear in my own objectives and intent. It also enables me to add to my explanations if I receive a question from my students (within announcements on the Black Board); no one has to wait for an answer until next week. This has helped me in courses I teach face-to-face because I have become more *articulate* and I tend to "waste" less time. The content I teach does not get so lost in the explanations of "stuff."

Also, using technology has allowed me to look at a topic from another perspective and to realize that I **MUST** provide interesting ways to access the content. Just lectures—in an online context, this might mean posting a linear lecture—will not work. So I have learned the value of graphics, video, and audio to enhance learning. This has helped me to present material differently also in my face-to-face classes. I have become aware that students do not necessarily find me scintillating enough to listen to me for two and one-half hours nonstop!

Related to the theme of *growth*, the interactive quality is much deeper in some ways now. I have students doing more weekly by listening to a reading and reacting, or visiting a web site, or doing an activity online, then participating in discussions about their learning. Since one of my course objectives is to help students see how their own students need to be active in their own learning and to take charge of it as soon as possible, the technology has helped me to demonstrate this aspect of learning. This has helped me in my face-to-face classes, because now I also incorporate those activities; and I have witnessed, just this semester, how much better the discussions now are, and how much less they rely on me. Before, I think students just came to class and abdicated responsibility to me to "stuff the content" in them. Now they see better the impact of study skills and interaction. (I hope). The social quality of threaded discussions (Mead, 1934; Moore, 1993) is now much more applied in my threaded discussions.

Related to the themes of *concerns*, I think that we may lose as much as 80% of the communication in threaded discussions where we have only the written word, with no facial expressions, no intonations, etc. That is why I ask students to consider an audio or video before participating in some discussions, as Holt et. al. (1998) suggests. But, there are simply times when the personal contact is very important. This is the time when a distance education environment can be helpful (people at remote locations all tuned in at the same time) or when visits to the instructor are necessary.

Charlene Fleener: During my first semester of asynchronous instruction the planning, reading and reflecting on threaded discussions, as well as participating with my colleagues in our own threaded discussions, served as a valuable learning experience for me. Lessons learned included appropriate question construction, role clarification, trust, and connections to synchronous instruction.

Related to the theme, *types of information*, I quickly discovered that threaded discussion questions that inspire rich interaction must be thoughtfully constructed. Questions that encouraged problem solving, affective connections, or reflection on literacy issues in the news worked well. However, in the beginning it seemed students still had a mindset that it was necessary for them to craft their answers to conform to an instructor's expectations. They used a lot of rhetoric and terms from the texts we were using.

Responses to questions varied in length and depth of thought but there was more time for reflection than would typically be available during a synchronous class period. Students could take as much time as they wanted to consider a peer's response and viewpoint before offering their own. This encouraged greater and more in-depth analysis resulting in more detailed answers and comments.

Another question related factor was the level of participation; this ties to the theme of instructor *responsibilities* and providing experiences for encouraging a sense of community. Since all my students were required to provide an answer to each posted question, as well as comments or questions to two of their peers' entries, each had an equal opportunity to express their own ideas. This level of active involvement and interaction for questions in a traditional setting is not possible. This "leveling of the playing field" may minimize the opportunity for one or two students to dominate a discussion, and consequently may serve to encourage some of the introverted students to share more freely.

My responsibilities in the threaded discussions included first posting a prompt and then shifting into the role of observer, clarifier, and sometimes, gentle guide. I found it took my students a while to adjust to this. Initially, they treated their responses as though I was their audience. When they began to understand that it was the other students in the class they were really "talking with" rather than me their answers became less didactic and more experienced-based and personal. I, too, had to adjust. Learning to step back and let the students dialogue without acting in the role of intermediary gave me a new respect for constructivism.

I learned from my colleagues that closure for a discussion thread could be facilitated if I took on the role of summarizer as each discussion concluded. This was accomplished by posting a few summary statements for clarifying issues and points. I especially liked learning about "facilitator wording." For example, I might say, "This is what I hear you saying..." In that way I provided another opportunity for students to clarify or explain anything that may have been unclear. Sometimes when answers are written absent intonation and expression common to oral communication misinterpretation may result.

A greater sense of trust was an unexpected lesson for me and I considered that a growth experience. Threaded discussions as described in the preceding paragraph require that students respond to one another without going through the instructor as is typically done in real-time classroom discussions. In this forum I found I really had to trust the students and the process to keep the discussions moving and connected. They had to learn to trust me as well as one another as they committed their thoughts and ideas to the Blackboard environment for all their peers to view and question. In so doing a type of learning community emerged. Students felt comfortable to share examples from their own experiences and those of their family members. They were not afraid to disagree but were careful to word responses in a tactful and professional manner.

Many of the technology tools I became accustomed to using in an asynchronous environment are appropriate for application and use in synchronous courses. I now use Blackboard tools for all my classes and particularly threaded discussions. Threaded discussions seem to increase the likelihood students will come to class having read and given some thought to the topics under study. This may allot more time for getting beyond surface level discussion. Threaded discussions also provide a forum for students who write more thoughtfully and eloquently than they speak, while giving practice to those who have difficulty clearly expressing their ideas in writing.

Linda Thistlethwaite: In relation to theme one, *types of information,* I learned that I had only brushed the tip of the iceberg in utilizing the potential of discussion boards. In my previous Internet ventures I had required students to independently submit to me answers for five questions for each of the four modules for the course. I responded individually to students as well as submitting to the course bulletin board my reflection on their collective answers. However, students did not have an opportunity to see one another's answers. Whereas I had used the discussion board as a place where students could pose questions and their reflections and also invited others to respond to what their classmates had to say, my online colleagues took a leadership role in posing key issues for discussion. (I did this via other course components rather than via the threaded discussions.) In the future, I plan to continue the individual submissions but to also pose a question on the discussion board myself for each module, requiring students to post their responses for classmates to read and, at the conclusion of the thread, summarizing key points made by students and sharing my own ideas. Perhaps this will better illustrate what Knowlton and Knowlton (2001) had in mind regarding student and teacher contributions to the educational dialogue.

For each module I provided students with a listing of 20-40 related web sites. I found that the majority of student-to-student responses on the discussion board focused on web sites that had been visited and evaluated. Participants shared ways they would utilize the information for themselves, for parents, or for students. The response of my students as well as the response of my online colleagues has encouraged me to refine this aspect of the online discussion. In the future I may divide the listing of sites into primary and secondary sites, providing students some direction regarding which sites they may find the most useful.

Related to theme five, *concerns,* I learned that other instructors also had concerns about the lack of face-to-face interaction but that they had discovered, as I had, that students were able to share ideas and did develop a sense of community without the face-to-face interaction. Students' first submission was biographical, including a reflection on their teaching experiences and their interest in participating in this language and literacy course. Although these personal sketches were submitted to the "Meet the Participants" page of the online course rather than to the discussion board, students used the information they learned about others in the class to share with and respond to one another.

Feedback about community discussion from students had been positive for the most part. Comments that my students made reflected the stand by Holt and his associates (1998) that this medium offers opportunities for broader participation and more dynamic interaction. Some of my students said they shared more online than they did in a traditional setting. They had time to think and reflect before responding rather than having to respond immediately. This type of format is effective for those who need more processing time. Others commented that often in a traditional class they didn't have time to respond because there was only so much class time that could be allotted to one issue before the instructor found it necessary to move to the next issue. Others appreciated that their colleagues' input was more specific and well thought out in an online response than in an in-class response. For example, in online responses class members would include complete titles for journal articles they wanted to comment on or would verify the author of an idea rather than sharing vague and incomplete information. Others students noted that being able to print the responses they were interested in was time-efficient. I want to further investigate the concept of exploring participant-to-participant interaction as an index of individual learning (Greenlaw & DeLoach, 2003).

I was pleased to find that my online colleagues who typically taught in a very interactive format and tried to develop a sense of community in the class through a variety of small-group activities were also finding that group discussion could be effective in an online course. I was looking for ways to "sell" this medium to my colleagues and my personal experiences were not sufficient.

Not all students have enjoyed this online print interaction. They missed "hearing" the words. However, I have learned that with the audio capabilities of the Internet that students can hear as well as read. I plan to utilize audio input to a greater extent in the future.

Related to *responsibilities,* clarity was important. Through my own experiences and those of my online colleagues, I learned that being clear with respect to assignment requirements, navigation of the course site, and particularly participation in the discussion board are imperative to course success. Holt (1998) referred to this type of moderator responsibility when he noted the importance of establishing ground rules for dynamic interaction. In some respects teaching an online course is more difficult when the course is a graduate course rather than an undergraduate course. Often graduate students have less experience with technology and find navigating through an online course, and particularly making submissions to the discussion board, to be a frustrating experience. The next time I teach an online course I will require an initial face-to-face meeting for all who can possibly attend. (The vast majority of persons who have enrolled in my online courses lived within two hours of the university campus.) During this first meeting, held in a computer lab, students should learn how to navigate the course site, how to submit a response to questions posed on the discussion board, and how to respond to the submission of a classmate.

I am presently creating modules for staff development that have more visual appeal. The presentation of the "lecture" includes graphics to "click" on to bring up related information. They also incorporate activities that students do online, such as "click and drag" matching activities. Without being too "cutesy," these activities provide learners with something more than simply reading the text. Visiting related web sites that themselves have visual appeal and interactive activities adds to the presentation of information.

Conclusions and Recommendations

Threaded bulletin boards CAN provide a higher level of comfort for students than the typical classroom environment and can be an environment where social interactions occur and peer learning takes place.

1. For online courses with a threaded bulletin board component, consider having a face-to-face introductory meeting for those who are able to attend. This is especially important for those who are unfamiliar with threaded bulletin boards. Focus on how to navigate the site, how to post initial responses, and how to respond to someone else's response. Even though all will not be able to attend, talking to those who do attend will greatly reduce the number of questions you have to respond to during the first part of the course. As students become savvier about Internet courses, this recommendation will be less important.

2. Think about your role, not as leader but as facilitator and as a member of the community. What kind of ice-breaking activities will you use? How will you encourage students to get to know one another? Submitting a biographical sketch is just one way. How involved will you be with the threaded bulletin board? What are the advantages and disadvantages of providing detailed prompts as opposed to giving students more latitude regarding their submissions? Many instructors find that developing good prompts and later bringing closure to the postings to those prompts is an effective framework for learning. You'll need to decide on what you believe is an effective ratio between teacher-directed prompts and student-directed ones.

3. Provide a variety of opportunities for students to respond to one another through submissions of their choice and through the submission of responses to common questions posed by the instructor. Include such avenues as discussion of theoretical issues, reflections on practical projects, and the review of a limited number of web sites related to the topic.

4. Opportunities for response should be based on more than simply reading text online (or from course textbooks) and responding. Instructors must creatively use graphics, audio, and video to make discussion prompts interesting. Incorporate "click" and "click and drag" interactive activities to supplement online lecture material related to the discussion prompts or have students complete an online activity in preparation for responding to the discussion prompt. Construct questions for student response that are thought provoking and require critical thinking rather than ones that simply require the student to summarize what has been read.

5. Clarify expectations regarding the expected length and depth of response. You may want to pose a sample question and response to illustrate your expectations. Also clarify expectations for student-to-student interaction and your desire for students to learn from one another. Involve students in the process of creating community. Early on solicit from students ways to make this happen most effectively (Holt, 1998).

6. Make sure directions regarding expectations for the content of the postings are clear. Directions for navigating the site and the "how to" of posting must also be clear. Part of using the threaded discussion should be accessing the announcement board for the site. No matter how clear you think you are being, you will find that points of confusion exist. Setting up the website so that the announcement board automatically comes up before students can access the threaded discussion will be a boon to getting information out to students in a timely manner.

7. Consider ways to address the concern that students may sift through the postings of others to "compose" their own rather than doing much independent critical thinking. Perhaps postings to an issue could be due one week with response to several postings made by other class member due the next week. Postings could be directed to the instructor with the instructor then posting them after the due date.

8. Recognize that learning to facilitate threaded discussions and encourage the trust necessary for effective communication (students to teacher, teacher to students and students to students) doesn't happen overnight.

9. Consider how you will evaluate responses. To what degree will you evaluate participant-to-participant interaction as an index of individual learning (Greenlaw and DeLoach, 2003)?

10. Lobby for teachers being as well-prepared as possible to use threaded discussions, either in partially or fully online courses. Per-

haps before moderating a bulletin board an instructor should be given the opportunity to participate in a miniproject with several instructors planning to teach online. Participating in an online discussion about issues related to online teaching and experiencing the threaded discussion as a student would be a valuable experience.

11. Recognize that teachers who effectively teach in the online milieu may spend much more time with the threaded discussions than with in-class discussion and activities, especially at first. Lobby for co-instructors the first time teaching an online course with a strong threaded bulletin board component.

12. Consider that threaded bulletin boards may be effective online components for a variety of types of reading courses, both theory-based ones and those that are more practice-based, e.g., the diagnostic and remediation courses. Although the medium can be effective for both, differences do exist in terms of the type of responses required of the students. In more theoretical courses responses might focus on prompts that are based on reading material while in practice-based courses the focus might be on sharing the effectiveness of using the test or strategy, what "lessons" were learned, and what modifications might be made. In truth, these two types of courses differ only in proportion. All theory courses have some practical application, and all practice-based courses are theoretically based.

Future Collaborations

In this project the three of us focused upon one aspect of online courses, threaded discussions. Although this component is one of the most difficult to implement, it is not the only component of an online course. As we continue to explore online teaching, we plan to address such issues as teacher preparation for online teaching and delve more deeply into the creativity issue—using video, audio, graphics, and interactive activities to enhance electronic instruction.

We would like to look at how threaded discussions and/or other online tools play out in "blended" courses—those face-to-face classes that include several online components. The three of us hope to find a few common topics/questions that may be appropriate to share in each of our classes. If so, we might have some threaded discussions among students in our courses.

References

Applefield, J.M., Huber, R.L., & Moallem, M. (2000). Constructivism in theory and practice: Toward a better understanding. *High School Journal, 84*(2), 35.

Fosnot, C.T. (1996). Constructivism: A psychological theory of learning. In C.T. Fosnot (Ed.), *Constructivism: Theory, perspectives, and practice*. New York: Teachers College Press.

George, L. (2002). E-communities in distance learning. *Library Mosaics, 13*(4), 14-16.

Gill, S., & Dupre, K. (1998). Constructivism in reading education. *The Reading Professor, 21*, 91-108.

Goldsworthy, R. (1999-2000). Collaborative classrooms. *Learning and Leading with Technology, 27*(4), 6-9.

Greenlaw, S., & S. DeLoach (2003). Teaching critical thinking with electronic discussion. *The Journal of Economic Education, 34*(1), 36-52.

Hanley, S. (2001). On constructivism. Retrieved July 21, 2001, from Maryland Collaborative for Teacher Preparation: http://www.towson.edu/csme/mctp/Essays.html.

Holt, M, P. Kleiber, J. Swenson, E. Rees, & J., Milton (1998). Facilitating group learning on the Internet. *New Directions for Adult and Continuing Education, 78*, 43-51.

Johnson, D., & R. Johnson (1991). *Learning together and alone: Cooperative, competitive, and individualistic learning*. (3rd ed.) Englewood Cliffs, NJ: Prentice-Hall.

Jonassen, D, Carr, C. & Yueh, H-P. (1998). Computers as mindtools for engaging learners in critical thinking. *TechTrends 4*(2), 24-32.

Knowles, M. S. (1990) *The Adult Learner. A neglected species* (4th ed.), Houston: Gulf

Knowlton, D. S. & Knowlton, H. M. (2001). The context and content of online discussions: Making cyber-discussions viable for the secondary school curriculum. *American Secondary Education, 29*(4), 38-52.

Lincoln, Y.S. & Guba, E.G. (1985). *Naturalistic inquiry*. Newbury Park, CA: Sage.

McComb, M. (1993). Augmenting a group discussion course with computer-mediated communication in a small college setting. *Interpersonal Computing and Technology, 1*(3). Retrieved January 8, 2004 from http://www.helsinki.fi/science/optek/1993/n3/mccomb.txt.

McDonald, J. (2002). Is "As good as face-to-face" as good as it gets? *Journal of Asynchronous Learning Networks, 6*(2), 10-23.

Mead, G. H. 1934. *Mind, Self, and Society: From the Standpoint of a Social Behaviorist*. Chicago: The University of Chicago Press.

Moore, M. (1972). Learner autonomy: The second dimension of independent learning. *Convergence, 5*(2), 76-88.

Moore, M. G. (1980). Independent Study. Redefining the discipline of adult education. In R. D. Boyd & J. W. Apps (Eds.), *Redefining the discipline of adult education*. (pp. 16-31). San Francisco: Jossey-Bass.

Moore, M. G. (1991). Three types of interaction. *The American Journal of Distance Education, 3*(2), 1-6. Retrieved from http://www.ajde.com/Contents/vol3_2.htm#editorial.

Moore, M. (1993). Three types of interaction. In K. Harry, M. Hohn, & D. Keegan (Eds.), *Distance Education: New Perspectives*. London: Routledge.

Pappas, M. (2002). Discussion forums: A tool for Collaboration. *Knowledge Quest, 31*(2), 17-19.

Pearson, P.D., & Stephens, D. (1994). Learning about literacy: A 30-year journey. In R.B. Ruddell, M.R. Ruddell, & H. Singer (Eds.), *Theoretical models and processes of reading* (4th ed.) pp. 22-42. Newark, DE: International Reading Association.

Roszak, Theodore. (1986). *The Cult of Information: A Neo-Luddite Treatise on High*

Tech, Artificial Intelligence, and the True Art of Thinking. Berkeley: University of California Press.

Slavin, R. (1994). *Cooperative learning: Theory, Research, and Practice.* 2nd Ed. Boston, MA: Pearson Allyn & Bacon.

Sotillo, S. M. (2002). Constructivist and collaborative learning in a wireless environment. *TESOL Journal, 11*(3), 16-20.

Tse, Alan C. B. (1999). "Conducting Electronic Focus Group Discussions Among Chinese Respondents." *Journal of the Market Research Society, 41*(4), 407.

Turner, L. (2003). Service learning and student achievement. *Educational Horizons, 81*(4), 188-189.

Turner, S., & V. Dipinto (1997). Peer collaboration in a hypermedia learning environment. *Journal of Research on Computing in Education, 29,* 392-402 .

Vermette, P., & C. Foote (2001). Constructivist philosophy and cooperative learning practice toward integration and reconciliation in secondary classrooms. *American Secondary Education, 30*(1), 26-37.

Weaver, C. (1994). *Reading processes and practices.* Portsmouth, NH: Heinemann.

Wickstrom, C. D. (2003). A "funny" thing happened on the way to the forum. *Journal of Adolescent and Adult Literacy, 48,* 414-423.

Williams, K. (1996). Cooperative learning: A new direction. *Education, 17,* 39-42.

Using Assistive Technology to Teach Content Area Literacy Strategies to Students with Disabilities

Kathleen Puckett

Arizona State University West

William Brozo

George Mason University

Abstract

This chapter explores the use of assistive technology applications and content area strategies for literacy support. A software toolkit, selected for its potential for literacy support, was paired with content area literacy strategies and obtained for teams of special and general education teachers. The teachers were trained to integrate these technology applications with literacy strategies and general curriculum content for students in inclusive environments. Examples of integration strategies and exploratory use of assistive technology resulting from a three-week workshop are offered.

Evidence abounds that teachers across the United States lack appropriate training and skills in content area literacy (Barry, 1997; Stewart & O'Brien, 1989). This situation may be especially detrimental to struggling readers and learners as well as students with disabilities. There are numerous indications that children of color (Jimenez, 1997) and special education students are not receiving adequate training in higher-level literacy skills (Brozo & Simpson, 2003). Nevertheless, these students can be taught to improve their reading and thinking abilities when knowledge of literacy, language development, and learning strategies is applied to them as it is to other students (Dole, Brown, & Trathen, 1996; Wood & Algozzine, 1994) and, when appropriate, strategies are adapted to meet their unique learning needs (Pearman, Huang, & Mellblom, 1997). Unfortunately, research also indicates that students at all achievement levels feel that they need adaptations that they are not getting

(Schum, Vaughn, & Samuell, 1991). Traditionally recommended adaptations, such as audio taping, text substitution, constructing abridged versions, or using multilevel materials, are time and labor intensive on the part of the teacher.

Technology applications provide a solution to this difficulty, and give both teachers and learners curriculum flexibility that was previously unattainable. Digital formats made possible by technology provide the means to adapt materials and strategies to suit the learners' needs. Text can be transformed (e.g., text to speech or text to Braille), transported (e.g., customized in size, color, or background; translated to another language) or recorded (e.g., saved for later use). Technology can offer students choices of scaffolding support in real time, increasing their learning independence. Designing lessons with strategic use of technology increases the probability that all students will be able to participate in the learning experience and reduces the need for elaborate adaptations and modifications of material later on (Rose & Meyer, 2002). This method of technology use, referred to as *universal design for learning,* can be paired with literacy strategies as an effective means of expanding content area knowledge for all students.

Although suggestions for the use of technology in the support of literacy learning strategies are appearing with increasing regularity in literature devoted to teaching students with disabilities, (Castellani & Jeffs, 2001; Edyburn, 2003; Hitchcock, Meyer, Rose, & Jackson, 2002), in the reading literature (International Reading Association, 2001), and in educational technology literature, (International Society for Technology in Education, 2002), few actual classroom examples are extant. In this article, we describe our attempts to operationalize the pairing of software for literacy support with content area literacy strategies. Technology-mediated content area strategy descriptions are supported by classroom examples developed by teams of classroom and special education teachers.

Technology: Assistive and Instructional

The use of instructional software has been reported in assistive technology literature for a number of years. (Behrmann & Jerome, 2002; Edyburn, 2000; Kaplan & Edyburn, 1998). Assistive technology (AT) is defined by the Individuals with Disabilities Education Act, or IDEA, (1997) as "any item, piece of equipment, or product system, whether acquired commercially off the shelf, modified, or customized, that is used to increase, maintain, or improve functional capabilities of individuals with disabilities" (20 U.S. C. 1401 [24]). This definition of AT can refer to a broad range of devices that may or may not be designed specifically with individuals with disabilities in mind. These devices may be very simple (e.g., pencil grips) or complex, such as mouse devices operated through a specialized straw. Many applications blur the distinction between technology use that is instructional (i.e., used for a teaching a variety of skills and learning strategies) and assistive (i.e., technology used to increase student performance). The key to referring to a device as assistive is the extent to which it allows the user to accomplish cognitive or physical tasks that would otherwise be difficult or impossible. Computer software, therefore, can be thought of as either a technology use that makes literacy tasks more efficient, or, in the hands of a student with a cognitive or physical disability, a form of assistive technology use that makes the literacy task possible. For the purpose of this discussion, we refer to assistive technology as software or equipment that could be used to support the literacy needs of students with disabilities, whether or not that software was originally designed for that purpose.

Background and Project Features

This project reports on the second year of funding from a Title II Improving Teacher Quality Grant, which focused on the use of content area literacy strategies with assistive technology applications. During the first year of funding, the project had emphasized assistive technology applications for all general curriculum standards (Puckett, 2004). We modified the data collection survey developed during the first year to reflect the current focus on content area literacy strategies. This survey was used at the start of this project and again at the end to document the extent of new knowledge. Pertinent sections of the survey and results are found in the Appendix.

Nineteen teachers from a southeastern state participated in three-week workshop during the summer of 2003. Each teacher was member of a school-based team consisting of at least one special education teacher and one general education teacher from the same elementary or middle school. Nine schools were thus represented, 4 elementary and 5 middle schools. Of the 19 teachers participating, age, experience and advanced degrees were evenly distributed. Seven teachers had less than 5 years experience, 4 teachers had over ten years experience, and 7 taught from 5-10 years. Eleven of the teachers had advanced degrees (i.e., Master's or above), 11 held certifications in special education, and 13 were certified in elementary education. Seventeen teachers were from high poverty schools serving children from inner city and rural Appalachian environments. The teachers were all volunteers and were recruited through principals and special education directors in their respective school districts.

The teachers were given purchased sets of an assistive technology toolkit, a collection of software products chosen by the authors for their value in literacy support, and were trained in the use of each application. They were also shown a variety of content area literacy strategies, along with ideas of potential assistive technology matches, and were then given the time and technological support to develop their own applications with current curriculum content. The teachers worked collaboratively, problem solving the technology applications within and among the teams. The project directors provided technical and content area assistance as needed. The teaching teams posted their lesson plans with an example of the related technology strategy to a database on the project website.

Training consisted of three two-hour sessions and five eight-hour sessions held over the three-week period in a university computer lab equipped with relevant software and curriculum materials. Project training was designed to familiarize teachers with current assistive technology software and ways this technology could be adapted to teach a variety of content area literacy strategies. For example, the workshop module for pre-reading strategies included: a) explanation and demonstrations of anticipation guides, KWL, and story impressions; b) explanation and demonstrations of relevant assistive technology, such as concept mapping, text to speech word processing, and scan and read programs, with content-area examples of the pre-reading strategies mediated by assistive technology; and c) guided practice in developing adaptations of the technology and strategies for specific content material.

The assistive technology used in this project was based on recommendations for learner productivity and a core assistive technology toolkit described by Edyburn (2000). The particular applications in this project were selected because they could be used to support the literacy needs of students with disabilities, whether or not the software was originally designed for that purpose. Selected programs are content neutral, have multiple features that support literacy within the curriculum, and are relatively easy to use. The software types, descriptions, and products selected are displayed in Table 1.

Table 1 also displays recommended content area literacy strategies for each software type. A brief synopsis of these strategies follows.

Table 1. Assistive Technology Descriptions and Suggested Content Area Literacy Strategies

SOFTWARE TYPE	DESCRIPTION, PRODUCT, AND SUGGESTED CONTENT AREA LITERACY STRATEGIES
Concept mapping	Concept mapping programs allow the brainstorming of multiple ideas or concepts on a computer screen, with tools to produce a visual map or diagram and an outline. This toolkit included Kidspiration for grades K-3 (2003) and Inspiration for grades 4-12 (2003). Suggested strategies included concept maps, Venn diagrams, word webs, KWL charts, and study guides.
Text to speech word processors	Text to speech word processors highlight text as it is read. Intellitalk (2003) also offers other literacy support features: templates, word prediction, graphic libraries and voiced dictionary support. Suggested literacy strategies include text impressions, gisting, possible sentences, anticipation guides, and word grids.
Multimedia	Multimedia programs combine visuals, sound, and external links in a presentation format. Intellipics Studio (2003) features an extensive instructional activity and template system for curriculum support, with drawings and backgrounds appropriate for most elementary and middle school classroom environments. Suggested strategies include word scavenger hunts, text impressions, and scrambled paragraphs.
Text to speech scan and read	Text to speech scan and read programs use optical character recognition (OCR) to digitize books and other print media, and then read the digitized text. Most text to speech scan and read programs also have an array of literacy supports: word prediction, dictionary and translation capacities. The *Kurzweil 3000* (2003) was paired with the question-answer-relationship strategy and study guides.

Anticipation Guides

This strategy involves giving students a list of statements about the topic to be studied and asking them to respond to them before reading and learning, and then again after reading and learning (Duffelmeyer, 1994; Duffelmeyer & Baum, 1992). Guides can activate prior knowledge of text topics and help students set purposes for reading and learning (Hurst, 2001).

Text Impressions

This strategy helps students activate prior knowledge by developing an impression of what the forthcoming reading and lesson will cover (Brozo & Simpson, 2003). Students are presented with a list of words and phrases taken directly from the material to be covered and asked to create a text using the words. As students encounter the actual content they compare what they wrote with what they actual read or encounter (Denner, Rickards, & Albanese, 2003).

Question-Answer-Relationship

This comprehension strategy is used to support students' abilities to recognize that information needed to answer questions can be processed at different levels of meaningfulness (Ezell, Hunsicker, Quinque, & Randolph, 1996). After reading a passage, students are presented with a series of questions and asked to determine if the answer could be found "right there" (textually explicit), or require "think and search," "author and you," (textually implicit), or "on my own" (scriptally implicit) processing (Raphael & Pearson, 1985).

Word Webs

Students create a graphic display of the interrelationships between key vocabulary and their own related associations. This strategy is useful for helping students activate relevant prior knowledge for content area topics (Johnson & Rasmussen, 1998).

Study Guides

This strategy is used to help students process content in an elaborative way. Study guides help students focus on important information and ideas and can be designed using novel and engaging response formats (Herber, 1978).

Scrambled Paragraphs

Students are presented with paragraphs separated from the original text. They are asked to arrange the paragraphs in a logical way, and then compare their arrangement with the original text. Practice with this strategy helps students become better able to perceive the interconnectedness of ideas (Brozo & Simpson, 1999).

"Gisting"

This is an excellent strategy for helping students paraphrase and summarize information (Vaughn & Klingner, 1999). Students are required to limit the gist of a paragraph to a set number of words. Individual sentences from a paragraph are presented one at a time while students create a gist that must contain only the set number of words.

Venn Diagrams

These simple interlocking circles can be used to promote close reading and focused listening and can be adapted to fit a variety of purposes (Baxendell, 2003; Bromley, Irwin-DeVitis, & Modlo, 1995). For example, students can use one circle to write what they already know about a topic. As they encounter information, they can write new items in the other circle. Where prior knowledge and the presented information is the same, students can place that information in the overlapping area of the circles.

Word Scavenger Hunts

Students are given a collection of content related terms and are asked to find visual examples of the terms from magazines, newspapers, and the computer. Scavenging for pictures that depict words is motivating for students and offers them an immediate context for newly learned vocabulary (Brozo & Simpson, 2003).

Possible Sentences

This is a pre-reading strategy that prepares students for the technical and general vocabulary they will encounter in a reading assignment and helps develop their contextual understandings of words (Stahl & Kapinus, 1991). Students are given key terms from the content and create sentences using the terms. As students encounter the actual content they compare the ways their words were used with the meanings of those words as used in context.

Word Grids

This strategy helps students differentiate related vocabulary by critical features (Johnson & Pearson, 1984; Stahl, 1999). In a grid, students write content related terms along the vertical dimension and key characteristics along the horizontal dimension. Words and characteristics are connected with checks or pluses, while those that are not related are given minuses or zeros.

KWL

In this acronym, each letter represents a column on a chart. Students fill in the *K*, or the "what I know," column with statements that represent their prior knowledge for a content area topic. In the *W*, or "what I want to learn," column students write statements and/or questions that they hope to discover or have answers to as they explore the content. And in the *L*, or "what I learned," column students write statements related to the *W* column (Ogle, 1986). This strategy helps students set purposes for reading and learning (Carr & Aldinger, 1996).

Concept Mapping

Concept maps are visual displays of the interrelatedness of key ideas and information (Boxtel, Linden, & Chen, 2002). These can be hand-drawn or created on a computer screen. Students are encouraged to use drawings and clip art as well as lines and arrows to make content connections explicit. This strategy encourages logical and inferential thinking (Chang, Sung, & Chen, 2002).

Results

Pre and post survey measures (see Appendix) document gains made by the teachers as a result of the workshop in knowledge and potential use of assistive technology and content area literacy strategies. Furthermore, the posting of lessons to a database instigated critical and purposeful dialog about the best uses and adaptations of assistive technology mediated content area literacy strategies. These measures were an expected outcome of the project and can serve to inform professionals involved with technology integration issues.

Of particular note were extremely low levels of reported technology use at the start of the workshop period, indicating that technology integration in general was not a common classroom occurrence for these teachers. Participants were asked to rate their use of twelve assistive technology applications on a 4-part Likert scale (i.e., categories designations of never, rarely, sometimes, or frequently). Before participation, over 75% of the teachers reported that they never or rarely used text-to speech word processors, voice recognition software, text scan and read programs, computer accessibility options, electronic concept mapping, or word prediction programs with special education students. After participating in the project, reports of potential use of instructional and assistive technology improved. Over 70% reported anticipating sometimes or frequent use of word processing, text-to-speech word processors, text scan and read programs, multimedia, computer accessibility features, electronic concept mapping, and commercial language arts programs (see Section 2, Appendix). Teachers also reported increases in knowledge of content area reading strategies. Post conference scores indicate over 90% reported practicing or proficient knowledge of content area reading strategies, whereas at the beginning of the sessions the practicing and proficient scores were consistently lower. Confidence in using technology to achieve reading standards increased from moderate levels of 26% to 84%, although high confidence levels remained essentially the same (see Section 3, Appendix).

Larger issues for the researchers were questions regarding curriculum integration, as in what would teacher generated examples of curriculum-referenced classroom applications of assistive technology and content area literacy strategies look like, and would these examples, when develop by school-based teams of special and general education teachers, improve access to general education curriculum content for student with disabilities? In the following sections, three examples of these technology and strategy pairings are discussed.

Text-to-speech-scan and read

Figure 1 depicts an example of text to speech scan and read programs with the question-answer-relationship reading strategy. In this example, the teachers used the *Kurzweil 3000* (2003) program to scan a paper-based selection from the novel *Holes* (Sacher, 1998), a reading selection from a seventh grade Language Arts class. In this example, the question-answer-relationship activities were typed into a text box, and students were directed to answer each question by typing the answer next to the question. In this figure, the typing cursor is placed at the end of question one, with the letter *R* typed. Note that the word prediction text box, located in the upper right had corner of the figure, lists ten potential words beginning with *r* that the student may select from. The student may complete the typing of the answer, or click on the item from the word predication box (i.e., The typing of the word *right* could be completed with one key-stroke and one mouse click). The student controls the literacy support needed to answer these questions: read controls are visible and may be selected for the passage or the questions. Definitions and synonyms may be obtained using either an English dictionary or as translations from a choice of dictionaries in several languages. Should the student have physical, perceptual or language difficulties that prevent typing the answer, a voice note may be added to this text area. The screen may be saved or printed as is with the scanned text, questions, and answers visible, or the questions and answers may be extracted.

Figure 1: Example of Question Answer Relationship Strategy Paired with a Scan and Read Program and Word Prediction Using Kurzweil 3000 (2003).

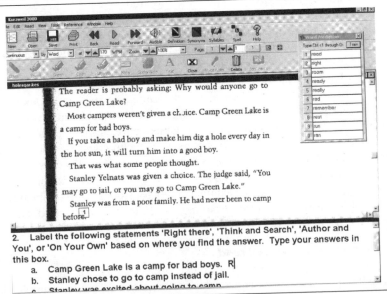

Not only is this an example of pairing a content area strategy with an assistive technology application, it can be offered as an example of accessing general curriculum content for a struggling reader. Students of differing abilities may use this software to read and respond to the same content as other members of the class.

Text to speech word processors

Figure 2 displays an example of a text to speech word processor paired with a text impression strategy. In this example, the teacher used the software program *Intellitalk II* (2003) to develop a template with words and phrases related to the story *Justin and the Best Biscuits in the World* (Walter, 1986), a selection read in a fourth grade class. After a brief introduction, but before reading the story, the student is directed to write about the main character, Justin, and his grandfather. As the student types the story, the words on the screen are read aloud according to selected feedback settings: word-by-word, letter-by-letter, or complete sentences. Template word banks are hidden or displayed (e.g., setting word bank, character word bank, etc.) by choice of the student. Students may click on selected words or on phrases in the templates to have them inserted into the story in lieu of typing the entire word. This particular template can be used in subsequent assignments by

Figure 2: Example of Text-To-Speech Word Processor Paired with a Text Impression Strategy Using *Intellitalk* (2003).

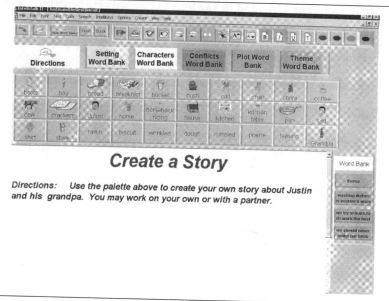

changing the initial directions (e.g., "Create a story" can be changed to a post-reading gisting strategy). In this example, as in Figure 1, the student has literacy support for access to the context of the general curriculum reading selection. Students are asked to develop the same assignment as the other members of this class; the task expression, not content, is adapted for the struggling learner. Note also that the student controls the extent of the assistance needed and has choice in typing using typical word processing composition tools or using the word templates.

Concept mapping software

The third example offered is that of using concept mapping strategy and software as a pre-writing activity. A concept map, whether produced by hand or by electronic means, is a visual display of ideas or information with lines or arrows showing relationships between the concepts. Figure 3 illustrates the use of the software program *Inspiration* (2003) in this capacity. In this example, the student is given three activities. The first activity is to write specific characteristics of sea animals on the concept map, and the second is to give two examples of each characteristic. Other than the convenience of typing or the novelty of using a computer, these activities function very similar to comparable activities using a paper and pencil diagram. The third activity in the top view, however, transforms this task into literacy support. The stu-

Figure 3: Examples of a Concept Map Using Concept Mapping Software in Diagram View and in Outline View Using *Inspiration* (2003)

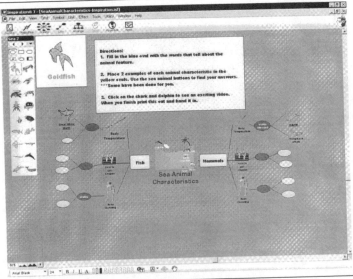

dent is directed to click on the shark and the dolphin to view a video. The teacher linked these images to an Internet site showing video clips that describe characteristics of sea animals. Student may use this site as well as the classroom material to add characteristics to the concept map. The diagram next be converted to an outline view, to provide a structure for note taking or for a written product. The outline view can be exported to a word processor for further development.

While this activity was based on general education content reading material, the relationship to actual reading material is not evident. This activity, therefore, could be used with advanced or struggling readers using differing reading or electronic source material.

Discussion

This project was limited by a small group of participants and a short time frame. Nevertheless, we offer its structure as a model for developing strategies to assist struggling readers in improving their access to the content, meaning, and richness of curriculum intent.

Classroom examples developed by the teachers demonstrated the viability of a productive link between assistive technology and content area literacy strategies. Moreover, the connections the teachers made to general curriculum content were most encouraging, even while these connections happened in different ways for different workshop participants. For instance, the teachers working with primary-age children became aware for the first time in some cases, that content area literacy strategies had relevance to their instructional contexts. These same teachers also discovered that assistive technology could provide not only their struggling learners, but also all novice readers, adaptive presentations of the strategies to ensure easier understanding and greater use. Teacher-participants of intermediate and middle school students, who came to the workshop with somewhat more knowledge of and experience with both literacy strategies and computer-assisted instruction, were quick to recognize the nexus of these two instructional tools. Within the supportive environment of the workshop context, the teachers were free to experiment with linkages between a variety of language-based strategies appropriate to the content and concepts of the subjects they taught and a variety of computer-mediated programs. For all participants, regardless of teaching level, we observed an increase in their knowledge and skills with content literacy strategies and an increase in their facility with technology to mediate the strategies. Helping teachers make these connections will continue to grow in importance as requirements for general curriculum access and accountability for students with disabilities are more stringently applied.

The clear impression from these findings was that the teacher-participants were highly motivated to explore legitimate applications of assistive technology for teaching literacy strategies and content information. The assistive technology programs were motivating for the teachers and were perceived by teachers to be motivating for their students. Indeed, advocates of technology-mediated instruction assert that it is worthwhile as a way of motivating many reluctant learners (Scheidet, 2003; Song & Keller, 2001). At the same time, the content area literacy strategies demonstrated in the workshop have been shown to increase student engagement for reading and learning (Brozo & Simpson, 2003). This knowledge suggests two fruitful areas of further research. One would be to explore whether technology supported content area literacy instruction might be more enticing to teachers who have been unsure about how or unwilling to employ these strategies. Another would be to examine student motivation and learning outcomes as a result of their use of technology-mediated content literacy strategies.

In order for students with disabilities to access the content and context of the curriculum, they must have fluid and flexible literacy skills. This laudable goal remains unattainable for many who struggle daily with basic levels of reading. Too often, these students are given a curriculum concentrating on remediation of basic skills rather than compensatory strategies that would allow them to unlock and use the meaning of the text based material they must learn. The projects highlighted here are offered as examples of how strategies and technology can be used together. These examples can inform the field in advancing a common vision of technology integration within literacy support that provides access to the curriculum of the general classroom, for which reading plays such a vital role. Follow-up studies could include validation of technology and strategy pairings in enhancing performance and effectiveness with students. Additional follow-up studies could document the actual extent of integration with curriculum standards and identify further support needed. Previous studies indicate that teachers who are familiar with technology will use it in classrooms with their students (Morrow, Barnhart, & Rooyakkers, 2002; Vannatta & O'Bannon, 2002). We are hopeful that follow-up data will support these findings.

References

Barry, A. (1997). High school reading programs revisited. *Journal of Adolescent & Adult Literacy, 40,* 524-531.

Baxendell, B. (2003). Consistent, coherent, creative: The 3 C's of graphic organizers. *Teaching Exceptional Children, 35* (3), 46-53.

Behrmann, M. & Jerome, M. K. (2002). *Assistive technology for students with mild disabilities: Update 2002.* Arlington Va.: ERIC Clearinghouse on Disabilities and Gifted Education. (ERIC Document Reproduction Service ED 463 595)

Boxtel, C., Linden, J., Chen, I. (2002). Collaborative concept mapping: Provoking and supporting meaningful discourse. *Theory Into Practice, 41(1),* 40-46.

Bromley, K., Irwin-DeVitis, & Modlo, M. (1995). *Graphic organizers: Visual strategies for active learning.* New York: Scholastic Professional Books.

Brozo, W. G., & Simpson, M. L. (2003). *Readers, teachers, learners: Expanding literacy across the content areas* (4th ed.). Upper Saddle River, NJ: Merrill/Prentice Hall.

Brozo, W. G., & Simpson, M. L. (1999). *Readers, teachers, learners: Expanding literacy across the content areas (3rd ed.).* Columbus, OH: Merrill/Prentice Hall.

Carr, E., & Aldinger, L. (1996). *Thinking works: Using cognitive process in the language arts classroom.* Ann Arbor, MI: Exceptional Innovations, Inc.

Castellani, J. & Jeffs, T. (2001). Emerging reading and writing strategies using technology. *Teaching Exceptional Children, 33(5),* 60-67.

Chang, K., Sung, Y., Chen. I. (2002). The effect of concept mapping to enhance text comprehension and summarization. *The Journal of Experimental Education,* 71(1), 5-23.

Denner, P., Rickards, J., Albanese, A. (2003). The effect of story impressions preview on learning from narrative text. *The Journal of Experimental Education,* 71 (4), 313-332.

Dole, J., Brown, K., & Trathen, W. (1996). The effects of strategy instruction on the comprehension performance of at-risk students. *Reading Research Quarterly, 31(1),* 62-88.

Duffelmeyer, F. (1994). Effective Anticipation Guide statements for learning from expository prose. *Journal of Reading, 37,* 452-457.

Duffelmeyer, F., & Baum, D. (1992). The extended Anticipation Guide revisited. *Journal of Reading,* 35 (May, 1992), 654-656.Edyburn, D. L. (2000). Assistive technology and students with mild disabilities. *Focus on Exceptional Children, 32(9),* 1-23.

Edyburn, D. (2003). Reading difficulties in the general education classroom: A taxonomy of text modification strategies. *Closing the Gap, 21(6),* 1, 10-13, 30.

Ezell, H.K., Hunsicker, S.A., Quinque, M.M., & Randolph, E. (1996). Maintenance and generalization of QAR reading comprehension strategies. *Reading Research and Instruction, 36,* 64-81.

Herber, H. (1978). *Teaching reading in the content areas.* Englewood Cliffs, NJ: Prentice Hall.

Hitchock, C., Meyer, A., Rose, D., & Jackson, R. (2002). Providing new access to the general curriculum: Universal design for learning. *Teaching Exceptional Children, 35(2),* 8-17.

Hurst, B. (2001). The ABCs of content area lesson planning: Attention to basics, and comprehension. *Journal of Adolescent & Adult Literacy, 44 (8),* 692-693.

Individuals with Disabilities Education Act, 20 U.S.C. § 1400 *et seq.* (1997).

Inspiration. (2003). [Computer software]. Portland, OR: Inspiration Software.

Intellipics Studio. (2003). [Computer software]. Petaluma, CA: Intellitools.

Intellitalk II. (2003). [Computer software]. Petaluma, CA: Intellitools.

International Reading Association. (2001). *Integrating Literacy and Technology in the Curriculum.* Retrieved November 5, 2003 from http://www.reading.org/positions/ technology.html.

International Society for Technology in Education. (2002). *National educational technology standards for teachers: Preparing teachers to use technology.* Eugene, OR: International Society for Technology in Education.

Jimenez, R. (1997). The strategic reading abilities and potential of five low-literacy

Latina/o readers in middle school. HtmlResAnchor Reading-Research-Quarterly, *32*(3), 224-243.

Johnson, A., & Rasmussen, J. (1998). Classifying and super word web: Two strategies to improve productive vocabulary. *Journal of Adolescent & Adult Literacy, 42 (3),* 204-207.

Johnson, D.D., & Pearson, P.D. (1984). *Teaching reading vocabulary.* New York: Holt, Rinehart, & Winston.

Kaplan, M. W., & Edyburn, D. L. (1998). Essential tools of the trade: An assistive technology specialist shares her tool kit. *Closing the Gap, 17(3),* 1, 8, 18, 24.

Kidspiration. (2003). [Computer software]. Portland, OR: Inspiration Software.

Kurzweil 3000. (2003). [Computer software]. Bedford, MA: Kurzweil Educational Systems.

Morrow, L. M., Barnhart, S. & Rooyakkers, D. (2002). Integrating technology with the teaching of an early literacy course. *The Reading Teacher, 56,* 218-230.

Ogle, D. (1986). K-W-L: A teaching model that develops active reading of expository text. *The Reading Teacher, 39,* 564-570.

Pearman, E., Huang, A., & Mellblom, C. (1997). The inclusion of all students: Concerns and incentives of educators. *Education and Training in Mental Retardation and Development, 32* (1), 11-19.

Puckett, K. (2004). Project ACCESS: Field testing an assistive technology toolkit for students with mild disabilities. *Journal of Special Education Technology, 19(2),* 5-17.

Raphael, T. E., & Pearson, P. D. (1985). Increasing students' awareness of sources of information for answering questions. *American Educational Research Journal, 22,* 217-235.

Rose, D. & Meyer, A. (2002). *Teaching every student in the digital age: Universal design for learning.* Alexandria, VA: Association for Supervision and Curriculum Development.

Sacher, L. (1998). *Holes.* New York: Farrar Straus and Giroux.

Scheidet, R. A. (2003). Improving student achievement by infusing web-based curriculum into global history. *Journal of Research on Technology in Education,* 36 (1), 77-94.

Schum, J. S., Vaughn, S., & Samuell, L. (1991). What teachers do when the textbook is tough: Students speak out. *Journal of Reading Behavior, 24,* 481-503.

Song, S. & Keller, J. (2001). Effectiveness of motivationally adaptive computer-assisted instruction on the dynamic aspects of motivation. *Educational Technology Research and Development,* 49 (2), 5-22.

Stahl, S.A. (1999). *Vocabulary development.* Cambridge, MA: Brookline Books.

Stahl, S.A., & Kapinus, B. (1991). Possible sentences: Predicting word meanings to teach content area vocabulary. *The Reading Teacher, 45,* 36-43.

Stewart, R., & O'Brien, G. (1989). Resistance to content area reading: A focus on preservice teachers. *Journal of Reading, 32*(5), 396-401.

Vannatta, R. & O'Bannon, B. (2002). Beginning to put the pieces together: A technology infusion model for teacher education. *Journal of computing in teacher education, 18*(4), 112-123.

Vaughn, S., & Klingner, J.K. (1999). Teaching reading comprehension through collaborative strategic reading. *Intervention in School and Clinic,* 34 (5), 284-292.

Walter, M. P. (1986). *Justin and the Best Biscuits in the World.* New York: Random House.

Wood, K., & Algozzine, B. (1994). *Teaching reading to high-risk learners: A unified perspective.* Boston: Allyn & Bacon.

Appendix. Using Assistive Technology to Access Content Area Literacy in Special Education

PRE-POST TRAINING EVALUATION INSTRUMENT AND RESULTS

Section 1. Knowledge of assistive technology
Please rate your level of familiarity and knowledge pertaining to the following assistive technology applications:

Application	None	Aware	Practicing	Proficient
Text to speech word processors				
Pre	7 (37%)	8 (42%)	4 (21%)	
Post			16 (84%)	3 (16%)
Voice recognition software				
Pre	7 (37%)	9 (47%)	3 (16%)	
Post		11 (58%)	7 (37%)	
Text scan and read programs				
Pre	10 (53%)	8 (42%)	1 (5%)	
Post			17 (89%)	2 (11%)
Multimedia				
Pre	1 (5%)	7 (37%)	10 (53%)	1 (5%)
Post			15 (79%)	4 (21%)
Writing Process: planning				
Pre	7 (37%)	8 (42%)	4 (21%)	
Post			14 (74%)	5 (26%)
Writing process: transcription				
Pre	14 (74%)	2 (11%)	3 (16%)	
Post		4 (21%)	15 (79%)	
Writing Process: Mechanics				
Pre	0	7 (37%)	8 (42%)	4 (21%)
Post		1 (5%)	5 (26%)	13 (68%)
Computer accessibility options				
Pre	7 (37%)	8 (42%)	4 (21%)	
Post		2 (11%)	14 (74%)	3 (16%)

Section 2: Use of technology with special education students
These questions are intended to measure your current level of use. Pre-Conference: Approximately how often do you use the following types of technology with your special education students? Post Conference: As a result of the training, how often do you intend to use the following?

Application	Never	Rarely	Sometimes	Frequently
Word Processing				
Pre	2 (11%)	3 (16%)	11 (58%)	3 (16%)
Post			6 (32%)	13 (68%)
Text to speech word processors				
Pre	14 (74%)	1 (5%)	4 (21%)	
Post	1 (5%)	1 (5%)	10 (53%)	7 (37%)
Voice recognition software				
Pre	14 (74%)	4 (21%)		
Post	3 (16%)	8 (42%)	8 (42%)	
Student draw and paint programs				
Pre	8 (42%)	6 (32%)	3 16%)	2 (11%)
Post	1 (5%)	3 (16%)	10 (53%)	5 (26%)
Text scan and read programs				
Pre	16 (84%)	3 (16%)		
Post	1 (5%)	1 (5%)	8 (42%)	9 (47%)
Student generated multi-media				
Pre	11 (58%)	2 (11%)	5 (26%)	1 (5%)
Post	1 (5%)	1 (5%)	9 (47%)	7 (37%)
Computer accessibility options				
Pre	16 (84%)	1 (5%)	2 (11%)	
Post	1 (5%)	4 (21%)	12 (63%)	2 (11%)
Concept mapping				
Pre	12 (63%)	3 (16%)	4 (21%)	
Post	1 (5%)	2 (11%)	9 (47%)	7 (37%)
Word prediction				
Pre	9 (47%)	6 (32%)	3 (16%)	
Post	1 (5%)	1 (5%)	12(63%)	
Commercial Language Arts Programs				
Pre	3 (16%)	3 (16%)	6 (32%)	7 (37%)
Post		3 (16%)	6 (32%)	10 (53%)
Commercial Multimedia Programs				
Pre	3 (16%)	4 (21%)	10 (53%)	2 (11%)
Post	1 (5%)	3 (16%)	9 (47%)	5 (26%)

Section 3: Knowledge of State and/or District Content Area Reading Standards and Strategies

A. Please rate your current familiarity and knowledge in content area reading strategies.

	None	Aware	Practicing	Proficient
Vocabulary Strategies				
Pre	3 (16%)	4 (21%)	10 (53%)	2 (11%)
Post		1 (5%)	14 (74%)	4 (21%)
Pre-reading Strategies				
Pre	8 (42%)	5 (26%)	5 (26%)	1 (5%)
Post		2 (11%)	11 (58%)	6 (32%)
Comprehension Strategies				
Pre	1 (5%)	5 (26%)	9 (47%)	4 (21%)
Post		1 (5%)	11 (58%)	7 (37%)
Study Reading Strategies				
Pre	1 (5%)	9 (47%)	5 (26%)	4 (21%)
Post		3 (16%)	12 (63%)	4 (21%)
Reflective Strategies				
Pre	10 (53%)	7 (37%)	2 (11%)	
Post		3 (16%)	13 (68%)	3 (16%)
Knowledge of State/District Reading Standards				
Pre	1 (5%)	6 (32%)	7 (37%)	5 (26%)
Post		3 (16%)	6 (32%)	13 (68%)

B. Please rate your confidence in your ability to help special education students to:

	None	Low	Moderate	High
Achieve reading standards				
Pre	1 (5%)	2 (11%)	9 (47%)	7 (37%)
Post			10 (53%)	9 (47%)
Achieve reading standards using technology				
Pre	5 (26%)	7 (37%)	5 (26%)	2 (11%)
Post			16 (84%)	3 (16%)

DATE DUE